Approaches to Peace

Approaches to Peace
An Intellectual Map

Edited by W. Scott Thompson and Kenneth M. Jensen
with Richard N. Smith and Kimber M. Schraub

UNITED STATES INSTITUTE OF PEACE
Washington, D.C.

The views expressed in this book are those of the authors alone. They do not necessarily reflect the views of the United States Institute of Peace.

United States Institute of Peace
1550 M Street, N.W.
Washington, D.C. 20005

Second printing 1992

Printed in the United States of America

Library of Congress Cataloging-in-Publication Data
Approaches to peace: an intellectual map/edited by W. Scott Thompson and Kenneth M. Jensen with Richard N. Smith and Kimber M. Schraub.
    p.   cm.
    Essays based on proceedings of a conference held at Airlie House, Airlie, Va., June 20-21, 1988.
    ISBN 1-878379-01-1
    1. Peace—Congresses.
I. Thompson, W. Scott (Willard Scott), 1942- . II. Jensen, Kenneth M. (Kenneth Martin), 1944- . III. United States Institute of Peace.
JX1933 1988
327.1'72—dc20

89-26871
CIP

United States Institute of Peace

The United States Institute of Peace is an independent, nonpartisan, federal institution created and funded by Congress to strengthen the nation's capacity to promote the peaceful resolution of international conflict. Established in 1984, the Institute has its origins in the tradition of American statesmanship, which seeks to limit international violence and to achieve a just peace based on freedom and human dignity. The Institute meets its congressional mandate to expand available knowledge about ways to achieve a more peaceful world through an array of programs including grantmaking, a three-tiered fellowship program, research and studies projects, development of library resources, and a variety of citizen education activities. The Institute is governed by a bipartisan, fifteen-member Board of Directors, including four members ex officio from the executive branch of the federal government and eleven individuals appointed from outside federal service by the President of the United States and confirmed by the Senate.

Board of Directors

John Norton Moore (Chairman), Walter L. Brown Professor of Law and Director of the Graduate Program, University of Virginia School of Law

Elspeth Davies Rostow (Vice Chairman), Stiles Professor of American Studies Emerita, Lyndon B. Johnson School of Public Affairs, University of Texas

Dennis L. Bark, Senior Fellow, Hoover Institution on War, Revolution, and Peace, Stanford University

William R. Kintner, Professor Emeritus of Political Science, University of Pennsylvania

Evron M. Kirkpatrick, President, Helen Dwight Reid Educational Foundation, Washington

Morris I. Leibman, Esq., Sidley and Austin, Chicago

Sidney Lovett, United Church of Christ Minister (retired), Holderness, N.H.

Richard John Neuhaus, Director, Institute on Religion and Public Life, New York

Mary Louise Smith, civic leader; former member, Board of Directors, Iowa Peace Institute

W. Scott Thompson, Professor of International Politics, Fletcher School of Law and Diplomacy, Tufts University

Allen Weinstein, President, Center for Democracy, Washington, and University Professor and Professor of History, Boston University

Members ex officio

J. A. Baldwin, Vice Admiral, U.S. Navy, and President, National Defense University

Stephen J. Hadley, Assistant Secretary of Defense for International Security Policy

Ronald F. Lehman II, Director, U.S. Arms Control and Disarmament Agency

Richard Schifter, Assistant Secretary of State for Human Rights and Humanitarian Affairs

Samuel W. Lewis, President, United States Institute of Peace (nonvoting)

Contents

Acknowledgments

The preparation of this volume was accomplished with the assistance of a large number of people, not the least of whom were the participants in the Airlie House Conference themselves. The editors owe a debt of gratitude to Priscilla Taylor of Editorial Experts, Inc., for her editorial work and to Lilly J. Goren and Aileen C. Hefferren for their work in preparing the manuscript. Thanks also goes to the Publications and Marketing Department of the Institute of Peace—most especially to Joan Engelhardt for production management and to Marie Marr-Williams for manuscript tracking.

This volume would not have been possible without the help of two individuals in particular. Many thanks go to Richard N. Smith, who administered the Intellectual Map Project, staged the Airlie House Conference, and began the design and editorial work on this volume. Kimber M. Schraub then took over supervision of substantive editing and manuscript preparation, made the authors and editors work hard, and brought the volume to fruition. On that account, we are most grateful to her.

Introduction
The United States Institute of Peace and the Intellectual Map Project

Kenneth M. Jensen and W. Scott Thompson

During its initial meetings in the spring of 1986, the Board of Directors of the United States Institute of Peace devoted considerable time to weighing the charge given it under the federal legislation establishing the Institute, considering how best to proceed in creating "an independent institution established...to strengthen the nation's capacity to promote peaceful resolution of international conflicts."

Although the directors cumulatively had extensive knowledge about international conflict and its management, all agreed that none knew with any certainty how best to proceed. The directors further agreed that even the sum of the existing experience and expertise available to them would not suffice to bring the Institute the type of definition and programs it needed to fulfill its broad mandate.

Accordingly, the Board decided that one of its first preoccupations—and one of the first formal projects of the Institute—should be an investigation of the salient approaches to the study of international conflict and peacemaking. The Board concluded that information and insights gathered from and about a large variety of scholars and practitioners was the best way to acquire the guidance necessary to set up the programs of the United States Institute of Peace.

From the beginning, Board members worked closely with the Institute's staff to push forward what came to be called the "Intellectual Map Project." Doing so offered several advantages. On one hand, the staff had Board experience and expertise to draw on. On the other, Board involvement—frequently daily—meant that the directors acquired information as it was being gathered, rather than having to wait until all the results were in. Thus it was possible to begin in earnest the Institute's program work in several areas—especially in making grants-in-aid for research, education, and information services.

As the Institute grew and the body of information gathered under the Intellectual Map Project increased, Board and staff members working on the project concluded that they should proceed in a more structured and coherent manner. They decided to do three things: first, to organize the approaches to understanding and managing conflict and peace into a coherent typology; second, to begin a series of formal colloquia during which the proponents of various approaches could gather and testify about the character and utility of their work; and, third, to refine project goals.

The Institute's early experience strongly suggested that, although an enormous body of literature already sought to delineate the most useful ways to attain a more peaceful world, considerable confusion and competition existed among proponents of various approaches. Furthermore—and precisely because of this confusion and competition—vital lines of communication among various schools of thought either had never existed or had broken down.

This breakdown was most notable in the gap between scholars and practitioners. Few diplomats, negotiators, and arms control policymakers seemed to find much utility in the theoretical writings of scholars; few scholars found much promise in the practitioners' experience. Although less apparent, the same could be said about relations between and among scholars, even those with seemingly related pursuits, such as deterrence and arms control theorists. In the main, the proponents of each approach seemed to the Institute to have staked their claims and, thereafter, to have withdrawn to work them—and to protect them from competing claimants.

These circumstances led the Institute to regard the Intellectual Map Project in new ways. Not only might it better inform the Institute regarding its purposes and work: the Intellectual Map might also directly serve the scholarly and policy communities it surveyed. It was clear that Intellectual Map activities in themselves could bring proponents of the various approaches to peace together immediately and help build and repair communications links. Further, exposure to one another might encourage a considerable amount of reflection and self-evaluation, for participants could not help measuring their claims against one another's.

The Institute was not alone in its appraisal of the conflict and peace field: contacts with scholars and practitioners showed that the field was indeed ready for the Intellectual Map. As one scholar said during an early discussion of the Institute's project,

> Developing an "intellectual map" takes place at the second stage of the evolution of a field, when work has begun but there remains overlapping and conceptual confusion. People then stop for a bit to see where different areas converge and diverge. Creating an intellectual map would have the additional advantage of demonstrating the historical progression of peace research and activity. Travelers on individual roads on the map would see their historical and analytical relationship to other travelers.

World Without War Council President Robert Pickus held a related view, which is echoed in his contribution to the present volume. According to

Pickus, there were too many "maps" of the conflict and peace field, and such maps—visions of the obstacles and means to peace—were most often constructed without knowledge of "past efforts, past assumptions, and...[past] consequences of acting upon them.... We need a better conceptual map to help people most likely to be caught in a single current of thought, unaware of even its history, let alone its relationship to other perspectives."

Taking these realizations into account, the goals of the Intellectual Map Project thus became

- to gather information on the various approaches to peace;
- to bring proponents of the various approaches into public fora designed to expose them to one another and to make it possible for them to interact;
- to encourage reflection and self-evaluation among scholars and practitioners involved with each of the approaches;
- to create new—and rejuvenate old—lines of communication between and among approaches; and
- to stimulate conceptual cross-fertilization and to encourage inter- and multidisciplinary (that is, multiapproach) efforts regarding international conflict and peacemaking.

The Intellectual Map Typology

During the winter of 1986–87, the Institute began the formal structuring of the Intellectual Map Project. The first order of business was to create a typology, which was necessary for the conceptual organization of the approaches to international conflict and peacemaking. Our intention was not to create a rigorous structure, but to begin to sketch the outlines of relationships between and among the various approaches. We did not intend to produce a definitive analysis, but to encourage thought about those relationships.

Initially, two main divisions suggested themselves: traditional approaches and newer approaches. "Traditional" implies those approaches, such as the study of treaty arrangements and alliance systems, that have been long since brought to bear and are most commonly referred to as part of the study of international relations. "Newer" implies those approaches, such as the psychological study of human conflict, that have only recently been applied in international affairs. It seemed to us that the principal difference between the two categories—apart from the fact that one preceded the other historically—lay in the emphasis placed on one or another sort of international actor. The traditional fields of international relations by and large emphasize interactions between and among sovereign nation-states, while the newer approaches tend to look to the interactions of individuals and subnational groups that cut across the psychological boundaries of nation-states.

Beyond this difference, the traditional and newer approaches seem to draw on different sorts of resources. For example, traditional approaches tend to make more use of history and the study of politics and diplomacy. They also tend to draw on those political philosophies that treat human beings and social institutions as rational actors. The newer approaches, on the other hand, seem to give far greater significance to the role of irrational forces. Regarding states—and to some extent their leaders and elites—as irrational actors, the newer approaches tend to seek insights into international behavior through means derived from the behavioral sciences, such as sociology and psychology, that study the irrational in individuals and subnational groups. Exponents of the newer approaches, when they go to political philosophers for assistance, are likely to find the work of those who deal with the role of impersonal forces in social organization most useful.

In preparing the Intellectual Map typology, we broke the general category of traditional approaches into three subcategories: collective security and deterrence, diplomacy and negotiation, and strategic management and arms control. The principles that guided this disaggregation were more complex than those used to divide the older from the newer approaches. What follows is not rigorous but is intended, rather, to portray some of the differences among the three traditional approaches, as we saw them.

The notion of collective security derives, by and large, from a classical liberal view of mankind—ranging from a Hobbesian to a Lockean view, if you will. Men—and nation-states made by men—are imperfect and will always be capable of producing evil. Nonetheless, most men, and nation-states, are rational enough to realize that it is in their best interests to live together in peace and order. When a nation-state deviates from this realization, it is in the best interests of the community to join together to discipline the deviant—that is, to create (or recreate) its security collectively.

The concept of collective security has its historical sources in the nineteenth-century Concert of Europe. Exponents of the concept regard the collective security arrangements of the nations of the Concert as responsible for the general peace that followed the French Revolution. They also regard the Concert's decline as a principal cause of World War I. Similarly, collective security proponents tend to regard the lack of "concert" (as expressed in the failure of the League of Nations) as an important cause of World War II. Accordingly, in essence they place their hopes of forestalling future major conflicts on collective efforts from large alliances like NATO and the UN.

Deterrence approaches were placed alongside collective security in the typology, for their proponents generally take a similar view of the ultimate source of world order and regard deterrence as the principal means of maintaining collective security against the threat of deviant nation-states.

One assumption here is that deviant nation-states are sometimes irrational actors and can be most readily and effectively encouraged to be otherwise by the threat of force. We chose not to subsume deterrence in collective security, for its proponents tend to regard other means of attaining collective security as only moderately useful when compared to deterrence.

Like other traditional points of view, diplomacy and negotiation presume that nation-states are, or can be made to be, rational actors. While exponents of the use of diplomacy and negotiation share many of the basic views of those who support collective security and deterrence, their concern with nation-state behavior lies less with the transcendent realm of collective interests than with the more limited (and more easily knowable) realm of the interests of immediate parties to conflict. While they may place their ultimate hopes in international institutions dedicated to collective security, proponents of this view tend to concentrate their efforts on understanding and building rational relationships among leaders and policy-making elites internationally, to exposing mutual interests among actual and potential parties to conflict, and to creating rational mechanisms by which agreements can be more easily reached.

Of the traditional approaches, those of strategic management and arms control are the most realpolitikal in character. Historically, they find their roots in the balance-of-power politics of eighteenth- and nineteenth-century Europe. Like collective security, these approaches presume that peace is a more orderly state of affairs than war, that war does not ultimately serve the self-interest of any nation-state party to it. In contrast to collective security, however, the balance-of-power schools presume that a peaceful, orderly world derives not from the surrender of national self-interest but from maximization of it. This maximization requires acute attention to forces without, to ensure sufficient strength to avoid tempting aggressors and to deal effectively with them when they arise. The guiding concept is derived from a view held in classical liberal economics—that self-interested forces, if effectively pursuing their self-interests, create a state of relative equilibrium. While they take a dynamic view of world order (that is, one in which the forces will constantly change and require constant rearrangement vis-à-vis one another), proponents of the balance-of-power approaches fear unlooked-for turns of events that seriously destabilize equilibrium. As we see in the area of arms control, they tend to feel that the world is safer when both parties to a potential conflict are endowed with similar means of maintaining their national interests. Similarly, they tend to feel safer when national interests are aggressively stated rather than obscured.

We broke the newer approaches down into transnationalism, behavioral approaches, and conflict resolution. We disaggregated this group based on principles different from those by which we disaggregated the traditional approaches. While proponents of the newer approaches share views that separate them from the traditional in the manner suggested previously, it is difficult to separate them from one another by examining their principles. It might be said that the three newer approaches differ from one another in focus more than in principle.

While the proponents of transnational approaches may be noticeably closer than the others to the traditionalists in their view of the nation-state and its institutions, for instance, their central interest lies in the role of the individual and the subnational group in creating international community and maintaining international order. In pursuing that interest, however, they are often less concerned with the effect of "transnationally disposed" individuals and groups on the nation-state than they are with the effect of such individuals and groups on one another. This concern brings the transnationalists very close to their behavioralist colleagues in anthropology, sociology, psychology, and political science, whose interest in the nation-state is minimal.

Conflict resolution, the newest approach to international conflict and peace, shows a tendency to embrace all other approaches—traditional as well as new—and more besides. Indeed, conflict resolution would itself be a sort of intellectual map of approaches to peace were it not for the fact that, as yet, it has not found the means to integrate all the other approaches. We have chosen to give conflict resolution a place apart from the transnational and behavioral among the newer approaches in respect to its intents. Nonetheless, the emphasis conflict resolution proponents currently place on bringing transnationalism and behavioralism into play in the study of conflict and into peacemaking puts them, for the time being, much closer to these fields than to others in the Intellectual Map and makes it difficult to discern the real differences between conflict resolution and the other newer approaches.

After looking at the traditional and new approaches, the Institute concluded that the categories established were too cut and dried and, further, that not all approaches could be subsumed within them. Among the first unsettling questions that the Institute asked itself at this juncture was what to do with international law. In many ways, it fit under the "traditional" rubric, both conceptually and historically. In many other ways, it did not. In the final analysis, international law seemed to us to be of interest and utility to the proponent of any approach to conflict and peace. Accordingly, we decided to create a third major category for international law and related fields. Our notion here was not to differentiate it from other approaches but to accord it a place in the Intellectual Map that was consonant with its importance to the whole.

Proceeding in this way, we were also able to find a suitable place in the Intellectual Map for interstate organization and third-party dispute settlement approaches to conflict and peace. Proponents of the salutary role of interstate organizations (that is, international bodies comprising official representatives of nation-states) share views equally close to those of the transnationalists and those of the collective security exponents. Nonetheless, they are by no means the same as either and play a sufficiently important role in international conflict management to entitle them to a category apart. Inasmuch as third-party dispute settlement may involve a wide variety of actors in mediating roles (including individual states, super-powers in condominium, interstate organizations of all shapes and sizes, and so forth), and as the mediators are disinterested parties and stand outside the self-interest of the traditional approaches, the approach fits much better with international law and interstate organizations than it does elsewhere in the Intellectual Map.

Our final quandary during the construction of the Intellectual Map typology came when we asked ourselves where the proponents of the most general, systemic, and philosophical approaches to peace and conflict fit. Where to put those who believe that the ultimate sources of conflict and the ultimate means to peace reside in fundamental understandings of such things as community, human nature, history, politics, economics, race and sex relations, and the like? Where do Gandhians, World Federalists, Marxists, and advocates of liberal democracy and the free market belong? As we considered this dilemma, we also realized that we had not found a place for that considerable school of political thought that holds that an important relationship exists between a society's political system and institutions and its international behavior. Where should we put those who believe that domestic tyranny and injustice are immediately and inextricably linked to interstate conflict? What about those who believe that freedom and social justice within states make them pacific international actors?

In the end, the Institute created a final major category called "Political Systems Approaches," which we subdivided into approaches that focus on the general character of domestic arrangements ("Internal Systems") and international behavior and approaches that focus broadly on worldviews ("Systemic Theories/World Systems"). In creating this category, we did not mean to differentiate those evincing such concerns from the proponents of other views so much as we meant to recognize the importance of political systems approaches to the understanding of international conflict and peacemaking. Proponents of these approaches have much to say to those traveling other roads. It can also be fairly said that the proponents of all approaches from time to time engage in the sort of reflections that the advocates of political systems approaches make their abiding concern.

The resultant typology appears in outline form below. Again, we emphasize that this Intellectual Map is provisional and intended to encourage reflection rather than conclusion. It should be taken in the same open and cautious spirit in which it was created. The outline nature of its form does not reflect the value or "weight" of any given approach.

I. Traditional Approaches
   A. Collective Security and Deterrence
   B. Diplomacy and Negotiation
   C. Strategic Management and Arms Control
II. International Law Approaches
   D. International Law
   E. Interstate Organizations
   F. Third-Party Dispute Settlement
III. New Approaches
   G. Transnationalism
   H. Behavioral Approaches
   I. Conflict Resolution
IV. Political Systems Approaches
   J. Internal Systems
   K. Systemic Theories/World Systems

The Intellectual Map Colloquium Series

In late 1986 the Institute began a series of seven colloquia under the Intellectual Map Project. The colloquia ranged in length from a morning or afternoon to two days. Although all but one event was held in Washington, D.C., participants came from throughout the country and, on occasion, from abroad. The first event was held on December 5, 1986: the last was on March 24, 1988.

Some colloquia addressed a single major division of the Intellectual Map (such as the session on Capitol Hill in July 1987 that was devoted to international law approaches). But in keeping with our goal of bringing together scholars from diverse fields, most of the colloquia were devoted to several subdivisions. Perhaps the best example of the latter was a session in Palo Alto, California, on February 19–20, 1987, where the Institute heard from scholars and practitioners in arms control, collective security and deterrence, systemic theories, transnationalism, behavioral approaches, and conflict resolution. Participants included both well-known and aspiring talents in international affairs, history, philosophy, behavioral theory, psychology, and peace activism.

A number of Institute Board members, including the Institute's president and other senior members, were present during each colloquium, as were Institute staff. The events were open to the general public, and, when time permitted, the audience was encouraged to take part in the discussions. By the end of the series, several hundred observers had benefited from the testimony of a total of forty-five scholars and practitioners (see appendix A).

While the colloquium series covered an enormous amount of ground, the Institute was nonetheless forced to conclude that its mapping effort had only begun. We learned that a great deal of work was being undertaken under the various approaches to peace and that the contact between and among approaches was all the more difficult and important given that fact.

Despite the often-demonstrated tendency of approaches to peace to diverge and go their own ways, the Institute became more than ever convinced that the task of strengthening "the nation's capacity to promote peaceful resolution of international conflicts" was a multidisciplinary approach. The experience of the colloquia demonstrated that each approach to international conflict management had virtue, but also that none could be dubbed "the answer" to the problem of achieving peace.

In addition, the more the Institute delved into the history of approaches to peace, the more apparent it became that this history was a story of waves of enthusiasm for one approach or another. In the nineteenth century, for example, the balance-of-power approach to the regulation of international conflict appeared to many to be a masterstroke. By the end of World War I, of course, the enthusiasm for the balance-of-power approach had been replaced by a new enthusiasm for multinational organizations such as the League of Nations. The twentieth century has brought a new rash of enthusiasms, most recently arms control, with a myriad of others vying to replace the old.

While this history shows that there are no "silver bullets," it also shows that the enthusiasms of the past were by no means wholly unwarranted. Our colloquia suggested that each approach clearly has something of merit to offer. In seeking to promote effective peacemaking, then, it was clear that those things ought to be sought out and combined. On this approach, peacemaking becomes quite naturally inter- and multidisciplinary.

This understanding came to inform nearly everything that the Institute attempted in the first two years of its existence.

The Airlie House Conference

As the Intellectual Map colloquium series drew to an end in the spring of 1988, the Institute concluded that an effort ought to be made to gather representatives of all of the approaches named in the Map typology into one large conference for extended discussion and interaction. Such a conference, we felt, would be a useful experiment. At the very least, we would learn the answers to several important questions, such as, Would proponents of widely variant approaches listen to one another, let alone interact? Would such a conference draw its disparate participants together or would it only serve to reinforce their prejudices regarding one another? Our hope, of course, was that the conference would serve to begin to pull the conflict and peace field together and to bring about a number of new, cooperative undertakings by proponents of the various approaches to peace.

To ensure the best possible chances of success, we planned the conference carefully. The Institute sought plenary papers from experts who could speak to the intentions, interests, and work of their respective general approaches to conflict management: the traditional, the international law, the new, and the political systems approaches. Other papergivers were chosen to represent approaches subsumed in each major category.

Each plenary session involved a paper presentation and a question-and-answer period. Thereafter, the conference broke into working-group sessions on each of the eleven Intellectual Map subdivisions. These sessions proceeded from a formal paper presentation to a critique by a formal commentator to a general discussion involving other participants. The moderators of the working-group sessions were carefully chosen for the contributions they might make to drawing out the papergivers and commentators and to encouraging participants with divergent views to get involved in the discussion.

The conference's general participants (that is, those who were not assigned papers or asked to make formal comments) were selected from the range of conflict and peace fields reflected in the Intellectual Map typology. The conference was also open to the public. In the end, more than eighty-five individuals took part in the proceedings. A look at the list of participants and their affiliations testifies to their diversity (see appendix B).

The conference was held June 19–22, 1988, at Airlie House outside Washington, D.C. This site was chosen to minimize distractions and to encourage participant interaction between sessions, over meals, and during the evenings. The conference principals—papergivers, commentators, moderators, and Institute Board members and staff—gathered on the first day to discuss conference intents and to go over details of the complicated schedule. Plenary and working-group sessions held on June 20 and 21 culminated in a dinner address by Ambassador Max Kampelman, followed by general discussion. The conference principals met again on the morning of June 22 to conduct an intense four-hour evaluation of the activities of the preceding days. They were joined at that time by many of the general conference participants.

The Airlie Conference was a splendid exercise. Discussion was abundant, surprisingly friendly, and, above all, intense. All participants showed a willingness to take seriously the need to acquaint themselves with work in fields foreign to them, and few were shy about giving detailed explications of their approaches and work. At many conferences, the most interesting and important things transpire informally, between sessions and during the relaxed times, when participants characteristically encounter one another as human beings rather than as advocates or professionals. Common ground is discovered indirectly and, often, quite by accident. While the Airlie Conference was no different in this regard, it can be fairly said that such encounters occurred as much during formal sessions as outside them.

The flavor of the discussions during the Airlie Conference is well captured by the following anecdote. During one of the sessions, one of the participants, to the astonishment of many others, made the suggestion that the Stinger missile be given the Nobel Peace Prize for its role in bringing Moscow to realize the futility of its war in Afghanistan. A longtime peace activist noted that "weapons are not exactly what the Peace Prize is about." She then went on to stress the limitations of realpolitik. A Foreign Service officer, in effect, synthesized the two views. While he agreed that the missile had played a vital role in "persuading" the Soviet Union to parley, little would have happened had the United Nations not already created a framework for peace negotiations to which President Gorbachev could turn without loss of face. The cease-fire and phasing down of that war could thus be seen as a consequence of the use of several roads to peace.

Perhaps the most fascinating—and successful—session at Airlie was one of the most ambitious in its intention of bringing together disparate intellects. Under the rubric of Systemic Theories/World Systems, classicist Michael Nagler, who teaches at Berkeley and resides in a Gandhian community, was asked to give a paper on "ideas of world order." Nagler's effort was a highly syncretic piece that drew on ancient Greek and Gandhian notions of social organization to produce a vision of world community without troublesome nation-states. The session was chaired by Board member W. Bruce Weinrod, a national security expert noted for his partiality to realpolitik and Hobbesian views of man. Nagler's commentator, A. Lawrence Chickering of the Institute for Contemporary Studies, is a student of ideology and a notable antiutopian. In his comments, Chickering quickly took the discussion in the direction of views of human nature. There followed a very rich and diverse interchange of views from a group that included everyone from psychologists and philosophers to former diplomats and arms control experts. By the end of the session, each had moved very far from his or her professional moorings and had eagerly indulged in serious conversation about an issue that is clearly basic to understanding human interaction in whatever form it might take. All agreed that it is a pity scholars and practitioners of international affairs could not take time out of their busy schedules to have more such discussions, for they deal with, as one participant put it, "the real stuff." When the evaluation session was held on the morning of June 22, conference camaraderie was still high and the participants were eager to speak about their experiences and the further implications thereof.

Nearly everyone at the evaluation session agreed that the conference represented a ground-breaking effort to bring together a variety of "cultures" that, for intellectual, ideological, and institutional reasons, had not traditionally interacted with one another. By fulfilling this "human" (as opposed to strictly "intellectual") function, the conference was deemed an important first step toward opening new lines of communication that had previously been considered closed or unproductive. It was, in effect, a "happening."

The postconference summaries given by the conference principals did not simply constitute a mutual admiration society. In fact, many participants shared concerns about the negative side effects of addressing too many topics within a limited timeframe. They feared that analytical depth was sacrificed for intellectual breadth. The conference organizers, however, maintained that such a sacrifice was warranted because this was the first time any organization had undertaken such an effort and in consideration of the enormously wide range of topics discussed.

It also should be acknowledged that some participants expressed concern for the underrepresentation of grassroots, social movement, and other activist organizations at the conference. The organizers pointed out that individuals from such organizations had been invited and expressed disappointment that few had chosen to attend. If the absolute numbers of such people at the conference was not great, there was nonetheless a significant and very much engaged representation.

With regard to the project's typology, many participants suggested that the Intellectual Map be made more specific and that further categorization ought to ensue. Although no one particularly objected to the basic structure of the typology, several participants doubted whether it was—or could be—sufficiently inclusive. As might be expected, this line of thought brought the participants to a discussion on the operative scope of the definition of "peace." As might also be expected, some felt that peace ought to be defined narrowly, as "the absence of war," and others felt that peace ought to be defined as the condition that remains when all the significant sources of social conflict have been dealt with. As one might imagine, there was no consensus on this issue at the end of the discussion. With regard to the definition that informed the Institute's Intellectual Map, the group agreed that, while still not fully formed, it fell somewhere between the poles and was distant enough from the first to satisfy some of those closer to the second. One of the reasons for this was a group consensus that if "peace" were left undefined, that is, without limits on its meaning, it could be regarded as synonymous with almost any social condition that some individual or group regarded as desirable, including social conditions disagreeable to most. Toward the end of this part of the discussion, everyone agreed that the problem of defining "peace" must be addressed by every scholar and practitioner in the field. They affirmed that, because there is no simple formula for peace, the Map served its intended purpose to sketch the array of possibilities.

The two subject areas of religion and economics were seen as needing increased attention in the Intellectual Map. Many participants felt that, because religious conviction and economic necessity are often given as rationales for going to war, it is essential that these forces be studied further to determine their causal relationship to peace. The organizers acknowledged the omission and explained that had conference papers been assigned on these topics, they would have come under either the transnational subdivision or the systems subdivision, depending on what angle the authors took.

Another notable criticism voiced at the evaluation session concerned what some participants identified as an overemphasis in the conference papers on superpower relations and the matter of nuclear weapons. Their view was that, while these issues are of critical importance, concentrating on them obscures the problems posed by other matters, such as regional conflicts and politically generated internal violence. The same participants made the additional observation that greater superpower rapprochement, if it became a reality, would significantly increase the importance of regional and internal conflicts, especially in terms of the possibilities for superpower cooperation in peacekeeping efforts.

As the group turned to the future of the peace field beyond the Airlie Conference, several responses were evoked by the question of how best to synthesize a number of approaches into new and more effective means to address future conflict situations. While some argued that much could be accomplished by intellectual cross-fertilization—through the study and adoption of useful theories and data developed in other fields—most felt that the most promising approach might be what was referred to as an "integrated" or "multidisciplinary working-group" approach. Under such an approach, a group of scholars and practitioners from various fields might be brought together to address what ought to be done in a particular case of international conflict or crisis. The principal advantage here lies in the circumstance that all members of the group would have to deal with the same, finite case. In the end, the participants enthusiastically recommended that the Institute consider sponsoring an experimental version of such an undertaking.

After the Airlie House Conference

In evaluating the Intellectual Map Project in the wake of the Airlie House Conference, the Board and staff of the Institute concluded that it had been an important exercise in every regard. We were well satisfied with the beginning we had made in gathering together the approaches to peace. The responses of the various participants convinced us that the Intellectual Map approach was sound. The pursuit of peace is indeed a multipart, multi-approach endeavor that would benefit from dialogue as well as from the self-reflection of its exponents. There were no "silver bullets" and, as important, no obsolete approaches.

At the same time, we were less than satisfied with what we thought we knew. The principal effect of the Intellectual Map Project on the Institute in the period following the Airlie Conference was to cause us to reconsider the sorts of projects we were undertaking ourselves and sponsoring through grants and fellowships. The Map experience served to expand the number and variety of individuals and groups that came to work with and be served by the Institute. We also learned much during the colloquium series and Airlie Conference about where unusually promising, yet under-supported, work was being done under a wide variety of approaches.

Looking back from late 1990, then, we have a strong sense that the Intellectual Map Project has borne substantial fruit. Not only has the community of experts working with the Institute broadened in its scope, but we have also noticed that work being done under all the Map rubrics has benefited from increased cross-fertilization and communication among the approaches to conflict and peace.

Although we would like to think that the Institute played at least a modest role, we cannot make any substantial claim to having brought more coherence and cooperation to the peace fields. Most responsible for the new coherence and cooperation have been the remarkable changes in international life over the past few years. Whether one refers to them as "the end of the Cold War," "the end of History," or "the victory of liberal democracy," recent changes have brought innumerable assumptions into question and made much more porous the boundaries between approaches to international conflict and peacemaking. For many, 1989—the year following the Airlie Conference—marked the point at which it was no longer possible for any reasonable observer to believe that anything less than great historical changes were afoot in the Soviet Union.

The period since then has been marked by one remarkable change after another and a steady increase in optimism. At the same time, a sense of uneasiness has developed regarding how the world will be post-Cold War, or after "the end of History." As one commentator recently noted, it is difficult for states long accustomed to steady-state adversarial relationships to operate in a world without their customary enemies. As the great conflict between East and West is being transformed, much intellectual reordering and reorienting is required for scholars and policymakers—as well as advocates of peace—to find a new way. The recent crisis in the Persian Gulf reminds us that world conflict in the post-Cold War era will be, if anything, more violent, more difficult to deal with, and much less easy to ignore. In each of the various approaches to peace, proponents could not ultimately avoid focusing on superpower relations, no approach could be validated without dealing effectively with the East-West conflict, and that took considerable time and effort. Needless to say, the possibility of a world without superpower conflict has shaken the foundations of most of the work on conflict and peace undertaken over the past forty years.

In a sense, then, the Institute's Intellectual Map Project may have been ahead of its time even while its organizers and participants thought of it as something long overdue. We attempted to encourage students of conflict and peace to "group" at a time only shortly before they would need to "regroup." It is the Institute's hope that the lessons of the past that caused us to bring approaches together will not be lost as that regrouping goes forward. Dealing with conflict and peacemaking in the post–Cold War era will be increasingly complex and difficult. A return to the past, when approaches and disciplines went their own ways, seems to be among the least productive ways of dealing with the uncertain future.

The Present Volume

This volume presents material generated at the Airlie House Conference in sixteen chapters organized after the fashion of the Intellectual Map typology.

Part I (chapters 1–4) is devoted to traditional approaches to peace and conflict study. Edward Luttwak's plenary paper is followed by essays on deterrence, diplomacy, and arms control.

Part II (chapters 5–8) presents international law approaches. After a plenary presentation by Oscar Schachter, essays follow on international law, interstate organizations, and international third-party dispute settlement.

Part III (chapters 9–12) addresses new approaches, with Robert Pickus's plenary remarks followed by essays on transnationalism, behaviorism, and conflict resolution.

Part IV (chapters 13–16) is devoted to political systems approaches. Following Scott Thompson's plenary effort are essays on the international behavior of various political systems and ideas of world order. We have printed Ambassador Max Kampelman's keynote address here also. While it focuses on the broad problems of peace among nations, expressing ideas shared with most of the other contributors to this volume, this address stresses the importance of political systems approaches.

We provide the reader with introductory summaries of each chapter. All chapters containing papers given in working-group sessions include summaries of the formal commentary and discussions that followed them at the Airlie Conference. While brief, these summaries are intended to give the reader access to some of the richness of the discussion and the interaction among representatives of the various approaches.

The essays in this volume are written in a variety of styles and for a variety of purposes. Some (for example, that on law and peace by Myres McDougal) offer detailed and thorough arguments on difficult but vital principles and understandings. Others are wide-ranging and provocative, such as those by Edward Luttwak on traditional understandings of conflict and peace and Michael Nagler on ideas of world order. Several authors, such as Richard Bilder and James Laue, offer extensive bibliographies that give readers new to their approaches easier access.

In all instances, the authors offer considerable substance and clear perspectives. While no single volume dedicated to approaches to peace can do justice to the subject, we believe that this one may be ideal for several kinds of readers. For the neophyte inclined to enter the study of international conflict, *Approaches to Peace: An Intellectual Map* reflects a good part of the diversity of the field and a good deal of the seriousness with which scholars and practitioners pursue their work. It also reflects the fact that not everyone agrees with everyone else. For the veteran student of international conflict, perhaps frustrated with the confusion and lack of communication among fields and disciplines, the volume will suggest any number of new ways in which the exponents of the various approaches to peace might be brought together. Finally, and perhaps most important, *Approaches to Peace: An Intellectual Map* provides ready access to the various ways students of international peace and conflict think—that is, to their assumptions, their values, and their absorbing concerns. It will be the rare reader who comes away from this volume with the view that the attempt to understand conflict and peace is anything less than a serious and worthwhile endeavor pursued by capable and imaginative intellects.

Part I: Traditional Approaches

Introduction to Chapter 1

Generally speaking, modern concepts of war and peace evolved primarily from the tradition of the European Enlightenment and philosophers such as Jean-Jacques Rousseau, who saw man as a uniquely "perfectible" being, not condemned to "instinctual fixity" and the intellectual stasis that it implies. From this perspective, war should be viewed not as a constant, inevitable, or natural human condition, but as a phenomenon that can be purged from human experience by removing the causal factors.

In contrast, as Edward Luttwak points out in this first chapter, the ancients viewed conflict much more organically. Rather than being the exception to the rule, conflict—potential, incipient, or actual—was seen as the natural state of human affairs, interrupted by occasional outbreaks of peace. It was therefore essential for the society that sought peace to be always prepared for war. *Qui desiderat pacem, praeparet bellum* (Let him who desires peace prepare for war).

This apparent contradiction underscores what Luttwak terms the "paradoxical logic of conflict," a logic in which to obtain a given result one must strive for its opposite. Luttwak believes this transposition of ends, although classical in derivation, remains valid today and permeates all levels and modes of conflict. For example, the paradoxical logic of conflict dictates that a military force must take the more difficult and circuitous route to a hostile objective because it is less likely to be defended than the most obvious route, and so the assault is more likely to be met with limited resistance.

In its dynamic form, the paradoxical logic of conflict contradicts the generally accepted linear notion that continued progression and accumulation are profitable and maintains, instead, that in conflict, unqualified advance on an objective ultimately results in the defeat of the advancing, and heretofore considered superior, force because of the inevitable weakening of strategic lines of resupply. Luttwak believes that many policymakers have trouble adapting to this seemingly convoluted decision-making process and thus perceive the U.S. defense policy as lacking coherence.

Using ancient Rome as his example, Luttwak suggests that the greatest benefit of preparing for war is that once a state is capable of waging war, it can then pursue peace through a variety of means, particularly diplomacy. Furthermore, the security that a war capability conveyed allowed the ancients not only to consider appeasement as a legitimate policy option, but also to believe it to be the cornerstone of classical diplomacy. In Luttwak's words, "More cold-blooded than ourselves, the Romans would have deemed it foolish to proffer millions for defense while refusing even a penny for tribute." Both war and tribute entailed the achievement of certain benefits at the expense of certain costs, with neither to be preferred over the other until a comparative calculation could be made.

In many instances, however, such calculations were neither warranted nor feasible because at least one party to the potential conflict deemed the decision to go to war as nonnegotiable. In other words, in cases in which the decision not to go to war would be considered a sin (for example, the Druids then, the Muslim jihad today) or would involve an irrevocable loss of honor, a fate considered worse than defeat on the battlefield (for example, the Afghani freedom fighters), conflict could not be avoided and the necessity of being able to wage war was of even greater importance. The only other available option was surrender—a viable, albeit costly, strategic choice.

Relating this analysis to the modern era, Luttwak believes that the experience of World War I resulted in the delegitimation of conflict and an increased emphasis on collective action to remedy social and economic evils. At present, however, the delegitimation of conflict has, in Luttwak's opinion, devolved to the point at which collective action is giving way to individualism, and the desire for peace has come to mean a move toward "debellicization"—a state wherein no conflict, not even that meant to avoid conquest, is deemed acceptable. But, as Luttwak hastens to add, the traditional approach to the preservation of peace is implicitly collectivistic, and a rejection of that concept leaves surrender as the only possible alternative to *praeparatio belli*.

1. The Traditional Approaches to Peace

Edward N. Luttwak

The traditional approaches to peace all assume that it must be actively preserved; peace was not viewed as a natural state—that being rather the attribute of conflict, in the meaning of potential, incipient, or actual war. The varied traditional methods for the preservation of peace all imply the moral and political acceptability of war, for each requires preparation for it. As the axiom advises, *Qui desiderat pacem, praeparet bellum* (Let him who desires peace prepare for war)[1]—that is, do not plan to wage deliberate war, but rather, be in readiness for war, so as to dissuade bellicose antagonists.

The paradoxical logic of conflict, with its seemingly contradictory prescriptive implications, was thereby fully recognized, as contrary to the direct causality of linear logic—the Hellenic inheritance the prescriptions of which we now regard as mere common sense, oblivious as we are to the ancestral prevalence of theist and magical origins. We are taught from childhood that, to obtain a given result, we should act straightforwardly by providing its constituent elements (for example, plant to reap) rather than rely on propitiatory dances or the succor of the gods. And of course that is the logic of everyday life, which rules all that is constructive, notably agriculture, commerce, and industry, as well as the consensual governance of states, voluntary communities, and families. The implied prescriptions are too familiar to be labored, from the alignment of promoted causes with desired effects to the open communication that is the prerequisite of cooperation.

Only conflict, the state characterized by the presence of an adversarial will, is ruled by the pervasively contradictory paradoxical logic, so that to obtain a given result we should strive for its exact opposite.[2] Classical elites, both Hellenic and Roman, universally practiced in war or otherwise well familiar with it, could intuitively grasp the implications of the paradoxical logic, whether in static form in which opposites are reversed *ab initio* (for example, to advance upon an enemy, the narrow, circuitous, uphill road is better than the broad, straight, level road because the narrow road is worse, and its use is thus less likely to be anticipated, yielding surprise) or in dynamic form, wherein straightforward action eventually evolves into its opposite (for example, the stronger, victorious army that keeps advancing long enough without a pause will become the weaker army, set for defeat[3]).

The paradoxical logic is equally manifest at every level of conflict, from the simple fight (the tactical level, in modern parlance), in which the direct assaults that the linear logic would prescribe must be costly if not fatal, and circumvention should be favored instead; to the level of the battle (operationally, we would say) in which all forms of maneuver are responses to the negating effect of the paradoxical logic; or to the level of the theater of war, in which the attempt to defend every segment of the front by spreading the forces thinly defends nothing against an enemy that concentrates its own forces; or, finally, to the level of the highest war and peace decisions (our grand strategy), in which straightforward action to achieve a given result, notably by providing its constituents, also obtains the opposite result. For example, if Visigoths are destroyed to secure the Danube frontier, the result is not security on the Danube but rather the unresisted arrival of the Huns who were pressing behind them. Or, to revert to our initial example, if military forces are disbanded and swords hammered into plowshares, those constituents of peace themselves invite aggression and war.[4]

Hence, there is no reason to suspect that the paradoxical war-peace prescription was ever disingenuous, mere rhetorical camouflage for aggressive purposes. Certainly it was honestly meant in its surviving textual form,[5] which dates from the late fourth century, when successive emperors were fully content to defend what their empire already had, having neither the means nor the desire for further expansion.

Peace by Diplomacy

Before it became contaminated by modern connotations, "appeasement" was not only a respectable term but actually the core of classical diplomacy, encumbered as it was by the varied commercial and financial concerns of its modern counterpart. The purposes of appeasement, then as now, were to uncover the incentives to war and to offer, if possible, such benefits as would outmatch their attraction, while advertising with due discretion the disincentives as well. Such negotiations, to remove at least the proximate motives of war, were, of course, already an ancestral practice when Thucydides wrote; his text simply takes it for granted that readers would be familiar with negotiating procedures, notably, the role of heralds even in the midst of war and the absolute immunity of visiting negotiators.[6]

There were no permanent ambassadors, which were a sixteenth-century Venetian invention, but there were instead *proxenoi*, "official friends," prominent citizens who acted as spokesmen and intermediaries for other city-states while retaining all the rights and duties of their own citizenship. Demosthenes, for example, was the *proxenos* of Thebes. (Contemporary Washington, D.C., lawyers who act as registered agents for foreign governments have revived this institution.) Another interesting practice of the

Hellenes was the direct access of visiting negotiators to the citizen assemblies of democratic city-states. Instead of dealing only with the (elected) officials, foreign negotiators could present their case to the citizens as a whole and try to sway them with their rhetoric; many fine examples were preserved or perhaps improved by Thucydides.

But the diplomacy of appeasement was never an alternative to *praeparatio belli* in the traditional scheme of things; instead, it was viewed as another of its benefits, often its greatest benefit. For negotiation can only be such (that is, an exchange of what is deemed valuable) in conjunction with the ability to wage war whenever the other party is itself *capax belli* (that is, if war is possible in the first place). When only one party is *capax belli*, there can be no negotiation but only concession—although the Romans, at least, were not opposed to concessions, even some that the Hellenes, or we ourselves, would find humiliating, notably, payments meant to purchase the good conduct of potential aggressors.

More cold-blooded than ourselves, the Romans would have deemed it foolish to proffer millions for defense while refusing even a penny for tribute. Rejecting romanticism (the glorious agony of the concealed death wish) even in, let alone matters of state, they regarded war as a tool of statecraft and not as an expression of martial virtue.[7] Thus war was not to be valued above its objective worth, in dollars and cents as we would say. War, like tribute, entailed certain costs to yield the probability of certain benefits. Although neither was to be preferred in principle, tribute, it was noted, could often yield greater benefits at lower cost than war. (Contrary to legend, the practice of paying off bellicose tribes was not a manifestation of late-Roman Empire decadence; it was frequent even at the height of imperial strength,[8] whenever, in fact, there was a calculated reason to avoid war.)

Still, even if tribute was paid, peace could not be secured without *praeparatio belli* as well, for it was only the conjunction of that incentive with the disincentive of resistance or retaliation that could secure the good conduct of potential aggressors. Tribute alone could merely evoke demands for more tribute, until the ultimate point when a war of resistance would remain as the only alternative to enslavement—meant literally in this case, slavery being the final mode of payment in classical times.

Hence the paradoxical rule applies in all cases, notwithstanding the priority accorded to negotiation, the emphasis that might be placed on appeasement, or even the willingness to pay tribute.

When Peace Is Impossible

All the foregoing are prescriptions for people and nations that are not bellicose, that truly desire peace—not a preference taken for granted in the traditional scheme of things, or today for that matter.

Peace as Sin

Along with the great variety of nations and tribes that calculated the costs and benefits of war and peace (or rather, resistance versus collaboration) more or less as they did, the Romans also encountered some who refused to calculate at all, because they held all compromise with Rome to be sinful. Most religious leaders could cheerfully accept Roman rule, which was almost always respectful of local faiths and sometimes positively enthusiastic (for example, the popularity of the Egyptian Isis cult in Rome). It was significant, too, that by standard operating procedure, the Romans allocated tax revenues for priestly salaries and liturgical expenses.[9] Other religious leaders might prefer to avoid such outright collaboration but were at least willing to concede to Caesar what they deemed to be Caesar's, that is, secular matters, including taxation.

But here and there some religious castes or factions interpreted their allegiance to their deities in ways that excluded all compromise with the ever-flexible Romans. So it was for both the Druids and sundry ultras among the Jews, notably the zealots who were dominant from the sixty-sixth year of the common era and Bar-Kosiba's movement two generations later. For them, it was contrary to their religion to calculate the strength of Roman arms and act accordingly, for that was merely an earthly power, while their self-set duty to resist the Roman presence was transcendental. With dissuasion, negotiation, and even tribute all ineffectual, war was inevitable, and it was pursued in Roman fashion until complete victory.

Neither Druids nor Jews were active proselytizers; hence, their religious bellicosity did not extend without geographic limit. But others who came later were, and are. If the salvation of the soul can be obtained only by correct religious practice, the nonpropagation of that practice by any means available, including force, is a crime against as yet unconverted humanity.

Exclusivity in salvation persists in Christian theory, but not in practice. Elsewhere the two have yet to diverge. Thus Iran's minister for the Haji, Wakf, and Charities said of the pilgrimage negotiations in 1987: "The House of Saud should cooperate with Iran and all Muslims in their performance of the rites and political duties of the pilgrimage, which consist of disavowing infidels."[10]

In this context, "disavowal" means the termination of all cooperative dealings with unbelievers. It is not, however, an expression of hostility toward infidels as human beings. On the contrary, it is the greatest act of disinterested benevolence, for peaceful dealings with infidels might be highly profitable for such Muslims as engage in them. Still, they must be avoided, for such selfishness would mean condoning unbelief, thus delaying the conversion that alone can grant the serenity of Islam on earth and the eternal joys of the Islamic heaven.

Sundry obfuscating glosses notwithstanding, the conversion of the infidel by any means, including war, remains a positive duty in Islam, just as the conversion of Muslims to other faiths remains a crime punishable by death. Islamic law allows truces with infidels, but not an indefinite peace, which remains a sin.

Peace as Dishonor

Even when calculations of costs and benefits would greatly favor peace over the alternative of war, peace may be rejected because it cannot be reconciled with the regnant ideals (or self-image) of the political community, or merely of its leaders. *Pax est tranquilla libertas. Servitus postremum malorum omnium non modo bello sed morte etiam repellendum* (Peace is freedom with tranquillity. Servitude is the worst of evils, to be averted not only by war but by death itself.)[11] Thus said Cicero, after having praised not war but peace.[12] Weak, changeable, and excessively vain as he was, Cicero acted on his words on this occasion; having spoken those lines against Mark Antony in the summer of 44 B.C., he died in great dignity on December 7 of the following year, when Mark Antony in triumvirate had him proscribed.

Servitudinem was neither an abstraction nor a memory for Cicero, who owned plenty of slaves. Slaves might live very well, own property, and raise families. Many could also enjoy a broader liberty than serving soldiers, normally subject to much more detailed discipline; for that matter, slaves might be freer than the sons and daughters of any *pater familias* who happened to exercise all the powers accorded to him by strict laws. But slaves were in a different category. However scant their obedience might be in practice, it was neither an honorable duty within functional limits as with soldiers, nor a highly honorable filial duty. Hence the *servus* could not have *dignitas* or honor—for that conflation of self-respect and self-definition could not coexist with the slave's implied acceptance of any humiliation that the master might choose to impose. Slaves might live out their lives, as many no doubt did, without ever being humiliated, but that did not alter the fact that their own willingness to live on as slaves was dishonorable, because of the implicit acceptance of humiliation that it entailed.

Cicero's *servitudinem* is thus the condition of the *servus*, defined not by the lack of liberty (a condition shared by many nonslaves) but by an irrevocable loss of honor, which nothing could redeem, not even manumission. Hence the dishonorable status of the numerous freedmen in Roman society, including those who acquired vast powers in the imperial service.

Oddly enough, the rejection of *servitudinem* even at the cost of death, let alone war, is one strand of the heroic canon that is still likely to receive widespread approval in our own age, which knows nothing of slavery as a defined status in society.

On the face of it, this insistence ("give me liberty or give me death") is blatantly illogical, for life is a precondition of liberty; but an implicit purpose of dissuasion can provide the missing logical link, inasmuch as an advertised intention to resist at all costs is meant to discourage those who might otherwise try to oppress. If such dissuasion fails, however, the costs of a war of resistance, including its deaths—plural and actual as opposed to the romantic abstraction of the singular—could be evaluated unfavorably against the costs of oppression or even outright servitude, which might then be conveniently viewed as no more than liberty deferred.

No such calculation is admissible, however, if the acceptance of oppression, let alone servitude, is believed to cause an irrevocable loss of honor, and if honor, in turn, is regarded as an essential attribute of all human life worth living. Thus logic is restored, for honor rather than life then becomes the first precondition and life can therefore be advantageously sacrificed in resisting the would-be oppressor, for the alternative (dishonored life) is deemed worse than death.

The persistence of such reasoning in our nuclear age is of course a remarkable tribute to the power of that earliest of ideologies. We deprecate the murder of errant daughters and sisters for the sake of the "family's honor" (a crime still not uncommon in some traditional societies), yet we would safeguard our own honor, as we define it, with an equal extremism.

Certainly the rejection of *servitudinem* is not an uncommon cause of war; one is even tempted to speak of victim-caused wars. At the end of December 1979, the Soviet Union's leaders ordered their armed forces to enter Afghanistan. At the start of the invasion on December 28, a Soviet commando unit apparently broke into the presidential palace to kill President Hafizullah Amin and his guards; other such units also killed some Afghans at sundry headquarters, the telephone exchange, and so on. All in all, Afghan deaths on that night might have reached a thousand, although a smaller number is more likely.

But the hundreds of thousands of killings that followed, by bombardment, gunfire, mines, and execution, were caused by the decision of many Afghans to resist the Soviet Union. It was the Afghan resistance that chose war and not the Soviet leaders, who would most certainly have preferred a peaceful, unresisted invasion.

In April 1940, the Danish government faced the same choice. The German invasion also began with a *coup de main* that immediately engulfed the capital city, the royal palace, and the seats of government. But despite the shock of surprise, Danish leaders were able to come to a coolly deliberated decision: they calculated that the Danish people would suffer less if there were no resistance, and the nation's cohesion was such that the order to refrain from any provocative acts, let alone armed struggle, was universally obeyed.

The final outcome fully vindicated the sound calculation of the Danish leaders of 1940: the Danes suffered very little during the war. While other peoples fought and died all over Europe, no Danes died in combat, except for a few who volunteered to serve in the British armed forces and a slightly larger number who joined the German SS. While cities were devastated all over Europe, Danish cities were not bombed by either side. And, because there was virtually no armed resistance, there were virtually no German reprisals either. Even food remained abundant. In consideration for their good behavior and high racial quality under Nazi criteria, the Danes were exempted from the confiscations that starved much of Europe. Of all the countries under German occupation, Denmark alone was allowed its own local rationing, on scales far more generous than in Germany itself. There was much good eating in Denmark throughout the war—so much so that when German evacuees arrived from East Prussia and Silesia in early 1945, many became dangerously ill when suddenly fed on fat-rich Danish rations.[13] For Denmark, therefore, *servitudinem* was most salutary, much more so than the wars of resistance that engulfed other Europeans.

In 1940 the Belgian, Dutch, and Norwegian leaders had the same opportunity to surrender peacefully to the Germans but chose to fight instead. As a result, many people of these three nationalities died in combat, more were executed or killed by exposure and starvation in captivity, and many children and elderly people died because of food shortages. In 1941 the Yugoslav government chose war, and the subsequent resistance of many Yugoslavs was violent indeed, at commensurate cost in German reprisals.

Yet after World War II, the vast majority of Danes repudiated the well-tested remedy of a peaceful surrender to aggression, endorsing instead the country's potentially war-attracting membership in NATO. And of course the Danes so decided at a time when war could be nuclear and might therefore result in the extinction of the Danish nation.

Thus it seems that postwar Danish electorates have agreed with Cicero that *non modo bello sed morte etiam* was justified to avoid another *servitus*, which must have grievously wounded Danish souls indeed, even while sparing their bodies. Now, of course, the generation of Danes who lived through World War II is passing from the scene, and so is their learned preference for *libertas* over a peaceful subjection.[14]

Peace as Social Evil

Finally, peace, or at least a prolonged peace, may be considered incompatible with the moral economy of society, as Juvenal wrote, in *Sateris, Nunc patimus longae pacis mala* (We are now suffering the evils of a long peace).[15] War demands sacrifice and bravery, tempering character; without it, the argument goes, the human spirit is corrupted, and so is society.

Actually, that view was not yet the establishment view in Juvenal's day. In deliberate contrast to the Hellenic cult of entirely personalistic heroics in the Homeric style, Roman magnates were contemptuous of all idealistic notions of war. But the notion that fairly frequent wars were essential for society's well-being certainly became a received idea of wide authority thereafter, through all the ages until our own. Thus the much-published Friedrich von Bernhardi wrote in 1911,

[Ignoring] the value of war for the political and moral development of mankind...whole strata of our nation seem to have lost that ideal enthusiasm which constituted the greatness of its history. With the increase of wealth they live for the moment, they are incapable of sacrificing the enjoyment of the hour to the service of great conceptions, and close their eyes complacently to the duties of our future and to the pressing problems of international life which await a solution at the present time.

He also wrote,

All petty and personal interests force their way to the front during a long period of peace. Selfishness and intrigue run riot, and luxury obliterates idealism. Money acquires an excessive and unjustifiable power, and character does not obtain due respect.[16]

A double contrast is presented in this societal argument for war, of which this example is only one among many: first, between the self-indulgence of peace and war's stimulation of manly virtues considered altruistic; and second, between the mean scope of life in peacetime civil society and the great endeavor of the nation at war. The first was the basis for the claim that war was salutary for society, while the second justified war as a collectivist enhancement of the nation's life as a whole.

Conclusion

By the end of World War I, the notion that war provided healthy exercise for society had become entirely discredited within the European cultural sphere. Left-wing opinion rejected the entire authoritarian world view from which it sprang, while right-wing opinion had discovered a new equation, not "war equals social discipline" but rather "war equals revolution."

It is not surprising, therefore, that an aversion to war became an organic element of the Western tradition after 1918. From then on, deliberate war for aggrandizement was delegitimated; only self-defense remained a valid justification. Even Adolf Hitler, prone to challenge a good many other established notions, felt compelled to fabricate the excuse of a prior Polish attack to justify his war of September 1939.

Yet World War I greatly increased the appeal of collectivism and specifically seemed to validate collectivist remedies for economic and social evils. In the trenches, men learned not only that war was unhealthy, if not deadly, but also that an elemental solidarity could bind them together, cutting across class lines. On the home front, people discovered that unemployment could simply cease to exist, while resources could be centrally allocated for common purposes by industrial and consumer rationing schemes. Both the ephemeral fascism of the interwar period and the economic collectivism of all Communists and many socialists were nourished by those twin discoveries.

In our own times, the post-1918 delegitimation of war has progressed much further, sometimes reaching the ultimate stage that has been described as "debellicization,"[17] in which even defensive war is no longer deemed acceptable. Moreover, the widespread suspicion that the ship of state is fated by its very nature to be steered periodically into morally dubious but always deadly fights has engendered a novel countercollectivism, manifest, for example, in the refusal to credit the pronouncements of the state institutions in charge of foreign affairs, intelligence, and the armed forces.

Even the notion of the ship of state is becoming obsolete in the most advanced societies, the citizens of which increasingly refuse their assigned role as well-disciplined sailors, even if the captain and officers are of their own choosing and follow exactly the course electorally approved. Periodic evidence indicates that patriotism is as intense as ever; the citizen-sailors are perfectly willing to defend the ship if it is attacked. But nowadays they are disinclined to sail the ship on any steady course set by strategy, aimed at the only port that statecraft knows: the enhancement of the power of the state.

Yet even while many people repudiate the goal that alone gives meaning to the voyage, only a few choose to reject outright their assigned place in the ship, to swim on their own as absolute pacifists. The reason, no doubt, is narrowly technical: weapons of mass destruction are prominent among the contemporary instruments of war, and they would hardly discriminate between obedient sailors and defecting swimmers.

The traditional approach to the preservation of peace is itself implicitly collectivistic—it ignores the possibility of an individual's absolute rejection of war. But the disavowal of all forms of power, including the power to avert servitude, remains the only alternative to *praeparatio belli*.

Notes

1. This common saying has many variants but is usually cited from Flavius Renatus Vegetius, *Epitoma de Rei Militaris*, book 3, prologue: *Nec minus Hannibal petiturus italiam Lacedaemonium doctorem quaesivit armorum; cuius monitis tot consules, tantasque legiones, inferior numero ac viribus, interemit. Ergo qui....* This text comes from ex officina Iohannis Maire (Louvain: Lugduni Batavorum, 1645), p. 65.

2. According to this logic, for example, secrecy and deception will obtain the most desired behavior of the other, which is a vulnerable passivity rather than informed cooperation.

3. Given the technological stasis of the Romans, they had little chance of observing the clearest manifestation of the paradoxical logic nowadays, the familiar process whereby the more new weapons are successful, the greater is the countermeasure effort they evoke, eventually reducing their net effectiveness below that of

weapons originally less capable and therefore less contested (for example, the countermeasured antiaircraft missile versus the gun).

4. For a fuller description, see Edward N. Luttwak, *Strategy: The Logic of War and Peace* (Cambridge, Mass.: Belknap/Harvard University Press, 1987).

5. See note 1.

6. This principle survived until the very end of antiquity. When U.S. diplomats were long held hostage in Iran, there was reason to reflect on Attila's treatment of the East Roman delegation to his court, whose immunity withstood the discovery that it included Vigilas, secret agent of the eunuch chamberlain Chrysaphius, sent to procure Attila's assassination. Priscus of Panium, who was there, cites Attila as saying that only the inderogability of ambassadorial rights prevented him from impaling Vigilas and leaving him as carrion for the birds. See *Priscus* (Exc.de.Leg. Rom., 3) p. 11, line 185.

7. When criticized for not being more aggressive, Scipio Africanus replied, *Imperatorem me mater, non bellatore peperit* (My mother bore me a general, not a warrior). Sextus Julius Frontinus, *Strategematon*, book IV, sect. vii.

8. Colin D. Gordon, "The Subsidization of Border Peoples as a Roman Policy of Imperial Defense." Ph.D. diss., University of Michigan, 1948.

9. From the time of Augustus, one of the three daily sacrifices at the Temple in Jerusalem was paid for directly from the emperor's household treasury.

10. Teheran Domestic Service, April 14, 1988.

11. From an oration against Marcus Antonius, *Philippicae* II, p. 44, line 113 [author's translation].

12. *Et nomen pacis dulce est et ipsa res salutaris* ("The very name of peace is sweet and it is itself the healthiest condition") [author's translation], ibid.

13. Ingemar Dorfer of Stockholm, personal communication.

14. Matters may evolve in the opposite direction as well: twenty years after Cicero's death—years of civil war and military tyrannies—Romans up to then as devoted to republican principles as Cicero himself welcomed the advent of Augustan rule, holding *pax et servitudinem* preferable to more civil war. Ronald Syme cites M. Favonius to that effect, as reported by Plutarch, *Brutus*, p. 12.

15. *Satires* VI, l., p. 223.

16. [General] Friedrich von Bernhardi, *Germany and the Next War*, tr. Allen H. Powles (London: Edward Arnold, 1914), pp. 9, 26, continuing with the apposite Schiller quotation from *Braut v. Messina*, "Law is the weakling's game."

17. The word was coined by Norman Podhoretz.

Introduction to Chapter 2

Continuing with Edward Luttwak's classical interpretation of the traditional approaches to peace, Gregory Treverton points out that Thucydides taught us most of what we know today about the concept of deterrence: namely, that smaller states do not usually attack larger, more powerful states. But history provides notable exceptions to that maxim, some successful, others nearly so, with World Wars I and II exemplifying the consequences of reliance on Thucydides' wisdom.

The commonsense notion of classical deterrence—in modern parlance, deterrence by denial or conventional deterrence—remains a cornerstone of defense planning, but it is not, as Treverton points out, sufficient to deter *all* aggression. Technology has ushered in the era of deterrence through punishment, characterized by the ability to threaten to wreak unacceptable levels of death and destruction on a would-be aggressor, at a low cost.

But here, too, the calculus becomes muddied. As nuclear weapons became the shared domain of the postwar superpowers rather than the exclusive prerogative of the United States, so did the unacceptable consequences of the use of nuclear weapons. Thus, the bipolar balance-of-power system was created based on the controversial premise of mutual assured destruction (MAD).

To Western Europe, MAD posed a vexing problem: Was it credible that the United States would use its nuclear deterrent in defense of European territorial integrity, if to do so implicitly suggested an escalatory step that would expose the United States to large-scale nuclear retaliation?

This "crisis of credibility" surrounding what amounted to a murder-suicide pact between Western Europe and the United States was inherently unstable and, in Treverton's words, "began a series of cyclical adjustments that has continued to the present. Changes in the central deterrent relationship—in this case, American vulnerability and the onset of parity—were reflected in concern about extended deterrence [that is, the U.S. nuclear guarantee to Europe] which, in turn, spawned changes in the essential American deterrent."

This seemingly unresolvable question highlights Treverton's surprise at the longevity of NATO, particularly in light of the inherent difficulties of sustaining collective security agreements in the nuclear age.

As he notes, smaller powers have traditionally sought to form alliances to counterbalance larger rivals. Because the smaller states in an alliance tend to undercontribute to the collective effort, a defensive, necessarily precarious, arrangement results. Another complicating factor is the psychological abrasion created by the reliance on others for one's security. Treverton notes that this is a particularly difficult problem in modern alliances, for "drives to national assertion seem likely to make alliances more tactical or fleeting."

NATO is, no doubt, a special case. It enjoys an unprecedented level of social, cultural, and political commonality; a common, visible enemy; and the vivid representation of World War II as testimony to the dangers of division. But Treverton points out, "even now it suffers the divisive forces, strategically, of the diminished credibility of extended deterrence and, politically, of the simple fading into memory of the reasons that called it forth." After more than forty years of peace in Western Europe, and in light of potential changes in Soviet security policies, NATO is now facing its most formidable political challenge to date. Whether it will continue in its current form is subject to debate, but there can be no doubt that fiscal and political pressures will result in some modification in the future.

2. Deterrence and Collective Security

Gregory F. Treverton

Thucydides taught us most of what we know about strategy, it seems, and Bernard Brodie and Thomas Schelling brought his conclusions into the nuclear era. Although deterrence and collective security are separable instruments for preventing war, they are connected in many ways. Most notably, they are joined in what is perhaps the most successful American and Western strategy for keeping the peace in the postwar period, NATO, an alliance that has explicitly relied on (nuclear) deterrence. Thus, a central question about my twin subjects is whether that success can and will continue. Another question concerns uncertainties about the future of deterrence and collective security.

The Fact of Deterrence

If most of what we know about deterrence was known by Thucydides, we have added the jargon. Throughout most of history, deterrence has been more a fact than a strategy. Weaker powers did not attack stronger ones unless they were driven to desperation or led by desperados; understanding that commonsensical proposition, groups, then states, arranged their forces and policies accordingly. This arrangement was what we now call "deterrence through denial"; groups were deterred from attacking by the knowledge that they would be defeated on the battlefield. (Interestingly, though, Thucydides was no stranger to other notions of deterrence. He tells of ancient powers threatening a region to kill all the young men in its villages if it did not submit, then reinforcing the threat by carrying it out in one village. The aggressive power was trying to exercise what Schelling later called "compellance," and it recognized that its threat—against societies, not just their soldiers—would not be credible unless it was reinforced.[1])

Deterrence through denial is now often called "conventional deterrence," with "conventional" construed to mean both the traditional military operations on the battlefield and the use of conventional, not nuclear, weapons. It was not always so, for various schemes for denying the enemy the battlefield through the use of nuclear weapons circulated in the United States and Europe into the 1970s. Such schemes may return again, but for now, whatever their military attractions, the political arrangements necessary to implement them seem out of the question.

Looking at the history of deterrence through denial, an observer can see either that the glass is much more than half full or that it is a little empty. Most of the time, weaker powers do not attack stronger ones not because they are explicitly deterred but, as Schelling noted in a different context, for the same reason that we do not step blithely into busy streets: they simply know better.[2]

The rub is that the glass is a little empty. Weaker powers sometimes do attack, and sometimes they succeed, at least in the short run. The list is long enough even in our own time—most notably and disastrously, Germany against France and then against the Soviet Union. This history is at the root of Western Europe's distaste for too much conventional force; having seen conventional deterrence fail twice this century, Europeans shun exclusive reliance on it. At least there is no proof that nuclear deterrence can fail.

If deterrence through (conventional) denial is not foolproof, it does seem safe to say that too little attention to conventional defense can tempt would-be aggressors. If desperados do not do their calculations, their adversaries usually do; Hitler's generals kept finding pretexts to defer the invasion of France. More recently, one calculating politician, Saddam Hussein of Iraq, was lured into attacking Iran by the perception that his enemy was weak and in turmoil. Like Hitler or the leaders of Japan, he counted on a decisive quick victory; like them, he miscalculated.

Technology seems unlikely to change the conclusion that conventional deterrence is necessary but not foolproof. New weapons do not seem likely to confer decisive advantages on the defense, especially because any attack is a mixture of offense and defense, whereas any defense is a mixture of holding positions and counterattacking.[3] New technology is making it easier to detect and engage targets at a distance. This technology should help a defender engage the follow-on forces of an attacker, but so should it also help an attacker frustrate the mobilization of a defender's reserves.

It is interesting to speculate about how conventional forces might have developed had nuclear weapons never been invented.[4] Surely, "strategic" weapons would be differently defined; in the absence of nuclear weapons, conventional weapons would have been assigned to "strategic" missions and would have been emphasized accordingly. Yet I am skeptical about how much difference that emphasis would have made. Before World War II, airpower was thought by many to have altered warfare decisively: "strategic" bombing would take the war over the front to the adversary's people and economy; the adversary's war-making capacity could be destroyed and its people perhaps demoralized.[5]

The evidence of the war, however, disproved this theory. As the Allies' Strategic Bombing Survey showed, Germany's war economy continued to grow until war's end, and popular demoralization was not apparent, even once it should have been clear that the country was being led by a demonic leader into certain defeat.[6] The U.S. war against North Vietnam was another case that seemed to underscore the lesson that inflicting conventional pain on an adversary's citizens is more likely to stiffen their resistance than to demoralize them. In the absence of nuclear weapons, conventional weapons might have developed much more than they have into weapons of mass destruction. But that prospect strains the imagination; if feasible, the implementation of it would have strained budgets.

Nuclear Deterrence

Nuclear weapons resurrected the idea of strategic bombing and ushered in the era of "deterrence through punishment." The simple destructiveness of the weapons meant that their possessors could threaten, cheaply, to wreak unacceptable damage on a would-be aggressor. Bernard Brodie, writing in 1945, set out in a paragraph the basic calculus of nuclear deterrence:

> It seems hardly likely, at least as among great powers at some distance from each other, that an attack can be so completely a surprise and so overwhelming as to obviate the opponent's striking back with atomic bombs on a large scale. For this reason, the atomic bomb may prove in the net a powerful inhibition to aggression. It would make little difference if one power had more bombs and were better prepared to resist them than the opponent.[7]

Once the Soviet Union had nuclear weapons and delivery systems to match, MAD was a fact. It never was a strategy.

Assured destruction, unilateral or mutual, is hardly appealing, and so it is no surprise that the entire logic of nuclear deterrence has been controversial. For some, deterrence is an illusion because the Soviet Union, like the United States, never intended to use nuclear weapons in any case. Deterrence only provided a rationale for building arms beyond reason. The fact that the United States never came close to using nuclear weapons, even when it had a monopoly and then overwhelming superiority, might be cited in particular support of this theory.

Yet, finally, this theory, like its opposite—that deterrence has worked—is unprovable. Because, happily, we have had no nuclear wars, we cannot know whether nuclear deterrence has been effective or superfluous. Notice, however, that the deterrence-is-an-illusion argument begins to edge back toward the logic of deterrence if it holds that part of the reason neither superpower intended to use nuclear weapons was that no prize was worth the risk.

Technology has not yet upset the fundamental advantage of offense over defense that nuclear weapons conferred. Specific targets, such as missiles or political leaders, can be protected against nuclear attack by sheltering them or making them mobile. But Brodie's logic still holds for cities: they cannot move, and a few nuclear weapons will destroy them. In all the furor over the Reagan administration's Strategic Defense Initiative, it is increasingly clear that the basic logic has been left standing. Technology eventually may upset that logic, but that time is not yet, nor near.

It is worth noting that nuclear deterrence through punishment is like other forms of deterrence, even though it relies on the ascendancy of the offense: it reinforces the status quo. By definition, deterrence seeks to deter another party from acting; if the party does not act, there is no way to know whether action was deterred or simply was never intended. Compelling the other party to act in a way that the compeller desires is harder, as the ancients knew, for it means visibly submitting to another's will, not merely remaining inactive.

Deterrence is a means of safeguarding peace to the extent that maintaining a status quo is peaceful; most of the time disruptions of the status quo lead to tension or war. But to the extent that the existence of particular regimes is itself regarded as a threat to peace, deterrence protects them as well, be they Stalin's or Hitler's or Idi Amin's.

Extending Nuclear Deterrence

From the start, the destructiveness of nuclear weapons brought with it an awkward question: How could threats to use them ever be credible? Once both superpowers acquired nuclear weapons, for either to threaten to use them was to threaten murder-suicide, for who could be sure that the other side would not retaliate, despite the manifest irrationality of doing so? As time passed, nuclear arsenals grew in numbers, but using them became less thinkable. The temporal distance from Hiroshima and Nagasaki made the idea of using them more and more alien to international affairs even as their destructive capacity grew.

The murder-suicide threat was, and is, credible enough as a threat to deter another power's nuclear—and, probably, conventional—attack on the possessor's homeland. If the physical integrity of the nation-state were at stake, who could be sure that it would not carry out its suicidal threat? If the threatened punishment were great enough, even a small probability that the punishment might be inflicted should suffice. Moreover, the destructiveness of nuclear weapons simplified the would-be aggressor's calculations and so seemed to impose a rationality across a wide range of leaders: no longer could an outnumbered attacker hope to succeed by surprise or superior tactical skill.[8]

This problem of credibility shrank the area over which nuclear deterrence could operate. That was true in principle even before the Soviet Union had nuclear weapons: Would its leaders really believe that the United States would inflict massive nuclear destruction in response to, say, a minor

Soviet incursion into Iran? Hence, strategists pronounced the Eisenhower administration's strategy of massive retaliation incredible on arrival.

These concerns were acute in the American nuclear guarantee to Western Europe, reflected in debates over "coupling." If deterring attack on the first kilometer of West German territory meant threatening to use American strategic weapons, could Washington be relied on to do it? In the early nuclear years, however, strategic logic muted the force of these concerns. The fact that American bombers could not reach the Soviet Union from the continental United States, and so had to be based in Europe, imposed a kind of strategic unity on NATO. More important, as long as the United States was invulnerable to a Soviet nuclear attack, there was no difference between what later came to be called "central deterrence" and "extended deterrence." Deterrence *was* central deterrence and could, in principle, operate all the way to the inner German border.

Or such was the strategic logic. The political facts were different. Throughout the 1950s, American leaders did not feel so invulnerable as the United States now looks in retrospect, and they behaved with commensurate caution—which should caution analysts now against looking back too fondly on a golden age of American nuclear invulnerability.[9]

By strategic logic, in the 1950s doubts about massive retaliation arose not because Europeans feared that an American president would not trade Chicago for Hamburg, as it was later put, but because presidents did not yet face that choice. Rather, massive retaliation seemed less and less credible because of the incommensurate escalation it implied. Would a president really unleash massive nuclear destruction in response to any Soviet adventure in the world? The doctrine put the United States in the position of having "to put up or shut up."[10]

When vulnerability converted nuclear deterrence in Europe into extended deterrence, NATO began a series of cyclical adjustments that has continued to the present. Changes in the central deterrent relationship—in this case, American vulnerability and the onset of parity—were reflected in concern about extended deterrence, which, in turn, spawned changes in the essential American deterrent.[11] The concern over extended deterrence led to British, and then French, independent nuclear forces and to proposals for a NATO nuclear force in Europe—the famous, now infamous, Multilateral Force.

That concern led Americans to a series of changes in the central deterrent. First came the Kennedy administration's innovations in the doctrine identified with Defense Secretary Robert McNamara—city avoidance, damage limitation, assured destruction, and, ultimately, flexible response.[12] Then came the rapid nuclear buildup of the 1960s. Finally came the innovations of another defense secretary, James Schlesinger, and his emphasis on selective options, outlined in 1974.[13] The new strategy—less new, in fact, than a continuation of trends a decade old—was a negative answer to the question President Nixon had asked of MAD in 1970: "Should a president, in the event of a nuclear attack, be left with the single option of ordering the mass destruction of enemy civilians, in the face of the certainty that it would be followed by the mass slaughter of Americans?"

By the time the selective options strategy was articulated, American strategists were already worrying about the next phase in the central strategic relationship, vulnerability to intercontinental ballistic missiles (ICBMs). They were contemplating the point, a few years hence, when the Soviet Union would have the theoretical capability to destroy all American land-based ICBMs in a first strike—the famous "window of vulnerability" that three American administrations tried without success to close.[14] And so the cycle began again.

The question for NATO's future is whether this cycle of concern and adaptation has come to an end. Will the next cycle of change in central deterrence and doubt about extended deterrence produce not a new strategic adjustment, but something very different from the alliance as it has existed for forty years? Put differently, how much longer can NATO sustain the fig leaf of credibility covering its deterrent threat to use nuclear weapons first if need be—to say, in effect, that Europe is important enough to the United States for the latter to commit murder-suicide on the former's behalf?

In other areas, such as the Persian Gulf, this shrinkage of the area over which nuclear deterrence can be extended makes nuclear threats all but incredible. Yet nuclear deterrence operates indirectly to limit superpower military options through what is now called "existential deterrence": simply because both sides have nuclear weapons in large numbers, *any* direct confrontation between them might lead to nuclear war, and so both behave with extreme caution if such a confrontation might ensue. When the superpowers send nuclear signals, such as the American nuclear alert during the 1973 Middle East war, they seek to enhance that deterrence by reminding their rival of it and by underscoring their interest in the stakes at play.

Collective Security or Self-Help?

Extended conventional deterrence means alliance or at least a security guarantee, an intersection of my two subjects; in the first several postwar years, the European states sought to deter Soviet attack by an alliance among themselves without military structure. As before, an attack on one would be considered an attack on all. Their expectations about the United States in those years were similarly limited; they sought, in the 1949 North Atlantic Treaty, an automatic mutual assistance treaty on the model of the 1947 Anglo-French Treaty of Dunkirk. In contrast, American thinking first ran to some sort of unilateral American guarantee as a backstop to defense arrangements established by the Europeans themselves.[15]

This history is a reminder that collective security covers a variety of arrangements. NATO is the most complete and formal of such arrangements, since it has been given form through an integrated military command and the stationing of foreign forces on the territory of the alliance partners to be defended. As such, it is a historical rarity. The U.S. commitment to Japan is another sort of security guarantee, in which diplomatic propriety precludes use of the term "alliance" and nuclear threats lurk in the background. That nuclear promise is less manifest than in the case of Europe; its credibility depends in part on the value of the stakes being defended, and in part on the fact that any aggression against Japan, as an island, would necessarily be clear.

The credibility of the U.S. commitment to Korea has been beset since the war there. Thus, more effort is required in the form of ground forces to sustain the security arrangement, especially because the power to be deterred is North Korea, not the Soviet Union. The U.S. commitment to Israel is at least as strong as that to Japan, with a similar shunning of "alliance" and even less pronounced nuclear influence. Nonetheless, it is clear, especially to the other superpower, that the United States will ensure Israel's survival, at least to the extent that the other superpower can control *its* clients.

American security guarantees to conservative Arab states, while vague and sometimes even denied but nevertheless backed by military presence, seem to have played a role in deterring an expansion of the Iran-Iraq War, although, in the nature of deterrence, it is impossible to know whether the result was success or happenstance. At the other extreme, Mexico falls within the security umbrella of the United States whether it likes it or not, as Finland falls within that of the Soviet Union.

Classically, small powers sought alliances to counterbalance larger rivals. The process is inherently unstable, as most of the work on alliances has noted.[16] Small powers have built-in incentives to undercontribute to the alliance—what economists call "free riding"—for they know that no matter how great their effort, it will be small in comparison with that of their larger ally(ies).[17] The dependence implied by these alliances is also chafing for small states, perhaps all the more so when there is no obvious alternative to it.

After the Congress of Vienna, the European powers managed for a century to keep the peace, Crimea excepted, through a shifting set of alliances. Their task was facilitated, perhaps, by the fact that the powers had roughly similar political systems that understood each other relatively well: ideology did not complicate their calculations. Yet even their arrangement could not be sustained; when it collapsed it led, if not to a war none of them wanted, at least to a disastrous kind of war none sought.

Modern alliances seem harder to sustain. The available evidence indicates that small states still seek to balance larger powers more than they are tempted to "bandwagon" by joining those powers.[18] Ideology, or at least a drive to national assertion, seems likely to make alliances more tactical or fleeting: witness the disarray among the Arab states in the Middle East despite the presence of a common bugbear.

These complications make the longevity of NATO all the more surprising. NATO had the special advantages of a vivid experience to drive home the dangers of division—World War II—plus a visible adversary, and a high degree of commonality in political systems, even if its members probably did not understand each other as well as the European powers before World War I. Yet even NATO now suffers the divisive forces: strategically, of the diminished credibility of extended deterrence; and politically, of the simple fading into memory of the reasons that called the alliance forth.

Looking to the future, older forms of collective security may be replaced by newer ones. Already, many of the alliances are quasi-alliances, the guarantees tacit, not explicit. It is worth remembering that the UN was to have its own military command; is it out of the question that warming superpower relations and, in particular, their shared awareness of the danger of regional instability might lead them from tacit cooperation to explicit common action?

Conversely, the difficulty of both extending deterrence and sustaining explicit collective security arrangements augurs for more self-help by individual nations. So far, few of them have resorted to nuclear self-help; despite incentives for doing so, the nuclear taboo has remained strong.[19] The states that have broken the taboo—Israel, South Africa, and India, in particular—have done so by creating nuclear options rather than explicit nuclear arsenals.

They have discovered what the superpowers knew: nuclear weapons may serve as ultimate guarantors of national survival, but they cannot be compellers. The neighbors of Israel or South Africa can never be sure that those countries would not unleash nuclear havoc if their survival as nations were threatened, but short of that point, the fact of their nuclear status makes almost no difference. Indeed, the Arab states have come close to a tacit acceptance of a nuclear Israel, having little choice in the matter.

Might American allies, West Germany or even Japan, be tempted to nuclear self-help? The prospect strains the imagination. But General de Gaulle's logic was impeccable, even if he was careful not to take it to its conclusion: if Europeans (or Japanese) doubt that the United States would push the nuclear button on their behalf, they need buttons of their own, with nuclear weapons to match. And, inadvertently, the United States is underscoring that logic—having at last understood how robust central deterrence is, it seems to be forgetting how fragile extended deterrence can be, a forgetfulness reflected particularly in its recent arms control choices.

Conclusion

The main points of this chapter may be summarized as follows:

- Conventional deterrence is not foolproof, but sustaining credible defenses is a necessary, if not sufficient, condition for deterring aggression.
- Nuclear deterrence is robust but limited: robust in deterring a nuclear, and probably conventional, attack on one's homeland, but limited elsewhere.
- The United States has sought to sustain extended nuclear deterrence through a series of cycles of concern and adaptation, especially in Europe.
- A central question for the future is whether that extended deterrence can be sustained.
- Alliances seem harder to sustain in the modern world, given ideology and drives for national assertion, but new forms of collective security may arise.
- Over a longer time period, nuclear self-help is a real prospect—particularly in the Third World, but also in Europe—and such a prospect seems, on balance, likely to be unstable.

Discussion

In commenting on Treverton's presentation, Bruce Russett raised some important questions concerning vital aspects of deterrence about which little is known:

- What percentage of every successful deterrence effort is attributable not only to coercion and credibility, but also to reassurances and nonprovocative action? Russett noted that just as appeasement may lead to aggression, so, too, can "bullying or excessive coercion." He also indicated that successful deterrence requires a delicate mixture of toughness and conciliation.
- What are the more important differences between general deterrence (which prevents a crisis from happening in the first place) and immediate deterrence (which contains a crisis once it has occurred)? For instance, why is it that for 150 years no significant crisis occurred between Britain and Argentina over the Malvinas/Falkland Islands?
- Are deterrence crises always the result of aggressive behavior? Can it be argued that the most notable failure of deterrence in this century—namely, the Japanese attack on Pearl Harbor—was the direct result of a perception on the part of the Japanese that they could not otherwise

successfully prosecute their war against China and so, for reasons of self-defense, had to attack the United States?

- To what extent do domestic influences create benign or aggressive images of potential adversaries? Did domestic issues lead European politicians to take a more benign view of Hitler in 1938? Under what domestic political conditions, if any, are decisionmakers likely to be more adventurous, tougher, and less willing to concede even small points?

Russett concluded by noting that a key problem in analyzing the success of deterrence, particularly nuclear deterrence, is that we have few examples of its outright failure. Hence, much of the analysis of deterrence is "deductive, rational analysis, and selectively empirical." The best way to overcome this obstacle, Russett said, is to engage in large-scale comparative studies or smaller focused comparisons and to attempt to "systematically draw out similarities and differences."

In the discussion, Myres McDougal challenged Treverton's characterization of peace—"the absence of war"—as too narrow and suggested that peace could be more accurately defined as the absence of unauthorized coercion. The real problem, he continued, is how to make protection from such coercion more collective.

Robert Pickus suggested that a possible mechanism for new forms of collectivism might be the plethora of individuals, organizations, and institutions that operate beyond national boundaries and seek to broaden the international public's vested interest in a more peaceful environment. Russett suggested that a logical application of this theory would be to use the United Nations as a forum for resolving any future nuclear crisis.

Treverton responded that, at least on the nuclear level, the trend seems to be away from new collective action and toward nuclear "self-help" measures; for example, nonsuperpower states (such as South Africa and Israel) seek to obtain nuclear weapons not to compel other states to act in a specific fashion, but to ensure their continued national survival by deterring potential adversaries from engaging in aggression. As the general credibility of nuclear threats wanes, he added, this might be the only type of nuclear deterrence that will be workable in the future.

This assertion raised another problem inherent to the study of conflict: What are the appropriate boundaries of self-defense? Oscar Schachter suggested that the notion of self-defense needs substantial clarification. Reminding the audience of Russett's point that the Japanese considered their attack on Pearl Harbor to be an act of self-defense, he emphasized the need for clear definitions and suggested that a more precise understanding of what objectively constitutes self-defense is a critical component of any discussion of deterrence and collective security.

Russett agreed, noting that because of the anarchic nature of the international system, nations still have to rely on self-help measures for their own security; hence, definitions of self-defense tend to be individualistic. The problem is, however, that weapons systems and alliances that look, and are intended to be, defensive to one state may appear to be provocative to another. The result is what has been termed the security dilemma: sometimes what nations do to try to make themselves more secure has the opposite effect.

Notes

1. Thomas C. Schelling, *The Strategy of Conflict* (New York: Oxford University Press, 1960).

2. Thomas C. Schelling, "What Went Wrong with Arms Control?" *Foreign Affairs* 62, no. 4 (Winter 1985–86): p. 233.

3. There are many reviews of new technology and conventional defense. For a good one, see *New Technology and Western Security: Parts II–III*, Adelphi Papers Nos. 197–9 (London: International Institute for Strategic Studies (IISS), Summer 1985).

4. For an intriguing analysis, see Carl Builder, *The Prospects and Implications of Non-Nuclear Means for Strategic Conflict*, Adelphi Paper No. 200 (London: IISS, Summer 1985).

5. The most influential of these theorists was Giulio Douhet, whose work is excerpted in Philip Bobbitt, Lawrence Freedman, and Gregory F. Treverton, eds., *U.S. Nuclear Strategy: A Reader* (New York: St. Martin's Press, 1988).

6. The survey is excerpted in Bobbitt, Freedman, and Treverton, *U.S. Nuclear Strategy*; the conclusion is, for understandable reasons, more between the lines than on them.

7. Bernard Brodie, *The Atomic Bomb and American Security*, Yale Institute of International Studies Memorandum No. 18, November 1945, reprinted in Bobbitt, Freedman, and Treverton, *U.S. Nuclear Strategy*.

8. The worry that the presumption of rationality, in the sense of value-maximizing behavior by a unitary decisionmaker, was being stretched too far led to at least two streams of work. One concentrated on perception and misperception; see Robert Jervis, "Deterrence and Perception," in Steven E. Miller, ed., *Strategy and Nuclear Deterrence* (Princeton, N.J.: Princeton University Press, 1984). The other was renewed emphasis on the role of organizations and politics in decision making, for which the best-known summary is Graham T. Allison, *Essence of Decision* (Boston: Little, Brown, and Co., 1971).

9. Richard K. Betts, "A Nuclear Golden Age? The Balance Before Parity," *International Security* 11, no. 3 (Winter 1986–87): p. 3–32.

10. This phrase is from an early, influential critique of massive retaliation by William W. Kaufmann, published in 1956 but circulated two years earlier. See his "Requirements of Deterrence," in William W. Kaufmann, ed., *Military Policy and National Security* (Princeton, N.J.: Princeton University Press, 1956), reprinted in Bobbitt, Freedman, and Treverton, *U.S. Nuclear Strategy*.

11. This argument is spelled out thoroughly and provocatively in Philip Bobbitt, *Democracy and Deterrence* (New York: St. Martin's Press, 1987).

12. McNamara's famous speech to the NATO ministerial meeting in Athens, May 5, 1962, where he foreshadowed flexible response, is now declassified. It is reprinted in Bobbitt, Freedman, and Treverton, *U.S. Nuclear Strategy*. The best formulation of the argument for restraint in nuclear war remains Thomas C. Schelling, *Controlled Response and Strategic Warfare*, Adelphi Paper No. 19 (London: IISS, 1965). For a public articulation of mutual assured destruction, see McNamara's speech on September 18, 1967, reprinted in *U.S. News and World Report* (October 2, 1967): p. 106–11.

13. See Schlesinger's *Annual Defense Department Report, FY 1975* (Washington, D.C., 1974) p. 25ff., reprinted in Bobbitt, Freedman, and Treverton, *U.S. Nuclear Strategy*. For a thoughtful discussion of the strategy, see Lynn Etheridge Davis, *Limited Nuclear Options: Deterrence and the New American Doctrine*, Adelphi Paper No. 121 (London: IISS, 1976).

14. In the end, President Reagan's panel, the Scowcroft Commission, named after its chairman, Gen. Brent Scowcroft, declared the "window" unimportant. See *Report of the President's Commission on Strategic Forces* (Washington, D.C., April 1983).

15. On this early history, see Alan K. Henrikson, "The Creation of the North Atlantic Alliance, 1948–1952," *National War College Review* 22, no. 3 (May–June 1980).

16. For a summary of this work, see Ole R. Holsti, "International Alliances: A Survey of Theories and Propositions," in Ole R. Holsti et al., eds., *Unity and Disintegration in International Alliances* (New York: Wiley, 1973). See also chapter 1 of Gregory Treverton, *Making the Alliance Work: The United States and Western Europe* (London and Ithaca: Macmillan and Cornell University Press, 1985).

17. Mancur Olson, Jr., and Richard Zeckhauser, "An Economic Theory of Alliances," *Review of Economics and Statistics* (August 1966).

18. For evidence from the Middle East, see Stephen M. Walt, *The Origin of Alliances* (Ithaca, N.Y.: Cornell University Press, 1987).

19. For an argument that nuclear proliferation may not be destabilizing, see Kenneth N. Waltz, *The Spread of Nuclear Weapons: More May Be Better*, Adelphi Paper No. 171 (London: IISS, 1981).

Bibliography

The now-classic works on nuclear deterrence are associated with the names of Thomas Schelling, Bernard Brodie, and Herman Kahn. See Brodie, ed., *The Absolute Weapon: Atomic Power and World Order* (New York: Harcourt Brace, 1946); *Strategy in the Missile Age* (Princeton, N.J.: Princeton University Press, 1959); Schelling, *The Strategy of Conflict* (New York: Oxford University Press, 1960); *Arms and Influence* (New Haven, Conn.: Yale University Press, 1965); and Kahn, *On Thermonuclear War* (Princeton, N.J.: Princeton University Press, 1960), *On Escalation: Metaphors and Scenarios* (Westport, Conn.: Greenwood Press, 1965).

On the interaction of central and extended deterrence, see Philip Bobbitt, *Democracy and Deterrence* (New York: St. Martin's Press, 1987).

On perception and misperception, see Robert Jervis, "Deterrence and Perception," in Steven E. Miller, ed., *Strategy and Nuclear Deterrence* (Princeton, N.J.: Princeton University Press, 1984).

For a broad survey on alliances, see Ole R. Holsti, "International Alliances: A Survey of Theories and Propositions," in Ole R. Holsti et al., eds., *Unity and Disintegration in International Alliances* (New York: Wiley, 1973).

For an argument from the perspective of rational self-interest, see Mancur Olson, Jr., and Richard Zeckhauser, "An Economic Theory of Alliances," *Review of Economics and Statistics* (August 1966); Chapter 1 of Gregory F. Treverton, *Making the Alliance Work: The United States and Western Europe* (London and Ithaca, N.Y.: Macmillan and Cornell University Press, 1985), which applies some of these propositions to the European-American alliance.

For an intriguing argument about alliance formation applied to the Middle East, see Stephen M. Walt, *The Origin of Alliances* (Ithaca, N.Y.: Cornell University Press, 1987).

Introduction to Chapter 3

Although many people view diplomacy and negotiation as synonymous terms—interchangeable in usage, identical in content—David Newsom considers negotiation but one component of the broader mosaic of diplomacy and, for most diplomats, a limited one at that. The problem stems, in part, from what Newsom sees as an attempt by negotiation and conflict resolution theorists to apply the principles of domestic conflict resolution—with its agreed set of norms, rules, and laws—to the international environment, where these elemental characteristics do not exist. Furthermore, Newsom adds, the rather high success rate of domestic conflict resolution efforts leads to over optimistic estimates of the utility of international negotiations, as well as the erroneous assumption that the United States is uniquely suited to intervene diplomatically in all international disputes.

Defining diplomacy as "the maintenance of relationships with foreign governments in the pursuit of the interests of the United States," Newsom sees the primary role of the diplomat as identifying and gaining access to the key persons in the decision-making structure of the foreign government in question. Only then can the issues and terms of any potential negotiation be defined and the skills of the able negotiator properly used.

There can be little doubt, Newsom points out, that conflict emerges from the profound historical depths of a society and that decisions to initiate or to end conflict are made within the power structures of that society. Therefore, the ability to prevent conflict from occurring, or to manage it once it begins, depends on a clear understanding of those structures and of the leaders within them. The secrets of who holds power, who favors peace and who does not, who makes decisions and how they can be influenced are the key questions that diplomats must answer, according to Newsom.

In other words, Newsom sees the current debate between the diplomat as practitioner and the negotiation specialist as theorist as a classic case of putting the cart before the horse. The debate should not be framed around the issue of whether negotiating processes can be studied and taught to potential negotiators. Failure to analyze, dissect, and learn from experience is a liability in any endeavor. The discussion of negotiation as it relates to diplomacy should first emphasize the intricate steps leading up to the point at which negotiation has a legitimate chance of influencing an outcome. Otherwise, one runs the serious risk of overemphasizing a symptom while ignoring the root cause of the malady.

3. Diplomacy and Negotiation

David D. Newsom

This chapter analyzes current historical scholarship and practice in diplomacy and negotiation, as reflected by the relevant literature and policy trends, and relates this analysis directly to the purposes of the United States Institute of Peace. A review of the literature currently available is followed by suggestions for research that could contribute additional insights into the ability of the United States to play an influential role in the resolution of conflicts around the world.

The United States Institute of Peace defines itself as "an independent institution established by Congress to strengthen the nation's capacity to promote peaceful resolution of international conflicts." The emphasis in its work to date has been on diplomacy through negotiation. James Laue, in the first issue of the United States Institute of Peace *Journal,* stated, "Most of us working in the field [of diplomacy] generally see negotiation as the core of it." To the diplomatic practitioner and the experienced policymaker this approach to the problems of conflict resolution is excessively narrow, yet it tends to be perpetuated by much of the current literature. To assume that the road to peace lies largely in the technique of mastering the art of bargaining is to rule out the intricate problems involved in bringing disputing parties to the table in the first place.

Inevitably, in any approach to matters of diplomacy, definitional problems arise. In *Modern Diplomacy: The Art and the Artisans,* Elmer Plischke lists six "interpretations" of diplomacy: international relations, foreign relations, conduct of foreign relations, implementation of foreign policy, communications, and negotiation.[1] Each of these interpretations embraces several arts beyond that of negotiating: analyzing, reporting, persuading, and relating to individuals and institutions. For the purposes of this chapter, diplomacy is defined as the maintenance of relationships with foreign governments in the pursuit of the interests of the United States. One of those interests historically has been to use the influence of the United States to prevent and resolve conflict, particularly in areas that are directly tied to the security of this country and in areas where regional conflict may carry the risk of wider war through confrontation with the Soviet Union.

The Literature

At least six categories of published material can be identified as relating directly to the purposes of the United States Institute of Peace. These categories do not include works in other disciplines that also bear on the international issues and techniques involved in diplomacy and negotiation. A full list would include, at a minimum, studies in comparative politics, geography, economics, sociology, anthropology, history, and psychology. In assessing the capacity of the United States to exercise influence abroad, analyses of the attitudes and politics in the United States also become relevant.[2]

The first of the six categories includes books and articles that concentrate on the theories and practices of international negotiations. Such works include *The Practical Negotiator* by I. William Zartman and Maureen R. Berman,[3] *How Nations Negotiate* by Fred Iklé,[4] and *The Art and Science of Negotiation* by Howard Raiffa.[5] Other books, such as Roger Fisher and William Ury's *Getting to Yes*[6] and Herbert Cohen's *You Can Negotiate Anything*,[7] are written for wider audiences and suggest that the principles that resolve domestic conflicts can be applied to international problems.

In recent years, efforts have been made to build a body of case studies based on actual negotiations. Six schools of international affairs—Columbia, Georgetown, Harvard, Pittsburgh, Princeton, and the University of Southern California—are involved in such a project under the auspices of the Pew Charitable Trusts. The Institute for the Study of Diplomacy at Georgetown University has published case studies that relate to the processes of diplomacy and negotiation.[8] Similar works have been produced by the Center for the Study of Foreign Affairs of the State Department's Foreign Service Institute.[9] Some scholarship is also directed at future negotiations; an example is the Council on Foreign Relations study *The Philippine Bases: Negotiating for the Future*.[10]

A second category includes a growing set of works on the negotiating styles of individual cultures and states. The Center for the Study of Foreign Affairs at the Foreign Service Institute has made a specialty of this aspect. The book published by the center in 1987 under the editorship of Hans Binnendijk titled *National Negotiation Styles* is an example.[11]

Third are books, some of them centuries old, on the processes of diplomacy, such as the work of François de Callières, *The Art of Diplomacy*, written in 1715.[12] These books reflect the traditional styles by which official representatives of government conduct their business. They also touch on the art of negotiation and, in the case of Harold Nicolson's *Diplomacy*,[13] on national styles as well. Nicolson, for example, has this to say about the diplomacy of the United States:

> The Americans…are convinced that all diplomatists are determined to ensnare, entangle, and humiliate all those with whom they negotiate. They enter a

conference as Daniel entered the den of lions, conscious that it is only their own bright faith and innocence which will preserve them from the claws of the wild beasts by whom they are surrounded.[14]

Three other books currently available are essentially handbooks for the conduct of relations between and among nations. *The Guide to Diplomatic Practice*, first published in 1917 by Sir Ernest Satow, has now been revised and reissued under the editorship of Lord Gore-Booth.[15] R.G. Feltham, for many years head of the diplomatic training program at Oxford, has published *Diplomatic Handbook*, covering virtually every aspect of the organization and practices of diplomacy.[16] R.P. Barston, of the Department of Politics at the University of Lancaster in England, has sought to bring the literature on diplomacy and negotiation up to date in his *Modern Diplomacy*.[17]

Fourth, a series of books on international business negotiation contains useful insights that apply to the political and diplomatic realms as well. More than many of the books directed at political negotiation, a business-oriented book by Frederick Posses, *The Art of International Negotiation*, stresses important cultural aspects.[18]

Fifth are the memoirs of diplomats, which can be mined for valuable and instructive experiences in the conduct of affairs with other countries and the resolution of conflict, but tend at times to be too anecdotal and self-serving. Three that do not fall into these traps but instead contain both entertaining and pertinent comments on the practices of diplomacy and negotiation are Charles Thayer's *Diplomat*,[19] Ellis Briggs's *Farewell to Foggy Bottom*,[20] and George Kennan's *Memoirs*.[21]

Finally, books and studies on the structure of power, not always related in bibliographies to the discipline of conflict resolution, are valuable guides to the assessment of other societies. Two that have a direct bearing on the ability to predict the conduct of individuals and governments in a conflict situation are Harold Lasswell's *Power and Personality*[22] and James Mac-Gregor Burns's *Leadership*.[23]

If the task of the United States Institute of Peace were only to train negotiators, the literature that concentrates solely on negotiation might be adequate. But the Institute's broader goal of conflict resolution requires more focus on how the United States acquires the necessary knowledge of other societies and, with that knowledge, establishes the degree of influence necessary to prevent conflict or to influence the course of conflict when it occurs.

Conflict springs from the most profound emotional and historical depths of a society. Decisions to initiate and to end conflict are made within the power structure of a nation-state or movement; understanding the possibilities and limitations of intervention for peace depends on a knowledge of that structure and its leading personalities. In the countries involved in conflict today, gaining such knowledge often requires penetrating a closed, authoritarian, suspicious, and sensitive environment. Academic studies and language proficiency are important, but the essential secrets of who holds power, who makes decisions, who favors peace, and who does not may often be locked in the closeness of the society. Several recent events illustrate the problems facing U.S. diplomats who seek to penetrate the curtain protecting that society.

In Iran, before the fall of the shah, portents in the thoughts of the ayatollahs of Qom were expressed primarily in the Friday sermons at the mosques. Not only were foreigners excluded from the Shiite mosques, but the shah also specifically forbade foreign diplomats from having contact with the religious leaders. The restrictions were understood to apply also to contacts with all opposition political elements. In his book on the United States and the Iranian revolution, *All Fall Down*, Gary Sick speaks of these restrictions:

> For at least a decade the United States had viewed its relations with Iran almost exclusively as relations with the person of the shah. There probably never was a formal order to avoid contacts with Iranian opposition groups, but there was a clear awareness that the shah was annoyed and suspicious about such contacts and they gradually dried up.[24]

The ability of the United States to influence Iran's attitude toward conflict was clearly limited by the absence of access to significant levels of society in the shah's day, and it remains so now.

The United States has faced similar problems more recently in other important countries. An understanding of the society of Saudi Arabia is necessary for a full assessment of the prospects of both peace and economic stability in the Middle East and beyond. In April 1989, the U.S. government was asked to replace its ambassador in Riyadh, an experienced diplomat, who sought actively to broaden the contacts of the embassy and the knowledge of that society.[25] Two months later, a U.S. diplomat was asked to leave Singapore, a nation of both strategic and economic interest to the United States, because of his contacts with the political opposition.[26]

A cliché popular among those who seek a better assessment of foreign societies is that the U.S. government needs more diplomats fluent in foreign languages and familiar with foreign cultures. It is true, yet our experience in Iran and Saudi Arabia shows the limitations of this wisdom. One of the most fluent Farsi speakers among U.S. hostages held by the Iranians in the 1970s, Michael Metrinko, received the harshest treatment.[27] And Ambassador Hume Horan, who was recalled from Riyadh at Saudi request, is one of the most fluent Arab speakers in the foreign service.

Areas for Research

These and similar incidents suggest at least six areas for further research relating to the access of the United States and its diplomats to other societies. This knowledge is essential if the Institute is to achieve its objective of enhancing the capacity of the United States to intervene effectively in international conflicts.

First, it is important to study the problem of access for U.S. officials, scholars, businessmen, and journalists to leaders and potential leaders in closed societies whether in non-Communist authoritarian governments or in those under Communist rule. What obstacles have been encountered? What approaches have worked? Do some Americans have easier access than others? What role does sympathy for a regime play in access? If access is provided to nonofficial Americans through such sympathy, can or should they share their insights with official Americans?

Second, a study of the possibilities of clandestine access in closed societies would provide a balance sheet of the risks and benefits. Much attention is given to covert political action, but less to the techniques and results of the clandestine collection of intelligence, often vital to an understanding of the possibilities of negotiation and conflict resolution. This subject is obviously a difficult one for unclassified research, yet it might be possible, without involving a knowledge of sources and methods, to compare the relative value and accuracy of information on such societies acquired by clandestine methods and information obtained through open contacts.

Third, today's diplomats are constrained by the need for greater diplomatic security.[28] American diplomats today work in a fortresslike environment that is inhibiting to politically sensitive visitors; the Americans also move conspicuously in convoys with security guards in a manner that is offensive to indigenous pride. The push to eliminate national employees from U.S. embassies in Eastern Europe and to restrict their activities in other parts of the world further reduces Americans' contact with local populations abroad. In the Middle East, apprehension over risk has resulted in the elimination of any effective U.S. observation of two key Arab states: Libya and Lebanon.

Fourth, access is affected not only by security concerns but also by the unpopularity of U.S. foreign policies. In some parts of the world—the Arab world, for example—nationals of a country are reluctant to associate with U.S. diplomats and to attend events at their embassy for this reason. This unpopularity of U.S. policies certainly inhibits the acquisition of the knowledge necessary to make the United States an effective actor in conflict resolution in some regions of the world. These policies cannot, however, be reshaped solely to provide access for diplomats. A study of the relationship of local attitudes to diplomatic access is, nevertheless, essential to an assessment of the U.S. capacity to influence the course of a regional conflict.

Fifth, many sources of information do not require personal access; the information media, for example, even in a closed society can reveal much about the circumstances of that society. A pertinent question for study would involve how one reads between the lines of a controlled press to predict changes in policies or leadership. The Foreign Broadcast Information Service (FBIS) is an important source for information of this kind and has demonstrated its ability to predict important political change through observing subtle changes in the output of an official broadcasting service. FBIS was the first, for example, to predict the Chinese-Soviet split, solely on the basis of unclassified intercepts of Chinese broadcasts. Scant literature appears to exist on this aspect of societal analysis.

Sixth, information is only as good as the use made of it. The intelligence gap, in the experience of many officials, seldom exists because of a lack of some knowledge about a given region or its potential for peace or war. The problem is more likely to be the unwillingness of officials to accept information that was contrary to conventional wisdom or would require politically embarrassing changes in announced positions. Bad news is unwelcome and the diplomatic messenger often suffers.

John Stempel, in his book *Inside the Iranian Revolution*, speaks of several elements that should receive closer attention if the United States is to avoid further miscalculations in foreign affairs:

> If policy makers had been sensitized in 1976 and 1977 to the increasing likelihood of instability [in Iran], the outcome could have been different. Encouraging a healthy dose of suspicion is another [example of how the United States might have better reacted to the situation], especially since too many policy and decision makers rejected out of hand analyses opposed to established American policy.[29]

Any study of this aspect should include the problems that arise in communicating information from the field and in handling that information in Washington. This subject obviously is not an easy one for a nonpartisan study, but numerous examples illustrate the point. *International Conflict Resolution*, by Edward Azar and John Burton, has a pertinent paragraph:

> Problem solving often involves consideration of decision-making processes. Frequently parties in conflicts assume that the other side acts rationally, that what it does it intended to do and that a whole theory of its behavior can be built in a coherent logical way. At home, of course, things are not like that at all. At home it is a mess, it is chaos, it is short-term fixing. Things happen which were never intended to happen and decision makers are trapped into a framework from which they would like to escape, but do not know how. Actions frequently have unintended consequences that are deplored, but that cannot be wished away. To help people understand the process of decision making by the different parties is a frequent task of a facilitator. Furthermore, it is important to see how political leaders often get riveted into, and entrapped by, a particular policy which they

cannot abandon despite its obvious cost and lack of success. Once good money has been spent on a bad option it is very difficult politically to give up that option.[30]

In addition to research into questions of diplomatic access, more study is needed on the means by which the United States establishes its influence in areas of conflict, particularly in the Third World. Because the United States is a superpower, many foreigners, for their own reasons, urge U.S. involvement in conflict situations, often exaggerating the actual influence that Washington might exert. The result can be unpleasant surprises, frustrations, and prolonged involvement in conflicts where U.S. interests may be minimal or at least debatable.

Factors Affecting U.S. Influence

The influence of the United States in any conflict is determined by at least six factors: the national objective, U.S. credibility abroad, imposed conditions, degree of U.S. leverage, degree of U.S. persuasiveness, and the alternatives. Each of these factors deserves more study.

The establishment of a national objective toward the resolution of a conflict requires the creation of a national consensus. That consensus was lacking in the debate over foreign policy objectives that was especially virulent during the Reagan administration. For example, does the United States perceive Third World conflicts as primarily regional problems or as extensions of the confrontation with the Soviet Union? From these differing perceptions flow different objectives. Where cases are perceived to be primarily regional, Americans are prepared to accept compromise in the interest of a solution. That is less true where regional conflict is seen as an episode in a superpower competition; the objective in such situations is generally to try to impose an American solution.

The effectiveness of intervention in the interest of conflict resolution relates directly to the degree that a national consensus emerges from an internal domestic debate. U.S. effectiveness is clearly diminished if one side views the possibility of division in the United States as beneficial to that side.

Americans generally supported covert action in Afghanistan because a national consensus existed in favor of such action. Such was not the case in Nicaragua, where differing voices within and outside that nation resulted in a polarization of views in the United States. Robert Pastor, in his book about the United States and the Nicaraguan revolution, *Condemned to Repetition*, writes,

Carter's policy may have been hitched to certain moral principles, but it was not made in a political vacuum. From the beginning, the Administration was subject to stinging criticism from Somoza's friends and enemies. While trying to heal the divisions of Nicaragua, the United States found itself contracting the same dreaded disease of political polarization.[31]

Closely related to national consensus at home is the question of U.S. credibility abroad. The possibility of successful intervention in the resolution of conflict is enhanced by the degree to which the United States is seen by the contesting parties as a thoroughly objective mediator. In recent years, U.S. credibility as an impartial intervenor in the Middle East has been lost as the United States came to be perceived as a party to a conflict rather than as a neutral outsider. In 1958, when the United States sent marines to Lebanon, the intervention was followed by a successful mediation of Lebanon's internal political quarrel; peace in that complex country existed for a decade thereafter. The 1982 U.S. intervention was seen as partial to Lebanon's Christian leadership, backed by Israel, and disaster resulted.

The credibility of a peacemaker is also related to the conditions imposed before negotiations begin. If, as in the case of the U.S. opposition to the participation of the Palestine Liberation Organization in the Middle East peace process, such conditions are identified with one of the contesting parties, U.S. credibility suffers. Certainly, a realistic position requires that a peacemaker relay the conditions that one party may impose on the other; but there is an important distinction between relaying conditions and defining them, as a precondition to mediation.

A study of U.S. leverage is also needed. Current literature seems to provide little information, for example, on the usefulness of economic or military assistance programs in establishing U.S. influence in conflict regions. It is common to say that official programs provide leverage, but, in fact, the inflexible process of legislating and administering aid makes such programs ineffective in this context. Furthermore, the amount of U.S. assistance in relation to total assistance these countries receive from other sources is often too small to give Washington any degree of influence. In Israel and Egypt, where large U.S. aid programs exist, Washington is reluctant to use those programs as leverage.

The power of the United States to gain leverage in a situation also depends on the degree to which parties to the conflict seek U.S. intervention. Is the initiative generated in Washington in order to meet domestic pressures for action, or does it come as the result of credible requests from the parties? On what basis does the United States accept an invitation to intervene? Secretary of State Alexander Haig believed that U.S. interests required his active mediation of the Malvinas/Falkland Islands crisis between Argentina and Britain. Although both sides expressed an interest in U.S. intervention, it became increasingly clear that Argentina was reluctant to place its interests in U.S. hands. Without that degree of confidence, mediation had slim prospects for success.[32]

When the United States does not, by virtue of other relationships, possess leverage, can influence be created through powers of persuasion? This question suggests a study of the links between so-called public diplomacy and conflict resolution. Every effort can be made, as Secretary of State George Shultz attempted in the Middle East in the closing days of the Reagan administration, to gain acceptance of intervention through normal diplomatic channels. In a day of rapid public communication, however, such an approach is often not enough. The official diplomacy must be supplemented by public utterances—President Reagan's constructive speech of September 1, 1982, on the Middle East is an example. It provided, briefly, a window of opportunity, but events in both Washington and the region precluded the follow-up that was necessary. A related question is the degree to which citizens' groups in contact with counterpart groups in conflict areas can enhance the effectiveness of a U.S. official role through their conferences and visits. In general, experience suggests that such groups can provide useful insights to another side, but that private groups or individuals can seldom substitute for official channels.

Finally, a complete coverage of the possibilities of U.S. action in conflict resolution must include a look at the alternatives. The objectives of the United States Institute of Peace appear to emphasize a unilateral role for the United States. The low regard in which the UN is held by the United States has, until recently, at least, made Washington less receptive to a UN role. Yet a look around the world today at successful conflict resolution efforts—Afghanistan being one example—suggests the effectiveness of the UN umbrella and the usefulness of Security Council resolutions as a basis for negotiations. As this chapter is being written, opportunities for the resolution of conflict appear to exist in the Iran-Iraq War, Cyprus, Cambodia, the Sahara, and southern Africa. Only in the last is the United States a central player. Although U.S. policies may have contributed to the movements toward peace in these areas, future studies should examine why the warring nations have turned elsewhere for the significant role of mediator.

Conclusion

In this assessment of the literature, I may have overlooked relevant scholarship. I agree with the Institute's position that the United States should play a constructive role in the resolution of conflict. At the same time, I believe that the focus of the Institute, and of much of the current academic literature of which I am aware, oversimplifies how the necessary knowledge and influence are to be achieved.

My specific conclusions are as follows:

- The principles of conflict resolution as they have developed under the umbrella of an agreed body of law in the United States cannot be applied easily to international conflicts where no such body of law exists.

- Negotiation is not the core of the problem but the final stage in a process that involves profound understanding of other cultures, sensitivity to the internal politics of one's own country as well as those of others, and a judgment of the relative effectiveness of unilateral and multilateral intervention. As de Callières said of a diplomat in 1715, "To have a particular knowledge of the interests of the Princes and States of Europe, it is necessary that he learn exactly wherein the strength, the revenue, the power of each Prince, and of each Commonwealth, does consist and how far it extends."[33] That applies today to the diplomat who must work, not only in Europe, but in all the world.

- We as a nation cannot assume that we are ordained by our position or our judgment to be effective in the resolution of conflict unless we are ready to meet with any representatives, no matter how repulsive; to recognize our limitations in understanding other societies; and to welcome the participation of other nations and organizations in regions where we cannot play an effective role.

Discussion

For commentator William Zartman, negotiation may be the end point of a much more fundamental process, as Newsom indicated, but it also represents the point at which the success or failure of most diplomatic efforts is ultimately determined. It is therefore only logical that negotiation be analyzed more critically and scientifically than it has been in the past, and that every effort be made to impart the results of that inquiry to people who may need the information in the future.

Unlike diplomacy, which has been formally studied for centuries, only in the past thirty years has negotiation been scrutinized by theorists as a distinct subject of study. In that time, significant progress has been made in building a coherent foundation for the future study of negotiation by drawing on the work of many scholars from a wide spectrum of fields. The purpose of this research has not been to supplant the diplomat or to reduce the craft of diplomacy to the art of negotiation, but to build a body of generalized knowledge, to examine the dynamics of negotiator interaction, and to discover how certain outcomes were obtained.

One of the most important outcomes of this research has been an enhanced appreciation for what Newsom referred to as "assessment." Although Zartman preferred the terms "prenegotiation" or "diagnostic stage," he shared Newsom's belief that, unless the proper groundwork is laid, there is little chance that any negotiation will be successful.

But negotiation analysts can go further. Whether it is the structuralist, behaviorist, or contextual school, each attempts to answer the basic question of power: What is it that determines or causes specific outcomes and under what conditions do those outcomes evolve? For Zartman, negotiation is still very much a trial-and-error process of trying to find the optimal outcomes for the largest number of parties. But as the field matures and more is learned from a variety of sources, diplomats will be able to draw on that knowledge and, using it in conjunction with the information gained in the prenegotiation stage, greatly enhance the prospects for a successful outcome.

Much of the general discussion generated by the Newsom-Zartman exchange concerned the question of negotiator training. Can diplomats, with the assistance of negotiation theorists and practitioners, be taught the skills necessary to conduct high-level diplomatic negotiations?

Both panelists agreed that training in negotiation is possible and useful, at least to some extent. In response to a question from John McDonald, Newsom said that the concepts of access, assessment, and persuasion can be examined in the classroom and that it is important to do so. People can even be trained to have a sense of negotiating technique—taught, for example, what to look for, how to anticipate the other side's position, and how to prepare fallback positions. But, he said, it is important not to oversimplify the process. More often than not, the problem is not so much what to do when one gets to the negotiating table, but how to get there. On the one hand, this concept is more difficult to teach because it is so situation specific; on the other hand, negotiation techniques are easier to teach because they can be dramatized. The important point to remember is that training in negotiating does not necessarily make negotiating any easier.

Responding to a comment from the floor concerning a perceived antipathy on the part of some State Department officials toward negotiator training, Zartman noted that, as in any other field, it is important for a new generation to build on the experiences of others. To say that certain negotiating techniques cannot be taught, or to deny that certain signposts occur over the course of a negotiation, is contrary to common sense. Negotiator training is not an end in itself; it must be combined with practice and experience.

When queried on the issues of different national negotiation styles and the different forms that negotiation can take (for example, multilateral as opposed to two-party), both panelists agreed that much research is needed in these areas. Domestic constraints and cultural traditions place limitations on even the most sophisticated diplomat. It is therefore essential for the negotiator, diplomatic or otherwise, to be able to identify and distinguish the attitudes and basic instincts of contending parties to lessen the chance of misinterpretation, particularly in dealing with closed or totalitarian societies and in multilateral negotiations, in which the emphasis tends to become more political than diplomatic.

In recent years, a certain amount of support has been given to unofficial or track-two diplomacy as a possible means by which to avoid cross-cultural miscommunication. The theory supporting this view is that unofficial and nongovernment contacts are not nearly as constrained by considerations of political propriety as official ones. With this theory in mind, a member of the audience suggested that such contacts, particularly between parallel nongovernment institutions such as churches, might be used to facilitate official diplomatic negotiations. This approach is especially appropriate in cases in which a stalemate has developed or the subject matter is too politically sensitive for open discussion.

Both panelists were skeptical of this approach. Newsom, citing experience during the course of a long diplomatic career, said that although private citizens and organizations have a role to play in furthering international relations, it was primarily a role of communication, not negotiation. He cautioned against accepting at face value the statements of unofficial actors concerning official negotiating positions. All too often, he said, negotiation breakthroughs communicated through unofficial actors prove inaccurate when explored through official channels.

These sentiments were echoed by Zartman, who added that state conflicts must be state solved; therefore, private efforts can, at best, be adjuncts to official state diplomatic efforts. Unofficial contacts should not be ignored, however; their usefulness in some cases has been documented. But much research remains to be done, Zartman said, to determine the full extent to which such efforts can be useful.

In concluding the session, panel chairman Morris Leibman broadly compared the current methods of professionally training law school students with those that were popular when he entered the profession fifty-five years ago. In those days, he said, the conventional wisdom was that young law school students who wanted to become trial lawyers could not be trained; either they "had it" or they did not—it was an art. Now, however, trial lawyers are trained—tutored in rhetoric, psychology, and the dynamics of personal interaction. They are videotaped and criticized by their peers. They are, in fact, better prepared attorneys. The times have changed and so have the requirements for success.

What Leibman seemed to be suggesting was that any attempt to separate diplomacy from negotiation and negotiation from diplomacy sets up a false dichotomy. Negotiation theorists are better preparing the diplomats of the future, and diplomats are providing the negotiation specialists with the raw data derived from their valuable experiences and their finely tuned persuasive abilities. Both are working toward the same goal: enhancing the ability of the United States to play a strong and positive role in the world of the future.

Notes

1. Elmer Plischke, "Diplomacy—Search for Its Meaning," in *Modern Diplomacy: The Art and the Artisans* (Washington, D.C.: American Enterprise Institute Studies, 1979).

2. See David Newsom, *Diplomacy and the American Democracy* (Bloomington: Indiana University Press, 1988).

3. I. William Zartman and Maureen R. Berman, *The Practical Negotiator* (New Haven and London: Yale University Press, 1982).

4. Fred Iklé, *How Nations Negotiate* (New York, Evanston, and London: Harper and Row, 1964).

5. Howard Raiffa, *The Art and Science of Negotiation* (Cambridge, Mass.: Belknap/Harvard University Press, 1982).

6. Roger Fisher and William Ury, *Getting to Yes*, with Bernice Patton, ed. (Boston: Houghton Mifflin, 1981).

7. Herbert Cohen, *You Can Negotiate Anything* (Secaucus, N.J.: L. Stuart, 1980).

8. Edwin M. Martin, ed., *Conference Diplomacy: A Case Study: The World Food Conference, Rome, 1974* (Washington, D.C.: Institute for the Study of Diplomacy, 1979); Jean M. Wilkowski, *Conference Diplomacy II: A Case Study: The UN Conference on Science and Technology for Development, Vienna, 1979* (Washington, D.C.: Institute for the Study of Diplomacy, 1982); Audrey Bracey, *Resolution of the Dominican Crisis, 1965: A Study in Mediation* (Washington, D.C.: Institute for the Study of Diplomacy, 1980).

9. Robert B. Houghton and Frank G. Trinka, *Multinational Peacekeeping in the Middle East* (Washington, D.C.: Center for the Study of Foreign Affairs, Foreign Service Institute, Department of State, 1984); Diane B. Bendahmane and John W. McDonald, Jr., eds., *International Negotiation: Art and Science* (Washington, D.C.: Center for the Study of Foreign Affairs, Foreign Service Institute, U.S. Department of State, 1984).

10. Fred Greene, ed., *The Philippine Bases: Negotiating for the Future: American and Philippines Perspectives* (New York: Council on Foreign Relations, 1988).

11. Hans Binnendijk, ed., *National Negotiating Styles* (Washington, D.C.: Center for the Study of Foreign Affairs, Foreign Service Institute, U.S. Department of State, April 1987).

12. François de Callières, *The Art of Diplomacy*, ed. H.M.A. Keens-Soper and Karl W. Schweizer (New York: Leicester University Press, Holmes and Meier Publishers, 1983).

13. Harold Nicolson, *Diplomacy*, 3d. ed. (New York: Oxford University Press, 1963; Washington, D.C.: Institute for the Study of Diplomacy, 1988).

14. Nicolson, *Diplomacy*, p. 69.

15. Lord Gore-Booth and Desmond Pakenham, *Satow's Guide to Diplomatic Practice*, 5th ed. (London and New York: Longman, Second Impression, 1981).

16. R.G. Feltham, *Diplomatic Handbook*, 5th ed. (London and New York: Longman, 1988).

17. R.P. Barston, *Modern Diplomacy* (London and New York: Longman, 1988).

18. Frederick Posses, *The Art of International Negotiation* (London: Business Books, Ltd., 1978). See especially chapter 2, pp. 25–53.

19. Charles W. Thayer, *Diplomat* (New York: Harper and Brothers, 1959).

20. Ellis Briggs, *Farewell to Foggy Bottom* (New York: McKay, 1964).

21. George Kennan, *Memoirs, 1925–1950* (Boston, Toronto: Little, Brown and Co., 1967).

22. Harold Lasswell, *Power and Personality* (New York: Harper and Row, 1978).

23. James MacGregor Burns, *Leadership* (New York: Harper and Row, 1978).

24. Gary Sick, *All Fall Down: America's Tragic Encounter with Iran* (New York: Random House, 1985), p. 32.

25. *Washington Post*, 1 April, 1988.

26. *New York Times*, 2 June, 1988.

27. Sick, *All Fall Down*, p. 261.

28. *Report of the Secretary of State's Advisory Panel on Overseas Security* (The Inman Report) (Washington, D.C.: U.S. Department of State, June 1985).

29. John D. Stempel, *Inside the Iranian Revolution* (Bloomington: Indiana University Press, 1981), p. 305.

30. Edward E. Azar and John W. Burton, eds., *International Conflict Resolution, Theory and Practice* (Boulder, Colo.: Lynne Reinner Publishers, Inc., 1986), p. 89.

31. Robert A. Pastor, *Condemned to Repetition: The United States and Nicaragua* (Princeton, N.J.: Princeton University Press, 1987), p. 98.

32. Alexander Haig, *Caveat* (New York: Macmillan Publishing Co., 1984), pp. 261–302.

33. De Callières, *The Art of Diplomacy*, p. 91.

Introduction to Chapter 4

Since the Hague Peace Conference of 1899, there have been more than one hundred proposed or ratified major arms control agreements involving the United States, Western Europe, and the Soviet Union, dealing with all types of weapons in most regions of the world. There have also been, however, two world wars; countless devastatingly destructive limited and protracted wars; numerous ethnic, religious, and revolutionary wars; and, since the end of World War II, the development of the largest and most lethal inventory of weapons ever.

Yet even in the face of this rather damning evidence, arms control agreements remain the Holy Grail of advocates of all political stripes, and the question Steven Miller poses in chapter 4 is appropriate: Is arms control a path to peace?

One way in which arms control agreements might, and perhaps someday will, lead to a more peaceful world is if they significantly constrained military capabilities in ways that would make war less likely to occur. But for such a scenario to come about, arms control agreements would have to be not only a fundamental determinant of military policy but an essential constraint on it as well. Experience indicates, however, that there are many internally and externally driven determinants of military policy, and, although arms control agreements do influence the policy-making process, they do so in a rather minor way. Rarely is an arms control agreement concluded that is fundamentally at odds with a state's long-term national security strategy.

Many people have also held out the hope that arms control agreements could further the cause of peace as a function of the dramatic increase in diplomatic exchanges that inevitably occur over the course of arms control negotiations. But, as Miller points out, when perceptions of hostility between countries stem from causes unrelated to arms control, as most do, arms control negotiations have little or no bearing on those perceptions. Furthermore, this negation of an otherwise attractive notion is compounded when one considers that the longest period of peace Europe has ever witnessed is attributed to the presence of nuclear weapons.

In sum, Miller cautions against adopting the intuitively compelling argument that arms control agreements necessarily further the development of a more peaceful international system and suggests instead that they can have the opposite of the intended effect. The problem, however, is that proponents of arms control have for too long allowed the wish to be the father of the thought, at the expense of more rigorous empirical analysis.

4. Is Arms Control a Path to Peace?

Steven E. Miller

One of the distinctive features of diplomacy in the twentieth century, beginning with the Hague Peace Conference of 1899, has been the emergence of arms control as an accepted and common activity among rival powers. This development reflects, at least partially, the belief on the part of publics and policymakers that arms negotiations and agreements represent means by which a safer and more peaceful world might be achieved. The yearning for a less dangerous world is certainly understandable, and the linkage of this yearning to interest in and hopes for arms limitation is both natural and intuitively compelling.

But wishing that arms control will contribute to international peace does not make it true; aspiration need not become reality. Indeed, an important (and even necessary) step in refining our understanding of the role and potential for arms control is to take a hard look, in the light of evidence available now, at such formative propositions underlying support for and the pursuit of arms control. And so the aim of this chapter is to provide at least the beginnings of an answer to the question posed in its title: Is arms control a path to peace?

To address this question, it is necessary to examine the effects of arms control in three distinct, albeit interrelated, contexts:

- What effect does arms control have on the military environment?
- What effect does arms control have on the international political scene?
- What are the domestic consequences of arms control?

In what follows, each of these questions is examined in turn. The theme developed here is that the historical record makes it difficult to entertain or sustain an affirmative response to the basic question under consideration. In other words, there is much evidence to suggest that arms control has been overrated as a path to peace. Here I propose to sketch the broad contours of the arguments and evidence that lead to this conclusion.

Arms Control and the Military Environment

Arms control is most directly an instrument for influencing the military environment. It could, in theory and perhaps in fact, serve as a path to peace by constraining military capabilities in ways that make war less likely.[1] One problem that arises immediately, however, is the wide disagreement over which configurations of military power and policy best serve the interests of peace.[2] Hence, there exist varying, and even contradictory, views about what arms control should seek to accomplish as it acts on the military environment. It is difficult for arms control to serve as a path to peace without at least some consensus on which arms control outcomes contribute to that end.

Even if the goals of arms control were clear, however, it is not inevitable that arms control would serve as an effective path to peace. The idea that arms control can regulate or dampen the "arms race" implicitly posits that it can serve as a major determinant of the military policies of the participants in an arms control process. It is this fundamental proposition that permits the belief that arms control can establish levels of military capability and effort, shape the character of the military environment, or manage the process of military modernization. And although in theory there is no reason why this proposition cannot be true, few indications in the history of arms control suggest that it is.

At the least, it is important to note that arms control will be only one determinant among many of a nation-state's defense efforts. As the literature on arms race behavior readily attests, a number of internal and external factors influence (or might influence) the size and composition of a state's military posture.[3] Among the internal factors, organizational interests often receive great emphasis. The military services are held to possess deeply rooted preferences for certain kinds of capabilities (the U.S. Navy's attachment to aircraft carriers, for example); in addition, the services will, like all large organizations, seek to maximize their wealth by working for the largest possible budget. Related arguments focus on the vested interests of the military industry in certain levels of military effort or in the production of certain kinds of military capabilities.[4]

In addition, some potentially significant domestic political considerations may bear on the level of military effort found in any given society. For example, defense issues figure in electoral politics; in general, it is politically expedient to be in favor of national strength (although occasionally, as in the United States during the latter stages of the Vietnam War, it can be popular to support military cuts).[5] Because large sums of money are involved, defense issues can also be caught up in pork barrel politics: members of Congress have every incentive to keep defense-related businesses or installations open in their districts, even if so doing violates their personal views or contravenes the wishes of the Defense Department.

Beyond these organizational and domestic political influences on military policy, several other internal factors are evident as well. One is budget inertia: next year's budget is almost always this year's budget plus or minus a few percentage points. Another is technological dynamics: improvements and pressures for technological modernization can arise from within.[6]

Many scholars have come to the conclusion that these internal factors constitute the predominant influence on the military effort of the state.[7] This fact has important implications for arms control, because it is essentially an instrument for dealing with the interactive dimensions of arms race behavior. To the extent that the sources of this behavior are internal, arms control may not address the most important determinants of the size and character of the military environment.

But there may be external factors at play as well. The classic arguments, of course, have to do with the behavior of a state's potential adversaries. Put crudely, each side reacts to the military effort of the other, and hence the magnitude or character of each side's effort is determined at least to some extent by the magnitude or character of the other side's effort.[8] This so-called action-reaction dynamic is thought by some analysts to result in needless and perhaps dangerous accumulations of military power; many who advocate arms control do so in the belief that it can interrupt and prevent the action-reaction cycle.

It has also been pointed out that the foreign-policy behavior of an adversary can trigger arms race reactions; adventurous or bellicose foreign policies can have the same effect on an opponent as worrisome moves in military policy.[9] The contributions of allies also can help shape the military posture of any given state.[10] And finally, the character of the military environment itself—the perceived ease or difficulty of attaining security—can dramatically influence the efforts that states take on behalf of their own defense. For example, it has been suggested that the arms race will become more intense when the offense-defense balance favors the offense, because in this case the danger of aggression is greater, and protection against aggression more difficult.[11]

In short, many internal and external influences affect the military behavior of states. Furthermore, they are not mutually exclusive, but complementary or even reinforcing. My aim here is not to provide an exhaustive survey of such influences or to judge their relative effects. Rather, it is to make the point that arms control, viewed as a major determinant of the military environment, must be seen as competing with all these other potential determinants. History suggests that arms control is a relatively weak determinant compared with these other factors.

This point brings us to a basic question about arms control: Does it constrain military policy, or does military policy constrain it? My conclusion is that the only possible arms control is that which is compatible with the military policies and requirements of the participating states.[12] The policy-making process, as well as the structure of domestic politics, makes it very unlikely that a government would offer or accept a proposal that is at odds in some significant way with its existing military policies. The reason is that the people who make military policy and choose military doctrines are usually (and perhaps inevitably) key players in making arms control policy, and hence they can enforce compatibility between the two. Obviously, this relationship between the military and arms control policy does not mean that arms control is impossible, because a number of agreements have been reached, but it does mean that the potential for arms control to reshape, restructure, or otherwise fundamentally modify the military environment is quite limited. Ironically, both supporters and critics overrate the military importance of arms control. Its effect has been marginal rather than central.[13]

To summarize, we began with the proposition that arms control could serve as a path to peace because of its capacity to shape the military environment. This discussion has suggested that there are two reasons for doubting the power of this proposition. First, there is no agreement on how arms control should be used to shape the military environment to serve the ends of peace. And second, arms control has a limited capacity to serve as a determinant of the character of the military environment.

Diplomatic Consequences of Arms Control

Even if arms control does not play a large or decisive role in military terms, it could perhaps serve as a path to peace by virtue of its diplomatic effects.[14] It could contribute to a more peaceful international environment by reducing tensions, improving relations between potential adversaries, and perhaps even by ameliorating the hostile images that potential enemies typically have of one another. Viewed from this perspective, it is not difficult to imagine that arms control could foster greater international harmony, but it often has not; so, at a minimum, although feasible, arms control is not a reliable "path to peace."

This point can be illustrated by examining the answers to three questions. First, does arms control make international environments more peaceful or resistant to war? Little evidence exists to suggest that the answer is yes. The twentieth century has been marked by three great waves of arms control activity. The first was the Hague Peace Conferences of 1899 and 1907; the third conference was to be held in 1915 but was canceled because of World War I. The second wave took place between 1921 and 1936, during which time there were a series of negotiations and agreements on naval arms control as well as the World Disarmament Conference of 1932-34.[15] But again, as was the case before 1914, an era of extensive arms control activity eventually gave way to mounting frictions, an intensifying arms race, and eventually to war. Indeed, in September 1939, almost exactly four decades after the opening of the first Hague Peace Conference in 1899, war erupted in Europe. Once again, the outbreak of war demonstrated conclusively that arms control had been inadequate as a barrier to armed conflict. Furthermore, many historians claim that arms control was not merely inadequate but counterproductive, in that it weakened the powers seeking to maintain the status quo relative to their eventual enemies in war by lulling public opinion and undermining building programs, while the aggressor states strengthened themselves through tough bargaining, cheating, and finally abrogating the treaties.[16]

Thus, the first forty years in which arms control occupied a prominent place on the diplomatic agendas of the major powers witnessed some of the most intense arms races in history and were interrupted by two world wars. This result is hardly testimony to the ability of arms control to preserve the peace, reduce the war-prone nature of the international environment, or increase international comity.

Nevertheless, the nuclear age has also been marked by extensive arms control activity, and the period since the beginning of Strategic Arms Limitation Talks (SALT) in 1969 can be described as the third great wave of arms control. Although the nuclear age certainly cannot be called peaceful, there has been no war between the superpowers. Ironically, however, this fact is often attributed not to arms control but to the existence of large numbers of nuclear weapons, which are thought to have induced sobriety and caution in the statesmen of the age.[17] Thus, grounds certainly exist for doubting whether periods marked by arms control activity are more peaceful or less war prone than those that are not.

It is possible, however, to attempt to gauge the potential positive diplomatic effects of arms control by asking a second, somewhat different, question: Does arms control improve relations between potential adversaries? Certainly it can have this effect, but the reality is that it often does not. A particularly illuminating illustration is the Geneva Naval Disarmament Conference of 1927.[18] The U.S. government, which initiated the conference, hoped that the ratios established in the Washington agreement of 1922 for capital ships could simply be applied to other types of naval vessels. But the apparent simplicity and attractiveness of this scheme was deceptive; it failed to take into account the differing strategic requirements of the conferees. The American position put the United States at odds with Britain, which held that it could not accept parity in cruisers because it required larger numbers of vessels to ensure the security of its global empire. This stalemate could not be overcome, and the conference ended in failure, with Anglo-American relations significantly worsened as a result. In the aftermath, the U.S. Congress passed a cruiser construction bill that seemed to guarantee increased Anglo-American naval rivalry; only changes in the governments of both countries prevented that outcome. The Geneva Conference is at least one case in which arms control, unsuccessfully pursued, made relations between two basically friendly powers considerably worse.

In other cases, arms control may not have made matters worse, but it did not improve relations either. For example, the naval arms control regime in the interwar years had no positive effect on the friction-laden relations between Japan and the United States and certainly did not reverse the drift toward war in the Pacific. If anything, Japan's expansionism, and hence its conflicts with the United States, was exacerbated by Japanese resentment of the treaty regime.[19] In the nuclear age, arms control seems to have contributed to only temporary, not enduring, improvements in Soviet-American relations.[20] Thus, the heyday of arms control and détente in the early 1970s turned out to be merely a prelude to a long period of worsened relations between the two superpowers. By the end of the decade, relations had deteriorated to the point that it was common to talk in terms of a "new Cold War," and the U.S. presidential election in 1980 brought to power a leader whose basic instincts were deeply hostile to the Soviet Union. The signing of an arms control agreement tends to be hailed as a turning point or a signal that relations have been or are being transformed. However attractive this thought may be, it is rarely true.

In short, it is much too simple to assume that arms control is somehow related to improved relations between potential adversaries. It may make things worse, it may have no effect, or it may provide only temporary improvement in relations. Once again we see that arms control is not a reliable route to a more harmonious international environment.

It is possible, finally, to attempt to gauge the beneficial diplomatic effects of arms control by asking yet a third, related, question: Does arms control influence the perceptions that potentially hostile states have of one another? Or, more specifically, does arms control cause adversaries to view one another as less hostile? If so, this would be a quite significant consequence, because perceptions of hostility have a number of malign effects;[21] they can result in increased expectations of war, for example, which in turn raise the risk of preemptive and preventive attacks.[22] They can also fuel the arms race and promote aggressive foreign-policy behavior.[23] And they can provoke dangerous upward spirals of hostility because they affect the way all adversary behavior is interpreted.[24] As Charles Glaser explains,

> Once decision makers develop a hostile image of the adversary, they tend to focus on the threatening components of the adversary's policy while overlooking defensive and cooperative behavior. As a result, states come to see the adversary as far more threatening than the ambiguities in the international environment require.[25]

For all these reasons, if arms control could moderate the images that adversaries hold of one another, it would be facilitating a more benign world. Furthermore, it seems plausible that arms control could and should have this effect: by constraining or reducing military forces or by eliminating certain troubling categories of military capability, arms control could make opponents look less threatening to one another.[26]

It is not obvious, however, that arms control actually has this effect. In several prominent instances—with the United States and Japan in the interwar years and with the United States and the Soviet Union in the nuclear age—fundamentally hostile images endured despite years of arms control negotiations and the achievement of several major agreements. Furthermore, some of the reasons why states develop and retain hostile images of one another are not undone in any direct or certain way by arms control. For example, states' perceptions of one another may be deeply colored by ideological differences or conflicts.[27] Or, to cite another illustration, some scholars believe that images of hostility are rooted in the self-interested inclination of military organizations—which tend to play a major role in shaping national perceptions of the external environment—to see a dangerous and threatening world.[28] When hostile images originate in phenomena not addressed by arms control, arms control cannot have much of a role, if any, in moderating those images.

To summarize, it has been suggested here that arms control does not certainly or invariably make the international environment more peaceful, that it does not certainly or enduringly contribute to improved relations between potential adversaries, and that it cannot easily or predictably reduce perceptions of hostility between states. Arms control can have the desired beneficial effects, but, if viewed from a diplomatic as opposed to a military perspective, arms control cannot be confidently pronounced a path to peace.

Domestic Effects of Arms Control

It follows inexorably from the foregoing discussion that arms control cannot be counted on to provide "peace-promoting" effects within participating nation-states.[29] After all, it can influence the military or diplomatic environment only by shaping, influencing, or constraining the policies of individual states. If arms control were having peace-promoting domestic effects, these effects ought to be manifested in the military or diplomatic realm. Consequently, the inability of arms control to modify the international environment dramatically or enduringly in peace-promoting ways suggests quite strongly that internal coalitions favoring benign approaches to military and foreign policy are not inevitably or powerfully strengthened by the pursuit or the success of arms control.

In theory, of course, it is possible that the process of arms control—including the achievement of agreements—could contribute to a more benign international environment by altering the distribution of political power within a society in ways that were conducive to peace: political fortunes could be advanced or hindered, popularity of policies or leaders increased or decreased, organizations strengthened or weakened. Advocates of arms control, for example, often hope that it will cause voices of restraint to be strengthened; public opinion to be tempered; détente policies to be validated; doves to be advantaged relative to hawks in the national security bureaucracy; and governments, parties, and factions favoring cooperative approaches to have their political fortunes improved.[30] Thus, a winning domestic coalition favoring military restraint, cooperation between potential adversaries, and benign foreign policies could perhaps be created, strengthened, and sustained by arms control.

Once again, however, history does not sustain the belief that arms control regularly or routinely has these effects. There are several possible reasons: First, arms control almost always provokes opposition from within. This result is not surprising, because arms control deals with one of the most sensitive areas of public policy, the national security of the state, and it involves an exercise—negotiation and cooperation with potential adversaries—that is usually politically difficult and controversial. Because of the wide disagreements that commonly exist about national security policy and the deep suspicion of potential adversaries that normally resides in any polity, it is to be expected that there will be domestic opponents of arms control who work against arms control policies and who want to neutralize politically, and supplant, the procooperation coalition. Moreover, the more prominent arms control becomes, and the more it seems to be succeeding, the more it may provoke a domestic mobilization against it. When this dynamic is taken into account, it becomes evident that arms control can provoke an internal political struggle, the outcome of which cannot be determined in advance and which may or may not contribute to the cause of peace.

In extreme cases, arms control can have dramatically adverse domestic consequences, as was vividly illustrated by the reaction in Japan to the London Naval Agreement of 1930. Opposition to the treaty was so intense that it served as a catalyst for a wave of political assassinations, for the replacement of civilian with military government, and for the abandonment of moderate policies. These developments contributed to the rise of Japanese expansionism in the 1930s and may be said to have accelerated the drift toward war in the Pacific.[31] In this case, obviously, arms control had the reverse of the desired effect; this example is a reminder that the full universe of possible domestic effects of arms control includes some that are very negative.

More commonly, however, domestic opposition to arms control does not reach such an extreme. Nevertheless, a countermobilization against arms control is often visible, and then come efforts to sway public opinion, alter policies, and affect electoral or political outcomes. For example, in the highly polarized debate in the British government in 1927 over policy toward the Naval Disarmament Conference, some opponents of the government's policy, alarmed by what they believed were excessive and unacceptable concessions, mounted a campaign to prevent further progress in the negotiation, gradually gained ascendancy, and eventually caused acrimonious collision between London and its own delegation. The conference ended in failure, and the chief British negotiator, feeling betrayed by his own cabinet, resigned from government.[32]

More recently and more publicly, the SALT II negotiations during the late 1970s provoked strong and determined opposition in the United States, and critics labored explicitly and purposefully (and with considerable success) to turn public opinion and Congress against the SALT II treaty. One of the most prominent and articulate of the opponents was the Committee on the Present Danger, of which one of its members has written, "Until President Carter withdrew the SALT II Treaty in the Fall of 1979 when it was clear that the Senate would not ratify it, the SALT II negotiations and the emerging treaty became the principal preoccupation of the Committee."[33]

The effort to achieve a treaty galvanized opposition, and that opposition in the 1970s was able to foster an atmosphere in which it ultimately proved impossible to ratify the SALT II treaty. Instead, there emerged a widespread political consensus that a large American buildup was required.[34] The likelihood of such opposition, and the evident possibility that the opponents will prevail in the domestic debate, clearly means that, at a minimum, the domestic consequences of arms control are not predictable and cannot be relied on to produce peace-promoting results.[35]

A second category of evidence concerns the effects of arms control on internal bargaining power. Advocates of arms control often claim or hope to give advantage to restraint—or cooperation-oriented domestic forces—at the expense of the national security bureaucracy. Presumably, this cooperative restraint ought to lead to a self-sustaining and even an ever-growing arms control process. Here, too, history casts doubt on this proposition, for several reasons. For one, the national security bureaucracy tends to dominate arms control policy-making, for the obvious reason that arms control intersects directly and dramatically with the bureaucracy's area of expertise and responsibility. Furthermore, some level of support from the national security bureaucracy is usually—across different polities and different time periods—critical to the political viability of a negotiation of an agreement. This fact often increases the leverage of the national security bureaucracy; the necessity to obtain its support provides the bureaucracy with a de facto veto over arms control policies, proposals, and treaties because it must be satisfied or it can refuse its support.

Political leaders seeking some sort of progress in arms control are often extremely sensitive to this reality. President Nixon, for example, seemed to be substantially constrained from pursuing a ban on multiple warhead missiles in SALT I because of the strong opposition of the Pentagon.[36] Another illustration of this point is President Carter's comment about his awareness of the importance of the Joint Chiefs of Staff to the success of his arms control policy: "I knew that when the SALT II treaty was submitted to the Senate for ratification, the testimony of these men would be most important...I needed them with me."[37] This political exigency will often limit arms control to that which is acceptable to the national security bureaucracy.

In addition, the arms control process may strengthen the domestic bargaining power of the national security bureaucracy by providing it with a potent rationale for weapons: the bargaining-chip argument. According to this argument, arms control itself becomes a justification for investment in weapons on the grounds that continued or additional expenditure and acquisition will strengthen one's position in the negotiation. This argument, of course, has some merit, because participants in a negotiation do need sources of bargaining leverage.[38] But often the bargaining-chip rationale serves to support programs, weapons, and levels of effort that turn out to be unrelated to arms control outcomes; weapons that are not traded away are not chips. In such instances, the arms control process ironically—some would say perversely—helps to facilitate rather than to constrain military programs.

Thus, Henry Kissinger reports in his memoirs, for example, that in the strongly antimilitary atmosphere of the Vietnam War period, the bargaining-chip rationale was critical to the preservation of the Nixon administration's military policy: "If it wanted to maintain an adequate defense program, the Administration was increasingly pushed into the 'bargaining chip' rationale for individual weapons programs—that is, arguing that it was building them not to fulfill strategic purposes but in order to give them up in arms control negotiations. This may have helped save minimum programs."[39] More recently, in 1984 and 1985, when the MX missile appeared headed for defeat in Congress, it was widely and explicitly observed by participants in that melodrama that only the linkage of MX to the ongoing strategic arms negotiations saved it.[40]

There is yet another way in which arms control may strengthen the domestic position of the national security bureaucracy or facilitate the development and acquisition of weapons: the "payoff" phenomenon, whereby potential opponents are offered compensations in return for their support of an agreement or proposal. In one well-known instance, President Kennedy agreed to a vigorous program of nuclear testing in order to secure the support of the Joint Chiefs of Staff for the Limited Test Ban Treaty.[41] Similarly, during the ratification process for the SALT I agreements, Secretary of Defense Melvin Laird made it explicit that his support of the treaty was conditioned by the Nixon administration's pursuit of, and Congress's support for, a comprehensive strategic modernization program.[42] The Carter administration sought in 1977 to "buy" the support of Senator Henry Jackson and his influential aide, Richard Perle, both outspoken critics, by including them, at least initially, in the policy-making process. Naturally, this action gave Jackson and Perle an unusual opportunity to influence directly the contents of the new administration's negotiating position.[43]

In conclusion, this discussion began with the proposition that arms control might strengthen domestic support of military restraint and cooperative behavior. It has been suggested that this domestic effect, in turn, could help arms control play a larger role in producing "peace-promoting" effects in the military and diplomatic environments beyond the state. In this chapter, I have examined significant historical evidence of arms control, indicating that this proposition is not always true, and is, indeed, generally doubtful.

Discussion

Commentator Janne Nolan took Steven Miller's argument one step further. Why, she asked, if there is a rough consensus among strategic analysts that arms control agreements are only modest instruments of national policy and nuclear strategy, is this fact not mentioned in the extensive public debate and rhetoric that accompany every arms control proposal? In other words, why does the political debate over arms control seem to go on unabated, completely disconnected from its real operational implications or consequences?

Nolan saw a partial answer in the fact that the threat of nuclear war—or, more precisely, the fear of nuclear annihilation inherent in the "non-doctrine" of mutual assured destruction—is an emotional issue that transcends political identifications. Although where one stands within the political spectrum tends to color one's assessment of how best to avoid this eventuality, she noted that no human being can advocate nuclear war and still be considered rational.

As a result, Nolan said, successive presidential administrations have come into office with promises of sweeping, peaceful change, usually with arms control playing a central role, to mollify the fears of their nation that Armageddon is at hand. But this radical oversimplification of nuclear strategy building is inevitably self-defeating and results, by the end of each administration's political tenure, in much less ambitious, if not diametrically opposite, policies. The fact remains that from a political point of view, policy propositions based on a best-case scenario are far more advantageous than those based on the difficult choices that reality offers.

It is important for every U.S. administration to appear willing to discuss the possibility of an arms control agreement with the Soviet Union. Using the Reagan administration as an example, Nolan noted that even in light of the Soviet intractability on arms control issues during his first term in office, President Reagan was clearly aware of the public pressure to get the Soviets back to the negotiating table. When he did, and the Intermediate-

Range Nuclear Force (INF) Treaty was concluded, a palpable and positive shift in public opinion was the result. But once again, the relative success of this agreement might best be analyzed in terms of its political and psychological benefits rather than its military merits.

In the general discussion, Geoffrey Kemp suggested that the political and psychological goodwill that arms control talks kindle in the public has effectively narrowed the debate over potential arms control agreements to the point that the most serious threats to nuclear peace are rarely considered. Kemp argued that the most likely area in which a political crisis could escalate into a superpower nuclear conflict was in the Third World, not in Europe, and that the failure to deal with this issue not only lessens the relevance of most arms control treaties but also severely reduces the possibilities of preventing such an occurrence.

The notion that Third World conflict results, in part, from the displacement of the Soviet-American rivalry into areas perceived by many to be less volatile and therefore less likely to lead to undesired escalation has gained currency in the minds of many analysts. Furthermore, maintenance of that "spillover" rivalry with the goal of avoiding direct Soviet-American military confrontation in the Third World has been, to date, one of the more successful efforts of policy-makers on both sides of the Atlantic. The possibility of a breakdown in that relationship sometime in the future, however, remains both plausible and dangerous.

Edward Luttwak added another dimension to this debate by suggesting that nuclear arms control negotiations are another variant of this phenomenon—a new stage on which the superpower drama could be played out without directly threatening the peace. The enormously destructive capability of nuclear weapons has made them into largely symbolic instruments. Because using them implies unacceptable and irreparable ends, negotiations over whether the United States and the Soviet Union should maintain arsenals of five thousand versus six thousand warheads are largely symbolic as well.

The advantage that such negotiations can confer, however, is that they provide a relatively safe forum for ideological posturing that allows the parties to the negotiations to be perceived as "keepers of the peace" to their domestic populations and international allies. Luttwak added that if this type of dialogue could be redirected to the conflict in the Third World and other more immediate security concerns, the tensions inherent in the current superpower relationship might be eased.

The idea that arms control negotiations could be broadened to the point of altering the structure of the Soviet-American relationship elicited some opposition. Miller argued that because arms control serves important purposes related to domestic politics, alliance management, and symbolic ideology, it is unlikely that a major contextual change is possible. But David Pabst countered that, whatever the military significance of the INF Treaty, the treaty did tackle two previously bedeviling issues: asymmetric cuts in arms levels and on-site inspections of weapon facilities. At the very least, he added, this achievement was a major improvement over the past and might even lay the groundwork for the more difficult problem of conventional and strategic arms reductions. Patrick Glynn cautioned that, particularly with respect to strategic weapons, on-site inspections could lead to a false sense of security, based on inaccurate intelligence assessments resulting from dishonest Soviet practices or significant technological losses due to espionage.

The audience and the panel remained skeptical that accurate verification of any arms control treaty could ever be possible in the absence of a major technological breakthrough or the development of an enforceable compliance mechanism.

Bruce Weinrod noted that democracies have a long record of not responding forcefully to violations of arms control treaties; democracies tend to "wish away" or rationalize violations so as not to disrupt the status quo. Pabst suggested that one of the reasons for this is that compliance and verification issues have traditionally been the domain of middle-level officials, rather than of people who are in a position to see that specific requirements are met. He suggested elevating the level at which compliance and verification issues are considered, preferably to the office of the secretary of state.

Notes

1. As Seyom Brown puts it, arms control involves "efforts to make military balances less war prone." See *The Causes and Prevention of War* (New York: St. Martin's Press, 1987), p. 173.

2. See, for example, Charles Glaser's chapter, "Why Do Strategists Disagree About the Requirements of Deterrence," in his *Analyzing Strategic Nuclear Policy: Theories, Alternative Worlds, and Choices in MAD* (Ann Arbor: University of Michigan Press, forthcoming), which examines in detail the large disagreements over the desirable character of the strategic nuclear balance. Also illustrative here is Michael Krepon, *Strategic Stalemate: Nuclear Weapons and Arms Control in American Politics* (New York: St. Martin's Press, 1984), which argues that the collision of opposing views about nuclear weapons policy often produces stalemate in arms control.

3. For a recent survey, see Matthew Evangelista, *Innovation and the Arms Race: How the Soviet Union and the United States Develop New Military Technologies* (Ithaca, N.Y.: Cornell University Press, 1988). See also the analysis by Colin Gray, "The Urge to Compete: Rationales for Arms Racing," *World Politics* (January 1974): pp. 207–33.

4. This statement, of course, refers to a family of arguments having to do with what is often called the military-industrial complex. For a concise survey of this notion, see Bruce Russett, *The Prisoners of Insecurity: Nuclear Deterrence, the Arms Race, and Arms Control* (New York: W.H. Freeman, 1983), pp. 80–86. More generally, see Russett's discussion of "Domestic Influences" in the same chapter.

5. For discussion of this point, see Miroslav Nincic, *The Arms Race: The Political Economy of Military Growth* (New York: Praeger, 1982), pp. 25–33. Nincic comments,

"U.S. security from foreign threats is a matter with considerable emotive content and is well suited to political rhetoric and debate—particularly at election time. From the point of view of both the public and the political opposition, incumbents can err in either of two ways: by overreacting or by underreacting to perceived external challenges, but the punishment meted out is likely to be much harsher for the second type of error than for the first" (p. 27).

6. As Graham Allison asked, "Can't technology trigger itself?" See his discussion in "Questions About the Arms Race: Who's Racing Whom? A Bureaucratic Perspective," in Robert L. Pfaltzgraff, ed., *Contrasting Approaches to Strategic Arms Control* (Lexington, Mass.: Lexington Books, 1974), p. 39. See also Evangelista, *Innovation and the Arms Race*. The implications for arms control of the "technological imperative" are directly addressed in Harvey Brooks, "Potentials for Curbing the Qualitative Arms Race," ed. Burton H. Weston, *Toward Nuclear Disarmament and Global Security: A Search for Alternatives* (Boulder, Colo.: Westview Press, 1984), pp. 416–28.

7. See, for example, Russett, *Prisoners of Insecurity*, p. 92; Nincic, *The Arms Race*, chapter 1; Allison, "Questions About the Arms Race," passim; as well as Nazli Choucri and Robert North, *Nations in Conflict: National Growth and International Violence* (San Francisco: W.H. Freeman, 1975), p. 218.

8. An excellent discussion is George Rathjens, "The Dynamics of the Arms Race," *Scientific American*, April 1969. Also suggestive is Thomas Schelling's discussion of what he calls "The Dialogue of Competitive Armament" (by which he means "the continuous process by which the U.S.S.R. and the United States interpret each other's intentions and convey their own about the arms race") in *Arms and Influence* (New Haven, Conn.: Yale University Press, 1968), pp. 260–86. About the interaction of adversary military programs, Schelling comments, "Implicitly…, if not explicitly, each of us in his own program must influence the other in some fashion. The influence is surely complicated and uneven, indirect and occasionally irrational, and undoubtedly based often on inaccurate projections of each other's programs. But the influence is there" (p. 271). But for a critique of simple action-reaction dynamics, see Allison, "Questions About the Arms Race"; and Graham Allison and Frederic A. Morris, "Armaments and Arms Control: Exploring the Determinants of Military Weapons," *Daedalus* (Summer 1975): pp. 99–130.

9. On this point, see, for example, Colin Gray, "The Arms Race Phenomenon," *World Politics* (January 1972): pp. 2–73. Gray also calls attention to other "political triggers," such as changes in leadership on the other side, that may influence perceptions of the necessary military posture.

10. As Kenneth Waltz notes, allies represent an external source of power that can supplement, and in some instances even replace, internally generated military capability in the effort to offset an opponent's or an opposing coalition's capability. See *Theory of International Politics* (Reading, Mass.: Addison-Wesley, 1979), pp. 167–69.

11. This argument is made by Stephen Van Evera in *Causes of War*, Ph.D. diss., University of California, Berkeley, 1984, pp. 108–14.

12. I can sketch this argument only briefly here. I have developed it more fully in "The Viability of Nuclear Arms Control: Domestic and Bilateral Factors," *Bulletin of Peace Proposals* 16, no. 3 (1985): pp. 263–76; and in "The Limits of Mutual Restraint," processed ms., MIT, June 1988.

13. For an even more pessimistic argument, which suggests that arms control neither truly controls arms nor is a self-sustaining process, see Bruce D. Berkowitz, *Calculated Risks: A Century of Arms Control, Why It Has Failed, and How It Can Be Made to Work* (New York: Simon and Schuster, 1987), pp. 20–68. Berkowitz comments, "Arms control generally has not limited arms, has not limited the development of military technology, and has not reduced defense spending. It would probably be an overstatement to say that arms control in the twentieth century has been a complete failure, but it has at least been sorely disappointing by most objective measures" (p. 26).

14. This subject rarely receives careful analysis. One of the few analyses I know is found in chapter 10 ("Why Arms Control in MAD?") of Glaser, *Analyzing Strategic Nuclear Policy.* Glaser writes, "Arms control may have greater potential for providing political benefits than strategic benefits" (p. 2). Glaser argues that arms control is important because it may moderate the superpower rivalry, rather than because it can shape the military balance.

15. For accounts of arms control activity in this period, see Christopher Hall, *Britain, America, and Arms Control, 1921–1937* (New York: St. Martin's Press, 1987); and Robert Hoover, *Arms Control: The Interwar Naval Limitation Agreements,* Monograph Series in International Affairs 17, no. 3, Graduate School of International Studies, University of Denver, 1980.

16. For example, Berkowitz, *Calculated Risks,* p. 149, concludes that the interwar naval treaties failed to restrain Japan effectively. Raymond O'Conner, *Perilous Equilibrium: The United States and the London Naval Conference of 1930* (Lawrence, Kan.: University of Kansas Press, 1962), also reaches a negative conclusion.

17. A notable example is found in John Gaddis's superb essay, "The Long Peace: Elements of Stability in the Postwar International System," in his *The Long Peace: Inquiries Into the History of the Cold War* (New York: Oxford University Press, 1987). Gaddis writes: "Statesmen of the post-1946 superpowers have, compared to their predecessors, been exceedingly cautious in risking war with one another.... It seems inescapable that what has really made the difference in inducing this unaccustomed caution has been the workings of the nuclear deterrent.... The development of nuclear weapons has had, on balance, a stabilizing effect on the postwar international system.... They have had a sobering effect upon a whole range of statesmen of varying degrees of responsibility and capability" (pp. 230–31). But for a thoughtful dissent, see John Mueller, "The Essential Irrelevance of Nuclear Weapons: Stability in the Postwar World," *International Security* 13, no. 2 (Fall 1988): pp. 55–79. Mueller argues that "it is not at all clear that [nuclear weapons] have had a significant impact on the history of world affairs since World War II" (p. 56).

18. For an interesting account, see David Carlton, "Great Britain and the Coolidge Naval Disarmament Conference of 1927," *Political Science Quarterly* (December 1968): pp. 573–98.

19. See Hoover, *Arms Control,* p. 101.

20. I sidestep here the question of whether improved relations contribute more to the prospects for arms control than arms control contributes to improved relations. It is possible that both propositions are true. For an early and interesting analysis of this puzzle, see J. David Singer, "Threat Perception and the Armament-Tension Dilemma," *Journal of Conflict Resolution* (March 1958): pp. 90–105.

21. What is problematic here is primarily false or exaggerated perceptions of hostility. Accurate images of hostility, that is, correctly perceiving the aggressive intentions of an adversary, can lead to appropriate defensive or deterrent measures. But an accurate image of hostility will still probably increase the likelihood of war.

22. On these points, see Van Evera, *Causes of War*, Part I.

23. On the consequence of hostile images of a potential opponent, see, for example, Robert Jervis's discussion in *Perception and Misperception in International Relations* (Princeton, N.J.: Princeton University Press, 1976), pp. 68–113, passim; and Glaser, *Analyzing Strategic Nuclear Policy*, chapter 3.

24. This is the result of what Robert Jervis describes as "the tendency for people to assimilate new information to their pre-existing beliefs." See his "Deterrence and Perception," *Strategy and Nuclear Deterrence*, ed. Steven E. Miller (Princeton: Princeton University Press, 1984), pp. 78–83.

25. Glaser, *Analyzing Strategic Nuclear Policy*, chapter 3, pp. 6–7. Also relevant here is Robert Jervis's discussion in his "Perceiving and Coping with Threat," in R. Jervis, R.N. Lebow, and J. Stein, eds., *Psychology and Deterrence* (Baltimore: Johns Hopkins University Press, 1986), especially pp. 18–22. Jervis suggests that: "The decision maker who thinks that the other side is probably hostile will see ambiguous information as confirming this image, whereas the same information about a country thought to be friendly would be taken more benignly" (p. 18). See also Klaus Knorr, "Threat Perception," *Historical Dimensions of National Security Problems*, ed. K. Knorr (Lawrence, Kan.: University of Kansas Press, 1976), pp. 112–16.

26. Glaser, *Analyzing Strategic Nuclear Policy*, chapter 10, pp. 23–36, explores this argument.

27. See Knorr, "Threat Perception," p. 113.

28. See, for example, Van Evera, *Causes of War*, pp. 254–73. Van Evera observes, "Militaries tend to exaggerate the hostility of other states. The more hostile others appear, the stronger the case for organizational growth and the greater the prestige of the military" (pp. 254–55). For a related point, see Jervis, "Perceiving and Coping with Threat," pp. 26–27.

29. For a review of theories linking internal affairs and war, see Jack Levy, "Domestic Politics and War," *Journal of Interdisciplinary History* 18, no. 4 (Spring 1988): pp. 653–73. Most of this discussion, however, has to do with the relationship between political or economic structure and the likelihood of war; or, as I.F. Stone recently put it, with the idea that "internal regimes [are] not just a domestic matter but could themselves become a menace to world peace" (from "The Rights of Gorbachev," *New York Times Review of Books*, February 16, 1989, p. 3). In what follows, I have in mind also the possibility of shifts in the distribution of power among internal coalitions—in whatever sort of regime—that have implications for the aims and policies of the states concerned.

30. Critics of arms control, generally those with a different conception of what causes peace, *fear* rather than hope it will have these effects. See, for example, Zbigniew Brzezinski's discussion of "the threat of arms control," in which he expresses concern that the arms control process "corrupts" discussion of strategic issues in the United States, prevents the formulation of sound nuclear policies, and blinds arms control advocates to the harsh realities of the Soviet-American competition, by causing an excessive preoccupation with restraint, cooperation, and compromise: "The contamination of strategy by pacifism is the key danger for the United States inherent in crusading arms control." *Game Plan: How to Conduct the U.S.-Soviet Contest* (New York: Atlantic Monthly Press, 1986), pp. 148–50. For Brzezinski, the effects described here lead not to peace but to "strategic impotence" (p. 148).

Those who believe passionately that power is the key to peace view arms control itself as a threat to peace. For a vivid example of this argument, see Malcolm Wallop and Angelo Codevilla, *The Arms Control Delusion: How Twenty-five Years of Arms Control Has Made the World Less Safe* (San Francisco: Institute for Contemporary Studies, 1987). They write, "By all measures, the danger of war is greater now than when the arms control process began.... The so-called 'arms control process'...has produced very nearly the opposite of what the American advocates of arms control have said they meant to accomplish" (p. 4).

31. See Hoover, *Arms Control*, p. 101; and Berkowitz, *Calculated Risks*, pp. 64–65. Berkowitz comments that the militarization of Japan in the 1930s "was partly a result of the constitutional crisis that the second naval treaty precipitated there.... The treaty became a bloody shirt for the militarists to wave" (p. 65).

32. See Carlton, "Great Britain and the Coolidge Naval Disarmament Conference of 1927," pp. 584–90 and passim.

33. Kampelman, "Introduction," in Tyroler, ed., *Altering America*, p. xix. The committee's position on SALT II was that "in the short run, it is unlikely that a comprehensive and safe SALT agreement can be negotiated." What was desired and required instead was a unilateral build-up (from "Where We Stand on SALT," in *Alerting America*, p. 20). For a detailed and extremely critical discussion of the activities of the committee, see Jerry W. Sanders, *Peddlers of Crisis: The Committee on the Present Danger and the Politics of Containment* (Boston: South End Press, 1983), especially pp. 191–317.

34. The opponents of SALT II were not, of course, the only cause of the change in American opinion on defense and arms control issues—the Soviets, for example, deserve some blame for their adventurous foreign policy in this period—but the Committee on the Present Danger and other like-minded groups rightly claim credit for having influenced both the policy debate and the trend in public opinion. And after the 1980 election the committee boasted about the extent to which its members—including the new president, Ronald Reagan, who was a member of the board of the committee—had supplanted the previous national security elite. About the success of the SALT critics, former president Carter complained in his memoirs, "It is almost inevitable that the voices heard most loudly are those of the opposition— and the more strident their attacks on the Soviets or on our own negotiators, the bigger the headlines." Jimmy Carter, *Keeping Faith: Memoirs of a President* (New York: Bantam Books, 1982), p. 213.

35. For a broader discussion, including but not limited to defense and foreign policy issues, of what I have here termed countermobilization, see Sidney Blumenthal, *The Rise of the Counterestablishment: From Conservative Ideology to Political Power* (New York: Times Books, 1986), especially pp. 122–65. Blumenthal suggests that one of the things the American "neoconservative" movement feared most was "a debilitating arms control agreement with the Soviets, the moral equivalent of appeasement" (p. 160).

36. See Gerard Smith's account, *Doubletalk: The Story of SALT I* (New York: Doubleday, 1980), especially pp. 157, 169–71. Smith describes the U.S. military as "flatly opposed" to a Multiple Independently-Targeted Reentry Vehicle (MIRV) ban (p. 169).

37. Carter, *Keeping Faith*, p. 222.

38. For a thoughtful discussion of this issue, see Robert J. Einhorn, *Negotiating From Strength: Leverage in U.S.-Soviet Arms Control Negotiations* (New York: Praeger,

1985). Einhorn's careful analysis suggests that the effects of bargaining chips are conditional: "What the record shows is that the issue of negotiating leverage is more complicated than categorical assertions either that U.S. programs promote arms control agreements or that such programs stimulate arms races" (p. 8).

39. Henry A. Kissinger, *White House Years* (Boston: Little, Brown, and Co., 1979), p. 538.

40. For unambiguous evidence on this point, see Miller, "The Viability of Arms Control," p. 270. For a detailed discussion, which argues that the MX missile cannot be defended as a bargaining chip, see William Rose, "MX as a Bargaining Chip," *Arms Control* 5, no. 1 (May 1984): pp. 60–70.

41. See Glenn T. Seaborg with Benjamin S. Loeb, *Kennedy, Khrushchev, and the Test Ban* (Berkeley: University of California Press, 1981), pp. 229, 269–71. Seaborg concludes sadly of President Kennedy's support for an aggressive program of underground nuclear testing, "While this support may have obtained the favorable testimony of the Joint Chiefs, it was a very heavy price for the cause of disarmament" (p. 271).

42. See Smith, *Doubletalk*, p. 30.

43. See Strobe Talbott, *Endgame: The Inside Story of SALT II* (New York: Harper, 1979), pp. 52–54. In this case, however, the attempted buyoff failed, largely because Senator Jackson's preferred treaty was unacceptable to the Soviet Union. President Carter writes bitterly of Jackson in his memoirs: "There was no possibility of support from Scoop Jackson for any treaty which the Soviets were likely to sign; he was already doing everything possible to defeat the agreement even before its final terms could be known" (p. 225).

Part II: International Law Approaches

Introduction to Chapter 5

In this chapter, Oscar Schachter analyzes the theoretical underpinnings of international law, with a special emphasis on how that theory pertains to the use of force in international relations as stipulated by the UN Charter. The Charter not only sought to outlaw war but also to add substance and structure to the notion of international government by basing itself on the principles of territorial integrity, juridical equality, and political independence of states.

The fundamental test of any legal system, international or otherwise, is the extent to which that system is able to control the unauthorized and impermissible use of force by one member of the community against another. For the UN, this means anticipating, preventing, and resolving a wide variety of conflicts to which any combination of members could be parties. The particular problem, however, stems from the lack of an effective central authority capable of enforcing agreed-upon norms pertaining to the use of force, as well as getting member states to seek UN intervention routinely when conflicts are brewing.

This situation has led some skeptics to conclude that, having failed to meet this test in any number of conflicts, international law is not in fact law at all, but simply a system of rules and regulations with which states comply only when doing so benefits them. Schachter acknowledges that international law is not perfect, but rather it is an ideal—the result of the complex interplay of interests, powers, and ideas that characterize relations among states. Furthermore, he says, when examined broadly, the UN system in general and international law in particular not only fulfill their intended purposes but also are actually expanding as a function of the dramatic increase in interaction among states in the areas of commerce, communication, transportation, health management, and environmental protection.

Schachter is primarily concerned here with the prohibition against the use of force as set forth in Article 2, paragraph 4 of the UN Charter:

> All Members shall refrain in their international relations from the threat or use of force against the territorial integrity or political independence of any state, or in any other manner inconsistent with the Purposes of the United Nations.

Although this clause is fairly straightforward in intent, its application and interpretation have been widely debated. The lack of a central enforcement authority to implement UN-generated decisions is exacerbated by the relative ineffectiveness of the Security Council, which stems from partisan voting behavior caused by the unanimity requirement. But these problems are structural, subject to structural modifications.

The interpretive questions raised by Article 2(4), however, are more subjective and therefore less easily resolved. The term "armed force," for instance, was intentionally used rather than the more ambiguous term "war," in order to reduce the contentious political issues raised by the definition of that term. But the inclusion of the prohibition against the "threat of force" has created unforeseen confusion over what form those threats must take before they are considered unlawful.

Under terms of the Charter there are only two cases in which armed force may be employed: (1) self-defense from an illegal armed attack and (2) armed action authorized by the UN Security Council as an enforcement measure. A number of attempts have been made to increase the allowable exceptions. Schachter dissects these attempts and shows how they violate the Charter's intent and are therefore unacceptable. The only possible exception (one he believes needs further rigorous review) concerns armed intervention on humanitarian grounds—for example, the restraint of a despot such as Pol Pot of Kampuchea—regardless of the political differences among the permanent members of the Security Council.

5. The Role of International Law in Maintaining Peace

Oscar Schachter

International law in its ideal sense promises a world without war. It aims to coordinate and constrain state conduct so as to reduce conflict and minimize violence among states. Often referred to as a "system," the corpus of international law consists of an interrelated and elaborate set of rules, obligations, procedures, practices, and institutions. It is global in scope, accepted as such by all nation-states—that is, by all territorial communities recognized as sovereign and independent. Because the system was not imposed by a superior authority, it is often viewed as basically contractual and consensual in character. It is important to recognize, however, that no state has, or has had, an option to remain outside the international legal system, and, indeed, no state has professed to do so.

The very claim of a community to statehood presupposes a normative order that defines the conditions of sovereignty and prescribes rules (together with processes) for the interaction of states in the pursuit of their separate and common goals. Many such rules are considered necessary to the coexistence of independent states. They include, for example, principles that recognize the territorial authority of states and their right to govern themselves. They also include rules to ensure and protect the processes for interaction among the states, particularly international agreements and diplomatic intercourse. In addition, as in any legal system, international law distinguishes between permissible and impermissible uses of force and provides means for giving effect to the restraints it seeks to impose.

This chapter is concerned primarily with international law on the use of force, because that aspect bears most directly on the maintenance of international peace. My aim is to explain and clarify the proclaimed restraints on force and the conditions under which armed force may be legitimately used. This approach may be seen as the contemporary version of the *jus ad bellum*, the traditional law governing the right to war. The central legal principle today is the broad prohibition of force in international relations. The effort to sustain this principle and to determine permissible exceptions to it has proved to be a formidable task. Almost every armed conflict since 1945 has exemplified this difficulty. Yet few, if any, governments are prepared to abandon the attempt to impose the rule of law on the use of force. They recognize, to be sure, that this effort must go beyond the formulation of abstract principle and that it must take account of the conditions of conflict, the role of power, and the limits on enforcement. Law, inescapably, is part of the broader political process. Although it sets normative limits, those limits are determined by political goals and they are applied in political contexts. Space constraints here prevent me from doing justice to these complexities, but my treatment of legal issues in this chapter indicates my awareness of these considerations.

Before I begin to discuss the law on force, it may be helpful to add a few general comments about the way in which international law operates at a time of great disparity in the power of states combined with profound ideological differences. The basic postulates of international law remain principles of the nation-state system, usually said to have begun with the Peace of Westphalia in 1648. Foremost among these principles are the political independence, the territorial integrity, and the juridical equality of states. All states are subject to the law of nations, but that law is not imposed by a superior authority. That law results from agreement of states (generally but not always in written form) and from "state practice" that is accepted as law. Practice alone does not create law; it must be accompanied by *opinio juris sive necessitatis* (evidence of a belief that the practice is rendered obligatory by the existence of a rule requiring it),[1] a point that is discussed later. Recourse to a judicial body for interpretation and application of law is essentially voluntary, but is often stipulated in advance in treaties and acceptances of compulsory jurisdiction.

These basic features of the international legal system have not been displaced by the UN Charter or by other contemporary legal developments. Far-reaching societal changes and new perceptions of interdependence and common interest, however, have significantly affected the operation of this legal system. One conspicuous consequence has been the enormous expansion of international law in response to the increased interactions among governments and peoples, advances in technology, demands on resources, the birth of new states, ideas of human rights, and felt needs for cooperation. Virtually every sector of political, social, and economic activity has become subject, in some measure, to international rules and procedures.[2]

Much of this expansion has occurred through deliberate lawmaking in the form of negotiated multilateral agreements on a global or regional scale. The UN and other international organizations have been important factors in the negotiation and adoption of these international treaties.

Alongside the body of international *lex scripta*, unwritten customary law also has expanded. This expansion, too, is attributable to needs identified by international bodies and to standards of conduct followed by common practice. Treaty and custom are not separate; they are often entangled. Treaty law, both multilateral and bilateral, generates practice and interpretations that are then accepted as customary law. A good example is the UN Convention on the Law of the Sea, which is widely accepted as binding customary law, although it is not in force and some of its major provisions are rejected by important states such as the United States.

The striking expansion of international law has been barely noticed by skeptics who see the world as lawless and anarchic. In contrast, the individuals and communities affected by these developments—those concerned with international trade investments, finance, transportation, environmental damage, humanitarian aims—are naturally aware that international law is directly relevant to the orderly conduct of their affairs.

The evaluation of conduct by individual states as customary "practice" and the appraisal of the "subjective" element of *opinio juris* are often controversial. Reaching agreement on the applicable rule of law is especially troublesome when state interests sharply clash or when changing conditions seem to require new law. International judicial decisions on such issues are rare in comparison with the frequency of the problems; but when such decisions are made by the International Court of Justice (ICJ) or even by an arbitral tribunal, they tend to be regarded as authoritative.

The infrequency of judicial recourse has resulted in a much greater role for professional international lawyers as an authoritative source of evidence of the law. Although their individual opinions may reflect national bias or political attitudes, the process is multinational and open to critical analysis of reasoning and facts. It is not farfetched to regard recognized experts as forming an invisible college of international law, whose collective judgments are given great weight as interpretations of existing law. Hence, although official behavior and government attitudes are at the center of the international lawmaking process, international legal scholars have a significant role. Other nongovernment entities such as business enterprises, professional bodies, and information media also influence the formation and interpretation of new law. The contemporary expansion of international law to many areas not previously covered by it is the product of these many diverse influences. The law has become a dense, intricate body of rules and procedures. In many respects, it is accessible only to specialists.

Is international law "real" law? This question is often raised on the grounds that the questions at issue are not subject to the compulsory adjudication of courts and that enforcement for violations tends to be uncertain and weak. These deficiencies are doubtless important, especially in highly controversial areas, but they should not obscure the important fact that international law is observed most of the time. There are many reasons for this observance. In general, the system is accepted—one might say "internalized"—so that officials routinely ascertain and follow the rules. In some cases, national interests may seem to call for noncompliance; in such cases, the consequences are considered. A violation may bring countermeasures, such as the suspension of treaty obligations by the injured state or, in some cases, by other states. The credibility of the violating government as a state that purports to honor its obligations will be at stake.

Only rarely do governments repudiate obligations that they have accepted and reaffirmed. They may seek means of exit in other ways—for example, reinterpretation of the rules or reliance on the doctrine of changed circumstances (*rebus sic stantibus*). Whatever the reason, outright violations of treaty or customary law are not without cost, even to powerful states.

What role does power play in international law? Power, here, refers to the ability to impose one's will on others, or, more precisely, to control contested outcomes. In international affairs, as elsewhere, that ability is relative—a matter of degree. (To refer to power as if it were a commodity can mislead.) States obviously differ greatly in their ability to prevail over others. Military, economic, political, demographic, and psychological conditions determine differentials in power, and the effects of these conditions vary with the situation. It is not always clear which state prevails in a specific context, although relative strength is manifested in many ways. States strive to augment their power for instrumental reasons (as means to increase freedom of action or to attain other objectives); but power is also perceived as an end in itself.

The striving for power and the use of power in international relations are conspicuous facts of international life. They necessarily have important effects on the international legal system, for the law is not an ideal construct based solely on predetermined ends and a logical structure. It is the product of state interaction, demands, claims, resistances, and alliances. The fact that common ends have been recognized in general terms (as in the UN Charter) does not mean that specific rules and obligations can emerge from within the system by legal logic alone. Inevitably, the law that emerges embodies numerous contested outcomes that result from clashes of interest and values.

Power undeniably plays a significant, if not decisive, role in this process. It does so, most clearly, in the formation of law. States are expected to pursue their interests when they create or modify law. It would be a mistake, however, to regard such lawmaking as unaffected by general international law. For even on this largely political level, some constraints are imposed by law—that is, by the basic postulates of the state system embodied in the law. These postulates include, as we observed earlier, the principles of sovereignty, territoriality, observance of treaties, diplomatic relations, and limits on force. As long as states accept an international legal system based on the coexistence of interdependent states, limits are imposed on their freedom to legislate. They are compelled to recognize that, in this sense, power is both restrained by the legal system and legitimated by it.

If this point holds true for the lawmaking process, it is even more evident with respect to the application of law to particular cases. If a powerful state is free to disregard the existing rules, law vanishes, except as rhetoric. Rules are the product of politics and power, but the application of them cannot be reduced solely to politics and power without negating the very idea of law. Law must therefore be accorded its own relative sphere of autonomy. International law falls short of ensuring such autonomy insofar as it lacks, for the most part, compulsory third-party adjudication and effective enforcement. In their absence, the application of law is left in large measure to the states concerned and, to some degree, the reactions of the larger community of states. Hence, the impact of power and political interests in resolving legal disputes can be substantial in many areas.

But here, too, restraints are imposed by the necessities of the legal system. Most states, and especially the more powerful, recognize their interest in maintaining that system. They could not do so if they treated the agreed principles and rules as subject entirely to political application. This reasoning does not exclude the possibility that a state, especially a great power, may seek to avoid the law in a particular case or seek, by violating it, to change it. It may be able to absorb the negative consequences of violation. But occasional violations do not mean that the rules generally lose their effect. All states still find it necessary to function within the system and to accept its obligations.

One of the restraints on power, apart from law, is countervailing power. In the absence of a hierarchical superior or an all-powerful hegemony, even relatively strong states must take account of the power of other states. It is a reasonable inference that parity of power between states with conflicting interests is supportive of stability and observance of the law. As some historians have observed, the nineteenth-century Concert of Europe, the exemplar of the balance of power, sustained international law.[3] Many observers today consider an equilibrium of power in regional contexts or between the two superpowers an important factor in restraining serious violations of international rules.

Although a balance of power is generally supportive of international law, it is not a substitute for international law. States, even if equal in power, still must know what is permissible and impermissible. They must have a fairly clear conception of actions that are considered unacceptable and that would justify counteraction by other states. The so-called balance-of-power system does not meet that need. It helps to support the legal system; it cannot replace it.

We can all agree that the proclaimed ideal of the equality of states under law is substantially qualified by the actual disparities in power. Powerful states do influence legal rules more than the weak, and power may impose limits on the equal application of the law. But powerful states have a stake in maintaining a system that gives a necessary measure of stability to the existing order. In a broad sense, their power sustains the legal system. Although international society may be called an "anarchical order of power"[4] because it lacks a supreme authority, it is far from being a lawless society.

The UN Charter's Prohibition on the Use or Threat of Force

When the UN Charter was adopted, it was generally considered to have outlawed war. States accepted the obligation to settle all disputes by peaceful means and to refrain from the use or threat of force in their international relations. Only two exceptions were expressly allowed: force in self-defense when an armed attack occurred, and armed action authorized by the UN Security Council as an enforcement measure. These provisions were seen by most observers as the heart of the Charter and the most important principles of contemporary international law. They have been reaffirmed over and over in unanimous declarations of the UN, in treaties, and in statements of political leaders.

Yet, as we are all acutely aware, there is widespread cynicism about the effect of these provisions. Reality seems to mock them. Wars take place; countries are invaded; armed force is used to topple governments, seize territory, impose settlements. Threats of force, open or implicit, pervade the relations of states. The menace of a nuclear holocaust hangs over all nations, great and small. Collective security as envisaged in the Charter has had little practical effect. Our personal lives are deeply affected by the expectations of violence, by the vast resources devoted to armaments, and, perhaps most insidiously, by the belief that little can be done to replace force as the ultimate arbiter in conflicts between nations.

It is no wonder that the obligations of the Charter are seen as amounting to mere rhetoric—at best, as idealistic aspirations, and at worst, as providing a pretext, a "cover," for aggression. This evaluation, devastating as it may appear for international law, cannot be dismissed or minimized. However, there is another aspect of reality. Never before in history has there been such widespread and well-founded recognition of the costs and horrors of war. That awareness and its objective basis are powerful factors in strengthening conscious self-interest in avoiding armed conflict.

It does not follow, of course, that rules of law must be seen as an effective remedy. Peace is often perceived today as "secured" by the balance of power between West and East and by the deterrent of nuclear arms. It is widely maintained that these factors count, not the legal rules of the UN Charter. But even if countervailing power and fear of nuclear devastation restrain the use of force, it is abundantly clear that they have not prevented many armed conflicts, nor have they led to effective prohibition on the use of force. We do not, for our present purposes, have to consider in detail why this point is so. It is sufficient to recognize that in numerous situations governments are not deterred from the use or threat of force by considerations of power, by fear of destruction, or, for that matter, by law. We generally attribute such decisions to judgments of self-interest and rational assessments of probable gains and costs. We may also recognize that nonrational factors—emotions, drives for power, ignorance—have an important role.

The influence of law and morality on such decisions is less certain. Yet the reasons for this uncertainty do not arise from an absence of reference to legal and moral rules; on the contrary, every time a government uses force or responds to such use by others, it invokes the law along with considerations of morality and humanity. This very fact generates cynicism, because it seems possible for every action to find support in law and there appears to be no effective higher authority to settle the matter. These facts understandably lead many people to conclude that the legal rules on the use of force may be used to rationalize and justify almost any use of force; therefore, they can have little if any influence on the actual decision to use force.

Before entering into a detailed analysis of the rules and the use of them, I want to comment on a related question. The absence of an authoritative body to decide conflicting positions objectively and to enforce them has led to a commonly held suspicion that rules, however clear their meaning, are only paper rules, for they may be disregarded or violated to a degree that renders them no more than nominal. This rather sweeping assertion requires further examination. We need to consider first the rather complicated situation with respect to third-party judgments about the use of force. It is true that the absence of compulsory jurisdiction means that the ICJ (or any other nonpolitical tribunal) has been rarely used to decide the legality of the use of force. Exceptions occurred in the case brought in 1949 before the ICJ by Britain against Albania concerning the use of force in the Corfu Channel[5] and in the case brought by Nicaragua against the United States, decided by the ICJ in 1986.[6]

In addition to the ICJ, the UN Security Council is competent under the Charter, particularly under Article 39, to render a decision on whether aggression has occurred. The Security Council is also empowered to adopt enforcement measures under Chapter VII against an aggressor (or, in fact, against any state) if it considers such measures necessary for peace and security. The authority of the Security Council applies to all states, regardless of whether they "consent" to it or participate in the Council's proceedings. In that sense, the Security Council has compulsory jurisdiction, namely, the formal authority to judge violations of the rules on force and to enforce its decisions. Its legal authority is virtually unlimited except for the implicit requirement that it conform to the principles and purposes of the Charter. But the Security Council can make decisions in nonprocedural matters only with the concurrence of the five permanent members,[7] a requirement that, in practice, has prevented the Security Council from reaching many decisions concerning alleged violations of the Charter. The use of the veto is a crucial factor—although not the only one—in the Security Council's failure to exercise the authority given to it under the Charter.

The General Assembly, which may decide important questions by a two-thirds majority, has on occasion adopted decisions that involve judgments on the use of force. Although those decisions are not binding under the Charter, they do not lack "authority," for such resolutions may be regarded as expressing the "general will" of the international community and as being persuasive evidence of legal obligation. It is true that the authority of such resolutions cannot be determined merely by the fact of their adoption. To assess their authority, we would need a more complete consideration of many factors, including the intent and circumstances of the adoption of the resolution, the composition of the supporting majority, the effect on state behavior in both the short and the long run, and the impact on attitudes of relevant publics.[8] There is no simple generalization or formula to enable us to evaluate the effect of such General Assembly decisions, but it is sufficient for our present inquiry to note that they may be (and have been) treated as authoritative in the sense indicated.

Can a political body have authority without power? Perhaps not, but in this context it is appropriate to consider a political body's influence as an aspect of power. Thus, when the General Assembly has condemned force as illegal in a particular case, its decision may be cited in opposition to such conduct by other governments and nongovernment entities of some significance. Consider, for example, how the UN resolution criticizing the use of force by the Soviet Union in Afghanistan[9] affected those Islamic countries and European Communist parties that had previously supported the Soviet position. The resolution in itself cannot be said to have determined the attitude of these bodies, but that it was widely used to underline and record the condemnation is evidence of its effect. At the very least, it was viewed as a political setback for the Soviet Union, with a potentially long-term negative effect on its claim to champion national sovereignty. An effect of this kind is not always a consequence of a resolution, but it shows that such resolutions may have authority irrespective of any formal legal authority they may lack.

In sum, the UN political organs provide an institutional mechanism for authoritative judgments on the use of force, but only under some circumstances can they obtain the requisite authority and consequential compliance to endow their decisions with effective power.

Third-party judgments are made not only by UN and other international institutions but also by governments and peoples throughout the world. When force is used today in international relations, the issue of legal and moral justification is invariably raised. Whether or not a UN organ can reach a decision, individual governments often take positions. Their positions may be expressed as censure, and they may take measures to impose sanctions on the offending government. Similarly, the public and influential nongovernmental organizations react in words and deeds. We need only recall the widespread criticism of force used in Hungary, Czechoslovakia, Vietnam, Cambodia, Angola, Afghanistan, Lebanon, and Nicaragua to see that along with, or sometimes without, UN action, the "world" in its diverse parts passes judgment on the legality of force and on the claims seeking to justify its use. Some observers consider such judgments of minor significance because they do not effectively restrain illegal conduct. The question then is not whether we have authoritative judgments, but whether such judgments are efficacious.

Admittedly, judgments of illegality have not stopped states from continuing to use force in several important cases. Nor can we assert with confidence that governments have actually refrained from force because they expect such use to be declared illegal by others. But these observations do not fully respond to the question, because they give too narrow a focus to the elements of decision. If we take the realistic view that governments deciding for the use of force take into account the diverse considerations referred to earlier—the probable costs and benefits, the responses of other states and publics, the effect on future claims by other states, the value of law compliance to international order—we may conclude that the issue of permissibility under the law is a factor that would normally be considered.

That it is often so is shown, at least in some degree, by the fact that in virtually every case in which force is used, states seek to justify their action by reference to the accepted Charter rules. Although such justification may be no more than a rationalization of an action decided solely on grounds of interest and power, the felt need to issue a legal justification is important. It demonstrates that states require a basis of legitimacy to justify their actions to their own citizens and even more to other states whose cooperation or acquiescence is desired. The fact that claims of legitimacy are also self-serving does not mean that they do not influence conduct by the actors or by those to whom they are addressed. Even if we label those claims as hypocritical (the tribute that vice pays to virtue), they require credibility and for that reason must be confirmed by action. Although not a necessary relationship, the link between conduct and the perceived restraints of law can be easily identified in a great many situations. Power and interest are not superseded by law, but law cannot be excluded from the significant factors influencing the uses of power and the perception of interest.

With these general observations on the relevance of law, let us turn to the question, Does international law lay down sufficiently clear rules governing the use and threat of force to make judgments about the permissibility or impermissibility of such force? Or are the principles in the UN Charter so vague and flexible as to enable states to advance a plausible legal basis for virtually any use of force?

The Meaning of Article 2(4)

The basic provision restricting the use or threat of force in international relations is Article 2, paragraph 4 of the Charter:

> All Members shall refrain in their international relations from the threat or use of force against the territorial integrity or political independence of any State, or in any other manner inconsistent with the Purposes of the United Nations.

The paragraph is complex in its structure, and nearly all its key terms raise questions of interpretation. We know that the principle was intended to outlaw war in its classic sense, that is, the use of military force to acquire territory or other benefits from another state. Actually, the word "war" is not used in Article 2(4). It was used in the League of Nations Covenant and in the Kellogg-Briand Pact of 1928, but it had become evident in the 1930s that states engaged in hostilities without declaring war or calling it war. The word "force" was thus a broader and more factual term to embrace military action.

"Force" has its own ambiguities. It is sometimes used to embrace all types of coercion: economic, political, and psychological, as well as physical. UN members have from time to time sought to give the prohibition in Article 2(4) this broader meaning, particularly to include economic measures that were said to be coercive. Although many states in the Third World expressed support for this broader notion, the Western states strongly resisted it. Other instruments (such as the Charter of Economic Rights and Duties of States)[10] were used to express opposition to economic coercion directed against sovereign rights, but this issue is marginal to the central problem with which Article 2(4) is concerned: the use and threat of armed force.

Even if limited to armed force, the term raises questions of interpretation. Some center on the notion of "indirect" force. Does a state use force when it provides arms to outside forces engaged in hostilities and when it trains troops? Does a state indirectly employ force when it allows its territory to be used by troops fighting in another country? These questions have usually been treated under the rubric of "intervention," a concept that has often been dealt with independent of Article 2(4) and defined as "dictatorial interference by a state in the affairs of another state." Article 2(4), however, remains the most explicit Charter rule[11] against intervention through armed force—indirect and direct—and it is proper to consider such action as falling within the scope of the prohibition. I therefore consider later the question of the indirect use of force by a state in hostilities between other states or internal conflicts.

What is meant by a "threat of force" has not received much consideration. Clearly, a threat to use military action to coerce a state to make concessions is forbidden. But in many situations, the deployment of military forces or missiles has unstated aims and its effect is equivocal. But the preponderance of military strength in some states and their political relations with potential target states may justifiably lead to an inference of a threat of force against the political independence of the target state. An examination of the particular circumstances is necessary to reach that conclusion, but the applicability of Article 2(4) in principle can hardly be denied. Curiously, it has seldom been invoked as an explicit prohibition of such implied threats.[12] The explanation may lie in the subtleties of power relations and the difficulty of demonstrating coercive intent. Or, perhaps more realistically, it may be a manifestation of the general recognition and tolerance of disparities of power and of their effect in maintaining dominant and subordinate relationships between unequal states. Such tolerance, wide as it may be, however, is not without limits. If the words "threat of force" are to have any meaning, a blatant and direct threat of force compelling another state to yield territory or to make substantial political concessions (not required by law) must be seen as illegal under Article 2(4).

Although these interpretive questions concerning the meaning of "force" and "threat of force" are important and indicate that the article requires further definition, they are, nevertheless, essentially peripheral questions. They do not raise questions as to the core meaning of the prohibition, nor do they, therefore, require us to conclude that Article 2(4) lacks determinate content.

A more basic question of interpretation is presented by the peculiar structure of the article. It is generally assumed that the prohibition was intended to preclude all use of force except that allowed as self-defense or authorized by the Security Council under Chapter VII. Yet the article is not drafted that way. The last twenty-three words contain qualifications. The article requires states to refrain from force when it is "against the territorial integrity or political independence of any State" or "inconsistent with the purposes of the United Nations."

These words have given rise to various interpretations. Some have argued that they allow force to be used for benign purposes consistent with the Charter as long as the territory of the state target is not permanently taken and its government continues to function. Accordingly, it has been claimed that states may use their armed force as a self-help measure to secure legal rights threatened by the action of a foreign government, when other means of protection are not available. The British-French attack on Egypt in 1956 in response to the allegedly illegal expropriation of the Suez Canal by Egypt was defended on that ground.[13] Similarly, military interventions of a temporary character to rescue hostages or to put an end to atrocities have been argued as legal, because they are consistent with the human rights purposes of the Charter and do not involve any permanent loss of territory or overthrow of the government in power. These arguments, if accepted, would go a long way to cut down on the scope of Article 2(4). Force would be legitimated as long as it fell short of conquest or the imposition of a puppet government and the attacking state could credibly claim that its motivation was in accord with the purposes of the Charter.

One answer to this line of argument is that the Charter itself requires that disputes be settled by peaceful means (Article 2, paragraph 3) and that the first declared purpose of the Charter is to remove threats to and suppress breaches of the peace. Consequently, any use of force in international relations would be inconsistent with a Charter purpose. The only exceptions would be those expressly allowed by the Charter for self-defense under Article 51 or Article 42 on military enforcement measures.

A second line of argument is that any coercive incursion of armed troops into a foreign state without its consent impairs that state's territorial integrity, and any use of force to coerce a state to adopt a particular policy or action must be considered as an impairment of that state's political independence. On these premises, it does not matter that the coercive action may have only a short-term effect, nor does it matter that the end sought by the use of force is lawful and consistent with the stated purpose of the Charter. As long as the act of force involves a nonconsensual use of a state's territory or compels a state to take a decision it would not otherwise take, Article 2(4) has been violated.

This position has been taken by the great majority of states and by most international lawyers.[14] It finds support in the two decisions of the ICJ concerned with the legality of the use of force. In the *Corfu Channel* case of 1949 between Britain and Albania, the British had used naval vessels for minesweeping in Albanian territorial waters after explosions of mines had killed forty-four British sailors and damaged naval warships. The minesweeping was claimed to be a self-help measure to obtain evidence to support the British claim for damages and therefore as an aid in administering justice. The ICJ held that notwithstanding its aim, the British action was a derogation of Albanian territorial sovereignty.[15] Whatever the intent, the fact that territorial sovereignty was impaired was sufficient for the application of the rule against forcible intervention. It did not matter in that case that derogation of territorial sovereignty was limited in time and intended to "assist" the administration of justice.

In its 1986 judgment in the *Nicaragua* case, the court held that an illegal intervention, short of an armed attack, did not justify the use of force in collective self-defense.[16] It is noteworthy that no judge or state involved in that case suggested that the text of Article 2(4) allowed armed force in the absence of legitimate self-defense.

Arguments have been made, however, that Article 2(4) allows force to be used independent of self-defense in the following circumstances:

- to intervene in a foreign state with the consent of the *de jure* government of that state (referred to sometimes as "intervention on invitation"),
- to recover territory illegally occupied by a foreign state,
- to prevent or suppress atrocities and massive violations of human rights (humanitarian ends),
- to assist a people struggling for national liberation,
- to assist a people struggling for democratic rights against a repressive regime, or

- to protect or secure legal rights when no other means are available.

The arguments for each of these exceptions to the general prohibition are considered in the sections that follow.

Intervention by Invitation

Governments have from time immemorial requested foreign military assistance, usually in response to attacks or threats of attack from without. Governments have also invited foreign forces to combat internal opposition or to secure law and order within the country. Prior to the UN Charter, it was generally argued that the invited state had a legal right to send its forces into the requesting state in accordance with the consent of the latter. Under the UN Charter, the question arises whether Article 2(4) imposes a limit on such "intervention by invitation" in the absence of a legitimate self-defense claim by the inviting state. Does Article 2(4) require a state to refrain from using its armed forces in another country when the purpose is to aid the inviting government in suppressing an insurrection or in maintaining order? These questions may be answered by referring to the last twenty-three words of Article 2(4). When a recognized government invites foreign armed forces to help it maintain internal security, the foreign troops would not, as a rule, be used "against the territorial integrity" or "political independence" of the inviting state, nor would their role normally be inconsistent with any of the purposes of the UN. If those stated conditions are met, there is no violation of Article 2(4).

In some cases, however, questions have arisen as to whether those criteria have been satisfied; for example, when officials purporting to act in the name of the inviting state lack the requisite authority to do so. The clearest case of such questionable authority has occurred when the invitation to a foreign government to intervene was made by officials who had been imposed by the "invited" state. Thus, the claims of the Soviet Union that its troops were invited by the Hungarian government in 1956 and by the Afghanistan government in 1978 were rejected by most states and by world opinion.[17] Clearly, a puppet regime installed by the foreign power cannot validate its armed intervention. On the contrary, the intervening state must be considered as having used force against the territorial integrity and political independence of the state in question.

Whether an "authority" is empowered to consent on behalf of the state may be the key issue, especially when facts and internal law are disputed. A controversy of this kind arose with respect to the claim by the United States that its armed intervention in Grenada in 1983 was undertaken in response to an invitation by the governor-general of Grenada. This claim was challenged in the UN on the ground that the governor-general (an appointee of the queen of England) lacked the constitutional authority to request an intervention. Some observers also believed that U.S. intervention had been set in motion before any request had come from the governor-general.[18] The debate in the UN and the ensuing decision that condemned the U.S. action as illegal showed that most states (including close allies of the United States) were skeptical about the claim that intervention had been "invited" by Grenada.[19]

A more complex issue of consensual "intervention" arises when the government extending the invitation is opposed by a large part of the population, for example, in a civil war. Such situations have not been uncommon. A request for outside military forces made by the government can be questioned on two grounds. First, a government beset by civil strife, the outcome of which may be in doubt, cannot speak for the state or its people as a whole.[20] Second, substantial military aid must be regarded as impairing the right of the people to decide their own political destiny. For these reasons, international law has prohibited states from intervening on either side in a civil war, defined as an internal conflict in which the insurgents are supported by a large number of people or occupy a substantial part of the territory.[21] An important qualification of this position is that foreign intervention may be legally justified as a response to a prior unlawful intervention by another state; this point is considered later in the section on collective self-defense.

Although most international lawyers accept an even-handed noninterventionist rule as existing general international law, it appears that states generally accord the *de jure* government the benefit of the doubt as to its right to receive military aid to be used against internal opponents. Accordingly, an outside state is rarely accused of unlawful conduct when it provides arms, or even forces, to a government as long as that government appears to control most of the territory in its country.[22] For example, neither the supply of arms to Nigeria in its civil war nor the actual sending of troops to a number of former colonial countries to enable the governments to put down attempted coups or local rebellions was condemned as illegal by any international body. In contrast, aid to insurgencies has been regarded as violating the Charter and customary law. An exception to the latter practice appears to be implicit in recent U.S. acts and declarations referred to as the Reagan Doctrine, a subject that is considered in a subsequent section.

Military assistance to a government inviting aid may also be questioned when the inviting government uses the aid for purposes incompatible with the Charter.[23] Providing military aid to a regime engaged in genocide or in systemic denial of basic human rights would surely constitute a use of armed force inconsistent with the declared aims of the Charter. Obviously, no invitation by the regime could legitimate such assistance.[24] UN resolutions barring military aid to South Africa are in keeping with this conclusion.[25] The issue of whether foreign states may use armed force to aid liberation movements fighting colonialist, racist, or repressive regimes is a related issue that requires separate treatment.

Use of Force to Recover "Lost" Territory

One of the most controversial issues concerning the meaning of Article 2(4) has arisen in some cases of territorial disputes. In such cases, states have used force or have threatened to use it in order to take territory that they considered rightfully theirs. Their legal position with respect to Article 2(4) has been that the use of force is not against the territorial integrity of the target state for the simple reason that the area is legally part of the state using force. Thus, India maintained in 1961 when it sent its troops into Goa, then under Portuguese authority, that it was merely moving its troops into a part of India that had been under illegal domination for 450 years. The Indian representative in the Security Council said, "There is no legal frontier—there can be no legal frontier—between India and Goa."[26] Argentina made a similar argument in 1982 in support of its use of troops to "recover" the Malvinas/Falkland Islands.[27] Iraq also took this position in 1981 to support its forcible attempt to regain an area it considered as unlawfully taken by Iran in 1937.[28]

In all these cases, Article 2(4) was at least implicitly argued as inapplicable on the ground that the forcible taking of the territory did not violate the other state's territorial integrity. It was not necessary, under this theory, to assert self-defense as a justification, but an argument based on self-defense was also made as a subsidiary point. It was contended that the allegedly illegal occupant had maintained its authority by armed force, and that this situation should be regarded as a continuing "armed attack" against the rightful sovereign.

In view of the considerable number of territorial disputes in the world at present, the claim that Article 2(4) does not apply to the use of force to recover territory (at least not against the rightful owner) would, if sustained, go a long way toward reducing the scope of the prohibition against force. Therefore, it is of some importance to consider whether the international community as a whole has accepted the legal position asserted by Argentina, India, and Iraq. The record is ambiguous. Many states expressed sympathy for the territorial claims advanced by the states using force. Some, like Venezuela and Guatemala, had similar irredentist claims; others had political ties or strong anticolonial views. A substantial number deplored the use of force, however, and many among them asserted the inconsistency with Article 2(4).

Thus, it cannot be said that most states would agree that the prohibition against force does not apply when a state seeks to recover territory that may have been illegally taken from it. Most states regard such cases as disputes that, under Article 2(3) of the Charter, should be settled by peaceful means. Even if such means are unsuccessful, there is no legal right to use force to rectify the wrong. Underlying this interpretation is a general awareness among governments that making an exception for recovering "illegally occupied" territory would render Article 2(4) nugatory in a large and important group of cases involving threats of force.[29]

To avoid the ambiguity arising from conflicting territorial claims, it would be useful to make it clear in authoritative instruments that the expression "territorial integrity" in Article 2(4) refers to the state that actually exercises authority over the territory, irrespective of disputes about the legality of that authority. The generality of that rule could be sufficiently qualified to cover situations in which actual authority over a disputed area has resulted from hostilities that are still taking place; in such cases, the territorial sovereignty has not been established, and so the use of force against the occupant should not be regarded as "against the territorial integrity" of the state.

It is evident from the interpretation put forward that, in cases of conflicting territorial claims, the prohibition against force is a strong normative support of the status quo. The aggrieved claimant finds "justice" sacrificed to "peace," especially when peaceful means of resolving the territorial issues have been exhausted or are futile. We are probably more conscious of this point today than we were in 1945, when it seemed as though the UN and the ICJ (supplemented perhaps by arbitral settlement) would be generally effective in resolving disputes. That they have not been successful in the cases that burst into violence has undoubtedly influenced the tendency to regard Article 2(4) as an ineffective restraint. Clearly, Article 2(4) cannot in itself restrain force when deeply felt rights to territory are claimed and peaceful means of dispute settlement have been unavailing. Yet, unfortunate as this situation may be, it cannot be an argument for opening a large exception to Article 2(4). Doing so would legitimate the use of force on a scale that cannot be tolerated, because force tends to escalate and spread. On the whole, the international community has recognized this fact. The most recent events show no significant support among states for so far-reaching an exception to Article 2(4).

Use of Force for Humanitarian Ends

Apart from self-defense, the strongest argument for an exception to the prohibition on armed force is the use of force to save populations that are threatened by massacres, atrocities, widespread brutality, and deprivation of elementary human rights. The UN Charter has not ended the sorry historic record of such inhumanity. Internecine wars, mass persecutions, forced expulsions, disappearances, and the breakdown of order have been strongly condemned in international forums and by world opinion, generally. Nonetheless, atrocities have continued, giving rise to a humanitarian demand for armed intervention to end the slaughter and degradation.

In support, it has been argued that the renunciation of armed force could not have been intended to prevent such humanitarian interventions when other means, short of force, had proved ineffective.[30] The interventions, if limited to humanitarian ends under conditions of necessity and proportionality, could not be against the territorial integrity or political independence of the state in question, nor could they be inconsistent with the purposes of the Charter. If neither the UN nor any other international body took effective action, elementary humanitarian principles would obligate states capable of taking protective measures to act, including, if necessary, to employ armed forces in the troubled countries.

These arguments, appealing as they seem to be, have not won the explicit support of the international community of states nor of any significant segment of that community. No UN resolution has supported the right of a state to intervene on humanitarian grounds with armed troops in a state that has not consented to such intervention. Nor is there evidence of state practice and related *opinio juris* on a scale sufficient to support a "humanitarian" exception to the general prohibition against nondefensive use of force.[31]

It is true that, in a few cases, the action of an army intervening beyond its borders was seen as serving a humanitarian end in saving innocent lives from death or injury. Whether these cases can be considered as practice is dubious, especially because no intervening state (with perhaps one exception) contended that its intervention was intended for humanitarian ends alone or claimed that its intervention was a right based on that ground. Thus, when Indian troops acted to protect Bengalis in East Pakistan in 1971 from Pakistani troops, India asserted that the action was necessary to protect its borders. While reference was made to the plight of the Bengalis and the benign effect of Indian protection, the UN General Assembly declined by a large majority to support the Indian arguments, calling on India to withdraw its forces. Despite much sympathy for the East Pakistani Bengalis, the states of the world were clearly unwilling to legitimate India's armed action as a permissible exception to Article 2(4).[32]

A second case that some lawyers have viewed as humanitarian intervention occurred when Tanzanian troops moved into Uganda following a Ugandan frontier incursion repulsed by Tanzania.[33] Tanzania claimed self-defense rather than a right of humanitarian intervention, but its subsequent occupation of Uganda for some months helped to reduce the disorder and atrocities that had been common under the prior Ugandan regime. Whether Tanzania's continued occupation was justified as self-defense is debatable.[34] Understandably, many governments were not disposed to challenge Tanzania's relatively benign occupation, but this reluctance can hardly be regarded as *opinio juris* accepting a broad rule of forcible intervention for human rights ends.[35]

Another claim of humanitarian intent was made by Vietnam to support its armed action in Cambodia in 1978. The main legal claim of Vietnam, however, was that its armed forces had been requested by the Cambodian government in power. That claim was itself questionable, because the Cambodian regime in the country owed its authority to Vietnamese military support. The majority of states in the UN rejected Vietnam's contentions and called for the withdrawal of its troops.[36]

One recent intervention that was generally accepted as unequivocally humanitarian in intent and effect was the French action in 1979 to depose an egregiously brutal leader, Emperor Bokassa, of France's former colony, the Central African Republic. The personal atrocities committed by the leader and the necessity to use force without delay were seen as adequate justifications for French intervention.[37] France's explanation that it had acted solely for humanitarian ends and that such action was necessary was not challenged in international organs.

This exceptional case and one or two others like it should not obscure the reluctance of most states to proclaim a "humanitarian intervention" exception to Article 2(4).[38] Such reluctance should be considered in an assessment of existing law; it is not merely a matter of denying that the one or two cases are evidence of state practice and *opinio juris*. The more important point is the skepticism about the motives of states sending troops abroad on allegedly humanitarian grounds. Past armed interventions, going back to nineteenth-century incursions by imperial powers, are reasons for such skepticism. Intervening states have had their own political interests and often a tendency to impose conditions that were not freely chosen by the people of the country in question. It is not surprising that governments have refrained from adopting a general rule for humanitarian intervention. Indeed, I believe that no government has actually declared itself as favoring so broad an exception to the rule against force.

That no government has done so should not mean, however, that mass killings, genocide, and other egregious violations of elementary principles of humanity should be tolerated or that protective force should never be used by external powers. Safeguards against abusive intervention should be sought. But it is unlikely that this goal can be accomplished merely by formulating legal principles or guidelines on a general level. What is needed is institutional machinery for inquiry and assistance, even in the incipient stages of threatening atrocities. A Hitler, Pol Pot, or Idi Amin should not be tolerated until it is too late. If necessary, the UN should call on individual states to carry out armed action under international auspices. The Security Council has the legal authority to request such action if it can be reasonably held that the inhumane conditions are threats to peace and security. True, experience shows that consensus among the permanent members of the Security Council is not easily attained even when atrocities are extreme and inconvertible. Given this dilemma, the use of force by individual states would have a strong moral justification and be widely condoned. Nonetheless, recognizing this probability—and, in effect, acknowledging the limits of the rule against force—does not require a new rule that could provide a pretext for abusive intervention. It may well be better to acquiesce in a violation of Article 2(4), when it is necessary and desirable in the particular circumstances, than to open a wide gap in the barrier against unilateral use of force.[39]

Use of Force for National Liberation

The anticolonial movement in the UN and the related attacks on "alien rule" and "racist regimes" have been accompanied at times by an argument that force may be used by a foreign state to assist in the liberation of people under colonial or other alien rule. On occasion, the argument has resorted to interpreting Article 2(4) to say not only that the use of force for national liberation was consistent with the purpose of self-determination (expressed in Article 1 of the UN Charter) but also that such use could not be "against the territorial integrity or political independence" of the target state, inasmuch as its occupation by a colonial or "alien" regime was unlawful.[40] As stated earlier, this argument ignores the goal stated in the first paragraph of Article 1: the prevention of breaches of the peace. Clearly, the use of force, for whatever laudable aim, would be inconsistent with the primary purpose of the Charter. That inconsistency does not disappear because armed force is used for one of the other purposes listed in the Charter. Thus, the attempt to find an exception for national liberation movements in the text of Article 2(4) does not withstand analysis. It would be absurd to suggest that prohibiting force "inconsistent with the purposes of the UN" could mean allowing force on the ground that it was consistent with one purpose of the Charter, even if contrary to other purposes.

Despite the weakness of the textual argument, the legitimate use of force in "national liberation" cases has, some have argued, received the approval of the UN General Assembly. The record of the UN deliberations, however, does not support this conclusion, although some isolated speeches may seem to. Commentators who have found such speeches to be an expression of a contemporary "just war" doctrine have given them more significance than they merit. The argument usually relies on General Assembly resolution 2625 (XXV) of 1970, which proclaims the "Declaration of Principles of International Law concerning Friendly Relations and Cooperation among States in Accordance with the Charter of the United Nations." The Declaration of Principles, the result of many years of debate and negotiation, was adopted by consensus, that is, without a vote or any expression of dissent. It has since been referred to by governments as an authoritative declaration of the law of the Charter and pertinent customary law. Its provisions on the right of self-determination (which were the subject of much negotiation) are an amalgam of positions, with subtle shadings of meaning. A key paragraph declares that the subjection of peoples to alien domination and exploitation is contrary to the Charter and that such peoples have the right to resist the "forcible action" that deprives them of their right of self-determination. This provision is compatible with the general understanding that customary law and the Charter do not purport to limit use of force by peoples against their own government or rulers. Civil wars and internal revolutions as such do not fall within the prohibition of Article 2(4), which bars force only "in international relations."

But the UN Declaration of Principles does declare that "every state has the duty to refrain from any forcible action which deprives people of their right to self-determination and freedom and independence." Moreover, it goes on to say that peoples resisting forcible action in pursuit of their right of self-determination "are entitled to seek and receive support in accordance with the purposes and principles of the Charter." It follows that if peoples are entitled to receive "support" by external powers, the latter have a right to extend "support." A key point, however, is that such support cannot be contrary to the Charter principles, which include, of course, Articles 2(3) and 2(4). A number of governments emphasized Article 2(4) when the Declaration of Principles was formulated. The record shows that they voted for it with the understanding that the Charter prohibits the use of armed force by an outside state even if that force is intended to assist the struggle for self-determination and independence.[41] In short, the General Assembly did not adopt a "self-determination" exception to the prohibition of force.

Whether the Declaration of Principles legitimates "support" for struggles of self-determination that fall short of armed force but were previously regarded as illegal intervention remains uncertain. Uncertainty also exists as to the implication of the provision in the Declaration of Principles relating to self-determination:

> Every state shall refrain from any action aimed at the partial or total disruption of the national unity and territorial integrity of any other state or country.

This provision reflects the apparent ambivalence of governments that oppose colonialism and some alien rule but even more strongly oppose support by foreign powers of national, ethnic, and religious communities that seek separation or autonomy. In fact, states of all kinds share a common interest in opposing self-determination that might threaten their own national unity.

Use of Force Against Repressive, Nondemocratic Regimes

Even more contentious than the issue raised by the national liberation movements has been the controversy regarding military aid given to insurgent forces seeking to topple allegedly repressive regimes. In these cases, Soviet-American antagonism has been in the forefront. Communist movements have often received military aid from the Soviet Union and its allies, while resistance forces opposed to leftist governments have obtained arms, training, and advice from the United States and occasionally from other governments that support U.S. positions. A recent U.S. position, known as the Reagan Doctrine, is construed as a general policy to support "freedom fighters" in their armed resistance to pro-Soviet regimes.[42]

From both a political and legal perspective, the Reagan Doctrine in its broad formulation seems to go beyond prior U.S. positions that had involved military aid to anti-Communist forces. Under the Truman policy announced in 1947 (and later elevated to "doctrine"), the United States undertook to give military and economic support to governments of "free peoples" that were resisting "subjugation by armed minorities or by outside pressure."[43] In political terms, the Truman Doctrine supported existing regimes friendly to the United States against Soviet-supported revolutionary movements. From the standpoint of international law, the doctrine was no more than aid to a government at its request for the purpose of maintaining law and order within the country; consequently, it did not involve force against the territorial integrity or political independence of the state.

U.S. military aid to Greece and Turkey, in accordance with the Truman Doctrine, was not widely challenged on legal grounds. However, governments and legal commentators who criticized the Truman Doctrine contended that U.S. aid involved intervention in the Greek civil war, thus violating the political sovereignty guaranteed to every state by international law. From the U.S. perspective, the Soviet Union's support of Yugoslav insurgents in Greece justified U.S. aid to Greece under the principle of collective self-defense.[44]

These legal and policy issues became more controversial when, in the 1960s, the United States expanded its military aid to the South Vietnamese government into a massive military action against both the internal insurgents (Viet Cong) and the government of North Vietnam, which heavily supported the insurgency. Critics condemned the United States on several grounds: for aiding an unpopular government, for seeking to determine the political destiny of South Vietnam, and for "internationalizing" a civil war by carrying it to North Vietnamese territory and neighboring countries.[45] The principal U.S. legal argument asserted the right of collective self-defense on behalf of the independent state of South Vietnam.[46] The U.S. bombings of North Vietnam and Cambodia were claimed to be a necessary and proportionate defense of the Republic of South Vietnam, which had been subjected to armed attack by North Vietnam and the Viet Cong.[47] The judgments on these factual and "categorical" differences have been left to the historians.

The Reagan Doctrine of the 1980s went beyond the principle of aiding established regimes against Communist subversion. It was a response to the increase in the number of Third World governments that had been supported by the Soviet Union and were regarded as under its influence.

A potential threat to U.S. security and a concern over denial of basic democratic rights were given as reasons for U.S. action against the governments in question. Action to overthrow "unfriendly" governments had been taken by U.S. officials on previous occasions (Iran in 1953, Guatemala in 1954, and Chile in 1970), but they were meant to be covert acts supporting internal coups d'état.[48] The United States made no serious attempts to justify them as legal. Indeed, the United States continued to maintain strongly that subversion and indirect aggression were contrary to international law. The Reagan Doctrine, in contrast, openly proclaimed the legitimacy of foreign military intervention to overthrow leftist "totalitarian" governments.

Proponents of the Reagan Doctrine have advanced a variety of legal arguments in its support. One such line of argument, especially favored by nonlawyers, considers the international law rules against unilateral use of force as relatively unimportant. They emphasize the "higher" values of national security and freedom and minimize the prohibitions of international law as dead-letter rules ignored by many states.[49] In addition, they argue that violations by the Soviet Union and others, plus the failure of the UN to protect states by collective action, have destroyed the underlying premises of the Charter principle renouncing the use of force.[50] (These latter arguments warrant separate treatment and will be dealt with later, but it is appropriate to note here that unlike such commentators, the U.S. government has never argued that Article 2(4) is legally defunct; on the contrary, it has condemned others for their violations and defended its own record of compliance.[51])

Other arguments for the lawfulness of the Reagan Doctrine attempt to find support in the Charter itself. One argument relies on those Charter principles that support self-rule and political freedom and maintains that a "contextual" interpretation supersedes a "restrictive" or "textual" reading of Article 2(4).[52] Another argument claims Article 2(4) to be simply a "means," and therefore subordinate, to the Charter's ends. Although these arguments are based on "higher purposes," they are the same as those made to support the right to use force for national liberation or for humanitarian ends. As noted earlier, they ignore the primary purpose of the Charter—to prevent breaches of the peace—and they would deprive both Article 2(3) and Article 2(4) of nearly all their effect.

A further argument for the Reagan Doctrine maintains that governments that deny political freedoms and democratic rights cannot be considered to be based on "the consent of the governed" and, consequently, they lack legitimacy in a political and legal sense.[53] They are said to be no more than de facto regimes that should not represent the state or its people under international law. Accordingly, the use of force against such regimes by an outside power would not be against the territorial integrity or political independence of the state. This argument, standing alone, has never been presented as the official U.S. position, although it has been suggested in statements of supporters of the Reagan Doctrine.[54] The argument, if applied consistently, would have profound implications for the international system, because many, if not most, governments of the world do not meet the main conditions of political democracy. To consider that deficiency as a sufficient basis to deny their legitimacy and thereby to allow other states to use force against them would be a radical departure from the present rules of the state system.

Implementation of the Reagan Doctrine has been more limited than its rhetoric would suggest. It has been confined thus far to providing military arms, supplies, and some military advisers to insurgent movements. Aid has been given only to resistance forces fighting regimes that have been heavily supported with Soviet Bloc military and economic aid.[55] It may be argued (although not absolutely demonstrated) that the resistance forces receiving U.S. aid have had significant popular support. Assuming these propositions are factual, they provide grounds to present the U.S. action as a "counterintervention" against a prior illegal use of force by Soviet Bloc states. This hypothesis supports the lawfulness of the U.S. intervention, prima facie, as collective self-defense or a lawful countermeasure to the delictual conduct of the Soviet Union and its allies. Although the issue of counterintervention qua defense is discussed later in consideration of self-defense, it should be said here that the Reagan Doctrine has been expressed and construed more as a defense of ideology or morality than as a defense against military aggression.

The United States has not submitted the Reagan Doctrine, as such, to the UN or any other major international forum. Any such proposal would most likely be rejected by most states. The debate and vote on the Grenada invasion is indicative;[56] hardly any democratic governments supported that intervention, despite their antipathy to tyrannical and brutal governments. Nor have they argued that because such governments lack "political legitimacy" they may be overthrown by foreign powers.

The idea that armed invasions could make the world "safe for democracy" has had little appeal to governments. Memories of past invasions and seizures of power in the name of self-determination and freedom are still fresh in many parts of the world. "People's democracies" have been imposed on unwilling peoples. Even states deeply committed to democracy have grounds to fear the manipulative and tendentious use of self-determination as a ground for foreign intervention. Governments of various shades of opinion have a common interest in rejecting a principle that would encourage internal opposition movements to seek foreign military support to topple their allegedly nondemocratic regimes. Moreover, the world in general has good reason to worry about the risks of escalation resulting from ideological wars, particularly those involving major powers.

For all these reasons, it is unlikely that the strong rhetorical version of the Reagan Doctrine will be accepted as part of contemporary international law. However, collective self-defense, as recognized in Article 51 of the UN Charter, still provides a legal basis for counterintervention by a third state against illegal military intervention by a foreign power. This point is discussed later in our consideration of collective defense.

Use of Force to Safeguard the Legal Rights of States

Prior to the UN Charter, customary international law was often understood to allow states to take forcible measures of self-help to safeguard or vindicate their legal rights.[57] A state could therefore respond with force to an unlawful action that injured or threatened a protected legal interest, regardless of whether the unlawful act involved a threat or use of force. Although such forcible self-help was subject to requirements of necessity and proportionality, a state violating its legal obligations to another state opened itself to armed measures by the aggrieved state. "Gunboat diplomacy" by the more powerful states was justified as self-help against lawless acts. (An exception, known as the Drago Doctrine, purported to exclude forcible self-help to collect debts; it was recognized by a number of states, including the United States, in a multilateral treaty of 1907.)[58]

After 1945, forcible self-help, other than self-defense, was generally considered incompatible with Article 2(4) of the Charter. Moreover, after 1945, there was also reason to regard it as contrary to customary law. In the *Corfu Channel* case referred to earlier, the British claimed that its use of naval vessels to obtain evidence needed for its legal claim against Albania was justified as self-help. However, the ICJ characterized the British action as the "manifestation of a policy of force," and it was held to be illegal.[59] Because the ICJ made no reference to the Charter, its decision can be regarded as an application of the customary law that evolved after 1945.

The issue of forcible self-help to protect a legal right came before the UN in 1956 after the British and French invaded Egypt in reaction to the Egyptian expropriation of the Suez Canal Authority, a company owned jointly by British and French nationals. The two invading states argued that the Egyptian expropriation had violated their legal rights under the law of state responsibility, that efforts at peaceful resolution had failed, and that no other recourse was available. The Security Council members, other than the two accused states, considered the invasion to be unlawful under the Charter.[60] The United States concurred with that view, as did the great majority of UN members, and most, but not all, international lawyers.

The question of using force to safeguard legal rights remains contentious. Concern is often expressed that the inability of an aggrieved state to employ armed force as a last resort encourages states to evade their legal obligations when such evasion serves their interest. It is argued that the absence, or at least the weakness, of collective enforcement machinery means that in many cases only unilateral forcible action could be effective. Although self-help measures short of force (such as suspending trade or financial benefits) may be used, experience shows they do not always provide adequate remedies. Hence, the argument continues that a denial of the right to use force leaves law-abiding states at the mercy of the lawless. This argument, often eloquently stated, has had a strong appeal in militarily powerful countries that have felt injured or threatened by the illegal acts of weaker states.

Some international lawyers, responsive to this argument, have proposed legal grounds to permit forcible self-help against injurious breaches of law. They emphasize the interdependency of the Charter provisions for collective action and the renunciation of force in Article 2(4). Accordingly, illegal conduct harmful to important state interests should release the injured state from its obligation to refrain from force in such cases.[61]

I do not find this argument persuasive. Nothing in the Charter or in its negotiating history suggests that the renunciation of unilateral recourse to force in Article 2(4) was intended to be conditioned on measures to give effect to legal rights. In fact, the Charter provisions for collective measures—especially those of a mandatory character—were designed to maintain peace and security; they were not intended to protect legal rights. Such protection is left to optional judicial recourse and to measures to be developed by agreement of states. Whereas this arrangement may be considered a deficiency of the Charter, it expresses the position taken in 1945 by the major powers, including the United States. This position was well known at the time of the Charter's entry into force, and it has remained true. Thus, there is no factual basis to maintain that the prohibition of force was meant to depend on collective enforcement of legal rights. So drastic a conclusion—in effect, licensing the use of force against a wide area of international wrongs—would surely have been expressed or at least referred to if it had been contemplated when the Charter was adopted.

A different line of argument seeks to legitimate forcible self-help by placing it under a broad conception of self-defense.[62] Before 1945, some scholars fused (or perhaps confused) self-help and self-defense; they treated measures to safeguard legally protected interests interchangeably as self-help or self-defense. This rather vague way of broadening self-defense is neither Charter law nor customary law. Self-defense requires an attack, or at least an imminent threat of attack, against the territory or political independence of the state. The breach of a legal obligation in itself would not be a ground for the use of force, even if that breach involved considerable injury to the state in question.

This interpretation does not mean that force is always barred when legal rights are threatened. Because a state may lawfully exercise a legal right in a peaceful manner, it may do so in appropriate ways to support its claim of right. An example is the passage of a vessel through territorial waters of another state within the legally permissible limits. In the *Corfu Channel* case, the ICJ recognized this right with regard to the passage of the British warships, which was intended to vindicate their right of passage.[63] (This action was permissible, but the later minesweeping, which had a military character, was held to be illegal.) Such naval passage is lawful, although it may be undertaken as a "demonstration." If another state resorts to force against the lawful exercise of a right, that act of force is unlawful and it gives rise to the right of forcible self-defense to the extent necessary and proportionate.

In sum, a state may deploy its military forces (within the limits of international law) to assert and secure a legal right. If another state uses force to prevent that exercise of right, the aggrieved state may respond with proportionate force. To that extent the Charter and customary law allow a state to take forcible action to protect its legal rights.

Has Article 2(4) Lost Its Legal Force?

Some proponents of a right to use armed force for purposes other than self-defense and UN enforcement measures have not only argued for exceptions (as we have seen) but have also maintained that conditions that have developed after the Charter's entry into force have rendered Article 2(4) legally defunct.

One such argument proceeds from the premise that the prohibition on force in Article 2(4) was part of the comprehensive agreement contained in the Charter for maintaining international peace and security. States would not have agreed to renounce unilateral recourse to force, it is argued, if the Charter had not provided a collective security system with enforcement measures. One eminent advocate of this position claimed that the prohibition against the use of force was intended to be "organically dependent on the effective establishment of collective institutions and methods."[64] Inasmuch as the UN has not been effective in ending international lawlessness and violence, he concluded, states should be released from their commitment to renounce the use of force. Otherwise, Article 2(4) becomes a shield for the lawless.

This argument rests on several assumptions. One concerns the "original intent" of the parties to the Charter. It is claimed that governments would not have given up the right to use force if the new international organization had not been given enforcement powers to maintain peace. This argument is not implausible, particularly in view of the importance attached to the Security Council's enforcement powers when the Charter was adopted. It does not follow, however, that the parties intended that the obligation of Article 2(4) restraining force would be conditioned on "effective" collective measures. It is hard to believe that, if that were the case, so basic a point would not have been discussed and referred to in the Charter itself or in the preparatory work. There is no hint of such intent. The ban on force had already emerged as nascent customary law prior to the Charter. Its inclusion in the Charter was not accompanied by any qualification arising from the failure to adopt collective measures. Such a condition would make little sense in the light of the voting requirements for Security Council decisions (particularly the veto). For those requirements would lose their importance if the absence of Security Council action released a state from the restriction on use of force. Nonaction by the Security Council cannot confer a new legal right on a state. The right to use force in that case depends only on whether the conditions of legitimate self-defense have been met in accordance with Article 51 and customary law. Nothing in the Charter or in general international law provides any ground for inferring an independent right to use force because the Security Council has failed to adopt collective measures.

It is also incorrect to conclude that "collective security" has failed when legal rights have been infringed and no remedy, short of force, is available in a particular case. The Charter makes it clear that UN enforcement measures were intended to be taken only to maintain or restore international peace and security. They were not meant to ensure compliance with the law or to bring about justice.[65] True, the Security Council may, at its discretion, decide that a state should comply with a legal obligation, but it has the responsibility to do so only if such a decision would serve peace and security. It cannot be maintained, therefore, that collective security, as established by the Charter, has failed because it has provided no remedy for a legal violation.

A somewhat different line of argument for denying legal force to Article 2(4) is based on the charge that the article has been violated on many occasions. That there have been violations is undeniable. The violations have varied greatly in their extent, intensity, duration, and modality. None of the violations compares with the Nazi and Japanese aggression of World War II. Most of the armed conflicts that have occurred since the Charter was adopted have been relatively minor clashes or interventions into internal conflicts. In nearly every case, the states concerned have claimed their use of force to be self-defense.

The legal argument that Article 2(4) has been nullified by violations has been advanced on three distinct legal grounds. One has focused on the general principle of reciprocal observance.[66] A state should not be bound by a rule that others flout or ignore. A second argues on the basis of *rebus sic stantibus*, namely, that infringements of Article 2(4) have so radically changed the positions of states that any party may invoke the violations as a legal reason to disregard or suspend its obligations to refrain from force. Still a third argument contends that the violations are evidence of state practice sufficiently widespread to be taken as evidence of a general interpretation of the Charter and customary law. Each of these points has some basis in political reality and legal principle. No doubt, a minimal level of observance over time is an essential condition for maintaining the force of law. Nor can it be denied that changes in international relations, manifested in new configurations of power and threats of destructive weapons, may affect attitudes toward rules on force and perhaps lead to changes. However, the question here is whether actual conditions have reached a stage at which the basic prohibition on use of force can be regarded as a nullity. The crux of the matter seems to be that no state, however powerful or resentful, has been prepared to argue that Article 2(4) should no longer be in force. No state is ready to propose sweeping exceptions to the prohibition.

The very states that have used force, arguably violating the rule, have claimed that the rule has not been abrogated or modified. Instead, they have relied on exceptions or justifications contained within the rule itself, or, most frequently, self-defense under Article 51. The ICJ took note of this in its judgment on the merits in the case of *Nicaragua* v. *United States*:

> If a State acts in a way incompatible with a recognized rule but defends its conduct by appealing to exceptions or justifications contained within the rule itself then, whether or not the State's conduct is justifiable on that basis, the significance of that attitude is to confirm rather than to weaken the rule.[67]

This observation should not be taken as giving priority to verbal rationalization over deeds. What is significant is the current reluctance of states to abandon Article 2(4). When governments declare, as they have repeatedly, that Article 2(4) is the fundamental precept of the current state system, they are rejecting the conclusion that violations, even if serious, can nullify the law. They are not practices "accepted as law." Nor, for that matter, can such violations be regarded as state "practice"; they are relatively few in comparison with the large number of disputes and conflicts between states that do not involve force.

The basic reality is that a stable society of independent notions cannot exist if each is free to destroy the independence of the others. The legal constraint on the use of force reflects this reality. Neither the failures of the UN nor the violations of the Charter justify a conclusion that would allow states to wage war freely. It would be foolish and dangerous to conclude that infringements by some have, under principles of reciprocity or "changed circumstances," released all from a rule so fundamental for world order.

Self-Defense in Law and Policy

Self-defense has been characterized as the modern equivalent of "just war." It is the only generally accepted legal ground for the use of force by one state against another, apart from collective enforcement ordered by the Security Council. States that have resorted to force in recent years have nearly always claimed self-defense—individual or collective—as their legal ground and motive. Such claims have often been controverted, for reasons of fact or law, but no government or legal scholar has denied that every state is entitled to act in self-defense when necessary.

In international law, self-defense is the permissible use of force in response to an illegal use of force. It is generally agreed that self-defense is not legitimate unless it meets the requirements of necessity and proportionality. Beyond these broad conditions, significant areas of disagreement exist as to their application. Before we consider those issues, however, it seems appropriate to consider a basic threshold issue, namely, whether self-defense can and should be governed by international law. That question has more than theoretical importance.

Dean Acheson, a former U.S. secretary of state and eminent lawyer, put the issue sharply when he declared in 1963 that "the survival of states is not a matter of law."[68] Acheson was then admonishing international lawyers for debating the lawfulness of the U.S. threat of force in 1962 to compel the removal of Soviet missiles from Cuba. To Acheson, the missiles threatened destruction of the American way of life. Acheson's conclusion would, as he recognized, leave it to each state to decide whether its survival as a state or of its "way of life" was at stake.

An essentially similar, if less aphoristic, emphasis on the ultimate self-judging character of a claim of self-defense was advanced by the U.S. counsel in the case brought by Nicaragua against the United States in the ICJ. Counsel argued then that the claim of self-defense made by the United States was not justiciable, because only the defending state could determine its need to use force and the extent and means required. Although the ICJ did not agree, the United States has maintained its position. In explaining why the United States would not and should not submit to the ICJ's jurisdiction in regard to its use of force in self-defense, the legal adviser of the State Department declared to congressional committees that the exercise of self-defense cannot be subject to the decision of any external body, inasmuch as the national security of the United States was involved:[69] "Such matters are the ultimate responsibility assigned by our constitution to the President and the Congress."[70] The implication was that every state was free to determine the necessity of self-defense without being subject to the decision of an "external body." This argument, it must be recognized, has a powerful political appeal. How can a state faced with a perceived imminent threat to its independence or territorial integrity leave it to others to decide on the need to use force in its defense, especially when international institutions are unlikely to extend adequate protection?

To allow an entity—state or person—that claims a legal right to decide exclusively and finally on the lawfulness of the exercise of law, however, brings law to the vanishing point. International tribunals faced with claims of self-defense have implicitly recognized this danger. In 1946, counsel argued on behalf of the Nazi leaders before the International Military Tribunal in Nuremberg that Germany had acted in self-defense and that every state must be the judge of whether, in a given case, it has the right of self-defense. The tribunal rejected that contention, however, observing that "whether action taken under the claim of self-defense was in fact aggressive or defensive must ultimately be subject to investigation or adjudication if international law is ever to be enforced."[71]

The ICJ in *Nicaragua* v. *The United States* took a similar position in rejecting U.S. arguments that a claim of self-defense was not justiciable. Even the American member of the ICJ, Judge Stephen Schwebel, who dissented on other points, concurred with the ICJ that the right of self-defense was, in principle, justiciable.[72] Schwebel placed much weight on the analysis of Sir Hersch Lauterpacht, rejecting the claim that self-defense is not amenable to evaluation by the law. Lauterpacht had concluded, "Such a claim is self-contradictory inasmuch as it purports to be based on legal right and as at the same time, it dissociated itself from regulation and evaluation by the law."[73]

Lauterpacht's analysis, as presented in his classic work, *The Function of Law in the International Community*, likened self-defense in international law to the corresponding right in municipal law. In both cases, Lauterpacht said, the right was "absolute," in the sense that no law could disregard it. Moreover, a state, like an individual, would have to decide in the first instance whether immediate use of force in defense was necessary. However, the right was also "relative," inasmuch as it is presumably regulated by law. "It is regulated to the extent that it is the business of the courts to determine whether, how far, and for how long, there was a necessity to have recourse to it."[74]

Lauterpacht was aware, of course, that, on the international level, most states resisted submitting disputes regarding their use of force to judicial process. That state of affairs, he emphasized, was in contradiction to the emerging law regulating the use of force.[75] States could not have it both ways: if they did not accept the principle of justiciability, the legal dimension of self-defense disappears and with it the regulation of force by law.

Since Lauterpacht wrote, the UN Charter and related instruments approved by all states have affirmed that self-defense is regulated by law, but they have not brought about the judicial control he considered essential. International courts have passed judgment on self-defense in the two cases mentioned: the Nuremberg judgment of 1946 and the ICJ judgments of 1985 and 1986 in the *Nicaragua* case. The Tokyo war crimes judgment of 1948 is a third example. These decisions indicate that a claim of self-defense can be judicially evaluated by a tribunal empowered to pass on the issues. But it is more significant that the cases are so few in relation to the numerous disputes over the legality of use of armed force. The contradiction noted by Lauterpacht persists: states claiming a legal right to use force continue to resist judicial scrutiny of their claim. This point was dramatically confirmed by the U.S. withdrawal from the *Nicaragua* case when the court assumed jurisdiction on the basis of the acceptance of compulsory jurisdiction by the United States in 1946.

The resistance to review by an international organ is also evidenced by practice in the UN. States that have resorted to force, claiming self-defense, have rarely complied with the requirement of Article 51 that such measures "shall be immediately reported to the Security Council." The failure to report has not precluded the Security Council from considering, and in some cases passing judgment on, such claims when the matter was raised by states that questioned the legality of the use of force.[76] The Security Council has rejected claims of self-defense in several cases (nearly all of which were taken against states whose policies were generally disapproved by large majorities.)[77] No resolution that explicitly upholds a claim of self-defense has been adopted, although in a few cases (for example, the Malvinas/Falkland Islands conflict)[78] a Security Council resolution or its nonaction has been construed as acceptance of the self-defense claim. The veto has precluded the Security Council, more often than not, from reaching formal decisions on the validity of such claims. Most of those cases were then considered by the General Assembly, which, unfettered by the veto, condemned the alleged self-defense action as a Charter violation. In no such case, however, has the target state accepted the UN decision as binding.

This situation could be said to show that each state remains the judge of its own cause in matters of self-defense; it also shows, however, that the decisions of a court are not the only way to determine lawfulness. In fact, appraisals of legality of state conduct, especially in regard to the use of armed force, are made in a variety of nonjudicial contexts. Since 1945, each time a state has used armed force outside its borders, lawfulness has been subject to third-party judgment. Such judgments have been made by other governments, expressed individually or in collective political bodies. They have also been made by the community of international lawyers, by organs of opinion, by political parties, and by other nongovernmental organizations. There is, in this sense, no escape from the judgments of the interested communities. They vary, to be sure, in their quality, objectivity, and impact on the conduct of the state in question. The processes as well as the results are uneven. Yet it is clear that, in the end, no state is actually the sole judge of its own cause when it claims to have used force in self-defense.

It is true that these various judgments are not binding or enforceable in the way judicial judgments are supposed to be, and their objectivity may be questioned because they often appear to be influenced more by political attitudes than by legal standards. But these deficiencies are not the whole story. Votes in international bodies show that the reactions to use of force are not always dictated by political affinities in disregard of facts and law. States that are friendly to, or even closely allied with, an accused state have not hesitated to cast their vote against that state when the issues were clear. Even the most powerful states have not been immune to censure by states that normally would follow their lead. The overwhelming majorities that have censured the Soviet Union for its Afghanistan invasion and have condemned the United States for its actions in Grenada and Nicaragua are notable examples.

Clearly, international violence is not a matter of indifference to the world; nor is it considered to be solely a political problem. States accused of illegality take pains to show their conduct as legitimate self-defense. They are mindful of the political costs of adverse opinion, even though they may persist in the questionable use of force. Significantly, accused states do not deny that they are bound by international rules; they rest their justification on factual assessments or interpretations that would bring them within the law. The ICJ took note of this tendency in its 1986 judgment in the *Nicaragua* case, declaring that the case confirmed the general acceptance of the rules on force as binding law.[79]

Of course, such "acceptance" does not fully answer the perennial question of whether legal principles significantly influence states in their planning or use of force. Political analysts often regard legal justifications as after-the-fact rationalizations that have little if any effect on the actual decisions. They maintain that, at bottom, such decisions are based on considerations of power and interest, which nearly always prevail over contrary legal restraints. This broad generalization, which is probably widely accepted, raises more questions than it answers. In particular, it leaves open the critical issue of whether the limitations on the use of force serve the national interests and the security of states. To counterpoise "interest" and "law" as conflicting factors in this context is misleading. Even on the premise of an essentially anarchical, Hobbesian conception of international society, the coexistence of independent states and their mutually beneficial intercourse are seen to require some restraints on the unilateral recourse to force.

Therefore, the agreement of states is that self-defense—defined by international law as the only ground for unilateral use of force—is not in itself inconsistent with the "realist" thesis of national self-interest. This thesis recognizes that international violence has not been eliminated by the legal prohibitions in the UN Charter or by its collective security provisions and, consequently, a right of self-defense must be legitimated. It also recognizes, through the right of collective self-defense, that the targets of aggression may require armed assistance by other states.

Recognizing these rights as exceptions to the general prohibition on force necessarily presupposes that exercise of the right is limited by law. If it were not and each state remained free to decide for itself when and to what extent it may use force, the legal restraint on force would virtually disappear. It surely cannot be said that this result is perceived to be in the national interest of states generally or, for that matter, in the interest of the most powerful states. Neither the United States nor the Soviet Union can realistically consider recognizing the unlimited right of each to use force to be in its national interest. They cannot, therefore, accept a self-judging conception of the right of self-defense without, in effect, licensing the other state to resort to force whenever it chooses to do so.

To say that self-defense must be regulated by law does not assume that general rules are sufficient in themselves to ensure the security of all states. The UN Charter and other relevant agreements make it quite clear that the maintenance of peace and security requires more than agreement on principles of law. Decisions must be taken in specific cases. States must react in words and deeds to claims of self-defense when force is used. Such responses are not automatic or foreordained; they involve acts of will and, therefore, assessments of interest and power. Governments rarely, if ever, make such decisions solely on legal grounds; they are not expected to behave like a court. But whatever factors determine such decisions, once made they become part of the law-shaping process, influencing expectations as to the acceptability of future actions affecting use of force. Most governments recognize this fact. Regardless of whether they are themselves involved in the particular conflict, they are aware of the implications for other conflicts and, often, of their own interest in avoiding the spread of hostilities. Legality matters to them, not only as rhetoric to win support but also as a factor to be taken into account as part of the effort to contain violence and reduce the risks of the escalation of force.

A critical question affecting both law and policy on self-defense concerns the degree of uncertainty or indeterminacy that is inherent in the proclaimed legal limits. Some indeterminacy results from the key standards of necessity and proportionality, concepts that leave ample room for diverse opinions in particular cases. Other sources of uncertainty are differing interpretations of the events that would permit a forcible defensive action. Governments and scholars have advanced varying views relating to the kinds of illegal force that would trigger the right of an armed defensive response. Although nearly all states have taken strong positions against "preventive" or "preemptive" war, some uncertainty remains as to the justifiability of threats of force against what is perceived as an imminent attack. Other issues, highlighted by the *Nicaragua* case, involve the illegal use of force through subversion, supply of arms, and logistic support of armed forces as sufficient ground for defensive response. It is not entirely clear to what extent self-defense responding to an armed attack embraces the use of force as a deterrent to future attacks. Nor is there agreement on the circumstances that would permit a state to intervene (or "counterintervene") in an internal conflict under the principle of collective self-defense. Even more unsettling is the uncertainty concerning the first use of nuclear weapons, the targeting of civilian centers, and the proportionality of retaliatory action.

These controversial issues indicate that the rules of self-defense fall far short of a code of conduct that would provide precise "hard law" for many cases likely to arise. Even though governments have a stake in securing clarity as to what is permitted and forbidden, there are obvious limits to achieving that objective. General formulas accepted as law are subject to continuing interpretation and, therefore, fresh arguments as to what the law should be. Concrete situations create new perceptions and "accomplished facts." At times the line between violations and emerging law may be difficult to draw because of the absence of judicial authority and the great disparities in power in the international community. Lawmaking authority does not reside in majorities in international assemblies, even though large majorities cannot usually be ignored.

Powerful states—that is, those with the ability to control the outcome of contested decisions—may determine patterns of conduct for other states as well as for themselves. But their ability to do so is limited by the checks and balances inherent in the distribution of power and, in particular, by the nuclear standoff. Clearly, the two superpowers are not all-powerful hegemonies; they are not able to exercise complete control over the use of force by weaker states, not even by those close to their borders. The rough parity of power between them undoubtedly contributes to restraint. It does not eliminate, however, the struggles within states that erupt beyond their borders or the localized hostilities between neighboring states that threaten to spread. The application of legal rules in these cases and the formulation of new rules derived from practice "accepted as law" are not decided by the great powers alone. Bipolarity of power is a significant structural feature of current international society, but it is only one of the many factors that affect the positions of states on the lawfulness of force used in self-defense.

Notwithstanding its relative indeterminacy, self-defense as a legal norm has an ascertainable relationship to the policies and actions of governments. The "defensist" principle, namely, that self-defense is the only legitimate reason to use force against another state, has been expressed as the strategic policy of most states.[80] Evidence for this defensist doctrine is not only found in government statements to international bodies where they may be expected, but recent studies by political scientists and students of military strategy also confirm the practical implications of defensist doctrine. When states proclaim the principle of self-defense as governing their use of force, they have a stake in its credibility to other states and to their own citizens.[81] To be credible, a defensist policy should be evident in their weapons, training, and contingency planning.

Moreover, a defensist doctrine practically affects a state's way of reducing threats and resolving conflicts without the use of force. The doctrine not merely restrains, but serves as a policy source that goes beyond the law's essentially negative rules. It has obvious implications for such protective activities as monitoring and inspection. It also calls for limitations on weaponry and balance among adversaries. The danger is that systems purporting to be defensive may be perceived as offensive and, therefore, "destabilizing" becomes a matter of central concern. An obvious consequence of defensist doctrine is that states no longer consider that they may invade other states for objectives that were considered legitimate and appropriate in prior periods. Thus, the naked use of force to gain economic benefits, avenge past injustices, civilize "inferior" people, vindicate honor, or achieve "manifest destiny" is no longer asserted as national policy. Historically speaking, this change in the relations of states is a profound one.

I do not mean to suggest that power—or, more precisely, relative power differentials among states—no longer matters. Acceptance of the legal norm of self-defense as the sole legitimate use of force has not eliminated military strength as a major factor in the relations of states. States will react, as they have in the past, to perceived power imbalances that are seen as threatening their present position and vital interests. Disparities in power may involve implied or sometimes expressed threats of force to influence behavior of other states. Armaments and military alliances are considered necessary and legitimate responses to such threats. Neither the Charter nor customary law imposes limits on the size or composition of armed forces or on military pacts for defense. States are legally free to deploy their forces as they choose within their territories or in the territories of consenting states. They are also entitled to deploy armed force in areas beyond national jurisdiction (notably, the high seas) except insofar as they have entered into treaties to limit their activity. The military establishments and the protective measures of states are governed, by and large, by national defense policies and the "politics of security," rather than by the international law governing use of force and self-defense.

Even so, international law is not entirely excluded. It becomes relevant to national security policy in different ways, all of which are rooted in the idea that force should not be used or threatened except in self-defense. States that accept this defensist principle—as nearly all do (although future exceptions cannot be ruled out)—are faced with heavy political and economic costs when they seek security by unilateral action. Such costs may be reduced by mutual arrangements with possible adversaries. But the choice may involve the so-called security dilemma, namely, the likelihood that unilateral measures intended to increase a nation's security decrease the security of others; whereas joint measures, although less costly, involve a measure of insecurity because of the fear of violations by the other parties.[82] The risks contribute to the complexities of international negotiations concerning mutual security. Whatever the dynamics of such negotiations and the obstacles encountered in particular cases, we now find many arrangements, bilateral and multilateral, that involve reciprocal restraints on national military activity. They extend to kinds of weapons; deployment of forces; military exercises; testing; and, in some cases, size of forces.

When these arrangements are embodied in treaties, they are readily seen as part of international law, as instances of a *lex social* is governing specific activities for the states that are parties. States may, of course, also agree on restraints in instruments that are not treaties, such as political declarations or gentlemen's agreements, or by tacit understandings expressed in reciprocal practices. Although these arrangements are not regarded as legal commitments, they are observed and relied on as long as the states concerned have a common interest in maintaining them. Violations in these cases may be treated substantially the same as they are treated with respect to treaties: they may be grounds for protest, termination of the arrangement, or countermeasures. The difference between nontreaty regimes and treaties may be important for domestic constitutional processes, but the distinction may make no significant difference in the observance of the rules and restraints. In some cases, nontreaty practice becomes "special" custom, recognized as legally obligatory customary law for the states concerned. Even apart from these cases, in which nontreaty practice becomes customary law, the distinction between the formal treaty obligations and the "rules of the game," based on tacit understandings and practice, may not have much practical significance.

The point I wish to emphasize is that national security policies, premised on defense, have produced a variety of international arrangements that enable states, particularly potential adversaries, to impose limits on their military establishment and activities in the well-founded expectation that others will do the same. The costs of self-defense are thereby reduced, although states still have to seek means of dealing with the risks of violation. Provisions may be made for verification, consultative procedures, countermeasures, and settlement of disputes. Such measures strengthen the understanding that the restraints are not simply arrangements of convenience to be broken at will. It is surely appropriate for governments as well as international lawyers to treat these regulatory arrangements as part of the body of international law, as rules of conduct, and not merely as transient power bargaining.

The more controversial questions of self-defense have been raised by actions and claims that would expand a state's right to use force beyond the archetypal case of an armed attack on its territory or instrumentality. Such expanded conceptions of self-defense are exemplified by the following uses of force by states claiming self-defense:

- to rescue political hostages believed to face imminent danger of death or injury;[83]
- to retaliate against officials or installations in a foreign state believed to support terrorist acts directed against nationals of the state claiming the right of defense;[84]
- to attack troops, planes, vessels, or installations in an effort to forestall imminent attack by a foreign state with declared hostile intent;[85]
- to retaliate against, and thereby deter, renewed attacks by a foreign government or military force;[86]
- to retaliate against a government that has provided arms or technical support to insurgents in a third state;[87]

- to retaliate against a government that has allowed its territory to be used by a hostile third state for its military forces;[88] or
- to act in the name of collective defense against a government imposed by foreign forces and faced with large-scale military resistance by many of its people (counterintervention).[89]

As indicated by the footnote references, these categories summarize situations that have occurred in recent years. The list is not complete; governments have asserted other extended self-defense claims to justify their use of force or to threaten such use in some situations. Nearly all such cases have been discussed in UN bodies, and, although opinion has been divided, it is clear that most governments are reluctant to legitimate expanded self-defense actions that go beyond the paradigmatic case. Thus, no UN resolution has approved the use of force in any of the cases referred to. In the few cases in which resolutions passing judgment on the legality of the action were adopted, they denied the validity of the self-defense claim. In many cases, resolutions were not adopted, but the majority of states that addressed the issue of lawfulness criticized the actions as contrary to the Charter. Few ventured to defend the legality of the self-defense claim.

Of course, political sympathies influenced the votes of many states; as we observed earlier, however, in several notable cases, states joined in condemning the actions of allied or friendly states. In at least some of these cases, and perhaps in all of them, the opposition to the self-defense claims appeared to be based in part on a difference of view about the facts. In many cases, assertions of the state claiming self-defense were simply not believed; in some cases, the factual claims of both sides to the dispute were treated with the utmost skepticism. The uncertainty surrounding the factual claims, together with significant political motivations, are reasons why condemnation by governments in the UN bodies cannot always be accepted as conclusive on the issue of lawfulness. Nor, conversely, can condemnations be ignored; they warrant consideration as relevant appraisals.

In a broader perspective, the general reluctance to approve uses of force under expanded conceptions of self-defense is itself significant. Such reluctance is evidence of a widespread perception that widening the scope of self-defense will erode the basic rule against unilateral recourse to force. The absence of judicial or other third-party determinations relating to use of force adds to the apprehension that a more permissive rule of self-defense will open the way to further disregard of the limits on force. The refusal of the United States to take part in the proceedings of the ICJ on the merits in the *Nicaragua* case, and its noncompliance with the judgment against it, give new emphasis to this point.

Some international lawyers and governments argue for a more "flexible" interpretation, stressing that the absence of effective collective remedies against illegal force makes it necessary, indeed inevitable, for states to take defensive action on the basis of their own perceptions of national interest and capabilities. They emphasize both the imperatives of national security and the responsibilities of power to maintain international law.

The legal arguments for a broader interpretation of self-defense have sought support in the usual criteria of legal interpretation: The words of the text are to be interpreted "in context" so as to yield "reasonable" meanings required by the "purpose and object" of the text. The various meanings of "purpose" are brought into play: original intent, expectations, complementary ends, "deeper" or "higher" aims, systemic goals, and so on. The plasticity of "purpose" opens up a range of interpretive supports for contextual (as against textual) construction by lawyers. Lawyers' arguments may cite "subsequent practice" as evidence of contemporaneous construction by the relevant community of states. Hence, acts that appear to violate text and earlier interpretations can then be viewed as new or emerging law based on the efficacy of accomplished facts in shaping the law.

People who take the issue of lawfulness seriously cannot dismiss these legal arguments, however transparent their political intent. The arguments fall sufficiently within the accepted premises of legal discourse to warrant consideration. At this point, I do not propose to consider the application of these various legal arguments to particular cases. Instead, I want to suggest some general ideas that may be helpful in seeking solutions. These ideas are more concerned with ways of thinking about the problem than with specific answers.

To begin with, a clear distinction should be maintained between law as an expression of common policy and purpose and the use of law for rationalization of state action. If law is to operate as a limit on national power, it will lead to judgments of legitimacy that diverge from perception of national interest by a particular state at a given time. True, such divergence may be reduced by redefining or widening the conception of national interest to include the long-term interest in stability and order. However, we must bear in mind that this "dialectical" solution is not always realizable and that, in the concrete case, national leaders and their citizenry may hold to their particular view of state interest, even though it is clearly incompatible with the law. To conclude that law must yield to such judgments of national interest, however, negates the idea of law as a restraint on state conduct. But international law cannot replace the continuing task of defining national interests and the defense needs of a state, and we must acknowledge that national goals and the restraints of international law may be in conflict. Recognizing such tension is an important step toward reconciliation of the competing interests.

One path toward reducing the tension between defense needs and legal rules of restraint lies in the specific agreements that were referred to earlier as the *lex specialis*. Such agreements may be explicit or tacit. They may even be legally nonbinding (like gentlemen's agreements) and still be relied on for mutual compliance. By moving from the abstract level to the concrete, states can achieve rules of behavior that are perceived to support common interests in security and reduced defense costs. Such agreements, it is true, may be frangible, but, while they last, they add to the sense of security. De Gaulle once remarked that "treaties are like roses and young girls; they last while they last." That they do not last forever is no reason to minimize them. Indeed, like some fashions, they would be intolerable if they did not change.

Specific agreements concerning defense rarely go beyond reciprocal negative restraints when the parties are adversaries. In contrast, agreements among states that share a common defense interest tend to involve more positive cooperation. But adversarial states that are apprehensive about the threat of others may also benefit by arrangements that entail cooperation, such as exchanges of information and other confidence-building procedures. Some of the recent arms limitation agreements between the superpowers are steps in that direction. Other agreements between former adversaries provide for exchange of data, free movement of persons, and freer trade. Agreements of that kind can create a sense of "diffuse reciprocity" (in Robert Keohane's phrase) that strengthens compliance. In the current parlance of political science, they may become "security regimes."

The adoption of such treaties and regimes for particular areas or activities would not exclude a continuing reference to the general requirements of self-defense set forth in the Charter and authoritative customary law. If such principles are to be treated as law rather than as after-the-fact rationalization, they must be applied to concrete cases in a disciplined and consistent way. This process entails analysis that takes rules seriously and does not "deconstruct" them so that all meanings are permissible. Legal reasoning helps to limit purely subjective interpretation. Exegesis, original intent, relevant context, evolving purposes, and practice "accepted as law" are elements in such reasoning, as are applicable doctrine and basic postulates of law. These elements cannot be reduced to a single governing factor. Every legal analysis, moreover, must take into account the complexity of the particular situations and their relationship to the dominant ends of the law in question. Yet the factual uniqueness of each case cannot obliterate the limits set by the general rules. If law is to be relevant, a state's right of self-defense in a particular situation must have as its necessary corollary recognition of the right of all other states in comparable cases.

Not only is this proposition implicit in the idea of juridical equality, but also it underlines the need for criteria that are generally recognized and accepted as authoritative. Ad hoc judgments that are purportedly based entirely on the facts and an undefined standard of "reasonableness" tend to be largely determined by crypto-criteria that reflect particular preferences and values. Such judgments are not likely to help clarify the line between permissible and impermissible conduct carried out in the name of self-defense. Moreover, these judgments will be perceived as lacking justification based on norms that the whole community of states—not just part of it—has accepted.

The standards for determining legitimacy of defense will necessarily be somewhat abstract; they will not be fully determinate, for they will have to be interpreted and applied to individual cases. Facts, analysis, and deliberation will be required to reach appropriate conclusions that take into account both standards and circumstances. A process of reasoning involving the interaction of principle and situation (casuistry in its favorable sense) is required. Moreover, that process and the continuing reflections of governments and international lawyers extend beyond the elaboration of established doctrine. They involve, as they should, the development (or construction) of more specific standards appropriate for changing circumstances. To some extent, this process occurs through the responses of states faced with new situations. This type of ongoing law-generating process calls for continuing appraisal by international lawyers as well as by governments.

Of equal importance to the elaboration of standards are the processes for application of the standards to particular cases. Traditionally, international lawyers have focused attention on the ideal goal of judicial determination, particularly the extension of compulsory jurisdiction of the ICJ. As already noted, the war crimes cases at the end of World War II and the *Nicaragua* case against the United States are recent examples of such cases. The controversies about the *Nicaragua* judgment should not lead us to rule out the possibility of future cases, especially those arising from specific incidents such as the shooting down of a plane or vessel (which the United States sought to bring to the ICJ some years ago).

More important, the necessity of strengthening the procedures for review and application of self-defense claims must go beyond judicial procedures. At the heart of such endeavor is the accountability of states to the international community, particularly the UN, for the use of force against another state. Accountability requires respect for the Article 51 obligation to report armed action claimed to be defensive. To give effect to that obligation, governments must report the facts openly and truthfully. Limits on secrecy would thus be imposed, although in some cases, military necessity may be a ground for limited reporting. Accountability can also be given effect in many situations by monitoring and verification arrangements, particularly by international agencies.

I referred earlier to treaties that provide for verification and monitoring. Surely ample room exists for a more extensive use of observers, truce supervisors, and peacekeeping forces to help determine the facts in disputes about the use of force and self-defense. Institutional procedures, such as those of the UN Security Council, the regional organizations, and the international secretariats, require strengthening to ensure that factual reporting and monitoring are effective. The deliberative processes of these organs require adaptation for the appraisal of facts and the claims of the disputing parties.

These various steps are not the exclusive province of international lawyers. They involve a much wider range of competence and expertise. However, the special concerns of international law in the formation of new normative standards, in the furtherance of stability and consistency, and in the establishment of procedures for applying and enforcing rules are good reasons why international lawyers can contribute to strengthening the restraints on the illegitimate uses of armed force.

The Requirement of an Armed Attack and Anticipatory Defense

The question of whether action in self-defense is legitimate only in response to an armed attack or whether it is permissible in anticipation of an armed attack has given rise to controversy among international lawyers. The text of Article 51 does not answer the question directly. It declares that "nothing in the Charter shall impair the inherent right of individual or collective self-defense if an armed attack occurs." In one reading, this statement means that self-defense is limited to cases of armed attack. An alternative reading holds that because the article is silent as to the right of self-defense under customary law, the article should not be construed by implication to eliminate that right. The drafting history shows that Article 51 was intended to safeguard the Chapultepec Treaty, which provided for collective defense in case of armed attack.[90] The relevant commission report of the San Francisco Conference declared, "the use of arms in legitimate self-defense remains admitted and unimpaired."[91] It is therefore argued that Article 51 has left unimpaired the right of self-defense as it existed prior to the Charter.

The main difficulty with this interpretation is that the words "if an armed attack occurs" become redundant. But without convincing evidence that such redundance was intended by the drafters, this interpretation is dubious. Moreover, as a matter of common sense, it is hard to believe that the drafters would have specified "armed attack" as a condition of defense (the obvious case) while leaving unspecified the far more uncertain and controversial matter of anticipatory or preventive war.[92] Most international lawyers and most governments have therefore rejected the contention that self-defense is permitted in the absence of armed attack.[93]

Much of the debate in recent years has focused on the consequences of adopting one or the other interpretation, especially in the light of the apprehension over nuclear missiles. Even as far back as 1946, the U.S. government stated that the term "armed attack" should be defined to include not merely the dropping of a bomb but "certain steps in themselves preliminary to such action."[94] In recent years, the fear that nuclear missiles could, on first strike, destroy the capability of defense and allow virtually no time for defense has appeared to many observers to render a requirement of armed attack unreasonable. States faced with a perceived danger of immediate attack, it is argued, cannot be expected to await the attack like sitting ducks.[95] In response to this line of reasoning, other observers argue that the existence of nuclear missiles has made maintaining a legal barrier against preemptive strikes and anticipatory defense even more important. These people concede that states facing an imminent threat of attack will take defensive measures irrespective of the law, but it is preferable to have states make that choice governed by necessity than to adopt a principle that would make it easier for a state to launch an attack on the pretext of anticipatory defense.[96]

Both of the foregoing positions express reasonable apprehensions. It is important that the right of self-defense should not freely allow the use of force in anticipation of an attack or in response to a threat. At the same time, we must recognize that there may well be situations in which the imminence of an attack is so clear and the danger so great that defensive action is essential for self-preservation. It does not seem to me that the law should leave such defense to a decision *contra legem*. Nor does it appear necessary to read Article 51 in that way, that is, to exclude completely legitimate self-defense in advance of an actual attack. It is surely reasonable to consider that an armed attack may be launched or mounted before the target state has been hit or its frontier crossed.

This interpretation would be in line with the well-known formulation by Daniel Webster in the *Caroline* case. Webster, as secretary of state in 1842, responded to a claim by the British that they had a legal right to attack a vessel (the *Caroline*) on the American side of the Niagara River in 1837 because the vessel carried armed men intending to use force in support of an insurrection in Canada. Secretary Webster denied the "necessity" for self-defense in those circumstances, asserting in his note that self-defense must be confined to cases in which "the necessity of that self-defense is instant, overwhelming and leaving no choice of means and no moment for deliberation."[97]

The Webster formulation of self-defense is often cited as authoritative customary law. It cannot be said that the formulation reflects state practice (which was understandably murky on this point when war was legal), but it is safe to say the formulation reflects a widespread desire to restrict the right of self-defense when no attack has actually occurred. A recent case in point concerns the Israeli bombing of a nuclear reactor in Iraq in 1982, which the Israeli government sought to justify on the ground of self-defense.[98] Israel cited the Iraqi position that it was at war with Israel and went on to claim that the reactor was intended for a nuclear strike. Many governments and the UN Security Council rejected the Israeli position. In the debates in the Security Council on this question, several delegates referred to the *Caroline* case formulation of the right of anticipatory defense as customary law.[99] We may infer from these official statements recognition of the continued validity of an "inherent" right to use armed force in self-defense prior to an actual attack, but only where such an attack is imminent, "leaving no moment for deliberation."

The Requirements of Necessity and Recourse to Peaceful Means

The requirement of necessity for self-defense is not controversial as a general proposition. Application of it in particular cases, however, calls for assessments of intentions and conditions bearing on likelihood of attack or, if an attack has taken place, on the likelihood that peaceful means may be effective to restore peace and remove the attackers. As a matter of principle, there should be no quarrel with the proposition that force should not be considered necessary until peaceful means have been found wanting or unless proven futile. To require a state to allow an invasion to proceed without resistance on the ground that peaceful settlement should be sought first, in effect nullifies the right of self-defense. One is compelled to conclude that a state being attacked is under a necessity of armed defense, irrespective of potential effectiveness of peaceful settlement. A similar conclusion is reached in the case of an imminent threat involving danger to the lives of persons, coupled with unreasonable demands for concessions. It would be hard to deny the necessity for forcible action in such a case on the ground that a peaceful means might succeed.

The question of necessity was also at issue with respect to the U.S. rescue action in Iran in 1980. Let us assume for the present purpose that the attack on the U.S. embassy in Tehran and the seizure of the U.S. hostages constituted an armed attack on the United States. From the outset, the United States was faced with the question whether an armed rescue action was necessary to liberate the hostages.[100] For about six months (November 1979 to April 1980), the United States sought without success to bring about release of the hostages through peaceful means. The fact that such efforts were futile was cited as evidence that armed action was "necessary" to effect a rescue. Does this mean that, at any time after the seizure of the embassy and hostages, the United States was free to use armed force to liberate them?

Note that the phrase "at any time" raises two separate questions. First, the question arises whether the attacked state has a right to use force immediately or soon after the attack, or whether it must seek peaceful solutions first. This issue was clearly presented in the Tehran hostage case after the seizure. The second question related to the timing of defense is whether the right remains available for a substantial period after the attack, when peaceful means have failed to achieve a solution acceptable to the attacked state. This issue was also presented by the Tehran hostage case and, in a much more far-reaching way, by the Argentine claim to a right to use armed force to recover the Malvinas/Falkland Islands. It is interesting that the issues concerning the "temporal" aspects of self-defense had received little attention in the legal writings prior to these events. They are of some importance, as we can now see, and they merit further analysis.

When an attack occurs against a state (including state instruments such as warships, planes, and embassies), armed force may be used to repel the attack. Such force must, of course, be proportional (this requirement is considered later), but, except for very unusual circumstances, the "necessity" of defense to an armed attack requires no separate justification. It is enough that an attack is taking place for armed defense to be permissible. It would be wrong to say that a warship or a frontier guard is prohibited from repelling an attack on the grounds that such defense is unnecessary because diplomatic steps might be taken instead. There is no legal rule that a state must turn the other cheek because of its obligation to seek peaceful settlement under Article 2(3).

The issue becomes more complicated if the attack succeeds in the capture of territory, property, or persons. Must we then consider whether available peaceful means offer the possibility of a just solution and, if so, conclude that there is no necessity for armed force as defense? The answer may seem to be implied by the question, namely, if peaceful solutions are available, armed force is not needed to rectify the wrong. The logic may be compelling, but experience suggests caution in accepting the full conclusion. History and common sense tell us that an aggressor that has seized territory or people might enjoy the fruits of the aggression while forestalling peaceful solutions through dilatory tactics or unreasonable conditions. The absence of compulsory adjudication on a general basis may be cited as a reason for such behavior, but even when compulsory judicial settlement is legally required (as in the Tehran hostage case, by virtue of treaties in force), it is possible for the recalcitrant state to avoid effective compliance. It is true that, under Article 39 conditions, the Security Council may seek to bring about compliance by requiring the aggressor to yield the fruits of its aggression and to provide reparations for its wrong. Prevailing political differences and the requirement of unanimity of the permanent members of the Security Council, however, render such enforcement measures unlikely.

These considerations indicate the legal dilemma faced in cases in which an attack has already occurred and the victim state has a choice between using force and seeking redress through peaceful means. I believe that a categorical answer to the problem is not warranted. It would be unreasonable to lay down a principle that armed action in self-defense is never permissible so long as peaceful means are available; it would also be unreasonable to maintain that self-defense is always a right when an attack has occurred, irrespective of the availability of peaceful means or the time of attack.

The difficulty in proposing a general rule does not mean that a reasonable answer cannot be given in particular cases. In a case involving imminent danger to the lives of captured persons, as in the Israeli raid on

Entebbe or, arguably, in Tehran, it would be unreasonable to maintain that the continued pursuit of peaceful measures must preclude armed rescue action. In contrast, the "necessity" of armed action to recover long-lost territory (as in the Malvinas/Falklands case) does not have a similar justification. In such cases, there is no emergency (as evidenced by the danger of irreparable injury), nor can it be said that all reasonable avenues of settlement had been exhausted.

The Requirement of Proportionality

Proportionality is closely linked to necessity as a requirement of self-defense: Acts done in self-defense must not exceed in manner or in aim the necessity provoking them. This general formula obviously leaves room for differences in regard to particular cases, but uncertainties in some situations do not impair the essential validity or practical application of the principle in many conflicts. Governments typically observe the requirement when they are faced with isolated frontier attacks or naval incidents. A "defending" state in such cases generally limits itself to force proportionate to the attack; it does not bomb cities or launch an invasion. We tend to see such restraint generally as political or prudential, but that fact does not detract from its legal relevance. Thus, when defensive action greatly exceeds provocation, as measured by relative casualties or scale of weaponry, international opinion will more readily condemn such defense as illegally disproportionate. Some of the Security Council decisions that have declared the use of force to be illegal reprisals rather than legitimate defense have noted the much higher number of casualties resulting from the defense in relation to those caused by the earlier attack.[101]

Geography may also be a significant factor in determining proportionality. An isolated attack in one place—for example, in a disputed territorial zone—would not normally warrant a defensive action deep into the territory of the attacking state. The situation may change, however, when a series of attacks in one area leads to the conclusion that defense requires a counterattack on the "source" of the attack and on a scale that would deter future attacks. Thus, the United States responded to threats to its naval vessels in the Gulf of Tonkin by strikes deep into North Vietnam.[102]

When Israel extended its "Peace for Galilee" action in 1982 deep into Lebanon rather than limiting it to a forty-kilometer zone (as originally announced), it asserted its right of self-defense to eliminate the Palestine Liberation Organization (PLO) in Beirut and other cities as the "source" of continuing PLO attacks on northern Israel.[103] International opinion, as expressed in the UN, rejected the Israeli contention.[104] A contrary view maintained that the continued state of hostilities in the area and the declared intent of the PLO and its governmental supporters to destroy Israel justified retaliation beyond the area of attack.[105]

Regardless of whether the Israeli action was excessive in execution, it seems reasonable as a rule to allow a state to retaliate beyond the immediate area of the attack when that state has sufficient reason to expect a continuation of attacks (with substantial military weapons) from the same source. Such action would not be "anticipatory," because prior attacks occurred; nor would it be a "reprisal," because its prime motive would be protective, not punitive. When a government treats an isolated incident of armed attack as grounds for retaliation with force, the action can be justified as self-defense only when it can be reasonably regarded as a defense against a new attack. Thus, "defensive retaliation" may be justified when a state has good reason to expect a series of attacks from the same source and such retaliation serves as a deterrent or protective action. But a reprisal for revenge or as a penalty (or "lesson") would not be defensive. UN bodies or third states may legitimately condemn such retaliatory actions as violations of the Charter.

Collective Self-Defense

Although the right of "collective self-defense" recognized in Article 51 has given rise to much controversy among legal scholars, it has nonetheless emerged as a major legal justification for military action by states outside their own territories. It is also the declared legal basis of the principal military alliances—NATO and the Warsaw Pact—as well as a significant element in regional security arrangements. Some jurists (notably, Hans Kelsen)[106] considered collective self-defense a contradiction because, in their view, the right of self-defense could only be the right of the attacked or threatened state. Others (for example, Derek Bowett)[107] accepted the basic premise of self-defense as an individual right and concluded that collective self-defense properly applied only when two or more states act in concert for defense in response to an attack on each. In contrast, if only one state has been attacked, another coming to its aid can be said to act not in collective self-defense, but on the more dubious ground of a common duty to maintain international peace and security.

This narrow view of collective self-defense is at variance with the positions taken by many governments in their declarations and treaties. When Article 51 was adopted in 1945, it was intended to legitimate the security arrangement of the Chapultepec Act of 1941,[108] which declared, in effect, that aggression against one American state should be considered an act of aggression against all. This arrangement was expressly referred to at the San Francisco Conference as the reason for collective self-defense in Article 51.

In 1949 the North Atlantic Treaty provided that an armed attack on one or more parties would be an armed attack against them all, and consequently, that action could be taken in accordance with Article 51.[109] Although it has been suggested that this provision still recognizes that the limits of Article 51 must apply to use of force (hence, there is no right of armed defense unless that state is attacked or threatened), that interpretation does not seem consistent with the key provision that an attack on one is an attack on all. The Warsaw Pact follows the North Atlantic Treaty in that respect.[110] Thus, the two major military groupings are founded on a liberal interpretation of collective self-defense as allowing armed action by any state when another member of the group is attacked.

Bilateral treaties also have applied the concept of collective undertakings by one state to come to the aid of another in case of aggression or armed attack. Such treaties do not require that the state providing aid to a victim of an attack be a victim itself. Moreover, some states have, from time to time, given aid to a government under attack by external forces when there was no existing treaty. In such cases (which have been rare), the two states have had political and strategic links as well as a common perception that the attacking state was a threat to both. It is highly unlikely that state A would defend state B against an attacker C unless A regarded C's attack as a threat also to A.

We are bound to conclude that the collective security system of the UN Charter has now been largely replaced by the fragmented collective defense actions and alliances founded on Article 51. When a state comes to the aid of another, the legal issue is not whether the assisting state has a right of individual defense, but only whether the state receiving aid is a victim of external attack and has requested military support from the assisting state.

Although NATO and the Warsaw Treaty Organization have a defined geographical scope and in that sense are regional, they are not "regional arrangements" within the meaning of Chapter VIII of the UN Charter. Thus, they do not inform the Security Council of their activities as required by Article 54. The regional arrangements falling within Chapter VIII include organizations such as the Organization of American States (OAS), the Organization of African Unity (OAU), and the League of Arab States. With regard to the use of force, these treaty organizations may act under two separate grants of legal authority. They may take armed action in collective self-defense in case of armed attack on a member, whether that attack is by a state inside or outside the region.

The Inter-American Treaty of Reciprocal Assistance of 1974 (the Rio Treaty) imposes an obligation on its parties to assist in meeting an attack on a member at the request of that member.[111] The use of force in that event is legally based on the collective self-defense provision of the Charter. But the treaty also provides that in cases of aggression, threats of aggression, and situations that might endanger peace, the parties, through an Organ of Consultation, may take measures in the common defense to meet the danger. Such measures may include the use of armed force in some circumstances, even though the aggression is not an armed attack. These measures would therefore not come within Article 51, but would instead be considered as "enforcement action" within the meaning of Article 53 of the UN Charter. Such enforcement action is permissible, but only if authorized by the UN Security Council. In the Cuban missile crisis of 1962, the crucial legal issue turned on this article. All states recognized the requirement of such authorization, but they differed on whether Security Council "inaction" constituted an implicit authorization. With arguments that were less than convincing to most governments and legal commentators, the United States took the position that the authorization was implicit.[112]

In the Grenada intervention of 1983, the United States responded to a request for assistance from members of the Organization of Eastern Caribbean States (OECS) acting under various articles of their constituent treaty of 1981.[113] The OECS members noted the "anarchic conditions, the serious violations of human rights, and bloodshed" on Grenada, and "the consequent unprecedented threat to the peace and security of the region created by the vacuum of authority in Grenada."[114] They also declared that foreign military forces were likely to be introduced, that "the country [could] be used as a staging post for acts of aggression against its members," and, therefore, posed a threat to the "democratic institutions" of the neighboring countries. The U.S. statement, referring to Article 52 of the UN Charter and Articles 22 and 28 of the OAS Charter as legal authority for the right of a regional security body to act to ensure regional peace and security, asserted that, "in taking lawful collective action, the OECS countries were entitled to call upon friendly States for appropriate assistance and it was lawful for the United States, Jamaica and Barbados to respond to this request."[115]

The thesis that neighboring states may be entitled to use military force and to legitimate the use of military force by others in order to meet a threat to their security by a country perceived as potentially aggressive and dangerous to the peace of all goes far beyond the right of collective self-defense or international "peacekeeping" as generally understood. Such action would have been legally valid if undertaken pursuant to a Security Council decision under Chapter VII or in response to an armed attack. But a regional arrangement under Chapter VIII of the Charter does not have the right to use armed force coercively or to license others to do so without authorization of the Security Council or consent of the *de jure* government of the state in question.

To maintain that the U.S. action was legitimate because there was "a vacuum of authority" in Grenada (hence, "force" was not used against Grenada) assumes a right to "police" another country to restore law and order.[116] As we observed earlier, foreign military intervention may be requested by the country itself through a legitimate governing authority. But when outside states use armed force in the absence of such request, the action is presumptively a violation of the territorial sovereignty of that state inconsistent with Article 2(4). That its purpose is benign and its effect on the country desirable would not constitute a legal justification under the

Charter. Consequently, the action in Grenada, insofar as it extended beyond the rescue of Americans, would have been permissible only on the grounds that the United States and the others responded to an invitation by the governor-general on the premise that he was the sole source of government legitimacy on the island after the violent overthrow of the previous regime. As we observed earlier, this premise was denied by most governments, including Britain and other West European states.[117]

The ICJ in its *Nicaragua* judgment produced another controversial issue concerning the nature of collective self-defense. The ICJ held that collective self-defense did not apply unless the victim of an alleged attack declared itself to have been attacked and requested armed aid from a third state.[118] A dissenting opinion by Judge Robert Jennings observed that these require- ments might be unrealistic.[119] It is easy to see why: an attacked state might lack a government because of the attack, or its government might be unable to communicate with potential sources of aid.

Jennings also raised a more basic point. He suggested that collective self-defense does not mean "vicarious defense" as if the third state were a "champion" of a victim in a kind of contractual relation. He observed that collective self-defense involved the defense of the "self" of the third state.[120] The premise, in his view, is that every act of aggression is an aggression against all other states. Consequently, there is no need for the victim of the direct attack to ask for a champion. Every state is, so to speak, a victim of the aggression, and the security of all is jeopardized. This position may be seen as an application of the *erga omnes* theory, under which certain inter- national obligations are owed to the community of states. Violations, therefore, give rise to a right of each state to respond. In this approach, collective self-defense is essentially an application of collective security under which the security of each is involved with the security of others.

The ICJ imposed a further limit on collective self-defense in its *Nicaragua* decision. It held that collective self-defense did not apply when the victim state was injured by illegal acts involving force short of armed attack.[121] Hence, the United States could not use armed force against Nicaragua, which had illegally intervened in El Salvador by providing arms and logistic support to insurgent guerrilla forces in that state. Some observers regarded this limitation on collective self-defense as the most important substantive ruling in the case. Let us consider it now in connection with intervention in internal conflicts.

Intervention by Armed Force in Internal Conflicts

Foreign military interventions in civil wars have become so common in our day that the proclaimed rule of nonintervention may seem to have been turned on its head. Talleyrand's cynical quip comes to mind: "Noninter- vention is a word that has the same meaning as intervention." Indeed, virtually all interventions that occur today are carried out in the name of nonintervention—they are justified as responses to prior interventions by the other side. No state today would deny the basic principle that the people of a nation have the right under international law to decide for themselves what kind of government they want and that this right includes the right to revolution and to armed conflict between competing groups. For a foreign state to support, with force, one side or the other in an internal conflict is to deprive the people in some measure of their right to decide the issue by themselves. It is, in words of Article 2(4), a use of force "against the political independence of a state."

The states that intervene do not challenge this legal principle; they generally proclaim it as the basis for their "counterintervention." They are often able to do so with some plausibility because, in almost every civil war, the parties have sought and received some outside military support. A preeminent difficulty in applying the rule of nonintervention in these circumstances arises from the equivocal position of the established government. The government is the legitimate authority under international law. As a general rule, other states are free (in the absence of contrary treaties) to furnish arms, military training, and even combat forces to that government at its request. But they may not do the same for an opposing force; such action would clearly violate the sovereignty and independence of the state.

Consequently, governments commonly receive foreign military aid, and they may request more such aid when faced with an armed insurrection. At that point, two questions arise: Is there an obligation to cease aid to the established regime because doing so now involves taking sides in an internal conflict? And, if such aid to the government constitutes foreign intervention, does it permit counterintervention to support the other side? Concretely, if the Nicaraguan Sandinista regime received Cuban and Soviet military supplies and advisers, was the United States free to support the armed opposition by training, arms, and technical advice? An answer to the first question involves an assessment of the particular circumstances and of the presumption that the government is entitled to continued aid. A relevant general principle in keeping with the concept of political independence and nonintervention would be that when an organized insurgency occurs on a large scale, involving a substantial number of people or control over significant areas of the country, neither side—neither government nor insurgency—should receive outside military aid.[122] Such outside support would be contrary to the right of the people to decide the issue by their own means. It would be immaterial whether the insurgency was directed at overthrow of the government or at secession (or autonomy) of a territorial unit.

The second, more difficult, question is whether an illegal intervention on one side permits outside states to give military aid to the other party (whether government or insurrection). Such counterintervention may be justified as a defense of the independence of the state against foreign intervention; it may then be viewed as "collective self-defense" in response to armed attack. However, it may also further "internationalize" a local conflict and increase the threat to international peace. The Vietnam War is an outstanding example. Despite the danger of internationalization, the law does not proscribe such counterintervention; the grave violations of the restraints on force allow a defensive response.

Of course, a strict application of a nonintervention rule applied to both sides would make counterintervention unnecessary. To achieve such a strict application, it is probably essential in most cases to have international mechanisms (peacekeeping forces or observer teams) to monitor compliance with a *cordon sanitaire*, as well as to have a ban on military assistance in cases of civil war.

A related problem of practical importance is to clarify what kinds of military aid qualify as illicit intervention. The UN resolutions on nonintervention leave this matter to ad hoc judgments, but a strong case can be made for specification of impermissible acts. Such specification would give more determinate content to the principle of nonintervention and, in that respect, strengthen it. In line with this view, the resolution on nonintervention[123] of the Institut de Droit International has designated the following acts as impermissible when done to support either party in a civil war:

- sending armed forces or military volunteers, instructors, or technicians to any party to a civil war, or allowing them to be sent;
- drawing up or training regular or irregular forces with a view to supporting any party to a civil war, or allowing them to be drawn up or trained;
- supplying weapons or other war material to any party to a civil war, or allowing them to be supplied;
- making territories available to any party to a civil war or allowing them to be used by any such party as bases of operations or of supplies, as places of refuge, for the passage of regular or irregular forces, or for the transit of war material.

The last-mentioned prohibition includes transmitting military information to any of the parties. The Institut also declared that outside states should use "all means to prevent inhabitants of their territories, whether nationals or aliens, from raising contingents and collecting equipment, from crossing the border or from embarking from their territories with a view to fomenting or causing a civil war."[124]

States also have a duty to disarm and intern any force of either party to a civil war that enters their territory. However, the Institut's resolution does not prohibit humanitarian aid for the benefit of victims of a civil war, nor does it exclude economic or technical aid that is not likely to affect the outcome of the civil war substantially. Although these declarations of the

Institut do not clearly reflect existing law in every detail, they are a persuasive interpretation of the general rule against nonintervention and should influence state practice.

Governments have suggested various limitations on counterintervention in civil wars. One suggestion is that the counterintervention should be limited to the territory of the state in which the civil war takes place. In this view, the fact that the prior intervention was illegal (that is, in violation of the rule of nonintervention) would not legally justify the use of force by a third state in the violator's territory. This territorial limitation on counterintervention has been observed in some recent civil wars, but it is hard to say it has become an accepted legal rule. The United States in its "counterintervention" on the side of the El Salvador regime has aided anti-Sandinista forces fighting on Nicaraguan soil. The United States sought to justify this action under the collective self-defense provision of Article 51, on the grounds that Nicaragua had engaged in an armed attack on El Salvador. The United States also "counterintervened" against Nicaragua by mining approaches to Nicaraguan ports. As noted earlier, the ICJ found that Nicaragua's illegal acts did not amount to an armed attack; hence, the U.S. justification of collective self-defense was not applicable.

The ICJ went on to say that a victim of illegal intervention short of armed attack could resort to countermeasures (including forcible measures) against the wrongdoer. Such measures constituted permissible self-help. "Collective" countermeasures, however, were not permitted; hence, a third state could not aid the victim by action against the wrongdoer, which is illegal under general international law.[125] The ICJ's decision on these points has been criticized on several grounds. One such argument is that the ICJ went too far in declaring, as if it were a rule of law, that the provision of weapons or logistical or other support to rebels does not constitute an armed attack. Critics charge that this conclusion ignores the real possibility that such support may well be so substantial in its scale and effect as to be justifiably seen as an armed attack.[126]

The point is well taken. The complexity of civil wars and the past involvements of outside states indicate that intervention cannot be assessed on the basis of an abstract formula alone. The scale and effect of outside support, whether by arms or logistics, must be taken into account. But it seems unwise, as a rule, to allow outside states to use armed force against a state that does no more than provide arms to insurgents in an internal conflict. To do so would give a very wide meaning to collective self-defense and armed attack. Yet the vague exclusion of some "acts of force" as grounds for self-defense is questionable, insofar as it leaves the right to an armed response to such unlawful acts uncertain.

Apart from the issue of armed attack, the ICJ also dealt with the question of whether a third state should be permitted to take other countermeasures against an illegally intervening state. It held that although the victim state itself could take countermeasures (including use of force) against a state that has illegally intervened short of an armed attack, the right of self-help does not extend to collective countermeasures, that is, to third states.[127] Hence, third states cannot take action against an illegal intervenor under a principle parallel to that of collective self-defense.[128] The ICJ's judgment did not fully explain this conclusion. Nor did it consider whether an illegal intervention short of armed attack but still violating Article 2(4) might be a wrong against the international community that falls within the *erga omnes* principle.[129] If that were so, the outside state could consider the illegal act as if it were a delict against all states, allowing each to take self-help action that was not disproportionate to the wrong. Under this principle, a third state could impose a trade embargo or deny transit rights to a wrongdoer, even if such measures would be inconsistent with its treaty or other international obligations.

It remains debatable whether "collective countermeasures" inconsistent with legal obligations are permitted in response to illegal intervention short of armed attack. The *erga omnes* category of international delicts has not been extended to "intervention" under any international rulings. Governments do not seem inclined to open a Pandora's box allowing every state to enforce international obligations in any cases short of armed aggression or extreme violations of human rights, such as genocide and apartheid. Over time, collective countermeasures against illegal intervention might result from UN or regional organizations' resolutions calling on states to join in sanctions. To be effective, such measures would almost surely require the support of the major powers, preferably expressed through formal decisions of the Security Council under its enforcement authority. This requirement could provide some safeguard against a double standard or other unwarranted uses of sanctions. For the present, illegal interventions, especially those involving arms and covert subversive activities, pose a serious challenge to the international institutions charged with maintaining peace and security. The ICJ's decision in the *Nicaragua* case has not provided a definite answer to the questions of legal principle, but it has stimulated thought on the issues.

Conclusion

International law, as this survey indicates, is not an ideal construct. It is the product of a complex interplay of interests, power, ideas, and ideals. Governments seek to restrain power and to control violence, not for reasons of morality, but as a felt necessity. An international order that does not distinguish between permissible and impermissible use of force would be unstable and dangerous. The legal restraints on force respond to this reality. These restraints are important as well for the independence and self-rule of nation-states in an incorrigibly pluralistic world. These widely shared interests are the basis for the international rules on force.

Only a raving optimist would expect the international legal system to ensure a nonviolent world. Verbal agreement on restraints, solemnly affirmed, may dissolve under the pressure of divergent interests and perceptions. Neither governments nor their peoples are ready, by and large, to entrust their security and vital interests entirely to foreign judges or international organs. The nation-state, whatever its deficiencies, represents for most peoples the primary source of identity and protection. The legacies of history and the long precivilized past have left a common "syndrome of parochialism"[130] in which distrust of strangers and expectations of violence contribute to a climate of mutual fear. In that climate, armed defense carries with it the threat of offense. Clashes of interest or ideology can turn into covert or open tests of force. Rules of law are bound to appear fragile in the face of these brutal facts.

Yet a stable society of sovereign states cannot exist if each is free to destroy the independence of another. In the present conditions of power, we cannot reasonably contemplate that either superpower could impose its rule by coercion on the rest of the world or that together they would establish a condominium of shared authority over the globe. The superpowers' ruling elites are aware of the supreme risks to their survival in the event of a major clash of arms. The legal constraints on unilateral force reflect those risks; they are not solely the product of moral sentiment.

The efficacy of international law remains limited because it lacks effective central authority and because vast discrepancies exist in the power of states. Fear of nuclear devastation has not eliminated the Hobbesian element in that system. Powerful and not-so-powerful states still violate international obligations. They may do so with relative impunity or they may suffer the cost; but they also have a stake in stability, and most have an acute sense of countervailing power. The largely decentralized legal system functions mainly because of the perceived self-interest and reciprocal reactions.

Moreover, the system is not wholly decentralized. As I have indicated, collective judgments are continuously being made both inside and outside formal institutions. Decisions of international bodies add to the specificity and density of agreed law; they also increase the negative consequences of unlawful conduct. However inadequate this international system may seem in comparison with a mature national legal system, it should not be scorned as an element in maintaining peace. To consider its inadequacy a reason for ignoring the restraints can only add to the present insecurity. A world in which power and self-interest by themselves are expected to restrain force is not a safer world. We may move dangerously in that direction by weakening existing law on the grounds that it lacks impartial organs of application and enforcement. The best would then become the enemy of the good.

Notes

1. International Court of Justice, North Sea Continental Shelf Cases, *ICJ Reports* 1969, p. 44, para. 77.

2. For general treatment of development of international law, see Oscar Schachter, *International Law in Theory and Practice.* Hague Academy of International Law, *Collected Courses,* vol. 178 (1982-V), especially chapters I–VII, pp. 21–132.

3. F.H. Hinsley, *Power and the Pursuit of Peace* (1963).

4. Raymond Aron, "The Anarchical Order of Power" in Stanley Hoffman, ed., *Conditions of World Order* (1968), pp. 25–48.

5. "The Corfu Channel Case," *ICJ Reports* 1949, p. 4.

6. "The Case Concerning Military and Paramilitary Activities in and Against Nicaragua (Merits)," *ICJ Reports* (1986), p. 14, hereafter referred to as the *Nicaragua* case.

7. United Nations Charter, Article 27.

8. Schachter, *International Law,* pp. 110–23.

9. United Nations General Assembly (UNGA) Res. 37/37 (1983).

10. UNGA Res. 3281 (xxix) (1974).

11. I. Oppenheim, *International Law,* 5th ed. (Hersch Lauterpacht, 1955), p. 305.

12. Sadurska, "Threats of Force," 82 *American Journal of International Law* (1988): p. 239.

13. See references to Security Council discussions in Rosalyn Higgins, *The Development of International Law Through the Political Organs of the United Nations* (1963), pp. 201, 221.

14. Ibid., pp. 210–22. See also *Year Book of International Law Commission* Vol. 2 (1980): pp. 52–53, notes 174–75.

15. *ICJ Reports* 1949, p. 35.

16. *ICJ Reports* 1986, paras. 211, 249.

17. See UNGA Resolutions on Soviet Intervention in Hungary, 10004 (ES-II 1956), and on Intervention in Afghanistan, UNGA Res. 37/37 (1983).

18. See *Economist* March 10–16, 1984, p. 34. The British government said it regarded the United States action as clearly illegal because "the invitation had come from those not entitled to make such a request on behalf of Grenada." Rosalyn Higgins, in *The Current Legal Regulation of the Use of Force,* ed. Antonio Cassese, 1986, p. 440.

19. UNGA Res. A/Res. 38/7 (1983), adopted by a vote 108 in favor, 9 against, with 27 abstentions. UN Doc. A/38 PV43, pp. 45–50. A strong criticism of this resolution can be found in John Norton Moore, *Law and the Grenada Mission* (1984).

20. William E. Hall, *A Treatise on International Law,* 8th ed., 1924, p. 347; Quincy Wright, *The Role of International Law in the Elimination of War* (1961), p. 61; Wolfgang G. Friedmann, *The Changing Structure of International Law* (1964), pp. 265–67.

21. Resolution of Institut de Droit International on the Principle of Non-Intervention in Civil Wars, 56 *Ann. Inst. Dr. Int.* (1975): pp. 544–49; Ann V. Thomas and A.J. Thomas, Jr., *Non-Intervention* (1956), p. 215. *Contra,* see John Norton Moore, "The Lawfulness of Military Assistance to the Republic of Vietnam," 61 *Am. J. Int. L.* (1967): p. 31.

22. Thomas and Thomas, *Non-Intervention,* p. 220. See also Doswald-Beck, "The Legal Validity of Military Intervention By Invitation of the Government," 56 *British Year Book of International Law* (1985): pp. 190–91.

23. See Oscar Schachter, *United Nations and Internal Conflicts in Law and Civil War in the Modern World*, ed. John Norton Moore, pp. 401–45.

24. See Lloyd Cutler, *The Right to Intervene*, 64 *Foreign Affairs* (1985): p. 96.

25. United Nations Security Council (UNSC) Res. 418 (1977).

26. UNSC Off. Rec., 987th Meeting (1961), pp. 10–11.

27. 37 UNGA Off. Rec., 51st Meeting (1982), p. 7.

28. T. Ismael, *Iraq and Iran* (1982), pp. 24–27.

29. See Thomas M. Franck, "Dulce et Decorum Est: The Strategic Role of Legal Principles in the Falklands War," 77 *Am. J. Int. L.* (1983): p. 109.

30. Support for use of force as humanitarian intervention can be found in Richard B. Lillich, "Humanitarian Intervention" in *Law and Civil War in the Modern World*, ed. John Norton Moore, (1974), pp. 229–51; Bazyler, "Reexamining the Doctrine of Humanitarian Intervention in Light of Atrocities in Kampuchea and Ethiopia," 23 *Stanford Journal of International Law* (1987): pp. 547–619; Fernando R. Teson, *Humanitarian Intervention* (1988), pp. 130–37.

31. See N. Ronzitti, *Rescuing Nationals Abroad and Intervention on Grounds of Humanity* (1985), pp. 89–113. Rescue of nationals, such as hostages threatened with execution, has been justified legally as self-defense by governments and by international lawyers. See statement of U.S. Representative to Security Council on Israeli rescue action in Entebbe, in *Digest of U.S. Practice in International Law* (1976): pp. 150–151. See also Schachter, "International Law in the Hostage Crisis: Implications for Future Cases," in *American Hostages in Iran*, ed. P. Kreisberg (1985), p. 325.

32. N. Ronzitti, *Rescuing Nationals Abroad*, pp. 95–97. See also Thomas M. Franck and Nigel S. Rodley, "After Bangladesh: The Law of Military Intervention By Military Force," 67 *Am. J. Int. L.* (1983): p. 275.

33. See Ronzitti, *Rescuing Nationals Abroad*, pp. 102–06.

34. The president of Tanzania declared that the sole reason for the Tanzanian attack on Uganda was Uganda's prior attack and its claim to have annexed Ugandan territory; ibid, p. 105.

35. In fact, the heads of state of the two largest African countries—Nigeria and Sudan—condemned Tanzania's intervention as unacceptable; ibid., pp. 105–06.

36. UNGA Res. 37/6 (1982). See also Ronzitti, *Rescuing Nationals Abroad*, pp. 98–101.

37. See F. Teson, *Humanitarian Intervention*, pp. 175–79. French troops took part in a bloodless coup to depose the "Emperor" Bokassa; only three African states protested the French action.

38. Ronzitti, *Rescuing Nationals Abroad*, pp. 89–114; Ian Brownlie, *Humanitarian Intervention in Law and Civil War in the Modern World*, ed. J.N. Moore, (1974), p. 217.

39. See also Franck and Rodley, *After Bangladesh*; and Brownlie, *Humanitarian Intervention*, p. 217.

40. See statement of representative of India, UNSC Off. Rec., 987th Meeting. See also Rafquil-Islam, "Use of Force in Self-Determination Claims" 25 *Ind. J. Int. L.* (1985): p. 424.

41. See Stephen Schwebel, "Wars of Liberation as Fought in United Nations Organs," in *Law and Civil War in the Modern World*, ed. J.N. Moore, (1974), p. 446. The same conclusion is supported by more recent statements of governments, especially in connection with the argument of Argentina that force was permitted to liberate the Falkland Islands. See Rubino, "Colonialism and the Use of Force By

States," in *The Current Legal Regulation of the Use of Force*, ed. A. Cassese, (1986), pp. 133–146.

42. Reagan declared in his 1984 State of the Union address: "We must not break faith with those who are risking their lives on every continent, from Afghanistan to Nicaragua, to defy Soviet-supported aggression and secure rights which have been ours from birth. Support for freedom fighters is self-defense." For comments in support of the Reagan Doctrine, see Jean Kirkpatrick, *Legitimacy and Force*, Vol.2, (1988), pp. 422–46. For critical views, see Stuart S. Malawer, "Reagan's Law and Foreign Policy," 29 *Harvard Journal of International Law* (1988): p. 85; Robert W. Tucker, "Intervention and the Reagan Doctrine" in *The Reagan Doctrine: Three Views*, ed. Kenneth W. Thompson, (1985).

43. The Truman declaration was made in a message to the Congress on March 12, 1947. For text, see *The Public Papers of the Presidents: Harry S Truman 1947* (Washington, D.C.: U.S. Govt. Printing Office, 1963), pp. 178–79.

44. Edwin C. Hoyt, *Law and Force in American Policy* (1985), pp. 14–16.

45. See Richard Falk, ed., *The Viet Nam War and International Law*, (1968), especially articles by Quincy Wright (p. 271), Wolfgang Friedmann (p. 292), and Richard Falk (pp. 362, 445).

46. John Norton Moore, "The Lawfulness of Military Assistance to the Republic of Viet Nam," 61 *Am. J. Int. L.* (1967): pp. 1–34, reprinted in R. Falk, ed., *The Viet Nam War and International Law*, pp. 237–70.

47. Ibid. See other articles by Moore in *The Viet Nam War and International Law*, pp. 303–17, 401–45.

48. Gregory Treverton, *Covert Action: The Limits of Intervention in the Post War World* (1987), pp. 49–80, 133–147; Stansfield Turner, *Secrecy and Democracy: The C.I.A. in Transition* (1985), pp. 75–85; Hoyt, *Law and Force*, pp. 102–05, 132–37.

49. See Jean Kirkpatrick, "The Limits of International Law," *Proceedings of the American Society of International Law* (1984): pp. 59–68. Also in J. Kirkpatrick, *Legitimacy and Force*, Vol. 1, (1988), pp. 241–52; Norman Podhoretz, *The Present Danger* (1980), pp. 96–101.

50. Eugene Rostow, "The Legality of the International Use of Force by and from States," 10 *Yale J. Int. L.* (1985): pp. 286, 290.

51. Statement by President Reagan, *U.S. Department of State Bulletin*, March 1986, p. 36; Secretary of State George Shultz, Address January 15, 1986 in *U.S. Department of State Current Policy* No. 783.

52. See Julius Stone, *Aggression and World Order* (1958), pp. 10–11; and Myres S. McDougal and Florentino Feliciano, *Law and Minimum World Public Order* (1961), pp. 151–53.

53. Kirkpatrick, *Legitmacy and Force*, pp. 432–37; W. Michael Reisman, "Coercion and Self-Determination," 74 *Am. J. Int. L.* (1984): p. 642.

54. Kirkpatrick, *Legitimacy and Force*.

55. Ibid.

56. See note 132. See also Cassesse, ed., *Current Legal Regulation*, p. 440. *supra* note 18 on West European positions.

57. Hans Kelsen, *Principles of International Law*, rev. ed., Robert W. Tucker, (1966), pp. 64–65, 84–87.

58. Charles C. Hyde, *International Law*, rev. ed., p. 1008.

59. *ICJ Reports* 1949, p. 35.

60. See Higgins, *The Development of International Law*, pp. 218–19.

61. Stone, *Aggression and World Order*, pp. 98–101; Thomas and Thomas, *Non-Intervention*, p. 209; *Contra*, H. Kelsen, *Principles of International Law.*

62. Derek W. Bowett, *Self-Defense in International Law* (1958), pp. 270–71.

63. "The Corfu Channel Case," *ICJ Reports*, 1949, pp. 31–32.

64. Stone, *Aggression and World Order*, p. 96.

65. Hans Kelsen, *The Law of the United Nations* (1950), pp. 15–16.

66. For references to commentators advancing these arguments, see Oscar Schachter, "In Defense of International Rules on the Use of Force," 53 *University of Chicago Law Review* (1986): pp. 128–31.

67. *ICJ Reports* 1986, p. 98, para. 186.

68. *Proc. Am. Soc. Int. L.* (1963): p. 14.

69. A. Sofaer, Statement in Hearing Before Subcommittee on Human Rights and International Organization of the House Committee on Foreign Affairs, 99th Cong., 1st Sess. (1985), pp. 27–28.

70. Ibid., p. 30.

71. Judgment of the International Military Tribunal for the Trial of German Major War Criminals, Nuremberg, 1946.

72. Stephen Schwebel, "Dissenting Opinion to Judgment 27, *Nicaragua* v. *United States* (Merits)," *ICJ Reports* 1986, p. 285, para. 46.

73. Hersch Lauterpacht, *The Function of Law in the International Community* (1933), pp. 179–80.

74. Ibid., p. 180.

75. Ibid., p. 181.

76. Combacau, "The Exception of Self-Defense in U.N. Practice," in *The Current Legal Regulation of the Use of Force*, ed. A. Cassese (1986), p. 9.

77. For example, self-defense claims made by Israel for attacks against Palestinian organizations based in Jordan and Lebanon were rejected by the Security Council in the following resolutions: S/Res. 228, November 25, 1966; S/Res. 265, April 1, 1969; S/Res. 270, August 16, 1969; S/Res. 279, May 12, 1970; S/Res. 313, February 28, 1972; S/Res. 332, April 21, 1973, S/Res. 347, April 24, 1974. See also S/Res. 488, June 19, 1981 (condemning Israeli air attack which destroyed the Osirag nuclear reactor in Iraq in 1981). The General Assembly rejected the Soviet Union's self-defense claim to justify its intervention in Afghanistan in 1980 (A/Res. ES. 6/2, January 14, 1980). In addition, South Africa has been condemned for its attacks against neighboring states (S/Res. 393, July 30, 1976; S/Res. 387, March 31, 1976). See Cassese, *Legal Regulation*, pp. 16–18.

78. The Security Council resolution noted reports of an invasion of the Falkland Islands by Argentina and demanded the immediate withdrawal of all Argentine forces from the Falkland Islands. No reference was made to the withdrawal of British forces. The resolution was adopted by 10 votes to 1 (Panama) with 4 abstentions (S/Res. 502, April 3, 1982).

79. *ICJ Reports* 1986, p. 98, para. 186.

80. Martin Ceadel, *Thinking About War and Peace* (1987), pp. 72–88.

81. See, for example, Frank Carlucci, "Is Moscow Really Tilting to Defense?" *New York Times*, May 6, 1988.

82. Robert C. Jervis, *Security Regimes in International Regimes*, ed. Stephen Krasner, (1983), pp. 173–94. See also Jed C. Snyder, "The Balance of Power and the Balance of Terror," in *The Balance of Terror in the Balance of Power*, ed. Paul Seabury, (1965).

83. Rescue actions were undertaken by Israel in Entebbe, Uganda, in 1976 and by the United States in Iran in 1980. Belgium carried out an earlier rescue mission in what was then Stanleyville in the Belgian Congo. For a discussion of legal issues see Oscar Schachter, "The Right of States to Use Armed Force," 82 *Mich. L. Rev.* (1984): pp. 1620, 1629, 1632. See also note 213.

84. For example, the U.S. Bombing of Libya. See 86 *U.S. Department of State Bulletin* no. 2111 (1986); UNGA Res. 41/38 (1986); Statement of U.S. Representative to U.N. Security Council, excerpt in "Contemporary Practice," 80 *Am. J. Int. L.* (1986): pp. 632–36.

85. For example, the Israeli action against Egypt in 1967. See Y. Dinstein, "The Legal Issues of Paramilitary War and Peace in the Middle East," 44 *St. John's L. Rev.* (1970): pp. 466, 469–70.

86. Israeli Military Invasion of Lebanon in 1982. See UNSC Res. 509 (1982) and UNGA Res. ES-75 (1982). See also Feinstein, "The Legality of the Use of Armed Force by Israel in Lebanon," 20 *Israeli Law Rev.* (1985): p. 362.

87. For example, the U.S. support of the contras in Nicaragua, see *Nicaragua* case, note 119. See also John Norton Moore, "The Secret War in Central America and the Future of World Order," 80 *Am. J. Int. L.* (1986): p. 568; J. Rowles, "Secret Wars, Self-Defense and the Charter," 80 *Am. J. Int. L.* (1986): p. 568.

88. For example, the U.S. blockade of Cuba in 1962. See M.S. McDougal, "The Soviet-Cuban Quarantine and Self-Defense," 57 *Am. J. Int. L.* (1963): pp. 597–604; Quincy Wright, "The Cuban Quarantine," 57 *Am. J. Int. L.* (1963): pp. 597–604.

89. A recent example is the military aid to the resistance in Afghanistan given by Pakistan and the United States. See Joseph J. Collins, *The Soviet Invasion of Afghanistan* (1985). On the legal claim of the Soviet Union, see Doswald-Beck, "The Legal Validity of Military Intervention by Invitation of the Government," 56 *Brit. Y.B. Int. L.* (1985): p. 189.

90. See Derek Bowett, *Self-Defense in International Law* 183 (1958).

91. Ibid., p. 182.

92. Y. Dinstein, *War, Aggression and Self-Defense* (1988), pp. 174–75.

93. Ibid., p. 175. Among the leading scholars who consider that self-defense is permitted only in the event of an armed attack are Judge R. Ago, W. Eric Beckett, Ian Brownlie, Louis Henkin, Philip C. Jessup, E. Jimenez de Arechaga, Hans Kelsen, Josef L. Kunz, Hersch Lauterpacht, K. Skubiszawski, and Hans Wehberg. For references to these writers see Dinstein, *War, Aggression, and Self-Defense*, p. 175, note 48; and T. Gill, "The Law of Armed Attack in the Context of the Nicaraguan Case," *Hague Y.B.I.L.* (1988): pp. 30–33, note 21. The opposing view that armed attack is not a requisite is taken by a small minority, notably Derek Bowett, Myres S. McDougal, Stephen Schwebel, and Humphrey Waldock. See Schwebel, "Dissenting Opinion," para. 173.

94. Quoted in Philip C. Jessup, *A Modern Law of Nations* (1948), pp. 166–67.

95. McDougal, *Am. J. Int. L.*, pp. 597–604.

96. Louis Henkin, *How Nations Behave*, 2d ed. (1979), pp. 141–45.

97. For the *Caroline* case, see L. Henkin, R. Pugh, O. Schachter and H. Smit, *International Law*, 2d ed. (1987), pp. 662–63.

98. U. Shoham, "The Israeli Aerial Raid upon the Iraq Nuclear Reactor and the Right of Self-Defense," 109 *Mili. Law Rev.* (1985): pp. 191–223.

99. 36 UNSCOR (2285-88th Mtg.) (1981).

100. For further discussion of legality of U.S. rescue mission in Iran, see P. Kreisberg, ed., *American Hostages in Iran*, p. 325. In the author's opinion the conditions for armed rescue missions are: the action must be for rescue and protection, not punishment; it must not continue beyond its necessity; an action legal in its inception can become illegal if prolonged or used for political purposes. See also the statement of U.S. Representative in Security Council on the Israeli rescue action in Entebbe, *Digest of United States Practice in International Law* (1976): pp. 150–51.

101. See Derek Bowett, "Reprisals Involving Recourse to Armed Force," 66 *Am. J. Int. L.* (1972): pp. 33–36.

102. Letter of President Lyndon B. Johnson, 1967, reprinted in R. Falk, ed., *The Viet Nam War and International Law*, pp. 604–07.

103. Israeli communication to Security Council, UN Doc. S/15271 (1982).

104. UNSC Docs. Res. 508, 509, 517, (1982) and UNGA Res. ES-7/9 (1982).

105. See Feinstein, *Israeli Law Rev.* (1985): p. 362.

106. H. Kelsen, *The Law of the United Nations* (1950), pp. 792, 797.

107. D. Bowett, *Self-Defense*, pp. 216–18.

108. 12 *U.S. Depart. of State Bull.* no. 297 (1945), p. 339.

109. North Atlantic Treaty, 1949, Article 5, *T.I.A.S.* no. 1964.

110. Warsaw Treaty, 1955, Article 4, 219 *UN T.S.* 3.

111. Rio Treaty, 1947, Article 3, 21 *UNTS* 77.

112. Abram Chayes, "The Legal Case for U.S. Action in Cuba," 47 *U.S. Dept. State Bull.* (1962): p. 763; Leonard Meeker,"Defensive Quarantine and the Law," 57 *Am. J. Int. L.* (1963): pp. 515, 524; *Contra* Wright, *Am. J. Int. L.* (1963); L. Henkin, *How Nations Behave*, 2d ed. (1979), pp. 291–92.

113. See 20 *Int. Legal Materials* (1981), p. 116.

114. This quotation and others are from the statement of K.W. Dam, Deputy Secretary of State to the Committee on Foreign Affairs of the House of Representatives, November 2, 1983, excerpted in 78 *Am. J. Int. L.* (1984): p. 200. See also Moore, *Law and the Grenada Mission*.

115. K.W. Dam, 78 *Am. J. Int. L.* (1984): p. 203.

116. The actual use of force in the Grenada invasion is distinguished from the "quarantine" in the Cuban missile case which was authorized (as a recommendation) by the OAS. An invasion undertaken pursuant to a decision of a regional organization would be permissible as an "enforcement measure" if it had been authorized by the Security Council, as required by Article 53. It might also have been permissible as "peacekeeping" if it had received the consent of the governing authority of Grenada. See J.N. Moore, "Grenada and the International Double Standard," 78 *Am. J. Int. L.* (1984): pp. 145, 154–59, and discussion, notes 130–138.

117. See notes 131 and 132.

118. *Nicaragua* case, *ICJ Reports* (1986), para. 199; ibid.

119. Judge Robert Jennings, "Dissenting Opinion," *Nicaragua* case, *ICJ Reports* (1986), pp. 544–45.

120. Ibid.

121. *Nicaragua* case, *ICJ Reports* (1986), pp. 103–04, 126–27, paras. 195, 247.

122. See references note 134.

123. See note 134.

124. See note 134.

125. *Nicaragua* case, *ICJ Reports* (1986), and pp. 103–04, 110, 126–27, paras. 210, 249.

126. Judge R. Jennings, "Dissenting Opinion," note 232; J.L. Hargrove, "The Nicaraguan Judgment and the Future of the Law of Force and Self-Defense," 81 *Am. J. Int. L.* (1987): pp. 135–43.

127. *Nicaragua* case, *ICJ Reports* (1986), pp. 110–111, 127, paras. 211, 249.

128. See Hargrove, *supra* note 124, pp. 139–140.

129. The principle of *erga omnes* obligations was recognized by the ICJ in its judgment in the Barcelona Traction Case *ICJ Reports* 1970, p. 32. The ICJ said all states had a legal interest in the observance of "obligations of a State to the international community as a whole." The ICJ gave as examples the outlawing of aggression and genocide and principles respecting the basic rights of the human person, including protection from slavery and racial discrimination. See Schachter, *supra* note 21, pp. 182–84.

130. Harold Lasswell, "Introduction: Universality Versus Parochialism," in M.S. McDougal and F. Feliciano, *Law and Minimum World Public Order* (1961), p. xxi.

Introduction to Chapter 6

Hugo Grotius, the father of international law, wrote one of the monumental works of his profession in 1625. Entitled *De jure belli ac pacis* (*The Rights of War and Peace*), Grotius's book set forth not only the fundamental humanitarian rules of warfare, but also the principle that would become the guiding legal postulate of the nation-state system as well: *Quod tibi non vis, alteri non facias* (What one does not wish done to himself, he should not do to others).

But this system of international law, based on reciprocity secured through the threat of retaliation, has lost its vitality as a result of the ever-growing interdependence of states, according to Myres McDougal. International law must now be seen as an integral part of a global community process, a universal system rather than one based on the nation-state. It is myopic, writes McDougal, to confine the discussion of peace to the coordination of the activities of nation-states, when it is more important to protect individuals from the random application of violence and coercion and to secure their access to the values that they most cherish.

The striking irony of the global community is that while demands for freedom from violence and access to values increase, so, too, do the incidences of violence and deprivation of human rights. This situation underscores the disutility of the traditional view of international law as an agreed-upon body of rules and norms. The basis of law must be rooted in values, not rules, because rules are necessarily complementary, ambiguous, and incomplete. A relevant concept of international law must have as its foundation not only an appreciation for the effective power process of the global community, but also for the means by which that process can be most realistically channeled into the service of the individual.

The global process of effective power is characterized by two types of decisions: those that rely on the exercise of naked power, violence, and coercion; and those that are based on the rule of law or the exercise of legitimate authoritative determinations. This latter type is further divided into two parts: considerations of the constitutive process by which recognized representatives and institutions, and the goals and values they symbolize, are identified and secured; and public order decisions that determine how best to protect those values and to distribute them throughout the community.

With these definitions in mind, any viable concept of international peace must encompass a two-pronged effort: to minimize the application of violence and coercion to the individual, and to provide for the freedom of access by individuals to all treasured values. Peace, therefore, must be defined as much more than the simple absence of armed conflict. In McDougal's words, "The peace demanded by contemporary humankind is not the peace of the concentration camp." Even when peace is conceived of in the minimum sense, as freedom from arbitrary violence, it depends on maintaining people's expectations that the effective decision-making processes concerning public order will be responsive to their demands for reasonable access to the values of human dignity. When peace is conceived of in a more optimal sense, as "security in position with expectation and potential access to all basic community values," the organic relationship between peace and human rights becomes striking.

The challenge then, as McDougal sees it, "is to work out ways of improving and of asserting authority into the effective power process that will increase the probabilities of outcomes that dispense with unauthorized violence and improve the sharing of human rights." In other words, how can we better collectivize and, to some degree, centralize the role of authority in the existing processes?

Clearly, Article 2(4) of the UN Charter and the emerging body of formal human rights declarations attempt to do just that. But both these efforts often still rely on the black-and-white application of rules rather than value-relevant considerations and, therefore, do not necessarily assist either cause. Furthermore, worsening environmental conditions, overpopulation, poverty, and resource depletion continue to make the expectation of violence and the denial of human dignity the norm in many regions of the world. True peace, McDougal asserts, cannot occur until these conditions are ameliorated and international emphasis on human freedom is renewed.

6. Law and Peace

Myres S. McDougal

The establishment and maintenance of a comprehensive peace, through law rather than by arbitrary violence and coercion, is today commonly regarded as one of humankind's most urgent and difficult problems. To achieve a productive understanding of what law may contribute to peace, of the inextricable interrelations of law and peace, it is necessary that we observe the larger context of global processes of interaction that contain and condition both law and peace. We must formulate appropriate conceptions of law and peace, note the inadequacies in our inherited theories and procedures designed to serve peace, and, finally, apply to the general problem, and numerous particular problems of promoting peace, certain relevant intellectual tasks. These tasks, extending beyond the unsystematic, anecdotal pursuit of random strategies in effective power, or the traditional logical derivation from allegedly autonomous legal rules, include the postulation and clarification of basic community goals, the examination of past trends in the achievement of such goals, the exploration of the factors that affect degrees in achievement, the projection of possible futures, and the recommendation of alternatives in the decision process and particular decisions that promise a higher degree of success.

We proceed to explore these points of inquiry and intellectual tasks *seriatim*.

The Larger Context

In realistic perspective, it can be observed that the whole of humankind today constitutes a single comprehensive community, entirely comparable to its many internal territorial and other communities, in the sense of interdetermination or interdependence in the shaping and sharing of all values.[1] This larger community is composed, not merely of an aggregate of nation-states, but of expanding billions of individual human beings who create, in addition to nation-states, a whole host of other groupings and associations, such as international governmental organizations, political parties, pressure groups, and private associations specialized to all demanded values, in activities increasingly transcending all territorial boundaries. The interdependences that characterize this larger community process, and all its internal component communities, include both those within any, and every, particular value process and those that cut across all value processes. The interdependent activities within, and across, all value processes stimulate, affect, and are affected by all decision processes, lawful and unlawful.[2]

A most important component in this larger community process is an ongoing, all-pervasive process of effective power, totally global or earth-space in reach, in which decisions are in fact taken and enforced by severe deprivations or high indulgences, oftentimes irrespective of the wishes of any particular participant.[3] For some centuries nation-states have been, and remain, through the resources and people within their boundaries, the principal institutions by which people wield effective power and have engaged in a continuous balancing of such power. In a world in which people and goods are in continuous and increasing movement, the bases of power are no longer hermetically sealed within the boundaries of particular nation-states. Resources are important only as potential values, dependent upon transnational activity; and as science and technology advance and universalize, enlightenment and skill, as well as conceptions of rectitude and responsibility, become of increasing significance as bases of power.

Upon close examination, it may be observed that the decisions taken within this comprehensive process of effective power are of two different kinds.[4] Many decisions are of course taken through sheer naked power or from considerations of expedience, without regard for common interest. Goliaths do not always live, or balance power, easily with pygmies. Many other decisions, however, may be observed to be taken from perspectives of authority, in the sense that they are made by the persons who are expected to make them, in accordance with criteria expected by community members, in established structures of decision, with enough bases in effective power to secure consequential control, and by authorized procedures. The continuous flow of this second type of decision may be realistically described as a comprehensive process of authoritative decision by which the effective elites of the global community, after the fashion of elites in lesser communities, seek to clarify and secure their common interests. The decision processes of the most comprehensive global community affect the shaping and sharing of values both as between and within all its constituent communities, of whatever geographic or functional reach. The decision processes of the lesser regional, national, and local communities in turn affect the distinctive decision processes and value allocations of the larger community that they comprise. The two different kinds of decisions that comprise the global process of effective power, those that employ arbitrary coercion and violence and those that seek through authority to minimize such coercion and violence, are obviously in continuous interaction and struggle. The most comprehensive global community process thus moves incessantly through a continuum between two polar extremes: that of the most intense violence and coercion, sometimes described as "war," and that which emphasizes persuasion and community-organized coercion, sometimes described as "peace."

It can be observed, further, that the most comprehensive process of authoritative decision exhibited in the global community, as in lesser component communities, is also composed of two different though closely interrelated types of decision. The first are the constitutive decisions that establish and maintain a process of authoritative decision. These are the decisions that identify and characterize decision makers, postulate and specify basic community policies, establish appropriate decision structures, allocate bases of power for decision and sanctioning purposes, authorize procedures for the making of different kinds of decisions, and secure the performance of all the different decision functions (intelligence, promoting, prescribing, invoking, applying, terminating, and appraising) necessary for clarifying and securing the more detailed policies of the larger community.[5] The second type of authoritative decisions are those that continuously emerge from global constitutive process to establish and maintain a public order: these are the decisions that determine how resources are allocated, planned, developed, and employed, how wealth is shaped and distributed, how human rights are promoted and protected or deprived, how enlightenment is encouraged or blighted, how health is fostered or neglected, how rectitude and civic responsibility to the larger community are matured or repressed, and so on through the whole gamut of demanded values.[6] The quality of the constitutive process that a community can establish tremendously affects the quality of the public order it can achieve; conversely, the quality of the public order a community achieves reciprocally affects the quality of the constitutive process it can establish.

A Relevant Conception of Law

The most relevant conception of law in the global community, as in lesser communities, is, as indicated above, in an ancient tradition revived by the American Legal Realists, that of a comprehensive process of authoritative decision.[7] It is the process, a component of the global process of effective power, by which the politically relevant members of the larger community seek to clarify and secure their common interests and to minimize and regulate the assertion of arbitrary, unauthorized violence and coercion, the other component of the global process of effective power. It will be observed that, as authoritative decision, the term "law" includes reference to both authority, in the sense of community expectations about the requirements of decision, and control, in the sense of actual participation in the making and enforcement of decision. It may need emphasis that the most minimal conception of law requires uniformities in decision in accordance with community expectation; law is the very opposite of the arbitrary, unauthorized use of violence and coercion. The members of the global community, as in lesser communities, who are concerned with the shaping and sharing of values will, further, focus attention, not upon isolated, anecdotal decisions, but upon the whole, comprehensive flow of authoritative decision.

A conception of law, whether for the global community or lesser communities, as a body of rules, though again of ancient origin, is hopelessly myopic. In pluralistic and rapidly changing communities, rules are always complementary, ambiguous, and incomplete. They do not apply themselves, and technology has yet to invent their automation. The only empirical reference, as faint as it sometimes is, of rules is to decision. For established decision makers, and others, the function of rules is to state community goals and to guide toward the factors in many varying contexts that may affect rational choice. Rules are, thus, but one component, however important, of a comprehensive process of authoritative decision.

The conception of "international law" as a body of rules regulating the interrelations of nation-states is doubly myopic.[8] Beyond the infirmities of its over-estimating of the potentialities of rules, it has infirmities in the scope of the activities it seeks to make subject to law. The activities of humankind in global community process today spill across the boundaries of nation-states in an ever accelerating and intensifying rate. The contemporary conception of "transnational law" takes only a beginning account of the importance of individual human beings, and their multiplicitous associations and groupings, in these new, transnational activities.[9] A rational concern for peace in either a minimum or optimum reference, must take these activities into still further account. The law relevant to peace cannot be confined to the coordination of the activities of nation-states. An appropriate law extends, must be extended, to the whole global process of authoritative decision that guides and regulates human activities across nation-state boundaries. In comprehensive conception this process of decision includes among its component features, and interrelates, all the various "roads" to peace indicated in the call for this symposium, such as international governmental organization, third-party decision making, the facilitation and protection of diplomacy and negotiation, conflict resolution, the organization of deterrence, the management of collective security, and so on.

A Relevant Conception of Peace

The most relevant conception of peace must make reference to the least possible application of violence and coercion to the individual human being and to the freedom of access of the individual to all cherished values. For community members and their decision makers alike, a viable conception of peace cannot today be limited to reference to a mere absence of armed, and international, conflict. The peace demanded by contemporary humankind is not that of the concentration camp (however large) or that of the living dead (whatever the community).

The conception of peace, as contraposed to war, in the historic literature of international law is most imprecise.[10] The words "peace" and "war" are characteristically employed, in high ambiguity, to make simultaneous reference both to the presence or absence of the facts of transnational violence and coercion and to the legal consequences to be attached by authoritative decision to different intensities in violence and coercion. The facts to which reference is made are those of the global process of effective power in which many different participants (state and nonstate), for many varying objectives in expansion or conservation, employ all instruments of policy (military, diplomatic, ideological, and economic), in alternative stages of acceleration and deceleration in intensity of violence and coercion, in attack upon the bases of power (people, resources, institutions) of other participants, and are themselves in turn the targets of attack. The legal policies and sanctioning consequences that the authoritative decision makers of the global community apply to the different aspects of this continuous process of violence and coercion vary with many particular problems, such as the minimization of major coercions, the conduct of hostilities, the termination of hostilities, the regulation of minor coercions, and so on. In a first effort to minimize major violence and coercion, through a law of "aggression" and "self-defense," authoritative decision makers seek to prevent alterations in the existing distribution of values among nation-states by processes of unilateral and unauthorized coercion and to promote value changes and adjustments by processes of persuasion or by community-sanctioned coercion. A second effort, when persuasive strategies fail and violence and coercion break out, is to reduce to a minimum the unnecessary destruction of values by defining with as much specificity as possible the permissible maximum of violence and destruction in particular types of situations. It has been many times documented that our inherited concepts of "peace" and "war," making such ambiguous reference to this vast maze of facts and legal policies, cast but a darkening light upon the difficult problems in public order that presently confront humankind.

It is suggested that a more relevant conception of peace can be found in a specification of contemporary notions of world public order. A distinction is sometimes made between "minimum order," in the sense of the minimization of unauthorized violence and coercion, and "optimum order," in the sense of the greatest access of the individual human being to the shaping and sharing of all the values of human dignity.[11] It would appear, however, that both these kinds of allegedly different public order goals are indispensable to any workable conception of peace. Even when conceived in the minimum sense of freedom from the fact and expectation of arbitrary violence and coercion, peace may be observed increasingly to be dependent upon maintaining people's expectations that the processes of effective decision in public order will be responsive to their demands for a reasonable access to all the values we today characterize as those of human dignity. When peace is more broadly conceived as security in position, expectation, and potential with regard to all basic community values, the interrelationship of peace and human rights quite obviously passes beyond that of interdependence and approaches that of identity. Hence, for reasons of interdependence or identity, there can be but one answer to President John F. Kennedy's question "Is not peace, in the last analysis, basically a matter of human rights?"[12]

The basic community policies that underlie conceptions of peace and human rights are in any democratic community the same policies that underlie all law. Hence, it is no metaphor to conclude that peace and law may appropriately be described as one side of the coin (of community process and effective power) of which arbitrary violence and coercion are the other side.

Formulating the Problem

The rising, common demands of peoples about the globe for increased protection from arbitrary violence and coercion and for greater participation in the shaping and sharing of all cherished values are written large in contemporary shared consciousness. Yet the expectation of impending major violence and coercion, employing weapons of apocalyptic destructive potential, continues to hang over the world, threatening and intimidating all peoples and in measure paralyzing "human rights" efforts to increase the participation of all individuals in the shaping and sharing of values. It is this disparity between the demands of the peoples of the world and responding community achievement that constitutes the most general problem in shaping a global legal process designed better to secure peace, whether peace is defined in minimum or optimum terms.

Utopian proponents of peace sometimes ignore that all efforts to improve authoritative decision for better securing peace, however defined, must take place within the context of the contemporary global process of effective power. This process of effective power, as we have noted, exhibits the major nation-states of the world, and especially those possessing nuclear weapons and the capabilities for chemical and biological warfare, engaged in a process of continually balancing power among themselves and others and taking all measures necessary to insure that no single state and its allies are able to secure a position of completely dominant, centralized power.[13] There is no way that peoples cherishing peace and common interest in all the values of human dignity can avoid direct confrontation with peoples employing violence and coercion for purposes of expansion in special interest and, when necessary, themselves employing military force and other coercion in defense of their values. Humankind has, unhappily, demonstrated down through the millennia that it is sometimes willing to employ the most destructive, unauthorized violence and coercion against others not merely for self-protection, but to secure demanded, though unwanted, changes in the others. The threats and horrors of the contemporary scene need no new depiction or emphasis.

Alleged realists, in contrast, sometimes ignore that authority, as community expectation, is itself a form of effective power, and a form that can be changed and improved. A most important base of power for the decision makers in any community derives from the expectations of the members of that community that these are the established decision makers and that they are authorized to make certain decisions, by specified criteria of common interest, and to invoke certain sanctioning consequences to secure compliance. In an age of instantaneous global communication, this form of effective power, with its appeal to world opinion and shared conceptions of rectitude, has enormous and increasing importance.

For perspicuous proponents of peace, the realistic and immediate challenge is that of introducing into the global process of effective power more collectivized, perhaps even more centralized, perspectives and operations of authority, sustained by control. It is not, however, to be assumed that humankind is limited in choice between an anarchy of allegedly equal, independent, and sovereign territorial communities and some fantasied omnicompetent universal state with all its threats to freedom and the values of human dignity. The words "federal," "confederal," "region," "alliance," and "coalition" are primarily meaningful in the present discussion in their suggestion of the infinite variety of potential modalities in organization. The parts may be related to the whole in many different, and changing, ways in a moving context. In the complex contemporary global community process, there can be no magical modality or gimmick for securing peace.

It is of course necessary in any effort toward improvement, to begin with the existing global process of authoritative decision, already collectivized in higher degree than many observers are aware. There is urgent need for reexamination of the competences accorded, in the United Nations and elsewhere, for minimizing resort to major violence and coercion and for the revision of these competences to make them accord more with a genuine democracy and the capabilities for responsibility in the enforcement of decisions. One promising alternative requiring consideration, as we will develop below, is that of enhancing the competence of regional organization and functional groupings. Many improvements could be made also in the multitudinous decisions emerging from global constitutive process in regulation of all the public order values other than power, such as wealth, enlightenment, health, and so on. It is the flow in outcomes of decision with respect to these values that constitute the subject matter of human rights and conditions the achievement of peace in both minimum and maximum conception.

The Inadequacies of Early Theories and Procedures

For some centuries the dominant conception of international law has been, as we are too often reminded, that of a body of rules that regulate the interrelations of nation-states.[14] Grotius, building upon a number of predecessors, established himself as the founder of modern international law by recognizing the increasing importance of the nation-state and by outlining a procedure by which an unorganized community of states (without centralized legislative, executive, and judicial institutions) could minimize the occurrence and devastation of major violence and coercion, through assertions of reciprocity and retaliation. In Grotius's eloquent words, *Quod tibi non vis, alteri non facias:* what one does not wish done to himself, he should not do to others.[15] This perception of common interest was built upon the fact, dubbed by later French scholars as *le dédoublement fonctionnel*, that the same states that are claimants in one case may be sitting as judges, through world opinion, in the next comparable case. In a community of a large number of states of relatively equal effective power, even so primitive a procedure could do substantial justice and maintain a modest peace. Grotius ransacked many versions of natural law, sacred and profane, and a great range of prior practices by states and other participants in search of appropriate authoritative rules.

In a recent book, *Visions of World Order*, the late Julius Stone reviews the major historic frames of jurisprudence and considers their past and potential contributions to world public order.[16] It is clear from Stone's presentation, and other surveys, that none of the major frames of jurisprudence either recognize the degree of collectivization in the contemporary global process of authoritative decision or escape from the shackles of the limited conception of international law as a body of rules regulating the interrelations of states. In some frames the notion of community is truncated or imprecise, not permitting either comprehensive or detailed description. Many conceptions of effective power stop short with the nation-state as participant, and ignore authority as an important base of power transnationally. Most frames define authority either in transempirical (religious or metaphysical) terms or in ambiguous, tautological syntactic reference, encouraging endless verbal disputations about the true source of the "obligation" or "binding force" of international law. Many frames can conceive of control as emanating only from organized and centralized governmental structures, thus foredooming inquiry at both international and national levels. The futility of each major, inherited frame may be noted.

The oldest frame of jurisprudence, commonly described as that of "natural law," deriving from times when religion and notions of physical nature were often merged with law, did achieve conceptions of a larger community of humankind and of a common human nature and, hence, make immense contribution to the development of transcommunity perspectives of law. The conception of authority propounded by this frame was, and is, however, characteristically in terms of religious or metaphysical references, admitting of diametrically opposite interpretations, and, on the rare occasions when the control dimension of power is addressed, the conception of control put forward is observable only in appeals from naked power. The frame does not focus squarely upon common interest as a guide to decision and characteristically makes unverified assumptions about human nature (social or asocial) and by logical derivations from such assumptions seeks to establish a body of prescriptions relating to world public order, including peace. The greatest difficulties for world public order are created by this frame when assumptions about the nature of individuals are transposed to territorial communities and such entities are believed to have absolute, unmodifiable attributes of equality, independence, and sovereignty.

The positivist frame, in contrast with natural law, assumes that the several nation-states constitute the principal communities of humankind and that whatever transnational community exists, if any, is composed only of these nation-states. The conception of law propounded by this frame, in an ill-defined confusion of both authority and control, is in terms of rules established by nation-state officials, as developed from an earlier version of the commands of the sovereign. Since the devotees of this theory can observe no global "sovereign," with centralized legislative, executive, and judicial institutions and officials, their theories by definition preclude a conception of international law as law. Indeed, the more bold devotees of this frame flatly assert, in obedience to John Austin's specifications, that international law is not law. A second version of this frame, described as "dualist," asserts that, though both national law and international law are equally law, they have a completely different set of decision makers, policies, structures, and procedures. A third version, known as "monism," finds authority, not in a "sovereign" decision maker, but in some postulated global *grundnorm,* located in either agreement or custom, and asserts that this grundnorm, by some mysterious derivational magic, without regard for effective power, dictates the content of the law both of the larger community and of all its lesser communities. It will be noted that these two latter versions of the positivist frame both build upon the assumption that international law is merely a body of rules that govern the interrelations of states. These rules are to be found, in theory, largely in the *past* practices of states. The goofus bird flies backward because, though it has no care for where it is going, it likes to know where it has been.

The historical frame, with its emphasis upon the parochial uniqueness of every particular territorial community, has had great difficulty in achieving a conception of transnational community. Although this frame does, in contrast with that of natural law, seek to ground law in empirical social process, the conception of law with which it commonly works is that of some mysterious *geist* or spirit, which supposedly in any particular community emanates from its people as does their language, religion, poetry, and music. In such an approach, the lines between authority and control are completely blurred, and few proponents of the approach are able to isolate authoritative decision or a comprehensive constitutive process of decision from the whole flow of particular events in which values are shaped and shared. The deep and pervasive determinism in the notion that law is somehow forever fixed by an ineluctable fate at some point in the past discourages all effort toward innovation and change and renders sterile the various intellectual tasks indispensable to rational decision.

Similarly, the sociological frame, despite its characteristic concern for the scientific study of explanatory factors and social consequences, unhappily takes its basic conceptions of community and law largely from the positivist frame. Too often its notion of community process is confined to activities within the nation-state, in neglect of the whole hierarchy of interpenetrating community processes from local through national and regional levels to the global. It commonly finds authority in rules established by nation-state officials, and even the most realistic proponents of the frame, find control only in organized and centralized institutions. Hence, the conception of international law for this frame continues to be that of a supposed body of rules governing the interrelations of nation-states, in disregard of the role of other participants in transnational community and power processes and without clear focus upon authoritative decision transcending state lines. The scientific study in any community of the causes and consequences of "rules," without clear relation to decision, is a difficult task, and can scarcely be expected to contribute greatly to the maintenance or improvement of world constitutive process and public order.

The particular policies and procedures developed, under the aegis of these inherited theories about international law, for the control of major coercion and violence, sometimes called force, were most primitive.[17] There have, of course, for some centuries been reasonably observed policies for the protection of diplomats and facilitation of diplomacy; for the making, application, and termination of international agreements; for the protection of nationals abroad from abuses by other states; and for the peaceful settlement of disputes, as through conciliation, mediation, and arbitration. With respect to the more direct control of major coercions and violence, the policies and procedures developed were, however, far from being adequate or consistently observed. The most important effort to control major coercion and violence, with roots reaching far back into the Middle Ages, derived from a distinction between just and unjust wars.[18] The basic thrust of *bellum iustum* was that resort to major violence could be regarded as legitimate self-help only for certain objectives, such as redressing a received wrong, a wrong "serious and commensurate with the losses the war would occasion" and which could not "be repaired or avenged in any other way." The effective power of the Papacy made possible some centralized administration of so general a concept of necessity and consequentiality. Yet even this modest effort to control major coercion and violence fell before changes in community and effective power processes in the eighteenth century, and by the nineteenth century, the requirement of *bellum iustum* was brought to an unobtrusive demise.

In the nineteenth and early twentieth centuries, resort to coercion came to be regarded as a prerogative of sovereignty, the legitimacy of which nonparticipating states were not competent to judge. In the international law of the time, as Eugene Rostow has written, "war was the sport of princes and the privilege of states, and could be undertaken for power, glory, revenge, or many reasons beyond considerations of self-defense."[19] International law offered no general prohibition of violence and made no clear distinction between impermissible and permissible coercion. It attempted only the regulation and the humanitarization of violence once violence had in fact been initiated. Contending belligerents were regarded as upon a plane of "juridical equality" and third states that chose not to participate were said to be under a duty of "neutrality." In deep paradox, though states were said to have a fundamental right to independent existence, there was no prohibition against states waging war and destroying one another. Decisions were to be taken by the relative strength of states and violence was permissible, not only for self-help and self-vindication in the conservation of values, but also for effecting changes in the international distribution of values. In only less paradox, a few authoritative prescriptions purported to govern the employment of minor coercions, limited in dimension and objective, sometimes labeled as "retorsion," "reprisal," "intervention," or "pacific blockade," and so forth, and generally categorized as "measures short of war." Any such governance was of course illusory: the initiating state could at any time designate its operations as "war" and avoid the thrust of limitation.

The movement in the twentieth century toward a general prohibition of major coercion and violence, and toward a collectivized administration of that prohibition, is traceable through the Covenant of the League of Nations, the Pact of Paris, and the Nuremberg verdict, with culmination in the core provisions of the United Nations Charter.

It requires only brief note that for centuries international law purported to offer but little protection to the citizens of a state against that state. Traditional law exhausted its concern for human rights with the modest protection afforded aliens.[20]

The Contemporary Authoritative Postulation of Basic Public Order Goals

In 1945, spurred by the "rising, common demands" of individual human beings from every corner of the globe to be free from "the scourge of war" and for greater participation in the shaping and sharing of all the values of human dignity, the framers of the United Nations Charter effected two revolutionary changes in historic international law: in core provisions, the Charter postulated, and authoritatively prescribed, both a general prohibition of the unauthorized employment of major coercion and violence and a new protection of the fundamental human rights of individuals, even against their own states.[21] In its preambular clauses and the statement of goals in Article 1, the Charter clearly recognized the intimate interdependence, if not identity, of peace and human rights and made the protection of human rights coordinate with the maintenance of peace. In Article 2(3) the Charter prescribed: "All members shall settle their international disputes by peaceful means in a manner that international peace and security, and justice, are not endangered."

The most difficult problem for law in any community, a problem greatly magnified in the global community by gross inequalities in the distribution of effective power, is that of characterizing and minimizing unlawful coercion and violence. In Articles 2(4) and 51, and certain auxiliary articles, the United Nations Charter makes an indispensable distinction between impermissible and permissible coercion and violence and projects a set of complementary prescriptions, whose unitary and overriding policy is that of protecting and promoting peaceful change.

The most important of the new policies, that of a general prohibition of unauthorized major coercion and violence, is stated very broadly in Article 2(4), which reads:

All Members shall refrain in their international relations from the threat or use of force against the territorial integrity or political independence of any state, or in any other manner inconsistent with the Purposes of the United Nations.

It was, however, recognized that in the still primitively organized global community, offering only modest expectation of the capability of the general community for protecting its members, some right of self-defense by states is indispensable to the maintenance of even the most modest minimum order. Hence, Article 51 of the Charter reads:

Nothing in the present Charter shall impair the inherent right of individual or collective self-defence if an armed attack occurs against a Member of the United Nations, until the Security Council has taken measures necessary to maintain international peace and security....

The historic right of states to self-defense did not require them, like sitting ducks, to await armed attack, and it is clear, despite occasional literalist interpretations, that the framers of the Charter had no intent to preclude response to *imminent* attack and to impose suicide. The most rational construction of these complementary policies contraposed in Articles 2(4) and 51 would appear to be: the right of self-defense established by the Charter, as in traditional practice, authorizes a state which, being the target of activities by another state, reasonably decides, as third-party observers may later determine reasonableness, that such activities require it to employ the military instrument to protect its territorial integrity and political independence, to use such force as may be necessary and proportionate to its defense.[22] The employment of force that creates this expectation in a target state is in violation of Article 2(4) and is commonly characterized as "aggression," the unlawful complement to lawful self-defense.

Learning from the obvious difficulties in Grotius's *dédoublement fonctionnel* and the failures of the League of Nations, the framers of the Charter projected, for the detailed administration of this basic distinction between impermissible and permissible coercion and violence, a highly collectivized and centralized structure of decision making. Thus, in Article 24(1) the Security Council, with its veto for the protection of permanent members, was accorded "primary responsibility for the maintenance of international peace and security," and the members agreed that the Security Council, "in carrying out its duties under this responsibility," acted on their behalf. In other chapters of the Charter, elaborate provision was made both for the peaceful settlement of disputes and for employment of organized community force in the maintenance of public order. In Article 39 the Security Council was authorized to "determine the existence of any threat to the peace, breach of the peace, or act of aggression" and to recommend or take appropriate measures "to maintain or restore international peace and security." In other articles possible measures, of varying intensity in coercion, are outlined in detail. The capstone Article 25 provides: "The Members of the United Nations agree to accept and carry out the decisions of the Security Council in accordance with the present Charter."

The United Nations Charter, despite all its emphasis upon the importance of (and modest prescription about) human rights, does not itself project a comprehensive and detailed bill of human rights. This gap in constitutive prescription has, however, been remedied by a sequence of cumulative subsequent developments. Building upon the provisions of the Charter, the main features of a comprehensive global bill of rights have been prescribed, if not yet effectively applied, through a whole host of authoritative communications, including the Universal Declaration of Human Rights (now largely customary law); the Covenant on Political and Civil Rights; the Covenant on Economic, Social and Cultural Rights; the Genocide Convention; and multiple specialized and regional pacts; as well as by national constitutions and the vast flow of judicial and other decisions that create the expectations of customary law. The outcome is, thus, an authoritatively prescribed global bill of human rights entirely comparable in content and reach to that maintained in contemporary, more mature national communities.[23] It embraces the fundamental policies that underlie all law in any community that seeks a genuine clarification of the common interests of its members. A world public order of human dignity may endure many variations in the practices by which particular values are shaped and shared if major value goals are kept compatible and all practices are evaluated and accommodated by the criteria of common interest.

Trends in Past Achievement of Basic Goals

It is common knowledge that the highly collectivized and centralized structure of decision making projected by the United Nations Charter for characterizing and minimizing major coercion and violence was stillborn. So complex an administrative structure, requiring the careful coordination of member states, could not survive the vast disparities in the effective power and interests of the member states and the mounting intensity of the struggle between an expansive totalitarian public order and an opposing order at least aspiring toward the values of human dignity. As the horrors of worldwide war have receded, the perception and clarification of a common interest between the contending orders have become more and more difficult.

In consequence of this failure of the projected centralized structure of decision making, the larger community of humankind has been thrown back, for making the difficult distinction between impermissible and permissible coercion and violence, upon Grotius's ancient *dédoublement fonctionnel*, in which the several states themselves make the necessary evaluations and undertake appropriate sanctioning measures. In such a context it cannot be surprising that states commonly make the evaluations in terms of their own special interests, including the interests of the public order to which they adhere. It is not believed, however, that the great bulk of humankind, taken as individuals, have abandoned their demand to be free from the "scourge of war," or have lost the realistic expectation that some stable, uniform administration of the distinction between impermissible and permissible coercion and violence is indispensable to even minimum attainment of a law-governed global community. The states of the world, and the whole of humankind as expressed through the many media of world public opinion, do continue to challenge and evaluate the behavior of states by the criteria of Articles 2(4) and 51. The hope would appear to remain that more centralized and more effective procedures for the administration of an indispensable policy can still be achieved. In the light of such expectations and hope, it can scarcely be said, with realism, that Articles 2(4) and 51 are dead and that humankind is again without authoritative prohibition of major coercion and violence.[24] At least for the proponents of a public order of human dignity, the understanding remains that the application of major coercion and violence to the human person is fundamentally incompatible with basic human rights and that a global community that genuinely aspires toward the values of human dignity must continue to seek to minimize major coercion and violence as an instrument of change, or as an instrument obstructing peaceful change.

A principal obstacle to the uniform application of Articles 2(4) and 51 has been in the insistence, from the beginning, by the Soviet Union that "wars of liberation" are not subject to Article 2(4). This concept, designed to facilitate totalitarian expansionism, is derived from an earlier idiosyncratic distinction between just and unjust wars. The distinction reads:

> (a) *Just* wars, wars that are not wars of conquest but wars of liberation, waged to defend the people from foreign attack and from attempts to enslave them, or to liberate the people from capitalist slavery, or, lastly, to liberate colonies and dependent countries from the yoke of imperialism; and

> (b) *Unjust* wars, wars of conquest, waged to conquer and enslave foreign countries and foreign nations.[25]

In more modern formulation, the concept and its justification are thus stated by Professor Tunkin:

> Modern international law also provides for the right of colonial peoples and dependent countries to use armed force against metropolies interfering with efforts of the peoples of corresponding countries or territories to realize their right to self-determination. Such use of armed force is also a justified form of self-defence. While in a general form that proposition follows from the United Nations Charter itself, it finds more concrete expression in numerous international documents, including the Geneva agreements of 1954 concerning Indochina, and numerous resolutions of the United Nations General Assembly, especially in the Declaration on Principles of International Law of 1970.[26]

This alleged exception to Article 2(4) has, as is well known, been employed by the Soviets to justify interventions in many countries in Europe, Asia, Africa, and Latin America.

In supplement to this alleged exception from Article 2(4) of "wars of liberation," the Soviets have in relatively recent times sought to establish an allied exception known as the "Brezhnev Doctrine." This doctrine is designed to justify Soviet intervention in states already "socialist" to preclude their choice to become other than socialist. In its most authoritative statement, this doctrine reads:

> There is no doubt that the peoples of the socialist countries and the Communist Parties have and must have freedom to determine their country's path of development. However, any decision of theirs must damage neither socialism in their own country nor the fundamental interests of the other socialist countries nor the worldwide workers' movement, which is waging a struggle for socialism. This means that every Communist Party is responsible not only to its own people but also to all the socialist countries and to the entire Communist movement.

Whoever forgets this in placing sole emphasis on the autonomy and independence of Communist Parties lapses into one-sidedness, shirking his internationalist obligations.[27]

The statement adds:

Each Communist Party is free in applying the principles of Marxism-Leninism and socialism in its own country, but it cannot deviate from these principles (if, of course, it remains a Communist Party). In concrete terms this means primarily that every Communist Party cannot fail to take into account in its activities such a decisive fact of our time as the struggle between the two antithetical social systems—capitalism and socialism.[28]

The violence with which this doctrine has been applied in Eastern Europe and elsewhere needs no new description. The totality of these claims for exception from Article 2(4), through both wars of liberation and the Brezhnev Doctrine, that the Soviet Union asserts is aptly summarized by Professor Michael Reisman:

The Soviet claim was and continues to be that, the U.N. Charter notwithstanding, the Soviet Union maintains the right to support those struggling against existing governments if their struggle is consistent with historical laws, of which the Soviet government is the exclusively authorized interpreter. If the groups succeed, the Soviet Union has the additional right and obligation to make sure that their members and constituents do not change their minds in the future. A scholar of no less stature than Professor Tunkin has sanctified the doctrine as a *jus cogens.*[29]

Incredibly enough, the International Court of Justice in the recent *Nicaragua* case would appear, perhaps maladroitly, to have conferred its authority upon "wars of liberation."[30] At one point in its opinion, the Court in piety, as excessive as impossible, declares its complete neutrality between contending systems of world public order. It writes:

The finding of the United States Congress also expressed the view that the Nicaraguan Government has taken "significant steps towards establishing a totalitarian Communist dictatorship." However the regime in Nicaragua be defined, adherence by a State to any particular doctrine does not constitute a violation of customary international law: to hold otherwise would make nonsense of the fundamental principle of State sovereignty, on which the whole of international law rests, and the freedom of choice of the political, social, economic, and cultural systems of a State. Consequently, Nicaragua's domestic policy options, even assuming that they correspond to the description given of them by the Congress finding, cannot justify on the legal plane the various actions of the Respondent complained of. The Court cannot contemplate the creation of a new rule opening up a right of intervention by one State against another on the ground that the latter has opted for some particular ideology or political system.[31]

Yet in its holding the Court finds in the acknowledged hostilities of Nicaragua against El Salvador no "armed attack" against El Salvador or even threat of "armed attack" against El Salvador or any other state; hence, it denies the United States the right to participate in the collective defense of El Salvador and legitimates the factual intervention by Nicaragua. As Judge Schwebel writes, in dissent, this was in substance to honor "wars of liberation."[32] Judge Schwebel, finding the errors of the Court conspicuous, writes:

> The Court appears to reason this way. Efforts by State A (however insiduous, sustained, substantial and effective), to overthrow the government of State B, if they are not or do not amount to an armed attack upon State B, give rise to no right of self-defence by State B, and hence, to no right of State C to join State B in measures of collective self-defence. State B, the victim State, is entitled to take counter-measures against State A, of a dimension the Court does not specify. But State C is not thereby justified in taking counter-measures against State A which involve the use of force.[33]

He adds confirmation of his interpretation by noting a negative inference from an earlier reference by the Court to "wars of decolonization," a kind of war not involved in the case. Thus, while professing not to be able to create a double standard, by its decision the Court in fact creates a double standard in favor of an expansive totalitarianism.[34] The question before the Court was not whether Nicaragua's choice of a public order was "a violation of customary international law," but whether Nicaragua's attacks upon its neighbors were in accord with conventional and customary international law.[35]

The decision and opinion of the International Court of Justice in the *Nicaragua* case, most unhappily, raises grave questions about the capabilities of a judicial body, under the contemporary circumstances of contending world public orders, to make rational decisions in the common interest about the regulation of major coercion and violence. At the jurisdictional phases of the case,[36] the Court held, contrary to all prior law, that it had jurisdiction over a state that had not consented to such jurisdiction, and in favor of a state that had no standing to sue except by the most factitious creation of the Court. At the merits phase, the Court demonstrated that it had few capabilities for discovering or recognizing the facts relevant to rational decision, and even less capabilities for evaluating such facts by the criteria that much of the world regards as expressed in the United Nations Charter and customary international law.[37] Hersch Lauterpacht could have been right in his famous insistence that in the abstract no dispute between human beings is inherently nonjusticiable.[38] His conclusion can, however, have little relevance to a struggle between contending world public orders in which all common interest, beyond bare human survival, seems at times to have disappeared.[39]

It should be no cause for wonder, in an infectious deterioration of policies and procedures for the regulation of major coercion and violence, that the United States, as a principal proponent of a public order of human dignity, should begin in measure, for self-help, to adopt policies and procedures parallel to those employed by the Soviet Union. Through the Monroe Doctrine and participation in the Organization of American States, the United States has long of course sought to preclude outside states from acquiring territorial power in the Western hemisphere. More recently, presidents as diverse in general perspective as Kennedy and Johnson have made pronouncements, in content comparable to the later Brezhnev Doctrine, designed to justify interventions against totalitarian expansion into this hemisphere.[40] Even the House of Representatives joined in support of these pronouncements. It resolved that:

(1) any [international communist] subversive domination or threat of it violates the principles of the Monroe Doctrine, and of collective security as set forth in the acts and resolutions heretofore adopted by the American Republics: and

(2) in any such situation any one or more of the high contracting parties to the Inter-American Treaty of Reciprocal Assistance may, in the exercise of individual or collective self-defense, which could go so far as resort to armed force, and in accordance with the declarations and principles above stated, take steps to forestall or combat intervention, domination, control and colonization of whatever form, by the subversive forces known as international communism and its agencies in the Western hemisphere.[41]

In contemporary times Presidents Carter and Reagan have extended comparable doctrines to the Persian Gulf and Saudi Arabia.

Another important obstacle to the rational, uniform application of Articles 2(4) and 51 derives from the attempt, as illustrated by the International Court of Justice in the *Nicaragua* case, to cut down the reach of the historic right of self-defense.[42] It is not always recognized that in the global community Articles 2(4) and 51 are as wholly complementary as are the prohibition of violence and the permission of self-defense in mature national communities. Some state officials and scholars have taken the position that Article 51 imposes upon states a higher degree of necessity than that of customary international law and requires states to await the inception of actual armed attack, without option to respond to realistic expectations of imminent attack. This interpretation of Article 51 is based upon an allegedly literal interpretation of the words *armed attack* regarded as an isolated component of the article. It may be noted, however, that such interpretation introduces the words *only if* into the Article and is contrary to all the important canons for the interpretation of international agreements.[43] The negotiating record indicates that the framers of the Charter sought only, by introducing the words *armed attack*, to immunize regional security arrangements, and especially the Inter-American system envisioned by the Act of Chapultepec, from the jurisdiction of the Security Council. There was no expressed intent to forbid response to threat of imminent attack. The most relevant Committee Report reads: "The use of arms in legitimate self-defense remains admitted and unimpaired."[44] The principle of interpretation by the subsequent conduct of states obviously can give little comfort to those who urge new limitations. Most importantly, the principle of effectiveness in interpretation by major purposes makes the asserted limitation of self-defense to the actual inception of armed attack an absurdity. In an age of increasingly awesome instruments of destruction and highly sophisticated coercion by instruments other than the military, the state that awaits armed attack can expect only quick transition to oblivion. It defies not merely major purposes, but even common sense, to think that an alleged prescription in effect imposing suicide could either create the expectation, indispensable to law, of its enforcement, or that it could be enforced.

It may be recalled that the United Nations Charter makes the protection of human rights coordinate with, if not inclusive of, its prohibition of unauthorized coercion and violence. It is presently being greatly debated among scholars and others in what degree the core provisions about human rights are, like the provision for self-defense in Article 51, completely complementary with Article 2(4).[45] Most observers agree that the long enjoyed practice of humanitarian intervention, for the protection of a state's nationals and sometimes others, has not been outlawed by Article 2(4). It would thwart reason to hold that a constitutional Charter so greatly emphasizing human rights should be interpreted to abolish a historic remedy so effective in the protection of human rights, a remedy which does not in fact threaten territorial integrity and political independence.

The more intense contemporary controversy centers most directly upon whether it is lawful for one state to interfere (engage or assist in coercion and violence) in the internal affairs of another state for a range of objectives. Unhappily, the discussion is carried on in terms, such as "intervention," "counter-intervention," "civil war," "self-determination," "spheres of influence," "reprisals," "retaliations," and so on, which make so ambiguous a reference to both facts and legal policies that it is often difficult to know what is being asserted. One suggestion appears to be that the self-determination of states is the paramount policy of contemporary international law and that the proponents of human dignity may intervene in other states to protect or promote self-determination, even as totalitarian states do in promotion of totalitarian public order. In response, other commentators, not always taking a position upon the Soviet claims, insist that such intervention would be in clear violation of the allegedly literal and neutral words of Article 2(4). A counter-response is that the proponents of human dignity may lawfully intervene after, but not before, expansive totalitarians have intervened in a state. In such controversy it is sometimes forgotten that what is involved in all instances is the application of the larger community's fundamental policy, as embodied in Articles 2(4) and 51, against *change* by coercion and violence and that the objectives of a state, whether for expansion or conservation, are among the most important feature of the factual context for evaluating the lawfulness or unlawfulness of a state's action.

It has long been urged that the rational application of Articles 2(4) and 51, in clarification of common interest, requires in every instance of challenged coercion and violence, not mere logical derivation from allegedly autonomous (policy neutral) rules, but rather a careful, configurative examination and appraisal of the many relevant features of the larger context of the coercion and violence.[46] In an earlier statement, noting that the relevant features of the context in any instance of challenged coercion and violence were many and complex, we summarized:

> Even the most modest suggestion must include the varying characteristics of the participants, and of their allies and affiliates; the distribution of perspectives of attack and defense, expansion and conservation, deliberateness and coincidence, inclusivity and exclusivity, consequentiality and inconsequentiality; the *locus* of events, as within a single community or transcending different communities, and the geographic range of the impacts of events; the timing of events, and their continuity or discontinuity; the differential distribution of the bases of effective power; the variety and characteristics of the different strategies—diplomatic, ideological, economic, and military—employed; and the various outcomes in intensity and magnitude achieved, of the fact, and expectation, of coercion and destruction of values.[47]

It is no revolutionary idea, alien to the common interest that must be effected by all law, that the kind of public order demanded by a state be taken into account in appraising the lawfulness of its acts of coercion and violence. In endorsing this idea, more than twenty-five years ago, Florentino Feliciano and I wrote:

> Lest the contrary impression arise by default, it may be made clear that, in contrast with the quoted Soviet doctrine, we make no proposal for incorporation of a double or multiple standard in the conception of permissible coercion. The policy we recommend is, on the contrary, that of demand for effective universality, for the uniform application to all participants of a basic policy that excludes the acquisition or expansion of values by coercion and violence. In urging the explicit examination of the fundamental public order perspectives of participants, in particular their definitions of the legitimate purposes of coercion, the hope is precisely that decision-makers may thereby escape the double standard which in specific interpretations may be created against those who do not accept as permissible the use of coercion for expansion. We think of the interest to be clarified, the demand for change by noncoercive and nonviolent procedures only, as a general community interest, as the long-term interest of all individual states, and recognize that there must be a promise of reciprocity from states who reject totalitarian conceptions of world order.[48]

What the proponents of a public order of human dignity cannot accept is that a double standard be established that discriminates in favor of expansive totalitarianism.

The Conditions Affecting Achievement of Basic Goals

By considering the conditions that have affected past failures in humankind's achievement of a stable minimum public order, an observer may be able to feed back to the clarification of goals, enhance understanding of past trends, and prepare for the projection of probable futures and a more rational choice among policy options. The conditions that have affected past failures are commonly described, at high level abstraction, in terms, first, of the contemporary anarchy of multitudinous states, exhibiting both a most uneconomic relation of peoples to resources and immense differences in effective power, and secondly, of the continuing struggles between contending systems of world public order, expressing diametrically opposed conceptions of the relation of the individual human being to the state. To make this high level description of overriding conditions meaningful, however, it must be given operational indices in terms of a maze of interacting predispositional and environmental variables.[49] The predispositional variables are the subjectivities of individual human beings, including their demands for values, their identifications with others, and their expectations about the context of interaction; these relevant subjectivities may be organized by employment of the maximization postulate, that individuals adopt one response rather than another when they expect to be better off in terms of all their values by the response chosen. The environmental variables are the features of the larger community context, which both condition and constrain predispositions. These environmental variables may economically be described in terms of population, resources, institutions, and outcomes in value shaping and sharing. A most convenient way of achieving comprehensive description of any community process, it may be recalled, is in terms of individual human beings, with varying patterns of demand, identification, and expectation, employing resources, through institutional practices, for maximization of value outcomes.

It has already been noted that a most important variable in the contemporary global process of effective power is what is commonly referred to as "the rising, common demands" of peoples for greater participation in the shaping and sharing of all the basic values of human dignity. Different peoples, conditioned by differing cultural traditions and modes of social organization, may of course pursue and achieve the same basic values through different modalities and nuances in institutional practice. Unhappily, in a world of contending public orders and immense contrasts in development, peoples nurtured in differing parochial communities may tend to express special, rather than common, interests. Unable to clarify and agree upon common interests, peoples often become preoccupied with short-term, immediate payoffs rather than long-term consequences. It is possible that as the respect revolution accelerates, peoples' demand for new participation in the different value processes will become more realistic in recognition of the need for reciprocity and common interest. The universalizing demands of individuals for greater participation in all value processes can be expected to continue to affect all effective and authoritative decision.

The identifications upon behalf of which demands for values are asserted today range from the whole of humankind to small parochial groups. The earliest parochial identifications with the family and the tribe were broken, in part, by the advent of cities, facilitating the later identifications with larger states. In more recent times, the "nation-state" has been the symbol about which individuals could organize their collective identifications, and most states have of course sought to inhibit more inclusive identifications that might limit their power. It would appear, however, that the potentialities for individuals to acquire and sustain more inclusive identifications, at least for the promotion of minimum order, are strengthening. The increasing tempo of interaction in all value processes about the globe, facilitated by modern communication and transportation, allows an individual not merely to change geographic location, but also to change "place" through identifications with many different functional groups. Individuals who participate in a vast global network of territorial and functional activities may be able better to identify with a common humanity and to demand its common interest.

The expectations of the peoples of the world about the conditions that affect minimum public order and their individual security, the expectations that in turn affect all effective and authoritative decision, vary tremendously in comprehensiveness and realism. The greatest contemporary failure in realism is in the lack of appreciation of the comprehensiveness and depth of the interdependences, affecting both minimum and optimum order, of all peoples everywhere with regard to the shaping and sharing of all values. No less importantly, in a world in which the giant powers continuously balance weapons capable of instantaneous global destruction, most peoples, elite and rank and file alike, are obsessed by a pervasive expectation of violence that affects all choices among alternatives in value shaping and sharing. Fortunately, the spread of new techniques of communication and modern education make it possible for individuals everywhere to acquire a new realism about the conditions, not merely of continued existence, but of improved public order. As the network or interaction and the perception of interdependence expand, more and more peoples may come to perceive that the assertion of special interest, against common interest, is not compatible with survival.

Some of the more important environmental variables that characterize the contemporary global community process, affecting all public order, may be indicated in the following tabular, if somewhat anecdotal, form:[50]

- *Security.* Continuing confrontations of the major powers, with rising expectations of violence. Threats of nuclear destruction and of chemical and biological warfare. The acquisition of contemporary instruments of destruction by smaller powers. The rise and spread of private violence and terrorism.
- *Population.* The accelerating rate of increase in population growth. The uneven distribution of peoples in relation to resources and increasing barriers to migration.
- *Resources.* The spoliation, pollution, and exhaustion of resources at an accelerating rate. Increasing violation of physical and engineering unities in the use of resources. The growing monopolization of sharable resources, with restraint upon scientific inquiry about resources. The promise and threat of both deliberate and accidental climate and weather modification. The continuing diversion of important resources to destructive purposes.
- *Institutions.* The antiquated nation-state structures, with their disregard of physical, engineering, and utilization unities. The continuing weakness of international governmental organizations. The lack of development of functional transnational associations devoted to values other than power and wealth. The relative immunization of wealth and other private associations from transnational authority.
- *Particular Value Processes Within Global Community Process.*
  - *Power.* The increasing centralization, concentration, and bureaucratization of power even within nominally democratic communities. The increasing monopolization of the effective bases of power within different communities.
  - *Wealth.* The continued prevalence of individual poverty. Unequal distribution of wealth both within and across community lines. Inadequate regulation of transnational monetary units. Governmental interferences with private trade. Arbitrary seizures and confiscations of property rights. Irrational allocations of resources and unequal development. Continuing cycles of depression and inflation.
  - *Respect.* Widespread denials of individual freedom of choice about social roles. Increasing individual differentiations and group hatreds upon grounds (race, sex, religion, language, national origin) irrelevant to individual capabilities and contributions. Massive encroachments upon individual autonomy and privacy through modern technology and increasing governmental bureaucratization.

— *Well-Being (Health).* Continuing high mortality rate and low life expectancy in many parts of the world. Increasing threats of famine, epidemics, and disease. Indiscriminate mass killings in armed conflict and other interactions. Unexplained disappearances. The globalization of the practice of torture as a deliberate instrument of policy.

— *Enlightenment.* Continuing high rates of illiteracy and differential access to information in many communities. Deliberate fabrications and disseminations of misinformation. Wholesale indoctrinations and brainwashings. The withholding and suppression of the information necessary to independent appraisals of policy.

— *Skill.* The unequal distribution of skills in modern technology and the rapid obsolescence of skills by changes in technology. The brain drain from the developing countries to the developed. Restrictions upon the freedoms of skill groups to organize and to function.

— *Affection (Loyalties).* The requisition of loyalties in the name of the state and the undermining of more universal loyalties. Severe restrictions upon freedom of association. Governmental frustration of congenial personal relations and employment of social ostracism as sanctions.

— *Rectitude.* Denials of freedom to worship and choose secular criteria of responsibility. The politicization of rectitude. Restrictions upon association for religious purposes and intolerance and persecution of religious minorities. The rise of messianic religious fundamentalism.

The intense interdependences among all the predispositional and environmental conditions make it possible to effect changes in the larger global community process, including movement toward a more stable minimum public order, by making changes in, and managing, the various particular conditions.

Possible Future Developments

Law is interested in the past and the present in aid of inventing and making the future. Even in relation to a problem as difficult as that of establishing and maintaining a stable minimum world public order, the projection of possible futures, when inspired and disciplined by knowledge of past trends in achievement and their conditioning factors, may serve to stimulate creativity in the invention and evaluation of improved alternatives in decision. One procedure for inquiry about the future, invented by the late Harold Lasswell some fifty years ago, is that of deliberately formulating provisional maps of "developmental constructs" of future possibilities that range through a broad spectrum from the most optimistic to the most pessimistic.[51] When this method of inquiry is applied to the problem of minimum world public order, the contrast in rival constructs is stark.

The most optimistic construct projects increasing progress toward a wider and more responsible sharing of power and a greater production and wider sharing in all the values of human dignity among the peoples of the world. This construct builds upon various assumptions about predispositional and environmental variables and their interaction. It projects, thus, that the widespread demands of peoples for a greater and more rewarding participation in all value processes will not diminish, but will rather intensify; that the contemporary largely parochial identifications of peoples may, despite recurrent phases of fragmentation, expand toward recognition, not merely of common humanity, but of shared community; and that peoples will achieve increasingly realistic perception of, and expectations about, their indissoluble interdependences in relation to the shaping and sharing of all values. This construct, considering environmental variables, projects assumptions that the accelerating rate of population growth can be controlled, that the resource-environment of the world can be protected from exhaustion and spoliation, that science and science-based technology can create vast new resources, and that more economic governmental and value-functional institutions can be created, and so on.

The most pessimistic construct regards the direction of history as reversing itself and moving toward an aggregate of militarized and garrisoned communities, controlled from the center and modeled on the prison. This trend could culminate in an all comprehensive, single totalitarian state, with a system of public order that, when finally entrenched, organizes the global community into a vast hierarchical pattern under the rule of a self-perpetuating military caste. This construct builds upon the assumptions, among predispositional variables, that the peoples of the world will not be able to clarify their genuine common interests, but will rather pursue short-term special and exclusive advantages, that the identifications of peoples will remain territorially bound and parochial, rather than extending to a common humanity, and that peoples' expectations will in general remain diffuse, truncated, and unrealistic, and include, in particular, an anticipation that violence will be so high and pervasive as to provide a chronic justification for the continuing military mobilization of humankind. The assumptions made in this construct about environmental variables are of course largely the opposite of those that sustain the optimistic construct.

Whatever mid-abstraction constructs may be drawn between these two extremes, most observers today agree that contemporary world public order is undergoing transformations of unprecedented magnitude and scope and that such change is likely to continue at an accelerating rate. Happily, it is not necessary to regard any particular developmental construct as inevitable in outcome. The future may, in ways about which we do not yet know, be inevitable, but statements about the future, made in light of present knowledge, cannot fathom the inevitable and may be accorded differing degrees of probability, subject to change. It is this indeterminacy of the future that presents the proponents of a world public order of human dignity with the opportunity, as well as the desperate necessity, to refashion the global constitutive process of authoritative decision in modalities better designed to secure both minimum public order and other community demanded values.

Alternatives for an Improved World Public Order

It may aid understanding of the need for a comprehensive approach to recall the intimate interrelations within the global community process (interrelations emphasized in our opening paragraphs about the larger context) of effective power, the constitutive process of authoritative decision, and the public order achieved in the protection of demanded values. It is the global process of effective power that establishes and maintains, as one of its components, the global constitutive process and, hence, identifies the basic policies to be sought in authoritative decision. It is the global constitutive process that establishes and maintains the larger community's most minimum order, in the sense of prohibiting and regulating major coercion and violence, and aspired optimum order, in the sense of promoting the greatest production and widest sharing of all demanded values, and it is upon this existing, contemporary constitutive process that observers and decision makers who would promote peace, whether conceived in minimum or optimum terms, must eventually focus their recommendations for change and improvement. Yet, through a grip of converse determination, effective power in the global community may be based upon participation in any and all the value processes other than power (wealth, enlightenment, respect, well-being, skill, rectitude, loyalty), and the kind of constitutive process the larger community of humankind can achieve is highly dependent upon the kind of public order it can establish in relation to all values. In consequence of all these intense interdependences in effective and authoritative decision and in choices in particular value processes, movement toward (or away from) both minimum order and optimum order in global community process may be affected, and managed, by decisions and choices about any feature of the larger community process.

The task of highest priority, for all who are genuinely committed to the goal values of a world public order of human dignity, would accordingly, appear to be that of creating in the peoples of the world the perspectives necessary for accelerated movement toward a more effective global constitutive process of authoritative decision. It has already been indicated that it is in the conflicting, confused, and disoriented perspectives of peoples—

as manifested in exorbitant demands for special, rather than common, interests; in syndromes of parochial, exclusive identifications; and in chronically unrealistic expectations about the larger context—and not the inexorable requirements of technologically malleable environmental variables, that perpetuate the existing conditions of contending world orders and appalling threat to the whole of humankind.

The optimalization postulate (that individuals act within their capabilities to maximize their values), and the many historic successes of law as an instrument for the clarification of common interest, would suggest that by appropriate modifications in perspectives the peoples of the world can be encouraged to move toward both the establishment of more effective decision process and the making of more rational specific decisions about public order values. It is hardly a novel thought that the factors—culture, class, interest, personality, and crisis—which importantly condition peoples' perspectives can be modified to foster constructive rather than destructive perspectives. The distinctive perspectives that must be created in promotion of a more viable global constitutive process include, as indicated above, a trilogy of demands, identifications, and expectations. The demands that require strengthening are those that insist upon the greater production and wider sharing of all human dignity values and which emphasize the protection of common rather than special interests. The identifications that require enhancement are those that most nearly embrace the whole of humankind and achieve increasing pluralistic expression in both territorial and functional groupings. The relevant expectations must include the recognition that all peoples, everywhere, are irrevocably interdependent for securing all values, even survival, and that all peoples, without exception, have more to gain and less to lose, for themselves and all with whom they identify, by the establishment and maintenance of a secure global minimum order, rather than by exercise of unilateral coercion and violence. The task for proponents of a world public order of human dignity is, in particular, that of establishing credible expectations that they do genuinely accept the basic policy of minimum order, that coercion and violence are not to be used for change, or to obstruct peaceful change, and that they are willing reciprocally to accord the benefits of this policy even to those who do not share their vision of world order. The contemporary technology of communication and collaboration, fortunately, makes possible the widespread generation and communication of these relevant perspectives.

There are of course multitudinous modalities in institution and policy that might be employed, if appropriate perspectives could be created in the peoples of the world, to improve the existing global constitutive process of authoritative decision toward a more secure, free, and abundant world public order.[52] For centuries, philosophers, clerics, and kings have proffered plans for perpetual peace, and contemporary proposals abound for various forms of world government and lesser modifications of prevailing institutions and practices. The difficulty with the proposals envisaging grandiose transformations in existing structures and practices is that they seldom consider the means necessary to translate the vast changes they propose into reality. The difficulty with the more modest proposals is that they are fragmented and anecdotal in form, dealing with isolated features of rule or procedure or structure, and are not put forward in appropriate relation to the processes of effective power and authoritative decision, which they are designed to affect. What is urgently needed, in more rational approach, is the creation of competent agencies, both public and private, for undertaking a systematic canvass of every feature of effective power, constitutive process, and public order decision to ascertain a wide range of possible improvements and to establish priorities among potential improvements in terms of relation to human dignity values, temporal need and acceptability, economy, and effectiveness.[53]

It is most unlikely, so long as the contention between rival systems of world public order intensifies, that the major states of the world can be persuaded to take important steps by agreement toward the greater collectivization and centralization of the existing global constitutive process. It is too difficult to clarify a common interest between a public order dedicated to expansion by major coercion and violence and those who regard change by peaceful procedures only as indispensable to any law and stable public order. The most that the proponents of a world public order of human dignity may now be able to do would appear to be to achieve and promote enlightenment about the conditions of minimum order, the potentialities of an optimum world public order, and the policies and measures that might, through appropriate interpretations of existing agreements and the uniformities of customary law, gradually move humankind toward the necessary changes in global constitutive process. Such a stance may be criticized as mere incrementalism, in a situation of desperate need, but it could be made an incrementalism guided by a clear vision of basic goals and a realistic understanding of the conditions of their achievement.

In the absence of comprehensive and detailed studies, it is difficult to offer definitive illustration of the changes in policies and measures that might transform the existing global constitutive process into a more effective instrument of minimum and optimum order. It may be remembered that the existing, most comprehensive process includes all the decisions that identify authoritative decision makers, project the basic policies of the larger community, establish appropriate structures in aid of decision, allocate bases of power for sanctioning purposes, prescribe procedures for the making of particular decisions, and secure the performance of all the different types of decision functions (intelligence, promotion, prescription, invocation, application, termination, appraisal) that are necessary to the making and application of community policy. The significance of any change or improvement in a particular feature of this process must of course depend at any given time upon both the configuration of all other features of the process and impacts from protected features of value processes other than power. It may be possible, however, to make highly impressionistic, even cryptic, suggestions of the kinds of policies and measures that could, in appropriate context, point in the direction of a more secure, free, and abundant world public order.

The Global Constitutive Process

We proceed phase by phase through the existing global constitutive process.

Participation in Decision Making

- Seek a more genuinely representative and responsible balancing of power through the creation of more rational intergovernmental regional organizations.
- Encourage the creation of political parties, pressure groups, and private associations dedicated to all values for participation in transnational activities.
- Recognize the importance of the individual human being, as ultimate actor in all organizations, through provision of increasing access to all authoritative arenas.

Perspectives: Basic General Community Policies

- Reinforce commitment to minimum order, that no change be effected by coercion and violence, by explicit recognition of the complementarity of Articles 2(4) and 51 of the United Nations Charter, emphasizing a broad conception of self-defense.
- Interpret Article 2(4) of the Charter to prohibit "wars of liberation."
- Interpret Article 51 of the Charter to authorize states to take measures in self-defense when attack is imminent, without awaiting the fact of armed attack.
- Reinforce commitment to optimum order by consolidating the emergence of a global bill of human rights through appropriate interpretation of the Charter, the major covenants, national decisions, and customary behavior.

Arenas: Structures of Authority

- Establishment

— Balance structures of authority in geographic range between centralized and decentralized, and integrate in a way to take into account the intensity of impacts within different geographic areas.
— Expand the scope and authority of the executive within international governmental organizations.
— Staff parliamentary bodies more effectively in aid of intelligence and appraisal functions for the better clarification of policies.
— Multiply occasional conferences for employment of the diplomatic instrument in the clarification and projection of policies.
— Provide panels of skilled experts for the voluntary adjudication (mediation, conciliation, arbitration) of disputes. With modern technology, these panels could be moved quickly about the world for sessions in convenient locations.

- *Access*
  — In promoting policies of openness and responsibility, aggrieved individuals and groups might be allowed to represent themselves or to be represented by others (including institutionalized ombudsmen) in a wide range of structures of authority.
  — Compulsory jurisdiction for adjudication might be increased with respect to matters not involving state security.

Bases of Power

The promotion of minimum and optimum order might be enhanced by a more pluralistic distribution of both authority and effective control.

- *Authority*
  — Insofar as compatible with the genuine security interests of states, reject claims of "political questions" and "domestic jurisdictions" that immunize activities from legal evaluation.
  — For the protection of inclusive interests, accord inclusive institutions a more ample competence with respect to the intelligence, promotion, appraisal, and invocation functions: with respect to the prescription, application, and termination functions, accord a broad competence on matters that do not endanger the security of states.
  — Allocate to the separate states the competence necessary to protect their exclusive interests, and settle conflicts between states by the criteria of reasonableness as determined through a disciplined, systematic examination of the features of the larger context that affects interests.
- *Control*
  — Through coalition, alliance, and regionalization, seek a more rational organization of the control of the resource bases of the earth-space community.

— By agreement and unilateral action, reduce the resources being devoted to armaments and military purposes.
— Expand multiple networks of transnational associations, governmental and private, to increase the greater production and wider sharing of all the values that affect power, as well as the quality of life.
— Encourage educational institutions to increase their inquiries about the conditions, policies, and alternatives necessary to an improved world public order.
— Employ the technology of modern communication to promote a world public opinion that demands and sustains a public order of human dignity.

Strategies: Authoritative Procedures

- Seek an appropriate integration in support of public order of all strategies (diplomatic, ideological, economic, and military), with a strong emphasis upon persuasion rather than coercion.
- In revival of Chapter VII of the United Nations Charter, collectivize and centralize such coercion as may be necessary and proportionate to the maintenance of public order.
- Enhance the diplomatic instrument by minimizing the employment of special majorities and vetoes, other than in relation to matters endangering the security of states, and by rationalizing the law of international agreements.
- Maintain free transnational channels of communication for more effective employment of the ideological instrument.
- Employ the economic instrument to improve the channels of trade, financial assistance, and development in the greater production and wider distribution of goods and services.
- In performance of decision functions, employ the best available scientific procedures in exploration of facts and potential policies, and make findings as dependable, contextual, and creative as possible.
- In prescriptive and applicative decision, final characterization of facts and policies should be made deliberate, rational in relation to goals, and nonprovocative, employing contextual analysis in evaluation and choice of alternatives.

Outcomes in Particular Types of Decisions

The culminating outcomes of constitutive process include both the establishment and maintenance of the process itself and a continuous flow of particular decisions affecting all public order values.

- *The Intelligence Function* (gathering, processing, and disseminating information relevant to decision). Accord international governmental organizations the resources necessary to increase their role in inquiry and communication about the goals, trends, conditioning factors, possible futures, and alternatives relevant to improved minimum and optimum order.
- *The Promotion Function* (taking initiatives and mobilizing opinion toward prescription of community policies). Encourage, by according appropriate access to authority and other resources, a tremendous expansion of pressure groups and private associations dedicated to mobilizing the predispositions necessary to an improved world public order.
- *The Prescribing Function* (projection of community policy that is both authoritative and controlling).
  — Recognize the increasing role of international governmental organization in creating and communicating expectations about future decision.
  — Weight voting in international governmental organization and special conferences in ways to secure higher conformity with genuine democracy and responsibility.
  — Establish distinctive specialized institutions, manned by scholars and experts rather than by representatives of governments, for the clarification and recommendation of policies upon important particular problems.
  — Improve facilities and policies for the making of multilateral agreements for the projection of authoritative general community policy.
  — Recognize the dominating importance of uniformities in state decision and practice in creating expectations about the requirements of future decision.
  — Understand the interlocked, cumulative impact of communication from all sources in creating expectations about future decision.
- *The Invoking Function* (provisional characterization of events in terms of community prescriptions).
  — Aggrieved participants in global community process might be afforded opportunities in appropriate arenas to make timely, non-provocative initiations of the application function to redress putative wrongs.
  — A specialized invocation competence might be accorded the secretary-general of the United Nations or established ombudsmen.
- *The Applying Function* (authoritative characterization of events in terms of community prescription and management of sanctioning measures to secure conformity).[54]

— Encourage the resolution of controversies by the parties themselves through diplomacy, mediation, and conciliation.
— Maintain panels for third-party adjudication when participants
consent. Create specialized, perhaps mobile, panels for particular
problems.
— Within national constitutive processes, establish unequivocally
that international law is the law of the land, to be applied by all
branches of government; reduce to minimum effect all doctrines
of governmental immunity, act of state, political questions, and so
on.
— Whatever the arena of application, emphasize the importance of
procedures for inquiry that both employ a contextual examination
of facts in relation to major community goals and principles for the
interpretation of prescriptions that emphasize such major goals in
all factual contexts.

• *The Terminating Function* (putting an end to prescriptions and arrangements effected under prescriptions). Establish specialized agencies
for reviewing existing prescriptions and arrangements, identifying
the obsolete or obsolescent, and recommending measures for
ameliorating the destructive costs of necessary change.

• *The Appraising Function* (evaluating decision process in terms of
achievement of basic community goals and ascribing responsibility).
— Establish specialized agencies, insulated from immediate pressures of threat or inducement, for the continuous appraisal of
successes and failures in the management of authoritative decision
and for the recommendation of decision process and decisions
better designed for the realization of major goals.
— A comprehensive inquiry would of course add exploration of the
impacts of the protected features of the larger community's
various value processes upon the establishment and maintenance
of constitutive process.

Conclusion

An appropriate concluding note of restrained optimism may perhaps be
that voiced by my late colleague, Harold Lasswell, in closing his book on
The Future of Political Science:

It is impossible to contemplate the present status of man without perceiving the
cosmic roles that he and other advanced forms of life may eventually play. We
are, perhaps, introducing self-awareness into cosmic process. With awareness of
self comes deliberate formation and pursuit of value goals. For tens of thousands
of years, man was accustomed to living in relatively local environments and to
cooperating on a parochial scale. Today we are on the verge of exploring a habitat

far less circumscribed than earth. The need for a worldwide system of public order—a comprehensive plan of cooperation—is fearfully urgent. From the interplay of the study and practice of cooperation we may eventually move more wisely, if not more rapidly, toward fulfilling the as-yet-mysterious potentialities of the cosmic process.[55]

Discussion

Commentator Fred Morrison suggested that the problem facing international lawyers today is illustrated by the following question: Is international law a system of rules pertaining only to relations between nations or does international law derive its validity and authority from a broader, humanitarian sense of values?

This age-old dilemma for lawyers, domestic and international, pivots on the issue of whether the rule or letter of the law supersedes the underlying intent of the law. Can current international legal decisions be based on literal readings of laws that were conceived and written nearly forty-five years ago? Morrison did not think so, and he illustrated his case using the UN Charter articles pertaining to the use of force as an example.

When Articles 2(4) and 51 of the UN Charter were adopted in 1945, the concept of conflict was dramatically colored by the recent experience of World War II. In fact, the entire Charter was designed to prohibit or control the outbreak of widespread, conventional, and cross-border conflict, and to provide alternative and peaceful means by which nations could resolve their differences without threatening the security of the entire globe.

Morrison's view was that both the primary threat to international security and the international system itself have so radically changed that a mechanistic interpretation of those rules leads not only to their fragmentary misapplication, but also to the devaluation of their original intent. In the current international environment, the primary threat to international peace is not the outbreak of another world war. On the contrary, conflict today is more subtle and less easily defined; it operates at the "edges" of Article 2(4).

What this means is that the most likely, midlevel, types of conflict—such as terrorism, counterinterventions, and wars of national liberation—often fall short of what the ICJ would characterize as "armed attacks" under Article 2(4), even though they clearly constitute armed conflict meriting international attention and resolution. International legal scholars tend to apply simple and mechanistic legal responses to these types of conflicts, ignoring the underlying legal principles pertaining to the use of force and allowing these situations to "fall through the cracks" of the international legal system.

The solution to this situation is either the enactment of more specifically tailored principles that take into account a variety of types and levels of conflict or a paradigm shift in judicial interpretation that fully embraces these conflicts under existing laws—neither of which is very likely. Unfortunately, the only other alternative seems to be the one taken in the recent *Nicaragua* case, in which the United States removed itself from the compulsory jurisdiction clause of the ICJ.

Much of the discussion that followed the panel presentations carried forth the debate over formalism versus contextual analysis. Oscar Schachter noted that contextual analysis, if taken too far, bestows on the interpretive body complete freedom to determine what constitutes armed attack. If the sectoral notion of law in the nature of restraint is removed or neutralized, determinations might be based on purely subjective criteria, which would lead to arbitrary findings.

Morrison acknowledged that the lack of a final authoritative decision maker demands rigorous self-restraint in contextual analysis, but he disputed the assertion that anything can be justified, provided the right context exists, particularly if there has been an elaboration over time of a series of standards. McDougal concurred, and he added that refining the context of a case, if it is done within the bounds of legitimate legal inquiry, is anything but arbitrary.

Gregory Treverton agreed with the assertion that midlevel conflicts pose the greatest challenge to international law and security, adding that these conflicts are the ones that tend to have the most muddied and controversial contexts. Therefore, while taking the context of the conflict into consideration seems to be exactly correct, it also seems very similar to the inexact science of politics. How does one avoid bringing political considerations to bear on judicial issues?

McDougal noted that "politics" and "political considerations" are ambiguous terms that need to be clearly defined in reference to power, authority, and control. A balance among these three factors must be struck within the context of a given conflict to create an environment inclined toward peace. This can be accomplished without reference to politics, because the politics of conflict are often more aptly defined as control without authority.

Nazli Choucri asked the panelists to describe the mechanisms by which international law responds or adapts to the rapidly changing international environment. Is international law inherently slow and conservative and, if so, is that the reason why it seems unable to deal with these newer forms of conflict?

In response, Morrison said that the classical approach to international law as outlined by Grotius was remarkably conservative and supported the status quo rather than change. In the past thirty years, however, questions about how to adapt international law and make new laws have received increased attention. McDougal reminded the audience that one of the primary functions of all laws is to repress destructive change. Not all change is for the better or in the interest of human dignity; international law must act as the balance wheel of international change.

R. J. Rummel observed that one-third of the world's states have their ideological and political base in Marxism-Leninism, a doctrine that does not eschew the use of force as a legitimate policy option. How can the West, he asked, expect these states to function as equal partners in a system that has as its root the prohibition on the use of force except in cases of self-defense? Is the West not condoning the Marxist-Leninist view of international law as an expedient to overthrow the old and create a new society?

Many theorists, responded McDougal, maintain that they can clarify a common interest between totalitarian and democratic order, but such clarification is impossible because totalitarian states refuse to renounce violence and coercion as an instrument of change. That does not mean, however, that the West should seek the destruction of those who hold different values, but that the West should try, through education and persuasion, to change the Marxist-Leninists' point of view.

Morrison added that there seems to be some positive, gradual change of attitude inside the Soviet Union concerning international law in general and the ICJ in particular. Whether this change of attitude will ultimately be translated into policy alterations remains to be seen. Schachter, who had recently returned from a trip to the Soviet Union, echoed this sentiment and reported that he was convinced that the Soviets are seriously considering realigning their position on the use of force so that it would be more in accord with the UN position. This point was contested by Allan Gerson, who suggested that what the Soviets say they are going to do and what they actually do are often quite different. He added that he was quite skeptical that the Soviets would ever renounce "wars of national liberation" as a legitimate policy option.

Notes

1. Detailed description is offered in M. McDougal, W. Reisman, and A. Willard, "The World Community: A Planetary Social Process," 21 *U.C. Davis L. Rev.* p. 807 (1988).

2. These interdependences are minutely outlined in M. McDougal, H. Lasswell, and L. Chen, *Human Rights and World Public Order* (1980), ch. 1.

3. M. McDougal, W. Reisman, and A. Willard, "The World Process of Effective Power: The Global War System," in *Power and Policy in Quest of Law: Essays in Honor of Eugene Victor Rostow* p. 353, ed. M. McDougal and W. Reisman, (1985); G. Schwarzenberger, *Power Politics*, 3d ed., (1964); W. Reisman, "Private Armies in a Global War System: Prologue to Decision," 14 *Va. J. Int'l. L.* p. 1 (1973).

4. For descriptions of these two types of decisions and their interrelations, see M. McDougal and W. Reisman, *International Law Essays* (1981) and M. McDougal and W. Reisman, *International Law in Contemporary Perspective: The Public Order of the World Community* (1981), ch. 1.

5. The basic features of the existing global constitutive process are described at length in: McDougal and Reisman, *International Law Essays* and *International Law in Contemporary Perspective;* and McDougal, Laswell, and Chen, *Human Rights.*

6. For an outline of claims for the protection of public order values, see McDougal, Lasswell, and Chen, *Human Rights,* ch. 3.

7. Lasswell and McDougal, "Criteria for a Theory About Law," 44 *S. Cal. L. Rev* p. 362 (1971). Background is given in W. Reisman and A. Schreiber, *Jurisprudence: Understanding and Shaping Law* (1987).

8. This theme is documented historically in McDougal, Lasswell, and Reisman, "Theories about International Law: Prologue to a Configurative Jurisprudence," 8 *Va. J. Int'l. L.* p. 189 (1967).

9. P. Jessup, *Transnational Law* (1956).

10. For comprehensive review, see M. McDougal and F. Feliciano, *Law and Minimum World Public Order* (1961).

11. McDougal, Lasswell, and Chen, *Human Rights,* ch. 5.

12. The Independent Commission on Disarmament and Security Issues, *Common Security: A Blueprint for Survival* p. 8 (1982): A secure existence, free from physical and psychological threats to life and limb, is one of the most elementary desires of humanity. It is the fundamental reason why human beings choose to organize nation-states, sacrificing certain individual freedoms for the common good—security. It is a right shared by all—regardless of where they live, regardless of their ideological or political convictions.

13. Relevant historical perspectives are delineated in F. Hinsley, *Power and the Pursuit of Peace* (1963); C. Murphy, *The Search for World Order* (1985).

14. This history is stated in detail in McDougal, Lasswell, and Reisman, *Va. J. Int'l. L.* p. 189. See also R. Macdonald and D. Johnstone, eds., *The Structure and Process of International Law* (1983). In this volume, chapter 5, the essay by Morison, "The Schools Revisited," is especially insightful. See also W. Schiffer, *The Legal Community of Mankind* (1954).

15. H. Lauterpacht, "The Grotian Tradition in International Law," 23 *British Yearbook of Int'l. L.* p. 1 (1943), reprinted in H. Lauterpacht, ed., *International Law,* (1975); T.C. Asser Institute, "International Law and the Grotian Heritage 1985" (a commemorative colloquium held at The Hague, 8 April 1983 on the occasion of the Fourth Centenary of the Birth of Hugo Grotius).

16. J. Stone, *Visions of World Order* (1984).

17. McDougal and Feliciano, *Law and Minimum Order,* ch. 1 and 3; H. Waldock, "The Regulation of the Use of Force between States," 81 *Hague Recueil des Cours,* 1952-II, p. 455.

18. J. Johnson, *Just War Tradition and the Restraint of War: A Moral and Historical Inquiry* (1981).

19. Eugene Rostow, "Disputes Involving the Inherent Right of Self-Defense," in *The International Court of Justice at a Crossroads* pp. 264, 283, ed. L. Damrosch, (1987).

20. C. Amerasinghe, *State Responsibilitv for Injuries to Aliens* (1967).

21. The first of these developments is described in McDougal and Feliciano, *Law and Minimum Order,* ch. 3; the second in McDougal, Lasswell, and Chen, *Human Rights,* ch. 4.

22. The detailed application of this test is outlined in McDougal and Feliciano, *Law and Minimum Order,* ch. 3.

23. This thesis is documented in McDougal, Lasswell, and Chen, *Human Rights*, ch. 4.

24. The question is raised by T. Franck, "Who Killed Article 2(4)? or: Changing Norms Governing the Use of Force by States," 64 *Am. J. Int. L.* p. 809 (1970).

25. History of the Communist Party (Bolsheviks), Short Course 167–168, ed. Commission of the Central Committee of the C.P.S.U.(B): 1939, as quoted in McDougal and Feliciano, *Law and Minimum Order*, p. 186.

26. G. Tunkin, *Law and Force in the International System* 85 (1983).

27. Kovalev, "Sovereignty and the International Obligations of Socialist Countries," *Pravda*, September 26, 1968. Quoted in McDougal and Reisman, *International Law in Contemporary Perspective*, p. 176.

28. McDougal and Resiman, *International Law in Contemporary Perspective*. See also N. Rostow, "Law and the Use of Force by States: The Brezhnev Doctrine," 7 *Yale J. of World Public Order*, p. 209 (1981).

29. W. Reisman, "Old Wine in New Bottles: The Reagan and Brezhnev Doctrines in Contemporary International Law and Practice," 13 *Yale J. Int'l. L.* pp. 171, 188 (1988). A possible change in Soviet attitudes toward both "wars of liberation" and the Brezhnev Doctrine is indicated in M. Gorbachev, "Reality and Safeguards for a Secure World," September 17, 1987, UN Doc. A/42/574, S/194143 (September 18, 1987). Unhappily, there appears to be some dissension in the ranks. See "Gorbachev Deputy Criticizes Policy," *New York Times*, August 7, 1988, p. 11. Even Mr. Gorbachev himself sometimes wavers. See "Dissenters Stay Silent," *The Times* (London), July 15, 1988, p. 6. The changes underway appear to be in the direction of greatly improved world public order.

30. Case Concerning Military and Paramilitary Activities in and Against Nicaragua (*Nicaragua* v. *United States of America*) 1986 ICJ 14.

31. *Nicaragua*, ICJ 14, paragraph 263.

32. *Nicaragua*, Dissenting Opinion, paragraphs 174–81.

33. *Nicaragua*, Dissenting Opinion, paragraph 175.

34. *Nicaragua*, Dissenting Opinion, paragraph 178, referring to paragraph 206 of the Judgment of the International Court of Justice.

35. My criticism of the ICJ is both of its holding that an actual "armed attack" by Nicaragua upon El Salvador was necessary before the United States could come to the aid of El Salvador, and of its finding that what Nicaragua was doing did not amount to an armed attack upon El Salvador. In light of this holding and this finding, it does not matter that the ICJ did not explicitly state that it regarded "wars of liberation" as lawful; by its decision, it honored such an expansionist war in fact.

36. *Nicaragua*, Jurisdiction and Admissibility, 1984 ICJ 392. We should note that the writer was counsel to the United States Government at this phase of the case.

37. Norton, "The *Nicaragua* Case: Political Questions before the International Court of Justice," 27 *Va. J. Int'l. L.* p. 459 (1987); J. Moore, *The Secret War in Central America* (1987); R. Turner, *Nicaragua v. United States: A Look at the Facts* (1987). The decision is discussed, in varying terms of approval and disapproval, in a sequence of comments in "Appraisals of the ICJ's Decision: *Nicaragua* v. *United States* (Merits)," 81 *Am. J. Int'l. L.* p. 77 (1987). A particularly perceptive comment is that of J. Hargrove, "The *Nicaragua* Judgment and the Future of the Law of Force and Self-Defense," 81 *Am. J. Int. L.* p. 135 (1987). See also H. Almond, Jr., "The Military Activities Case: New Perspectives on the International Court of Justice and Global Public Order," 21 *Int'l. Law.* 195 (1987); Macdonald, "The Nicaraguan Case: New

Answers to Old Questions," 1986 *Can. Y.B. Int'l. L.* 127; Turner, "Peace and the World Court: A Comment on the Paramilitary Activities Case," 20 *Vand. J. Transnational L.* 53 (1987).

38. H. Lauterpacht, *The Function of Law in the International Community* (1933).

39. McDougal and Lasswell, "The Identification and Appraisal of Diverse Systems of Public Order," 55 *Am J. Int'l. L.* p. 1 (1959).

40. The various pronouncements of United States officials are summarized in Reisman, 13 *Yale J. Int'l L.*

41. As quoted in Reisman, 13 *Yale J. Int'l L.*, p. 177.

42. Rostow, *International Court;* O. Schachter, "In Defense of International Rules on the Use of Force," 53 *U. Chi. L. Rev.* p. 113 (1986).

43. This position is fully developed in McDougal and Feliciano, *Law and Minimum Order*, pp. 217, 232.

44. McDougal and Feliciano, *Law and Minimum Order*, p. 236.

45. See, inter alia, W. Reisman, "Coercion and Self-Determination: Construing Charter Article 2(4)," 78 *Am. J. Int'l. L.* p. 642 (1984); "The Use of Force in Contemporary International Law," 78 *Proc. Am. Soc'y. Int'l. L.* p. 74 (1984); "Criteria for the Lawful Use of Force in International Law," 10 *Yale J. Int'l. L.* p. 279 (1985); "The Emperor Has No Clothes: Article 2(4) and the Use of Force in Contemporary International Law," ch. 1 in *United Nations for a Better World*, ed. J. Saxena et al, (1986), p. 3; Schachter, "The Legality of Pro-Democratic Invasion," 78 *Am. J. Int'l. L.* p. 645 (1984); "The Right of States to Use Armed Force," 82 *Mich. L. Rev.* p. 1620 (1984); "International Law in Theory and Practice," 178 *Recueil des Cours* (1982-V), ch. VII, VIII; Cutler, "The Right to Intervene," 64 *Foreign Aff.* p. 96 (1985).

46. This position is believed to be established in McDougal and Feliciano, *Law and Minimum Order*, ch. 3.

47. M. McDougal, Foreword in J. Moore, *Law and the Indo-China War* (1972). For example, in relevant prescription, the customary right to use force in self-defense is limited by the criterion of *necessity* to defend against an imminent, or exercised, use of force against the territorial integrity of a state or its political independence, and by the requirement of *proportionality* of the action taken in self-defense. Thus, the action defended against has to be appraised in its entire context: the participants, their objectives (for example, whether they are expansionist or conservative in nature), the situation of decision, the bases of power behind the activities, the strategies employed, and their immediate outcomes in intensities of coercion. If the activities complained of would lead a disinterested third party reasonably to conclude that use of the military instrument is urgently required to protect the target country's territorial integrity and political independence, then the target country may employ force in a reasonably proportionate response—the proportionality of the defensive action, again, being determined through comprehensive contextual analysis.

Such a contextual examination of the events in the *Nicaragua* case would reveal the Soviet Union and Cuba along with the Sandinistas as participants and would note the expansionist nature of their objectives. For an outline of the necessary examination and appraisal in a comparable case, see M. McDougal, "The Soviet-Cuban Quarantine and Self-Defense," 57 *Am. J. Int'l. L.* p. 597 (1963).

48. McDougal and Feliciano, *Law and Minimum Order*, p. 187, note 156.

49. These variables are outlined, and described in some detail, in McDougal, Lasswell, and Chen, *Human Rights*, ch. 1.

50. This presentation is adapted from McDougal, "International Law and the Future," 50 *Miss. L. J.* p. 259 (1979).

51. H. Lasswell, *World Politics and Personal Insecurity* (1935); *The World Revolution of Our Time: A Framework for Basic Policy Research* (1951). See also Eulau, "H. D. Lasswell's Developmental Analysis," XI *Western Pol. Q.* p. 229 (1958); W. Ascher, *Forecasting: An Appraisal for Policy-Makers and Planners* (1978).

52. For an introduction to the literature, see B. Ferencz, *A Common Sense Guide to World Peace* (1985); The Independent Commission on Disarmament and Security Issues, *Common Security: A Blueprint for Survival* (1982); R. Falk, *The End of World Order* (1983); McDougal and Feliciano, *Law and Minimum Order*, ch. 4; J. Mikus, *Beyond Deterrence: From Power Politics to World Public Order* (1988); S. Mendlovitz, *On the Creation of a Just World Order: Preferred Worlds for the 1990s* (1975); J. Perkins, *The Prudent Peace* (1981); Falk, "A New Paradigm for International Legal Studies: Prospects and Proposals," 84 *Yale L. J.* p. 969 (1975).

53. It could have been in recognition of this need that the United States Institute of Peace was established.

54. Chapter 8 of this volume offers examples of alternatives that might be considered for improvement of the application function.

55. H. Lasswell, *The Future of Political Science*, p. 242 (1963).

Introduction to Chapter 7

> The United Nations embodies, as it were, the interests of different states. It is the only organization which can channel their efforts—bilateral, regional, and comprehensive—in one and the same direction. Fresh opportunities are opening before it in all the spheres within its competence: military, political, economic, scientific, technological, ecological, and humanitarian.

On December 7, 1988, those words were spoken not by a traditional advocate of the UN system, but by Soviet General Secretary Mikhail Gorbachev in an address before the UN General Assembly. Representing, at least in spirit, a radical departure from previous Soviet positions concerning international organizations, Gorbachev's words tend to support author Edward Luck's premise in this chapter: although the UN's record of success has been bleak for many years, new opportunities appear to offer legitimate cause for optimism about the organization's future role in enhancing international peace and security.

According to Luck, a number of related events over the past two decades have caused U.S. and world opinion to retreat from the enthusiasm of 1945. An urgent need now exists to rebuild bipartisan consensus that the UN can and must play a central role in securing and maintaining a more peaceful international environment.

As the UN system began to evolve and it became apparent that the UN would not function solely as an instrument of Western ideals and foreign policies, a number of Americans no longer considered it a useful international actor. At the same time, perceptions of the areas in which the UN could have the greatest effect shifted away from security- and conflict-related issues toward economic and social issues.

The unfortunate but understandable result of this shift in perception has been an increased emphasis on bilateral solutions to conflict-related issues, which has seriously undermined the intent of the UN's multilateral framework. This change in emphasis is demonstrated by the number of arms control and disarmament treaties negotiated and ratified under the auspices of the UN during the 1960s and 1970s versus the number of treaties attempted during the 1980s. Security- and conflict-related matters, particularly those concerning the United States and the Soviet Union, are now thought to be resolved best through face-to-face negotiations between representatives of the two governments. Limited success in these bilateral initiatives has led to increasingly negative assessments of the utility of the UN's multilateral system.

Recent UN successes in Afghanistan and elsewhere, coupled with a reduction in the level of Soviet-American tension, however, have led many Americans to believe that issues that fall through the cracks of national sovereignty—such as terrorism, narcotics trafficking, and AIDS—are best addressed in a multilateral framework such as that provided by the UN. If progress can be made in these areas and more rigorous research into the dynamics of the changing international environment is undertaken, Luck says, the UN might once again find itself at the center of the international peace initiative.

7. Interstate Organizations
Current Scholarship, Analysis, and Practice
Edward C. Luck

This chapter is about global and regional organizations and prevailing American views on their contributions to international peace and security. It offers a snapshot of the current state of the art in terms of scholarship, policy analysis, and practice. Its central premise is that the record has been bleak in recent years on all three fronts, but that promising new possibilities have begun to emerge at a surprising rate. The focus on past models and experiences when the UN was in decline, however, has left American analysts and policymakers ill-prepared for the unprecedented opportunities and challenges now facing global and regional institutions, particularly in the field of peace and security. Polarized policy debates have further soured the atmosphere for objective analytical work in this country. Although this chapter focuses on the importance of multilateral institutions for the maintenance of international peace and security, it recognizes that they serve as a supplement to, not a substitute for, sound national and bilateral security policies. Multilateral organizations have simply been the least understood and least appreciated tools of a well-rounded and successful security strategy.

This chapter has four parts. First, I look at trends in American scholarship in the area of interstate organization. Second, I consider the effect of political cycles. Third, I address weaknesses and gaps in policy analysis. And fourth, I present some ideas about a future agenda for research and analysis.

Trends in U.S. Scholarly Research

During the first two decades of the UN's existence, American scholarship on international organizations flourished. For Americans, this tended to be a time of optimism, of confidence in Western ideals, of the dominance of international bodies in policy-making, and of belief in the utility of international institutions for the implementation of U.S. foreign policy objectives. Americans had faith in themselves and their institutions: local, national, and international. The number, size, responsibilities, and budgets of international organizations were expanded throughout this period. And, there was no doubt in Washington, D.C., about the necessity of meeting American monetary obligations to the UN and other bodies.

More recently, however, a generation gap has emerged. As international organizations have evolved over the past two decades in directions that had not been anticipated by either the scholarly or the policy communities, American intellectual leaders and their theories have begun to age. Younger scholars, maturing at a time when international organization is a fact of life rather than an ideal to be nurtured, have drifted into abstract theorizing, much of it politically irrelevant even if intellectually challenging. But even among these scholars, much of the work about international regimes, hegemonic decline, and other elegant theories has focused on interstate and transnational interactions on humanitarian, functional, economic, and social issues rather than on questions of peace and security (the one exception being the nonproliferation regime, which seems to fit the theories a bit better than messier aspects of international security).[1]

Whereas much of the abstract theorizing may be useful in building an intellectual framework for understanding contemporary international relations, little has been done to bridge the gap between the scholarly and the policy communities. The result is theory without reference to practice, and practice without reference to theory.

True, there have been a few efforts in recent years to bring practitioners, policy analysts, and international organization theorists together.[2] Where they did exist, these efforts probably enhanced sensitivity on all sides, but they also served to illustrate how little each side understands the work of the other. In the peace and security realm, in particular, the theorists have not been fully informed of recent diplomatic and political developments, and the practitioners have had only the faintest inkling about what these theories are about.

The scholarly literature, on the other hand, has begun to shed two past intellectual encumbrances. The first is that the workings and politics of contemporary international institutions can be understood through a detailed analysis of their charters and the intentions that motivated the Founding Fathers. Many Americans have been reluctant to shed their essentially idealistic, structural, and legalistic assumptions about the nature of international organizations. Those who liked to think of the UN as somehow above the stresses and strains of international politics found it disconcerting when Jeane Kirkpatrick spoke of the UN as an inherently political organization, whose wheeling and dealing bears a stronger resemblance to national legislatures than a gathering of wise men.[3]

Although a handful of analysts have addressed the workings of the bloc system within the UN, most of them failed to anticipate or even to recognize the gradual crumbling of the nonaligned movement as a coherent, purposeful force within that global organization. As Americans began to sour on the UN after the repeated and misguided efforts in the 1970s of Third World states to force their agenda by sheer weight of numbers, a series of unfortunate stereotypes became so deeply ingrained in our thinking that we paid relatively little attention to the changing political landscape of the organization. A number of people simply stopped paying attention once the United States began to take its lumps in the General Assembly.[4]

The second tendency that has fortunately been shed in the scholarly literature was the attempt, particularly popular in the 1960s and 1970s, to apply quantitative analysis to the study of international political interactions. For example, scholars have at last recognized that examining the voting patterns of the General Assembly and other UN deliberative bodies yielded, at best, modest insights into the real workings of these organizations. Moreover, emphasis on General Assembly voting tended to yield a distorted picture of the politics and products of the UN system. The current congressional requirement for annual reports on the degree of each nation's voting concurrence with U.S. positions in the General Assembly may appear to represent something of a throwback to that earlier era. (This device, however, has been undertaken to make a political rather than an analytical point and has been used more for advocacy than for scholarship. Its methodologies, which ignore the 60 percent of General Assembly resolutions that are reached by consensus and which lump important and unimportant resolutions together, have been widely discredited.[5])

Political Cycles

It is important to bear in mind the historical context in reviewing scholarship and analysis about the contribution of global and regional organizations to international peace and security. The fifteen years from the 1973 Yom Kippur War to the early 1988 Afghan accords were hardly banner years for multilateral efforts to prevent and dampen conflict. The international political climate simply did not permit the UN or regional organizations to play an active role. During that period, international institutions, particularly the UN system, were subjected to repeated volleys of criticism from Western scholars, analysts, and policymakers for a variety of real and imagined wrongs.[6] Most of these complaints centered on the politics and management of the UN—things that might have been much easier to tolerate if the UN had been perceived as an effective actor in efforts to achieve a more peaceful world. In a politically unpropitious period, however, international institutions are caught in a vicious circle: because of their inability to achieve visible results as peacemakers, they are more vulnerable to criticisms of their politics and management, which, in turn, have a ripple effect on perceptions of their ability to handle future security issues effectively.

The 1970s and early 1980s was also an era of rising nationalism and of transnational religious and ethnic movements in many parts of the world.

Respect for international law and order had been at a low ebb, with unilateral intervention repeatedly appearing as a more attractive alternative, at least in the short run, to multilateral peacekeeping and peacemaking efforts. As a result, multilateral mechanisms in the security field for many years seemed to be playing an increasingly marginal role in the conduct of international life.

The perceptions that have guided scholarship, public commentary, and national policy-making have inevitably been affected by these trends. The study, like the practice, of multilateral diplomacy has become, at best, a secondary calling. The assumption that multilateral alternatives cannot work and should be considered only as a last resort in terms of policy choices has become deeply ingrained in our psyche, as well as in our writings and actions. Charles Krauthammer has gone so far as to postulate that those who entrust responsibilities to multilateral bodies are the true isolationists, because doing this constitutes nothing more than passing the buck to institutions incapable of achieving results on peace and security issues.[7]

The study of international mechanisms, in other than theoretical terms, simply has been out of vogue. Until the UN's dramatic diplomatic breakthroughs in the Afghanistan and Iran-Iraq conflicts, most of the policy-making community viewed the resort to regional or global institutions to address national security problems as softheaded and idealistic thinking. Whether the problem was peacekeeping in Beirut, peacemaking in the Malvinas/Falkland Islands, or escorting Persian Gulf shipping, it was deemed "realistic" and "tough-minded" to go it alone or, at most, with a few allies. Policymakers considered multilateral options unreliable, and not even scholars wanted to be labeled softheaded idealists.

Not only has the study of international institutions been out of vogue intellectually, but there have also been relatively few incentives for scholars or policy analysts to focus on these institutions. A number of problems exist:

- Grant support for work in this area had, until recently, largely dried up. In recent years, the Ford Foundation has renewed its former interest in international institutions, but so far, no other major foundation has followed suit in terms of making them a priority. The Carnegie Endowment for International Peace, once a leader in this field, abandoned its New York headquarters and its work on international institutions in the mid-1970s.

- With the UN and regional organizations cutting back their budgets and staffs, in part because U.S. dues were in arrears, few job opportunities existed within these institutions. Because multilateral diplomacy has not been a policy priority, neither the U.S. government nor private think tanks have offered significant employment alternatives. Even the United Nations Association (UNA) operates today with about half the staff it had in the mid-1970s.

- Academic editors and media editors alike have largely ignored developments in these institutions, so that relatively little space is available on op-ed pages or in scholarly journals for writings on, and hence visibility of, these issues.
- Because relatively few of the upcoming generation of scholars and analysts have a background in this area, they are reluctant to venture into uncharted territory. Considerable effort and some direct experience are required to understand the workings of international institutions, which involve quiet diplomacy and subtle political trade-offs; the outcomes are rarely clear-cut and generalizations are usually wrong.
- People are often more attracted to fields that appear to be opening new possibilities, rather than focusing on problems where the conclusions of their analysis are likely to be, or at least are expected to be, downbeat and pessimistic. In this country, at least, our political culture has treated international organizations as a dying breed, even though their numbers and functions have actually been on the rise.
- Scholarship tends to look backward rather than forward. Because of the nature of their materials and methodologies, scholars tend to tell us more about where we have been than about where we are going. In seeking lessons from the past, scholars are usually not in a good position to explain current trends and emerging factors that will shape the environment for future policy-making. Policy analysts are far better at explaining why things will not work rather than why they will.

In view of the record of international organizations over the past fifteen years, it is understandable that scholars and analysts would be pessimistic as they project experience into the future.[8] Few scholars, moreover, are close enough to the day-to-day developments within international organizations to have a good sense of current thinking and attitudes. Besides, their disciplines prefer historical rigor to subjective analysis of the contemporary environment. And, if analysts are dependent on voting records, the texts of agreements concluded, and public statements, much of the art of multilateral diplomacy will escape their analysis.

Policy Analysis

Global and regional organizations are dynamic, not static, enterprises. They change as the world changes, sometimes acting as catalysts and more often as reflections of developments over which they have little control. If scholarly treatments are unlikely, for the reasons previously cited, to capture the nuances of institutional evolution, this task is left to the media and policy analysts.

The problem, of course, is that the media and the policy-making community are particularly susceptible to prevailing political influences. American writings on the UN in recent years have come to resemble contributions to an ongoing debate rather than contributions to serious scholarship or policy analysis. The controversy surrounding U.S. policies toward the UN, fueled by the failure of the United States to pay its full sum of its dues as the world organization faces bankruptcy, has tended to polarize thinking and writing about every aspect of the institution's work. In the process, much of the policy work undertaken in recent years could be characterized as advocacy analysis: part preaching and part thinking.

The UN and other international organizations have not been of much help in encouraging rational, thorough, and objective analysis. Like the U.S. government, the various secretariats have relatively little capability for this kind of work; they are designed more for operational and short-term tasks, not for long-range strategic thinking.[9] Moreover, for years many people inside and outside the UN have treated the institution as if it should be immune to the rough and tumble of foreign policy debate. This trend was particularly evident in the Waldheim years; his successor, Secretary General Javier Perez de Cuellar, however, welcomes constructive debate.

There is an urgent need to try to rebuild a bipartisan consensus in this country about U.S. interests in international organizations and about the role of such organizations in the realm of peace and security. In recent years, even peacekeeping—to some extent an American innovation once thought to be above partisan criticism—has become the target not only of brickbats, but also of U.S. financial withholdings.[10] Now that UN peacekeepers are the recipients of the 1988 Nobel Peace Prize, the American ambivalence appears even more incongruous.

The polarized debate and divisions between Congress and the executive branch—not to mention the constant bickering within the administration in recent years—have made it difficult to develop or project anything close to a coherent American strategy toward international organizations. The result has been a large gap in American security policy. It is striking, for example, that the influential 1988 *Foreign Affairs* article by Henry Kissinger and Cyrus Vance, "Bipartisan Objectives for Foreign Policy," which addresses the central themes of a nonpartisan foreign policy for the next president, fails even to mention international organizations in passing.[11]

One need not be an enthusiast of international organizations to recognize both their importance in the world, and the necessity for American policymakers to have access to the best available data and analysis as well as to be presented with a range of sensible policy options. When there are voids in information and analysis, there are voids in our national policy-making. Two glaring examples are our failure to understand rapidly evolving Soviet policies toward international organizations and to grasp the long-term significance of global approaches to arms control and disarmament.

Paradoxically, the concept of seeking bilateral accommodation with our chief adversary, the Soviet Union, has become far more palatable than attempting to work with a broader coalition of states through multilateral organizations. An enormous literature and almost obsessive policy concern have been directed to bilateral relations with the Soviet Union, whereas almost no attention has been paid to possibilities of working with the Soviets in the UN. When General Secretary Mikhail Gorbachev published his now-famous September 1987 article on reviving the UN and rebuilding broad international cooperation on security issues, our policy-making, analytical, and scholarly communities were caught flat-footed. It has been twenty-five years—more than a generation—since the last book-length study of Soviet policy and motivations in international organizations was published in this country. The last two efforts were published in 1962 and 1963, and neither of these books focused on Soviet interests in using or abusing the international mechanisms for peace and security.[12]

Since Gorbachev first enunciated a radically new and far more positive Soviet approach to international organizations, the approach has received little serious treatment in scholarly or policy journals in this country.[13] The new Gorbachev approach, however, could have been foreseen, at least in its broad outlines, and the United States could have been much better prepared to react sensibly to it, if American scholars and analysts had been watching the signs of impending change in Soviet thinking on these matters over the past several years. But American observers had become so accustomed to the dreary monotony of the Soviet stance at Turtle Bay that these developments simply had not been monitored closely (at least not in the public domain).

Similarly, there has been remarkably little serious analysis of global arms control and disarmament efforts, particularly in contrast to the enormous amount of attention devoted to the faintest nuance in U.S.-Soviet negotiations. To a certain extent, this lack of analysis could be explained by the relatively meager results in terms of treaties concluded in the multilateral realm since the mid-1970s, as opposed to the series of nine global accords achieved in the 1960s and early 1970s. In addition, during the late 1970s and early 1980s, the bilateral arms control relationship was also barren. And, throughout this period, while all eyes were focused on Moscow and Washington, there was a significant yet quiet shift in military power toward the Third World—at least in terms of usable conventional and chemical weapons and the potential for building nuclear capabilities.

The proliferation of advanced conventional weapons and missile technology from the north to the south has, in a number of cases, narrowed military options for the global powers acting in the Third World, while considerably raising the risks and costs associated with the projection of direct military force in those regions.[14] This proliferation of advanced weapons beyond the superpowers may, in fact, be one of the important factors behind growing Soviet and U.S. reluctance to try to sustain military operations in much of the Third World (and for the Soviets to seek an orderly withdrawal from Afghanistan). While the United States and the Soviet Union have logically focused their negotiations on limiting unusable weapons of mass destruction, their relative position in terms of usable military power has declined, compared with that of a number of regional military powers in distant parts of the world, which have received advanced arms from a range of supplying countries or have developed their own arms production and expert capabilities.

In political and economic terms, as well as military, the past decade has witnessed a gradual shift toward a more truly multipolar world system in which neither the United States nor the Soviet Union can hope to dominate. This shift has been reflected in the politics of the UN itself, whose agenda is no longer dominated by any one bloc, as it was by the United States and its allies in the 1950s and 1960s and by the nonaligned countries through the 1970s and early 1980s. The UN has become, for the first time, a truly multilateral organization. For the future of arms control and disarmament, these trends suggest that as the United States and the Soviet Union make progress toward reducing their nuclear arsenals, the remaining arms control agenda will be composed largely of multilateral issues—such as conventional, chemical, and nuclear proliferation—and these will have to be pursued through multilateral institutions either regionally or. globally.[15]

Ideas for a Future Agenda

One thing is certain about political cycles, domestic or international: they are sure to turn sooner or later. In the case of international institutions, the cycle apparently bottomed out two or three years ago, and their fortunes—seen most vividly in the revived UN peace and security role—are again on the rise. We now have good reason to believe that these institutions will play an increasing role in our policy, analysis, and scholarship in the years ahead.

In the latter years of the twentieth century, global and regional organizations have become an integral part of the international landscape. They are not about to go away, so our only choice is to rebuild and reinvigorate them. Their presence, in fact, has become so commonplace as to be almost invisible. Thus, the fact that they are in crisis, financially and politically, is serving to spur renewed attention as to how they can be structured, managed, and used more effectively.

It is an important but little-noted paradox that nations are assigning greater and greater responsibilities to international organizations even as these bodies are beset by stinging criticism from many quarters. Perhaps international organizations were originally established in part to fulfill ideals about a world that could never be realized. Today, however, stripped of their idealistic facade, these organizations continue to multiply simply because of the realities of contemporary international life. The very functioning of the international system requires a wide range of daily cooperative interactions among nation-states. Some of these involve human security, others national security, and still others international security. The realities of interdependence have become so tangible that even skeptics in the Kremlin, who long rejected interdependence as an alien bourgeois concept, have now adopted it as a cornerstone of the new Soviet world view.

It has long been recognized that national sovereignty severely restricts the ability of international organizations to impose the collective will on recalcitrant nations or transnational groups. Rarely, moreover, have political conditions allowed the emergence of anything approaching a collective will on difficult security issues. Collective security remains a theory rather than a reality. But analysts have recently come to recognize that multilateral cooperation is essential to the preservation of sovereignty.[16] National leaders are discovering that they do not have the power, acting unilaterally or in concert with a few like-minded states, to control an enormous range of issues for which they are responsible. On issues as diverse as capital flows, the environment, drugs, trade, AIDS, terrorism, and nuclear war, national borders are less and less relevant. Whether we like it or not, international organizations serve to develop and project global norms on subjects as diverse as human rights, disarmament, decolonization, women's rights, conservation, and population. Each of these can have far-reaching effects on security, however narrowly or broadly the concept is defined.

For years, the common wisdom has been that security issues, because they seemed to have taken a back seat to economic and social issues on the agendas of international organizations for much of the 1960s and 1970s, will inevitably continue to slide down the list of priorities for years to come. As so often happens, however, the prevailing presumptions appear to have been dead wrong because they overlooked the subtle changes that were under way in national perspectives and global politics. A number of analysts have come to just the opposite conclusion. Although UN responsibilities in functional and humanitarian areas may well continue to grow, its economic and social structure seems to be less and less relevant to the macroproblems now facing the global system.[17] At the same time, conditions may well be ripe for a renaissance of peace and security work on the part of both regional and global institutions.[18]

A major factor in increased peace and security work, of course, is the new approach the Soviets are taking to a host of arms control and security issues at the UN. For many years, Soviet recalcitrance, as well as Soviet-American differences, limited the ability of the Security Council and the secretary general to function effectively on a wide range of issues. The depth of the new Soviet commitment to multilateral diplomacy remains largely untested, but it certainly raises the possibility of expanding the UN role in the future. Over the past few years, a multitude of signs have indicated that most Third World states are more inclined to moderation and less inclined to confrontation than they were in the 1970s and early 1980s. Thus, politically, the UN and other international institutions are becoming more hospitable places for U.S. business and for a realistic search for common ground on common problems. Consequently, in its second term, the Reagan administration took a far more positive view of the world organization and the possibility of involving it in major questions, such as Afghanistan, Iran-Iraq, and southern Africa, than it did during its first term in office.[19] Moreover, the Defense Department agreed that peacekeeping assessments could come out of its budget rather than out of State Department funds, and George Bush submitted to the UNA remarkably positive statements about the UN and its peacekeeping work.[20]

Positive interest in international organizations also appears to be rising on American campuses and among the general public. In recent years, public opinion polls have shown broad public skepticism about the effectiveness of the UN in securing international peace, coupled with strong support for finding ways to bolster the organization so that it can better carry out its founding mandate. By overwhelming and growing majorities, the American people favor continued U.S. participation in the world body. The widespread positive publicity that UN peacemaking and peacekeeping efforts have received in the last few years will undoubtedly increase public support.

In the scholarly community, there appears to be a revival of teaching and research on international organizations. A new organization, the Academic Council on the UN System, has been formed to foster research and training in the field; the Ford Foundation has sponsored two major conferences to encourage this trend; and, the international organization section of the International Studies Association is growing steadily. The participation of college and high school students in model UNs is expanding rapidly, with more than sixty thousand students a year now involved, and the membership of UNA-USA is growing steadily again after decades of decline.

In view of these upbeat observations, a number of subjects seem ripe for further research and analysis:

- Soviet motivations, interests, and theories vis-à-vis international organizations;
- the politics and future role of the nonaligned movement in international organizations;
- the nature of convergent and divergent interests among the Western allies in the UN system, and the role of middle powers in helping to shape the future of global and regional organizations;

- the definition of a dynamic and constructive role for multilateral institutions in the arms control and disarmament process;
- the possibilities for developing multilateral monitoring and verification capabilities in terms of existing or future multilateral arms control and disarmament agreements;
- ways of enhancing UN early warning, preventive diplomacy, and crisis-alert capabilities;
- the interrelationship and possibilities for coordination among arms control, peacekeeping, and peacemaking efforts in regions of high tension and conflict;
- the possibilities for developing a multilateral capability for monitoring, publicizing, and restraining—qualitatively and quantitatively—international arms transfers;
- the development of new forms of peacekeeping, for example, in terms of a modest international naval presence to clear mines, to internationalize disputed waterways, or to escort commercial vessels through international straits and waters in regions of high tension;
- U.S. interests in and strategies for the use of international organizations to help secure world peace and security;
- an analysis of nonfinancial means for the United States to exercise leverage in international institutions through the use of both carrots and sticks;
- more extensive polling and analysis of American public attitudes toward international organizations;
- consideration of ways to better coordinate the work of global and regional institutions in the effort to constrain regional conflict;
- the development of a better understanding of the likely future trends in the capabilities, politics, and functions of international organizations; and
- the consideration of ways to develop greater common ground among politically divergent approaches to assessing the work of international organizations and U.S. policies toward them.

Clearly, there is no lack of work to be done, if a new generation of scholars and policy analysts are persuaded that the study of international organizations will be an expanding, not contracting, field in the years ahead. The relative paucity of innovative and policy-relevant work in this field in recent years has left an enormous amount of room for important original contributions to scholarship, analysis, and policy-making.

Discussion

Commentator Roger Hansen took a more theoretical and general approach to the topic by discussing what role, if any, generic international organizations play in creating a more peaceful international environment. His conclusions were far less optimistic than Luck's.

There is, he said, an inherently intuitive appeal to the notion that international organizations and multilateral negotiations can provide answers to the many difficult questions raised by the increasingly interactive international system. Questions that transcend international borders logically require answers that do so as well. The problem is, however, that many of the issues that gave rise to this theory of the utility of international organizations—such as questions of international health, science, and communication—are essentially nonpolitical. Hence, they are not particularly applicable to the most vexing problem encountered by international organizations: the realignment of political loyalties away from the sovereign state and toward the international community. Politics in general, and political allegiances in particular, are more immutable than intuition can account for; and problems that are a function of the increased interdependence of states will be resolved on a multilateral basis only if it is in the interest of the states.

Furthermore, on questions of a higher political order—such as national security and international conflict—states are most unlikely to seek multilateral solutions to problems that they have not been able to resolve bilaterally, lest the very outcomes they rejected bilaterally be the end result.

Hansen suggested that two types of states are drawn to international organizations: the weak, who gain strength from unity in numbers; and the great powers, who can set the rules, control the agenda, and engineer outcomes. It is precisely because the United States was in a position to engineer outcomes in 1945 that there was so much enthusiasm for the UN. As the balance of power in the international system shifted toward multipolarity, U.S. support for the UN abated.

In short, the UN can play a greater role in securing and maintaining international peace only as long as such a role coincides with superpower interests. If there is no such overlap, the Security Council's provision effectively insulates the UN from becoming embroiled in a political conflict between the superpowers and lessens the possibility that the organization itself would become a casualty of such a conflict.

What is needed, Hansen continued, is a narrower and more realistic determination of what problems international organizations, and the UN in particular, are best suited to handle. Failure to make these determinations can only result in continuous cycles of optimism and disillusionment in American public opinion, as expectations rise and fall in the wake of political realities.

In the general discussion, Samuel Lewis posed two related questions: How can the Security Council be refined or strengthened in light of the apparent change in Soviet attitudes toward the UN, and what role can regional organizations, such as the OAU and the OAS, play in securing and maintaining peace in various parts of the world?

Luck responded that the Security Council has been the victim of misperception. It was never meant to be the "court" of first recourse; that role was intended for such groups as the OAU and OAS. But because the Security Council has attempted to be all things to all people, it has not been able to satisfy its primary mission as final arbiter in conflict situations. Moreover, it is almost impossible to have strong regional organizations in areas of conflict because the political cohesion needed to make them strong is lacking and the resulting divisiveness is often at the heart of the conflict in question. Increased Soviet participation in such efforts may ameliorate some of these tensions, but certainly not all of them.

Hansen concurred, but he cautioned that if the U.S. government's optimism over recent shifts in Soviet views on the UN outstrips the reality, a serious backlash against the UN will probably develop and lead to a weakening of the overall institution.

The discussion of regional organizations should not be restricted to the developing world, suggested Lily Gardner Feldman. The European Community (EC) represents much more than a simple economic union of states; it also plays an important international political and peacekeeping role. The United States may not have a particular interest in multilateral institutions, but by 1992, the world will be able to look at the EC as a model of the enormous international benefits such institutions can offer.

The panelists agreed (for somewhat different reasons), however, that the EC model was a difficult one to transfer to other regions of the world. Both panelists questioned whether the enormous historical and cultural homogeneity of Europe could be duplicated elsewhere. Furthermore, to what extent the success of the EC is a function of the security provided by a U.S. nuclear umbrella, and whether the "old" Europe would reappear if that umbrella were withdrawn, is difficult to determine.

Taking this analysis one step further, Hansen suggested that the EC experience did not obviate the original analytic question posed, namely, do international organizations necessarily have a positive impact on international peace? He suggested that perhaps all that was being accomplished in Europe was the exchange of twelve international actors for one, which reduced the potential for conflict on the already peaceful continent of Europe but did not significantly enhance international peace.

A common criticism of U.S. policy toward the UN and other international organizations is that it lacks the coherence of a strategy, is unpredictable, and is subject to fluctuation. The reason for these problems, one member of the audience suggested, was that the UN is not an end in itself, so to speak, but a tool by which certain objectives can be reached. Failure to appreciate this distinction, he added, leads many observers to conclude erroneously that if the United States only acted more consistently, the UN would be more effective.

The panelists agreed that this was a common misunderstanding. Hansen added that if the primary concern of states is the defense of their national interests, international organizations and regional organizations are, by definition, derivative issues. They become diplomatic instruments that are used to achieve certain ends. As situations and environments change, so, too, do the perceptions about how best to use the tools at one's disposal. It is impossible to design a blanket strategy to fit all contingencies.

Luck suggested, however, that certain baseline policies concerning fundamental issues, such as funding, could be made more predictable and reliable. The only way the United States can use the UN for constructive purposes, when the opportunity presents itself, is to maintain U.S. credibility as a central actor within the organization.

Elise Boulding suggested that one of the reasons why the United States seems less competent in multilateral environments is that it lacks historical experience in this area. Unlike our European allies, she said, multilateral diplomacy and internationalism have become matters of serious concern to the United States only since 1945; this "experience gap" needs to be closed. Furthermore, no state simply chooses a policy of bilateralism over multilateralism; rather, it acts between the two as extremes on a wide spectrum.

Hansen concurred, stating that the issue was not a choice between one policy or the other, but a matter of where on the spectrum a state finds itself at any given time. That is precisely why, he added, it is impossible to maintain an overarching strategy toward international organizations. Luck also noted that the State Department lacks well-trained multilateral specialists because professional diplomats are not particularly interested in the field. Instead, positions in Soviet affairs and arms control tend to be more highly coveted by Foreign Service officers. The fact remains that multilateral specialists are sorely needed.

In conclusion, John McDonald noted that the efficacy of the UN in a peacekeeping role is hard to measure because much of its activity is preventive. It is difficult to determine how many potential conflicts were avoided by virtue of the UN's mere existence, because such conflicts were resolved at a precrisis stage. This argument takes on even greater salience when it is remembered that 60 percent of General Assembly resolutions are agreed to by consensus.

Notes

1. For useful overviews of the literature, see Friedrich Kratochwil and John Gerard Ruggie, "International Organization: A State of the Art on an Art of the State," *International Organization* 40, no. 4 (Autumn 1986).

2. The Stanley Foundation conducts a series of annual conferences for policymakers, diplomats, and scholars to consider the future of the UN and ways to strengthen its peace and security work.

3. Speech of Ambassador Jeane Kirkpatrick to the 1985 National Convention of UNA-USA. This point is developed in Edward C. Luck, "The UN at 40," *Foreign Policy* 57 (Winter 1984–85).

4. See, for example, Edward C. Luck, "The Impact of the Zionism-Racism Resolution on the Standing of the UN," *Israel Yearbook on Human Rights*, University of Tel Aviv (Spring 1988).

5. As a result of legislation introduced by Senator Edward Kennedy, the State Department is currently considering modifications in the methodology of this report and has asked for the views of a number of scholars and policy analysts.

6. The series of critiques published by the Heritage Foundation under its UN Assessment Project have been the most outspoken and extreme.

7. See his columns in the *Washington Post* and his article "Let It Sink: The Overdue Demise of the United Nations," in *New Republic*, August 24, 1987.

8. Among the major analyses are Ernest B. Haas, "Regime Decay: Conflict Management and International Organizations, 1945–1981," *International Organization* 37, no. 2 (Spring 1983); Arthur R. Day and Michael W. Doyle, eds., *Escalation and Intervention: Multilateral Security and Its Alternatives* (UNA-USA and Westview Press, 1986); and Jock A. Finlayson and Mark W. Zacher, "The United Nations and Collective Security: Retrospect and Prospect," in Toby Trister Gati, ed., *The U.S., the UN, and the Management of Global Change* (New York: UNA-USA and New York University Press, 1983).

9. A new unit established in the UN, the Office for Research and the Collection of Information, is designed to help overcome the lack of early warning and policy planning capabilities.

10. Again, the harshest criticisms, although not necessarily the best founded, have come from the Heritage Foundation and its UN Assessment Project.

11. *Foreign Affairs* 66, no. 5 (Summer 1988), pp. 899–921.

12. Alexander Dallin, *The Soviet Union at the United Nations: An Inquiry into Soviet Motives and Objectives* (1962) and Harold K. Jacobson, *The U.S.S.R. and the UN's Economic and Social Activities* (1963).

13. The major exception so far is Edward C. Luck and Toby Trister Gati, "Gorbachev, the UN and U.S. Policy," *Washington Quarterly* (Autumn 1988).

14. The transfer of Chinese surface-to-surface missiles to Iran at the time that the U.S. Navy was escorting Kuwaiti tankers in the Persian Gulf is a recent example.

15. This point is developed more fully in Edward C. Luck, "A New Role for the UN in the Era of 'Multipolarity,'" *Christian Science Monitor*, May 26, 1988.

16. See, for example, the "sovereignty gap" concept developed by a high-level international panel on UN management and decision making convened by UNA-USA in its final report *A Successor Vision: The United Nations of Tomorrow*, UNA-USA (September 1987).

17. UNA-USA, *A Successor Vision*, September 1987.

18. This point is addressed in greater detail in Edward C. Luck, "Renewing the Mandate: The UN's Role in Peace and Security," in the *Successor Vision* project, UNA-USA (November 1988).

19. White House press release of September 13, 1988, and remarks of President Ronald Reagan to the 43rd General Assembly of the United Nations, September 26, 1988.

20. Statements on the UN submitted by George Bush to the United Nations Association during the presidential election campaign, October 1988, are available from UNA-USA.

Introduction to Chapter 8

Third-party dispute settlement—the process by which an individual or group not involved in a dispute between two or more entities tries to help the disputants reach a settlement or, in some cases, is authorized to determine a settlement on its own—is as old as society itself, as Richard Bilder points out in this chapter.

Furthermore, persons entrusted with discharging settlement duties—the arbiters, judges, or mediators—have been accorded a special place by every society in which they have operated, underscoring Bilder's assertion that third-party dispute settlement is not only a deeply rooted human experience but also is closely linked to the emergence of political order and law.

Why would sovereign states agree to submit their grievances with other sovereign states to settlement by an external or third party? Like adherence to international law, submission to a third-party settlement procedure is purely consensual and contractual; yet many states have agreed to submit to such settlement, bilaterally and multilaterally as well as under the UN Charter.

It is generally accepted that the best method for resolving disputes between states is through direct negotiation. However, states, like individuals, often find themselves unable to maneuver toward a constructive solution, although they may feel much internal and external pressure to do so. At such times, a third party can be most useful, providing, of course, that the disputing parties have no ulterior motives for submitting to a supplementary procedure.

Third parties themselves have a variety of motives. Some, like judges and the secretary general of the UN, are directly commissioned to settle disputes. Other states or individuals may volunteer their services out of a sense of altruism or in the interest of national prestige, while still others volunteer because they have a perceived interest in the resolution of a given dispute. Bilder notes that the options available to disputants are quite extensive and flexible. The methods may be used individually or in combination with one another and are therefore best viewed as a line on a continuum between the least intrusive (good offices) and most intrusive (judicial settlement) means of dispute resolution.

Although judicial settlement or adjudication plays a limited role in the overall scheme of third-party dispute settlement, Bilder says, it has an important symbolic role in the panoply of dispute resolution methodologies and is a useful prod to persuade states to accept less intrusive means of settlement.

Bilder identifies a number of potentially negative side effects of third-party dispute interventions as well as many benefits, indicated by empirical evidence. He notes that much of the best research in the field deals with nonlegal aspects of dispute settlement and is being conducted by social scientists rather than legal scholars.

8. International Third-Party Dispute Settlement

Richard B. Bilder

From earliest times, third parties have played an important role in attempts to resolve interpersonal and intergroup conflicts. Indeed, the concept of third-party dispute settlement and the roles of judge, arbitrator, and mediator pervade all human societies and are closely linked to the emergence of political order and law.

It is not practical here to review either the long history of international third-party dispute settlement or the extensive descriptive and analytical literature it has produced. Instead, this chapter is intended to suggest some basic questions and tentative answers that may help to provide a framework for further thinking, discussion, and research about the potential role of third-party intervention.[1]

Several introductory comments are in order. First, third-party intervention is not simply a "legal" means of dispute settlement but a subject relevant to many conflict resolution processes. International lawyers have tended to look principally at the more formal, institutionalized, and "legal" aspects of international third-party dispute settlement, in particular, international adjudication.[2] Current interest in the role of international arbitral tribunals and courts has certainly been heightened by the recent assertion of jurisdiction and ruling against the United States by the ICJ in the *Nicaragua* case,[3] and by the Reagan administration's related decision to withdraw the declaration made by the United States in 1946 submitting to the ICJ's compulsory jurisdiction.[4] In contrast, political scientists and social psychologists have focused their attention primarily on mediation and other nonbinding processes of dispute resolution; indeed, their writings have largely ignored the role of law or of formal legal techniques such as adjudication in international conflict resolution.[5]

Clearly, any approach to thinking about international conflict resolution should take account of all types of factors that may affect the usefulness and success of third-party intervention, including normative influences, power-political interests, and the parties' perceptions and attitudes. Our understanding is best served by pursuing legal and social science research and by combining a variety of disciplinary perspectives.

Second, third-party dispute settlement is only one way of trying to resolve international conflicts, and it can be understood only in the context of a more general study of dispute settlement problems and processes. An exploration of these broad underlying questions is beyond the scope of this chapter, but they include the following:

- What do we mean by *conflicts* and *disputes?*
- What causes conflicts and disputes?
- Do we need to settle conflicts and disputes, and, if so, which ones and why?
- Do states have an international obligation to settle their disputes peacefully?
- What are the kinds of international disputes?
- How frequently do they arise?
- Between or among what states?
- What kinds of claims do they involve?
- Do disputes or conflicts follow typical patterns or "life cycles"?
- What general techniques or procedures are available for settling international disputes?
- When is a dispute "settled"?
- How can disputes be avoided?
- What is the relationship between law, or normative considerations, and dispute settlement?[6]

What Is Meant by "Third-Party Dispute Settlement"?

A third party can be defined as an individual or group that is external to a dispute between two or more other individuals or groups and that either tries to help the disputants reach a settlement or, in some cases, is authorized to determine a settlement.[7] Thus, a third party may be another state or group of states (e.g., Algeria in the U.S.-Iranian hostage crisis); a governmental international organization (e.g., the UN or the OAS); an international court (e.g., the ICJ); or an arbitrator or arbitration panel (e.g., the U.S.-Iranian Claims Tribunal); a nongovernmental organization (e.g., the International Committee of the Red Cross); or an individual or group of individuals functioning either in a representative capacity (e.g., a UN-appointed mediator) or, conceivably, in a private capacity.

In the interest of impartiality, mediators, arbitrators, or judges (or at least most of the judges on an international court) are usually of a nationality other than that of the disputing parties. However, this need not be the case so long as the third party is perceived by the disputants as "external" to the dispute and capable of performing impartially and effectively the role of a third party. For example, the United States and Canada have frequently used binational panels in dispute settlement roles (e.g., the arbitral panels established under the Jay Treaty and the International Joint Commission of the United States and Canada).[8]

"Third-party intervention" has also been defined as "intervention into a dispute of a person or agency whose purpose it is to act as an instrument for bringing about a peaceful settlement of that dispute, while creating structures whereby the foundations of a lasting settlement may be laid,"[9] or, more broadly, as "any action taken by an actor that is not a direct party to the crisis, that is designed to reduce or remove one or more problems in the bargaining relationship and, therefore, to facilitate the termination of the conflict itself."[10] International lawyers and others sometimes appear to use the term "third-party dispute settlement" to refer not to the broad political processes of third-party intervention, but only to the more formal regularized structure of norms, institutions, arrangements, and procedures that are recognized parts of the international legal order—in particular, techniques and procedures for binding adjudication using arbitral tribunals or the ICJ. Here "third-party intervention" and "third-party dispute settlement" are used interchangeably, as meaning the same thing. It is important to note that third parties can play an important part in managing, de-escalating, or dampening disputes, even if such efforts do not result in a final resolution of the disputes. Any inquiry into the role of third parties should appropriately address and encompass their function in dispute management and processing, as well as in dispute resolution and settlement.

Do Nation-States Have an Obligation to Submit Their Disputes to Third Parties for Help or for Binding Settlement?

It is well established that, in the absence of special agreement, nation-states have no obligation to submit their disputes to third parties either for help in achieving settlement or, a fortiori, for binding settlement by such third parties.[11] Consequently, the use of most third-party dispute settlement techniques, and, in particular, resort to arbitration or judicial settlement, depends on the acquiescence of the disputing parties and cannot occur without their consent.

Members of the UN (in effect, almost all the nations of the world), however, have assumed treaty obligations under the UN Charter to accept at least limited types of third-party intervention, particularly regarding disputes whose continuation "is likely to endanger the maintenance of international peace and security."[12] In addition, Article 33(2) of the Charter directs the Security Council, when it deems necessary, to call on the parties to settle their dispute by the means (which include third-party means) listed in Article 33(1) of the Charter.

Nations also, of course, are free to enter into agreements with each other, which include so-called compromissory clauses or other obligations and arrangements to settle their disputes peacefully, and a great number—probably thousands—of such agreements are in effect.[13] Many such agreements not only include general obligations of peaceful settlement, but require, recommend, or provide procedures for the use of specific dispute settlement techniques, such as conciliation, arbitration, adjudication, or other third-party techniques.

It is an interesting question whether the international community's interest in peaceful settlement of disputes suggests the need for expanding the duty of states to resort to at least certain nonbinding methods of third-party dispute settlement, even in the absence of their consent.

Why Do Disputing States Turn to Third Parties?

Third-party dispute settlement is primarily a supplementary means of conflict resolution. Typically, it is used only when the disputing states are unwilling to reach a settlement themselves and wish the help of third parties to do so, or a third party is otherwise authorized or in a position to intervene to affect the settlement or outcome of the dispute.

Louis Sohn points out that "it is an axiom of international diplomacy that the most efficient method of settling international disputes is through negotiations between the two governments concerned, without any meddling of third parties, other states or international organizations," and that "in most instances negotiations lead to a solution."[14] Negotiation is the preferred means of resolving disputes for many reasons. Perhaps the most important reason is that negotiation is the least risky way the parties can try to resolve their dispute. Thus, negotiation permits each state maximum control over both the dispute settlement process and the outcome, because each state always has the option of simply walking away from the negotiation and *not* agreeing. In contrast, any third-party involvement carries a risk of reducing a disputing state's flexibility and freedom to do what it wants, and of somehow trapping it into an undesirable outcome.

Some other advantages of direct negotiation are as follows:

- Negotiation places responsibility for resolving the dispute on the parties themselves, who are in the best position to develop a sensible, workable, and acceptable solution.
- Negotiation works toward a freely agreed rather than imposed solution, which is likely to have maximum acceptability and stability.
- Negotiation favors compromise and accommodation, which are most likely to preserve good long-term cooperative relations between the parties.

- Negotiation is generally simpler and less costly than alternative dispute settlement methods.

As long as disputing states are making some progress toward solving their dispute themselves, they will normally have little reason to turn to third parties, and, conversely, third parties will have little reason to intervene.

Consequently, disputing states would be expected to seek or acquiesce in third-party intervention only when their own efforts to reach a negotiated settlement have been unavailing and are at an impasse, and when neither prefers such a failure to the alternative possibility of continuing to seek settlement through assistance by, or delegation to, third parties. In this case, both parties may choose to ask third parties for help in their attempts to reach an agreement or, at the extreme, they may simply ask or allow a third party to determine the settlement or outcome for them.

Presumably, in deciding whether to seek or acquiesce in third-party dispute settlement procedures, each party will weigh what it thinks it may gain from such intervention against the risks and constraints on its control of the situation and outcomes that the particular third-party techniques may involve. Typically, the party in the more powerful negotiating position might be expected to be particularly reluctant to accept third-party intervention, because such intervention may have the effect of counterbalancing or neutralizing its bargaining power. But sometimes, even for the stronger party, the risks of conflict, continued dispute, or unfavorable internal or external public opinion may outweigh even substantial risks from third-party intervention.

Of course, a state's apparent consent to third-party intervention may not be serious or sincere; a state may pretend to agree simply to appeal to internal or external public opinion or seem like a "good citizen," but without any real intention of compromise or cooperation in a good-faith effort to settle the dispute. Indeed, *both* disputing parties may find it useful to seem to be doing something by accepting third-party intervention, even though neither really expects such intervention to be successful, or at least to do any more than ratify the outcome that would have occurred anyway. In some cases, for example, agreements may contain nominal obligations, included solely to pacify an internal political constituency of one of the parties, which neither expects to be observed. If and when such "noncompliance" occurs, the party will complain and "dispute the matter," although it cannot in good faith insist on its position. By resorting to third-party dispute settlement techniques, including adjudication, the parties can delay and look as though they are trying to adjust the question while ultimately reaching the outcome they always intended.[15]

In practice, the context of each dispute and conflict is likely to be unique, and many factors may bear on the willingness of disputing states to seek or accept third-party intervention. First, such attitudes obviously will vary with the particular circumstances and stakes involved, the type of intervention contemplated, and the third parties themselves. For example, a state may be willing to accept nonbinding UN mediation but not a binding ICJ decision, or fact-finding by neutral state A but not by hostile state B.

Second, as a threshold condition, disputing states must believe that there are things third parties can do that are more likely to be helpful than harmful, and the disputing states must be willing, at a minimum, to let third parties try. This means that third-party intervention often has at least two stages or phases: an initial "jurisdictional" phase in which the parties are persuaded to seek or acquiesce in letting a third party have some role (or the third party otherwise establishes its right to do so); and a "substantive" or "merits" phase in which the third party actually attempts to help to settle the dispute.

Third, it may not always be easy to say when the disputants are in fact at an "impasse"; for example, a state in a weaker bargaining position may seek third-party intervention in the hope of thus obtaining an outcome better than it can obtain itself, even though it is prepared, if its efforts to involve third parties prove unsuccessful, to agree to a less favorable settlement.

Fourth, even when states are reluctant to accept third-party intervention, they may, as previously noted, have previously undertaken legal obligations to do so under the UN Charter, the ICJ statute, or other international agreements. Indeed, serious problems may arise when a third party, at the request of one party to a dispute, intervenes on the basis of what it construes as the other party's prior consent, only to find that the other party did not consent or is no longer willing to accept such intervention. Recent experience in the *Nicaragua* and other cases raises questions about the usefulness or effectiveness of third-party intervention in the absence of real and continuing consent on the part of all of the disputing parties.

Finally, third-party intervention may occur even in the absence of impasse between disputing states or, indeed, of real consent by one or both of them. Thus, the third state may have its own interest in promoting or preventing a particular outcome (e.g., helping an ally or hurting an enemy). Indeed, in some situations, the "selfish interest" of the intervening state may be so great that its role is better analyzed as that of a third party *to* the dispute, rather than as an *external* third party concerned only with helping the parties resolve the dispute. Or, as is often the case, the international community as a whole may be interested in resolving conflicts or preventing unjust or unstable settlements that might escalate to threaten other states. Much of the UN's interventionary authority, under Chapters VI and VII of the Charter, is based on this premise. Indeed, it is worth noting that the international community may wish to intervene even if the disputing states are themselves able to agree easily on an amenable settlement. For example, the UN or third states might wish to intervene in a bilateral settlement of a transfrontier pollution dispute in which the two states agreed to solve the problem by dumping large amounts of the pollutant into the ocean.

Why Are Third Parties Willing to Intervene?

Performing a third-party role in dispute settlement is not an easy task; it can be arduous and costly (e.g., the U.S. role in the various Middle Eastern crises), dangerous (e.g., the assassination of Count Bernadotte), or unrewarding (e.g., the U.S. role in the Malvinas/Falkland Islands War). Indeed, third parties may run serious risks of becoming caught up in, or "blackmailed" into, a continuing role in a long, drawn-out dispute or conflict, or of being blamed by one or both of the parties for unfavorable outcomes.

Reasons why third parties are willing to intervene include the following:

- The third party may have a legal or institutional responsibility to do so; it may simply be the third party's job or raison d'être. For example, serving as third parties in dispute settlement is what international judges, arbitrators, and the UN secretary general are paid for.
- The third party may have a sense of public responsibility, as well as perhaps a desire for the prestige and honor that may accompany a successful third-party role. Algeria's role in the Iran hostage dispute, the pope's role in the Argentina-Chile Beagle Channel dispute, and the Soviet mediation of the Kashmir dispute are examples.
- As previously noted, the third party may have its own interests or the interests of an ally at stake, which it believes will be protected or advanced by its intervention and third-party role.

Of course, several of these motives may be combined—as may be the case, for example, with U.S. intervention in the Middle East or the "Contadora" states' intervention in the Nicaraguan conflict.

What Kinds of Third-Party Techniques Are Available?

The most usual and accepted list of methods of peaceful settlement of international disputes, and the one most familiar to international lawyers, is the list set forth in Article 33 of the UN Charter: negotiation, inquiry, mediation, conciliation, arbitration, judicial settlement, resort to regional agencies or arrangements, and resort to the UN or other international organization dispute settlement procedures. In essence, this list of methods reflects a continuum of techniques ranging from so-called diplomatic means, which give control of the outcome primarily to the parties themselves, to so-called legal means, which give control of the outcome primarily to a third party or parties. That is, the principal difference among these techniques is the extent to which third parties can legitimately participate in helping to bring about or determine the settlement and, conversely, the extent to which the parties can reject a settlement proposed by the third party.

In practice, distinctions among these techniques may be more theoretical than real, and a particular process of dispute settlement may combine elements of various techniques. For example, international arbitration or adjudication may often embody compromises reflecting strong elements of negotiation or mediation among the arbitrators or judges, at least some of whom may see their role as safeguarding the interests, or representing the point of view, of one or the other party. Negotiators often have to make their bargaining decisions with the possibility of third-party intervention, or perhaps even resort to adjudication, in mind.

The traditional third-party methods of peaceful settlement, and their distinctive characteristics, are as follows.

Good Offices and Mediation[16]

Good offices and mediation are techniques by which the parties, who are unable to resolve a dispute by negotiation, request or agree to limited intervention by a third party to help them break an impasse. In the case of good offices, the role of the third party is usually limited simply to bringing the parties into communication and facilitating their negotiations. In the case of mediation, the mediator usually plays a more active part in facilitating communication and negotiation between the parties and is sometimes permitted or expected to advance informal and nonbinding proposals of his or her own. President Carter's mediation leading to the Egypt-Israel Peace Treaty is a recent example of successful mediation.

Fact-finding, Inquiry, and Conciliation[17]

These are methods of settlement in which the parties request or agree to the third-party intervention, usually on a more formal basis, for the purpose of determining particular facts or otherwise conducting an impartial examination of the dispute and, if the parties so agree, attempting to suggest or define the terms of a mutually acceptable settlement. Like mediation, the report of a fact-finding body or conciliation commission is normally nonbinding, although the third-party finding or recommendation may have an important influence on the settlement. A recent example of the successful use of a formal inquiry procedure is the 1961 "Red Crusader" inquiry into the facts concerning the stopping of a British trawler by a Danish fishery protection vessel. A recent example of successful conciliation is the special commission established by Norway and Iceland to make recommendations about their dispute over the apportionment of the continental shelf off Jan Mayen Island. The commission's report, recommending joint development of hydrocarbon production, was implemented with the conclusion of a 1981 Norway-Iceland treaty on the matter.

Arbitration[18]

This method involves the reference of a dispute or series of disputes, by the agreement of the parties, to an ad hoc tribunal for binding decision, usually on the basis of international law. The parties agree on the issue to be arbitrated and the machinery and procedure of the tribunal, including the method of selection of the arbitrator or arbitrators. Although arbitration is normally binding, the parties may stipulate that the tribunal's opinion will be only advisory. The arbitration in 1978 of a dispute concerning interpretation of the French-American Air Agreement is a recent example of a successful arbitration.

Judicial Settlement[19]

This method involves referring of the dispute, by the agreement or consent of the parties, to the ICJ or some other standing and permanent judicial body for binding decision, usually on the basis of international law. Again, if the rules establishing the court so allow, the parties may agree to an advisory or nonbinding opinion rather than a binding decision, or to a declaratory judgment specifying the principles that the parties should apply in the settlement of their dispute. The *Gulf of Maine* case between the United States and Canada is a recent example of successful judicial settlement under ICJ procedures.

Settlement Through the UN or Other Global or Regional International Organizations or Agencies[20]

In some circumstances, the parties may request the assistance of the UN, a regional organization, or another international organization in settling their dispute. Or, the UN or another organization (for example, a regional organization) may legitimately intervene in the dispute on its own motion, at least for the purpose of trying to bring about a peaceful settlement. Sometimes a third party may ask for the organization's intervention. This assistance may, inter alia, take the form of good offices, mediation, fact-finding, or conciliation. The rights and obligations of the parties and authority of each organization in these respects are in each case set out in their respective charters and other constitutive instruments, as well as developed through practice. The UN's various attempts to deal with Middle Eastern, Iran-Iraq, and many other problems are familiar examples of the attempted use of this technique.

The international system has developed a wide variety of institutions, arrangements, procedures, and norms through which these kinds of techniques can be invoked and implemented. These include more than a hundred international organizations; international courts such as the ICJ, the Court of the European Communities, and the European and American Courts of Human Rights; arbitral tribunals such as the Iranian-American Claims Tribunal currently sitting in the Hague; General Agreement on Tariffs and Trade (GATT) dispute settlement panels; and many binational commissions such as the Canadian-American International Joint Commission.

There are, of course, other distinctions that can usefully be drawn. For example, two social psychologists, Dean G. Pruitt and Jeffrey Z. Rubin, suggest the following broad types of third-party roles:[21]

- Formal versus informal role. Is the third party intervening pursuant to a formal understanding or legal precedents (for example, under UN authorization or the compromissory clause of an agreement), or is the intervention informal and without express legitimation?
- Individual versus representative role. Is the intervenor acting in a personal capacity, or in a representative capacity (for example, as a government or an international organization official)?
- Invited versus noninvited role. Is the intervenor acting pursuant to an express or implied invitation or with the parties' consent, or on its own or some other third-party initiative (or, conceivably, against the expressed wishes of one or both of the parties)?
- Impartial versus partial role. Is the intervenor impartial or neutral, or is it biased in favor of one party or a particular result?
- Advisory versus directive role. Is the intervenor's role wholly or primarily advisory, with the aim of helping the parties achieve their own solution, or can the intervenor determine all or part of the settlement or outcome?
- Content-oriented versus process-oriented roles. Does the intervenor's role focus primarily on the actual content of the dispute (the substantive issues under consideration) or primarily on the decision-making process (the way in which the discussions are taking place)?

How Can Third Parties Help?

As indicated, in the case of advisory and nonbinding techniques such as good offices, mediation, fact-finding, and conciliation, the third party's role is usually limited to helping the parties negotiate their own dispute settlement. In contrast, in the case of directive and binding techniques such as arbitration and judicial settlement, responsibility for settlement of all or part of the issues in dispute is removed from the parties' direct control, and the third party is authorized to decide the matter for them. In each case, of course, the actual, or even potential, presence and activities of a third party may have various effects on the dynamics of the disputing process and the disputing parties' relationships—some helpful, but some perhaps not.

How can third parties help the disputants achieve a settlement themselves? Much research has been done to identify the general functions that mediators and other nondirective third parties can perform and the specific kinds of things they can do that are likely to be most useful.

Pruitt and Rubin, for example, describe the type of negotiating impasse that may call for third-party assistance:

> Positions tend towards rigidity because the protagonists are reluctant to budge lest any conciliatory gesture be misconstrued as a sign of weakness. Moreover, the parties may lack the imagination, creativity, and/or experience necessary to work their way out of the pit they have jointly engineered—not because they don't want to but because they don't know how. Thus, for a variety of reasons, disputants are sometimes either unable or unwilling to move toward agreement of their own accord. Under the circumstances, third parties often become involved at the behest of one or more of the disputants, or on their own initiative.[22]

They suggest and discuss a variety of ways in which a third party can help the parties break out of such an impasse, including the following:[23]

- *Modifying the physical and social structure of the dispute* (e.g., by structuring communication between the principals, opening and neutralizing the site in which problem solving takes place, imposing time limits, and infusing resources).

- *Modifying the issue structure* (e.g., by helping the disputants identify existing issues and alternatives, helping them package and sequence issues in ways that lead towards agreement, and introducing new issues and alternatives that did not occur to the disputants themselves).

- *Increasing the disputants' motivation to reach agreement* (e.g., by facilitating their making concessions without loss of face, engendering mutual trust, encouraging their venting and coming to grips with irrational feelings, and respecting their desire for autonomy).

Another commentator, Jacob Bercovitch, divides third-party aims into "process objectives" and "outcome objectives," each of which he in turn subdivides into two categories: "information search" (e.g., establishing communication, searching for common principles) and "social influence" (e.g., persuading the parties to converge on an acceptable outcome). Bercovitch sees third-party behavior as implemented through certain tactics: "reflective behavior" (e.g., receiving, transmitting, and interpreting messages and signals reflecting and influencing how the parties perceive their situation); "nondirective behavior" (e.g., influencing the context and structure of the conflict by controlling publicity, controlling the environment, controlling resources, reducing pressure, and recasting issues); and "directive behavior" (e.g., influencing the parties' perceptions and motivation through making proposals, judiciously exercising power, and promising resources).[24]

Other commentators suggest other types of potential third-party contributions, or classify third-party objectives or functions somewhat differently. For example, Oran Young classifies third-party objectives as "informational" (e.g., offering information or increasing communication); "tactical" (e.g., offering services); "supervisory" (e.g., monitoring an agreement); and "conceptual" (e.g., offering new ideas for a settlement).[25] Indeed, there is now a rich literature suggesting imaginative techniques through which third parties may help parties in an impasse "get unstuck"—for example, by creating a "hurting stalemate," by providing "decommitting formulas" or "bypass solutions," by "changing or reframing the game," or by using "single text procedures."

I have suggested elsewhere that a principal reason why disputing parties may not be able to reach a settlement is that they distrust each other or are otherwise concerned with what they see as serious risks in such an agreement. In this case, a third party can play a crucial role in dispute settlement by helping the parties to manage these risks in a variety of ways, including by monitoring or verifying performance, serving as an escrow agent, or providing guarantees.[26] Third-party risk management devices of this kind may be particularly helpful when distrust is a serious obstacle, such as in armistice or peace agreements or agreements seeking to resolve complex and emotional racial, ethnic, or religious conflicts.

What about more directive techniques of third-party intervention such as adjudication, in which third parties have authority themselves to determine how the dispute is to be settled? The subject of adjudication is discussed in the next section, but two of the most important ways in which this kind of third-party technique can help disputing parties can be briefly mentioned here.

First, adjudication can dispose of the matter. It is often more important to the parties that a dispute be settled than that it be settled in a particular way. When negotiations are unsuccessful, adjudication or other third-party disposition of the matter provides an alternative way in which the parties can put the dispute behind them and move on to other things.

Second, adjudication can permit concessions without "loss of face" or bureaucratic risk. Because adjudication involves an impersonal decision by a third party, neither of the governments of the parties (or the officials involved) can be held directly responsible for the outcome. In a number of disputes, governments may be relatively indifferent as to the outcome and would normally be willing to negotiate a compromise settlement, but for internal political or other reasons, they are unable to concede or even compromise the issue in negotiations. Third-party settlement is a politically useful way by which foreign offices can dispose of such problems without taking direct responsibility for concessions. In effect, they can "pass the buck" for not "winning" the dispute to the third-party tribunal—"Don't blame us, blame the judge!"

Which Techniques Work Best?

Many people have described the relative advantages and disadvantages of various techniques and made suggestions about when and how each can best be employed.[27] For example, J.G. Merrills, assessing the value of conciliation as a dispute settlement technique, concludes as follows:

> Conciliation has proved most useful for disputes where the main issues are legal, but the parties desire an equitable compromise.... In cases of this type, conciliation would appear to offer two advantages over arbitration *ex aequo et bono*, the obvious alternative.
>
> First, because of the way conciliation is conducted—through a dialogue with and between the parties—there is no danger of its producing a result that takes the parties completely by surprise, as sometimes happens, in legal proceedings. Secondly a commission's proposals...are not binding and, if unacceptable can be rejected.[28]

Merrills and others have attempted similar assessments of other techniques. Moreover, a considerable body of theoretical and empirical research, historical and political analysis, and biographical and anecdotal reporting now exists concerning such "how to do it" questions as the most appropriate timing of intervention, characteristics of a third party, site selection, and the pros and cons of publicity in mediation. In this overview, however, only a few broad generalizations can be suggested.

First, different kinds of disputes obviously call for different methods of settlement. The craft of effective dispute settlement involves judging what method or combination of methods may be most useful in helping to resolve the particular dispute and how and when such techniques can best be employed. Among the factors affecting such a choice are

- the subject matter of the dispute;
- the characteristics of the dispute (for example, whether it involves a dispute about the facts, the law, what the law should be, the terms of a particular allocation, or procedural issues);
- the nature of the relationship between the parties (e.g., whether they are "repeat players" that have continuing relations with each other or only parties that infrequently have occasion to interact or deal with each other, and whether friendship and trust or enmity and distrust generally exist between them);
- the parties' perceptions and emotional attitudes concerning the importance of the dispute (e.g., whether it is considered a matter of "vital

interest" or national prestige, or whether either party feels it "cannot afford to lose");

- the history of this and other disputes between the parties (e.g., the stage of the dispute and extent to which positions have changed or hardened, and precedents as to how the parties have handled such problems in the past);
- the potential effect of the dispute on other states or the international community (e.g., whether it is a matter that might affect international peace and security);
- the availability or willingness of appropriate third parties to serve and the resources they are able or willing to deploy.

The second generalization is that the various techniques are not mutually exclusive, nor are the boundaries between them rigidly drawn. A number of them can be, and usually are, employed either seriatim (although in no fixed order) or in combination to supplement or complement each other. For example, the 1982 UN Convention on the Law of the Sea and the 1988 Convention on the Regulation of Antarctic Mineral Resource Activities, both of which used a variety of techniques to deal with diverse types of disputes, showed how these possibilities can be exploited innovatively and imaginatively. As Oscar Schachter has pointed out, "Flexibility and adaptability to the particular circumstances are the essential characteristics of these various procedures. There is little to be gained by seeking to give them precise legal limits or procedural rules as a general matter."[29]

Similarly, Judge Manfred Lachs, in his individual opinion in the 1978 *Aegean Sea Continental Shelf* case (Greece v. Turkey) commented as follows:

> There are obviously some disputes which can be resolved only by negotiations, because there is no alternative in view of the character of the subject-matter involved and the measures envisaged. But there are many other disputes in which a combination of methods would facilitate their resolution. The frequently unorthodox nature of the problems facing States today requires as many tools to be used and as many avenues to be opened as possible, in order to resolve the intricate and frequently multi-dimensional issues involved. It is sometimes desirable to apply several methods at the same time or successively. Thus, no incompatibility should be seen between the various instruments and fora to which States may resort, for all are mutually complementary.[30]

Third, it is often useful to develop structured institutions and arrangements, such as international courts or fact-finding agencies, and to have them in place, ready for use, and available if need should arise. In other cases, it may be better to deal with problems as they arise, on a pragmatic, flexible, and ad hoc basis, rather than to try to force dispute management efforts onto the Procrustean bed of some possibly unsuitable and inflexible already established dispute settlement institution.

Fourth, the choice of techniques and the way they are employed should, when relevant, take into account the particular dispute settlement experience of the states involved. Every bilateral or other international relationship has its own unique character and environment, which shape both the kinds of disputes that arise and the ways particular states tend to deal with them. Some states (for example, Canada and the United States) have developed special dispute management systems—a unique set of practices, procedures, techniques, and institutions—to deal with their particular quarrels.

Fifth, no specific list of techniques will exhaust the possibilities. Rather, the list will always be open to the disputing parties, or to third parties, to modify or adapt most of these techniques (except in the case of judicial settlement by an existing court with established rules), or to develop such additional methods as their needs and ingenuity suggest. Moreover, because every dispute or conflict will be unique, we must apply generalizations such as these, or particular "rules" or "formulas," with caution.

The Role of Adjudication

In view of current interest regarding the proper role of adjudication as a method of international dispute settlement, particularly in the wake of the ICJ's decision in the *Nicaragua* case, some remarks on this technique in particular may be appropriate. Again, it is not practical to review here the extensive literature analyzing the experience, procedures, role, and significance of international arbitral tribunals and courts, particularly the ICJ.[31] However, we can make several general suggestions.

As is true with respect to any method of dispute settlement, in deciding whether to use adjudication, the parties to a dispute will weigh its potential advantages against its disadvantages.[32] Potential advantages of adjudication include the following:

- As previously indicated, adjudication is dispositive. Ideally, at least, it puts an end to the dispute.
- It is impersonal, permitting the parties to pass responsibility for unfavorable outcomes to the tribunal.
- It is principled and impartial, ostensibly deciding the matter by neutral principles rather than power, bias, or whim.
- It is serious and demonstrates that the state instituting the suit really believes in its claim.
- It is orderly and can be useful in resolving complex factual and technical disputes.
- It can sometimes "depoliticize" a dispute, reducing tensions or buying time.

- It can provide rules socially useful for guiding conduct and resolving disputes more broadly.
- It can reflect and educate the community as to social values and interests of the international community more broadly, apart from those of the parties alone.
- It can be system reinforcing, supporting respect for and the development of international law.

Potential disadvantages of adjudication include the following:

- Adjudication involves the possibility of losing.
- Adjudicative settlement may be illusory or superficial, deciding the "legal" but not the "real" issues in dispute.
- It can be inflexible, resulting in a "win-lose" rather than a compromise decision.
- It can be judgmental, labeling one party as a "lawbreaker," rather than providing for a shared acceptance of responsibility as a face-saving way out of a conflict situation.
- It looks primarily to the past rather than to the future, possibly jeopardizing the maintenance of a useful ongoing relationship.
- It is conservative.
- Its results are unpredictable.
- It may not be impartial.
- It is imposed on the parties.
- It is adversarial and may escalate the dispute or conflict.
- It may freeze the parties' options and discourage settlement.
- It can be complex and costly.
- And finally, an adjudicative decision may or may not be enforceable.

As previously noted, adjudication has generally played only a limited role in the settlement of international disputes. Although nations often pay lip service to the ideal of judicial settlement, in practice they have entrusted relatively few significant disputes to international tribunals. Moreover, countries have been particularly reluctant to obligate themselves *in advance* to compulsory binding adjudication of their potential disputes with other countries—particularly disputes concerning issues that may involve what they consider "vital" national interests. In general, they have been willing to do so, at most, only when their commitment to such compulsory jurisdiction is restricted in terms of subject matter or otherwise carefully circumscribed.

I believe that this reluctance of states to submit disputes to arbitral or judicial settlement will continue for some time. Thus, for the near future at least, the prospects for widespread acceptance of the general compulsory jurisdiction of the ICJ, under the optional clause of Article 36(2) of the ICJ's statute, do not seem bright.[33] In particular, in the aftermath of the *Nicaragua* case, it seems unlikely that the United States will soon resume its acceptance of the optional clause, except possibly with very broad reservations— even though it appears to be in our national interest to do so.[34]

Although adjudication may not be the best way to resolve every dispute, there are clearly a number of situations in which adjudication, or at least the availability of adjudication, can perform a useful role in dispute settlement. In practice, most disputes do not involve issues of significant or "vital" national concerns. In such cases, although each party may prefer to "win" the dispute, the stakes involved are limited and each can afford to lose. Adjudication is one good way for the parties to achieve their most important objective in these situations—getting rid of the dispute. Indeed, to the extent that states can be assured that a commitment to adjudication will be restricted to less vital issues, they will be more willing to agree, even in advance, to adjudication. Thus, nations have frequently been willing to agree to compromissory clauses providing in advance for compulsory jurisdiction over disputes arising out of treaties concerned with specialized matters of clearly defined scope and limited import, such as commercial treaties.

Adjudication is likely to be particularly useful in three types of disputes:

- Disputes in which governments are indifferent to the outcome but, for internal political or other reasons, are unable to concede or even compromise the issue in negotiations (e.g., minor boundary disputes or substantively unimportant but emotionally volatile issues of title to small or insignificant areas of territory).
- Disputes involving difficult factual or technical questions in which the parties may be prepared for a compromise solution, but because of the complexity of the situation or because of internal political pressures, they cannot develop a basis for developing a workable compromise (e.g., again, certain complex boundary or maritime, continental shelf, or fishery resource zone delimitation issues).
- Some particularly awkward or dangerous disputes, in which resort to judicial settlement may be a politically acceptable way of buying time and containing a volatile situation while solutions are sought over time.

International tribunals, simply by being available, may help avoid, or may induce the settlement of, disputes. Even if states choose only infrequently to invoke the ICJ's jurisdiction under the optional or compromissory clauses in agreements, such commitments would not be useless. On the contrary, because each party to a dispute covered by such provisions knows that the other can resort to the ICJ, a party that wishes to avoid adjudication will have more incentive to reach a negotiated settlement. That is, when the parties have conferred potential jurisdiction on an international tribunal, their decisions and bargaining, like those of parties to domestic disputes, will be more likely to occur "in the shadow of the law." J.G. Merrills comments: "The value of arrangements for dispute settlement is not to be judged solely by the cases. For a provision for compulsory arbitration by its very existence can discourage unreasonable behavior and so may be useful even if it is never invoked."[35]

For many people throughout the world, international adjudication symbolizes civilized and ordered behavior and the rule of law in international affairs. Whatever the truth may be as to how the international legal system actually works, public judgments about the relevance and effectiveness of international law are at least in part based on whether the public sees international courts, particularly the ICJ, as playing a significant role in international dispute settlement. If many states, especially important ones, are willing to submit their disputes to impartial settlement and show respect for the ICJ, the public will assume that international law is in itself important and worthy of respect. In turn, the public will believe in and support international law. If, conversely, important states show indifference to or contempt for international adjudication and the ICJ, the public is likely to conclude that international law is meaningless and withdraw its support. Consequently, if a state believes that its national interest will be furthered by wider global respect for international law, it will arguably also have an interest in doing what it can to strengthen and support the role of international adjudication.

Even if the role of international adjudication is limited and there is no international court with general compulsory jurisdiction, there can still be effective dispute settlement and a workable international legal order. The international legal order is different from national legal orders in many respects, and it need not operate in exactly the same way.[36] Moreover, we are coming to realize that, even in the domestic legal system, adjudication plays a largely supplementary or "backup" role and that much of the work national courts do is, in effect, mediation or conciliation.[37]

In sum, because adjudication can be a particularly useful dispute settlement technique, it is important that it be kept at hand, easily available, and employed fully whenever its use is warranted. Even if adjudication is not a panacea for problems of world order, it makes sense to do all that we can to strengthen and encourage the greater use of judicial institutions, and to improve their ability to respond in flexible ways to nations' needs for dispute settlement.

The Soviet Union's recent apparent change of attitude and new receptiveness toward the compulsory jurisdiction of the ICJ, and toward multilateral conflict resolution techniques more generally, at least as stated in General Secretary Gorbachev's September 17, 1987, *Pravda* and *Izvestia* articles,[38] may represent a unique "window of opportunity" for strengthening international dispute management institutions, which the United States and other Western nations ought seriously to explore.

Some Limitations of Third-Party Dispute Settlement

Although third-party intervention is usually helpful and undertaken for benevolent motives, this may not always be the case.[39] Even well-meaning intervention may get in the way of or discourage the parties' own settlement efforts, making things worse rather than better. This may be particularly true when the intervention is premature or inept, or when the third party is an "officious meddler," butting into a situation without invitation and against the parties' wishes. But even if intervention is invited, things may somehow go wrong.

Third-party intervention will not necessarily produce a fair or stable settlement or outcome. Even when third-party intervention is ostensibly "neutral," it may have the effect of supporting the position and interests of one of the parties. Moreover, to the extent that intervention by third parties typically produces outcomes different from those that would have resulted from negotiations based on the effective power of the disputing states acting solely by themselves, the outcomes and "settlements" resulting from intervention may distort rather than reflect real underlying power relationships and be unstable. Indeed, when third parties artificially constrain real pressures, the result may be that over time the boiler will explode, producing even greater problems in the future.

As a corollary to the previous point, the possibility of third-party intervention may sometimes lead to or prolong disputes and conflicts by encouraging parties (particularly weaker ones) to be more aggressive or intransigent than they would otherwise dare to be. For example, it has been suggested that the Arab states have little reason to refrain from hostile actions against Israel, or to reach a definitive settlement with it, so long as they believe from experience that any severe Israeli sanctions or retaliation will always be nullified by UN or other third-party intervention.

Third-party intervention, or even its possibility in the future, can hinder or chill negotiations by encouraging an exaggeration or freezing of the parties' positions. Each will be aware of the tendency of mediators (and even arbitrators and judges) to split the difference and seek a compromise; consequently, rather than focusing on settling the matter themselves, they may seek to put themselves in the best position to "win" any third-party intervention.

In trying to help resolve a dispute or conflict, third parties can become enmeshed in it, thus widening, complicating, and prolonging the dispute. For example, one of the disputants may come to perceive the third party as really an ally or an enemy; may persuade, coerce, or trick it into taking sides; or may blackmail it into taking a continuing role in the dispute. In this event, the third party may become part of the problem rather than its solution.

Third parties often have their own interests at stake in intervening in a conflict or dispute, which may distort their settlement efforts or cause them to seek outcomes not in accord with the parties' desires or interests. Indeed, sometimes a third party may have a mischievous or malevolent purpose, seeking to prevent the conflict or dispute from being resolved or to keep the pot boiling to suit the third party's own purposes.

How Important Is Third-Party Dispute Settlement, and Does It Really Work?

It is difficult to measure precisely and objectively either the practical significance or the success of third-party dispute settlement. Clearly, any such judgments will vary with the situation under examination and the perspective of the observer. Moreover, in assessing importance or success, it may be necessary to answer the question, "third-party dispute settlement compared to what?" Four points can be made, however.

First, as indicated, most disputes are, and should be, settled through direct negotiations. Thus, third-party intervention will usually be less important, effective, or efficient than settlement directly by the parties themselves.

Second, although precise data are lacking, recent studies suggest that third-party intervention in international conflicts often plays a significant role—a result in accord with long human experience and intuition. In particular, there is evidence that, although third-party intervention does not always provide a final settlement to a conflict or dispute, it often seems to keep things from getting worse. For example, Bercovitch, analyzing data involving 310 conflicts between 1945 and 1974, found that in 235 or 82 percent of these conflicts, there was some form of official third-party intervention. This intervention was primarily in the form of mediation by the UN, and Berkovitch noted that in a substantial number of these situations, the intervention was useful in abating conflict.[40] In concluding that "third-party intervention seems to be an important method for managing international conflict," Berkovitch has this to say:

> Studies show that institutional third parties can be particularly useful in abating, insulating and restraining international conflict, though not in settling it. We do not know, however, whether conflicts in which the parties accept the intervention of an outsider are more, or less, likely to terminate in a settlement. Nor do we know whether a better, or even a similar outcome could not have been attained without the participation of a third party. Until we have some answers to these questions, third parties' contributions to successful outcomes should be kept in their proper, and critical, perspective.[41]

Similarly, Pruitt and Rubin conclude that, "in the last analysis,...third parties are enormously helpful and important in the reduction and resolution of differences."[42]

Certainly, there is much to be said for techniques that stop the parties from fighting and keep them talking, even if a definitive solution proves for the moment elusive. Sometimes, if matters can just be put on hold, time and changing attitudes, interests, and circumstances may provide opportunities for settlement not presently apparent.

Third, it is usually assumed, probably correctly, that third-party intervention is much more widely used in relatively "unimportant" rather than in "important" types of disputes. But it is also evident that third parties do, at least occasionally, help parties resolve "important" disputes. If third-party intervention is in fact useful in resolving a number of less important, and even a few important, disputes, it certainly seems to be performing a significant function, even if it cannot help in all disputes.

Fourth, regarding adjudication, it seems fair to conclude that despite the relatively small number of these cases—perhaps in all only several hundred intergovernmental arbitrations and fewer than eighty-five contentious cases in the World Court (thirty-three in the Permanent Court of International Justice and some fifty in the ICJ), many have involved disputes of considerable significance. Among these important cases are the *Alabama Claims, Bering Sea, North Atlantic Fisheries, Lake Lanoux, Island of Palmas, Trail Smelter, Rann of Kutch, Channel Islands,* and *Beagle Channel* arbitrations, and the *Gulf of Maine, North Sea Continental Shelf,* and *Iranian Hostage* cases. Moreover, these decisions have helped to establish principles and rules that have helped resolve or avoid other international disputes.

Summary and Recommendations

What is the proper role of third parties in managing international disputes, and what recommendations can be made to improve their usefulness?

First, negotiation between the parties themselves is the best way to deal with international disputes; usually the most important and useful contribution third parties can make is to assist this process. Consequently, efforts should be directed particularly to improving facilitative techniques such as mediation, fact-finding, and conciliation. The use of more directive techniques such as adjudication should be encouraged, but with awareness that arbitration and judicial settlement are likely to play only a limited role in international dispute settlement for some time to come.

Although third-party techniques may often be useful, we should avoid inflated expectations. For example, even the most skilled use of third-party techniques usually cannot succeed in bringing unwilling parties, who have fundamental differences, to agreement. But even if it does not bring about a final settlement, third-party intervention can be useful and "successful" simply by restraining or isolating conflict, buying time, or keeping a situation from getting worse.

Whereas it is certainly helpful to learn more about various methods of third-party intervention, such as mediation, and to improve our ability to use them effectively, we should not overemphasize the importance of mere technique or gimmicks. There are few secrets and little magic in successful dispute settlement. The crucial factor will continue to be whether the parties want—or can be persuaded to want—the dispute settled. The most important qualities of a third party will continue to be traditional, old-fashioned virtues—common sense, honesty, trustworthiness, patience, integrity, stamina, courage, intelligence, competence, sensitivity to the concerns of others, conscientiousness, impartiality, and goodwill. And luck always helps.

Also helpful are attempts to develop better dispute management systems between or among particular states or groups of states.[43] Dispute settlement is a complex process, in which a variety of techniques may appropriately be used. Each international relationship is unique and may require its own special approach or mix. Thus, the United States and Canada historically have developed and may be able to use one type of dispute management system, whereas Soviet-American relationships may appropriately call for a completely different kind of system.

In thinking about dispute settlement, however, we must not forget the importance of doing more to avoid disputes. Thus, the development and improvement of arrangements and mechanisms designed to keep disputes from occurring and to permit them to be dealt with at an early stage, before political interests become vested, emotions become involved, or positions harden, is important.[44] Such dispute avoidance measures might include prior agreement on clear rules and workable arrangements, prior notification and consultation, and the establishment of ad hoc or permanent binational commissions or joint agencies.

Also, sensitivity to the relevance of particular cultural attitudes and responses toward conflict and dispute settlement of the parties involved in a dispute should be increased. Such cultural perspectives should be taken into account when deciding on the appropriateness of different approaches or techniques. For example, Chinese, Japanese, and certain other non-Western societies appear traditionally to have given particular emphasis to nonadversarial techniques of mediation and mutual accommodation as a way of dealing with disputes; they have been particularly reluctant to use adjudication or other adversarial or "legally oriented" methods. Similarly, different societies may have different perspectives regarding the types of persons most worthy of respect and trust and most suitable to perform third-party roles; thus, in some cultures, eminent lawyers may be appropriate mediators or dispute resolvers, while in others, political or religious leaders may be more suitable.

At the same time, we must continue to study possibilities for improving old third-party institutions and procedures and developing new ones. Clearly, there is much to be said for having institutions or procedures in place, more easily available to parties if they wish to use them—although it is open to question whether new institutions in themselves will make much difference without some change in underlying state attitudes. Certainly, one of the most important things we can do is to foster an international atmosphere in which third-party intervention and efforts to promote peaceful settlement of disputes are considered routine, appropriate, legitimate, and acceptable. Some ideas worth exploring are as follows.

First, expand the availability and use of nonbinding conciliation processes and of the advisory jurisdiction of international tribunals. As indicated, governments have been reluctant to accept binding judicial settlement because they view legally binding judgments as posing special risks—even though their fears may be unrealistic. Conciliation and advisory or nonbinding adjudication, in contrast, can offer many advantages of impartial third-party factual and legal determination while reducing some of its most significant risks. In many cases, a recommendation or an advisory decision may actually provide a mutually acceptable basis for resolution of the dispute; however, each party will have the assurance that, should its worst fears be realized and the decision prove unacceptable, it can legally refuse to comply, incurring only limited public relations costs. Although binding adjudication may be preferable in principle, nonbinding conciliation or adjudication may be the most that one or both parties will agree to in some situations. In that event, it is better than nothing. The experience of the newly formed Inter-American Court of Human Rights with advisory jurisdiction, which has been successful so far, appears to bear out this statement.[45]

Second, develop a wider, more easily available, and more credible array of international fact-finding, monitoring, and verification facilities. For example, proposals have been made in the UN for the development of permanent fact-finding institutions, and even for the establishment of the International Satellite Monitoring Agency to help verify arms control or similar agreements. I have elsewhere suggested the possibility of establishing an essentially independent and neutral entity—a "Facility for International Risk Management"—outside the UN framework and free of direct government control, which would be available to states, at their request and with their sharing of costs, to perform verification, monitoring, escrow, or other risk management functions. Such a facility might take the form of an international corporation or a nongovernmental organization, such as the International Committee of the Red Cross.[46]

Third, explore ways of making international adjudication, and in particular the ICJ, more acceptable, accessible, and flexible.[47] As indicated, any substantial change in the willingness of states to use international adjudication or the ICJ is likely to require a fundamental change in their attitudes and in their willingness to face the risks inherent in binding third-party dispute settlement techniques. But some procedural innovations may help. For example, the recent expansion of the availability and use of the ICJ's chamber procedure is a useful step in this direction.[48] Louis Sohn's proposal for step-by-step acceptance of the ICJ's compulsory jurisdiction—the idea of slicing or fractionating types or degrees of commitment to adjudication into less risky and more acceptable packages—is another innovative suggestion.[49] Among others that have been made and debated are

- permitting wider access to the ICJ or other international courts by international organizations, nongovernmental organizations, or even individuals;
- restricting the types of reservations that can be made to acceptance of the compulsory jurisdiction of the ICJ under the "optional clause";
- completely discarding the concept of compulsory jurisdiction; and
- expanding the "law" the ICJ can draw on under Article 38 of its statute to include UN General Assembly declarations.

We might consider whether at least some of the so-called alternative dispute resolution techniques, such as "minitrials," currently being discussed and experimented with in the U.S. and some other national legal systems, are applicable to international problems and worth exploring.

Fourth, strengthen the ability of third parties in appropriate situations to intervene on a temporary basis in disputes and conflicts simply to keep matters from getting worse. Provide time or a "waiting period" in which the disputing states or third parties can seek solutions. Precedents include the power of the ICJ, under Article 41 of its statute, "to indicate, if it considers that circumstances so require, any provisional measures which ought to be taken to preserve the respective rights of either party," as well as the activities of various UN peacekeeping forces. We should explore whether there might be additional ways of temporarily restraining and preventing escalation of disputes to permit time and opportunity for settlement.

Fifth, develop ways of better using national legal systems to implement international dispute management objectives. Proposals to allow the ICJ to give advisory opinions to national courts on questions of international law would be an interesting step in this direction.[50] Other possibilities are agreements facilitating access to national courts or agencies by alien individuals, corporations, or even foreign governments seeking domestic remedies for particular kinds of transnational problems, such as transfrontier pollution disputes; or an agreement, similar to the New York Arbitration Convention, expressly providing for implementation by a respondent state and third states of the obligation of states under the UN Charter to comply with a judgment of the ICJ.

We should give more emphasis and support to innovative research about the international dispute process and techniques of international dispute management and settlement, particularly empirical and interdisciplinary studies.[51] This research should include investigations of the broad, underlying questions concerning the causes, characteristics, and "life cycle" of disputes noted at the beginning of this chapter. Particular questions relevant to third-party dispute settlement that might merit more attention and additional research include the following:

- What factors influence disputing states and perceptions of the acceptability, authority, and persuasiveness of third parties? What qualities really are most important? In particular, what do we mean by "neutrality," "impartiality," or "lack of bias"? How important are perceptions about the neutrality of third parties to the success of their efforts, and how can we best ensure that third parties are in fact neutral and unbiased? Even though every human being, inevitably, may have biases, cannot people still be counted on to perform conscientiously in roles that require them to act "neutrally"? How can we strengthen such traditions? What are the pros and cons of using an international institution, such as the UN, in a third-party role, in contrast to a state or individual?

- What do we mean by "settlement of a dispute" or an "acceptable outcome"? In particular, what affects the parties' perceptions as to the equity or fairness of a particular outcome? Is fairness primarily substantive or procedural? Against what baselines or by what criteria are the parties likely to judge it, and how can we best achieve it? More generally, how can we best define or measure the *quality* of dispute resolution processes and outcomes?

- Can we say anything about when is the "right time" for various types of intervention? How important are interpersonal relations between individual participants in settlement processes? Can nongovernmental organizations play a more useful role in dispute settlement?

- How can disputing parties best protect themselves against improper, overreaching, or counterproductive interference by a third party? How can a third party best protect itself from becoming enmeshed or blackmailed in the dispute?

- What affects third-party perceptions of the legitimacy and persuasiveness of the disputing parties' positions? Is there a difference between the type of argumentation the parties use in negotiation to try to persuade each other, and the type of argumentation they use in third-party contexts to try to persuade the third party?

- What role do international law, generalized norms, or general "public opinion" and the attitude of third parties play in dispute resolution? What does "social pressure" mean, and how does, or can, it affect dispute resolution processes? Are perceptions of legitimacy relevant only to adjudication or other "legal" techniques of settlement, or do they affect nonadjudicative methods of third-party settlement as well?

- In what kind of cases is it important to successful intervention that the third party be able to provide specific resources, particularly resources to help the parties manage the risks of potential settlement arrangements? How can such resources be made more available?

- What do we mean by "face"—the quality of respect or reputation that states (and officials) seem so concerned with "losing" by giving in to settlements? How can we reduce the obstructive influence of such considerations on settlement efforts?
- What is the effect of "trust" and "distrust" on dispute settlement efforts, and how can third parties help disputing states to overcome or counterbalance distrust?
- Is it desirable or undesirable for a third party to be "powerful" or have some independent basis of influence over the disputing parties? More generally, what is the role of power or force in third-party settlement? Can there be an appropriate role for "creative coercion"?
- In what respects do mediators or conciliators behave differently from adjudicators or judges? What makes them act and see their roles as different? What do the parties, or the "general public," expect of third parties entrusted with these different roles?
- How can third parties better contribute to the settlement of the complex and pervasive internal racial, ethnic, and religious strife that increasingly threatens international order (e.g., in South Africa, the Middle East, Cyprus, Northern Ireland, Sri Lanka, and elsewhere)? Clearly, it is becoming increasingly difficult to draw sharp lines between international (or external) and domestic (or internal) disputes. Do we need to develop new approaches or ways of thinking to help us to deal effectively with these "mixed" or "transnational" kinds of disputes?

In conclusion, the international community should be more assertive in insisting that parties accept third-party intervention in disputes that threaten international peace and security or, indeed, the international community's general welfare. It is now widely recognized that, for better or worse, the world has become an interdependent community and that serious disputes and conflict are now everyone's business. The idea that states are free to conduct their quarrels however they wish and without regard to the cost to others is outdated and has no place in a nuclear age.

We also should not forget that international third-party dispute settlement has symbolic significance as well as practical importance. The concept that disputes and conflicts within a group are not simply the business of those directly involved, but are concerns of every member, is at the root of civilized and ordered society. Consequently, third-party dispute settlement and institutions such as the ICJ, which implement its use, can encourage growing perceptions of international community and play a crucial role in the development of a more peaceful, just, and decent world.

Discussion

Jeffrey Rubin suggested that third-party intervention in international conflict is but a minor aspect in a much larger mosaic. Much of what is known today about this topic is the direct result of research and practice in areas such as divorce mediation, labor relations, community relations, and the increasing role of ombudsmen. But Rubin was considerably less optimistic than Bilder about the application of this increasingly large body of knowledge to international relations. The problem, Rubin said, was that nation-states may feel little or no need to go along with suggestions of third parties for resolving a conflict, and that such reluctance often leads to protracted and worsening crises.

When third-party intervention in relations between states works, Rubin said, it does so not because it imposes a binding settlement, but because it provides sound advice to the disputants as to how best they can resolve their differences in the prenegotiation phase of the dispute.

The paradox that third parties often encounter in international relations, however, is that their services are least likely to be utilized precisely where they are most needed. Third parties that try to facilitate political solutions in regions where political cohesion is lacking are usually frustrated in their efforts. Conversely, if regional and political conditions tangential to the conflict in question are suitable and all parties really desire to resolve the crisis at hand, a third party can assist that effort in a number of ways: it can encourage the disputants to come to the negotiating table, create a "hurting stalemate" that makes moving forward more attractive, clarify what both sides really need as opposed to what they want, and suggest procedures for ensuring implementation and follow-up of any signed agreements.

Third parties are limited in what they can do primarily by the willingness of the disputing parties to end the conflict and by the overall political conditions in the area of the conflict writ large. Internationally adjudicated and suggested third-party settlements lack the legal weight of enforcement that their domestic counterparts rely on and are therefore much more likely to fail as a result of outside pressure or the recalcitrance of one or more of the primary disputants.

In the discussion, Lawrence Chickering asked about the extent to which the formal, legal, and rational model of third-party dispute settlement is at odds with the less formal, emotional, and social scientific approach. Both panelists agreed that the issue is not a matter of friction so much as it is one of application. There are no ironclad rules as to the best methodology to adopt, nor are there formulas by which to determine who the most appropriate third party would be in any given case. The real advantage of third-party settlement lies in its flexibility to adapt to changing conditions.

Francis Deng suggested that cultural considerations play an important role in the choice of a third party, and that failure to recognize this results in unnecessary complications. Bilder agreed, with the qualification that it is important not to overemphasize the intuitive limitations that acceptance of this point places on objective third-party selection. Citing the example of wide-ranging Canadian-American dispute resolution efforts, Bilder noted that successful interventions have often been undertaken by citizens of one or both countries. This fact was instructive, he said, because it flew in the face of the conventional wisdom that appropriate third parties, by definition, cannot be nationals of the disputing countries. He said that almost anybody, with the proper tools, can serve as a third-party mediator.

This point was disputed by Maire Dugan, who argued that for a third party to be effective it must have no vested interest in the outcome of the dispute under consideration. Rubin responded that, although such a party might be found in the domestic realm of third-party settlement, there is no such entity in international relations. Every state, and every representative thereof, has a vested interest in seeing international conflict reduced. Given this assumption, the question becomes how to use that interest in the service of reaching an equitable and reasonable solution.

This point was further emphasized by Samuel Lewis, who said that in many instances, it is precisely because a potential third party has an acknowledged vested interest in the conflict at issue that the party is sought out. This is particularly true regarding the United States and is most clearly shown in the case of the Camp David Accords. Not only was the United States perceived as the only party with the requisite political strength to undertake such an awesome task, but the perceived pro-Israeli bias of past U.S. policy dramatically increased the pressure on President Carter and his subordinates to behave in an evenhanded fashion. This was a clear case of a third party with vested interests acting more impartially than was thought possible in the abstract. Furthermore, Lewis said, the history of the UN in providing impartial mediators to act as third parties has been terribly uneven and supports the hypothesis that powerful and influential mediators are not only appropriate but are usually indispensable on the international level.

Notes

1. Certain parts of this paper draw upon my two articles on dispute settlement and adjudication recently published in the *Emory Journal of International Dispute Resolution* and cited in the bibliography.

2. See particularly references cited in the first paragraph of the bibliography.

3. 1984 *ICJ Report* 392 (Judgment of Nov. 26, 1984 on Jurisdiction and Admissibility), 231 *I.L.M.* 468 (1984); 1986 *ICJ Report* 14 (Judgment of June 27, 1986 on Merits), 25 *I.L.M.* 1023 (1986). Among the many articles analyzing and discussing the decision and various aspects of the case, see articles and comments in 79 *Am. J. Int'l L.* pp. 373–404, 423–30, 652–63, and 992–1004 (1985) (dealing with jurisdictional phase), and 81 ibid. pp. 77–183 (Jan. 1987) (dealing with merits); Abram Chayes, "Nicaragua, the United States and the World Court," 85 *Colum. L. Rev.* 1445 (1985);

John Norton Moore, "The Secret War in Central America and the Future of World Order," 80 *Am. J. Int'l L.* 24 (1980); W. Michael Reisman, "Has the International Court Exceeded Its Jurisdiction?" 80 *Am. J. Int'l L.* 128 (1986).

4. See Secretary of State Shultz's letter to UN Secretary General, October 7, 1985; U.S. Department of State statement of Oct. 7, 1985; and Legal Adviser A. Sofaer's statement of December 4, 1985, all reproduced in 86 *U.S. State Dept. Bull.* No. 2106 p. 67 (January 1986) and 24 *I.L.M.* 1742 (1985).

5. See the references cited in the third paragraph of the bibliography.

6. For a discussion of some of these broader issues, see R. B. Bilder, "An Overview of International Dispute Settlement," 1 *Emory J. of Int'l Dispute Res.* 1 (1986).

7. Based upon D. G. Pruitt and J. Z. Rubin, *Social Conflict*, pp. 165–66.

8. See R. B. Bilder, *When Neighbors Quarrel: Canada-U.S. Dispute Settlement Experience* (the 1986–87 Claude T. Bissell Lectures, University of Toronto), Institute for Legal Studies, University of Wisconsin Law School, Disputes Processing Research Program Working Paper (DPRP) 8:4 (May 1987).

9. J. Bercovitch, *Social Conflicts and Third Parties*, p. 13, citing Michael Harbottle, "The Strategy of Third-Party Intervention in Conflict Resolution," 35 *Int'l. Journal* 118 (1979–80), p. 120.

10. O. Young, *Intermediaries*, p. 34.

11. See generally R. B. Bilder (1986), *supra* note 6, pp. 7–13. See also Louis Henkin et al., *International Law*, p. 910: "As long as a State does not resort to force, there has been no disposition to find a violation of law in failure to settle disputes peacefully, as by leaving them unsettled." Also see *Restatement*, bibliography, 902, comment (e): "It is well established in international law that no State can, without its consent, be compelled to submit its disputes with other states either to mediation or to arbitration, or to any other kind of pacific settlement." Eastern Carelia (*Finland* v. *Russia*), 1923 PCIJ, ser. B, No. 5, p. 27 (Advisory Opinion of July 23). Consequently, international claims "cannot, in the present state of the law as to international jurisdiction, be submitted to a tribunal, except with the consent of the States concerned." Reparation for Injuries, 1949 *ICJ Report* 177–78 (Advisory Opinion of April 11).

As to arbitration, see also the *Ambatielos* case, (Greece v. U.K.) 1953 *ICJ Report* 10, 19 (Judgment of May 19) ("a State may not be compelled to submit its disputes to arbitration without its consent").

12. See UN Charter articles 1(1), 2(3), 33; ch. 6 (articles 33–38); and ch. 7 (articles 39–51).

13. For example, there are some 250 agreements, bilateral and multilateral, conferring on the ICJ jurisdiction over disputes as to the interpretation or application of the agreements. See 1983–84 ICJ Y.B. 51–56, 92–108 (1984). See generally, Louis B. Sohn, "Settlement of Disputes Relating to the Interpretation and Application of Treaties," 150 *Recueil des Cours* (Hague Academy: 1976); and Fred L. Morrison, "Treaties as a Source of Jurisdiction for the International Court of Justice" in Lori F. Damrosch, ed., *The International Court of Justice At A Crossroads* (1987). Many additional agreements contain provisions for dispute settlement by means other than reference to the World Court. See L. Sohn, *Structure and Process of International Law*, and United Nations, *A Survey of Treaty Provisions for the Pacific Settlement of International Disputes* 1949–62 (1966).

14. L. Sohn, *Structure and Process of International Law*, p. 1122.

15. For an interesting discussion of such "latent" functions of adjudication, see Robert E. Hudec, "Transcending the Ostensible: Some Reflections on the Nature of Litigation Between Governments," 72 *Minn. L. Rev.* 211 (1987).

16. See J. G. Merrills, *International Dispute Settlement*, ch. 1; H. G. Darwin, "Mediation and Good Offices," in H. Waldock, *International Disputes*, p. 83; V. K. Raman, *Dispute Settlement*, ch. 3; and, generally, O. Young, *The Intermediaries: Third Parties in International Crises* (1967).

17. See J. G. Merrills, *International Dispute Settlement*, ch. 3 and 4; Fox, "Conciliation," in H. Waldock, *International Disputes*, p. 159; Nissim Bar-Yaacov, *The Handling of International Disputes by Means of Inquiry* (1974); Jean Pierre Cot, *International Conciliation* (1972); Firmage, "Fact-Finding in the Resolution of International Disputes: From the Hague Peace Conference to the United Nations," 1971 *Utah L. Rev.* 421.

18. See J. G. Merrills, *International Dispute Settlement*, ch. 5; Fox, "Arbitration," in H. Waldock, *International Disputes*, p. 101; Gillis J. Wetter, *The International Arbitral Process Public and Private* (1979); Stephen Schwebel, *International Arbitration: Three Salient Problems* (1987); Simpson and Fox, *International Arbitration* (1959); L. Sohn, "The Function of International Arbitration Today," 1 *Recueil des Cours* 108 (1963); Kenneth S. Carlston, *The Process of International Arbitration* (1946).

19. See J. G. Merrills, *International Dispute Settlement*, ch. 6; R. B. Bilder, "International Dispute Settlement and the Role of International Adjudication," 1 *Emory J. Intl. Dispute Res.* 131 (1987); Lori F. Damrosch, ed., *The International Court of Justice at a Crossroads* (1987); Thomas M. Franck, *Judging the World Court* (1986); Richard Falk, *Reviving the World Court* (1986); R. B. Bilder, "Some Limitations of Adjudication as an International Dispute Settlement Technique," 23 *Va. J. Intl. L.* 1 (1982); Allott, "The International Court of Justice," in H. Waldock, *supra* note 2, p. 128; Shabtai Rosenne, *The World Court*, 3d ed. (1973); S. Rosenne, *The Law and Practice of the International Court* (1965); W. Jenks, *The Prospects of International Adjudication* (1964); the excellent collections of articles in *The Future of the Internatinal Court of Justice*, ed. Leo Gross, 2 vols. (1976); and *Judicial Settlement of International Disputes*, ed. H. Mosler and R. Bernhardt (1979); O. Schachter, L. Sohn, references cited in notes 32 and 34, respectively, and the many additional articles cited in these works.

For a listing and brief description of the various present international courts, see L. Sohn, pp. 1127–30.

20. See J. G. Merrills, *International Dispute Settlement*, ch. 8 and 9; Derek W. Bowett, "The United Nations and Peaceful Settlement," in H. Waldock, *International Disputes*, p. 179; and V.K. Raman, *Dispute Settlement*.

Some international agreements empower the organizations established by them to render a binding decision. See *Restatement*, 902, Rept.'s Note 6, 176. See also L. Sohn.

21. Pruitt and Rubin, *Social Conflict*, pp. 166–69.

22. Pruitt and Rubin, *Social Conflict*, p. 165.

23. Pruitt and Rubin, *Social Conflict*, pp. 169–79.

24. J. Bercovitch, *supra* note 20, chapter 5, esp. pp. 96–108.

25. O. Young, in the bibliography, and O. Young, "Intermediaries: Additional Thoughts on Third Parties," 16 *J. Confl. Res.* 51 (1972).

26. See R. B. Bilder, *Managing the Risks of International Agreement* (1981).

27. See references in the bibliography. For excellent brief evaluations of various techniques from an international lawyer's perspective, see especially J.G. Merrills, *International Dispute Settlement.*

28. Merrills, *International Dispute Settlement,* p. 66.

29. O. Schachter, p. 205.

30. 1978 *ICJ Report* 52 (19 December 1978).

31. See R. B. Bilder, "International Dispute Settlement and the Role of Adjudication," 1 *Emory J. Int'l Dispute Res.* 131 (1987), and other references in the bibliography and in note 19.

32. For discussion of the advantages and disadvantages of adjudication, reasons why states may be reluctant to accept adjudication and, in particular, the compulsory jurisdiction of the ICJ, see R. B. Bilder, *Emory J. Int'l Dispute Res.,* pp. 144–65; Thomas M. Franck, *Judging the World Court* (1986); O. Schachter, pp. 207–11; I.A. Vallat, *Foreword* in H. Waldock, *International Disputes;* J. G. Merrills, *International Dispute Settlement,* pp. 107–13; F. S. Northedge and M. D. Donelon, pp. 321–29; Leo Gross, especially R. P. Anand, "Role of International Adjudication," and Rovine, "The National Interest and the World Court"; Robert E. Hudec, "Transcending the Ostensible: Some Reflections on the Nature of Litigation Between Governments," 72 *Minn. L. Rev.* (1987); Rosalyn Higgins, "The Desirability of Third Party Adjudication: Conventional Wisdom or Continuing Truth?," in *International Organization: Law in Movement* 37, ed. J. E. Fawcett and Rosalyn Higgins, (1974); Manfred Lachs, "After Thoughts on the Independence of Judges of the International Court of Justice," 25 *Colum. J. Transnat'l L.* 593 (1987); Owen, "Compulsory Jurisdiction of the International Court of Justice: A Study of Its Acceptance by Nations," 3 *Ga. L. Rev.* 704 (1969); Shihata, "The Attitude of New States Toward the International Court of Justice" 19 *Int'l. Org.* 203 (1965); J. Gamble and D. Fisher, *The International Court of Justice (1975); Dalfen, "The World Court in Idle Splendour: The Basis of State Attitudes,"* 23 *Int'l J.* 124 (1967); Brauer, "International Conflict Resolution: The ICJ Chambers and the Gulf of Maine Dispute," 23 *Va. J. Int'l L.* 463, 468–73 (1983); Charles de Visscher, "Reflections on the Present Prospects of International Adjudication," 50 *Am. J. Int'l L.* 467 (1956); Edward McWhinney, *The World Court and the Contemporary International Law-Making Process* (1979); Richard Falk, "The Role of the International Court of Justice," 37 *J. Int'l Affairs* 253 (1984); R. Falk, *Reviving the World Court* (1986); W. Jenks, *The Prospects of International Adjudication* (1964); and generally other sources cited in the bibliography and in note 19.

As indicated, explanations of why states are generally reluctant to agree to adjudicative, or "legal," techniques of dispute settlement often emphasize states' lack of confidence in the predictability of such procedures and their concern over their loss of control over outcomes. See Derek W. Bowett, "Contemporary Developments in Legal Techniques in the Settlement of Disputes," Hague Academy of International Law, 180 *Recueil des Cours* 177 (1983-II), p. 181: Although specific reasons change from state to state, the basic reason for avoiding legal settlement is simply that states prefer to retain control over the settlement process, so as to ensure that any settlement is acceptable to them, or, if that cannot be achieved, that no settlement is reached. With the political techniques they retain such control—though this is less true when the pressures of United Nations organs are brought to bear—whereas with legal techniques, states evidently feel that they lose control.

Some commentators suggest a distinction between so-called legal or justiciable disputes, on the one hand, and political, nonlegal, or nonjusticiable disputes, on the other; the implication is that some disputes have inherent characteristics that make them either particularly appropriate or inappropriate for the use of adjudication as a dispute settlement technique. Others commentators, including myself, believe that, although state attitudes toward accepting the risks of adjudication and the usefulness of adjudication will obviously differ in different circumstances, in principle *all* international disputes are "justiciable." See R. B. Bilder (1986), pp. 15–17. For discussion, see O. Schachter, pp. 211–15 and O. Schachter, "Compulsory Jurisdiction in Cases Involving the Use of Force" in L. Damrosch; Louis Henkin et al., 829–31; H. G. Darwin, "General Introduction" in H. Waldock, *International Disputes*, pp. 6–13; *Restatement*, 903, Rpts. Note 7; J. Gamble and D. Fischer, p. 20.

33. For comprehensive reviews and analysis of experience respecting the ICJ's compulsory jurisdiction (the so-called optional clause of Article 36(2) of the ICJ statute), see Lori Damrosch, ed., *The International Court of Justice at a Crossroads* (1987); J. G. Merrills, "The Optional Clause Today," 1979 *Brit. Y.B.I.L.* 87; Giustini, "Compulsory Adjudication of International Law: The Past, the Present and Prospects for the Future," 9 *Fordham Int'l L.J.* 213 (1985–86); Scott and Carr, "The International Court of Justice and Compulsory Jurisdiction: The Case for Closing the Clause," 81 *Am. J. Int'l L.* 57 (1987). On the ICJ jurisdiction under compromissory clauses, see Charney, "Compromissory Clauses and the Jurisdiction of the International Court of Justice," 81 *Am. Int'l L.* 855 (1987).

34. For recent discussions of U.S. attitudes regarding international adjudication and the ICJ's compulsory jurisdiction, see Lori Damrosch; Thomas M. Franck, *Judging the World Court* (1986); Symposium 81 *Am. J. Intl. L.* 1 (1987).

Suggestions have been made for various types of reservations to meet the administration's concerns and to permit resumed U.S. acceptance of the compulsory jurisdiction of the ICJ. Some proposals would exclude from ICJ jurisdiction matters involving national security or the use of force, matters referred to other dispute-resolution procedures, or matters under consideration by the UN Security Council; some proposals would exclude jurisdiction when the applicant party's declaration of acceptance of the ICJ's compulsory jurisdiction was made for the purpose of filing the individual suit; and some would provide for the possibility of denunciation of U.S. acceptance, taking effect immediately. Suggestions have also been made to modify or eliminate certain U.S. reservations in its 1946 declaration of acceptance, particularly the multilateral treaty (Vandenberg) reservation and the "self-judging" domestic jurisdiction (Connally) reservation. See, for example, Damrosch; Louis B. Sohn, "Suggestions for the Limited Acceptance of Compulsory Jurisdiction of the International Court of Justice by the United States," 18 *Georgia J. of Int'l and Comp. L.* 1 (1988); Anthony D'Amato, "Modifying U.S. Acceptance of the Compulsory Jurisdiction of the World Court," 79 *Am. J. Int'l L.* 385 (1985); D'Amato, "The U.S. Should Accept by a New Declaration, the General Compulsory Jurisdiction for the World Court," 80 *Am. J. Int'l L.* 331 (1986); Gardner, "U.S. Termination of the Compulsory Jurisdiction of the International Court of Justice," 24 *Colum. J. Transnat'l L.* 421 (1986); Morrison, "Reconsidering United States Acceptance of the Compulsory Jurisdiction of the International Court of Justice," 148 *World Affairs* 63 (1985); Comment, "Reaccepting the Compulsory Jurisdiction of the International Court of Justice: A Proposal for a New United States Declaration," 61 *Wash. L. Rev.* 1145 (1986).

35. J. G. Merrills, *International Dispute Settlement*, p. 88.

In this context, it is amusing to compare an ancient Chinese suggestion that a good way to encourage dispute settlement by the parties themselves is to provide only very *bad* courts. The 7th century Emperor K'ang Hsi is reported to have said: "Lawsuits would tend to increase to a frightful amount, if people were not afraid of the tribunals, and if they felt confident of always finding in them ready and perfect justice. As man is apt to delude himself concerning his own interests, contests would then be interminable, and the half of the Empire would not suffice to settle the lawsuits of the other half. I desire, therefore, that those who have recourse to the tribunals should be treated without any pity, and in such a manner that they shall be disgusted with law, and tremble to appear before a magistrate."

See Rene David and John E. Brierly, *Major Legal Systems in the World Today* (1978), p. 480; Sybille Van Der Sprenkel, *Legal Institutions in Manchu China* (1962), p. 77.

36. See discussion in R. B. Bilder (1987); Allott, in H. Waldock, *International Disputes*, pp. 128–32; O. Schachter, ch. III and pp. 207–11.

37. See references on dispute processing in the United States cited in the bibliography, and, particularly, M. Galanter, (1986) and (1983).

38. Mikhail Gorbachev, "The Realities and Guarantees of a Secure World," published in *Pravda* and *Izvestia* on September 17, 1987, USSR Mission to the UN Press Release No. 119, September 17, 1987, suggests that the ICJ's "mandatory jurisdiction should be recognized by all on mutually agreed conditions," that "the permanent members of the Security Council, taking into account their special responsibility, are to make the first step in that direction," and that "the international community should encourage the UN Secretary General in his missions of good offices, mediation and reconciliation" (pp. 11–12).

39. See also Pruitt and Rubin, *Social Conflict*, pp. 179–82.

40. Bercovitch, pp. 92–93 and 113–15, using data from Robert L. Butterworth.

41. Bercovitch, pp. 113–15.

42. Pruitt and Rubin, *Social Conflict*, p. 179.

43. See R. B. Bilder, *When Neighbors Quarrel: Canada-U.S. Dispute Settlement Experience* (1987).

44. See R. B. Bilder, pp. 29–31; Frederic L. Kirgis, *Prior Consultation in International Law: A Study of State Practice* (1983).

45. See Thomas Buergenthal, "The Advisory Practice of the Inter-American Court of Human Rights," 79 *Am. J. Int'l L.* 1 (1985); and, more generally, for arguments for more pragmatic, flexible, and nonbinding types of risk management and dispute resolution arrangements, R. B. Bilder, *Managing the Risks of International Agreement* (1981).

46. See R. B. Bilder, "An Institution to Monitor Treaties," *International Practitioner's Notebook*, Amer. Branch, Int'l Law Assoc., No. 18, April 1982, p. 13 and *Milwaukee Journal*, Part 9, March 14, 1982.

47. For recent discussions of the ICJ and suggestions for broadening its role, see the references cited in the bibliography and notes 19 and 32, and also Allott, pp. 134–58; Leo Gross, "The International Court of Justice: Consideration of Requirements for Enhancing its Role in the International Legal Order," 65 *Am. J. Int'l L.* 253 (1971); L. Sohn; U.S. Department of State, "Study on Widening Access to the International Court of Justice" (1976), reprinted in *Digest of U.S. Practice in International Law* 650, ed. Mcdowell (1976); Cornelius Murphy, "The World Court and the Peaceful Settlement of International Disputes," 7 *Ga. J. Int'l & Comp. L.* 551 (1977); Andrew Dillard, "The World Court: Reflections of a Professor Turned Judge," 27

Am. U.L. Rev. 205 (1978); Petren, "Some Thoughts on the Future of the International Court of Justice," 6 *Neth. Y.B.I.L.* 59 (1975).

48. See Stephen Schwebel, "Ad Hoc Chambers of the International Court of Justice," 81 *Am. J. Int'l L.* 831 (1987).

49. L. Sohn, "Step-by-Step Acceptance of the Jurisdiction of the International Court of Justice," 58 *A.S.I.L. Proc.* 131 (1964).

50. See Schwebel, "Preliminary Rulings by the International Court of Justice at the Instance of National Courts," 28 *Va. J. Int'l L.* 495 (1988); L. Gross, *Am. J. Int'l. L.* 253; L. Sohn, "Broadening the Advisory Jurisdiction of the International Court of Justice," 77 *Am. J. Int'l L.* 124 (1983); Goldklang, "House Approves Proposal Permitting ICJ to Advise Domestic Courts," 77 *Am. J. Int'l. L.* 338 (1983); McLaughlin, "Allowing Federal Courts Access to International Court of Justice Advisory Opinions: Critique and Proposal," 6 *Hastings Int'l & Comp. L. Rev.* 745 (1983).

51. For lists of academic and other study programs, institutes, and organizations involved in research relating to conflict resolution and dispute settlement, see Institute for World Order, *Peace and World Order Studies: A Curriculum Guide*, 3d ed. 1981), pp. 373–86. A number of these organizations, such as the Program on Negotiation at Harvard Law School and its Harvard Negotiation Project, expressly adopt an interdisciplinary approach. There is a need, in particular, to integrate the insights of legal and of social science research in this respect, and to provide more occasions for lawyers and social scientists interested in these problems to talk and work together.

Bibliography

For legally oriented overviews of international dispute settlement, see Richard B. Bilder, "An Overview of International Dispute Settlement," 1 *Emory Journal of International Dispute Resolution* 1 (1986); R. B. Bilder, "International Dispute Settlement and the Role of Adjudication," 1 *Emory J. Int'l Dispute Res.* 131 (1987); J. G. Merrills, *International Dispute Settlement* (1984); *International Disputes: The Legal Aspects*, A Report of a Study Group of David Davies Memorial Institute, ed. Humphrey Waldock (1972) (with supporting individual studies); F. S. Northedge and M. D. Donelan, *International Disputes: The Political Aspects* (David Davies Memorial Institute, 1971); Oscar Schachter, "International Law in Theory and Practice," 178 *Recueil des Cours* 10, esp. ch. III, X, XI; Louis B. Sohn, "The Future of Dispute Settlement" in *The Structure and Process of International Law: Essays in Legal Philosophy, Doctrines and Theory* 1121, ed. Ronald S. MacDonald and Douglas M. Johnston (1983); Derek W. Bowett, "Contemporary Developments in Legal Techniques in the Settlement of Disputes," Hague Academy of International Law, 180 *Recueil des Cours* 177 (1983); J. Laylin et al., "Outlines for Third Parties in International Disputes," 66 *Proc. Am. Soc. Int'l L.* 22 (1972); Charles de Visscher, *Theory and Reality in International Law*, trans. Corbett (1968) Book IV; *International Law: Cases and Materials*, ed. Louis Henkin, R. Pugh, Oscar Schachter, and Hans Smit (1980); Hersch Lauterpacht, *The Function of Law in the International Community* (1933); *Dispute Settlement Through the United Nations*, ed. Venkata K. Raman (1977); *American Law Institute, Restatement of the Law, Foreign Relations Law of the United States* 902 (1988); Manfred Lachs, "Some Reflections on the Settlement of International Disputes," 68

Proc. Am. Soc. Int'l L. 323 (1974); Lillian L. Randolph, *Third-Party Settlement of Disputes in Theory and Practice* (1973); Vratislav Pechota, *Complementary Structures of Third-Party Settlement in International Disputes* (UNITAR Study P.S. No. 3, 1971). See also, on dispute settlement in particular fields, Louis B. Sohn, "Settlement of Disputes Arising Out of the Law of the Sea Convention," 12 *San Diego L. Rev.* 495 (1975); R. B. Bilder, "The Settlement of Disputes in the Field of the International Law of the Environment," 1 *Recueil des Cours* 139 (1975).

Among recent legally oriented empirical or otherwise less-traditional studies, see Sidney D. Bailey, "Peaceful Settlement of International Disputes" in Raman, *supra;* Thomas M. Franck, *The Structure of Impartiality* (1968); J. Gamble and D. Fischer, *The International Court of Justice: An Analysis of a Failure* (1976); Gregory A. Raymond, *Conflict Resolution and the Structure of the State System: An Analysis of Arbitrative Settlements* (1980); Alexander M. Stuyt, *Survey of International Arbitrations* 1794–1970 (1972); F. S. Northedge and M. J. Grieve, *International Disputes: Case Histories 1945–70* (1973); William D. Coplin and J. Martin Rochester, "The Permanent Court of International Justice, The International Court of Justice, The League of Nations, and the United Nations: A Comparative Empirical Survey," 66 *Am. Pol. Sci. Rev.* 529 (1972); and L. Prott, *The Latent Power of Culture and the International Judge* (1979).

For recent overviews of international dispute settlement primarily from an international relations or social psychological perspective, see Dean G. Pruitt and Jeffrey Z. Rubin, *Social Conflict: Escalation, Stalemate, and Settlement* (1986) (esp. ch. 10, "The Intervention of Third Parties"); Martin Patchen, *Resolving Disputes Between Nations: Coercion or Conciliation?* (1988); Jacob Bercovitch, *Social Conflicts and Third Parties: Strategies of Conflict Resolution* (1984); I. William Zartman, ed., *The 50% Solution* (1976); I. William Zartman, *Ripe for Resolution* (1985); Gilbert R. Winham, ed., *New Issues in International Crisis Management* (1988); Dean G. Pruitt, *Negotiation Behavior* (1981); Jeffrey Z. Rubin, *Dynamics of Third-Party Intervention: Kissinger in the Middle East* (1981); J. Z. Rubin, "Experimental Research on Third-Party Intervention in Conflict: Towards Some Generalizations" 87 *Psychol. Bull.* 379 (1980); James A. Wall, "Third-Party Consultation as a Method of Intergroup Conflict Resolution," 27 *J. Confl. Res.* 301 (1983). Among many other useful political or social science-oriented works, see J. Z. Rubin and B. R. Brown, *The Social Psychology of Bargaining and Negotiation* (1975); Robert L. Butterworth, *Managing Interstate Conflicts 1945–1974* (1976); Daniel Frei, ed., *Managing International Crises* (1982); Nazli Choucri and Robert C. North, *Nations in Conflict* (1976); R. J. Rummel, Jr., *Understanding Conflict and War* (1975); Glen H. Snyder and Paul Dieseng, *Conflict Among Nations* (1977); John G. Stoessinger, *Why Nations Go to War*, 3d ed. (1982); Zeev Maoz, *Paths to Conflict: International Dispute Initiation 1816–1976* (1982); S. Roberts, *Order and Disputes* (1979); Christopher R. Mitchell, *The Structure of International Conflict* (1981); Oran R. Young, *The Politics of Force* (1968); Richard N. Lebow, *Between Peace and War: The Nature of International Crisis* (1981); Oran R. Young, *The Intermediaries: Third Parties in International Crises* (1967); Richard Smoke, *War: Controlling Escalation* (1977); Saadia Touval and I. William Zartman, eds., *The Man in the Middle: International Mediation in Theory and Practice* (1985); John W. Burton, *Conflict and Communication* (1969); J. W. Burton, *Resolving Deep-Rooted Conflict* (1987); M. H. Banks, ed., *Conflict in World Society* (1984); Roger Fisher and William Ury, *Getting to YES: Negotiating Agreement Without Giving In* (1981); Robert C. Jervis, *Perception and Misperception in International Relations* (1976). There are also many case studies of third-party intervention in particular conflicts or dispute, e.g., J. Z. Rubin, *supra* (1981); Max Hastings and Simon Jenkins, *Battle for the Falklands* (1983); Robert L. Kennedy, *Thirteen Days: A Memoir of the Cuban Missile Crisis* (1969); and Jimmy Carter, *Keeping Faith* (1982).

Among the leading scholarly journals relevant to these problems are the *American Journal of International Law*, the *Journal of Conflict Resolution*, and the *Negotiation Journal*.

For examples of the recent interesting and sophisticated empirical and theoretical research on dispute processing within domestic societies, and particularly the United States, see M. Galanter, "Adjudication, Litigation, and Related Phenomena" in Leon Lipson and Stanton Wheeler, ed., *Law and the Social Sciences* (1986) (with extensive bibliography); materials collected and cited in Special Issue on "Dispute Processing and Civil Litigation," 15 *Law and Soc. Rev.* 389–428 (1980–81); Stephen B. Goldberg, Eric Green, and Frank Sander, eds., *Dispute Resolution* (1985); Eric Green, Jonathan B. Marks, and Frank Sander, eds., *Disputing in America: The Changing Role of Lawyers* (1985) (all with extensive bibliographies). See also F. Sander, "Varieties of Dispute Processing," 70 *F.R.D.* 111 (1976); and M. Galanter, "Reading the Landscape of Disputes: What We Know And Don't Know (And Think We Know) About Our Allegedly Contentious and Litigious Society," 31 *UCLA Law Rev.* 4 (1983); Cathie J. Witty, *Mediation and Society* (1980); Sibley and Merry, "Mediator Settlement Strategies," 8 *Law and Policy* 7 (1987); Kenneth Kressel and Dean G. Pruitt, "Themes in the Mediation of Social Conflict," 41 *J. Social Issues* 179 (1985); Vilhelm Aubert, "Competition and Dissensus: Two Types of Conflict and Conflict Resolution," 7 *J. Conflict Res.* 26 (1963); T. Eckhoff, "The Mediator and the Judge," 10 *Acta Sociologica* 158 (1986); Owen Fiss, "Against Settlement," 93 *Yale L.J.* 1073 (1984); Mather and B. Ynvesson, "Language, Audience, and the Transformation of Disputes," 15 *Law and Soc. Rev.* 775 (1980–81); C. Menkel-Meadow, "Toward Another View of Legal Negotiation: The Structure of Problem Solving," 31 *U.C.L.A. Law Rev.* 754; S. Merry, "Disputing Without Culture," 100 *Harvard L. Rev.* 2057 (1987); L. L. Fuller, "Mediation—Its Forms and Functions," 44 *S. Cal. L. Rev.* 305 (1971); L. L. Fuller, "The Forms and Limits of Adjudication," 92 *Harv. L. Rev.* 353 (1979); Wagatswma and Rossett, "The Implications of Apology," 20 *Law and Soc. Rev.* 461 (1980); B. Yngvesson, "Reexamining Continuing Relations and the Law," 1985 *Wisc. L. Rev.* 623; S. Sibley and A. Sarat, *Dispute Processing in Law and Legal Scholarship*; DPRP Working Paper 8:9 (June 1988) (University of Wisconsin-Madison Inst. for Legal Studies); Deborah M. Kolb, *The Mediators* (1985).

On the growing interest among U.S. scholars and practitioners in nonjudicial or "alternative" dispute resolution, see previous references and Leo Kanowitz, *Alternative Dispute Resolution: Cases and Materials* (1985) (with extensive bibliography).

For interesting discussions of disputes and dispute processing from a broader cross-cultural and anthropological perspective, see Elie Abel, "A Comparative Theory of Dispute Institutions in Society," 8 *Law and Soc. Rev.* 217 (1973); S. Roberts, *Order and Disputes* (1979); Philip H. Gulliver, *Disputes and Negotiations: A Cross-Cultural Perspective* (1979); Laura Nader and Harry F. Todd, Jr., ed., *The Disputing Process Law in Ten Societies* (1978); F. G. Snyder, "Anthropology, Dispute Processes and Law: A Cultural Introduction," 8 *British J. of Law and Society* 141 (1981).

Part III: New Approaches

Introduction to Chapter 9

In this chapter, Robert Pickus attempts to sort out what the United States Institute of Peace has termed the "new approaches" to peace and to identify those most worthy of further development. Pickus observes that over the course of his lifetime, the "peace debate" has become hackneyed; characterized by polar, sterile, and inflexible positions and by internecine rivalries; and resistant to interdisciplinary methodologies, adaptations, and rejuvenation. The climate, however, appears to be changing.

One of the more divisive quarrels within the peace community is, ironically enough, over a workable definition of what constitutes peace. Should peace be narrowly defined as the absence and antonym of war, or should a broader, more inclusive definition be used, one that first requires the maximization of optimal values such as justice and the abolition of poverty? Noting that these all-inclusive definitions vitiate "the real horror of war, which is not simply the dying, but the deliberate organization for killing and engaging in indiscriminate slaughter," Pickus opts for a definition of peace as the absence of war, because he believes it establishes the correct order of priority.

Pickus then suggests that much of the work of peace organizations, scholar- and practitioner-oriented alike, lacks the creativity and historical perspective required to develop approaches that are genuinely new, and not simply variations on age-old recommendations that recognized the need for effective world political and legal authorities. Pickus suggests several lessons from the past that everyone engaged in the effort to create a more peaceful international community should learn, namely, that

- progress for peace will not come from a sudden break with human history, but through thoughtful and careful reflection on history;
- attention should shift from opposition to the weapons of war to an understanding of the causes of the political vacuum that make such weapons necessary; and
- the roles of freedom and democratic government in securing and maintaining international peace are too often ignored by people who are constructing proposals for the future.

9. New Approaches

Robert Pickus

I once heard Chief Buthelezi turn an old commonplace into fresh insight. He said, "The longest journey begins with a single step." He then added, "And the single step commences by facing in the right direction."

"Conceptual Roads to Peace," Scott Thompson's initial paper that launched the project from which this volume emerged, presented not one, but eleven directions. Proponents for each assert that *this* road leads to peace, or at least to the avoidance of war. But not even eleven directions suffice, as individual readers struggle to fit their own favored "roads to peace" into the typology. We begin, then, with the recognition that, at present, a conceptual map of approaches to peace charts an imbroglio, not an ordered understanding. That sense is reinforced as one reviews sixteen years of articles submitted to the *Journal of Peace Research*[1] or recent research in "quantitative international politics." Summarizing even one current of research (e.g., the Correlates of War Project) or the work of one serious scholar (like Ernst Haas or Kenneth Waltz) is daunting. To push the point to an extreme, try to discern and to order the conceptual assumptions underlying a typology of simply the kinds of nongovernmental organizations that claim that their work will help in the nonviolent resolution of international conflict.

Clearly, the United States Institute of Peace has set for us an immensely difficult and long overdue task. This book could represent the beginning of a continuing responsibility as the Institute defines its role. The pace of change, the flow of events communicated and experienced, besieges us in a television age. Shaped by "its" experience, a new "generation" now turns up every four years or so. People drawn to work for peace enter a field with a very spotty institutional memory—at least in its nongovernment dimensions—and no adequate overview of its work and problems. With inadequate charting of past efforts, past assumptions, and the consequences of acting on them, each generation repeats past errors. We need a better conceptual map to help people most likely to be caught in a single current of thought, unaware of even its history, let alone its relationship to other perspectives.

What follows are the observations of a nonacademic specialist who has traveled many of these conceptual and programmatic roads. In particular, I bring to these reflections thirty-five years of painful experience, of detours (often), dead ends (with every new war), and progress (rare) in "new" approaches to peace.

I begin by highlighting a change in the intellectual climate that augurs well for the Intellectual Map Project. Next, I present an overview of different definitions of peace that leads to the case for one being deemed worthy of priority attention. I then give my reasons for asserting that, although I can see no new "conceptual" approaches to achieving a world at peace, the world environment itself is, in many respects, radically new. New factors in the international equation, coupled with an explosion of intellectual and organizational creativity in imaginatively extending old concepts, lead to an optimistic judgment: new approaches to a world without war are now feasible. Finally, I list lessons from experience about how such efforts fail, as well as cautions that view such failure as being in the nature of the case—cautions from which we can also learn.

A Changed Climate

As we enter the 1990s, the time to begin such a project is auspicious. Weariness with too patterned a debate is widespread. A speaker or an essay begins, and most experienced auditors or readers can finish the argument and even accurately state the likely response. Sterile argument has produced a demand for fresh ground ahead of past polarities. Many today recognize the need for a developed perspective on progress toward peace, one that draws from more than one place on the political spectrum, from more than one discipline. A thoughtful overview of present currents of thought and action will significantly aid its production.

Then, too, a different wind is blowing in the often-enemy camps pitched on the differing roads to peace. Even quantitatively oriented scholars often rest their work on stated or unstated ideological ground.[2] That fact and the passions of recent wars over paths to peace in academic and organizational circles have blocked communication. Truths from the security and liberty end of the spectrum, for example, are seldom merged with those from the peace and disarmament end.

But that climate is changing. People at both poles of the argument are shaken. Those who predicted nuclear war as the result of President Reagan's foreign and military policy, and those who denied the possibility of change in a democratic direction in the USSR, are having second thoughts, or at least mustering new arguments. Where bumper stickers once sufficed, many people are now open to thoughtful discussion.

More profound, there is a growing rejection of the politicized climate that for many years dominated the war-peace public dialogue in academic centers. One senses a reaching for balance, for debate characterized not by eristic goals, but by a common effort to bring new knowledge to bear.

Proponents of competing perspectives are, at times, now engaged in useful dialogue.

Take, for example, the remarkable exchange between Stanley Hoffman[3] and his respondents about useful relations between traditional analytic political scientists and scholars committed to the study of the psychology of conflict. Their exchange is a contribution to mature thought—albeit, from my point of view, more of a contribution by the political scientists than by the psychologists. In any case, it is a model of clear exchange and response between differing schools of thought, a model this project could encourage in at least eleven areas.

Such a climate augurs well for the Intellectual Map Project and especially for that most difficult part of it: sorting out new approaches and identifying those worth developing, as distinguished from adequately describing traditional approaches to international relations and the problem of war.

In this section, three able exponents of new methodologies—and of what many people assert to be new concepts—explain their work. Conflict resolution and transnational and behavioral approaches occupy prominent places on the peace research agenda and, in varying degrees, in the ideas behind the programs of peace and world affairs organizations. The concern of Joseph Montville, Nazli Choucri, and James Laue is not so much to argue the novelty, as to argue the utility of their respective frameworks of thought and action.

Each of these three approaches in some degree challenges traditional "realist" understandings of world politics. Each offers an alternative analysis (and two offer prescriptions) for those policymakers ready to move from a focus on state power, legal institutions, and coercive authority to more optimistic assessments of the possibilities for agreement and the development of alternate security concepts.

My task here is threefold: to assess whether it is worth casting a still wider net to encompass a fuller range of new approaches; to present a view of what turns up in the net if we do; and to help focus the discussion by offering some judgments about which approaches are most likely—in ways that encourage the best in man—to move us toward the nonviolent resolution of international conflict. But a prior effort is needed.

Defining Peace

I have chosen a narrow definition of peace, as the nonviolent resolution of international conflict. I believe it is important to distinguish this narrower aim from other, broader definitions that include values and goals that should be pursued but that, when presented as prerequisites to the achievement of peace among nations, themselves become obstacles to that achievement. This is the familiar discussion in peace research circles of "negative" peace, the absence of organized mass violence, or war, versus conceptions of "positive" peace, the constructive integration of human society.

In fact, three distinctly different definitions of "peace" set conceptual frameworks for very different approaches to its achievement.[4] One refers to a spiritual tranquillity, an inner peace achieved through religious pursuits and found in the individual; it is not considered a proper object of political action. Yet it plays a crucial role in many peace cadres, even though it may be found as well in the midst of war. Some people offer this kind of peace and the change in the human condition it marks as both the essential definition of peace and as the major prerequisite to any significant change in a world dominated by war. Here, the essential condition for a peaceful world is located not in the mind of "man," as in the preamble to the UNESCO Charter, but in his soul.

The second definition is the "positive" peace referred to earlier. A world at peace is defined in this understanding as a world of justice and brotherhood, a world governed by compassion and the fulfillment of human need. For one sector of the religious community, it is a world that comes into being only after the religious conversion just described. It is a world in which human beings have given up selfishness and greed; it is a world of love and harmony. In terms more comfortable for sectors of a secular academic community, it is peace defined as an end to "structural violence." Economic and political structures of deprivation and oppression are the "first violence," which, ironically, is then seen in some formulations as the cause of and justification for the "second violence" of war and revolution. The irony of the "Peace Is Our Profession" sign at Strategic Air Command headquarters is replicated here in the embrace by some peace researchers of one more rationale for mass violence.

It is not, I believe, helpful in work for peace to dilute the concept of violence by stretching it to include other evils which, as in the cases of "oppression" or "starvation," have their own names. Something precious is lost when the word "violence" is blurred. The real horror of war—which is not simply the dying, but the deliberate organization for killing, for engaging in mass, indiscriminate slaughter—is vitiated.

Whatever the specific content of this "structural violence" concept as a guiding force in some peace research and peace action, the essential point is that only as the speaker's concept of social justice is realized does international peace become possible. For many people thinking in this perspective, it is not until this point that international peace even becomes desirable.

Another, often related, "positive" definition of peace posits certain "world order values" as essential to the search for peace. When these values are disentangled from Marxist assumptions and presented simply as worthy in themselves and helpful in establishing the conditions under which international conflict can be resolved without war, they constitute important elements in work for peace. When they are tied to concepts of "structural violence," however, they share in the criticism already presented.

A third definition of peace assumes that although a peace of universal love and harmony is not possible for imperfect man, it does not follow that war is inevitable. This definition sees the "positive" peace described earlier—the realization of the biblical promise of "shalom"—as an ultimate goal, ever to be sought but unlikely to be attained. It maintains that we experience another kind of peace daily, and have done so for generations, within many national political communities. This view defines peace as the antonym of war, peace as an end to mass organized violence. It is peace as public order, as security from mass violence, achieved in the governed community.

In this definition the pursuit of social justice, ecological balance, and economic well-being are seen as valid, necessary, and related to the achievement of world peace. However, it denies that they are prerequisites.

This narrow definition of peace as the absence of war is the definition I use in what follows. Most people who opt for this narrower definition couple the choice with an apology, assuring the reader that their reasons for making the choice are editorial and not intended to argue for a priority of attention to resolving the problems of achieving "negative" peace. I, however, *do* wish to make that argument—to assert that the narrower definition establishes the right order of priority; that some of the formulations of "positive" peace stand as obstacles to our first priority; and that such obstacles should be rejected. I decline here, although reluctantly, to make the case against perverse concepts of justice and equality that, short of war, have nevertheless filled the world with corpses in our century.

It is not simply the vision of nuclear war that prompts this focus on a narrower definition of peace. War is not the only problem we face; thus far it is not even the most lethal.[5] But it is the problem that most clearly embodies the attitudinal and behavioral barriers to a more humane future and to the functional cooperation needed to create that future. War—its structures and the beliefs that underlie them—occupies the ground that must be cleared if we are to build the needed institutions of a wider political community and to achieve the changed understandings required to sustain them.

The proponents of "positive" peace tell us that only after justice is achieved, hunger and poverty are ended, and a more rational equilibrium between population and resources is established may we expect progress on controlling the threat of war. In the narrower definition of peace used here, however, the order of concern is reversed. The commitment to mass violence itself is seen as a primary obstacle to the achievement of these goals. Establishing the minimal conditions for the nonviolent resolution and prosecution of political conflict becomes the first objective.

Those who assert that "wars will cease when men refuse to fight" assert a truth; but throughout the millennia that pacifist belief has stood against war, it has contributed little to actual progress toward ending it. That truth does not, however, warrant altering the priority just mentioned—ending war should be the first objective. Pacifist belief has been a powerful force in turning men and women to that task. The thought and action capable of defining and achieving those minimal conditions for international peace are not yet present. Difficult as it will be to bring them into being, that task is a narrower one than realization of the vision of "shalom."

Discerning the New

Given this narrower definition, is there anything new in concept of how to pursue the resolution of international conflict without war? Let us consider first the sense in which there is not.

Thirty-five years of experience with organizations whose stated purpose is progress toward peace leave little resonance in the word "new." Goethe's maxim catches one level of the experience: "General ideas and great conceit tend always to horrible mischief." Even at their best, peace organizations are rarely conceptually creative. Each of the ideas underlying activity in different sectors of the peace organization world has a long pedigree: some three hundred years before the American civil rights movement discovered Gandhi (and American peace groups initially acted out, and eventually corrupted, Thoreau's concept of civil disobedience), Etienne de la Boe'tie[6] was writing of the organized nonviolent withdrawal of consent as a necessary form of political power. The idea that an overarching authority is essential to keep sovereign social units from warring is an ancient one. Pierre Dubois (1307), Dante Alighieri (1309), Erasmus (1517), Sully (1595), Emeric Crucé (1623), Grotius (1625), William Penn (1693), Abbé de Saint-Pierre (1716), Rousseau (1761), Kant (1795)—each developed his own variation on the central concept of the need for effective world political and legal authorities.

Proposals for disarmament, arms control, economic and political development, strengthened people-to-people connections across national boundaries, regional approaches to international organization—a variety of symbolic and functional acts and structures deemed capable of making visions of world community more of a reality; these and some twenty other roads to peace have long been on the agenda of governments, let alone peace organizations.

A skeptical view of the new is justified by surveys of peace research, by efforts at theory building or codifying knowledge, or even by the quantitative study of international relations. This last method admittedly is one of the latest chapters in the development of behavioral studies of international politics and the parallel development of the peace research movement, both products of only the past fifty years. But there is a difference between an impressive flowering of more precise and replicable methodological practices, on the one hand, and new international relations concepts, on the other. New names such as decision making, crisis studies, deterrence, tacit bargaining, stability, misperception, dispute settlement, and systems approaches are helpful in carefully targeting research, but the concepts involved are not simply familiar—they are ancient, however impressive the new efforts to gather and codify data about them and to test hypotheses about these data in ways that enable scholars to build on one another's research.

No wonder Nicolas Murray Butler, introducing a 1932 edition of Immanuel Kant's *Perpetual Peace* and viewing then-current thought about war and peace, lamented, "How little that is being said and thought . . . is in any sense new."[7] Butler claimed that Kant's work, done when the United States was in its cradle, was a definitive discussion of the perennial problems that block the road to international peace.

Any experienced person surveying the latest journals and organizational reports of even, perhaps especially, the most advanced sectors of the field—those claiming to offer new approaches to peace—is more likely to reach for Ecclesiastes than to rush to inform colleagues of something new under the sun. Yet, if we focus not on concepts but on the world these concepts seek to understand and alter, a wealth of radically new factors *are* clearly present. Indeed, there are so many new ones as to change significantly the odds on the possibilities of creating a world that resolves international conflict without mass violence. What follows is intended to illustrate how some of these new factors can affect our conceptions of the roads to peace and the programs flowing from those conceptions.

World Interdependence

We need not review here the ways in which economics and advances in technology and communication have radically altered the impact of international factors on what were previously local, regional, or national patterns of human thought and behavior. I remember just thirty years ago when television news began broadcasting weather maps for all of the United States. What did we in California care about the weather in St. Louis? Today, world calendars that mark religious holidays in every country sell briskly to those planning to work abroad. My point is not that more people now travel to St. Louis or Egypt, but that such maps and calendars are now expected, are now part of our consciousness.

The initial use of the word "interdependence" to herald a world of cooperation has given way to a more accurate use, acknowledging a new, inescapable, and often threatening fact of life. Raymond Aron put it well, recognizing that our situation differs from familiar past worlds of combative states or broad reaches of empire. What we have, he said, is more complicated: "Quarreling states more subjected to asymmetric interdependence than they would like,...too different to agree, too interconnected to separate."[8]

Economic historians tell us that Europe on the eve of the Thirty Years' War was, in fact, more economically interdependent than the world is today. What I am suggesting here is not that the facts of our current interdependence in themselves will move us toward peace, but that they are now part of the consciousness of a significant portion of the human race. That fact alone must change the way we think about roads to peace. What possibilities, for example, were opened by the 1988 Olympics? We are told that almost two billion people watched the same pictures in the same brief time span and shared common waves of feeling and identification.

Transnational Nongovernmental Entities

Another new factor, beyond world interdependence, is the changed role of the nation-state in world affairs. The list of nonstate entities able to affect world affairs grows ever longer. Massive contacts across state boundaries, which are not controlled by the central organs of state power, now vitally influence governments' foreign and military policies. True, states remain the dominant actors in the international arena; states wage war and collect taxes. But that reality is increasingly constrained. It is not even literally true anymore, given the activities of terrorist political organizations. Transnational nongovernmental forces intrude now in world affairs in almost every area of human activity, and in some cases, in concentrations both older (e.g., the Roman Catholic church) and more powerful (e.g., General Motors) than most nation-states.

These transnational forces in world affairs have called forth bursts of optimism about the work of the most diverse entities. Some see multinational business corporations[9] as the single force most likely to create the conditions and the necessary dynamic for a more peaceful international order. Others respond similarly to the grassroots involvement of citizens around the globe in nongovernmental human rights, environmental, and peace organizations.[10] Whether attention is directed to functional international nongovernmental organizations (INGOs) like the International Airline Pilots' Association or the International Olympic Committee, or to transnational nongovernmental organizations (TRANGOs), which link members directly, rather than through national structures, few would deny the importance of these new actors in world affairs.

But again, there is nothing new in the concept. Transnational factors and organizations (for example, the migration of persons, the Olympic Games themselves) have a long history. What is new is their number and variety and, more significant, their challenge to the control that state actors have over world affairs. Thus Robert Keohane and Joseph Nye, Jr., deny Raymond Aron's earlier judgment of the relative unimportance of these actors in world politics. They accept some of his case but carefully demonstrate the increasing influence of transnational actors in world politics and intergovernmental relations.[11]

Operating from diverse institutional bases (foundations, non-governmental organizations, professions, universities, labor unions, corporations) and from the wonderful range of human interests (gardening, stamp collecting, knitting), these transnational groups influence world politics in many arenas. To take just one example, the World Psychiatric Association's planned expulsion in 1983 of the Soviet All-Union Society of Psychiatrists (the Soviets withdrew in advance of the decision) must surely be counted among the forces leading to current changes in Soviet society, changes that are, for the moment at least, significantly altering world politics. Viewed from the Soviet perspective, especially in recent decades, "nongovernmental" organizations like the World Peace Council and a host of international youth, women, lawyers, etc., federations have influenced foreign and military policy decisions in many states, despite their obvious service to Soviet propaganda efforts.

I pass over the familiar story of the massive growth in intergovernmental and transnational government agencies, except to note how radically they, also, have changed the arenas in which world political and economic decisions are made. Many of these agencies have now turned their attention, and their efforts at control, toward the activities of the nongovernmental, transnational agencies referred to earlier.

Qualitative Changes

It is beyond the scope of this survey (and unnecessary, given the now extensive literature) to further explore the ways in which ecological, economic, and nongovernmentally organized political currents have significantly changed the world arena and the possibilities within it. My point here is simply to focus on the degree of change. Quantitative change becomes at some point qualitative. A cat on my desk is just a cat. Multiply his size by a thousand and there is a qualitative change in my situation. Given the quantitative changes in communications alone, qualities in world interactions that simply were not present before, now exist.

These changes are harder to characterize than the changes in the nature of state power. They relate to fundamental concepts of identity, community, and responsibility that drive influential flows of thought and action such as those now present in the world human rights movement. They open new possibilities for the realization of old goals of human unity. People's expectations of what is possible and what is desirable have altered in ways that make new structures and relationships possible. The moral commitment to end war that arose in the shadow of Hiroshima and led to new attempts at world order is alive again. More of the conditions essential to its realization, if not present, are clearly coming into being.

Yet in thirty-five years of experience with organizations in this field, I often find reason to wish that more of the groups developing those expectations combined with their work the wisdom and mature judgment of, say, a Raymond Aron or a Jean-François Revel. Many of these hopeful developments have been corrupted, turned not to humane but to destructive ends. Most often it is chaos, not order, reflected in the tragic kaleidoscope of each night's newscast; chaos fed, not challenged, by forces that lay claim to being harbingers of human unity. The tragedy of Lebanon casts its shadow, reminding us how difficult it is to establish zones of peace within a nation, and how easy it is to destroy them. The gap between the UN Charter and the UN's actual role in past decades is sobering. The disorders in the entire international system are many and profound; the structures for resolving them are obviously inadequate; and the failure to deal with them is disastrous. In a time when the central problems can be resolved only by transnational cooperation, political separatism, both within and between nations, remains a powerful political current. The will to confront and change these realities has yet to be gathered, let alone applied. The realist's view of the human condition, which is too easily abandoned by many, remains the weightiest, time-tested perspective. Still, there *are* now new conditions—realities, not just visions—with which to confront and enlarge that view.

We have long known a familiar prescription for a world without war. It calls for a disarmed world, under law, in which economic and political development lessens the gap between the First and Third Worlds and a growing sense of world community opens the way for pluralistic, democratic societies in which political conflict replaces lethal conflict. Given agreement on these goals, the prescription is complete.

But no agreement exists. The reasons behind that fact remain. Yet changes like those cited earlier allow new hope. Disarmament proposals become more meaningful as technology makes inspection and verification more reliable. The dilution of state power and the increasing pluralization of decision-making centers, when allied with more encompassing institutions of both functional and political community, make nonviolent conflict resolution more likely. Economic pressures in an interdependent world, combined with the impossibility of a sufficient preponderance of power with which to make empire possible, push us toward cooperation. And most of all, travel and communication patterns like the Olympic example, along with the strength of the democratic idea of free societies, which defends the worth of each human being, begin to knit the common ties that make a community of humankind feasible.

New Approaches: Thought and Research

The massive explosion of new energy, both intellectual and organizational, centered on the problem of war constitutes one pivotal new reality, which is central to the task set for this United States Institute of Peace project. Agencies devoted to the study of international conflict and cooperation, and to developing alternatives to violence in the pursuit of both security and constructive change, are now legion. A whole new industry is engaged simply in cataloguing research and listing foundations, exchange organizations, precollegiate peace education programs, and policy centers. We currently have, for the first time, a coordinated plan to develop guides to these intellectual and organizational centers and to provide for their systematic updating. Despite these developments, I remain doubtful of the claim that new concepts now guide us in progress toward peace. But if we focus on the care and imagination with which old concepts are being developed, related, and applied, we find again that we now inhabit a different universe.

The development, for example, of behavioral science approaches to the study of international conflict and the parallel development of the peace research movement are clearly important. Wars occur periodically, but they are not necessarily present in every place where human societies interact. Nor do all nations engage in war. Research on past outbreaks of international violence may reveal patterns identifying the conditions and tracing the interactions that end in war. Two major objections have been raised to this work: that normative and ideological commitments have skewed the researchers' approach to and application of their studies; and that the study of war encompasses a field in which there are no demonstrable patterns or laws that would make adequate theory possible. Few would maintain that the product thus far resolves these doubts. Thoughtful scholars like Anatol Rapoport and Dina Zinnes[12] acknowledge how far the field currently falls short of presenting such theory. But the sheer volume and complexity of work undertaken in the past thirty-five years are impressive.

Thus, while retaining the judgment that little in the behavioral science approach presents a new concept, I recognize that systematic and analytic modes of inquiry are yielding new data. Researchers now work with those data in ways that enable them to build on each other's efforts, producing cumulative instead of piecemeal results, which add to our knowledge of war and peace: thus the work undertaken and progressively refined by Charles McClelland, Edward Azar, J. David Singer, and their associates.[13]

The serious entry of psychologists into the field is another example of a new approach. Some have rejected that entry, for they have seen it accompanied by charges of "paranoidal madness"[14] directed by publicists and scholars at national political leaders who must deal with the terrible dilemmas athwart the road to security in a nuclear age. Such charges often come from people who demonstrate little awareness of history, international politics, or even the nature of the dilemmas decision makers face. Another criticism of psychological approaches points to the dangers of easy transference of lessons learned from interpersonal therapy to the radically different arena of international politics.

But some political psychologists are long past those errors and are jointly developing with international relations specialists and historians new and more balanced approaches. The argument, as developed in Joseph Montville's response to Stanley Hoffman[15] and even in the exchange between those arguing "the need for enemies" and those pointing out that "even paranoids *have* enemies," shows promise. When ethical and ideological commitments are clarified, the possibility of useful synthesis exists. Able and experienced political scientists like James Rosenau have lent an ear to these new voices, and, as the psychologists have enlarged their own understanding, new insights and new practices of some promise have emerged. To those who say there is nothing of value in this approach, Herbert Kelman's recent judicious telling of its development since the 1950s, proceeding from Quincy Wright and Lewis Richardson's earlier work, is a reproof in itself.[16] But it would be salutary for those committed to psychological approaches to take seriously the critics who are skeptical of social science generalizations and to direct themselves more pointedly to the knowledge that comes with careful study of the particulars of history.[17]

Gene Sharp has developed a different focus of attention in his examination of socially organized nonviolent force as an alternative to mass violence. In studies of political power, national civilian defense, and movements for social change, he has given specificity and the weight of historical case histories to what before was more a discussion of ethical alternatives.[18]

Given James Laue's thorough exploration, in chapter 12 of this volume, of what is unfolding under the "conflict resolution" rubric, I pass over this subject, except to note how rich a set of possibilities for both study and practice has been developed, and how important is the critic's caution to beware of unwarranted transfers of intergroup conflict resolution to world politics. My final assessment is that the increasingly multidisciplinary character of peace research—although sometimes justly subject to criticisms in some disciplines (e.g., anthropology[19]) equivalent to those directed at the psychologists—can nevertheless produce a better understanding of what is required to end war. We would do well, though, to listen to critics who see social science-oriented peace research as simply "erod[ing] the forces of common sense, experience, and history that argue for a strong defense as a deterrent to war."[20] At points, this is an accurate description. But there are other possibilities. When this work is allied to serious study of international politics, it may aid in the search for peace and security. I have found James Rosenau's periodic overviews of the field helpful in fitting these new currents into a solid base of traditional international relations studies.[21]

Morality and War

I shift now to another intellectual arena—the most troubled one—in which moral reasoning confronts war. This is not a field in which new approaches should be expected, nor are they necessary. But recovery of the fully developed character of the moral argument is essential, for normative beliefs drive most of the approaches surveyed in this book. If that discussion is degraded, we remain divided and confused. For some time now, the phrase "a divided community" has accurately characterized our situation. Much of the blame belongs with those thinkers who have wrongly assumed that the moral choices are obvious. Add to that the further error of ignoring Julien Benda's caution,[22] to those who would bear moral witness, to beware entry into the struggle for political influence.

The Vietnam War years left a mixed history for anyone tracing the role of ethical intentions in American politics. In reaction to the war, the necessity of moral choice in matters of foreign policy powerfully entered many lives for the first time. That story has been widely and admiringly told. But the noble tradition of conscientious objection to war—openly held, nonviolently expressed, its adherents respecting the law in a democracy even when consciously refusing to obey it—was almost lost in the falsifications, disaffiliations, violence, and contempt for democratic processes and law that characterized some sectors of the movement that opposed, in many cases, not the war itself but only America's role in it.

The moral case for resistance to U.S. power led many who might have strengthened a moral witness against all war into the support of regimes engaged in less humane uses of government and military power than our own. More recently, mistaken moral equivalencies have been drawn in comparisons of Soviet and American societies and their roles in world affairs. Peace-oriented ethicists, to give just one example, now compare American shame—My Lai—with Soviet activity in Afghanistan, ignoring the fact (among others), that My Lai was a violation of government policy, whereas Soviet action in Afghanistan was an expression of it. Survivalism, a code that, as Sidney Hook put it, was fine for jackals but not for man, for a time swept the peace movement and made fear its central message. The fact that acquiescence in the spread of totalitarian power was one of the least likely roads to a world at peace was drowned in dangerous combinations of passion and ethical arrogance.

None of this is meant to excuse the moral obtuseness, the easy acceptance of "megadeath" calculations, or the denial of responsibility to others across national and ideological boundaries that have characterized some on the other side of the argument. I want only to mark the character of the public argument: a vulgarized discussion in a time when we most needed wise ethical common ground. Americans were for a time left without an acceptable moral compass by the earlier dominance of one "realist" current, which asserted that only the national interest and accurate assessments of power were needed as guides to national policy. But we are no better off when the case for moral principle in foreign policy decisions is fairly characterized as contemporary versions of the distorted discussions of the Vietnam period criticized earlier.

In line with the determined optimism of this essay, I believe that, with regard to the moral question also, new and better possibilities are unfolding. Consider, for example, the dialogue now developing in the American Catholic church. The work through which J. Brian Hehir guided the American bishops in their pastoral letter on war and peace, taken in conjunction with George Weigel's criticism of that work and his attempt to reestablish the Catholic tradition of rightly ordered political community as the essential requisite for peace, illustrates the kind of ethical discussion needed.[23] This discussion contains a new civility, a new reaching for connection between an old tradition and present realities, that gives promise of movement toward agreement in even this most difficult and important stage.

New Approaches: Practitioners

When we turn from old ideas and new developments in the study of international relations and world systems to the practitioners—the nongovernmental organizations that take a world at peace as their stated goal—the first thing to note is another massive, quantitative change.

If we exempt, for the moment, organizations with military, diplomatic, or legal approaches to preventing war, experienced observers usually put the number of U.S. peace organizations—or organizations that intend their work to contribute to achieving that goal—at some ten thousand. Many, perhaps most, of these have less than a two-year half-life. But if we look not at organizational titles, which change, but at their addresses, which often do not, we see persisting cadres of organized belief with roughly the same political perspective and strategy of work. The number of organizations, by my conservative estimate, has at least doubled and perhaps tripled in the past twenty years. Although some of these groups are ephemeral, a number of mainstream mass organizations (e.g., religious) now have branches in every community, with continuing programs in this field.

A recent guide to such organizations in the San Francisco Bay area alone needed fifty categories to order the universe surveyed.[24] The variety of groups, the concepts underlying their strategy of work, and the number and kinds of people involved represent a quantitative change that holds, again, the promise of qualitative alterations. Just as there are new actors in world politics, peace research, and international studies, so in even greater degree are there new organizational expressions of the intention to move toward peace. Intentions, of course, are not enough. Critics, with ample justification, charge that some of these groups can best be described as obstacles to peace and security. What is argued here, though, is that some of them do help to create the conditions, develop the structures and processes, and organize the vectors of influence and relationships that make for progress toward the nonviolent resolution of international conflict. That is why understanding them, and the ideas moving in them, is so important.

The guide, produced by ACCESS: A Security Information Service and the World Without War Council, attempts to build that understanding. The first step is to index the organizations now at work. The guide will make available data on the work of organizations in each region of the country and each sector of the field, cross-referenced to programs (and, if my hopes are realized, political perspectives) on each world geographic and problem area. Mapping the organizational universe of peace groups and other groups working on America's role in world affairs is not an exciting endeavor, but there is great interest in it now. People want to know who is out there, talking to whom, offering what kinds of programs. People wish to probe below the surface and current headlines to understand the ideas and strategies that characterize these groups. More of these organizations are now transferring their archives to libraries across the country. A listing of such organizational research archives and an analysis of their holdings is now available.[25]

Exchange Organizations

But are new conceptual approaches to peace visible in the work of these organizations? Again, for the most part, what we find are not new concepts but better developed and more extensive applications of old concepts. For example, the idea of person-to-person contact across national, cultural, and ideological barriers has a long history as a road to peace, but the number of organizations acting on that idea and on an understanding of the difference between effective exchanges and counterproductive ones is growing. To see how much we have to learn, we need only to reflect on our experience with fifty thousand Iranian students, for example, or to examine the many Soviet-American exchange efforts of the past decade. Many exchange organizations accepted Soviet restrictions without challenge, with no adequate effort to orient exchange participants to the political, as distinguished from cross-cultural, problems they would encounter. In consequence, many exchanges aided the Soviet World Peace Council's organizational efforts and confirmed, instead of challenged, the Soviet foreign and military policy agenda.

An example of a new approach in this field occurred when the president of the American Chemical Society (ACS), breaking with previous patterns, told Soviet officials the conditions under which Soviet delegates would be welcome at the ACS's annual meeting. (Had the Soviet scientist invited by the ACS not been allowed to attend, the American invitation would no longer stand.) In the end, the invited Soviet chemist was allowed to come. A new message went through the Soviet scientific establishment: if you want to meet with colleagues abroad, pursue serious science and do not, as before, seek political preferment by pleasing Communist party officials.

Another example of the more thoughtful development of this exchange road to peace was the recent cancellation of an exchange project with the Soviet World Peace Council by an American exchange organization when the Soviets canceled their agreement to share responsibility for choosing participants. Whereas exchanges previously served to confirm the Communist party's moral and political authority, they have now begun to be used in movement toward a more open and pluralized Soviet Union, surely one of the requisites for a stable peace.[26]

Precollegiate Curriculum

Developments in precollegiate education provide another example of organized peace efforts that have, in recent years, not just increased in number but improved in quality. The focus on precollegiate education by many peace groups and other nongovernmental organizations is, in part, the product of a significant change in our sense of time. The move away from a two-minutes-to-midnight approach, symbolized by the cover of the *Bulletin of Atomic Scientists,* toward attention to the precollegiate curriculum seems both important and desirable. This change gives us a more accurate sense of the time spans required for constructive change, and it offers protection against apocalyptic programs and movements.

Initially, this change of emphasis by peace groups produced what I would label "a great tragedy"—great in that a remarkable recruiting and organizing effort engaged precollegiate educators across the country in what was called peace education, but tragic in that what was taught were the least thoughtful ideas and programs in the peace movement. Educational standards were debased as political recruiting became the dominant mode in many classrooms. The Association for Supervision and Curriculum Development recently surveyed the ways in which "global education" was altering traditional international studies, and it marked as "most notable"[27] the development of the Alliance for Education in Global and International Studies (AEGIS), a new organizational coalition that attempts to reestablish sound educational standards and to address the problem of linking civic and global education. This quotation from the AEGIS charter demonstrates what I mean by the wiser development of new approaches:

> For some, a sense of world responsibility seems to require abandonment of a commitment to one's own nation. For others, a commitment to one's own nation precludes the pursuit of world responsibilities. We affirm the wisdom—indeed the necessity—of a commitment to both....[28]

Religious Programs

A third example of new practitioners who are improving our concepts of what is required in work for peace is the National Association of Evangelicals (NAE). My experience with the thinking that went into developing the *Guidelines*[29] for their Peace, Freedom, and Security Studies Program was heartening. In efforts to get a wide range of organizations to put intelligent work for peace on their agenda, I have had to put on many hats (those of Catholics, bankers, psychiatrists) to see a number of differing world views from within. Work in the evangelical world was a special challenge. Like many outside that world, I needed some time to learn that many of the most publicized television evangelists are exotics in the real world of American evangelicals, which is made up of eighty thousand local churches and is part of the backbone of this country. NAE's effort to create a continuing program of peace education breaks with much of the conventional wisdom brought to the discussion by parts of the religious community that have joined the current peace movement. Because the NAE includes both the most ardent military-patriotic currents and the oldest committed pacifist currents, its efforts to find agreement on useful approaches to world power realities is important. At the heart of the NAE program is the search for nonviolent approaches to the resolution of international conflict and a carefully considered alternative to a strategy of work that would have national churches function as lobbyists.

This NAE program also demonstrates a rebuttal to Edward Luttwak's charge that those working for peace often "disaffiliate"; people separate themselves, he charges, from the country they criticize.[30] That *is* a familiar pattern in some parts of the current peace movement, but it is not present in NAE's program. Far from teaching disaffiliation, NAE seeks to strengthen a sense of identity, of responsibility to our own community. NAE's *Guidelines* also give reasons why a country like ours has duties beyond its borders, and why it should lead progress toward peace.

Two Intellectual Currents: "Alternative Security" and "New Age" Thinking

These examples from exchange, precollegiate, and religious programs mark a merging of previously sharply opposed perspectives, but none involves significantly new intellectual approaches. Two currents that can claim that distinction are worth noting. One is the growth among peace organizations of programs rooted in concepts of "alternative security." Often, this is simply a rhetorical device, similar to the Strategic Air Command's "Peace Is Our Profession" slogan. In this case, some groups that can be counted on routinely for opposition to U.S. military programs prefer titles in which "national security" or "defense information" replaces the word "peace." (This mutual attempt to capture the opposition's moral and practical case could, when it does not mislead, move us toward wiser ground than either of the polar arguments has yet offered.)

The range of ideas proposed in these nongovernmental organization alternative security (or defense) programs includes military strategies, suggested as long ago as 1932 by the British military strategist Liddell Hart. These strategies call for efforts to make military programs "non-aggressive by rendering them incapable of attack but eminently capable of defense," and include "qualitative disarmament" proposals designed to achieve that result.[31] A radically different alternative security concept involves a variety of nonviolent, civilian resistance strategies designed to make invasion and occupation more difficult. Another concept, entitled "mutual security," seeks to enhance the security of both sides and change their political relationship by joint efforts to improve all parties' security (e.g., the Incidents at Sea Agreement includes proposals based on the hot line for jointly manned war-by-accident risk-reduction centers). The reaction to the most dramatic of such ideas, President Reagan's proposal that the Strategic Defense Initiative (SDI) constitute a mutual security approach to defense against nuclear attack, is instructive. All these mutual security and alternative defense proposals, imaginative and even feasible as some of them are, rest on strongly held ideological and analytical perspectives. In the instructive case of SDI, both the political Right, for its reasons, and the political Left, for its reasons, refused even to consider the dramatic lever of SDI for changed political and military relationships between the United States and the Soviet Union. Despite at least seven public repetitions of the idea by President Reagan and some reporting of his efforts to persuade General Secretary Gorbachev to join in launching it, I know of only two peace organizations, both out of step with ideological currents in the present peace movement, that sought to develop the idea. There was also one task group involving officials from the Pentagon and the U.S. Arms Control and Disarmament Agency, which explored the idea, but its work had little impact.

Recent attention devoted to Gorbachev's unilateral initiative in cutting Soviet military forces in Eastern Europe has revived interest in that route to progress toward effective disarmament. The idea of unilateral initiatives—action taken without prior agreement, but designed to bring pressure for reciprocation—has great potential for producing movement in previously frozen situations. Given the increasing importance of public diplomacy, the idea has considerable utility and an interesting intellectual history.

All these alternative security concepts have organized adherents and together may produce feasible new strategies. None is conceptually new, but exploring them in the current international climate deserves a high priority.

The second intellectual current that lays claim to new thought and sustains an amazing array of organizations, newsletters, and journals now engaged in developing peace programs, has been categorized under the rubric "New Age." A Nobel laureate, Roger Sperry, wrote as follows in the 1981 *Annual Review of Neuroscience*:

> Current concepts of the mind-brain relation involve a direct break with the long-established materialist and behaviorist doctrine that has dominated neuroscience for many decades. Instead of renouncing or ignoring consciousness, the new interpretation gives full recognition to the primacy of inner conscious awareness as a causal reality.[32]

This focus on "inner conscious awareness as a causal reality" seems to be the central concept of the New Agers. Richard Smoke and Willis Harman summarize the recent shifts in scientific thought as shifts from

> structure to process, from linear to multidimensional logic, from mechanistic to holographic models, from hierarchical to nonhierarchical ordering, from a focus on elements to one on "whole systems," and, most generally from an orientation toward matter-energy to one emphasizing relationships and connections.[33]

New Age efforts seek parallel shifts in thinking about war and peace.

In contrast to the Sperry quotation, New Agers, with their talk of transformation, images, courses in miracles, and so on, appall most scientists and other people engaged in work for peace. One smiles at the thought of high Soviet officials carrying the scars of thirty years of lethal bureaucratic battles into a typical gathering in an Esalen hot tub. But consider an article by Audrey V. Kozyrev, a close associate of Foreign Minister Shevardnadze, which appeared in the journal of the Soviet Foreign Affairs Ministry. In this article, Kozyrev berates his colleagues for pursuing the "anti-imperialist struggle" and thus being drawn into an arms race that sustains the barriers keeping the West's technology from the Soviet Union. On par with these bad consequences, he lists one other: accepting an "enemy image" in their view of the West.[34]

This latter idea, most likely transmitted through a New Age contact, is both an example of the effect this current of thought has had in many unlikely places and an example of what critics, sometimes reacting to only the most vulgarized mass media presentations, labeled "psychobabble."

Whether viewed as a source of genuinely fresh thought, translating into a mix of "depth" psychology, ancient religious truth, and the frontiers of science, or as a dangerous brew of vulgarized mysticism, egomania, and ill-conceived political perspectives and programs, there is a lot of life currently running in this river. Encounters with some New Agers who fit the negative descriptions should not turn us away from the serious work of some people with a New Age perspective. In a time when many can no longer speak the word "soul" but resonate to "psyche," these ideas have wide reach. Of the periodicals published by the Helen Dwight Reid

Foundation, which specializes in scholarly publications, the one with the widest circulation by far is a New Age journal.

I am not the best person to interpret these ideas. I commend to those interested Richard Smoke and Willis Harman's *Paths to Peace: Exploring the Feasibility of Sustainable Peace*, which thoughtfully explains how these ideas add new dimensions to approaches to peace.

Lessons Learned

Heraclitus's argument for change—eternal motion as the dominant metaphysical reality—usually wins in the short run, for the waters are ever running and, as he put it, you cannot, therefore, step into the same river twice. But any exploration of purported new currents in life drives us back to Parmenides and the unchanging. Much has changed, but people who are engaged in work for peace tend to take the continuities in human experience too lightly. Most leave the endeavor before learning the hard lessons, or, if they do learn them, find them reason enough to abandon a task whose true dimensions are now apparent. It is especially important to keep these hard lessons in mind amid the recent hopeful changes in the Soviet Union and world politics. Seasons of hope and despair regularly attend the tides of human yearning for peace.

We have yet to find a sure road. Can we learn anything from a survey like this of "New Approaches"? I have scattered some lessons throughout this chapter, but I would like to end by simply listing a few additional points. My short list of lessons to be learned by those attempting to travel new roads to peace follows.

1. *Those who try to go beyond Thucydides, do not.* Real progress will come not from any sudden break in human history, but from thoughtful reflection on it. It will come by adding to the realists' understanding of international politics, not by trying to find some path to peace that avoids traversing the fields of power. Everyone entering into serious work for peace should be required to read, and be examined on, the first chapter of Hans Morgenthau's *Politics Among Nations*—whatever later use they may make of these ideas.[35]

2. *Tranquillitas ordinis.* One requisite of progress will be a shift of attention from weapons to the political vacuum that makes them necessary. If all the effort and ingenuity that have gone into arms control, or for that matter, deterrence theory, had focused on the problem of the "tranquility of order"—the achievement of rightly ordered political community—we would be further ahead, because that achievement allows law and politics to flourish as alternatives to war.

3. *In defense of apathy?* The increasing role of "non-elites" in foreign and security policy drives some policymakers to consider the virtues of apathy. Although the dangers of ever-increasing numbers of ill-prepared people in

the policy arena are apparent, that reality in our country cannot be reversed. How well we work at improving American competence in world affairs is one crucial measure of the possibility of wise policy. We have a multitude of instruments. Their performance is seldom assessed; relations among them are ill-developed; many are motivated by dangerous combinations of passion and ignorance. Just as the U.S. Department of State, whose seventh floor is now replete with doors reading "Public Diplomacy," has begun to respond to this fact, so must an agency with the special mission of the United States Institute of Peace. In my judgment, its careful development of an appropriate approach to the world of nongovernmental organizations and public education will probably be of more consequence in progress toward peace than its research activities.

4. *Beyond the nation-state*. The fact of transnational forces, problems, and organizations, and the extent of their impact on national and individual life, are obvious central new realities. It is worth noting that, setting aside the politicized transnational organizational work, most groups in the field trace their beginnings to the United States. The most effective and lasting ideas will seek to relate this new transnational reality to the need of *tranquillitas ordinis*. The sorry record of the UN in the past thirty years has led many people to reject international organizations as a constructive force in world affairs. Why, they say, turn over decision making to such as these? It is a fair question, but a mistaken stance. The world *is* gathering; the question is in what frameworks, through what processes, and to what ends, not whether there will be world forums or, even more important, functional structures that limit national policy.

5. *Within the nation-state*. Approaches that combine a commitment to existing political community with a recognition of the need for new and wider forms of community will lay the broadest base for steps to peace and, in the case of our own country, do the least harm. As one educator put it when surveying the precollegiate scene, "If global education envisions a world in which the only enemies are ethnocentrism, patriotism, and nationalism, then global education is not something the American people much want or will long tolerate." But he went on to stress that "civics education and global education are not mutually exclusive."[36]

6. *Freedom*. The ease with which the cry for justice has been wed to the work for peace has not been matched in many sectors of the peace movement by a recognition of the relationship of the growth of democracy to progress toward peace. Too often the American peace movement has not only *not* been a friend of free societies or people reaching for democracy, it has been an enemy. This is as much a consequence of nonideological sectors of the movement as it is of the frankly ideological. The lesson to be learned is the danger of political innocence in work for peace. Contact across ideological barriers is necessary and important. When work billed as above politics is in fact turned to political—and antidemocratic—purposes, the results are counterproductive.

7. *The politics of eternity.* It is significant that Hans Morgenthau, the man who did so much to advance this country's understanding of the realities that shape the international arena, drew the title of his last book from an old Quaker imperative, "Speak truth to power." There is a politics of time and a politics of eternity. We must attend to both if we want progress toward peace.

8. *A return to the words of Chief Buthelezi.* We have a plethora of directions. Finding the right ones and advancing along them is the task. If the United States Institute of Peace accepts an overview responsibility, one that earns it sufficient trust as an honest broker, it can help to build common agendas and encourage necessary assessments. It can promote the synthesis of ideas from different places on the political spectrum and in the intellectual and research communities. My own recent experience attests to the difficulty of the task. Nevertheless, the Institute should have these responsibilities high on its agenda.

My list is a long one. I forgo completing it here in the interest of encouraging readers to begin drawing up their own. We at the World Without War Council have begun our own "Lessons Learned" lists and would be glad to share them.[37] The United States Institute of Peace is steadily gathering the people who have demonstrated some capability in this work. It is time for common reflection on lessons learned.

We live in a country distinguished from many others by its wealth, size, diversity, technological capability, and, most of all, by the idea that formed it. The idea that the people shall rule because of the innate dignity of every person has been progressively realized in our experience of building and sustaining our political community. Such a political community must address the problem of war. Such a country has a significant, perhaps the key, role to play in progress toward peace.

Notes

1. Hakan Wiberg, "What Have We Learnt about Peace?" *Journal of Peace Research* XVIII, no. 2 (1981).

2. Keith L. Nelson and Spencer C. Olin, Jr. in *Why War?* (Berkeley and Los Angeles: University of California Press, 1979) make the case for the importance of ideological factors in thought about war and its causes.

3. Stanley Hoffman, Presidential Address, "On the Political Psychology of Peace and War: A Critique and an Agenda," *Political Psychology* 7, no. 1 (1986): pp. 1–21. See also note number 15.

4. See Ben Seaver's *Three Definitions of Peace* for a useful, brief clarification of this definitional confusion (available from the World Without War Council, 1730 Martin Luther King Jr. Way, Berkeley, CA 94709).

5. See, for example, R.J. Rummel, "War Isn't This Century's Biggest Killer," *Wall Street Journal*, July 7, 1986; R.J. Rummel, "Deadlier than War," *IPA Review* (Institute of Public Affairs Limited, Australia) 41 (August–October 1987): pp. 24–30.

6. Etienne de la Boe'tie, *Anti-Dictator* (New York: Columbia University Press, 1942).

7. Immanuel Kant, *Perpetual Peace* (New York: Columbia University Press, 1939).

8. *Report from Aspen Institute Berlin* (Berlin: Aspen Institute for Humanistic Studies, 1976), pp. 31–36.

9. Frank Tannenbaum, "The Survival of the Fittest," in *Transnational Corporations and World Order*, ed. George Modelski (San Francisco: W. H. Freeman, 1979).

10. Chadwick F. Alger and Michael Stohl, eds., *A Just Peace Through Transformation: Cultural, Economic and Political Foundations for Change* (Boulder, Colo.: Westview Press, 1988).

11. Robert O. Keohane and Joseph S. Nye, Jr., eds., *Transnational Relations and World Politics* (Cambridge: Harvard University Press, 1972), p. 374.

12. Dina A. Zinnes, *Contemporary Research in International Relations* (New York: Free Press, 1976); "Why War, Evidence of the Outbreak of International Conflict" in Ted Robert Gurr, *Handbook of Political Conflict* (New York: Free Press, 1980); and Anatol Rapoport, *Fights, Games and Debates* (Ann Arbor: University of Michigan Press, 1974).

13. See J. David Singer's "Accounting for International War: The State of the Discipline," *Journal of Peace Research* XVIII, no. 1 (1981); "Confrontational Behavior and Escalation to War 1816–1980: A Research Plan," *Journal of Peace Research* XIX, no. 1 (1982); E. E. Azar and J. W. Burton, eds., *Facilitated Conflict Resolution: Theory and Practice* (Brighton, Sussex: Wheatsheaf, 1986). See also John A. Vasquez, "The Steps to War: Toward a Scientific Explanation of Correlates of War Project," *World Politics* XL, no. 1 (October 1987): pp. 108–45.

14. See James Blight's cutting comment on this current in "How Psychology Might Contribute to Reducing the Risk of Nuclear War," *Political Psychology* 17, no. 4 (1986): pp. 627–28.

15. Joseph V. Montville, "A Commentary on Stanley Hoffman's Presidential Address," *Political Psychology* 7, no. 2 (1986): pp. 219–22.

16. Herbert C. Kelman, "A Behavioral-Science Perspective on the Study of War and Peace," in *Perspectives on the Behavioral Sciences: The Colorado Lectures*, ed. Richard Jessor (forthcoming). For useful overviews of peace research, see also Dean G. Pruitt and Richard C. Snyder, *Theory and Research on the Causes of War* (Englewood Cliffs: Prentice-Hall, Inc., 1969) [1950s–60s]; Juergen Dedring, *Recent Advances in Peace and Conflict Research* (Beverly Hills, Ca.: Sage Publications, 1976) [1970s–80s]; C.M. Stephenson, ed., *Alternative Methods for International Security* (Lanham, Md.: University Press of America, 1982) [1950s–to date].

17. For a harshly critical article, which will be dismissed by many but which contains warnings worth heeding, see Donald Kagan, "The Pseudo-Science of 'Peace,'" *Public Interest* 78 (Winter 1985). For a positive but individual perspective, see Kenneth E. Boulding, *Stable Peace* (Austin: University of Texas Press, 1978).

18. Gene Sharp, *The Politics of Nonviolent Action* (Boston: Porter Sargent Publishers, Inc., 1973); and *Making Europe Unconquerable: The Potential of Civilian-Based Deterrence and Defense* (New York: Ballinger, 1985).

19. For positive views of the contribution that anthropologists are making, see *The Anthropology of War and Peace: Perspectives on the Nuclear Age*, eds. Paul Turner and David Pitt (Granby, Mass.: Bergin and Garvey Publishers, 1988); and Milton

Singer's *Nuclear Policy, Culture and History* (Chicago: Center for International Studies of the University of Chicago, 1988).

20. Kagan, "The Pseudo-Science of Peace," p. 61.

21. James N. Rosenau, *The Study of Global Interdependence* (New York: Nichols Publishing Co., 1980). For more recent work, see *Global Changes and Theoretical Challenges* (Lexington, Mass.: Lexington Books, forthcoming) and *Turbulence in World Politics* (Princeton: Princeton University Press, forthcoming).

22. Julien Benda, *Treason of the Intellectuals*, trans. Richard Aldington (New York: W. W. Norton and Co., 1969).

23. *The Challenge of Peace: God's Promise and Our Response: A Pastoral Letter on War and Peace*, National Conference of Catholic Bishops, May 3, 1983, publication no. 863 (Washington, D.C.: United States Catholic Conference); also George Weigel, *Tranquillitas Ordinis* (New York: Oxford University Press, 1987); and *The Peace Bishops and the Arms Race: Can Religious Leadership Help in Preventing War?* (Chicago: World Without War Publications, 1982). See also *International Ethics in the Nuclear Age*, ed. Robert J. Myers (New York: Carnegie Council on Ethics and International Affairs, 1987) for an excellent overview of the current discussion (note especially the essay by Joseph S. Nye, Jr., on ethics and foreign policy, pp. 39–84).

24. Marguerite Green, ed., *Americans and World Affairs: A Guide to Organizations and Institutions in Northern California* (Berkeley: World Without War Council of Northern California, 1988). The typology of organizations from this guide is available on request, as is a sampling of titles of other guides to special categories of organizations in the field.

25. Marguerite Green, ed., *Peace Archives: A Guide to Library Collections* (Berkeley: World Without War Council, 1986).

26. See, for example, the work in the early 1980s of Scientists for Sakharov, Orlov, and Shcharansky, and current work of the Center for Democracy in the U.S.S.R., a New York-based organization.

27. *ASCD Curriculum Update*, January 1986 (Arlington, Va.: Association for Supervision and Curriculum Development).

28. Charter for the *Alliance for Education in Global and International Studies*, "A Statement of Goals and Values for [AEGIS]," October 1987, p. 5. (Available from Ronald Herring, Institute for International Studies, Littlefield Center, Stanford University, Stanford, CA 94305-5013, or from the World Without War Council.)

29. *Guidelines*, Peace, Freedom, and Security Studies Program (Wheaton, Ill.: National Association of Evangelicals, October 1986).

30. See chapter 1 of this volume.

31. Christopher Kruegler, "Liddell Hart and the Concept of Civilian-based Defense," Ph.D. diss., Syracuse University, 1984.

32. Roger Sperry, "Changing Priorities," *Annual Review of Neuroscience* (Palo Alto, Ca.: Annual Reviews, Inc., 1981), vol. 4, pp. 1–15, quoted in *Paths to Peace: Exploring the Feasibility of Sustainable Peace*, Richard Smoke with Willis Harman (Boulder, Colo.: Westview Press, Inc., 1987), p. 93.

33. Smoke and Harman, *Paths to Peace*, p. 94.

34. Andrey V. Kozyrev, "Why Soviet Foreign Policy Went Sour," *New York Times*, January 7, 1989.

35. Hans Morgenthau, *Politics Among Nations*, 5th ed. (New York: Alfred Knopf, 1978). See especially "Six Principles of Political Realism," pp. 3–13.

36. Chester Finn, quoted in John O'Neil, "Global Education: Controversy Remains, But Support Is Growing," *ASCD Curriculum Update*, January 1989 (Arlington, Va.: Association for Supervision and Curriculum Development), p. 6.

37. See, for example, Gene Sharp's unusually succinct listing in his Wallach Award-winning essay, "Making the Abolition of War a Realistic Goal" (Chicago: World Without War Council Issues Center-Midwest Newsletter, 1980), which includes the following: conflicts of some type will always exist within societies and between societies, requiring use of some type of power; "human nature" need not, and most likely will not, be changed; people and governments will not sacrifice freedom or justice for the sake of peace; mass conversions to pacifism are not going to occur; brutal dictatorships and oppressive systems exist, will continue, may become more serious, and may seek to expand; the abolition of capitalism does not produce the abolition of war; and negotiations are no substitute for the capacity to struggle and apply sanctions.

Introduction to Chapter 10

In this chapter, Joseph Montville traces the evolution of the theory of transnationalism—people-to-people interaction outside the government context—from the formative years of its development to one of its most interesting and current applications, "track-two" diplomacy. Noting the radical growth in the number and size of international nongovernmental organizations over the past eighty years, Montville suggests that transnationalism is best understood not so much as a road to peace but as a process of long-term "peacebuilding." Critical to that process has been the increased focus on functionalism—a term used by Montville to define the study and development of "those international organizations arranged according to the requirements of the task to increase welfare rewards to the individual beyond the level obtainable within the nation-state."

Despite the optimism that has characterized the growth of these organizations, particularly the functionalists' centerpiece, the UN, their cumulative impact on the level of international peace has been limited. The reason lies, Montville says, in the failure of transnationalism, functionalism, and other such theories to address the fundamental issue of human psychology and its relationship to the causes of international conflict.

One of the many paradoxes of human interaction and organization is the need of individuals to seek the identity and security provided by the group, combined with the seeming inability of such groups to appreciate the motivations of others engaged in an identical process. The result is identity by negation: "I am an Israeli Jew, not an Arab"; "I am an Irish Catholic, not an Irish Protestant." This process, says Montville, naturally leads to competition between groups and often results in violent conflict. The task of the would-be peacemaker under these conditions is extraordinarily complex and requires a psychologically sensitive approach not usually included in traditional diplomatic training. Track-two diplomacy focuses on the direct interactions of members of adversarial groups or nations aimed at developing strategies to influence public opinion and marshal human and material resources to resolve the conflict at issue. It has shown early potential as a supplement to diplomatic and other government-to-government negotiations.

Montville describes the process, which works through small, intensive problem-solving workshops in which representatives of conflictive groups meet to distill their differences and come to terms with each other's essential needs. The aim is to rehumanize the relationship so that reason, rather than emotion, becomes the dynamic factor of interaction. Participants return to their own communities and share the lessons they learned from their meetings.

10. Transnationalism and the Role of Track-Two Diplomacy

Joseph V. Montville

"Transnationalism" is a term for "actions undertaken by entities larger than nations or smaller than nations and outside the framework of nation-states."[1] In its most positive conception, transnationalism aims to enhance the prospect of peaceful political relationships. It expresses the view that collaborative interaction between and among peoples outside the government context reduces the likelihood of war and strengthens the movement toward international community.

This view is apparently gaining increasing international support. Elise Boulding, professor emerita of sociology at Dartmouth College, reports that the number of international nongovernmental organizations (INGOs) grew from 176 in 1909 to more than 18,000 in 1988. They include not only churches, farmers' organizations, service clubs, and chambers of commerce, but also coalitions on disarmament, the environment, human rights, and Third World economic development.[2]

It is certainly the value-driven version of transnationalism that qualifies the concept for inclusion in "an investigation of the roads to peace," but when the subject came into fashion among American scholars in the early 1970s, its normative implications were addressed only marginally if at all. During this period, political science, such as it was, and the study of international relations tended to be essentially descriptive rather than prescriptive and to rely on the "physics" model of politics. Or, as Joseph Nye and Robert Keohane put it in their collection of essays entitled *Transnational Relations and World Politics*, .

> Students and practitioners of international politics have traditionally concentrated their attention on relationships between states. The state, regarded as an actor with purposes and power, is the basic unit of action; its main agents are the diplomat and soldier. The interplay of governmental policies yields the pattern of behavior that students of international politics attempt to understand and that practitioners attempt to adjust to or control. Since force, violence, and threats thereof are at the core of this interplay, the struggle for power, whether as an end or necessary means, is the distinguishing mark of politics among nations. Most political scientists and many diplomats accept this view of reality, and a state-centric view of world affairs prevails.[3]

It was the prevalence of the state-centric focus of analysis that inspired Nye and Keohane to provide evidence in support of their differing view of world politics. In their conception, the state remains the prime actor, but numerous other transnational actors significantly influence the context within which states act and inevitably undermine the ability of states to control events in the way they would like. The essays examined the roles of multinational corporations, private international finance, international terrorist networks, the Ford Foundation, airlines, scientific organizations, and the Roman Catholic church, among others.

In light of this enriched sense of global interaction of states and non-government forces, Nye and Keohane offered a definition of politics that referred "to relationships in which at least one actor consciously employs resources, both material and symbolic, including the threat or exercise of punishment, to induce other actors to behave differently than they would otherwise behave."[4] The world politics version of this definition included "all political interaction between significant actors in a world system in which a significant actor is any somewhat autonomous individual or organization that controls substantial resources and participates in political relationships with other actors across state lines."[5]

This was, in its time, a useful advance in the conceptualization of international politics. By using the term "relationships," rather than "international relations" or "affairs," Nye and Keohane were implying that politics was infinitely more complex than the physics- or power-oriented models previously held and that perhaps biology, with all those "official" and "unofficial" elements swimming around on the microscope's slide, was a more appropriate image. The even more elusive psychology model, as is shown later, was yet to establish a meaningful intellectual beachhead.

In 1973 Harvard scholar Samuel P. Huntington published an essay entitled "Transnational Organizations in World Politics."[6] Like Nye and Keohane, Huntington concluded that the proliferation of transnational actors had clearly limited the capacity of states to impose their will. But he muddied his argument by throwing into his collection of multinational corporations, international financial institutions, airlines, churches, and philanthropies the United States Air Force and the Central Intelligence Agency. Furthermore, Huntington insisted that "internationalism [the interaction of states, for example, at the United Nations] is a dead end."[7]

There was, of course, no way Huntington could know at the time that a Gorbachev would come along, pay up Moscow's back dues, and announce strong support for the UN's mission; that the UN secretary general would play an important mediating role in the Afghan and Iran-Iraq wars; and that an enlarged European Community (EC) would be on the verge of becoming the biggest internal market and trading bloc in the history of the world (in 1992).

In none of the essays just referred to did the authors contend that transnationalism was inevitably a "road to peace." Neither, indeed, do I in this chapter. But this chapter does belong in the normative category that sees an aspect of transnationalism—that is, the deliberate use of nongovernment, transborder interaction among individuals and groups—as part of a *process* of potential peace building. The remainder of this chapter is addressed to this subject. In light of this bias, we might turn to a related, and perhaps more focused, name for transnationalism, which is "functionalism."

In an introduction to *The Functional Theory of Politics* by the late David Mitrany, recognized widely as the father of functionalism, Paul Taylor of the London School of Economics described functionalism as the belief

> that man can be weaned away from his loyalty to the nation-state by the experience of fruitful international cooperation; that international organizations arranged according to the requirements of the task could increase welfare rewards to individuals beyond the level obtainable within the state; that the rewards would be greater if the organization worked, where necessary, across national frontiers, which may frequently cut into the organization's ideal working area. Individuals and groups could begin to learn the benefits of cooperation and would be increasingly involved in an international cooperative ethos, creating interdependencies, pushing for further integration, undermining the most important bases of the nation-state.[8]

In his award-winning study of international organization, *Swords Into Ploughshares*, Inis L. Claude, Jr., wrote that functionalism is based on a complex conception of the causes of war and the nature of peace, which he divided into three broad components. First, war results not from the instinctive nature of man or his innate sinfulness but rather from the objective conditions of state and society. War is a product of gravely flawed economic and social systems. Poverty, disease, economic and social inequity, and other systemic dysfunctions account for the moral and emotional breakdown leading to war. By promising to raise living standards in poor, underdeveloped countries, and by breaking down the political boundaries that inhibit economic developmental processes, functionalism will treat the basic ills of mankind.

Claude's second component is that functionalism holds the system of sovereign nation-states to blame for structurally promoting the conditions of mindless and destructive state competition.

> The state system imposes an arbitrary and rigid pattern of vertical divisions upon global society, disrupting the organic unity of the whole, and carving the world into segments whose separateness is jealously guarded by sovereignties which are neither able to solve the fundamental problems nor willing to permit them to be solved by other authorities.[9]

The third component is that functionalism aims ultimately to change the basic conditions of human existence. If people's attention is focused on the regions within which constructive economic and social tasks are performed rather than on artificial political boundaries, the habit of human cooperation will be developed. And the international organizations that help perform the tasks that assure the good life will be seen as natural and beneficent, far more deserving of support than traditional political units.

For students and proponents of functionalism, the UN and its related agencies were natural instruments of the concept. That these international organizations could not bear the burden of the tasks assigned to them by the theorists became clear soon enough. Writing in 1970, Claude made a trenchant assessment:

> The clearest lesson of United Nations experience is that functionalism's assumption of the preliminary separability of political and nonpolitical matters does not hold true—not in this generation, at any rate. We are not vouchsafed the privilege of warming up the motors of international collaboration in a sheltered area of concordant interests, getting off to an easy start, and building up momentum for crashing the barriers of conflicting interests that interpose between us and the ideal of world order. The dilemma of functionalism is that its ultimate impact upon politics may never be tested because of the immediate impact of politics upon functionalism.[10]

David Mitrany's own judgment on the virtues of functionalism was bleak as well as poignant. In the epilogue to *The Functional Theory of Politics*, written toward the end of his academic career in 1975, he said,

> Hope as one may, at this moment the political prospect looks like the slow inexorable march of a Greek tragedy—not at the ordering of the Gods, but in the making of man himself . . . having dethroned the Gods, subdued nature, and subjugated mechanical force, man is now the only ruler of man—and his chief enemy.[11]

There is the rub. Despite the best efforts of scholars, the clergy, and enlightened leaders in government, business, and the arts to develop rational theories, plans, and programs for the constructive governance and development of humankind beyond the quarreling state system, surges of humanoid irrationality persist, and states engage in hostile policies, acts of military aggression or terrorism, coups, assassinations, and brutal violations of the most fundamental human rights.

Without explicitly identifying the theoretical flaws of functionalism or, in fact, almost all international relations theory in the Western tradition, David Mitrany spotted the problem: Conflict theory based primarily on the dysfunction of systems or structures—whether legal, constitutional, economic, or social—leaves out the critical analytical component of human psychology.

Learning Political Psychology

When we consider how much scientifically sound scholarship in political psychology is available, it is remarkable to realize the extent of the resistance to learning it on the part of academics, journalists, political actors, diplomats, military officers, and others with varying degrees of responsibility for thinking about or assuring the security of nations. Yet the serious student of the science of individual and group behavior in politics—that is, political psychology—soon learns that the resistance to knowing is one of the principal subjects political psychologists have to study. Such resistance is a psychological defense against information or realities that, if acknowledged, could generate painful anxiety in some people about their personal fears or inadequacies or about external conditions that threaten or are seen to threaten their job security, dignity, self-esteem, or even their very survival.[12]

This and other forms of irrationality that make politics such a difficult subject to understand led scholars, psychotherapists, government officials, journalists, and others from five continents to form the International Society of Political Psychology (ISPP) more than a decade ago, with its headquarters in the United States. The scholars, in particular, shared the strong feeling that much of political and social science at the time was so preoccupied with methodology imitative of the natural sciences—the *Journal of the American Political Science Association* looked more like a textbook on physics—that it was making no contribution to the critical survival issues of the age, particularly the threat of nuclear disaster by design or by accident.

The formation of the ISPP, then, could be seen as a human adaptive response to a genuine and serious threat to the survival of the species. Man was indeed man's worst enemy, and the study of the enemy phenomenon became a major preoccupation of psychopolitical theory. In June 1988, an important new contribution on this subject—*The Need to Have Enemies and Allies: From Clinical Practice to International Relationships*[13]—was published by Vamik D. Volkan. Volkan is a medical doctor, psychoanalyst, and past president of the ISPP. He also collaborates with me on numerous political research and theory-building exercises inside and outside the Department of State. The exercises deal with the psychology of the Soviet-American relationship, the psychological tasks of Israeli-Palestinian peacemaking, and strategies to deal with the Greek-Turkish conflict on Cyprus, among other subjects.

Volkan's book is a pathbreaking analysis of the human need for identity, recognition, and acceptance as an aspect of security, and of the way the individual developmental process of identity construction expands to deeply rooted identification with the tribe, ethnic group, or nation. This identification is so profound that individuals readily lay down their lives for the defense of the group.

An important way that identity is established is by knowing who one is not. In stark political example note: in Northern Ireland, I am a Catholic and not a Protestant; in Israel, I am an Israeli (Jew) and not an Arab; in South Africa, I am an Afrikaner and not a black. These very examples demonstrate that the emotional distinction between identity groups can become brutal or, at least in the dreams of some, genocidal. The mutual fear and loathing that generate the dehumanization process between groups and nations in conflict, especially those with a history of bloody clashes or repression, is one of the greatest psychological tasks to confront political conflict resolution strategists or peacemakers. It is a fundamental part of the "politics" Claude deplores, which apparently makes it impossible to determine whether functionalism might ever work.

The Need to Have Enemies and Allies explains the nature of social and political stress and its effect on perceptions of enemy threat. It describes the various levels of intergroup relations possible, from playful competition in peacetime to rituals representing warlike possibilities, to the actual group transition to war preparedness, willingness, and, finally, eagerness to fight. After violent conflict and the losses sustained from it, mourning these losses—whether human, material, territorial, or related to a sense of identity or self-worth—becomes a psychologically obligatory process if the peoples involved are to adapt to new situations and get on with life. It is in the enduring conflicted political relationships such as those just noted that the mourning process has not been completed and the adversaries become locked in a perpetual negative symbiosis.

It is in cases like these—and the overwhelming majority of violent political conflicts around the world are long-standing ethnic and sectarian conflicts—that peacemaking strategies require rigorous analysis to identify the psychological tasks that must be completed before the more conventional business of traditional diplomacy and political negotiation can be undertaken. One of the great challenges in this regard is working with and through the psychopolitical phenomenon of victimhood.[14]

Throughout life, human beings experience varying levels of anxiety about their safety and survival. By adhering to the institutions of family, work, and society, human beings develop tangible and psychological defenses against unexpected negative events in life—the sudden death of the breadwinner, criminal assault, accident or disability, impoverishment, or war. Individuals have a protective superstructure of belief in safety through membership in a social system—tribe, ethnic group, or nation—that gives them a sense of personal power and self-worth.

Victimization destroys the defensive structure. It exposes the victim (or victim group) to unrelieved, conscious anxiety about real threats to its existence. This state of anxiety is extremely difficult to endure, and it produces a toleration of and need for constant defensive action—cynicism, militance, violence, or even terrorism—to assure survival in what is seen as a relentlessly hostile environment. Victims in the psychological sense have almost always suffered personal physical or emotional violence that has generated a sense of profound loss. They believe that there was no justification for the violence, by any standard of human justice, and they implicitly or explicitly fear that the perpetrator of the violence and loss will continue or resume the aggression at any time.

The psychological tasks generated by victimhood for would-be peacemakers are enormous. They defy the skills of traditional diplomacy and mediation and have not been part of the agenda of scholars of international relations, including the well-meaning architects of transnationalism, functionalism, and world order theory. There is strong evidence that dismantling the rigid, fear-based defenses of victimhood requires elaborate small-group leadership and large-group or nationwide processes of rehumanization of the adversary relationship; recognition of grievances past and present; offers and acceptance of forgiveness; and commitments to conduct relationships on new, higher levels of morality, intellect, and, where feasible, collaboration.[15]

The more recent the experience of violence, the more difficult the reconciliation process might be. Here, for example, is the conclusion of a 1988 report of an American group called Physicians for Human Rights, which documented thousands of deliberately inflicted limb, body, and head injuries in the West Bank and Gaza Palestinian uprising that began in December 1987:

> Serious and potentially long-lasting psychological damage may ensue for many segments of the Palestinian population, especially to children and adolescents, and for the Israeli population, especially the soldiers. The consequences of the present violence may well affect a whole generation and thereby further constrict the possibilities of peaceful resolution in the future. As injury and death become routine, there is a steady erosion of the basic principles that all human life should be protected and that Palestinian and Israeli lives are equally precious. We observed an accumulating burden of rage and mutual dehumanization in response to the unremitting toll of bloodshed. Impulses for revenge lead to further escalation. Violations of medical and human rights are increasing as both sides become habituated to violence and complex political conflicts are reduced to a daily body count.[16]

Creating Positive Public Attitudes

Stanley Hoffmann, one of the most internationally respected analysts of international relations and also a past president of the ISPP, has said flatly, "Politics is wholly psychological."[17] If we return to Claude's critique of functionalism as stymied by "politics," and substitute the word "psychology" for "politics" in his assessment, we get closer to the roots of the problem. Thus,

On the whole, the accumulated evidence tends to discredit, rather than confirm, the basic proposition that preliminary concentration on international cooperation in the areas designated by functionalism promises to heal the [psychological] cleavages that plague the international system. This judgement must be tentative, for functionalism has been presented as a long-term program of [psychological] therapy, not as an instant palliative.[18]

Then Claude introduces the concept of "neo-functionalism." He writes,

Whereas "classical" functionalism relies upon the cooperative pursuit of common interests in nonpolitical fields to generate political changes conducive to peace, neo-functionalism stresses the utility of such enterprises as elements in a program of political engineering, as contributors to the realization of political designs.[19]

If we substitute "program of [psychological] engineering, as contributors to the realization of [psychological] designs" in the quotation, we come face to face with my preoccupation with the development of psychologically sensitive, political conflict resolution theory and, just as important, action programs, as a basis for a new problem-solving diplomacy. One name for this phenomenon, which I suggested in 1981 and which since has gained some currency in the field, is "track-two diplomacy."[20]

In the simplest terms, track-two diplomacy is unofficial, informal interaction among members of adversarial groups or nations with the goals of developing strategies, influencing public opinion, and organizing human and material resources in ways that might help resolve the conflict. Although there has been a good deal of hubris on the part of citizen supporters of track-two diplomacy who wish to bypass government and let "the people" do the job, my concept of track-two diplomacy fully recognizes and accepts the exclusive authority of governments to negotiate and make binding agreements with leaders of political groups or with other governments. This power is in the hands only of duly constituted authorities.

But the theory of track-two diplomacy also recognizes that, for increasingly apparent psychological reasons, governments are constrained by the emotional attitudes of their constituencies, if not by the personality flaws of certain individual leaders, and thus the ability of governments to take risks for peace is limited by the degree of fear and loathing toward the adversary found in public opinion. This is particularly true in conflicts characterized by a strong sense of victimhood generated by fairly recent histories of violent confrontation. As noted by the Physicians for Human Rights, the Israeli-Palestinian crisis is an obvious and painful example. The Sinhalese-Tamil conflict in Sri Lanka is also particularly vulnerable to popular passions for revenge, as is the Armenian-Azerbaijani conflict in the Soviet Union.

Other protracted ethnic conflicts also place significant limits on their leaders' ability to explore strategies of reconciliation, for example, Northern

Ireland, South Africa, Cyprus, and Lebanon. Interestingly, the lack of a history of violent conflict between the Soviet Union and the United States may explain the relative ease with which President Reagan was able to lead American public opinion toward a more benign attitude concerning the Soviet Union, despite the long-standing "sectarian" conflict between the two superpowers.

Track-two diplomatic strategies place great importance on the instrument of unofficial, informal problem-solving workshops mediated or facilitated by psychologically sensitive third parties. The workshops bring politically influential representatives of parties in dispute together for three- to five-day sessions in which at some point the conflict comes to be seen as a shared problem requiring the cooperative contributions of both sides toward resolution. I have participated in seven major workshops as part of the third-party team and can attest that, when they are properly designed, they almost always succeed in developing meaningful levels of mutual confidence among the opponents and producing practical strategies for at least initial steps in a conflict resolution strategy.

The workshop instrument is vital and must be seen as the foundation stone for the process of peace building. But by itself, the workshop has a very limited chance of changing the conflict for the better. The workshop leaders must "reenter" their communities or nations where the people have had no facilitated learning experience. They still fear and hate, and they are quite capable of ignoring, rejecting, or even assassinating a leader who is trying to promote reconciliation rather than revenge. In such a situation, the demagogue pandering to these negative emotions always has the advantage.

Track-two diplomacy, therefore, has a critical second component, which is the development of grand strategies to create a public opinion environment in which it is safer for political leaders to take risks for peace. The goal of such strategies is to arrest the dehumanization process between the groups in conflict, and gradually to educate the population about the human dimension of the pain and loss all sides suffer from the conflict. It is a difficult cognitive and group psychological process.

My favorite example of an institutionalized action program to improve negative public attitudes is Neve Shalom/Wahat al-Salam, the voluntary Jewish-Palestinian village in Israel that is determined to demonstrate through day-to-day, year-to-year example, that the two peoples can live together in peace and mutual respect. The name of the village means "oasis of peace," and it contains a School for Peace that has trained approximately ten thousand Jewish and Palestinian young people in four-day workshops to learn to value each other as innately worthy human beings with a universal right to life and to the fulfillment of their developmental potential. In the tragic uprising in the occupied territories, this village stands as a lonely beacon of hope.

Clearly, the work of a place like Neve Shalom/Wahat al-Salam, which is now being studied in Northern Ireland and South Africa, must be supplemented with changes in education curricula, programs in the popular media, and, at some point, individual acts of moral and intellectual leadership by political and nonpolitical actors who command respect in the community.

There is reason to believe that the broader the voluntary participation among groups of citizens in the communities in conflict, the more successful the process of rehumanizing the relationship will be. Such activity could be classified as neofunctional. It would be nonofficial, nonspecifically political, "cross-border" interaction among citizens, but with a clear purpose of political (psychological) engineering.

The classic example is the extensive number of citizen initiatives that took place simultaneously with the development of the European Coal and Steel Community in the process of Franco-German reconciliation after World War II. Tens of thousands of French and German academics, businessmen, journalists, politicians, artists, schoolchildren, and young people participated in collaborative exchanges in their areas of interest. Activities included language instruction, summer camps, and joint performances of theater and music groups. All this activity literally and figuratively signified the reintegration of the two peoples on a positive, human psychological level.

One must admit that it is easy to romanticize the Franco-German reconciliation at the psychological level. The citizens in both countries who made the transformation from hatred to respectful engagement with the former enemy were probably a small minority of educated people high on the late Lawrence Kohlberg's scale of intellectual and moral development. And here is where the third component of track-two diplomacy, which Claude would call "developmental functionalism," comes into play. Those elements of society unaffected by purely moral and intellectual arguments might well be attracted by material incentives. And, for that matter, even moralists have to make a living.[21]

The Coal and Steel Community was a striking example of cooperative economic development or developmental functionalism, as were the thousands of other enterprises, many financed by the Marshall Plan, which allowed French, German, and other West European countries to do political good while doing well economically. The result was the "economic miracle"; the EC, now with twelve members; and with luck, in 1992, the actual common market in goods, services, and labor flowing unimpeded across political boundaries. This event should be at least the regional answer to the functionalist's dream.

The only other example of the second component of track-two diplomacy, or cross-group psychological engineering of which I am aware and which approaches the design and level of Franco-German citizen participation is the joint Northern Ireland–Irish Republic organization called Cooperation North. It was founded a decade ago at the initiative of Brendan O'Regan, the visionary entrepreneur and manager who led the development of the duty-free shop and industrial zone at Shannon, which became a worldwide phenomenon. Allied with Catholics and Protestants from the north and the south of the island, O'Regan has built an organization through which some ten thousand young people engaged in cross-border exchanges in 1987 and which involved almost half of the secondary-level schools in Northern Ireland.

Research, consultation, and information exchange are fostered by Cooperation North among businesses, north and south, to enhance the environment for joint ventures and to increase trade. But the major contribution to the practice of track-two diplomacy, in terms of creating a positive attitude in public opinion in both communities, is the organization's emphasis on "fun" activities for ordinary people. The most popular of these is the "Maracycle," in which thirty-five hundred people bicycled the hundred miles between Belfast and Dublin in 1987. In 1988, Cooperation North sponsored a "Marastroll," which attracted fifteen hundred people from each side of the border for a trek between the two capitals.

What is psychologically intriguing about the bicycling, but especially the walk, is that for thousands of Catholic and Protestant participants, the mental representation of the island will be of one place and, for a short time at least, of one community with two traditions. The exercise will symbolically do away with the idea of state sovereignty and political borders, of keeping people apart. And the image may well sink into many Irish minds.

In 1985, in Shannon and Londonderry, O'Regan founded the Irish Peace Institute (IPI), which is composed of faculty from Ulster University and the National Institute of Higher Education, now University of Limerick, in the south. And in 1987, the IPI spawned the Centre for International Cooperation, also at Shannon, which has major corporate business sponsors, to facilitate functional economic relationships across borders east and west, north and south around the globe. The center has hosted three international conferences on tourism, global communications, and trade, with Soviet, EC, North American, and some, but not nearly enough, Third World participation.

Cooperation North and its sister institutions make up an impressive infrastructure for the development of a genuine sense of community in Ireland. Unique in O'Regan's contribution to track-two diplomacy is his conviction that successful business leaders have a moral obligation to contribute to peace building, and that commerce is a logical engine to power constructive transformation in conflicted societies. What Cooperation North, the IPI, and the Centre for International Cooperation urgently need now is the funding that will allow them to approach critical mass in public opinion.

Collaborating for Economic Development

The work of the three institutions to help create positive public attitudes has now been joined by activities that approximate the third component of track-two diplomacy—collaborative economic development, or developmental functionalism.

Foremost among such activities is the International Fund, which was established by the U.S. Congress at the initiative of the former speaker of the House of Representatives, Thomas P. (Tip) O'Neill, and which has been increased by donations from other industrialized countries. The fund, devoted to investment in cross-border enterprise to increase Ireland's production, employment, and income, could be seen in design, if not scope, as a functional equivalent of the Marshall Plan.

Also in 1987–88, a potentially significant development in cross-border trade development linked to the U.S. market was led by an organization called Boston-Ireland Ventures. This initiative, in which the highly respected and increasingly psychologically sensitive political analyst Padraig O'Malley played a significant role from his base at the University of Massachusetts at Boston, links businesses in Londonderry (Northern Ireland), in Galway (Republic of Ireland), and in Boston.

The Derry organization is led by two businessmen, a former politically militant Protestant and a Catholic. Mayor Flynn of Boston is a vigorous supporter of the scheme, which is seen as a model for additional trade triangles linking U.S. and Irish (north and south) cities. O'Malley has told me that previously pessimistic Derry Catholics, who had a low sense of self-worth and a dependency mentality because of their disadvantaged minority status, have become psychologically empowered by the opportunity to take business initiatives and work for themselves. He said it was exciting to see how much people have changed for the better in only one year.

Conclusion

Unfortunately, this chapter cannot be concluded on such an optimistic note. Although there is much good work being done in the Irish case and even in the Israeli-Palestinian case, there continue to be clashes, bombings, and assassinations between the Irish Republican Army (IRA) and British troops, and between Palestinians and Israeli troops. Every new report of violence is a tragic reminder that political grievances, some centuries old, remain alive in the consciousness of the conflicting peoples. In terms of the psychology of victimhood, a British soldier killed by the IRA is a direct descendent symbolically of one of Oliver Cromwell's English soldiers who participated in the seventeenth-century repression of Catholic Gaels. A Palestinian killed by an Israeli soldier is, in terms of Jewish historic victimhood, a direct descendent of a Cossack or a soldier of the Spanish Inquisition who participated in pogroms, massacres, and executions in their Gentile contributions to a final solution to "the Jewish problem." And, in the tragic continuation of the cycle of violence, Israeli assertion of the right to a homeland has made a new group of victims of the Palestinian people.

The amount of work to do remains discouraging, and much remains to be discovered about the process of resolving violent political conflict. But as each day passes, more is being learned about man as enemy of man. If track-two diplomats continue to make thoughtful, prudent, but psychologically imaginative contributions, some day track-one diplomats may be better able to do their job. And perhaps one fine day, tracks one and two may converge in an enlightened, life-enhancing form of statecraft for the third millennium of the current era, which is just around the corner.

Discussion

With regard to Joseph Montville's presentation, commentator Juergen Dedring acknowledged that track-two diplomacy might play a useful role in the future, but as long as the nation-state remains the primary level of analysis, the effects of track-two diplomacy seem fleeting. What is needed, he suggested, are methods by which the international community can be weaned from its overreliance on the nation-state and moved toward multilateralism. The central role of the UN secretary general in negotiating the cessation of hostilities in Afghanistan and in the Iran-Iraq War showed the promise that such non-state-based intervention can play. The same holds true for UN activities in Cyprus and the Middle East, where security considerations and decisions have been made beyond the nation-state.

Dedring attributed the phenomenon—by which basic instrumentalities and key issues are handled without primary consideration given to the nation-state—at least partially to the worldwide revolution in communication and satellite technology that does not recognize state boundaries. It is no longer possible to keep information from the citizens of the world about what is happening in other regions of the globe. The international system is still dominated by sovereign states acting unilaterally, but the world is gradually coming to realize the enormous benefits that successful multilateralism can convey.

Similarly, just as modern communication devices do not recognize sovereign territories, neither do the most pressing problems facing the world today. Issues such as terrorism, drug abuse, environmental degradation, communicable disease, and economic desperation must be seen as global problems in need of multilateral solutions.

The subsequent open discussion reflected the same diversity that characterized the panel presentations. Myres McDougal agreed with Dedring that any discussion of transnationalism should concentrate on private associations rather than on government institutions, but he said that Dedring had vastly underestimated the role government institutions can play in lessening international conflict. He further asserted that Montville's focus on political psychology is essential, but that much of the work done in this field, beginning with Sigmund Freud's, has been ignored.

Lily Gardner Feldman endorsed the two-track approach, with its emphasis on actors rather than on issues, and suggested that more research is needed to determine how such actors influence nation-state sovereignty and how they can be more efficiently utilized.

Elise Boulding noted that, although vast amounts of pertinent information regarding INGOs has been accumulated and computerized, the information is rarely used. She said there is a clear need for a more structural analysis of the existing INGO networks.

The role of religion was the topic of two related questions. Jay Lintner, observing that religious differences are at the core of many protracted international conflicts, raised the question of whether governments foster rather than ameliorate the "enemy images" that Montville spoke of in his paper. This observation was followed by a suggestion from the floor that a more ecumenical approach is needed to deal with these conflicts, to break the cycle of violence that evolves.

Robert Rudney pointed out that INGOs are not a new phenomenon but have long played an important role in the history of civilization and will, no doubt, continue to do so in the future. However, some have been vastly more successful than others in achieving their goals. The question that must be addressed, he said, is what explains the difference between success and failure among various INGOs? How do their strategies and activities differ and what are the implications of those differences?

Montville concluded the discussion with two comments. Environmental degradation offers the best example of why transnational solutions to problems should be attempted. The destruction of the ozone layer, he noted, and general concern about air pollution indicate a growing awareness of the indiscriminate nature of environmental disasters. The entire population of the globe will be exposed to greater risk of skin cancer, not just people in the countries originally responsible for the problem.

With respect to wars stemming from religious conviction, Montville suggested that appeals must be made to the resources of reconciliation that exist in every faith. Otherwise, as history has shown, the likelihood of prolonged conflict is high.

Notes

1. William M. Evan, "Transnational Forums for Peace," in Quincy Wright, William M. Evan, and Morton Deutsch, eds., *Preventing World War III* (New York: Simon and Schuster, 1962), p. 395.

2. Elise Boulding, "The Rise of INGOs: New Leadership for a Planet in Transition," *Breakthrough* (Fall 1987/Spring 1988): pp. 14–17.

3. Joseph Nye and Robert Keohane, eds., *Transnational Relations and World Politics* (Cambridge: Harvard University Press, 1972), p. ix.

4. Nye and Keohane, *Transnational Relations*, p. xxiv.

5. Nye and Keohane, *Transnational Relations*.

6. Samuel P. Huntington, "Transnational Organizations in World Politics," *World Politics* XXV (April 1973): pp. 333–68.

7. Huntington, *World Politics* XXV, p. 368.

8. Paul Taylor, Introduction to David Mitrany, *The Functional Theory of Politics* (New York: St. Martin's Press, 1974), p. x.

9. Inis L. Claude, Jr., *Swords Into Ploughshares*, 4th ed. (New York: Random House, 1970), p. 382.

10. Claude, *Swords Into Ploughshares*, p. 399.

11. David Mitrany, *Functional Theory of Politics*, p. 267. Mitrany seems to have been overly pessimistic. Joseph S. Nye's *Peace in Parts: Integration and Conflict in Regional Organization* (Boston: Little, Brown and Co., 1971) is an excellent analysis of the weaknesses and the modest potential of regional functional organizations.

12. See John E. Mack, "Resistances to Knowing in the Nuclear Age," *Harvard Education Review* 54, no. 3 (August 1984): pp. 260–70.

13. Vamik D. Volkan, *The Need to Have Enemies and Allies: From Clinical Practice to International Relationships* (Northvale, N.J.: Jason Aronson, 1988).

14. The definition of victimhood is from Joseph V. Montville, "Psychoanalytic Enlightenment and the Greening of Diplomacy," a plenary address to the American Psychoanalytic Association in New York, December 19, 1986.

15. Montville, "Psychoanalytic Enlightenment," and Volkan, *Need to Have Enemies and Allies*.

16. Physicians for Human Rights, "The Casualties of Conflict: Medical Care and Human Rights in the West Bank and Gaza Strip," *Report of a Medical Fact-Finding Mission*, March 30, 1988, as quoted in John E. Mack, "T.E. Lawrence's Vision for the Middle East: How Does It Look Now?" Keynote address, T.E. Lawrence Symposium, Pepperdine University, Malibu, California, May 20, 1988, unpublished.

17. Stanley Hoffmann, "On the Political Psychology of Peace and War: A Critique and an Agenda," presidential address to the ISPP Washington, D.C., June 20, 1985, published first in *Political Psychology* 7, no. 1 (June 1986) and reprinted in Stanley Hoffmann, *Janus and Minerva: Essays in the Theory and Practice of International Politics* (Boulder, Colo.: Westview, 1987).

18. Claude, *Swords Into Ploughshares*, pp. 403–04.

19. Claude, *Swords Into Ploughshares*.

20. See William D. Davidson and Joseph V. Montville, "Foreign Policy According to Freud," in *Foreign Policy*, no. 45 (Winter 1981–82), and Joseph V. Montville, "The Arrow and the Olive Branch: A Case for Track Two Diplomacy," in John W. McDonald, Jr. and Diane B. Bendahmane, *Conflict Resolution: Track Two Diplomacy* (Washington, D.C.: Foreign Service Institute, 1987).

21. Claude, *Swords into Ploughshares*, p. 404.

Introduction to Chapter 11

The behavioral school of international relations, Nazli Choucri points out in this chapter, was formulated in the mid-1950s as a reaction to the realist approach to world politics, with its emphasis on power, and to the post-World War I Wilsonian idealism, which had shown itself incapable of preventing another world war.

Born of a desire to identify the causes of war more scientifically and reliably, the behavioral "revolution" was based on two primary assumptions: first, that wars do not simply break out or erupt, but are the result of "functional regularities" in the way nations organize their international relations; and second, that these regularities can be rigorously quantified and modeled to predict conflict more accurately as well as to formulate more appropriate responses to conflict.

Behaviorism rests on the assertion that national power is rooted in the relationship of three master variables—population, technology, and natural resources—all of which are subject to change as a result of government policy and intervention. The ranking of countries that results from this comparative profile measurement is a source of competition among states. As the levels of the three primary ingredients of power change within a state, so, too, does the competitive relationship that the state has with other countries. The resultant "conflict spiral" is a key element in predicting the likelihood of clashes between states.

The leap from a point of collision to full-scale violence is the hardest to predict, measure, and control. One of the essential indicators of this transition is the existence of an action-reaction-fueled arms race. Although it is clear that arms races exist to some extent before every conflict, not all arms races result in war. The problem is to determine the variables that prevent some arms races from escalating to the point of full-scale violence.

Choucri suggests three basic models for developing workable peace strategies: first, a pragmatic strategy, aimed at intervening on the margins of a conflict in an effort to de-escalate hostilities and bring about negotiations; second, a rule-seeking strategy, aimed at clarifying the rules of international interaction along the lines of international law, which involves development of regimes so cognizant of interdependence that the motivation to ignore rules unilaterally is no longer a consideration; and third, a strategy aimed at preventing conflict before it occurs, which entails getting at the root causes of what makes states perceive that their national security is at risk and recognizing the destabilizing effect of fluctuations in the levels of the three master variables.

11. Analytical and Behavioral Perspectives

Causes of War and Strategies for Peace

Nazli Choucri

The behavioral approach to the study of international relations is an important method of contemporary analysis with a strong tradition that has influenced many contemporary modes of inquiry. At the time of its inception, in the 1950s, this approach was considered revolutionary in method and orientation. Indeed, the "behavioral revolution" became the label most frequently given to that approach.[1]

This chapter summarizes some contributions of the behavioral approach to the study of war and peace, some drawbacks, and some more recent approaches that owe their origins to the behavioral perspectives. To a large extent, the term "behavioral" is largely passé. The dominant lines of inquiry have gone beyond the initial and, in retrospect, somewhat simplistic behavioral perspectives.

This chapter has four sections. The first focuses on the origins and characteristics of behavioral inquiry and summarizes important contrasts with other dominant perspectives. The second section presents an integrative theory of the major causes of war among nations, as a way of illustrating insights from behavioral analysis. The third section addresses the issue of peace and, on the basis of observations in the first and second sections, presents three alternative strategies or models of peacemaking. All three owe their origins to the behavioral revolution, and together they provide an outline of the contributions of behavioral inquiries to strategies for peace. The preferred strategy is highlighted accordingly, but in the interest of fairness, equal time and opportunity are given to the intellectual preferences of other scholars. The final section of this chapter places behavioral approaches in the context of contemporary modes of analytical inquiry.

The Origins and Characteristics of the Behavioral Revolution

The "behavioral revolution"—its origins and its consequences—has been widely studied.[2] To simplify what can appear to be an otherwise arcane debate, it is useful to contrast the behavioral approach with the other

272

important approaches to the study of international relations. Following a recent survey of international analysis,[3] we attempt to place the behavioral views in perspective, beginning with a discussion of the context and then outlining the characteristics of the behavioral approach.

The Context

The conventional approach to the study of international relations in the United States is the "traditional" approach, which represents the evolution of the field in major universities during the period between the two world wars and its consolidation with the emergence of the Cold War, and the succeeding decades. The conventional approach appears in two guises— political realism and political idealism. The dominant one, political realism, represents a hard-nosed reaction to the idealism of Woodrow Wilson and the legal and institutional emphasis in world politics between the wars. The second perspective, political idealism, differs on assumptions, views of politics, and policy implications, but the Wilsonian ideals remain at the core of this traditional form of inquiry. The failure of the League of Nations and the outbreak of war in 1939 (for the United States, in 1941) were unmistakable signals of the failure of idealism. The scholarship of E. H. Carr and Hans Morgenthau represents the most distinctive of the traditional approaches.[4]

Another major form of inquiry—the Marxist approaches—was European in origin. The Marxist approaches were (and continue to be) profoundly antitraditional, debating not only the essence of political power but its sources and consequences for international relations.[5] The logic of inquiry was dialectical. (In recent decades, a form of "non-Marxist" dialectics appeared in the United States, but this is getting ahead of our review.)

The behavioral sciences emerged as a challenge to both traditional and Marxist approaches. Some aspects of the behavioral sciences took root and developed as a corollary to research associated with the war effort. Within a clear appreciation for the limits of idealism, the behavioral revolution stemmed from a recognition that the tough-minded, power-emphasis realist approach rested on a soft intellectual foundation. The core concepts were poorly defined, scholarship was a form of storytelling, and elegant insights were obscured by ambiguous methodology.

The development of the behavioral sciences in the early 1950s, and the expansion of them in the 1960s, was an intellectual and scholarly innovation that was not aimed at, or driven by, an interest in international relations per se.[6] The root of the behavioral sciences was far removed from the world of nations. It was through the interest of political scientists in world policies that the new tools, methods, and orientations of the behavioral sciences were brought to bear on international realities.[7] With the benefit of hindsight and scholarly careers devoted to sustained methodological inquiries, the naïveté of earlier applications looks rather touching. But the intellectual base was sound, by methodological criteria, and the war effort clearly paid off.

The Characteristics

Behavioral approaches to war and peace are grounded in the behavioral sciences: anthropology, psychology, behavioral aspects of biology, economics, geography, law, psychiatry, and political science.[8] Without these sciences, which address the study of human behavior through the use of scientific methods of inquiry, there would have been no basis for behavioral approaches to world politics.

The development of behavioral approaches is due in part to Ford Foundation support in the late 1950s for research toward understanding peace and democratic institutions. The essence was, and continues to be, interdisciplinary orientation, irrespective of the particular subject matter. For analysis of international relations, this orientation meant bringing methods, theories, and insights from the social sciences to bear on aspects of relations among nations. For example, analysts used theories of psychology[9] to develop and test hypotheses about perceptions and actions of leaders in international crises. The near-classic studies are those of the pattern of decision making leading to World War I,[10] of Kennedy during the Cuban missile crisis,[11] and of the leaders' perceptions in the Arab-Israeli conflict.[12] Analysts who argued that leaders must be placed in the context of the entire system within which they operate used insights and methods from sociology and organization theory, differentiating between "role" and "personality" to determine how each leader's position shapes and constrains behavior and policy choices. The study of decision making during the Korean War illustrates this combined approach[13] and the extensive explanations offered by various social sciences.

The behavioral perspective of the late 1950s and early 1960s based its orientation on several assumptions—even strong suppositions—including the regularities in human behavior, the linkages across levels of analysis, the possibilities of systematic analysis, and the possibility of significantly reducing the role of random factors in explaining relations among nations.[14]

Each of these assumptions has important implications for how world politics and international events are analyzed. The "regularities" assumption means that forms of interaction can be identified through systematic inquiry and that particular kinds of states are likely to "behave" in some ways and not in others. Implicit is the notion of prediction, based on patterns of activity of states.

The "levels of analysis" assumption[15] placed heavy emphasis on differentiating among subnational, national, and international types of organizations and activities, identifying the characteristics of each and the connections among them. According to this assumption, countries were not "black boxes," and domestic factors could systematically influence international activities.[16]

The "systematic analysis" assumption provided a broader framework for incorporating regularities of behavior and levels of analysis. The effects of behavior are systematic, not erratic, random, or chaotic. This is an especially strong assumption since it was applied to all factors of inquiry and all elements in analysis of international relations—leaders, states, and international organizations. As a corollary, the "reduced randomness" assumption meant that the role of the erratic could be constrained, reduced, and perhaps even explained.[17]

The overarching characteristics of the behavioral sciences applied to international relations were methodological. The guiding concepts included analytical rigor, quantification, metricization, and modeling (to gain "predictive" power).[18] Theory binding and theory testing were the goals; the methods were to facilitate the goals.

Behavioral approaches sought to make order of seemingly chaotic factors; place "facts" in a broader context; build "models" of these contexts; and simulate, forecast, even "predict" outcomes. The vision was bold: it viewed politics as a form of social interaction; it treated perceptions and cognition as real and worthy of political analysis; and it argued that by understanding how the pieces fit together, one could identify the causes of war and delineate the conditions for peace.

Within the behavioral scientific tradition, the contention and differences appeared mainly methodological. The merits of different levels of analysis for inquiry were debated (state-centric, interstate, transnational, international, and so on). They involved different types of inferences (deduction, induction, and statistical analysis, among others), and they reflected different ways of defining the problem and proceeding with the analysis (whether causal modeling, world system modeling, gaming, decision-making analysis, or simulation). The debates were sharp[19] and the passions strong.[20] But the underlying commitment to the basic assumptions noted earlier was unshakable. Traditionalists (mainly realists) mounted powerful campaigns of criticism and contention,[21] and the battle lines eventually blurred as the antagonists on both sides of the divide adopted methods of analysis that were increasingly similar in style and substance.

In retrospect, it now seems clear that the behavioral perspective rejected the conventional distinction between "high politics" (referring to factors related to power, leaders, states, diplomacy, and war) and "low politics" (reflecting more aggregate of routine factors like economics, demography, and factors not conventionally thought of as political). By adopting a definition of "politics" as "who gets what, when, how,"[22] the behavioral approach effectively broadened the discourse of what was considered earlier as being important and worthy of political inquiry; and, by extension, power meant the ability to influence and determine who gets what, when, and how.

In this context, one of the major insights of the behavioral approaches clarifies the essence of the concept of power, so central to the traditional approaches. Differentiating between power as an attribute versus power as a relationship[23] paved the way for developing measurements of each and resolving what had earlier been considered a hopelessly ambiguous concept.[24]

This example points to the fact that the behavioral approaches to international relations, to questions of war and peace, focus on the same concerns of the traditionalists—the same issues, the same central themes, and the same worries. The methods were different; the way of defining the problem was different, as were the ways of marshaling evidence and mounting a persuasive case. Behavioral analysts viewed the tenets of scientific inquiry as most important. Traditional analysts viewed the modes of verbal, logical, or other forms of persuasion as most important. This difference accounts, in large part, for the near-polemical exchanges between behavioral and traditional scholars throughout the 1960s.[25]

The emphasis on methodological competence and scientific inquiry contributed to the charge that behavioral approaches could not address "important" problems, but only those that were quantifiable. This unfortunate development obscured the fact that methodological rigor was not necessarily contingent on quantification; it was contingent on congruence or consistency among the basic question, the theoretical directive, the hypothesis to be explored, the evidence to be marshaled, and the conclusions to be drawn. All behavioral approaches required (and shared) this basic sequence of inquiry. Quantification was usually important, but not always necessary.[26]

This critique of behavioral analysis was augmented by a "crisis of conscience" in the academic community with the worsening of the Vietnam War. Conscience dictated an appreciation for feelings, moral stances, and a concern for truth and justice in relations among nations. This reaction was, to a large extent, misplaced, for it implied that the tenets of scientific inquiry were somehow opposed to feelings, moral rectitude, or truth and justice. Behavioral scientists recognized that any methodological stance implied a value judgment and that "value-free" science was more a figment of misguided imagination than a reflection of reality. They agreed that the underlying guideline was to develop "value-explicit" inquiry.

A significant development toward the end of the 1970s in the study of international relations involved a convergence of realistic thought and behavioral orientations and led to a form of neorealism.[27] In this context, emphasis on "two-track" international relations led to the new focus of inquiry, labeled "transnationalism," and to a view of the world as composed of intrinsically interdependent parts.[28] The concept of interdependence became central to the analysis of relations among nations and to the "normal" view of world politics.[29] The oil crisis of 1973 had precipitated an appreciation of interdependence, and the scholarly community responded by developing the intellectual and analytical foundations of this very apparent international reality.[30]

By the end of the 1970s, behavioral analysis had become mainstream; it no longer elicited passionate attacks or heated defense. Attacks on the neorealists, in various forms and guises, now reflected the earlier traditionalist responses to the behavioral revolution. These critics also included neoidealists emerging from their earlier antirealist positions.

Throughout these years, the behavioral approaches generated a variety of insights and "findings" about the causes of war and the conditions for peace. Several distinguished edited volumes reflect this intellectual growth.[31] In addition, major research projects resulting from a decade of work provided evidence of the utility of many distinctive lines of research.[32]

The behavioral revolution had become quite established, and interdisciplinary scientific inquiry was now regarded as normal scholarly practice for examining evidence about causes of war and conditions for peace. The essential legacy of an intellectual tradition born some thirty years ago remains in force today: a respect for systematic and analytical modes of inquiry. The increasing use of systematic, even quantitative, methodological techniques by scholars in the field reflects the debt to the behavioral sciences and, at the same time, the extent of influence. Quantitative methods became respectable, worthy of use by the most realistic or idealistic of the traditionalists.[33]

The next section of this chapter identifies some specific contributions of behavioral analysis to international relations. These contributions are placed in the context of the theory of "lateral pressure," a theory of international conflict that evolved as a systemic explanation of causes of war and owes its origins and development to behavioral and interdisciplinary inquiry. The distinctive features of this theory of conflict are its basic assumption, the way the pieces are put together, and the types of prediction possible about prospects for war.[34]

Finally, the theory of lateral pressure provides the basis for differentiating among broad strategies for peace, the subject of the third section of this chapter. This theory reflects in part the intellectual history of the past decades by drawing upon the notion of regularities in behavior of states, combined with insights derived from systematic and quantitative inquiry. The theory identifies the two central obstacles to conflict resolution in international relations: the security dilemma and the obstacles to peace.[35] Resolving the dilemma and reducing the obstacles are essential conditions for a more "peaceful" international environment.

The Causes of Conflict Among Nations[36]

That there is rarely a single "cause" of war is seldom disputed. Traditionalists as well as behavioralists argue that the causes, and the antecedent conditions, are complex. The difference between the two approaches, however, rests on the extent to which causes can be identified systematically and a logic of war rendered accordingly. The behavioral sciences have contributed to determining the ways in which specific factors interact to generate hostilities that eventually lead to war. And behavioral analysts have a wide range of views about salient factors and the sequence of causation.[37] There is general agreement, as noted earlier, that war is not a random process, and that chance does not play a large role, compared with underlying systematic conditions and precursors.

Profiles of National Capabilities

We begin here with elements of "high politics," characterizing states in the international system conventionally in terms of "power." But the three essential features of states are population, resource base, and technological capabilities. The population variable includes all demographic features; technology encompasses both mechanical and organizational knowledge and skills; and resources refer to arable land, water supplies, minerals, metals, fibers, fuels, and other raw materials. National capabilities are based on these factors; government policies and actions are responsive to, and influence, these three "master variables." All other characteristic features of states are derived from these core variables.[38]

Although states are believed to "act" and "interact" in world politics, individuals in their local and institutional environments actually shape state priorities and influence state actions. These two conditions frame the behavioral orientation to international relations, linking individual factors to aggregate national attributes. Acknowledging the role of individuals stresses cognitive elements and their knowledge and the central role of their numbers. (By numbers we mean the size of the population along with various attributes, the level and characteristics of technology, and the types and volume of resources.) Clearly, national power[39] cannot be reduced entirely to these factors; however, population, resources, and technology shape the base of national power and define what a state can or cannot do at any point in time.[40]

To illustrate the salience of the population-resource-technology relationships as the core of national capability, imagine

- A China with the technology of the United States,
- A United States with the resources of Saudi Arabia,
- A Saudi Arabia with the technology of Israel,
- An Israel with the technology of Chad, and

- A Chad with the resources of Saudi Arabia.

The contingencies are simplistic, to be sure. The point is that countries are able to act the way they do—perhaps are even driven—by the characteristics of their national profile and by the disposition of their core variables. And governments, through instruments of public policy and modes of political bargaining, can and do influence their population features, resources, and technological capabilities.[41] The basic reality—an assumption as well as a fact—is that core elements of power are not static; they are always changing, contributing to the continual changes in relations among nations.[42]

Comparing profiles of states is a useful way of assessing the relative size and capabilities of states at any point in time.[43] The profiles sketched here suggest that actions of states can be inferred from their basic national attributes. These profiles are presented here as "ideals" or archetypes; they should not be taken too literally. Profiles, moreover, are high-speed snapshots of relationships at one cross section of time, whereas each of the major dimensions—population, technology, territorial size—is subject to almost continual change (each at its own rate). Time-series analyses of the changing profiles and behaviors of states of different profiles provide a useful mapping of the global system and a basis for estimating future growth, development, and conflict trends.[44]

Four profiles (or ideal types) are identifiable among the major powers, the large industrial states. Identifying a country as belonging in one or another of these profile categories will reveal some of the major constraints shaping its behavior.

First are the most powerful countries with high levels and commensurate rates of growth or development in population, technology, and resources. These "large" and advancing countries—in which technological advancement maintains a substantial lead over population growth—are typically expanding states, the most powerful and influential in the international system. Pursuing economic, political, and strategic hegemony, such countries extend their trade, diplomatic activities, and, increasingly, strategic actions beyond their national boundaries. During the colonial periods, the British, French, and other Western European empires expanded their activities and interests over much of the globe. Britain and France were increasingly challenged by a newly united Germany and, in terms of population growth, technological advancements, and demonstrated capacities for expansion, by the United States and Japan.[45] Historically powerful states have been challenged by new countries.[46]

Among the challengers—the second profile—are states with growing populations, advancing technology, and inadequate resources. When population is large (relative to territory) and technology is advancing commensurately but access to resources is perceived as significantly impeded, the foreign policy priorities are often shaped by the desire to expand resource access. Constraints exist because the domestic resource base appears to be limited or inadequately endowed, trade capacities seem inadequate to provide resources, and efforts to expand trade or the resource base (by exploration, conquest, purchase, or other means) remain inadequate. Such states feel economically insecure and under continuous pressure to expand their trade or, if that recourse is impeded or otherwise insufficient, to expand their territory by one means or another. Germany and Japan approximated this type of profile prior to and during early stages of their imperial expansion.

A third state profile is characterized by dense population, advancing technology, and constrained resources. Such states are distinctive in that, although their domestic resource base remains severely limited, their level of technology is developing rapidly. Since World War II, Japan has achieved such a profile by moderating its population growth, further developing its industrial technology, and expanding its imports, exports, and investments worldwide.

Finally, among the more "fortunate" states in the international system are those with low population density, advancing technology, and secure access to resources.[47] In such cases, populations remain low relative to advancing technology, and access to resources is consistent with the demand for resources. Such states may have developed these characteristics because of limited population growth combined with a resource-rich territorial base, an effective trade network, or a technology that has been used in considerable part for production and exports (as opposed to consumption and imports). Thus, new resources are generated. These countries rank at or near the top in quality-of-life indicators and tend to avoid war unless invaded. Modern Norway and Sweden approximate this profile, although historically both countries were major expanding powers.

On the other hand, the conventional "poor" profile of a newly developing state (such as Bangladesh, Honduras, and El Salvador) is one with dense and growing population, relatively poor technology, and limited access to resources either because the territorial base is limited or poorly endowed or because existing resources cannot be extracted (or even located, perhaps) with available knowledge and skills.

State profiles change dramatically when the population density is low. States with sparse population, primitive technology, and limited resources access have different development problems. In addition to the relative underdevelopment of knowledge and skills and their poor access to resources, sparsely populated societies of this sort—for example, Chad, Niger, and Gabon—possess an extremely limited labor pool and lack a critical mass of professional specialists to facilitate effective development. Possibilities for the expansion of activities and interests are severely constrained relative to other states, and starvation and disease are often endemic.

The modern international system has given rise to yet another distinctive type of state: the still developing and still industrializing one. This is the profile of states with sparse population, recently imported technology, and a rich resource base. Kuwait, Saudi Arabia, Libya, and the United Arab Emirates are examples. Such states differ from the Chads, Nigers, and Gabons in two critical respects: resources are abundant, and advanced technology and population have been imported from abroad. As a consequence, valuable and hitherto unavailable resources (such as oil), now accessible in large quantities, expand the gross national product to extremely high levels. These states are distinctive because resource abundance enabled large-scale importation of technology, therefore effectively changing their overall profile.[48]

The point of these brief sketches is to depict the types of interactions among populations, technology, and resources, and to show that such profiles provide a systematic way of characterizing states. The next step is predictive: different states are likely to (and will) behave and act internationally in some ways and not in others.

The same pattern of state profiles can be formulated within the context of economic "growth models," predicated on land, labor, and capital.[49] The critical difference is that economic growth models specify technology as an exogenous factor and infer the rate of growth (rather than measuring it directly); resources are implicitly derived from "land" and "capital," and only "labor" as a population variable is explicitly incorporated. Thus, while it is possible to specify national profiles in the functional forms of growth models, explicit information concerning the basis for national power and profiled differences will be rendered implicit, or lost.

The national profiles shown here illustrate two important propositions in the analysis of international relations. First, the types and patterns of international activities are systematically related to profiles of states: different profiles result in, or lead to, different forms of international actions, with different propensities for conflict and violence. Second, national profiles are not fixed: winning or losing in an international exchange can result in changes in profiles, and, as indicated, governments can and generally do influence any of the three master variables. For example, population can change through immigration policy; technology can be augmented through imitation, education, and innovation; and resources can be expanded through access to imports or exports. Much of what is done in the domain of public policy almost routinely affects population, technology, or resources. It is the interactive effects among the three master variables that matter, not the idiosyncratic or singular changes.

This characterization of states in the international system is based on an interdisciplinary orientation toward power, behavior, and capability. Demographic, technological, and resource factors—central to this view of states—provide strong clues as to how states are likely to behave and to the distribution of power in the international system. These clues are reflected (or presented) in the theory of lateral pressure.

The Theory of Lateral Pressure

Lateral pressure is defined as the extension of a country's behavior and interests outside its designated territorial boundaries. In some circumstances, lateral pressure results in the extension of the territorial boundaries themselves.[50] The theory of lateral pressure is an explanation of the determinants and consequences of external behavior and accounts for immediate as well as less proximate sources and outcomes. The theory relates the profile of states to types of external activities and the propensities that lead nations to war.[51]

The theory maintains that the behavior of nations is shaped by interactive effects of demand and capability, both of which are required for effective action. Demand and capability are conditioned, in turn, by population, technology, and access to resources—the master variables whose interactions define the essential characteristics, or basic profile, of each state in the international system. Within this framework, the only deciding and acting units are individual human beings.[52] The state and the international systems consist of individuals acting within formalized relationships identified as coalitions, organizations, and institutions.

The basic premise of this theory is that states with superior capabilities and power tend to use more resources, have a wider range of interests, and expand their activities further (and with greater impact) than weaker actors. If resources in demand are not domestically available or can be acquired cheaper from abroad, states either develop new technologies to obtain old resources at lower costs (or to find new and cheaper substitutions for old resources) or reach out for (and, if feasible, protect their access to) resources from abroad, through trade, investments, acquisitions, territorial expansion, or other means.[53]

The political assumptions embedded in the lateral pressure theory derive from bargaining and coalition formation: to strengthen the probability that their demands will be met, states increase their capabilities by using available capabilities or by persuading others, through bargaining, to assist or cooperate with them. This bargaining introduces volition and voluntarism and reduces an otherwise deterministic view of state action (that is, shaped uniquely by master variables).

Theories of bargaining and coalitions are among the most important contributions of behavioral analysis, and interaction—give and take—is formally specified to enable deductive reasoning or inductive analysis. Within some fairly restrictive outcomes or assumptions, results of bargaining—and efforts to induce compliance—can be clarified (even predicted) systematically.

Lateral pressure refers to the expansion beyond national borders of both private and governmental activities and interests. Some are motivated by the search for resources. Other manifestations of external behavior are exploration; territorial acquisition; establishment of overseas colonies; search for markets, investment, and cheap labor; extension of religious, educational, and scientific activities; economic and military assistance to other countries; dispatch and maintenance of troops and bases overseas; exploitation of the continental shelf; and exploration of the ocean depths or space.[54]

The large-scale movement of people across national borders is a particularly daunting case of lateral pressure. "Push" and "pull" explanations of international migrations exist.[55] Recent history has shown what happens when the process comes full circle: "push" out of the home community, to "pull" of the recipient region, to a subsequent "push back" from the recipient community to the home country, as in Western Europe or the Persian Gulf. In this process, profiles of states at both ends of the migration stream are affected by the movement of people.

For conceptual articulation, empirical analysis, and modeling, we have distinguished among *sources* of lateral pressure (demand and capabilities), *disposition* or tendency, *manifestation* of actual behavior, and *impacts* of activities on external actors or environments.[56]

Intersections of Spheres of Influence

A significant factor leading to escalation of hostilities among nations lies in the reality that the expanding activities and interests of powerful states have generally intersected, or "collided," with the activities and interests of other states of different sizes, capabilities, and power. Intersections of spheres of influence per se seldom trigger a violent conflict. Sometimes they do no more than bring two or more countries into closer relations with each other.[57] But intersections turn violent when relations between the states involved are already hostile or at least one of them (rightly or wrongly) perceives the in situ bargaining and leveraging activities of the other as dangerously competitive or overtly violent.

Territorial conflicts are among the most obvious forms of intersections, even if they are couched in ideological terms. The Vietnam War can be regarded as a notable intersection among major powers, although the direct antagonists were "clients" of the great powers. The Cuban missile crisis was also an intersection. President Kennedy's diplomacy was designed to push Soviet influence out of the U.S. domain in Latin America.

A new mainline behavioral analysis has recently been developed to systematically examine types and forms of territorial conflicts.[58] These conflicts can be powerful antecedents to war if they are accompanied by, and give rise to (or exacerbate), prevailing patterns of competition among nations. But the more immediate, or proximate, stimuli for crisis and war often emerge from subjectively generated perceptions, affects (fears, distrust, hostility, and so on), and human decisions (conditioned by and in response to situations shaped by processes of growth and competition).

The Conflict Spiral and the Paths to War

The "conflict spiral" refers to the processes that lead nations into warfare. It is labeled a "spiral" because levels of antagonizing increase and propensities of violence are enhanced accordingly; perceptions and cognitions become laden with hostility; and the actions of adversaries are interpreted in increasingly antagonistic terms.[59] The national profiles can be thought of as nations positioned at the "starting line," the initial stages of interactions, and the subsequent pattern of state interactions and activities as shaping the process that may lead to violence.[60]

The behavioral tradition has generated important findings about the nature of the conflict spiral and the factors that increase, rather than decrease, prospects for violent confrontation.[61] Some of these findings have become propositions, "near truths," about how and why nations go to war and what, if anything, can be done about it.

The arms race is a major feature of this process, although the evidence remains inconclusive as to whether an arms race is a precursor to war or a surrogate for it. Nonetheless, the fact remains that military competition is a near-universal prerequisite for violent conflict.

The evidence also points to two reinforcing factors that push arms races upward. One factor is a reaction process, whereby antagonists increase their own allocations in response to the arms investments of their adversaries.[62] The other is an internal process, whereby bureaucratic and budgetary forces interact to push for greater investments in the military. Internal forces do not necessarily respond to external forces (actions of others): they are endogenous, reacting primarily and sometimes only to internal pressures, budgetary imperatives, and domestic politics. Either of these two sources of arms competition is dangerous in its own right; the interaction of both is particularly destabilizing.

Well-developed models of arms races constitute the most important legacy of the behavioral approach, as well as the subsequent revisions and the intellectual traditions these have created.[63] This work has helped clarify which factors are responsible for an increased level of arms, and in what proportions and contexts—be they perception of hostility, actual military allocation, internal forces, memories of past hostilities, or other factors.[64] Although the model of armament competition is generic in form, the parameters are idiosyncratic, derived from analysis of unique circumstances and particular simulations of how nations respond to the actions of their adversaries.

From Escalation to Crisis and War

Action-reaction phenomena, such as arms races, can be viewed as escalations of negative leverages that are designed to induce compliance and are applied by two or more adversaries, wherein each side's expectations change as interactions develop; each side's expectations and intents are not fully known to the other; and cognitive and psychological processes "filter" actions and intents.[65] The arms race is a special type of escalation process in which an increase in country A's military capabilities, whether undertaken as a form of deterrence or as a routine defense measure, is viewed by the leadership of rival country B as a threat to its security. The behavioral tradition has created a body of evidence on the nature of arms races and hypotheses about points of intervention—what can be done to produce "de-escalation" and under what conditions such interventions are likely to fail.[66]

However the phenomenon of international crisis is defined, it almost always meets the criteria for an escalatory or action-reaction process.[67] Thus, in an international crisis, escalatory interactions come about in part because the leaders of one country, perceiving an action of another as aggressive or threatening, undertake counteraction in one form or other. This counteraction is then perceived as a threat by the other state, and it responds accordingly. If the response is perceived by the other as threatening, then each nation is likely to undertake further hostile action to deter the other and thus maintain security. Under the pressure of intense interchange, each response is likely to be automatic, legitimized by the view that "we have no alternative."

For every crisis that escalates into war, however, there are many others that cool down, or de-escalate.[68] Similarly, once initiated, a war will continue until at least one side decides that the risks and costs of further hostilities outweigh the gains. Except in the case of annihilation or surrender, war termination is, by definition, a function of this decision.

The following propositions emerge from this theoretical view of causes of war:

- There are several points in the process of lateral pressure at which effective policy interventions can influence outcomes, that is, when taking some action may produce the right result, one that could be more conducive to peace.
- Seldom are nations immune to the actions of others. The actions of one state, or the claims it makes on the international environment, affect others or the claims others make.
- States in the international system cannot fully accommodate all their objectives all the time without encountering resistance from other states. This condition necessitates institutional developments, regimes, and formalization of coordinated actions.[69]

The Security Dilemma as an Obstacle to Peace

The idea of "security" is at the core of all approaches to the study of international relations and is central to the realities of the international environment.[70] In strategic terms, the security dilemma is defined as "activities undertaken by one state to enhance its security [that] may itself be perceived as a dangerous threat to the national security of some other state."[71] The more general version of the security dilemma lies in the reality that normal behavior in the pursuit of legitimate ends can be viewed as hostile and lead to defensive, reactive actions by others.

The dynamics of interactions among nations lie at the core of the security dilemma. These interactions are obscured by any static view of the international system or relations among states. The national profiles sketched earlier in a comparative static framework represent a cross-sectional view at one point in time; however, interaction among nations—as nations grow and expand—influences the development of the security dilemma among nations. The dynamic perspective—the transformation of the comparative static over time—addresses the phenomena that are least well articulated in contending international relations theories: namely, change within a nation, change in relations among nations, change in the international system, and the effects of all three on national security (the fact itself and the security dilemma).

The dominant, or conventional, view of national security stresses the military threats to security and the military or defense elements in managing the threats.[72] The revisionist view argues that security of nations can be eroded by factors not generally military and that the threats to security need not be exclusively military in nature.[73]

The theory of lateral pressure highlights the essential commonality between the two views, arguing that security of states is, at a minimum, a triangular problem, or a three-dimensional concern: the military or strategic dimension, namely, the security of borders; the political dimension, namely, the security of the regime and mode of governance, including economic security; and the structural dimension, namely, the security of the society with respect to its population-resource balance, given its technological capabilities. Erosion or threats to security can come from outside or inside.[74] The theory of lateral pressure seeks to articulate the links among all three dimensions of national security and the implications for the specific security problems associated with different state profiles and modes of interaction.

Strategic security refers to the conventional and military view of security, the ability to defend and, if necessary, to assume an offensive posture. Regime security is the ability of government to govern and of regimes to elicit support, including meeting the imperatives of economics for the society. Structural security refers to the ability of society in a given environment to sustain viable population-resources-technology balances. In those terms, a state like Bangladesh is very insecure; it threatens to "crumble" from within, and the pressures of population on a scarce resource base are extensive.

The contribution of lateral pressure theory lies in the recognition that the roots of the dilemma are fundamentally generic. They are embedded in the characteristic features of states, in the master variables. These variables define the parameters of permissible behavior—what a state can or cannot do at any point in time.

The security dilemma is an obstacle to peace because of the inadvertent consequences of behavior: a defensive action can look offensive, and an act designed to reduce tensions can be viewed as hostile by others. The important factors are cognitive and perceptual rather than factual or empirical. The intervening lenses of interpretation, assessment, and evaluation often change the entire calculus of security and the moves toward peace.

Thus, since national security means protection of borders (strategic), stability of governance and regime (political and economic), and integrity of society (structural), ultimate national security means that a state's claims are honored and recognized by others. Effective strategies for peace must therefore address how the security dilemma frames prospects for peace in conflict situations, which is discussed in the next section.

Strategies for Peace

Changing the course of interactions from a conflict path to a peace path requires two simultaneous interventions: not making the security of a state threatening to others and not letting peace moves become opportunities for exploiting seeming weakness. A conciliation posture, which involves stressing the negatives in these conditions, by itself is insufficient to ensure moving along a peace path; it is necessary, but not sufficient.

Three Models

Three broad "peace strategies" are based on the behavioral, postbehavioral, and contemporary perspectives on international relations.

Model 1, the pragmatic strategy for intervening at the margins, is a strategy of incremental action. The Model 1 strategy attempts to identify moves that de-escalate hostilities and reverse the course of the conflict spiral (akin to turning a tanker around in a narrow strait). Model 1 acts on attitudes, cognition, and perception in the effort to influence behavior once the adversaries have traveled up toward violence in the conflict spiral.[75] Peace strategies of the Model 1 type are designed to de-escalate hostilities by the sequence of moves loosely characterized as "tit-for-tat" and "flexible response."[76] The essence of this model is to influence attitudes, actions, and reactions.[77]

Model 2, the rule-seeking and regime-making strategy, focuses on ways of reaching agreement for cooperation and institutional actions. Model 2 solutions are based on behaviorally induced rule-seeking arrangements.[78] This strategy involves the search for international regimes and institutions for rule-driven behavioral modification techniques; the strategy may address the conditions that lead states to avoid rules or to cheat. However, by focusing on rulemaking for cooperation, Model 2 solutions may obscure the very reality that engenders lack of cooperation, namely, perceived and actual inequalities in the positioning of states on the world scene.

Model 3, the strategy that addresses fundamentals, focuses on the core structural features that establish the positioning of states in antagonistic and hostile stances. Model 3 solutions recognize the inherently destabilizing elements generated by population-technology-resource balances (or imbalances). Model 3 solutions seek to address the structure of national profiles and the external behaviors engendered. This model directs peace-seeking efforts toward reducing problems, discomforts, and constraints created by the national characteristics of a state's profile and by attempts to change the profile).[79]

Models 1 and 2 obscure the fact that the tanker-in-the-strait is a structural condition, born of structural necessity and the imperatives of international politics. An improved strategy would reduce the necessity for turning the tanker around. This metaphor, inelegant as it may be, stresses the importance of the structural factors leading to conflict, those born of the national profile of states.

Model 3 is more comprehensive. Based on the theory of lateral pressure, it seeks to reduce the conflict inherent or manifested at every stage or mode of extension of behavior outside national boundaries. This strategy calls for a battery of moves, actual interventions, at each stage of the process of lateral pressure. It is inclusive of Models 1 and 2 but does not rely solely on either type of intervention. This stance views diplomacy and politics as the arts of creating and shaping workable conceptions of realities, not limited to de-escalating moves or reducing hostile interactions or to specific rule-seeking balances. The aim is to intervene in the fundamental structural conditions that lead to conflict. The peace strategy strikes at the roots of interactions among nations.

All three models are based on the view that policies are generally made in response to signals, or moves, rather than by careful consideration of goals and action toward these goals. All recognize the interactive politics of international relations. All appreciate the problem of unintended consequences of moves and countermoves. And all converge on the uses of bargaining, application of leverages, inducements for compliance, and political pressure. Beyond this convergence, however, the strategies differ fundamentally. The differences lie in the focus of the action and the points of intervention.

Intervening at the Margins versus Addressing the Fundamentals

The international system, at any particular time, is defined by the distribution of power among states; by competition among them; and by differentials in rates of growth of their population, resources, and technological capability. It is essential to understand the critical structural underpinnings that define power relations. Critical imbalances in power can threaten peace, as "dissatisfied" states seek to redress imbalances. Because all states are changing—many growing—over time, the mere fact of growth becomes an important political and strategic factor. The management of growth is at the core of effective choices: actions leading toward conflict or actions contributing to conditions of peace.

The choice between conflict and peace is seldom made explicitly: it is a consequence of discrete actions and decisions. Making this choice explicit at specific points in interactions among nations will be a major component of any peace strategy.

This choice derives from a more fundamental fact: the essential aspects of statehood, the master variables, are seldom considered "high politics"; they are usually thought of as falling in the realm of "low politics." This view is simply wrong. Countries come into conflict *because of* their population characteristics or their population-related objectives.[80] Resources are not socially or politically neutral; they are always central to a state's power.[81] Technology is the ultimate facilitator, making it possible for states to use their profile and to marshal resources in the pursuit of national objectives.[82] An imbalance among master variables is a serious problem for the state in question and often defines the priorities for national policy.

The fact that one state's objectives are often in conflict with the objectives of another is a basic reality of political life. Working to ameliorate conflicts in goals may be a worthy, even important, enterprise, but it is more important to address the structural factors that first shaped the goals. If these factors are fundamentally problematic, the task of peacemaking is harder—perhaps impossible. Diplomacy becomes relegated to the art of intervening at the margins rather than addressing the fundamentals. A more effective intervention point is before the emergence of a security dilemma and the need to consider obstacles to peace.

This stage is one in which national profiles become of great strategic importance. Recall the theoretical example of a China with the resources of Saudi Arabia (or with the technology of Israel or the United States); it would be a very different China indeed. However threatening Chinese posture could be perceived today, it is considerably less threatening than if China were able, as Japan has been able, to industrialize and modernize technologically in fairly short order and attain a level of technical capability roughly commensurate with that of the United States.

Of the three basic modes of peace strategies, I believe Model 3 provides the necessary conditions of a strategy for peace. In the absence of a credible

Model 3 type of strategy, the alternative models will not generate sufficient conditions for attaining or maintaining peaceful international relations.

Conclusion: Future Analytical Directions

The "behavioral revolution" has come and, for all practical purposes, it is here to stay. The tenets of scientific inquiry are no longer as disputed in international relations analysis as they were in earlier decades. The revolution has been institutionalized.

At this point in the development of the study of international relations, the intellectual approaches that owe their origins to the behavioral legacy can be characterized in the following terms.

First are the mainstream quantitative modes of inquiry focusing on behavioral manifestations of national attributes and centering on the question of causes of war and conditions for collaboration. These include activities among all facets of the conflict spiral, from the causes of initial antagonizing all the way to decisions for war. Mainstream analysts have developed the contemporary lines of modern political economy and the connection between wealth and power[83] in an increasingly interdependent world.[84]

Second are the mainstream contenders within the scholarly community, vying for intellectual recognition of their superiority. The contenders can be roughly characterized as the dominant "rational" approaches to international relations and institutions versus the "reflective" posture that questions the assumptions of rationalists, argues for context-specific cognition, and emphasizes perceptions and reflections.[85] Contemporary debate continues to center on basic assumptions about the nature of international relations. The behavioral legacy is well represented in the scholarship of these contending orientations. The rationalists owe to the behavioral revolution the interest in economic game theoretical precepts and epistemology and the eventual expansion of the rational choice model. The reflectivists owe their origins to the crisis of relevance; the postbehavioral (or antibehavioral) reaction, and the awareness of cultural, analytical, and cognitive diversity in shaping understanding of relations among nations. They share with the earlier behavioral tradition an emphasis on the psychological factors in the measurement and meaning of actions and the cognitive interpretation and determination of outcomes. The legacy pervades all these theoretical concerns. There are traditionalists in both camps: the realists and the neorealists are aligned on the rational side, the idealists and the neo-idealists along the reflective side. Both owe their intellectual origin to the behavioral sciences and the impact of those sciences on international relations.

Third are analytical developments based on the behavioral revolution's consistent emphasis on interdisciplinary approaches and integration of the insights from all the behavioral—and, by extension, the social—sciences. This new thrust involves the adoption of a global perspective in international relations, one that places interactions among units within the framework of the broader biosphere. Problems of environmental degradation, politicization of pollution, and global threats of nuclear war all fall within a global concern, one that is broader and beyond consideration of conventional international relations.[86] The importance of a global perspective is reinforced by a new Committee on Population, Resources, and Environment in the American Association for the Advancement of Science and its subcommittee on attendant transnational and international consequences.[87] The behavioral legacy is reflected primarily in the relationship among demographic, ecological, technological, and resource factors in shaping interactions among states, and in helping to define the evolving agenda of international organizations.

Against the background of the evolution of behavioral analysis over time and its origins in the traditionalist debate of realists versus idealists, the intellectual contenders are still those who insist on the differentiation between "high" and "low" politics and on the separation of the political sphere from other spheres of social activity or of international relations. Politics, from a behavioral perspective, consists essentially of "who gets what, when, how," at both the national and the international levels. The new emphasis on global issues simply broadens this basic precept by encompassing the biosphere as the framework of debates, conflicts, and modes of persuasion over who gets what, when, and how. In this context, the theory of lateral pressure summarized in this chapter provides the basis for differentiating states according to profile (attributes and capabilities) and for deriving testable propositions (or loose predictions) about who will do what, when, and how.

Discussion

Commentator Herbert Kelman used Choucri's presentation as a way to highlight six key assumptions and emphases of the behavioral approach.

1. Behaviorism represents the convergence of empirical and normative perspectives. Central to the development of both peace research and the behavioral approach is their emphasis on the symbiotic relationship between the empirical and the normative. Kelman challenged Choucri's assertion that this convergence occurs only at the postbehavioral stage.

2. Issues of war and peace must be examined at all levels of analysis. Choucri's presentation is unusual in that it emphasizes the relationship between structural (master variables) and individual factors. Most scholars tend to emphasize one or the other, but not the relationship between the two. A number of other levels of analysis, such as the collective national

(cultural) level and the organizational level, also are important, Kelman noted.

3. Just as there are a number of different levels of analysis in the behavioral approach, there are also a number of actors. For certain purposes, Kelman said, the individual is the central actor, particularly when one is trying to determine how the core variables of power are perceived and translated into policy decisions and actions. The key point, however, is that the perceptual and cognitive processes of the kind that lead to the "security dilemma" or the "peace paradox" are the normal results of the way in which decision makers and populations process information about their adversaries.

4. The behavioral school recognizes international conflict as an interactive process, the dynamics of which often lead to the escalation or perpetuation of conflict. But this view of conflict as an interactive process also suggests possible ways of reversing the process once conflict has been initiated.

5. The behavioral approach is acutely aware of the relationship between domestic and international politics, as is evident in Choucri's emphasis on the three master variables, which are domestic factors. As governments attempt to rectify perceived imbalances in the master variable equation, they make policy choices that inevitably have international ramifications. Furthermore, from both the peace research and the behavioral perspectives, conflict is seen as an international societal phenomenon rather than a state phenomenon, hence the role of the individual is central.

6. The most distinguishing characteristic of the behavioral approach is that it is particularly sensitive to change in the international system. As a result, the behavioral approach lends itself to the development of effective intervention models.

In the general discussion, R. J. Rummel suggested that the behavioral approach has added to the field of international relations a means by which adherents of the traditional school can test their basic assumptions about the nature of reality. In other words, he asked, by expanding the methodology, incorporating different and more precise data techniques, and making conclusions testable and reproducible, has not behaviorism had a greater impact on the reliability of results than on their content?

Expressing general agreement, Kelman emphasized that behaviorists have also been able to incorporate the notion of change into the overall equation; traditionalists have often been unable to do so. Choucri agreed, but she added that to view behaviorism as simply a corrective for the traditional school of thought is to ignore the dramatic expansion of knowledge that behavioral analysis has added to the field. Whereas traditionalists limit their considerations to "high" politics—notions of power and national interests—behaviorists draw attention to the wide variety of important social and political phenomena that constitute "low" politics and, hence, expand our understanding of the multiple factors inherent in every conflict.

David Hitchcock asked whether a country's size and geography might be considered another master variable, and whether all three models of peace strategies could be applied simultaneously to any given conflict. Choucri replied that although the size dimension is an important factor in any conflict analysis, location need not be considered another core variable because it is generally a fixed value, except in places such as the Middle East, where boundaries are not yet entirely agreed upon.

Choucri suggested that the three peace-strategy models are not mutually exclusive and, therefore, can be used individually or in combination with one another, but she questioned whether the diplomatic infrastructure would be able to operate under the strain of applying all three models simultaneously. She preferred Model 3 because she believed that the structural conditions in many conflict situtations are so problematic that they are most readily approached through that model. She also pointed out that Model 3 is the one about which the least is known, and thus it merits increased attention. Kelman added that unless policymakers are aware of what constitutes a Model 3 situation, they will be hard-pressed to implement the model when the time is ripe to do so.

Ivan Kaufman noted that a common failure of academics is to assume the rationality of individuals in conflict situations; he suggested that emotional and nonrational factors most frequently drive individuals in conflict. Choucri responded that irrational decisions (or what seem in hindsight to be irrational decisions) are often the product of rational calculations. Therefore, determinations of rationality are too subjective a level of analysis and should be avoided. Ted Gurr suggested that all analysis of conflict behavior of individuals or groups—and, by extension of nations—should encompass nonrational factors, rational calculations, and cultural influences. Otherwise, the analyst risks attributing undue weight to one factor over the others.

Notes

1. See Heinz Eulau, *Behavioral Persuasion in Politics* (New York: Random House, 1963).

2. See, for example, Herbert C. Kelman, *International Behavior: A Social-Psychological Analysis* (New York: Holt, 1965) for a collection of relevant studies.

3. For example, Hayward R. Alker, Jr., and Thomas J. Biersteker, "The Dialectics of World Order: Notes for a Future Archeologist of International Savoire Faire," *International Studies* 28 (1984): pp. 121–42.

4. E.H. Carr, *The Twenty Years' Crisis* (London: St. Martin's Press, 1946); Hans J. Morgenthau, *Politics Among Nations*, 4th ed. (New York: Knopf, 1966).

5. V.I. Lenin, *Imperialism* (Moscow: Progress Publishers, 1916); Mao Tse-Tung, "On Contradiction," in *Four Errors on Philosophy* (Peking: Foreign Language Press, 1964).

6. See Herbert C. Kelman, "International Relations: Psychological Aspects," in David L. Sills, ed., *International Encyclopedia of the Social Sciences, Vol. 8* (New York: Macmillan, 1968) for a brief survey.

7. For example, Kelman, *International Behavior.*

8. For a brief survey, see Bernard Berelson, "Behavioral Sciences," in David L. Sills, ed., *International Encyclopedia of the Social Sciences, Vol. 2* (New York: Macmillan, 1968), pp. 41–5.

9. For a recent study of the kind, see Lucian W. Pye, *Asian Power and Politics: The Cultural Dimensions of Authority* (Cambridge: Belknap Press, 1985).

10. See Ole R. Holsti, "The 1914 Case," *American Political Science Review* 59 no. 2 (1965): pp. 365–78; and Ole R. Holsti, Richard A. Brody, and Robert C. North, "Perception and Action in the 1914 Crisis," in J. David Singer, ed., *Quantitative International Politics* (New York: Free Press, 1968), pp. 123–58.

11. For example, see Ole R. Holsti, Richard A. Brody, and Robert C. North, "Measuring Affect and Action in International Reaction Models: Empirical Materials from the 1962 Cuban Crisis," Papers, Peace Research Society 2 (1965): pp. 170–90; and Graham Allison, *Essence of Decision* (Boston: Little, Brown and Company, 1971).

12. See, for example, Randolph M. Siverson, "International Conflict and Perceptions of Injury: The Case of the Suez Crisis," *International Studies* 14, no. 2 (1970): pp. 157–65.

13. Richard Snyder and Glenn D. Paige, "The United States Decision to Resist Aggression in Korea," *Administrative Science Quarterly* 3 (1958): pp. 341–78; Glenn D. Paige, *The Korean Decision* (New York: Free Press, 1968).

14. Kelman, *International Behavior.*

15. J. David Singer, "International Conflict: Three Levels of Analysis," *World Politics* XII (1960): pp. 453–61.

16. James N. Rosenau, ed., *Linkage Politics* (New York: Free Press, 1969).

17. The use of statistical and economic analysis involved trying to isolate—and then even account for—the nature of the random factor, identified statistically as the "unexplained variance."

18. See, for example, Nazli Choucri, "From Correlation Analysis to Computer Forecasting: The Evolution of a Research Program in International Relations," in James N. Rosenau, ed., *In Search of Global Patterns* (New York: Free Press, 1976), pp. 81–90; and Nazli Choucri and Thomas Robinson, eds., *Forecasting in International Relations: Theory, Methods, Problems, Prospects* (San Francisco: W.H. Freeman, 1978).

19. A typical debate was between Morton A. Kaplan, "The New Great Debate: Traditionalism vs. Science in International Relations," *World Politics* (1966) and Hedley Bull, "International Theory: The Case for a Classical Approach." *World Politics*, 18 (1966): pp. 361–377.

20. See Hayward R. Alker, Jr., "The Presumption of Anarchy in World Politics" draft manuscript (Cambridge, Mass.: MIT, Department of Political Science, 1966).

21. Stanley Hoffman, "International Relations: The Long Road to Theory," *World Politics* (1959).

22. Harold Lasswell, *Politics: Who Gets What, When, How* (New York: Meridian Books, 1964).

23. For the definitions of power, see Karl W. Deutsch, *The Analysis of International Relations*, 2nd ed. (Englewood Cliffs, N.J.: Prentice-Hall, 1978).

24. See James G. March, "The Power of Power," in David Easton, ed., *Varieties of Political Theory* (Englewood Cliffs, N.J.: Prentice-Hall, 1966), pp. 39–70.

25. The best collection of the contending articles was Klaus E. Knorr and James Rosenau, eds. *Contending Approaches to International Relations* (Princeton: Princeton University Press, 1969).

26. See, for example, J. David Singer, ed., *Human Behavior and International Politics* (Chicago: Rand McNally, 1965).

27. See, for example, Robert Gilpin, *War and Change in World Politics* (New York: Cambridge University Press, 1981).

28. Richard Cooper, *The Economics of Interdependence* (New York: McGraw-Hill, 1968).

29. Robert O. Keohane and Joseph S. Nye, *Power and Interdependence: World Politics in Transition* (Boston: Little, Brown and Company, 1977).

30. See, for example, Nazli Choucri, *International Politics of Energy Interdependence: The Case of Petroleum* (Lexington, Mass.: D.C. Heath, 1976).

31. For example, Bruce M. Russett, ed., *Peace, War, and Numbers* (Beverly Hills: Sage, 1972); James N. Rosenau, ed., *In Search of Global Patterns* (New York: Free Press, 1976); and Francis W. Hoole and Dina A. Zinnes, eds., *Quantitative International Politics: An Appraisal* (New York: Praeger, 1976).

32. Major examples are the Stanford Studies in International Conflict and Integration (Stanford University); the Correlates of War Project (University of Michigan); and the Dimensionality of Nations Project. See Hoole and Zinnes, *Quantitative International Politics* for the summaries of various projects.

33. The establishment of the *Journal of Peace Research* well represents the efforts shared by idealists and realists.

34. Nazli Choucri and Robert C. North, *Nations in Conflict: National Growth and International Violence* (San Francisco: W.H. Freeman & Co., 1975).

35. See, for example, Robert C. North, *War, Peace, Survival: Global Politics and Conceptual Synthesis* (Boulder, Colo.: Westview Press, 1990).

36. This section summarizes collaborative research with Robert C. North. The earlier statement is from Choucri and North, *Nations in Conflict*. For a more developed version, see Nazli Choucri and Robert C. North, "Lateral Pressure in International Relations: Concept and Theory," in Manus I. Midlarsky, ed., *Handbook of War Studies* (Winchester, Mass.: Hyman Unwin, Inc., 1989). The detailed theoretical and analytical underpinnings from an interdisciplinary perspective are in North, *War, Peace, Survival*.

37. See, for example, Nazli Choucri, *Population Dynamics and International Violence: Propositions, Insights, and Evidence* (Lexington, Mass.: D.C. Heath, 1974).

38. For a theoretical summary, see Choucri and North, "Lateral Pressure in International Relations."

39. See Klaus E. Knorr, *The Power of Nations: The Political Economy of International Relations* (New York: Basic Books, 1975).

40. Gabriel A. Almond and Bingham Powell, *Comparative Politics: A Developmental Approach* (Boston: Little, Brown and Company, 1966).

41. For an example of a changing profile—the case of Japan—see Nazli Choucri, Robert C. North, and Suzumu Yamakage, *Lateral Pressure and International Conflict: The Case of Japan* (forthcoming).

42. See North, *War, Peace, Survival.*

43. See Choucri and North, "Lateral Pressure in International Relations."

44. These observations are based on Choucri and North, "Lateral Pressure in International Relations." The theoretical behavioral underpinnings are in North, *War, Peace, Survival.*

45. Choucri and North, *Nations in Conflict.*

46. See, for example, A.F.K. Organski and J. Kugler, *The War Ledger* (Chicago: University of Chicago Press, 1980).

47. See Choucri and North, "Lateral Pressure in International Relations."

48. See, for example, U.S. Office of Technology Assessment, *Technology Transfer to the Middle East* (Washington, D.C., 1984).

49. See, for example Robert M. Solow, "Growth Theory and After," *American Economic Review* 78, no. 3 (1988): pp. 307–17.

50. See Choucri and North, *Nations in Conflict.*

51. North, *War, Peace, Survival.*

52. This proposition has been central to the Stanford Studies in International Conflict and Integration; it is also central to behavioral analysis.

53. The international oil and energy markets, and conflicts therein, are illustrative. For a simulation model of international exchanges in energy resources, see Nazli Choucri and David Scott Ross, *International Energy Futures: Petroleum Prices, Power, and Payments* (Cambridge, Mass.: MIT Press, 1981).

54. Choucri and North, *Nations in Conflict,* pp. 17–18.

55. These explanations have focused on domestic migration from the economic perspective and are largely based on wage differentials; therefore, treatment of international migration has been scanty. For a new interpretation of international migration from the vantage points of international relations and political economy, see Nazli Choucri, "International Relations and International Migrations: Theoretical Gaps and the Empirical Domain," unpublished monograph (Cambridge, Mass.: MIT, Department of Political Science, 1987).

56. See Choucri and North, *Nations in Conflict*; and Nazli Choucri and Marie Bousfield, "Alternative Futures: An Exercise in Forecasting," in Nazli Choucri, ed., *Forecasting in International Relations: Theory, Methods, Problems, Prospects* (San Francisco: W.H. Freeman, 1978).

57. Choucri and North, *Nations in Conflict,* pp. 18–20.

58. See K.A. Rasler and W.R. Thompson, "Global Wars, Public Debts, and the Long Cycle," *World Politics* 34 (1983): pp. 489–515.

59. See Ole R. Holsti, *Crisis, Escalation, War* (Montreal: McGill-Queens University Press, 1972).

60. Choucri and North, *Nations in Conflict.*

61. See, for example, Hoole and Zinnes, *Quantitative International Politics*; North, *War, Peace, Survival.*

62. See Choucri and North, *Nations in Conflict.*

63. See M.D. Intriligator and D.L. Brito, "Formal Models of Arms Races," *Journal of Peace Science* 2 (1976): pp. 77–96.

64. See Holsti, *Crisis, Escalation, War*; Robert Jervis, *Perception and Misperception in World Politics* (Princeton: Princeton University Press, 1976); and Choucri and North, *Nations in Conflict.*

65. See, for example, Jervis, *Perception and Misperception.*

66. See Lewis F. Richardson, *Arms and Insecurity* (Pittsburgh: Boxwood Press, 1960).

67. See Roberta Wohlstetter, *Pearl Harbor: Warning and Decision* (Stanford: Stanford University Press, 1962); and Holsti, *Crisis, Escalation, War.*

68. Choucri and North, *Nations in Conflict.*

69. See Stephen Krasner, ed., *International Regimes* (Ithaca: Cornell University Press, 1983); and Robert O. Keohane, *After Hegemony: Cooperation and Discord in the World Political Economy* (Princeton: Princeton University Press, 1984).

70. For a recent debate about the security dilemma in relation to the conceptual problem of anarchy, see Kenneth A. Oye, ed., *Cooperation Under Anarchy* (Princeton: Princeton University Press, 1986); and Hayward R. Alker, Jr., "Long Road to International Relations Theory: Problems of Statistical Nonodditivity," *World Politics* 18, no. 4 (1986): pp. 623–55.

71. Choucri, North, and Yamakage, *Lateral Pressure*, p. 2.

72. See, for example, Kenneth N. Waltz, *Theory of International Politics* (Reading, Mass.: Addison-Wesley, 1979).

73. See R. Ullman, "Redefining Security," *International Security* 8, no. 1 (1983): pp. 130–53; and Edward Azar and Chung-In Moon, "Third World National Security: Toward A New Conceptual Framework," *International Interaction* 11, no. 2 (1984): pp. 103–35.

74. See, for example, Nazli Choucri, *Structural Dimensions of National Security: The Case of Egypt* (prepared for the World Resources Institute, 1988); Nazli Choucri, Janet Welsh Brown, and Peter M. Haas, "Dimensions of National Security: The Case of Egypt," in Janet Welsh Brown, ed., *In the U.S. Interest: Resources, Growth and Security in the Developing World* (Boulder, Colo.: Westview Press, 1990), pp. 89–120; and North, *Peace, War, Survival.*

75. See, for example, Charles E. Osgood, *An Alternative to War or Surrender* (Urbana, Ill.: University of Illinois Press, 1962).

76. Robert Axelrod, *The Evolution of Cooperation* (New York: Basic Books, 1984).

77. For Charles Osgood's GRIT (Graduated Reduction in International Tension), see Osgood, *Alernative to War* and C.E. Mitchell, "GRIT and Gradualism—25 Years On," *International Interactions* 13, no. 1 (1966): pp. 73–86.

78. See, for example, Keohane, *After Hegemony*, and Krasner, *International Regimes.*

79. The Middle East provides a wide range of examples, however unfortunate these may be: declaration of intents for "peace" are seldom considered credible by the adversaries, as each party recognizes that its own national profile endangers its own national security. Peace-at-the-borders (and the Model I strategies) are singularly inappropriate to conditions where national identity and national security are threatened from "within." And because they do not embody the necessary conditions, they are too weak to produce altered situations and robust "peaceful" patterns of interstate behavior.

80. Witness the situation in the Middle East as an example.

81. The "oil crisis" of the 1970s amply illustrated this simple fact.

82. See, for example, Robert Gilpin, "Trade, Investment and Technology," in Herbert Giersch, ed., *Emerging Technologies: Consequences for Economic Growth, Structural Change and Employment*, Symposium 1981 (1982); and Raymond Vernon, *Two Hungry Giants: The United States and Japan in the Quest for Oil and Ores* (Cambridge, Mass.: Harvard University Press, 1983).

83. See, for example, Robert Gilpin, *The Political Economy of International Relations* (Princeton: Princeton University Press, 1987).

84. Keohane and Nye, *Power and Interdependence*.

85. For a recent theoretical synopsis of these two contending approaches, see Robert O. Keohane, "International Institutions: Two Approaches," *International Studies* 32 (1988).

86. See North, *War, Peace, Survival*.

87. Nazli Choucri, Robert C. North, and Peter Haas, *The State System and the Global Environment: Interactions Among Population, Resources, Technology* (Prepared for the Committee on Population, Resources, and the Environment, American Association for the Advancement of Science, 1990).

Introduction to Chapter 12

In this chapter, James Laue makes a convincing case for viewing conflict resolution as a separate and important field of intellectual inquiry. He also shows how continued progress in the field will add significantly to our ability to prevent future devastating conflicts.

According to Laue, conflict resolution is much more than conflict management, regulation, or even settlement. A conflict can be considered resolved only when the parties have reached a joint agreement that satisfies the interests and needs underlying the conflict, does not sacrifice any party's important values, meets standards of fairness and justice, is self-supporting and self-enforcing, and is an agreement that none of the parties will wish to repudiate in the future, even if they are in a position to do so.

Laue points out that a more complete understanding of the four main noncoercive and nonjudicial settlement techniques—conciliation, negotiation, mediation, and arbitration—is essential to the work of the United States Institute of Peace. Peace must be recognized as both a process and a goal; otherwise, it becomes impossible to uncover and address the core issues in conflicts.

Conflict resolution has a rich genealogy. Laue traces the development of the field from Aristotle and Plato through modern diplomatic institutions and techniques aimed at resolving conflict on a variety of levels: individual, community, national, and international. He also provides numerous bibliographies that illustrate the enormous amount of work that has already been done, and he suggests subjects for further research.

12. Contributions of the Emerging Field of Conflict Resolution

James H. Laue

Criteria for Constructing an Intellectual Map

The emerging field of conflict resolution was one of the major intellectual influences leading to the establishment in 1984 of the United States Institute of Peace. The first congressional action toward establishment of the Institute put in place the U.S. Commission on Proposals for the National Academy of *Peace and Conflict Resolution* [emphasis added]—the Matsunaga Commission. The United States Institute of Peace Act (Public Law 98-525), which faithfully reflected the draft legislation contained in the commission's report to the president and the Congress in 1981, found that creating such an institution "would be the most efficient and immediate means for the Nation to enlarge its capacity to promote the peaceful resolution of international conflict" (sec. 1702.a.8).

From its twelve hearings nationwide and extensive staff research, the commission also found that

- many potentially destructive conflicts among nations and peoples have been resolved constructively and with cost efficiency at the international, national, and community levels through proper use of such techniques as negotiation, conciliation, mediation, and arbitration (sec. 1702.a.4); and
- there is a national need to examine the disciplines in the social, behavioral, and physical sciences and the arts and humanities with regard to the history, nature, elements, and future of peace processes (sec. 1702.a.4).

From the first hearing on peace academy legislation in the U.S. Senate in May 1976, the linkage between peace and conflict resolution energized the deliberations and made it possible to do more, in the words of Senator Jennings Randolph, than "love peace to death." Three emphases in the legislation summarize this framework:

- The peaceful resolution of international conflict (sec. 1702.a.8), which is part of the Institute's mission statement on its letterhead and in its publications;

- The four basic techniques of nonjudicial conflict resolution: negotiation, conciliation, mediation, and arbitration; and
- The concept of peace processes. In that context, the question addressed by this chapter is this: What are the major boundaries of "conflict resolution" and what contributions can a framework based on these boundaries make to understanding the processes that lead to the peaceful resolution of international conflict?

Definitions and Boundaries: Peacemaking and Conflict Resolution

The operative terms here are "peace," "peacemaking," "conflict," "resolution," and "process." Their definitions prescribe the boundaries for a discussion of the contributions of conflict resolution approaches to international disputes.

Peace is both the goal and the object of study of the United States Institute of Peace. In its most general sense, it is made up of two elements. It is an idealized outcome—a state of relations between actors (both individuals and groups) characterized in all definitions by the absence of war and in some definitions by the presence of conditions such as economic well-being, social justice, and full human rights that serve fundamental human needs.

Peace also is a process of continuous and constructive management of differences toward the goal of more mutually satisfying relations, the prevention of escalation to violence, and the achievement of those conditions that exemplify the universal well-being of human beings and their groups, from the family to the culture and the nation-state. The focus of conflict resolution is on the processes of peace.

Peacemaking is the active process of peace, the behavior of actors and institutions that leads to more peaceful relations. It is subject to understanding and systematization through the standard tools of empirical analysis. Many scholars in the field have come to use the term as a way of linking conflict resolution techniques with the achievement of peace (National Conference on Peacemaking and Conflict Resolution 1983, 1984, 1986). Peacemaking is to be distinguished from peacekeeping, which is a more narrow and technically specified set of procedures for maintaining a cease-fire line, a demilitarized area, or buffer zone.

Conflict is a natural and inevitable part of all human interaction. It is not the opposite of order or the same as chaos, because it is patterned and in many instances, highly predictable. Conflict occurs at all levels of society—interpersonal, intercultural, and international. It is not deviant or pathological per se; it may be a healthy expression of injustices or strains in the social system that demand attention. In many instances, the origins of conflict are in the nonfulfillment or blockage of fundamental human needs. Conflict may then be defined empirically as escalated natural competition of two or more parties who believe they have incompatible goals, and whose aim is to neutralize, injure, or gain advantage over the other party or parties. Struggles over identity, values, power, and scarce resources are at the heart of all social conflicts (see Coser 1956; Kriesberg 1984).

Resolution is at the heart of the Institute's mission of "peacefully resolving international conflict." A conflict may be said to be resolved when all the parties freely accept a solution that has the following characteristics:

- By joint agreement, the solution satisfies the interests and needs underlying the conflict.
- The solution does not sacrifice any party's important values.
- The parties will not wish to repudiate the solution even if they are in a position to do so later.
- The solution meets standards of justice and fairness.
- The solution is sufficiently advantageous to all the parties so that it becomes self-supporting or self-enforcing (adapted from Azar and Burton 1986, p. 171).

Resolution is only one of a wide range of outcomes that may be preferred for a conflict. Any party's stance toward a given conflict depends largely on variables such as ideology, power (who has it), and goals (that is, who wishes to maintain or gain what). Low-power groups generally do not call for conflict resolution or peace; they want empowerment, change, and justice. Their more typical approach is to agitate conflict. More powerful parties are more likely to wish to deter, suppress, repress, or control conflict. Third-party intervenors may aim to resolve, manage, regulate, or settle conflicts, whereas academics analyze, teach, and predict (Laue 1982).

A conflict resolution approach to international or other disputes focuses, then, on the process of moving conflict presentation and escalation to resolution—and on the processes or behavior used by third parties to assist in this transformation. The most frequent complaint from scholars and practitioners in the more traditional approaches of international relations, formal diplomacy, or strategic studies is that the process by itself accounts for only a small amount of the variance in achieving the final outcome. Even if the contribution is only, say, 5 percent, attention to improving that 5 percent (which could be the difference between stalemate and resolution) is worthwhile for the peace practitioner and scholar. Furthermore, true and lasting resolution of conflicts requires attention in the process to improving the relationship between the parties as well as securing a substantive outcome. Agreements terminate conflicts; relationships implement agreements.

Emergence of the Field of Conflict Resolution

Mechanisms to deal with conflict are, of course, as old as human society. P.H. Gulliver introduced his cross-cultural study of *Disputes and Negotiations* (1979, pp. 1–2) by noting that "in all societies, regardless of their location in time and space, there is a wide variety of modes by which disputes are handled and resolution sought." The range and variation in these procedures, he argues, "can be comprehended in a few broad categories": the duel; violent self-help (including raids and war); avoidance; deflection (through such supernatural and symbolic activities as witchcraft accusations, sporting contests, or getting to the moon first); adjudication; and negotiation. Mediation systems in ancient China, the peace pipe, the Samoan circle—all are antecedents of current attempts to deal with differences more constructively.

In the West, James Schellenberg suggests, the roots of conflict management can be found in the convictions of Aristotle and Plato that social reality is subject to rational understanding; hence, some degree of control over capriciousness is possible (1982, pp. 237–41). Thucydides's narrative of the Melian dialogues in *The Peloponnesian Wars* offers one of the first detailed descriptions of the principle of "negotiating from strength" (1954, pp. 379–408).

We may point in the immediate premodern period to Hugo Grotius's effort to place the understanding of war and its termination on a natural law basis (Kossman 1968, p. 257), and to Adam Smith's attempt to understand the reasons behind naturally competitive human beings' willingness to engage in cooperative social relations beyond being coerced into participating in orderly society by a Hobbesian state. Smith focused on "sympathy," a quality of socialization in which one becomes able to understand the identities of others (Smith 1853; Shaner 1989).

Roots in Law, Diplomacy, and International Organization

As the nation-state emerged and technology permitted international as well as intra- and intertribal conflicts, there correspondingly developed a process of regulating such conflicts via the development of transsocietal norms and the codification of these norms into law (Shaner 1989, p. 16). The emergence of treaty law and international law in the West was institutionalized in the Geneva Conventions of 1864 and 1906, and The Hague Conventions of 1899 and 1907 (Akehurst 1984). The two-decade history of the League of Nations and its successful use of good offices and adjudicative forums, such as arbitration, continued the growing emphasis on international conflict regulation mechanisms, which culminated in the formation of the UN in 1945 with its provisions for broad uses of the secretary general's good offices under Articles 33, 98, and 99.

Parallel with the development of international law and organizations is the growth of the processes of international diplomacy, whose core process is bilateral negotiation. The Center for the Study of Foreign Affairs in the U.S. State Department's Foreign Service Institute is one of the best repositories of knowledge about the use of specific conflict resolution techniques in the history of diplomacy. In recent years, the new center has sponsored a series of training opportunities on negotiation for diplomats and has published a series of books on negotiating behavior and cases (see Bendahmane and McDonald 1984, 1986).

Labor-Management Disputes. Perhaps the most important roots of the conflict resolution field in the United States have been in the application of negotiation and mediation to labor-management and racial disputes. The well-known history of the growth of collective bargaining between management and unions in the 1920s and 1930s produced a continuous stream of cases and techniques of dispute resolution, as well as the passage of the National Labor Relations Act and the establishment of the Federal Mediation and Conciliation Service in the 1940s. Further evidence of the institutionalization of collective bargaining in the workplace is the operation of labor relations offices in more than thirty-five states, the aim of which is to provide ongoing dispute prevention and resolution services.

Racial, Community, and Environmental Conflict. There have been two recent waves of response to the ubiquitous racial tensions in the United States. Many human relations and human rights commissions, formed in the 1940s and 1950s to deal with racial conflicts and injustices, housed at least informal mediation and conciliation functions. Then, following the civil rights movement of the early 1960s and the urban racial disorders beginning with the bloody riots by blacks living in the Watts area of Los Angeles in 1965, public and private racial conflict resolution agencies were formed. Chief among these were the Community Relations Service of the U.S. Department of Justice in 1964, the National Center for Dispute Resolution (now the Community Dispute Services Division) of the American Arbitration Association (AAA), and the Institute for Mediation and Conflict Resolution in New York, both in 1970.

Formalization of dispute resolution mechanisms in communities and their neighborhoods began in the United States in the 1970s. Small, local dispute resolution centers and projects grew, as mediation was applied to everyday problems of community life. The Standing Committee on Dispute Resolution of the American Bar Association reports that fifteen such centers were operating in 1975. Under the leadership of President Jimmy Carter and Attorney General Griffin Bell, the Justice Department sponsored experimental neighborhood justice centers in three cities in 1976. By 1986, the number of community dispute resolution centers had grown to more than 350, with the predominance of sponsorship coming from the court system and local bar associations.

Experience at the small-group and neighborhood levels quite naturally led to applications of negotiation and mediation models to more complex, communitywide problems. Now a considerable practice and literature have developed around what are labeled "public disputes"—multiparty complex conflicts, usually played out in a community or metropolitan setting, such as conflicts over housing policy, highway location, zoning, planning, and the like (see Ball 1986; Susskind and Cruikshank 1987; Laue 1988).

Also in the 1970s there began a more formal application of negotiation and mediation to environmental disputes, with the first major intervention lasting more than two years and resulting in the resolution of a long-standing river and flooding dispute in the Snoqualmie Valley in Washington. By 1986, Gail Bingham could report more than 160 examples of the successful resolution of environmental disputes through mediation (Bingham 1986).

The Criminal Justice System. During the 1960s and 1970s, many components of the criminal justice system in the United States were experimenting with nonlitigative and noncoercive approaches—special family crisis intervention units in police departments (which dramatically reduced the incidence of officer deaths on domestic calls), the diversion of court cases to mediation, and the development of inmate grievance procedures in state and federal prison systems. During the 1980s, further applications were being tested, including face-to-face mediation between victims and offenders in property crimes and the training of defendants' lawyers in capital cases in negotiation skills.

Commercial and Consumer Disputes. For many years, the AAA and the Better Business Bureau have employed arbitration, mediation, and fact-finding to resolve commercial and consumer disputes. The AAA and a range of trade and professional associations have been involved in the application of arbitration in international business disputes. Recently, the AAA has signed agreements with a number of Eastern Bloc countries to administer arbitration in commercial disputes involving those nations and vendors and suppliers in the West.

International Relations in the Twentieth Century

International relations practitioners and scholars show increasing awareness of conflict resolution frameworks in approaching their tasks. The Carnegie Endowment for International Peace, when it was established early in the 1900s, specifically aimed to develop conciliation as the major tool for resolving international disputes (Carnegie Endowment 1985). The League of Nations and the UN both were premised on an appropriate and permanent forum for discussion and resolution of international disputes. The seminal works of Fred Iklé (1964), Roger Fisher (1964), Herbert Kelman (1965), and Oran Young (1967) brought insights to the negotiation process from people with direct involvement in international conflict resolution as public officials, consultants, and members of treaty delegations. In the late 1970s, the Foreign Service Institute of the U.S. Department of State began to introduce formal programs of training and study in negotiation and mediation. NATO has been regularly conducting training for its officials in conflict resolution. And now the United States Institute of Peace is available as a permanent institutional presence to bring the insights of the conciliation-negotiation-mediation framework to bear on international conflicts.

The Religious Community

Every major religion directs its adherents toward peace and harmony in human relations. The Judeo-Christian tradition, which has dominated the religious development of the United States, is no exception. In the current wave of development of conflict resolution, virtually every major Protestant denomination has prepared a statement on peacemaking, many have developed organizational capabilities in mediation and conciliation, and still others are using the services of conflict resolution specialists. From 1965 to 1980, the national social action board of the United Methodist Church provided staff mediators in many situations, including racial conflicts in the North and the South and at Wounded Knee, and in the Iranian hostage crisis. The Mennonite Conciliation Service, which was formed in 1979 on the model of the church's disaster relief service, has conducted extensive training in addition to direct mediation services in the United States as well as in Northern Ireland and Central America. Along with other historic peace churches—Quakers and Brethren—the Mennonites have also undertaken study and training in conflict resolution techniques in their congregations and colleges. In 1986, the Council of Bishops of the United Methodist Church advocated the use of conflict resolution techniques in the pursuit of peace and supported the role of the United States Institute of Peace (United Methodist Council of Bishops 1986). In 1989, all 100 bishops received training in "The Bishop's Role as Conflict Resolver." The United Church of Christ used mediators and facilitators to help deal with a range of conflict issues facing the church in its biennial general synod in 1989.

Among Jewish agencies, the American Jewish Committee and the Anti-Defamation League have been active for years in promoting the use of intergroup relations techniques in interreligious conflicts, and they have recently promoted dialogues on the protracted Arab-Israeli conflict.

Conflict Resolution Organizations and Journals

The growing formalization and direct experience that have led to the development of a new "field" of "conflict resolution" are reflected in the growth of organizations, associations, and journals. The Society of Professionals in Dispute Resolution (SPIDR), now fifteen years old, is the professional organization for mediators and arbitrators. SPIDR's code of ethics and set of standards for intervenors are indicators of the institutionalization of the field, as is the "arbitrators and mediators professional liability insurance" now available. The National Institute for Dispute Resolution and the Fund for Research in Dispute Resolution offer grants for development and research in the field. Dozens of university programs and hundreds of public and private mediation organizations are bringing the systematic application of conflict resolution techniques to every aspect of American life and building a legacy of case lore and trained intervenors that now brings increasing attention to the field in the general media.

The field produced its first journal in the United States more than thirty years ago at the University of Michigan, the *Journal of Conflict Resolution*. Recent additions have been the *Mediation Quarterly*, the *Negotiation Journal*, and the *Ohio State Journal on Dispute Resolution*. The first student journal, the *Journal of Conflict Intervention*, began publication in 1989 by master's and doctoral students at George Mason University.

Further description of the conceptual, practical, and institutional critical mass that has been achieved in conflict resolution appears in the concluding section of this chapter.

Emergence of the Field of Peace Research

The intellectual and public climate that has made possible the ascendancy of the conflict resolution framework for viewing international affairs—and the establishment of the United States Institute of Peace—has its most immediate roots in the growth of the peace research field as well as the conflict resolution movement.

One of the best historical treatments of the emergence of peace research is found in the 1981 report of the U.S. Commission on Proposals for the National Academy of Peace and Conflict Resolution: *To Establish the United States Academy of Peace* [1981] (hereafter referred to as Peace Academy Commission). The commissioners carefully distinguished between the peace *movement* (or the various peace movements) and the field of peace *research*, which grew largely from the work of social scientists and scholars in international relations. The assessment of the sources and present status of "the field of peace learning" was organized according to what the commissioners saw as three interrelated branches: peace as the absence of war, peace as social justice, and peacemaking techniques. Further analysis is provided in the follow-up book by Charles D. Smith, *The Hundred Percent Challenge* (1985).

In testimony to the commission's first hearing in March 1980, Kenneth Boulding, one of the founders of the Center for Conflict Resolution at the University of Michigan in 1957, told the commission that

In its origin, conflict studies owes much to an American historian, Quincy Wright, whose classic work is entitled *A Study of War*, and to an English meteorologist, Lewis F. Richardson, whose two great works, *Arms and Insecurity* and *Statistics of Deadly Quarrels*, were circulated in manuscript for many years before they were finally published in 1960. The two "founding fathers" in some sense symbolize two sources of the field, ... one coming out of the study of war, the other coming out of the quest for peace. The first goes into the arms control movement, as reflected, for instance, in the foundation of the Arms Control and Disarmament Agency in the early 1960s. The second goes into the peace research movement, symbolized perhaps in the formation of the International Peace Research Association, under the sponsorship of UNESCO, again in the early 1960s (U.S. Commission on Proposals for the National Academy of Peace and Conflict Resolution, 1981, pp. 124–25).

The phrase "peace research" first gained currency in the United States in St. Louis when Theodore Lentz founded the Peace Research Laboratory in 1954 and published *Towards a Science of Peace*, with a foreword by Julian Huxley, in 1955. The book advocated intensive systematic application of the methods of the physical sciences to the causes of war and peace.

In its treatment of the peace-as-the-absence-of-war branch of peace research, the Peace Academy Commission's report focused on questions of arms control, the role of science in leashing the technology of warfare, the work of J. David Singer and his Correlates of War Project (Singer 1979), and the work of Gene Sharp in nonviolence and nonmilitary civilian defense (Sharp 1970).

The Peace Academy Commission's approach to peace as social justice describes the World Order Models Project with its focus on economic well-being and social justice (Mendlovitz 1975), the substantive components of a peaceful society and world (for example, international order, arms control, development, human rights—see pp. 136–37), the work of Commissioner Elise Boulding on futurism, and the seminal contributions of Johan Galtung. The most influential contribution of Galtung, the first holder of the Chair in Conflict and Peace Research at the University of Oslo and the founder in 1959 of the Peace Research Institute of Oslo, has been his work on the distinction between and the connections among direct violence (between individuals as well as states) and structural violence. He ties structural violence to asymmetric power relationships and has conducted numerous studies to demonstrate that such relationships will always lead to violence (1979, p. 135). Galtung's thinking has provided the stimulus for three decades of work on peace as a state that requires the presence of justice rather than simply the absence of war or violence.

The Peace Academy Commission report's treatment of peacemaking techniques as the third branch leads directly to the conflict resolution portion of the intellectual map. The focus here is on studies of "the four basic peacemaking techniques—negotiation, conciliation, mediation, and arbitration" (p. 139); their teachability; their use and success in intranational disputes; the work of the AAA and the Federal Mediation and Conciliation Service in tens of thousands of disputes in the United States; and the scholarship and practice of such persons as Richard Pipes and Diego Ascencio. Pipes contended that diplomacy schools are "not really training diplomats" but rather are "training people in international relations," noted the superior and highly specific training of Soviet diplomats in negotiation theory and skills, and called for greater attention to training their American counterparts in negotiations analysis and techniques (pp. 141, 144–45).

The Peace Academy Commission's report pointed to a number of annotated bibliographies including the thousand-entry (most of them since 1960) *Bibliography on World Conflict and Peace: Second Edition* (Boulding, Passmore, and Grassler 1979). A number of works on conflict resolution were cited; those focusing specifically on conflict resolution are included in the next section of this paper.

Testimony from former UN Ambassador Andrew Young and Coretta Scott King highlighted, with specific examples, the utility of negotiation and conciliation in resolving conflicts and pointed to the history and skills of Americans in social movements and the resolution of everyday disputes. Other witnesses described the use of mediation in environmental, urban planning, and other disputes.

The groundbreaking and synthesizing work of the Peace Academy Commission's staff—especially the director, William Spencer, and the special assistant to the chairman, Charles D. Smith, who organized and wrote the final report—has formed the foundation for an assessment of the status of the conflict resolution field's current contributions to the peaceful resolution of international conflict.

Peace Research Organizations and Journals

The first organization devoted to "peace research" was the Peace Research Laboratory, founded by psychologist Theodore Lentz in St. Louis in 1945. Two of the premier peace research organizations were born in the Scandinavian countries—the Peace Research Institute of Oslo in 1959, and the Stockholm International Peace Research Institute in 1966. They remain among the world's leaders in the field today. Founded in 1970, the Consortium on Peace Research, Education, and Development (COPRED) now counts some 160 institutional members, most of them in the United States, some in Canada and in Europe. The International Peace Research Association has more than 100 institutional members from throughout the world. Leading journals include *Cooperation and Conflict* (Norway), *Current Research on Peace and Violence* (Finland), *Gandhi Marg* (India), *Journal of Peace Research* (Norway), *Peace and Change* (COPRED), *Peace Research* (Canada), and *Peace Research Reviews* (Canada). Barbara Wien has compiled a comprehensive listing (1984, pp. 699–707).

It is significant that more national governments have recently formed peace research capabilities, chief among them the Canadian Institute for International Peace and Security, in 1984, and the United States Institute of Peace, also in 1984. It is also significant that the link between peace research and conflict resolution was made early, when Lentz of the Peace Research Laboratory secured a major contribution to start the Center for the Study of Conflict Resolution and its *Journal of Conflict Resolution* at the University of Michigan in the late 1950s.

The Literature of Conflict Resolution and International Peacemaking: The Search for Models and Matrices

The most difficult task of this chapter is to construct a productive matrix for reporting the substantial contributions of the growing conflict resolution field to the "peaceful resolution of international conflict." A "figure-ground" problem exists, for rather than conflict resolution being viewed as one "strand" of the intellectual map, it could reasonably form the very matrix from which the mapping takes place. Many strands of this book relate directly: the interplay between deterrence and diplomatic strategies, international law and organizations, behavioral analysis, and third-party dispute settlement, to name a few. Given the centrality of the conflict resolution field to the Institute's mission and, therefore, to its intellectual map, I have chosen to organize its contributions around approaches and methods of conflict resolution rather than around other frameworks that could provide equally logical ways of viewing the field (for example, by system level, substantive nature of the conflict, region, level of violence, goals of the intervenor, or outcome).

There are a number of bases on which a matrix of approaches and methods of peaceful resolution of international conflicts could be constructed:

- Article 33 of the UN Charter urges parties to pursue the pacific settlement of disputes through "negotiation, enquiry, mediation, conciliation, arbitration, judicial settlement...or other peaceful means."
- Christopher Moore (1986, p. 67) describes five general conflict strategies: competition, avoidance, accommodation, negotiated compromise, and interest-based negotiation.
- Dean Pruitt and Jeffrey Rubin (1986, pp. 25–26) organize their strategies of conflict as follows: contending, yielding, problem solving, withdrawing, and inaction.
- Joseph Folger and Marshall Poole (1984, p. 40) identify five distinct styles of conflict behavior: competitive, accommodative, avoiding, collaborative, and compromising.

- Donald Bassett (forthcoming) combines the dimensions of strategy/style and process, creating a matrix with cells that run Moore, Pruitt and Rubin, and Folger and Poole against eight third-party intervention processes, arranged from the highest degree of disputant control to the highest degree of third-party control:

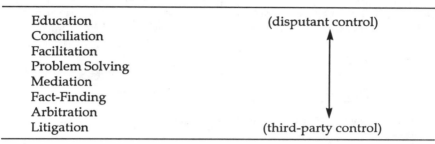

Education	(disputant control)
Conciliation	
Facilitation	
Problem Solving	
Mediation	
Fact-Finding	
Arbitration	
Litigation	(third-party control)

Bassett further reminds us that resolution is only one of a range of potential goals of conflict intervention, and he relates resolution to the solution of underlying issues and the satisfaction of fundamental human needs of the parties. He also notes that other major goals of conflict intervention (which can form a helpful matrix with the processes continuum illustrated above) are prediction, prevention, causing, avoidance, containment, and settlement.

We need to be reminded often that resolution is different from each of the other goals listed here—and from regulation, management, termination, coercion, and other modes of cessation of conflict symptoms.

The matrix building implied in these categories presents important challenges, but the scope of this paper does not allow for the in–depth analysis required to match specific examples and methods with matrix cells. The mapping exercise is intended to lay the groundwork for the Institute to carry on that task.

Instead, I have chosen to arrange bibliographies of what I consider to be the most important contemporary literature—largely American, to be sure—chronologically around the three major noncoercive intervention approaches that appear in most treatments of the field: negotiation, conciliation, and mediation. Enforcement approaches (for example, arbitration, litigation, and armed force) are omitted; they may frequently result in settlement or termination of a dispute, but rarely in true resolution. As I reviewed the literature, I assumed that an education category (including fact-finding, analysis, and technical assistance) would be included, but I found that, with the field's inherent orientation toward application and resolution, very few offerings stand alone as "education." In addition, most treatments of the major methods include education and analysis in their early sequence of resolution stages. Accordingly, the work of Elise Boulding and Betty Reardon, for example, is included under the conciliation category, for education—however general or specific—is a crucial part of getting to the table for resolution.

In this section are six bibliographies. Bibliography 1 lists theoretical or methodological overviews. Bibliographies 2, 3, and 4 list works on the three major conflict resolution approaches—negotiation, conciliation, and mediation, respectively. Bibliography 5 lists works on applications of these approaches to specific disputes or problems, and bibliography 6 lists major frameworks and bibliographies.[1]

Bibliography 1: Theory and Method Overviews

1941 Commission to Study the Organization of Peace, *International Conciliation*

1961 Anatol Rapoport, *Fights, Games, and Debates*

1964 Roger Fisher, ed., *International Conflict and Behavioral Science*

1965 Herbert Kelman, *International Behavior: A Social Psychology Analysis*

1969 Roger Fisher, *International Conflict for Beginners*

1971 Sidney Dawson Bailey, *Peaceful Settlement of International Disputes: Some Proposals for Research*

1971 Adam Curle, *Making Peace*

1973 Robert F. Randle, *The Origins of Peace: A Study of Peacemaking and the Structure of Peace Settlements*

1973 Lillian I. Randolph, *Third Party Settlement of Disputes in Theory and Practice*

1974 Morton Deutsch, *The Resolution of Conflict: Constructive and Destructive Processes*

1976 Barbara Stanford, ed., *Peacemaking: A Guide to Conflict Resolution for Individuals, Groups, and Nations*

1978 Gordon Bermant, Herbert Kelman, and Donald Warwick, eds., *The Ethics of Social Intervention*

1979 Paul Wehr, *Conflict Regulation*

1981 C.R. Mitchell, *The Structure of International Conflict*

1981 Report of the U.S. Commission on Proposals for the National Academy of Peace and Conflict Resolution, *To Establish the United States Academy of Peace*

1982 Maire A. Dugan, ed., *Conflict Resolution: Theory and Practice*, special issue of *Peace and Change*

1982 Daniel Frei, *Managing International Crises*

1984 Robert Axelrod, *The Evolution of Cooperation*

1984 Michael Banks, ed., *Conflict in World Society: A New Perspective on International Relations*

1984 John Burton, *Global Conflict: The Domestic Sources of International Crises*

1985 Stephen Goldberg, Eric Green, and Frank E.A. Sander, eds., *Dispute Resolution*

1985 Arthur S. Lall, ed., *Multilateral Negotiation and Mediation*

1986 Duane K. Friesen, *Christian Peacemaking and International Conflict*

1988 Martin Patchen, *Resolving Disputes Between Nations: Coercion or Conciliation?*

Bibliography 2: Negotiation in International Conflicts

Negotiation is defined as the patterned exchange of information, ideas, and promises by two or more parties with differing interests, with the aims of, first, developing a mutually acceptable resolution of their differences that is stable over time and, second, improving their ongoing relationship. Negotiation may be highly cooperative or highly adversarial. Solutions are more likely to improve if the mode is collaborative.

1964 Fred Iklé, *How Nations Negotiate*

1973 Daniel Druckman, *Human Factors in International Negotiations*

1974 Otomar J. Bartos, *Process and Outcome of Negotiations*

1975 Jeffrey Z. Rubin and Bert R. Brown, *The Social Psychology of Bargaining and Negotiation*

1976 I. William Zartman, ed., *The 50% Solution: How to Bargain Successfully with Hijackers, Strikers, Bosses, Oil Magnates, Arabs, Russians, and Other Worthy Opponents in This Modern World*

1978 Anselm Strauss, *Negotiations: Varieties, Contexts, Processes, and Social Order*

1978 I. William Zartman, ed., *The Negotiation Process: Theories and Applications*

1979 P.H. Gulliver, *Disputes and Negotiations: A Cross-Cultural Perspective*

1979 Charles Lockhardt, *Bargaining in International Conflicts*

1981 Dean Pruitt, *Negotiation Behavior*

1982 I. William Zartman and Maureen R. Berman, *The Practical Negotiator*

1983 Paul Pillar, *Negotiating Peace: War Termination as a Bargaining Process*

1984 Diane B. Bendahmane and John W. McDonald, Jr., eds., *International Negotiations, Art and Science*

1984 Jimmy Carter, *Negotiation: The Alternative to Hostility*

1986 Diane B. Bendahmane and John W. McDonald, Jr., eds., *Perspectives on Negotiation, Four Case Studies and Interpretations*

1987 Han Binnendijk, *National Negotiating Styles*

Bibliography 3: Conciliation in International Conflicts

Conciliation covers a range of intervention techniques used to create a climate for negotiation and eventual resolution. A blend of education, organization, party identification, process advocacy, and analysis, conciliation's major function often is to help shape a table for negotiation or mediation—to arrange incentives to get the parties there. Two examples of highly promising work in this realm—the analytical problem-solving workshops of John Burton and Herbert Kelman and track-two diplomacy as defined by Joseph Montville and John McDonald—are the subject of further analysis in the final section of this paper.

1941 Butler, Nicholas Murray, *International Conciliation*

1967 Oran R. Young, *The Intermediaries: Third Parties in International Crises*

1969 John Burton, *Conflict and Communication: The Use of Controlled Communications in International Relations*

1972 Herbert Kelman, "The Problem-Solving Workshop in Conflict Resolution," in A.L. Merritt, ed., *Communication in International Politics*

1977 Maureen R. Berman and Joseph E. Johnson, *Unofficial Diplomats*

1978 C.H. Mike Yarrow, *Quaker Experiences in International Conciliation*

1979 Johan Galtung, *The True Worlds: A Transnational Perspective*

1979 Martin Herz, ed., *Contacts with the Opposition*

1986 Don Carlson and Craig Comstock, *Citizen Summitry*

1986 John W. McDonald, Jr., and Diane B. Bendahmane, *Conflict Resolution: Track Two Diplomacy*

1987 John W. Burton, *Resolving Deep-Rooted Conflict: A Handbook*

1988 Elise Boulding, *Building a Global Civic Culture: Education for an Interdependent World*

1988 Betty Reardon, *Comprehensive Peace Education: Educating for Global Responsibility*

Bibliography 4: Mediation in International Conflicts

Mediation is the process in which a third party, accepted by all the direct parties to a conflict, assists the parties in their negotiations or other problem-solving interaction. A mediator operates with the voluntary consent of the parties and has no authority or control over the parties or the outcome of the dispute. Mediation is somewhat more focused than conciliation, generally referring to the role third parties play with disputants once they have agreed to attempt to resolve their dispute. Although there is considerable debate about appropriate terminology, I include here processes variously labeled "facilitation" or "analytical problem solving" (or, in some cases, "conciliation") because the basic structure is similar: a third party without decision-making authority assisting the direct parties in resolving their dispute.

1971 Frank Edmead, *Analysis and Prediction in International Mediation*

1978 Roger Fisher and William Ury, *International Mediation: A Working Guide*

1983 Deborah Kolb, *The Mediators*

1984 Jacob Bercovitch, *Social Conflicts and Third Parties: Strategies of Conflict Resolution*

1984 Jay Folberg and Alison Taylor, *Mediation: A Comprehensive Guide to Resolving Conflicts Without Litigation*

1985 Pierre Casse and Surinder Deal, *Managing Intercultural Negotiations: Guidelines for Trainers and Negotiators*

1985 Saadia Touval and I. William Zartman, eds., *International Mediation in Theory and Practice*

1986 Christopher Moore, *The Mediation Process: Practical Strategies for Resolving Conflict*

Bibliography 5: Applications to Specific International Disputes and Issues

A number of items included in this section could have been assigned to one (or more) of the first four categories, for they represent the application, and, in some cases field testing, of negotiation, conciliation, or mediation. Their placement here is intended to make them more accessible for readers with area or topical specialties. Examination of the results of the application of conflict resolution techniques to specific international disputes or issues should also help set the context for the next important step in the development of the field: systematic assessment of outcomes.

1965 Harold Nicolson, *Peacemaking 1919* (original 1920)

1970 Leonard W. Doob, ed., *Resolving Conflict in Africa: The Fermeda Workshop*

1971 Vratislav Pechota, *Complementary Structures of Third-Party Settlement of International Disputes*

1974 Indar Jit Rikhye, Michael Harbottle, and Bjorn Legge, *The Thin Blue Line: International Peacekeeping and Its Future*

1975 D. Smith and L. Wells, *Negotiating Third World Mineral Agreements*

1977 K.V. Raman, *Dispute Settlement Through the United Nations*

1978 International Peace Academy, *The Peacekeeper's Handbook*

1979 International Peace Academy, *Negotiating the End of Conflicts: Namibia and Zimbabwe*

1981 Jeffrey Z. Rubin, ed., *The Dynamics of Third-Party Intervention: Kissinger in the Middle East*

1982 International Peace Academy, *Managing Africa's Conflicts*

1982 Lucian Pye, *Chinese Negotiating Style*

1984 Ann Florini and Nina Tannenwald, *On the Front Lines: The United Nations' Role in Preventing and Containing Conflicts*

1984 Robert Houghton and Frank G. Trinka, *Multinational Peacekeeping in the Middle East*

1984 James Sebenius, *Negotiating the Law of the Sea: Lessons in the Art and Science of Reaching Agreement*

1985 Jimmy Carter, *The Blood of Abraham: Insights into the Middle East*

1985 William Ury, *Beyond the Hotline*

1986 William B. Quandt, *Camp David: Peacemaking and Politics*

1986 Harold Saunders, *The Other Walls: The Politics of the Arab-Israeli Peace Process*

1986 Leon M. Sloss and Scott Davis, eds., *A Game for High Stakes: Lessons Learned in Negotiating with the Soviet Union*

Reported uses of mediation and other third-party conflict resolution techniques in international disputes have proliferated in the 1980s, and we can look forward to case-related publications soon. Already the Quandt and Rubin books have brought us in-depth analyses of the Camp David process, mediated by President Carter, and of Secretary Kissinger's shuttle mediation in the Middle East in 1973–75. Bendahmane and McDonald report detailed debriefings of American dispute intervention roles in the Panama Canal treaties, the Malvinas/Falkland Islands dispute, Cyprus, and Zimbabwe. Research projects funded since 1986 by the United States Institute of Peace should cover much of the range of recent case examples (see *USIP Biennial Report 1987*).

We can expect analyses of some of the following recent applications of conflict resolution techniques:

- Central America (the Contadora and Arias peace processes, and the attempts of Cardinal Obando to mediate);
- the Middle East (Secretary Shultz's attempts to get to the table with Israeli and Arab parties);
- Afghanistan (Diego Cordovas's six-year mediation resulting in settlement and Soviet withdrawal);
- Soviet-American summitry in the 1980s;
- the INF Treaty;
- successful negotiation, mediation, and conciliation roles in the Tehran and TWA-847 hostage situations;
- negotiation of the release of French hostages in Lebanon;
- mediation and conciliation attempts in South Africa;
- mediation and conciliation attempts in Northern Ireland; and
- the UN Environmental Agency's successful mediation of fluorohydrocarbon production conflicts among more than thirty nations.

We also await, when the parties determine the time is appropriate, extensive analysis of the processes and achievements of ongoing conciliation and confidence-building activities such as the Dartmouth Conferences (now expanding to include Chinese as well as Soviet working groups), the Processes of International Negotiation project at the International Institute for Applied Systems Analysis in Vienna, and myriad other systematic and regular points of contact among nongovernmental scholars, commercial interests, clergy, and the like.

Bibliography 6: Frameworks and Bibliographies

Frameworks for mapping and cataloguing scholarship on international conflict resolution are proliferating. The most recent one is published in this volume; another is forthcoming in a six-volume series in preparation by John Burton. Burton is working as a Jennings Randolph Distinguished Peace Fellow of the United States Institute of Peace to develop a map based on a human needs theory of conflict and its resolution. Some of the more recent and influential frameworks are listed here:

1969 Hanna Newcombe and Alan J. Newcombe, *Peace Research Around the World*

1976 Juergen Dedring, *Recent Advances in Peace and Conflict Research: A Critical Survey*

1979 Elise Boulding, J. Robert Passmore, and Robert Grassler, *Bibliography on World Conflict and Peace*

1980 UNESCO, *UNESCO Yearbook on Peace and Conflict Studies* (latest edition published in 1985)

1981 Berenice Carroll, Clinton Fink, and Jane Mohraz, *Peace and War: A Guide to Bibliographies* (since 1785)

1982 Robert S. Woito, *To End War: A New Approach to International Conflict*, 6th ed. (bibliographies, frameworks, organizations, networks)

1984 Barbara Wien, *Peace and World Order Studies: A Curriculum Guide*, 4th ed. (World Policy Institute)

1986 Chadwick F. Alger, "The Quest for Peace," in *Quarterly Report of the Mershon Center*

1986 Liparit Kiuzadjan, Juberta Hogeweg-de-Hart, and Werner Richter, *Peace Research: A Documentation of Current Research, 1983–85* (Europe)

Cases: Recent Examples of Conciliation and Mediation in International Conflicts

Finding the forum—or "getting to the table" (Laue, Burde, Potapchuk, and Salkoff 1988)—is among the most difficult problems in international conflict resolution. As in intranational or intercultural conflicts, the higher the stakes and the deeper the issues, the less likely there is to be an existing legitimated forum with the characteristics that can help support movement toward a lasting resolution. These characteristics are as follows:

- a collaborative rather than adversarial process, with principled negotiation at the core;
- a protected environment, away from the immediate pressures of back-home constituencies, media, and the courts;
- a skilled person or team helping to manage the process; and
- an orientation toward analysis and problem solving rather than fault finding or adjudication.

Creating this type of forum is at the heart of the conciliation or "pretable" process. Before constructive negotiation can occur—with or without the assistance of a third party—an acceptable venue must be found or created. Recent examples of successful resolution of international disputes have involved a dedicated and patient person (or persons) in an appropriate institutional setting, first to help set the table, and then to assist in managing the process. Instructive cases include Jimmy Carter at Camp David, recent efforts to establish a Middle East peace process (by the United States, Sweden, and private parties), Diego Cordovez in Afghanistan, Chester Crocker in Namibia, Mustafa Tolba in the successful ozone treaty negotiations, and Oscar Arias and Miguel Obando in Central America.

Jimmy Carter at Camp David

Perhaps the best example of successful mediation in a contemporary international conflict is the role played by President Carter in fashioning the

Camp David Accords in 1978. Former National Security Council official William Quandt writes as follows:

> The Camp David Accords, signed by the President of Egypt and the Prime Minister of Israel on September 17, 1978, were an event of historic importance in the modern Middle East. These agreements, hammered out in lengthy negotiations over a period of eighteen months, set the stage for the signing of a formal treaty of peace between Egypt and Israel on March 29, 1979. With these two states at peace, and both closely tied to the United States, the strategic map of the Middle East was fundamentally changed (Quandt 1986, p. ix).

For students of international conflict resolution, Camp David is as instructive for process considerations as it is for the outcome produced. The major lesson is the intense personal commitment and attention invested by President Carter over a long period of time, guided by a well-honed but flexible strategy and bulwarked by massive staff work. Numerous private meetings with Sadat and Begin and their emissaries shaped the mutually agreeable conditions under which they would talk. A thirteen-day marathon commitment by President Carter in a private setting, unhampered by media or clamoring constituencies, was the carefully controlled, and highly productive, venue. A long period of "relationship building" between Carter and the two adversaries accompanied the development of a mutual plan for the summit and made the Camp David Accords possible.

Carter played a classic mediator's role: bridging hostilities between two parties through the building and modeling of a good relationship with each, committing time and attention to them and to the problem, developing an intelligent strategy, and structuring a protected environment in which serious and continuous dialogue was possible (see Carter 1985; Saunders 1986; Quandt 1986). The political staying power of the agreements produced at Camp David was demonstrated in President Reagan's "Address to the Nation on the West Bank and the Palestinians" September 1, 1982, in which he said, "With respect to the Arab-Israeli conflict, we have embraced the Camp David framework as the only way to proceed" (Carter 1985, p. 229).

Contemporary Conciliation Efforts in the Middle East: Getting Back to the Table

During the second half of President Reagan's administration, Secretary of State George Shultz conducted intensive efforts to restart Israeli-Arab peace negotiations—an attempt at what is defined in this chapter as conciliation. In 1987–88 Secretary Shultz carried out several lengthy shuttle missions among top Israeli and Arab leaders to promote both an American peace process and an American peace plan. At the height of the efforts early in

1988, it was "not at all clear" to three former Middle East diplomats from the United States "that the ground has yet been well prepared for peace negotiations" in the Middle East (Elits, Lewis, and Quandt 1988). Shultz had been publicly pressing the U.S. formulation of both a process and a set of outcomes, including media attacks on Prime Minister Yitzhak Shamir of Israel for stubbornly refusing to accept the American plans. The framework was never accepted, floundering at least in part because, as former assistant secretary of state for Near Eastern and South Asian Affairs Harold Saunders put it, "We were pushing both for a particular plan and a peace process at a time when the parties hadn't even decided they wanted to talk" (Saunders 1985).

A tightly choreographed series of moves in the fall of 1988 included Secretary Shultz's refusal to grant Yasser Arafat, leader of the PLO, a visa to address the UN on potential negotiations among Israel, the PLO, and the United States; intervention by Sweden's foreign minister and moderate American Jewish interests in the form of a meeting with Arafat; and the start of direct PLO-American talks in the face of stiff opposition from Israel. The American presidential transition put the process on ice early in 1989, but this getting-to-the-table process was expected to continue to gain momentum under the Bush administration—an example of the complexity of prenegotiation negotiations in international conflicts.

The UN as Mediator: Good Offices in Afghanistan, Iran-Iraq, and Cyprus

Personal commitment, patience, staying power, intelligent and continuous assessment, a strong and legitimate base of support—all these conditions have been present in the recently intensified "good offices" activities being conducted from the offices of the UN Secretary General Javier Perez de Cuellar. Under the secretary general's auspices, Under Secretary Diego Cordovez mediated the Soviet withdrawal from Afghanistan and other accords (signed in Geneva on April 14, 1988) in six years of stop-and-start talks with representatives of Afghanistan, Pakistan, Iran, the Soviet Union, and the United States. In the face of many discouraged calls for ending the talks, Diego Cordovez said his major duty was "not to give up" (*Washington Post* 1988a).

Perez de Cuellar brought Iranian and Iraqi representatives to the table for direct negotiations on their long-standing conflict and acceptance of a UN-sponsored cease-fire in July 1988.

The secretary general's office has been conducting proximity talks in the Cyprus dispute, as well as providing peacekeeping forces. Under his leadership, the UN is increasingly capitalizing on its base to play third-party roles as convener, fact-finder, and mediator—functions specified in Article 33 of the UN Charter but not fully employed until now. Further evidence of the growing attention of the UN to the great potential of its role as a third-party peacemaker was the focus of the 1988 annual conference of nongovernmental organizations on "The Role of the United Nations in Conflict Resolution, Peacekeeping, and Global Security" (*Peace Institute Reporter* 1988, 1).

Further strengthening of the role of the secretary general's office in peacemaking appears under way. In November 1988, Perez de Cuellar reorganized the Secretariat to take direct control of such efforts, with a particular focus on implementation of the Afghan accords, the Cyprus dispute, and the Iran-Iraq War (*New York Times* 1988, 1).

Chester Crocker in Namibia

The recent peace accord for Namibia is one of the most clear-cut demonstrations of the ability of a superpower to serve as a base for a mediator—and of the desired characteristics of a successful international mediator. U.S. Assistant Secretary of State Chester Crocker conceived, conciliated, convened, and ultimately mediated to conclusion the agreement signed by Cuba, Angola, and South Africa, which secured independence for Namibia after seventy-three years as a South African colony, removed fifty-two thousand Cuban mercenaries from neighboring Angola, and created conditions for national reconciliation in Namibia. Crocker began in 1980 by writing an article in *Foreign Affairs* on "constructive engagement" with South Africa, then worked through South Africa's objections to UN Resolution 435 calling for supervised free elections in Namibia, spent 1985 through 1987 in "talks about talks," and finally was able to convene all the parties (under the eyes of some of their patrons) for a year-long mediated negotiation that led to the signing of the agreement in Brazzaville, Congo, on December 13, 1988 (*Washington Post* 1988b; 1988c).

Crocker's work was praised by President Reagan, Soviet Deputy Foreign Minister Anatoly Adamishin, South African Defense Minister Roelof Botha, and others. Botha told a cheering Congolese host delegation at the signing that the pact is "fundamentally an African agreement." He called for the "brotherhood" of African blacks and whites, adding, "A new era has begun. My government is removing racial discrimination.... We want to be accepted by our African brothers. We need each other" (*Washington Post* 1988b). The Namibia agreement may become a model for interstate conflict resolution in Africa for years to come.

Mustafa Tolba and the Ozone Treaty

The development of the 1987 Montreal Protocol to eliminate production of ozone-depleting fluorocarbons by the year 2000 illustrates, in yet another setting, the peacemaking power of a patient and committed mediator with a legitimate base. Mustafa Tolba of Egypt, executive director of the UN Environmental Program, conceived and coordinated a two-year mediation process under the auspices of his agency that produced the agreement among the major producers of fluorocarbons. Sixteen have already signed the agreement (Benedick 1988), and the success of the endeavor is assured. Tolba had strong assistance from Richard Benedick, the assistant secretary of state representing the United States in the negotiations; from Lee Thomas, administrator of the U.S. Environmental Protection Agency; and from a range of environmental groups. But it was Tolba's vision, and strong and persistent leadership, that produced what a representative of the Environmental Defense Fund said could be a "signal event—a watershed in human history." Tolba got the parties to the table. His agency provided technical support. He kept them at the task and provided the protected environment where the interests of nations, fluorocarbon producers, and environmentalists could be heard by one another without excessive playing to the press (Laue 1987).

Tolba has demonstrated the potential of the UN agency structure for service as a convener and mediator in difficult international disputes.

Oscar Arias and Miguel Obando in Central America

President Oscar Arias Sanchez of Costa Rica won the 1987 Nobel Peace Prize for his authorship and mediation, which led to the signing of the Central American Peace Plan by five Central American presidents on August 7, 1987. Attempts to implement the plan have been less successful, although progress has been made through national oversight commissions established in Guatemala, El Salvador, Nicaragua, and Panama, and through the mediation attempts of indigenous Roman Catholic Cardinal Miguel Obando y Bravo. Whether the plan results in peaceful change depends on myriad internal and external factors (not the least of them being the roles of the United States, the Soviet Union, and Cuba). High-level attention by a mediator with the intensity of a Carter, a Diego Cordovez, or a Crocker, sponsored by the UN or the OAS, may be required to move the plan forward.

Related Activities

The work of other third parties could be added: Roman Catholic intellectuals who helped to gain recognition for Solidarity as a legitimate bargaining agent for Polish shipyard workers in a country where unions were not recognized at all; a long history of assistance through unofficial, or track-two diplomacy (see Berman and Johnson 1977; McDonald and Bendahmane 1987); the role of the International Peace Academy in developing the techniques of peacekeeping; recognition of the UN peacekeeping forces— the "blue helmets"—with the 1988 Nobel Peace Prize; the attempt of U.S. Secretary of State Alexander Haig to "mediate" the British-Argentine dispute over the Malvinas/Falklands Islands. Historical and comparative research on these interventions within a framework of the conflict resolution process will add substantially to our understanding of international peacemaking techniques.

Lessons and Needs in International Conflict Resolution

The literature and direct experience of conflict resolution at the international level have expanded dramatically in the past decade or two: the Dartmouth Conferences, Camp David, track-two diplomacy, the good offices role of the secretary general of the UN, the formation of the United States Institute of Peace. The field is poised for further expansion and application, and a stock-taking and projection are in order. The final section of this chapter addresses that task in two parts: lessons we have learned about international conflict resolution and needs for further development of the field.

Lessons

1. Critical mass is being achieved in the United States, as should be clear from the array of books, articles, institutes, case examples, and other indicators noted in this chapter. COPRED counts more than 400 academic programs in peace and conflict studies in American colleges and universities alone. The Ford, Rockefeller, Carnegie, and MacArthur foundations all have declared themselves heavily committed to funding international peace projects, and the Hewlett Foundation has given more than $500,000 to each of a dozen American universities to build conflict resolution theory programs over three- to six-year periods: Colorado, George Mason, Harvard, Hawaii, Michigan, Minnesota, Northwestern, Penn State, Rutgers, Stanford, Syracuse, and Wisconsin. The United States Institute of Peace is in place, with a new five-year authorization from Congress. It has already created significant spin-offs in the Iowa Peace Institute, the Kansas Institute for Peace and Conflict Resolution, and the Hawaii Institute for Peace. The latest development on the institutional front in the United States is the formation of the International Negotiation Network at the Carter Presidential Center to apply mediation expertise early to brewing international conflicts.

2. Scholarship and practice are diverse, rich, innovative, of varying quality (from eclectic and often unexamined theoretical bases), and largely unevaluated. As Roger Fisher has commented, "We know it works in practice, but does it work in theory?" (Fisher 1978).

3. Conflict resolution in international affairs is rooted in domestic conditions such as the back-home political importance of the conflict and the influence of constituencies with ties to the dispute. Many conflicts are, in fact, intercommunal or interreligious conflicts that began within a national

border and spilled over. The tribe, clan, religion, community, or ethnic group may be a more accurate unit of analysis than the nation-state in many transnational conflicts (see especially Burton 1984).

4. Conflict resolution efforts in international affairs take place in a context of ongoing political relations and acts, and therefore should not be treated as isolated "summits" or as determinate of outcomes in themselves. Nonetheless, there is a good deal to learn about the effects of variations in important elements such as venue, mediator characteristics, process, and party alliances.

5. Nonofficial diplomacy and the getting-to-the-table stages are receiving considerable attention from scholars and practitioners in conflict resolution at the international level. These methods point to the limitations of traditional, formal diplomacy and to the limitations of any analysis that begins only when the parties meet for face-to-face negotiations. Reports of the long and careful preparation of Carter, Diego Cordovez, and Crocker have opened a rich area for research on the creative potential of informal approaches, including prenegotiation conditions and behavior.

Needs

1. Research is needed to build a body of empirically supported findings on gaping areas of knowledge such as these:

- the causal relationship (if any) between interventions and outcomes (see Bercovitch 1986);
- the nature of resolution, compared with management, compromise, settlement, deterrence, containment, and so on;
- the dynamics of the third-party role;
- getting to the table (Laue et al. 1988);
- relationships between system levels (e.g., intra- versus international, intercultural versus international); and
- regional cases.

2. A coherent theory and the criteria underlying concepts of desirable outcomes and conceptual organization of the field need to be developed. For example, is a control and deterrence orientation to international conflict more hospitable to settlement or to management as an outcome goal? Does a framework stressing human needs presage resolution or management as a logical and desired outcome?

3. Networks need to be developed with a range of non-American institutions, among them the Canadian Institute for International Peace and Security, Jean Freymond's International Institute for the Advanced Study of Negotiation in Geneva, the Peace Research Institute of Oslo, the Stockholm International Peace Research Institute, the USA-Canada Institute for

Applied Systems Analysis in Vienna (that published a new volume in 1989 tentatively titled *International Negotiations: Problems and New Approaches*).

But by far the most important tasks facing the United States Institute of Peace are further development and refinement of the mapping project begun with the July 1988 Airlie House Conference and this volume. The need is exemplified in the close and overlapping relationship between this chapter and chapter 3, "Diplomacy and Negotiation" by David Newsom, and chapter 8, "International Third-Party Dispute Settlement" by Richard Bilder. Perhaps all of these should become categories under the general rubric of "Negotiation and Mediation" or "Third-Party Peacemaking."

This volume and the mapping work of John Burton as Jennings Randolph Distinguished Peace Fellow of the United States Institute of Peace have made a significant beginning in that direction.

Discussion

The figure-ground problem was also addressed by commentator Geoffrey Kemp, who questioned whether conflict resolution is a separate and distinct field. It may be, he said, but much of the existing literature on the subject suggests that conflict resolution is a euphemism for a radical-liberal critique of the more traditional methods of studying the field of international relations.

Kemp commented that all the institutions and think tanks around the world in which he has worked would characterize at least part of their mission as seeking the resolution of international conflict, yet they do not seem to be included in Laue's list of organizations working in the field. He asked how traditional institutions of both the Left and the Right can be incorporated as components of conflict resolution.

The question is important, Kemp continued, because it is indicative of the false dichotomy drawn between the fields of peace studies and security studies. Why is it assumed that people interested in security studies cannot be interested in peace and vice versa? Unless conflict resolution as a field broadens its approach, he said, it is in danger of perpetuating and exacerbating this fallacy.

The true test of any academic or intellectual theory is its relevance to the real world. How does conflict resolution fare in this regard? Kemp suggested that the field of international relations is overpopulated with experts. The government has its experts, such as the National Security Council, the State Department, and the intelligence agencies; Congress has its foreign policy specialists and their staffs; and there are the diplomats on the front lines who are exposed to conflict daily. These groups, in turn, are under the watchful eye of the print and electronic media, the think tanks, and academe, each with a particular view about solving the problems of the world. How does conflict resolution fit into this equation?

Because the amount of data that people can process is limited, familiarity with conflict resolution cannot immediately change the perspectives of policymakers. But the academic or journalist of today may well be the government policymaker of tomorrow, and future policymakers can become informed about problems of resolving international conflict through experiences such as this. It is important for conflict resolution theory and practice to be discussed and challenged in forums such as this, so that we will have more qualified people when we need them.

The group discussion following the Laue and Kemp presentations focused on two broad areas of interest: the need to operationalize the theory of conflict resolution to make it more relevant and accessible to the practitioner; and the supplementary role of power and coercion in the resolution of protracted conflict, particularly in the Third World.

According to Janne Nolan, the conceptual breakthroughs that Laue suggests are so important that they are actually secondary to the need to forge political coalitions that can implement solutions. There is, she said, a glaring need to mesh theory and practice.

Richard Smyser agreed, adding that although the advocates of conflict resolution as a field of study deserve credit for being the first to formalize the idea that negotiating positions are often reflections of enduring emotional beliefs rather than mere political tactics, it is now important to shift the emphasis away from academics to practitioners in the field. This is particularly true, added another member of the audience, because conflict resolution, if it is not studied in the context of a specific conflict, tends to get intellectually "mushy."

Richard Bilder raised two related issues: whether a third-party mediator must be an expert in the field under mediation, and what role differing cultural perspectives of mediators and protagonists play in the mediation process.

Laue agreed that conflict resolution must incorporate theorists and practitioners of all philosophical persuasions and acknowledged that often the problem is not so much getting parties to sit down at the negotiating table as it is getting them to discuss the issues realistically. The main task of conflict resolution specialists is to adapt the framework of discussion to make innovative solutions feasible. Cultural considerations play a part, but it does not follow that a potential mediator must share the culture of either of the disputing parties.

The question of whether mediators must be functional experts in areas under mediation is somewhat more problematic, Laue said. Although it can be helpful for mediators to have a working knowledge of the issues under debate, specialists in the field might have preconceived ideas of a proper solution and thus neglect to explore some avenues that they have already intellectually rejected.

Max Singer observed that conflict resolution theorists seem to assume that the protagonists share a desire to see a negotiated end to the conflict.

But if one side believes it has a chance to win an all-out victory, Singer said, a negotiated settlement is unlikely. The situation is further complicated by the tendency of disputing parties to have contradictory perceptions about the balance of power between them.

Laue agreed, noting that power considerations drive most conflicts; when a gross disparity of power exists, the result is usually an imposed, unilateral solution. But this is not always the case. The Soviets are vastly more powerful than the Afghani resistance, yet they were unable to impose a unilateral settlement.

Alberto Coll expressed the view that a diplomatic settlement was reached in Afghanistan primarily because of the effort by the United States and other countries to make the resistance groups a more modern and effective fighting force through the provision of Stinger missiles and other military technologies. Without such support, Coll said, it is unlikely that the Soviets would have retreated when they did.

David Pabst suggested that, although the Stinger missile was an important component of the Soviet decision to withdraw, the key to the process was the timing of the missile's introduction. If the United States had not let the diplomatic process mature over a number of years and if certain other events (including Mikhail Gorbachev's rise to power) had not come to pass, the introduction of the Stinger missile would probably have had the reverse effect.

The important point here, Laue said, is that conflict resolution is not a panacea for international violence but a process to achieve a more positive outcome by reexamining the framework of the dispute. It is but one of many tools to be employed in combination with one another, depending on the circumstances of the conflict under consideration.

In his summation of the discussion, Samuel Lewis noted that one of the major functions of the United States Institute of Peace is to facilitate the flow of ideas between the academic and practitioner communities. Conflict resolution is a good example of a relatively new academic discipline that contains valuable insights that the practitioner could use; however, the transference of those ideas and experiences from the domestic to the international arena is problematic. It is clear that traditional approaches to maintaining peace have been unsatisfactory when they are applied to the Third World, so it is important to see whether these new approaches, combined with the knowledge and experience of diplomats in the field, offer new hope.

Note

1. I am especially indebted to George Lopez, William Potapchuk, Miranda Salkoff, Charles D. Smith, and Peter Swanson for their written works and direct assistance in developing these materials.

Bibliography

Akehurst, Michael. *A Modern Introduction to International Law*. 5th ed. Winchester, Mass.: Unwin Hyman, 1984.

Alger, Chadwick F. "The Quest for Peace." *Quarterly Report of the Mershon Center* II, no. 2. Columbus: Mershon Center (Autumn 1986): 1–7.

Axelrod, Robert. *The Evolution of Cooperation*. New York: Basic Books, 1984.

Azar, Edward E., and John W. Burton, eds. *International Conflict Resolution: Theory and Practice*. Boulder, Colo.: Lynn Reinner, 1986.

Bailey, Sidney Dawson. *Peaceful Settlement of International Disputes: Some Proposals for Research*. New York: United Nations Institute for Training and Research, 1971.

Ball, Geoff. *When Controversy Comes to the City*. Palo Alto, Calif.: Geoff Ball and Associates, 1986.

Banks, Michael, ed. *Conflict in World Society: A New Perspective on International Relations*. New York: St. Martin's Press, 1984.

Bartos, Otomar J. *Process and Outcome of Negotiations*. New York: Columbia Press, 1974.

Bassett, Donald A. "Selecting Intervention Goals, Strategies and Processes," in James H. Laue and Robert K. Reed, eds. *The Conflict Resolution Handbook*. Forthcoming.

Bendahmane, Diane B., and John W. McDonald, Jr., eds. *International Negotiation, Art and Science*. Washington, D.C.: Foreign Service Institute, U.S. Department of State, 1984.

_____. *Perspectives on Negotiation, Four Case Studies and Interpretations*. Washington, D.C.: Foreign Service Institute, U.S. Department of State, 1986.

Benedick, Richard. Presentation at School of Advanced International Studies, Johns Hopkins University. Washington, D.C., November 1988.

Berman, Maureen R., and Joseph B. Johnson, eds. *Unofficial Diplomats*. New York: Columbia University Press, 1977.

Bermant, Gordon, Herbert Kelman, and Donald Warwick, eds. *The Ethics of Social Intervention*. Washington, D.C.: Halsted Press, 1978.

Bercovitch, Jacob. *Social Conflicts and Third Parties: Strategies of Conflict Resolution*. Boulder, Colo.: Westview Press, 1984.

_____. "International Mediation: A Study of the Incidence, Strategies and Conditions of Successful Outcomes." *Conflict and Cooperation* (December 1986): 155–67.

Bingham, Gail. *Resolving Environmental Disputes*. Washington, D.C.: Conservation Foundation, 1986.

Binnendijk, Han. *National Negotiating Styles*. Washington, D.C.: Foreign Service Institute, U.S. Department of State, 1987.

Boulding, Elise. *Building a Global Civic Culture: Education for an Interdependent World*. New York: Teachers College Press, 1988.

Boulding, Elise, J. Robert Passmore, and Robert Grassler. *Bibliography on World Conflict and Peace*. 2d ed. Boulder, Colo.: Westview Press, 1979.

Burton, John W. *Conflict and Communication: The Use of Controlled Communications in International Relations*. London: Macmillan, 1969.

_____. *Global Conflict: The Domestic Sources of International Crises*. Brighton, Eng.: Wheatsheaf Books, 1984.

_____. *Resolving Deep-Rooted Conflict: A Handbook*. New York: University Press of America, 1987.

Butler, Nicholas Murray. *International Conciliation*. New York: Interpay, 1941.

Carlson, Don, and Craig Comstock, eds. *Citizen Summitry*. New York: St. Martin's Press, 1986.

Carnegie Endowment for International Peace. *Beginnings: Carnegie Endowment for International Peace: 1910–1985*. Washington, D.C., 1985.

Carroll, Berenice, Clinton Fink, and Jane Mohraz. *Peace and War: A Guide to Bibliographies*. Santa Barbara, Calif.: ABC-Clio Press, 1983.

Carter, Jimmy. *Negotiation: The Alternative to Hostility*. Macon, Ga: Mercer University Press, 1984.

_____. *The Blood of Abraham: Insights Into the Middle East*. Boston: Houghton Mifflin, 1985.

Casse, Pierre, and Surinder Deol. *Managing Intercultural Negotiations: Guidelines for Trainers and Negotiators*. Washington, D.C.: SIETAR International, 1985.

Commission to Study the Organization of Peace. *International Conciliation*. New York: Carnegie Endowment for International Peace, 1941.

Coser, Lewis. *The Functions of Social Conflict*. Toronto: Free Press, 1956.

Curle, Adam. *Making Peace*. New York: Barnes and Noble, 1971.

Dedring, Juergen. *Recent Advances in Peace and Conflict Research: A Critical Survey*. Beverly Hills, Calif.: Sage Publishers, 1976.

Deutsch, Morton. *The Resolution of Conflict: Constructive and Destructive Processes*. New Haven, Conn.: Yale University Press, 1973.

Doob, Leonard W., ed. *Resolving Conflict in Africa: The Fermeda Workshop*. New Haven: Yale University Press, 1970.

Druckman, Daniel. *Human Factors in International Negotiations*. New York: Academy for Educational Development, 1973.

Dugan, Maire A., ed. "Conflict Resolution: Theory and Practice." Special Issue of *Peace and Change* 7, no. 2/3 (Summer 1982).

Edmead, Frank. *Analysis and Prediction in International Mediation*. New York: UNITAR, 1971.

Elits, Hermann F., Samuel W. Lewis, and William B. Quandt. "Why Mideast Talks Go Nowhere." *Washington Post*, March 20, 1988.

Fisher, Roger, ed. *International Conflict and Behavioral Science*. New York: Basic Books, 1964.

Fisher, Roger. *International Conflict for Beginners*. Magnolia, Mass.: Peter Smith Publishers, 1980.

Fisher, Roger, and William Ury. *International Mediation: A Working Guide*. New York: International Peace Academy, 1978.

Florini, Ann, and Nina Tannenwald. *On the Front Lines: The United Nations' Role in Preventing and Containing Conflicts*. New York: United Nations Association of the USA, 1984.

Folberg, Jay, and Alison Taylor. *Mediation: A Comprehensive Guide to Resolving Conflicts Without Litigation*. San Francisco: Jossey-Bass, 1984.

Folger, Joseph P., and Marshall Scott Poole. *Working Through Conflict: A Communication Perspective*. Glenview, Ill.: Scott, Foresman, 1984.

Frei, Daniel, ed. *Managing International Crises*. Beverly Hills, Calif.: Sage, 1982.

Friesen, Duane K. *Christian Peacemaking and International Conflict*. Scottdale, Pa.: Herald Press, 1986.

Galtung, Johan. *The True Worlds: A Transnational Perspective*. New York: Free Press, 1980.

Goldberg, Stephen, Eric Green, and Frank E. A. Sander, eds. *Dispute Resolution*. Boston: Little, Brown, 1985.

Gulliver, P. H. *Disputes and Negotiations: A Cross-Cultural Perspective*. New York: Academic Press, 1979.

Herz, Martin, ed. *Contacts with the Opposition*. Washington, D.C.: Georgetown University, 1979.

Houghton, Robert, and Frank G. Trinka. *Multinational Peacekeeping in the Middle East*. Washington, D.C.: Foreign Service Institute, U.S. Department of State, 1984.

Iklé, Fred Charles. *How Nations Negotiate*. New York: Harper and Row, 1964, 1982.

International Peace Academy. *Managing Africa's Conflicts*. New York, 1982.

_____. *Negotiating the End of Conflicts: Namibia and Zimbabwe*. New York, 1979.

_____. *The Peacekeeper's Handbook*. New York, 1978.

Kelman, Herbert, ed. *International Behavior: A Social Psychology Analysis*. New York: Holt, Rinehart and Winston, 1965.

_____. "The Problem-Solving Workshop in Conflict Resolution," in A. L. Merritt, ed. *Communication in International Politics*. Hobson: University of Illinois, 1972.

Kiuzadjan, Liparit, Juberta Hogeweg-de-Hart, and Werner Richter. *Peace Research: A Documentation of Current Research 1983–85 (Europe)*. Moscow: Inion, 1986.

Kolb, Deborah. *The Mediators*. Cambridge, Mass.: MIT Press, 1983.

Kossman, E. H. "Hugo Grotius," in Davis L. Stills, ed. *The International Encyclopedia of the Social Sciences*, Vol. 6. New York: Free Press, 1968.

Kriesberg, Louis, ed. *Research in Social Movement, Conflict and Change*, Vol. 7. Greenwich, Conn.: Jai Publishers, 1984.

Lall, Arthur S., ed. *Multilateral Negotiation and Mediation: Instruments and Methods*. New York: Pergamon, 1985.

Laue, James H. "The Future of Community Conflict Intervention." *The Journal of Intergroup Relations* 10, no. 2 (Summer 1982).

_____. "The Subject Is Peacemaking." Radio Commentary, KWMU, St. Louis, Mo., May 14, 1987.

Laue, James H., ed. "Using Mediation to Shape Public Policy." Special edition of *Mediation Quarterly*, no. 20 (Summer 1988).

Laue, James H., Sharon Burde, William Potapchuk, and Miranda Salkoff. "Getting to the Table: Three Paths." *Mediation Quarterly*, no. 20 (Summer 1988): 7–21.

Lentz, Theodore F. *Towards a Science of Peace*. London: Halcyon Press, 1955.

Lockhardt, Charles. *Bargaining in International Conflicts*. New York: Columbia University Press, 1979.

McDonald, John W., Jr., and Diane B. Bendahmane, eds. *Conflict Resolution: Track Two Diplomacy*. Washington, D.C.: Foreign Service Institute, U.S. Department of State, 1987.

Mendlovitz, Saul. *On the Creation of a Just World Order*. New York: Free Press, 1975.

Mitchell, Christopher R. *The Structure of International Conflict*. London: Macmillan, 1981.

Moore, Christopher. *The Mediation Process: Practical Strategies for Resolving Conflict*. San Francisco: Jossey-Bass, 1986.

National Conference on Peacemaking and Conflict Resolution. Conference Reports. Fairfax, Va.: George Mason University, 1983, 1984, 1986.

Newcombe, Hanna, and Alan J. Newcombe. *Peace Research Around the World*. Oakville, Ont.: Canadian Peace Research Institute, 1969.

New York Times. "U.N. Shuffles Peacekeeping Operations, Giving Power to Secretary General." April 4, 1988.

Nicolson, Harold. *Peace Making 1919*. New York: Grosset and Dunlap, 1920, 1965.

Patchen, Martin. *Resolving Disputes Between Nations: Coercion or Conciliation?* Durham, N.C.: Duke University Press, 1988.

Peace Institute Reporter. "U.N. Helps Negotiate Afghan Peace Accords." Washington, D.C.: National Peace Institute Foundation (June 1988): 1–2.

Pechota, Vratislav. *Complementary Structures of Third-Party Settlement of International Disputes*. New York: UNITAR, 1971.

Pillar, Paul. *Negotiating Peace: War Termination as a Bargaining Process*. Princeton, N.J.: Princeton University Press, 1983.

Pruitt, Dean. *Negotiation Behavior*. New York: Academic Press, 1981.

Pruitt, Dean, and Jeffrey Z. Rubin. *Social Conflict: Escalation, Stalemate, and Settlement*. New York: Random House, 1986.

Pye, Lucian. *Chinese Negotiating Style*. Cambridge, Mass.: Oelgeschlager, Gumm, and Hain, 1982.

Quandt, William B. *Camp David: Peacemaking and Politics*. Washington, D.C.: Brookings Institution, 1986.

Raman, K. Venkata. *Dispute Settlement Through the United Nations*. New York: UNITAR, 1977.

Randle, Robert F. *The Origins of Peace: A Study of Peacemaking and the Structure of Peace Settlements*. New York: The Free Press, 1973.

Randolph, Lillian I. *Third Party Settlement of Disputes in Theory and Practice*. Dobbs Ferry, N.Y.: Oceana Press, 1973.

Rapoport, Anatol. *Fights, Games, and Debates.* Ann Arbor, Mich.: University of Michigan, 1961.

Reardon, Betty. *Comprehensive Peace Education: Educating for Global Responsibility.* New York: Teacher's College Press, 1988.

Rikhye, Indar Jit, Michael Harbottle, and Bjorn Legge. *The Thin Blue Line: International Peacekeeping and Its Future.* New York: International Peace Academy, 1974.

Rubin, Jeffrey Z., ed. *The Dynamics of Third-Party Intervention: Kissinger in the Middle East.* New York: Praeger, 1981.

Rubin, Jeffrey Z, and Bert B. Brown. *The Social Psychology of Bargaining and Negotiation.* New York: Academic Press, 1975.

Saunders, Harold. *Other Walls: The Politics of the Arab-Israeli Peace Process.* Washington, D.C.: American Enterprise Institute, 1985.

Schellenberg, James A. *The Science of Conflict.* New York: Oxford Press, 1982.

Sebenius, James. *Negotiating the Law of the Sea: Lessons in the Art and Science of Reaching Agreement.* Cambridge, Mass.: Harvard University Press, 1984.

Shaner, George R. "The Field of Conflict Resolution Emerges," in James H. Laue and Robert K. Reed, eds. *The Conflict Resolution Handbook,* 1989.

Sharp, Gene. *Exploring Nonviolent Alternatives.* Boston: Porter Sargent, 1970.

Singer, J. David. *Explaining War: Selected Papers From the Correlates of War Project.* Beverly Hills, Calif.: Sage, 1979.

Sloss, Leon M., and Scott Davis, eds. *A Game for High Stakes: Lessons Learned in Negotiating with the Soviet Union.* Cambridge, Mass.: Ballinger Press, 1986.

Smith, Adam. *The Theory of Moral Sentiments.* First published 1853. Reprinted New Rochelle, N.Y.: Arlington House, 1969.

Smith, Charles D., ed. *The Hundred Percent Challenge.* Washington, D.C.: Seven Locks Press, 1985.

Smith, D., and L. Wells. *Negotiating Third World Mineral Agreements.* Cambridge, Mass.: Ballinger Press, 1975.

Stanford, Barbara. *Peacemaking: A Guide to Conflict Resolution for Individuals, Groups, and Nations.* New York: Bantam, 1976.

Strauss, Anselm. *Negotiations: Varieties, Contexts, Processes, and Social Order.* San Francisco: Jossey-Bass, 1978.

Susskind, Lawrence, and Jeffrey Cruikshank. *Breaking the Impasse.* New York: Basic Books, 1987.

Thucydides. *The Peloponnesian Wars.* Original printing circa 401 B.C. New York: Penguin, 1954.

Touval, Saadia, and I. William Zartman, eds. *International Mediation in Theory and Practice.* Boulder, Colo.: Westview Press, 1985.

UNESCO. UNESCO Yearbook on Peace and Conflict Studies. New York: United Nations, 1980.

United Methodist Council of Bishops. *In Defense of Creation.* Nashville: Cokesbury, 1986.

United States Institute of Peace. *USIP Biennial Report, 1987.* Washington, D.C.: U.S. Government Printing Office, 1987.

The United States Institute of Peace Act. U.S. Congress, (P.L. 98–525), 1984.

Ury, William. *Beyond the Hotline*. Boston: Houghton Mifflin, 1985.

U.S. Commission on Proposals for the National Academy of Peace and Conflict Resolution. *To Establish the United States Academy of Peace*. Washington, D.C.: U.S. Government Printing Office, 1981.

Washington Post. "U.N. Mediator Relies on Humor, Persistence." April 9, 1988a.

Washington Post. "Cuba, Angola, South Africa Sign Accord." December 14, 1988b.

Washington Post. "For Crocker, Accord Was Long Time Coming." December 14, 1988c.

Wehr, Paul. *Conflict Regulation*. Boulder, Colo.: Westview Press, 1979.

Wien, Barbara J. *Peace and World Studies: A Curriculum Guide*. New York: World Policy Institute, 1984.

Woito, Robert. *To End War: A New Approach to International Conflict*. New York: Pilgrim, 1982.

Yarrow, C. H. Mike. *Quaker Experiences in International Conciliation*. New Haven, Conn.: Yale University Press, 1978.

Young, Oran R. *The Intermediaries: Third Parties in International Crises*. Princeton, N.J.: Princeton University Press, 1967.

Zartman, I. William, ed. *The 50% Solution: How to Bargain Successfully with Hijackers, Strikers, Bosses, Oil Magnates, Arabs, Russians, and Other Worthy Opponents in This Modern World*. New Haven, Conn.: Yale University Press, 1976.

_____, ed. *The Negotiation Process: Theories and Applications*. Beverly Hills, Calif.: Sage, 1978.

Zartman, I. William, and Maureen R. Berman. *The Practical Negotiator*. New Haven, Conn.: Yale University Press, 1982.

Part IV: Political Systems Approaches

Introduction to Chapter 13

In his classic study, *Man, the State, and War,* Kenneth Waltz wrote, "Peace programs, whether they would rely for their efficacy upon irenic diplomacy, armed crusade, moral exhortation, or psychic-cultural readjustment, are all based at least implicitly on the ideas of the causes of war we entertain." Chapters 14 and 15 of this volume seek to put the relationship between the causes of war and efforts for peace into perspective by approaching the issue from opposite ends of the intellectual spectrum.

In chapter 14, R. J. Rummel addresses the issues of war and peace as a function of a state's adopted form of political organization. Can the relative bellicosity of states, he was asked, be measured and predicted as a function of their internal political system? His answer is an unequivocal yes.

In chapter 15, Michael Nagler takes a holistic approach to the search for international peace. How can the entire world, in both the philosophic and geographic senses, be organized in such a way as to lessen and eventually preclude the possibility of violence? His answer lies in the interesting concept of "unity in diversity."

In an effort to reconcile these two very different approaches to peace, Scott Thompson suggests, in this chapter, that their differences can best be argued as functions of various antinomies, particularly "in terms of philosophical approaches to free will and determinism, mutatis mutandis utopianism and realism."

Citing noted scholar E. H. Carr, Thompson characterizes the utopian as one who seeks to supplant reality with an idealized vision of the way things should be, rather than the way they are. The imposition of good intentions on faulty evidence often results in the wish being father to the thought.

The pure realist, in contrast, makes an equally erroneous assumption by concluding that relevant events are predetermined in such a way as to make conflict and war an inevitable consequence of international relations. The hope that progress can be made toward reducing international violence through the application of new ideas and instruments is, at best, misplaced and, at worst, dangerous.

But neither of these extremes adequately explains our situation today along the continuum between peace and war. We live in neither a perfect nor a perfectly flawed world. Violence and conflict are a part of our universe, and theories of causes and solutions must be viewed through the philosophical lens that colors each approach.

In Thompson's view, the lens most often adopted by the present-day peace movement is colored by at least one of the three main historical branches of utopianism. The first of these strands, best represented by Plato's *Republic*, constitutes purely intellectual efforts to achieve a better ordered universe without, however, prescribing how it is to be achieved. This brand of utopianism is still accepted by philosophers today, yet rarely has any noticeable influence on the activists or practitioners in the field.

A much more salient—and in Thompson's view, passionate—version of utopianism stems from what he sees as "an ineradicable and necessary search for the millenium [that is] built into human nature." This historic quest for a more peaceful world order, usually under the auspices of one imperium, is primarily responsible for the many tragedies associated with chiliastic movements and lays the theoretical groundwork for the third, and most relevant, branch of utopianism: modern millenialism.

Citing the work of Bernard Yack, Thompson argues that the defining characteristic of modern millenialism, which sets it apart from others, is the "longing for total revolution." This approach, although first formulated by the philosophers of the late eighteenth century, is most closely associated with the work of Karl Marx, who emphasized the notion that the major obstacle to social perfection was the "dehumanizing spirit of modern society, symbolized by the capitalist system." For Marx, movement toward international peace was contingent on a total Communist revolution and the destruction of the capitalist system.

Marx viewed society as a utopian totality, but he was forced to repudiate this premise in order to argue that the capitalist sickness he diagnosed as plaguing society actually existed. As a result, his teachings have come to assume a quasi-religious and transcendental quality that incorporates a sense of consistent "longing" with the paradoxical notion of a social totality. This explains why empirical facts cannot destroy the myth of Marxism: it has become a moving target with changing objects of hope; the search for its true manifestation, therefore, continues.

Modern peace researchers confront the antinomy between people who optimistically believe that nuclear weapons can be wished away or somehow abolished, and those who are prepared to negotiate step by step toward a safer world. The first of these positions represents the quasi-Marxist approach adopted by some members of the peace movement, while the latter is more representative of traditional diplomatic initiatives.

The major difference between the two methodologies is this: In the former, Western-style democracies are viewed as the most serious obstacle to international peace, and a value-oriented, utopian world government is substituted for revolutionary communism as the universal antidote for the world's ills. The latter approach features a diplomatically and politically enhanced version of the traditional superpower relationship. Neither methodology, however, includes prescriptions for resolving some of the persistent problems identified by the theorists—most notably, the question of power as it is exercised by the sovereign state.

This problem of state power points to another of Thompson's key antinomies. In the aftermath of World War II, the modern notion of the sovereign state was attacked as a leading cause of international violence, to the extent that the state was no longer deemed privileged to wage war except in self-defense. In place of the state, optimistic theories of regionalism, functionalism, world federalism, and other "one-world" conceptions emerged. As a unit of analysis, the state came to be viewed as an anachronistic and destabilizing international force.

Ironically, at the same time this intellectual movement was gaining momentum in the West, the number of sovereign states in the international system radically increased as a result of the dissolution of the European colonial system. By sheer weight of numbers, the nation-state is in the ascendancy, not on the wane. Furthermore, as these states are just beginning to consolidate their "nationhood," it is highly unlikely that many of them will endeavor to restrict their new-found sovereignty in the international system, particularly on behalf of a Western theory of world peace.

Therefore, as Thompson points out, at least for the foreseeable future, the state is sure to remain the legal representative of the peoples and nations of the world, and efforts to effect peace through state-to-state diplomacy are hardly misplaced. Transnational political, social, and economic forces will continue to play an active role in facilitating conflict avoidance between states, but such efforts will probably remain within the framework of the modern nation-state and the traditional context of diplomatic relations.

Thompson notes that people searching for peace tend to seek answers based on ever larger associations and schemes. Yet higher loyalties to smaller units cause conflict, and large associations and grand schemes dissolve under the weight of international realities. For progress to be made, peace researchers must shed some utopian ideals, and the realists must abandon preconceptions that U.S. power alone can solve every conflict.

13. The Antinomies of Peace

State-Oriented and Holistic Views

W. Scott Thompson

Where does peace start and from what does it issue? Two essays in this last section approach the subject from opposite perspectives: first, from the perspective of the individual state and the role of its internal organization on its peace policies; and, second, from the perspective of the entire world, in both philosophic and geographic senses.

The difference can be argued as a function of various antinomies, for example, in terms of philosophical approaches to free will and determinism, mutatis mutandis utopianism and realism. No one has stated it better than E. H. Carr:

> The utopian is necessarily voluntarist: he believes in the possibility of more or less radically rejecting reality, substituting his utopia for it by an act of will. The realist analyses a predetermined course of development which he is powerless to change.

So for the realist, Hegel's owl of Minerva, of course, always comes too late to cause improvements in our lot. "The complete realist," Carr adds with contemporary relevance, "unconditionally accepting the causal sequence of events, deprives himself of the possibility of changing reality."[1]

This dichotomy drives the scholars of the field, not just the practitioners—whether negotiators, international lawyers, or peace demonstrators. Today, idealists often look through the lens of psychology to find the key to peace—changing the minds of men—and sometimes making another kind of mistake: setting the wish and hope above reality. They impose their own good intentions on the insusceptible data; or they hope that the quality of their work will demonstrate the possibility of quick results in a field of deeply ingrained habits, driven by historic competitions. Realists, faced with examining bewildering and often abstruse studies of conflict resolution, often consider these studies mere quackery and may fail to recall the difficulty besetting the establishment of all the social sciences during the past 150 years as, slowly, good research drove out bad. We do not have to accept the world as it is, but let us assume that we must work with it as it is to change it—and bend our efforts to understand where and how it is susceptible to a learning process in the interest of peace. Thus, we need to find where we are, today, between utopia and reality in constructing a more peaceful world.

The Peace Movement and Utopia

At least three major historical strands of utopianism bear on holistic solutions to the problem of war and peace. Plato's *Republic* is the most striking of the first strand—purely intellectual efforts to construct universes of order, without instructing how order is to be achieved. These efforts still inform philosophers today, but they are not generally the source of slogans in the street.[2]

A much more passionate tradition is the search for the millennium. Apparently, an ineradicable search for the millennium is built into human nature and tied directly to the historical search for a peaceful world order, usually under one imperium; Karl Marx did not start it. John of Leyden went to Munster in the sixteenth century and, in his own miniholocaust, proposed the paradise of God on earth within the town's walls; his glint of steel was more than matched by the bishop's forces outside. John's destruction of the existing foundations of communal life was nearly total. But "King" John's extraordinary life-style, set against the starvation of the town's masses and executions by the thousands,[3] reminds us of what all too often happens in chiliastic situations—there is always a *nomenklatura*. Long after, in our own day, came the Jonestown tragedy in Guyana, which was all too reminiscent of the Munster millennial tragedy.

But there are differences in historic and modern millennialism, which brings us to the third strand of modern utopianism—by far the most important one. As Bernard Yack has reminded us, when we confront the vulgar aspects of human life, "we long to escape the limitations of our social existence." He has brilliantly traced a change in that longing to the philosophers at the end of the eighteenth century, who longed for "total revolution." The notion of "longing" itself is critical; it is, Yack points out by quoting Immanuel Kant, "the empty wish to overcome the time between the desire and the acquisition of the desired object."[4] Yack convincingly argues that Marx's longing for a Communist revolution "represents a new species of the longing for total revolution," arising out of his belief that the obstacle to social perfection is the dehumanizing spirit of modern society, symbolized by the capitalist system.[5] Marx, of course, saw society as a totality, based on an idealist premise that he must, however, "immediately deny, in order to argue that his conception corresponds to the way things are."[6]

There is something in Marxism that transcends the present lessons of "Marxism" by glasnost-minded "Marxists" in Moscow. It is, as Lawrence Chickering put it, "Communism's Elusive Holy Grail."

> The demise of the Soviet Incarnation of Marxism does not eliminate the longing. The search thus continues for Marxism's true manifestation.... It is a moving target, with changing objects of hope.... This explains why empirical "facts" cannot deter the search or destroy the myth.[7]

It is in this longing, and the ensuing but contradictory Marxist notion of a social totality, that we see part of the dichotomy in modern peace research—between people who, longing for a total revolution with respect to nuclear weapons, demand total abolition of those weapons based on a belief that they can be wished away, and people who are prepared to negotiate step by step toward a safer world.

It is important to note here that some members of the so-called peace movement, according to Johan Galtung, one of the most distinguished writers in the movement, are willing to hold "a relatively symmetric perception of the two Superpowers, seeing both as responsible for the present predicament." This is, of course, the same phenomenon that Rummel identifies as "two-partyism" in chapter 14 of this volume, and what contemporary neoconservatives decry as the Left's insistence on "moral equivalence" between the two superpowers.[8]

But beyond that, Galtung argues, more has to be asked: Which power has driven the arms race with new, qualitative improvements in weapons systems, supported repressive regimes around the world, and so forth? His answer is, of course, the United States. So from the notion of "moral equivalence" (or two-partyism), Galtung goes much further. People around the world, he claims, "seem to be much more afraid of what a reckless United States could start doing, and are certainly more afraid of nuclear war as such, than of the much-touted Soviet attack."[9]

This view is not limited to Europeans. Sidney Lens, editor of the *Progressive*, wrote in 1982 about how quickly so many Americans had "recognized the danger of the nuclear arms race.... On this issue, it now seems clear, the government of the United States no longer represents the American people." He noted the vast demonstrations in Central Park at the time of the UN disarmament conference, omitting, however, the simultaneous arrest in Red Square of a handful of would-be peace demonstrators.[10]

The sharp leftward turn in the West German Social Democratic Party's national defense consensus in the 1980s, despite the INF agreement of 1988, is but one consequence of this attitude. David Gress has noted that

> Behind the revival of utopian pacifism and the belief that the main obstacle to true peace in Europe is NATO and not the Soviet Union, there lies in fact a profound denial of the legitimacy, specifically the legitimate authority, of democratic Western governments. In the world view of the peace movement [sic], governments, whether in Bonn or in Washington, are seen as hostile entities opposed to the true interests of the people.[11]

Thus NATO's INF buildup, a response to the previous, much larger Soviet buildup, and designed to cause a withdrawal of both Soviet and American weapons (the so-called zero option), was viewed only with hostility. No matter that it was predictable, indeed it had been predicted,[12] that the peace movement's opposition would delay consensus on history's first great arms reduction agreement, probably by several years. Today it is obvious that this was the case.

But the peace movement went further: it questioned the structures of authority, which were seen at best as "negative elements of past history that must be eliminated if the 'soft' society of peace and ecological balance is to be achieved."[13] The old Marxist notion that these structures are but instruments of ruling-class control appears barely beneath the surface in much of the peace movement literature.

Galtung, in effect, made the same argument, going beyond the mere abolition of nuclear weapons to attack the quality of world order by locating the "deep and destructive inclinations in Occidental civilization, trying to get the softer aspects up to the surface, trying to rid ourselves of the harder, expansionist, even extremist aspects."[14]

Thus, we find the "world order" theorists, whose impetus has been well summarized by Juergen Dedring:

> As a consequence of rising concern about the future of the globe and of mankind, symbolized in the current food, population, resources, and environmental crises, a growing number of scholars have begun to view the world as a whole in a value-oriented manner and to formulate relevant utopias for a new world order over the long range rather than to concentrate on conventional interstate relations.[15]

So many of the aims of these theorists are obviously supported by all people of goodwill—who advocate cleaning up the global environment, reforestation, raising energy efficiency, to cite some examples from the *Worldwatch* list[16]—that it seems unchivalrous to pick a quarrel. And yet we do so because, as is so often the case, the only references to current international political issues in the Sage Library volume appear in a highly critical chapter on the Reagan administration's SDI, an initiative intended to take the war business a long step away from provocation to defense. The Sage chapter on SDI is wedged between chapters on "Controlling Toxic Chemicals" and "Planning the Global Family."

An additional problem exists with such theories, namely, the means by which the intractable problems of power in the international system can be settled. The numerous global crises of which we are rapidly becoming aware—Third World (and American) debt, the environment, arms races— have not changed the primary source of control for the solution of these problems: the state. Once again we find the antinomy, or, as Albert Sorel put it, "the eternal dispute between those who imagine the world to suit their policy, and those who arrange their policy to suit the realities of the world."[17]

The State

The state has been with us in its current form since 1648; there is nothing inherent in world systems requiring the presence of states as such, and the utopian animus against the state is understandable, given the crimes most of them have perpetrated at one time or the other. Indeed, as R. J. Rummel argues in the next chapter, states are responsible for more deaths against their own people than the wars of this century.

The philosophical upshot of World War II, in addition to the secularization of European society that had proceeded swiftly in the previous century, was the tendency, as written by David Gress, to "deny the state the metaphysical legitimacy and privileges of sovereignty that older philosophers and political thinkers, above all Hegel, had been generally willing to grant."[18] Above all, this tendency meant that the state was no longer deemed privileged to wage war, except in self-defense.

In the aftermath of World War II, schools of functionalism, regionalism, world federalism, and "one-world" conceptions came to the fore. The forces of transnationalism and the early successes of regional associations— economic and political—gave force to their arguments and encouraged their adherents. But after a time, the argument of "peace in parts" turned sour, too—with the conspicuous, yet still partial, exception of Western Europe. The early achievements came up against what in retrospect seems like an irreducibly ironclad tenacity of the nation-state.

Some of the early idealists learned quickly. A useful organizational example is that of the world federalists, who had their "fifteen minutes" in the aftermath of World War II. Their hope was to bring the world together in a sovereign unity, perhaps making the mistake Michael Nagler, in effect, identifies as simply enlarging the aperture for violence. In the meantime, many of the prominent adherents realized that "one world" was not a practical possibility and converted their organizations to useful lobby activity for a strengthened United Nations and international adjudication. World federalists did not get what they wanted, but they got something.

During this time, a contradictory tendency operating against one-world philosophies emerged: the independence of more than a hundred new states as a consequence of the breakup of the West European empires. And whether states are good or bad, or whether the assumption that states cause wars is true, it is obvious that, at certain levels, the state is on the ascendancy, not on the wane, particularly in the Third World. It is also worth noting that, almost without exception, wars waged since World War II have been in the Third World.

This ascendancy is true despite the academic theorizing and fashion of "the rise and demise of the territorial state," as the academic argument of the 1950s put it. It is true despite the imminence of the 1992 deadline for economic unification of Europe, a date of far greater significance than most Americans have realized, for the new states are only beginning to consolidate their nationhood and their hundredfold number ensures that (as a rule) they will successfully resist any attempt to limit state sovereignty in the international system. It is interesting to note that in Africa, the least developed regional Third World system—where there was the most sophisticated "Pan" movement for regional unification in addition to the largest number of (internal) ethnic conflicts—the process of legitimating the system of individual states has gone furthest. Yet Robert Jackson and Carl Rosberg argue,

> It is a paradox of Africa's multi-ethnic states that internal division and discord [have] resulted not in their civil disintegration, but rather in their jurisdictional protection. The map of Africa has remained virtually unchanged since the end of colonialism, and every state has enjoyed, and has been upheld by, international legitimacy.[19]

The state, then, is unlikely to be on the way out, save perhaps in post-1992 Europe; but in Europe a cultural imperium exists, and indeed, a political order, the successor to a Roman one that lasted at least in outward form until the Napoleonic Wars. And, even in Europe, the state is surely with us as the legal representative of the people and the nation at least for our lifetimes.

The state's resilience exists independent of transnational political, social, and economic forces. These may, as we see with "track-two diplomacy," ameliorate conflict and introduce channels through which resolution can eventually be found; so, too, may trade ties, through which states develop incentives to avoid conflict.[20] Still, some of the peoples who know each other best fight the longest—witness the Iran-Iraq War.

This line of reasoning suggests that efforts to effect peace through state-to-state diplomacy are hardly misplaced. Furthermore, efforts by countries to introduce or reinforce the norms of freedom and liberty in other countries also point toward peace. American efforts in Chile or Poland, either through diplomacy or semigovernment channels (for example, the National Endowment for Democracy), are, then, inherently in the cause of peace. Rummel's chapter and recent work by Samuel Huntington[21] and others give powerful testimony to this judgment.

Indeed, what has happened in the past decade in this regard is parallel to what happened in the previous decade in the economic sphere. It became obvious that market economics worked in the Third World; state planning did not. By the 1980s, the argument was largely settled because the evidence was so overwhelming. Something of the same thing is now happening in the debate over democracy. It takes time for the weight of new ideas to be felt, but the realization that democracy and peace are correlates is spreading widely as supporting evidence comes from so many different directions.

The Current Choice

The choice between utopia and reality continues to confront us. It is seen recently in the debates between Soviet and American representatives in international forums. There, characteristically, the Soviet delegate will urge an audience to accept the complete nuclear disarmament of the world as a goal, whereas the American will urge a step-by-step approach. The Soviets have a beguiling siren song, particularly for some audiences. In West Germany, for example, an American delegate[22] and a representative of the Soviet Union's USA-Canada Institute, Sergie Rogov, each recently attempted to present his own country's best position. The Soviet delegate belittled American approaches as "nickel-and-dime," when what the world needed were "cosmic," "historic," total solutions—for example, an end to all "alienation," let alone nuclear arms.

Whereas the American delegate routinely registered skepticism, the French delegate flatly said, "We will not go to complete nuclear disarmament—never so long as we inhabit the tip of a huge land mass otherwise dominated by the Red Army." Or, as his conference paper stated, the "nuclear threshold will remain necessary" so long as conventional defense is not "sufficient to resist . . . a military blackmail in Europe."

The artifice was grander. To the question of why the Soviet Union would not allow emigration, the Soviet delegate responded, as if to shame the questioner, that the Gorbachev revolution was doing something vastly more important—removing the causes of why people wish to emigrate. Another American delegate asked whether, in the meantime, in good faith, Moscow might let people who wish to leave do so. The French delegate simply noted that a French request of the Soviet delegation to respond, whether negatively, positively, or neutrally, within two months to the question of placing emigration on the agenda, had elicited no response whatsoever. It seems the nirvana where no one seeks emigration is still a long way off. The belittled step-by-step approach at least yields some product (for example, the INF agreement). Thus, as the French delegate said, he might be dealing with nickel-and-dime material, but it was at least intended to accomplish something.

My point is not to question the direction of Soviet society; in fact, it is obvious that revolutionary changes are afoot. My point is rather to note that, with respect to foreign policy, precisely the same proposals that accompany glasnost have been around before. And it is obvious that, however close the relationship between foreign and domestic policy, state interests dictate and maintain at least a partial separation. After all, a generation ago, Nikita Khrushchev called for complete and total nuclear disarmament and then, soon after, detonated a fifty-megaton test weapon, the largest nuclear blast ever. Although the sweeping reforms of Soviet society now being attempted go far beyond what most Sovietologists might have expected—and far beyond what Khrushchev attempted—the Soviet general staff has not been disbanded, and the profoundly destabilizing SS-18 intercontinental ballistic missiles remain in place. Should Gorbachev falter, it seems unlikely that the Brezhnev status quo ante would be restored, but the prospect of a military takeover—to put a tight lid on the boiling pot—would increase international tension, and the great verbal encouragement toward arms control, in addition to the partial achievements thus far, would not have any particular standing in a saber rattling contest over a strategic point of conflict between superpowers. "War lurks in the background of international politics, just as revolution lurks in the background of domestic politics," Carr wrote—an apt sentiment for the present situation, in which seething demands from a long-stifled Soviet populace could make external aggressiveness the only satisfying alternative to a return to the old order.

Power and Peace

We can search the "peace literature" for the magic wand that will exorcise power from the universe and bring the kingdom of heaven to earth, or merely a warless world; or we can search, in fact, for a serious discussion of power.[23] We find, for example, purportedly serious studies of the search for peace that aver that a peaceful world could be achieved through educating Americans toward a yearning for peace. In one such article, the notion of similarly educating the Soviet *nomenklatura*, without taking into account the military power and experience of the Strategic Rocket Force, was given as a central prescription for arms control between the superpowers.[24] But as Carr wrote on the eve of World War II, this failure to deal with power "has hitherto vitiated all attempts to establish international forms of government, and confused nearly every attempt to discuss the subject.... Power is an indispensable instrument of government. To internationalise government in any real sense means to internationalise power."[25]

It is not just the massive search for power (what Bertrand Russell so economically defined as "I talk, you listen") that we need to take into account in the international system. Our naiveté about power must be shed at every level. David Newsom has reminded us that in our search for the resolution of conflict we must know the locus of power in individual societies. The location of power inside a society is not always obvious, especially in unstable Third World states with revolving leaderships and ethnic instability.

People searching for peace tend to assume it can come only through larger associations and larger schemes. This is natural, given the ever-larger entities that can be involved in general war during the nuclear age. But it is precisely because of higher loyalties to smaller units on the part of so many people that conflict does ensue, and the grand schemes fall apart.

Two recent illustrations make this point. A UN official from Africa expressed irritation at an American's question as to his "tribe," a term of opprobrium to educated Africans. "It is a 'divide and conquer' colonial-era term," he noted, not unjustly. But when asked whether he could bring home to his village a wife from a different "ethnic group," he replied, instinctively and naturally, that he could not: "No one in my tribe would receive her." And then his face turned red. While traveling in France, I once heard a Breton blame Paris for a recent decision regarding his province, which he bitterly attributed to Queen Anne's trade with the king of France of a marriage bed for the kingdom's independence—almost four centuries ago. Celtic signs throughout Brittany remind the traveler that a sixth-century invasion is still a pervasive cultural fact.

This human predilection is at the root of much suffering in this century. Germans, with their romantic tradition, fell prey to a messianic message, and Russians bought a more systematic program, but one still intrinsically flawed in its chiliasm; tens of millions of deaths ensued from each attempt to impose a total order on society. So many of the people involved in what has been loosely called "peace research" have indicated a certain intolerance for anything but utopian solutions to war that we are inclined to wonder whether they are all in fact seeking real solutions. At the same time, David Newsom has correctly criticized Americans (and the United States Institute of Peace, too) for being unable to envision solutions in which Americans are not at the core. For the former error, let us remember E.H. Carr's last line, that "those elegant superstructures must wait until some progress has been made in digging the foundations."[26] For the latter, we Americans need to learn that much, maybe most, of the digging will be done by others, with whom we might well learn to work more productively.

Notes

1. E.H. Carr, *The Twenty Years' Crisis 1919–1939: An Introduction to the Study of International Relations* (New York: Harper and Row, 1964). Throughout the ensuing essay, Carr is cited for his piquant ability to state compellingly the central dichotomies of this essay, not necessarily out of agreement with his overall message. For a brilliant analysis of Carr's own confusions, see Whittle Johnson, "E.H. Carr's Theory of International Relations: A Critique," in *Journal of Politics*, vol. 29, 1967.

2. I was interested to find, in the midst of the 1973 Thai student revolution, the famous quotation from St. Augustine's *City of God,* "What is a state but a band of robbers if there be no justice?"

3. See Norman Cohn's excellent study, *The Pursuit of the Millennium* (Oxford: Oxford University Press, 1970), especially ch. 13. Marguerite Yourcenar's novel, *L'oevre au Noir (The Abyss)* (New York: Farrar, Straus, and Giroux, Inc., 1976) has a brilliant literary rendition of King John's reign.

4. Bernard Yack, *The Longing for Total Revolution: Philosophic Sources of Social Discontent from Rousseau to Marx and Nietzsche* (Princeton N.J.: Princeton University Press, 1986), pp. 3–5.

5. Yack, *Longing for Total Revolution*, p. 253.

6. Yack, *Longing for Total Revolution*, p. 304.

7. A. Lawrence Chickering, "Communism's Elusive Holy Grail," *Wall Street Journal*, May 16, 1986.

8. See Jeane J. Kirkpatrick, "Doctrine of Moral Equivalence," *U.S. Dept. of State Bulletin*, August 1984, pp. 57–62.

9. Johan Galtung, "Will the Peace Movement Become a Liberation Movement?" *On the Brink: Nuclear Proliferation and the Third World*, ed. Peter Worsely and Kofi Hadjor (London: Third World Communications, 1987), pp. 244–45.

10. Sidney Lens, "Revive the Ban-the-Bomb Movement," in *The Apocalyptic Premise: Nuclear Arms Debated*, ed. Ernest Lefever and Stephen Hunt (Washington, D.C.: Ethics and Public Policy Center, 1982).

11. David Gress, *Peace and Survival: West Germany, the Peace Movement, and European Security* (Stanford, Calif.: Stanford University Press, 1985), p. 113.

12. By me, among others, in numerous speeches made in my capacity as a member of the Reagan administration.

13. Gress, *Peace and Survival*, p. 114.

14. Worsely and Hadjor, *On the Brink*, p. 247.

15. Juergen Dedring, *Recent Advances in Peace and Conflict Research: A Critical Survey*, vol. 27, (Beverly Hills, Calif.: Sage Library of Social Research, 1976), p. 53.

16. See Lester R. Brown, et. al., *State of the World, 1988: A Worldwatch Institute Report on Progress Toward a Sustainable Society*, (New York: W.W. Norton and Co., 1988).

17. Albert Sorel, *L'Europe et la Revolution Francaise*, p. 474, cited in Carr, *The Twenty Years' Crisis*, p. 11.

18. Gress, *Peace and Survival*, p. 109.

19. Robert Jackson and Carl Rosberg, "Popular Legitimacy in African Multi-Ethnic States," *Journal of Modern African Studies* 22, no. 2 (June 1984): p. 198.

20. It is also worth noting that the issue of international debt has sharply limited the sovereignty—and the range of action—of numerous Third World states, as well as of the United States. But this is a different order of problem.

21. See Samuel Huntington, "Will More Countries Become Democratic?" *Political Science Quarterly*, vol. 99 (Summer 1984): pp. 193–218.

22. I was the delegate to the conference of the German Lutheran Church Academy in Loccum, West Germany, June 3–5, 1988.

23. Chapter 12 of this volume is a conspicuous exception.

24. See Paul C. Warnke, "Apes on a Treadmill," *Foreign Policy*, no. 18 (Spring 1975): pp. 12–29.

25. Carr, *The Twenty Years' Crisis*, p. 107.

26. Carr, *The Twenty Years' Crisis*, p. 239.

Introduction to Chapter 14

What is the relationship between a state's adopted form of political organization and its propensity to engage in collective violence and international war? According to R. J. Rummel, recent theoretical and empirical research confirms that the more democratic a regime, the less likely it is to participate in foreign or domestic violence. Furthermore, in relationships between democratic states, violence and war are precluded all together.

Although, as Rummel points out, these findings are based on relatively new material, the belief that the democratic form of government is an inherently peaceful one has been a tenet of classical liberalism for centuries. For the past fifty years, however, this notion has fallen prey to a host of ideological and methodological misperceptions that have resulted in its being widely ignored or dismissed.

Kant, Paine, Montesquieu, Bentham, Mill, and many others shared the essential idea that the more freedom people have over their lives and the more government leaders are directly responsible to their people, the more restrained those leaders will be in waging war. Although democracies are formidable opponents once the decision to take up arms has been made by the political leadership and embraced by the populace, democracies find it harder to muster the consensus necessary to pursue foreign aggression than do totalitarian regimes. Absolutist governments inevitably cause society to polarize into what Rummel terms "command and obey classes." Therefore, he says, "who commands and what is commanded are matters of grave concern" because "a loss on one issue may result in a loss on all. . . . With so much at stake, therefore, violence comes easily, especially to the rulers who must use repression and terror against possible dissent or sources of opposition."

Rummel's data indicate that totalitarian regimes are more likely than democracies to engage not only in international violence but also in domestic violence. Compared with the 36 million casualties from wars in the twentieth century, 119 million people have died at the hands of their own governments, through acts of genocide, massacres, and other mass killings. Of this figure, 115 million, or 96 percent, were the victims of totalitarian regimes, 95 million of those in Communist countries.

What caused this apparent crisis of faith in classical liberalism? Rummel suggests that the retreat from classical liberalism was spurred on by the early excesses of capitalism during the nineteenth century. Before the economic and social reform legislation that protected the rights of industrial workers, capitalism was viewed by many intellectuals and scholars as fundamentally exploitative of labor at home and dependent on a repressive colonial system abroad.

Socialist critics of democratic capitalism usually fell into one of three categories: democratic socialists, state socialists, or Marxist-Leninists. Both the democratic and state socialist models call for a nonviolent and peace-loving governmental system. Marxist-Leninists, however, view only the final, Communist stage of development as inherently peaceful, and although interstate war is to be avoided if at all possible, all other means short of war are to be pursued with vigor.

By the mid-twentieth century, the "protracted socialist assault on capitalism" had resulted in a move toward reform or welfare liberalism that could hardly be differentiated from the platforms of the early socialists. Furthermore, by the mid-1960s, a large percentage of the Western intellectual and scholarly communities had generally come to believe that war was "caused by the existence of haves and have-nots, rich and poor countries, exploitative multinational corporations, armament merchants, and the military-industrial complex." As the social sciences, and peace research in particular, became more internationalized, this relatively mild modern liberal approach was radicalized by "the global growth of the European socialist and neo-Marxist view" that democratic capitalism not only does not foster peace, it fosters war. This shift in thinking was primarily responsible for the evolution of a middle-of-the-road, value-neutral approach to peace research that posits that both capitalism and socialism are sources of conflict, with neither one being particularly peaceful. But this "two-partyism," as Rummel refers to it, obscures the powerful dynamic of classical liberalism—that freedom, above all else, has a positive and enduring role in preserving and maintaining international peace.

Rummel also cites a number of methodological errors by peace researchers and social scientists that contributed to the demise of classical liberalism:

- "Selective attention" has been paid to a few major democracies, such as the United States and Britain, while the larger population of democracies and their very limited involvement in conflict are ignored.
- The relative intensity of the conflicts in question has been ignored, so that, for example, the invasion of Grenada by the United States is equated with the invasion of Poland by Nazi Germany that precipitated World War II.
- Screening correlations theoretically and ignoring low correlations when they exist have led researchers to overlook the consistent and significant, albeit low, negative correlation between democracies and the collective violence predicted by classical liberal thought.
- The tendency to view nations as isolated entities rather than in relationship to one another has caused countries to be seen as wealthy

or poor, large or small, powerful or weak; and, as Rummel suggests, "history is generally studied for the relationship between a nation's political system and its bellicosity," (monadically) rather than in comparative terms with other states (dyadically).

Rummel concludes that once peace researchers take these ideological and methodological factors into consideration, they will realize that they can, in fact, define a policy to minimize collective violence and war and to enhance and foster democratic institutions, civil liberties, and political rights.

14. Political Systems, Violence, and War

R. J. Rummel

> By the end of the eighteenth century a complete [classical] liberal theory of international relations, of war and peace, had...developed. ...Peace was...fundamentally a question of the establishment of democratic institutions throughout the world.[1]

Are political systems related to collective violence and war? This question is now fundamentally answered in one of three ways: yes, democracies are the least prone to violence; yes, socialist egalitarianism assures peace; or no, political systems and violence are unrelated.

Recent theoretical and empirical research confirms the first answer: those political systems that maximize and guarantee individual freedom (democracies) are least prone to violence; those that maximize the subordination of all individual behavior to state control (totalitarian systems) are most prone to violence, whether socialist or not; and wars do not occur between democracies.

Known for centuries as a tenet of classical liberalism, the pacific nature of democracy has become largely forgotten or ignored in the past half-century. That democracy is inherently peaceful is now probably believed by no more than a few prominent peace researchers. In part, this situation has been due to the intellectual defection of Western intellectuals from a classical liberalism to some variant of socialism, with its emphasis on the competitive violence and bellicosity of capitalist freedoms. Many intellectuals, and in particular European and Third World researchers, have come to believe that socialist egalitarianism is the answer to violence; others, particularly American liberals, believe that if the socialists are wrong, then democracies are, at minimum, no better than other political systems in promoting peace.

Socialism aside, there has also been a rejection of Western values, of which individual freedom is prominent, and an acceptance of some form of value-relativism (thus, no political system is better than any other). In some cases, this rejection has turned to outright hostility, particularly anti-Americanism, and thus opposition to American values, such as freedom. Therefore, to the value-relativist, to accept the proposition that democratic freedom is inherently most peaceful is to say the unacceptable—that it is better. Moreover, to accept the proposition that this freedom

350

promotes nonviolence seems to take sides in what is perceived as the global ideological struggle or power game between the United States and the Soviet Union.

Independent of different ideological or philosophical perspectives, several interacting methodological errors have blinded intellectuals and peace researchers to the peacefulness of democracies. One of these errors is the strong, general tendency to see only national characteristics and overall behavior. Therefore, a nation is rich or poor, powerful or weak, belligerent or pacific. Most important for identifying the relationship between freedom and violence, however, is an examination of the similarities and differences between two states and their behavior. Thus, we can observe a lack of violence and war between democracies while observing the most severe violence between those nations with the least freedom.

Another methodological error has been the selective focus on the major powers. These powers include not only several democracies that have engaged in many wars, but also Britain, which has participated in the most. A systematic comparison among all the belligerents and neutrals in wars, however, would uncover the greater peacefulness of democracies.

Along with this selective attention is the tendency to count equally against democracies all their wars, no matter how mild or small. Thus, the American invasion of Grenada would be one mark against democracy; Hitler's invasion of Poland initiating World War II would be a similar mark against nondemocracies. This tendency stacks any such accounting against democracy.

Finally, although a systematic survey of the literature shows significant support for the inverse relationship between democracy and violence, researchers have done little theoretical testing of this relationship. Thus, they tend to overlook or ignore this phenomenon when it appears in their results.

Democracies Promote Nonviolence

The organizers of this conference asked me to write a taxonomic paper on the question, "Can the relative bellicosity of states be measured and predicted as a function of their internal political system?" The answer derived from most current empirical research is decidedly yes.[2] Indeed, the empirical relationship is even more profound and comprehensive than the question implies. In theory and fact, the more democratic the political systems of two states, the less violence between them; and if they are both democratic, violence is precluded altogether.[3] That is, democratic states do not make war on each other. Moreover, the more democratic a political system, the less likely it is that such a state will engage in foreign *and* domestic collective violence; the more totalitarian, the more likely such violence.[4]

Perhaps the most surprising finding is that the less democratic a government is, the more likely that the government will kill its own citizens, independent of any foreign or domestic war. War is no longer the most deadly form of violence. Indeed, whereas 36 million people have been killed in battle in all foreign and domestic wars in our century, at least 119 million more people have been killed by government genocide, massacres, and other mass killing. Of this figure, 96 percent, or about 115 million persons, were killed by totalitarian governments, as many as 95 million of those by Communist governments alone. There have been no recorded cases of democracies killing, en masse, their own citizens.[5]

The inverse relationship between democracy and foreign violence, collective domestic violence, or government genocide is not simply a correlation, but a cause and effect. In a nutshell, democratic freedom promotes nonviolence. These results are worthy of the greatest attention and analysis, for, if they are true, which I am now convinced they are, peace researchers have in fact defined a policy for minimizing collective violence and eliminating war: enhance and foster[6] democratic institutions—civil liberties and political rights—here and abroad.[7]

The Classical Liberals

The fundamentally inverse relationship between freedom and violence is truly a matter of insight and knowledge gained and lost among political philosophers only to be rediscovered through rigorous theoretical and empirical research by peace researchers. In fact, as long ago as 1795, in his now virtually forgotten *Perpetual Peace*, Immanuel Kant systematically articulated the positive role of political freedom in eliminating war and proposed that constitutional republics be established to assure universal peace. This proposal has various nuances, such as those involving the difference between republics and democracies and between political and economic freedom, but the essential idea was this: the more freedom people have to govern their own lives, government power is constitutionally limited, and leaders are responsible (through free elections) to their people, the more restrained the leaders will be in making war. In Kant's words,

> The republican constitution...gives a favorable prospect for the desired consequence, for example, perpetual peace. The reason is this: if the consent of the citizens is required in order to decide that war should be declared (and in this constitution it cannot but be the case), nothing is more natural than that they would be very cautious in commencing such a poor game, decreeing for themselves all the calamities of war. Among the latter would be: having to fight, having to pay the costs of wars from their own resources, having painfully to repair the devastation war leaves behind, and, to fill up the measure of evils, load themselves with a heavy national debt that would embitter peace itself and that can never be liquidated on account of constant wars in the future. But, on the

other hand, in a constitution which is not republican, and under which the subjects are not citizens, a declaration of war is the easiest thing in the world to decide upon, because war does not require of the ruler, who is the proprietor and not a member of the state, the least sacrifice of the pleasures of his table, the chase, his country houses, his court functions, and the like. He may, therefore, resolve on war as on a pleasure party for the most trivial of reasons, and with perfect indifference leave the justification which decency requires to the diplomatic corps who are ever ready to provide it.[8]

Through the writings of Kant, Montesquieu, Thomas Paine, Jeremy Bentham, and John Stuart Mill, among others, it became an article of classical liberal faith in the eighteenth and nineteenth centuries that "Government on the old system," as Paine wrote,

is an assumption of power, for the aggrandizement of itself; on the new [republican form of government as just established in the United States], a delegation of power for the common benefit of society. The former supports itself by keeping up a system of war; the latter promises a system of peace, as the true means of enriching a nation.[9]

These liberals believed that there was a natural harmony of interests among nations, and that free trade would facilitate this harmony and promote peace. Most important, they were convinced that monarchical aristocracies had a vested interest in war. It was, in contemporary terms, a game they played with the lives of the common people. Empower the common people to make such decisions through their representatives, and they would always oppose war.

Lacking a historical perspective, the classical liberals obviously had too much faith in the masses. They failed to anticipate the rise of nationalism, despite the presaging the by French Revolution and the Napoleonic Wars of what our century would behold in full glory: the entire nation at arms, total mobilization, and total war. They did not appreciate how the super-heated hatred and vengefulness of majorities can drive democratic nations to war. The Crimean and Boer wars, as well as the Mexican-American and Spanish-American wars, were yet to occur. The clamor for war can be irresistible to ambitious politicians.

But much to their peril, popular leaders have also discovered the flip side to "popular will." The people can be aggressive today, pacific tomorrow. We need only contrast the popular support for American involvement in Vietnam from 1963 to 1966 with the vigorous hostility among intellectuals and opinion leaders against continuation of that war in 1969. Of course, it is also true that the people can be stubbornly opposed to what they perceive as bellicose policies, no matter what their merits may be. Thus, because of isolationist public opinion, President Roosevelt felt constrained from giving all-out military aid to America's fraternal ally, Britain, in 1940–41, at the very time that Britain's survival of air and submarine attacks by Nazi

Germany was questionable indeed. In deference to massive public opposition to American involvement, Roosevelt could only aid this final European bulwark against Nazi tyranny, aggression, and genocide indirectly, discreetly, or illegally.

In the eighteenth century, classical liberals had to write about the pacific nature of democracies in the abstract, by hypothesis. Of course, the bellicose history of emperors, kings and queens, and aristocracies was clear. History could not tell them, however, how free peoples would behave. This behavior could only be derived from reason and was ultimately based on faith. No wonder, then, that their associated theory was simplistic. Leaving out the invisible hand and harmony of interests, free majorities would refuse to pay in their blood and property for such wars.

As mentioned, the historical record now shows that the people are not only willing, but sometimes demand to go to war. The problem with the classical liberal theory is that it provides an incomplete and superficial explanation and, for that reason, is only correct part of the time (e.g., the theory explains why the United States did not declare war on Hitler in 1940, but not why the United States did declare war against Spain in 1898). A proper theory of democratic peacefulness must allow for both these aggressive and pacific sides of popular will. It must go beneath public opinion and popular majorities and deal with the social forces involved. These social forces should be examined in terms of social field, cross pressures, and polarization.

Why Democracies Are Less Violent

The civil liberties and political rights of a democratic system foster and maintain an exchange society. This is a social field, whose medium is composed of a people's loyalties (symbolized by the flag or a cross), values, and norms. The social forces of the system are imbedded in this medium and flow one way or another, forming various equilibriums among what people want and will try to get. Conflict or cooperation within this field, violence or peace, depends on the congruence between these equilibriums and the expectations people have about the outcome of their actions.

Democratically free people are spontaneous, diverse, and pluralistic. Many, often opposing, interests push them in different directions. Individuals belong to independent and overlapping occupational, religious, recreational, and political subgroups, each having its own interests; people are also moved by the separate and even antagonistic desires of different age, sex, ethnic, racial, and regional strata.

Freedom thus creates a social field in which social forces point in many different directions, and in which individual interests, the engine of social behavior, are often cross-pressured. Like the Catholic political conservative who cannot decide whether to vote for the Episcopalian Republican conservative or the Catholic welfare Democrat, many people in a free society must balance wants that are often contradictory. This means that the very strong interests that drive people in one direction to the exclusion of all others, even at the risk of violence, do not develop easily. And if such interests do develop, they are usually shared by relatively few persons. That is, the normal working of a democratically free society in all its diversity is to restrain the growth across the community of that consuming singleness of view and purpose that leads, if not frustrated, to wide-scale social and political violence.

Consider, by contrast, a centralized society with a totalitarian government. In the main, behavior is no longer spontaneous, but commanded; in its most significant outlines, what people are and what they do are determined at the center. The totalitarian model is familiar and need not be elaborated. Such a system turns a social field into an organization with specific tasks to achieve, such as equality, communism, social justice, development. A management-worker, command-obey class division cuts across all society, and the system has all the characteristics of an organization (coercive planning, plethora of rules, lines of authority from top to bottom) needed to direct each member's activities.

The consequence of the totalitarian model is to polarize major interests. If the satisfaction of individual interests always depends on the same "them," and if "they" are responsible for everyone's job, housing, quality and cost of food, and even life and death—then almost everything important depends on whether a person is in the command class or the obey class. In effect, these are two poles to which interests become aligned. Thus, and most important for the argument here, because most vital interests depend on one center, it is easy to see that the interests related to this center—who commands and what is commanded—are matters of grave concern. In a democracy people can shrug their shoulders over losing: "Win some, lose some, I'll do better next time." But in a highly centralized system, a loss on one issue may result in a loss on all, even including one's life.

With so much at stake, therefore, violence comes easily, especially to the rulers who must use repression and terror against possible dissent or sources of opposition; the gun, prison, and concentration camp are the major tools of social policy. And, as happened in Lech Walesa's Solidarity movement in Poland in 1980–81, in such a polarized system, conflict and violence involving local interests soon expand to the whole society. The split between those who command and those who obey is a fault line: slippage in one place moves along the whole fault and causes a social quake—wide-scale conflict and, given the importance of the issues, quite possibly violence.

What about foreign violence? By virtue of the same cross pressures restricting violence within democracies, the unification of public interests needed to pursue foreign aggression is usually missing. Given the lack of general public support, and perhaps the outright opposition of certain social or interest groups, a democratic leader would pursue a costly foreign conflict at great risk to his or her political future, even if the leader could get the government's counterbalanced machinery to work in the same perilous direction. A leader can do this, especially when some external threat of attack unites public opinion (as in Britain's military response to Argentina's invasion of the Malvinas/Falkland Islands), but not with anything like the political freedom with which a dictator or small ruling group can make war. And, among democracies, each with its own pluralism, cross pressures, and politically constrained leaders, and each quite possibly having a variety of political and commercial ties and transactions that create their own pro-peace interest groups, the forces opposing violence overwhelm any tendencies toward severe conflict.

A totalitarian ruler has no such natural constraints. True, there will be cross pressures among the elite. Calculations must be made about the cost in lost trade, aid, allies, and the like, not to mention resources and manpower. But such cross pressures are usually within a particular direction (Should we invade today or wait? Should we squeeze them into submission?) and often among handpicked subordinates. Real, fundamental opposition is lacking in a totalitarian state, whereas in a democracy even the basic constitutional laws governing the making of war are open to debate and political contest.

In all this I am simplifying to essentials, as in universally describing a falling body by a simple equation that ignores wind, body shape, and air friction. And the heart of this pure explanation is the difference between a social field of cross-pressured interests and politically responsible leaders versus a tightly organized society of polarized interests and dictatorial rulers. I am describing pure types, recognizing that there are many gradations between them. In sum, encouraging democratic institutions promotes a deeper and more durable peace, because encouraging democracy also promotes a social field, cross pressures, and political responsibility, plus pluralism, diversity, and groups that have a stake in peace.

The Socialist Critique of Classical Liberalism

Contemporary theory aside, the classical liberal's view of the peacefulness of democracy was insightful. But by the middle of the twentieth century, this insight had become almost completely ignored or forgotten.

How did we fall off the classical liberal path to peace, to find it again only recently? There are several answers, some ideological, some methodological. First, the classical liberal view itself fell into disrepute among intellectuals and scholars. Essentially, classical liberals believed that the government that governs least, governs best. Adam Smith's *An Inquiry into the Nature and Causes of the Wealth of Nations* was their economic bible. And, in current terms, they preached democratic capitalism. But beginning in the nineteenth century, capitalism came under increasing attack by socialists of all flavors. First, the socialists agreed with the classical liberals that the people had to be empowered and that this empowerment would bring peace. But what the socialists saw when the liberal creed was enacted into law, especially in Britain, was that the bellicose aristocracies were replaced by equally bellicose capitalists. Democracies and their attendant free markets appeared to foster exploitation, inequality, and poverty and to enable a very few to rule over the many. Most important here, capitalism was seen not just to promote, but also to require, colonialism and imperialism, and thereby war.

But what was to be done? Here the socialists divided mainly into democratic socialists, state socialists, and Marxists. The democratic socialists argued that true democracy means that both the political and economic aspects of people's lives must be under their control, and this is done through representative government and government ownership, control, and management of the economy. The capitalists would thus be replaced by elected representatives, who would oversee economic planners and managers and, above all, be responsive to popular majorities. Because the aristocratic and capitalistic interests rest in war, these interests would be eliminated. Peace would be assured when peace-oriented workers and peasants were democratically empowered.

The state socialists, however, would simply replace representative institutions with some form of socialist dictatorship. This would assure the best implementation and progress of socialist egalitarianism, without interference by the bourgeois and other self-serving interests. Moreover, the people cannot be trusted to know their own interests, for they are easily blinded by procapitalist propaganda and manipulation. Burma—which has renamed itself Myanmar—today is a good example of state socialism in practice.

While agreeing on much of the socialists' analysis of capitalism, the Marxists added to it a deterministic, dialectical theory of history, a class analysis of societies, an economic theory of capitalism, and the necessity of the impoverishment of the workers and the inevitability of a Communist revolution. However, the Marxists disagreed with the socialists on the ends. Never far from the anarchists, the Marxists, especially the Marxist-Leninists of our century, looked at the socialist state that would come into being with the overthrow of capitalism as nothing more than an intermediary dictatorship of the proletariat through which the transition to the final stage of communism would be prepared. And stripped of its feudal or capitalist exploiters and, thus, its agents of war, communism would mean not the natural harmony among nations, as in the liberal creed, but harmony among all people, as all work according to their ability and receive according to their need. The state then would wither away, and the masses would then live in true, everlasting peace and freedom.

It should be underlined that whereas democratic or state socialists believe that socialist governments will be peace loving and nonviolent, the Marxist-Leninists believe this to be true of only the final, Communist stage of stateless anarchy. The socialist transition period may well involve war with capitalist states, but although this war between nations is to be avoided (if at all possible in this age of nuclear weapons) the worldwide struggle against capitalism must be pursued by all means short of war between nations. Such means include not only the arts of deception, disinformation, subversion, and demoralization against capitalist states, but also terrorism and domestic wars through "national liberation fronts." For the Marxist-Leninists then, it is the ultimate Communist system that is inherently peaceful, not the socialist intermediary state. This socialist stage means the purposeful, aggressive use of force and violence to pursue the final, global stage of Communist peace and freedom.

In any case, regardless of the brand of socialism from which the critique of capitalism ensued, the protracted nineteenth-century socialist assault on capitalism had a profound effect on liberalism and especially the theory of war. Falling into disrepute with its program seen as utopian or special pleading for capitalists, pure classical liberalism mutated among Western intellectuals into a reform or welfare liberalism that is little differentiated today from the programs and views of the early socialists. This modern liberalism, which has been heavily influenced by the socialist view of war, became widely influential in scholarly research on international relations, and thus war and peace. It must be recognized that, until the 1960s, such research was largely the preserve of the social sciences, and that, by the mid-twentieth century, an overwhelming number of social scientists were modern liberals or socialists in their outlook.

Peace research began to take off in the early 1960s, and today it is a full discipline. In its early years, it was very much an American phenomenon, and it was very liberal in its view of war. When researchers focused on real factors, as apart from psychological ones, war was generally believed to be caused by the existence of haves and have-nots, rich and poor nations; by poverty, unrestrained competition, and the maldistribution of resources; by exploitative multinational corporations, armament merchants, and the military-industrial complex. But peace research soon became internationalized, and with this global growth, the European socialists' and neo-Marxists' view of capitalism and war soon dominated. The milder, American peace researchers' modern liberal view soon became passé, and in its place we began to read about Western (capitalist) imperialism and dominance; about world capitalist economic control, manipulation, and war making; and about the promotion of nonviolence through material equality and a socialist world economy. Positive peace and social justice became central concepts in peace research, both meaning some kind of socialist egalitarianism.[10]

But what happened to the idea that individual freedom promotes non-violence?[11] With the protracted socialist attack on the classical liberal's fundamental belief in capitalism, coupled with the apparent excesses of capitalism, such as sweatshops, robber barons, monopolies, depressions, and political corruption, classical liberalism eventually lost the heart and minds of Western intellectuals. And with this defeat went its fundamental truth: that democracy promotes peace. Interestingly, there was a conservative resurgence of classical liberalism in the 1980s. Former President Ronald Reagan and former Prime Minister Margaret Thatcher exemplify this resurgence; their often expressed views on the positive role of free institutions for peace are straight out of classical liberalism. This popular resurgence has yet to percolate through to those in the social science and peace research communities.

This is not to say that most peace researchers generally view capitalist political-economic systems as the cause of war, as hard-line socialists assert. Many European and Third World peace researchers generally view capitalism as one cause among several, although some theoretical emphasis may be given to capitalism, as in Johan Galtung's influential center-periphery theory, which clearly lays the major blame for war on a capitalist type of competitive system.[12] Indeed, many peace researchers, especially Americans, have moved to a middle position: both capitalism or socialism can be a source of peace or war, depending on the circumstances, but neither is a general factor in war.

Now, capitalism and democracy are not the same thing. Democratic socialist systems exist, as in Sweden and Denmark, and so do authoritarian capitalist systems, like Chile and Taiwan. Why then have the peacemaking effects of democratic freedoms been tossed out with capitalism? As mentioned, these freedoms were part of an ideology emphasizing capitalism; as the ideology retreated, so did its belief in the positive role of freedom in peace. But there are other factors at work here that are at least as important.

Methodological Blinders

One of the factors causing scholars and peace researchers to reject democracy's peacefulness is a misreading of history. Kant and the classical liberals were writing theoretically about freedom and war; they had virtually no historical evidence. But by the middle of the twentieth century a sufficient number of democracies had existed for more than a half-century—enough for a historical judgment to be made. This evidence was believed to show that democracies not only do go to war but can also be very aggressive. Americans alone could easily note their wars against the American Indians; the Mexican-American and Spanish-American wars; and, of course, the Civil War, the most violent war during the century between the Napoleonic Wars and World War I. And even if one argues that the United States was dragged into both world wars, there are the invasion of Grenada and the Vietnam War, which many peace researchers view as cases of American aggression. Then, of course, there is Britain, which between 1850 and 1941 fought twenty wars, more than any other state. France, also a democracy for most of this period, fought nearly as many—eighteen. The United States fought seven. These three nations alone fought 63 percent of all the wars during these ninety-two years.[13] Of course, Britain did not become a true democracy until 1884 with the extension of the franchise to agricultural workers, but thereafter, Britain remained the aggressor in numerous European and colonial wars. The historical record of democracies thus appeared to be no better than that of other regimes; and the classical liberal belief in the peacefulness of democracies seemed nothing more than bad theory or misplaced faith.

But all other types of regimes seemed equally bellicose. The supposed peacefulness of socialist systems was belied by the aggressiveness of its two major totalitarian variants, that of the Soviet Union and Nazi Germany;[14] and other types of regimes, whether authoritarian dictatorships like Japan before World War II or absolute monarchies like czarist Russia before World War I, appeared no less warlike. The verdict is an easy one: all types of political, or politico-economic, systems make war, and none is especially pacific. Clearly articulated in Kenneth Waltz's widely read *Man, the State, and War*,[15] this critique is today the consensus view of American peace research, and in peace research elsewhere, it is the major alternative belief to that of the inherent bellicosity of capitalist systems.

A number of methodological errors account for the misreading by the peace researchers of the recent history of democracies, as well as the misleading nature of the history of wars. First is the problem of selective attention. The many wars of a few democracies are the subject of attention while the total population of democracies and wars is ignored. A true comparison should involve all democracies and nondemocracies, and all wars, at least in this century.

Second is the error of improper weighing. Even where such systematic comparison is done, the intensity of wars is ignored.[16] In such comparisons, the American invasion of Grenada and the British war with Argentina over the Malvinas/Falklands Islands, two of history's least violent wars, are counted as wars and put on a par with the American and British participation in, say, World War II. The proposition that democracies are more peaceful than other political systems really means that they engage in less violence, where violence is understood as a continuum, from low intensity to high. To say that democratic freedom reduces violence is like saying that aspirin reduces pain. It is not a question of the presence or absence of war, but of the degree of killing involved.

Another error, one that I admit to being guilty of in my earlier work, is the atheoretical screening of correlations (and the ignoring of low ones)—in other words, to claim that low correlations between political systems and violence simply show that no meaningful relationship exists. This is simply a matter of seeking the mountains and ignoring the hills. In truth, as a systematic screening of all the empirical and quantitative literature shows,[17] there is a consistent and significant, but low, negative correlation between democracies and collective violence, as predicted by classical liberalism. The reason for this low correlation is that freedom is not both necessary and sufficient for nonviolence to occur. That is, like democracies, authoritarian and totalitarian systems can be without violence for many years.[18] The problem here is an almost endemic one in the social sciences: drawing conclusions about a theory from exploratory data analysis in which the theory is not explicitly tested.

Even if these errors caused a historical misinterpretation of the relationship between freedom and violence, how could peace researchers have failed to see that democracies do not make war on each other, if this is true? After all, this is a prediction of data points on a graph, the historical truth or falsity of which should be obvious. The problem is just that social scientists and peace researchers do not ordinarily think dyadically. They think of nations as developed or undeveloped, strong or weak, democratic or undemocratic, large or small, belligerent or not. That is, they think monadically. Thus, history is generally studied for the relationship between a nation's political system and its bellicosity.[19]

Like so much in science, this is a matter of perspective, as in looking endwise at a cylinder and seeing only a circle. A simple change in perspective would show a cylinder; similarly, a simple shift to dyadic relations would show that when two nations are stable democracies, no wars occur between them.[20] In all the wars from 1814 until the present, there has been no war between stable democracies, even though the number of democracies has grown to number fifty-one today—31 percent of all nations, governing 38 percent of the world's population. Among all the large or small wars since 1945, not one has involved democracies against each other; in a world where contiguous nations often use violence to settle their differences or at least have armed borders between them, democracies like the United States and Canada have long, completely unarmed borders; and in Europe, the historical cauldron of war, once all West European nations became democratic they no longer armed against each other, and the expectation of war among them is now zero—that these observations should be overlooked by peace researchers shows how powerfully misleading an improper historical perspective or model can be.[21]

Internationalism and Two-Partyism

So the socialist critique of capitalism, combined with a monadic view of history and a failure to test these beliefs empirically and properly, has led peace researchers to accept the view that capitalist freedoms were, in fact, the cause of violence, or at least that there was no relationship between democratic freedoms and collective violence. But besides socialism and these methodological errors, still other factors are at work. Since World War I, there has been a strong rejection accelerated by World War II among intellectuals of any hint of nationalism. Many nonsocialists viewed nationalism as the fundamental cause of war, or at least of its total national mobilization and total violence. Internationalism, rising above one's nation, seeing humanity and its transcending interest as a whole, and furthering world government became their intellectual ideal. Social scientists and peace researchers, who, after all, are usually intellectuals with doctoral degrees, have almost universally shared this view. In fact, one of the attractions of socialism for many was its inherent internationalism, coupled with its rejection of the nation and patriotism as values.

Internationalists generally have refused to accept that any one nation is really better than another. After all, cultures and values are relative; one nation's virtues are another's evils. It is best that we treat all nations equally to better resolve conflicts among them. As Hans Morgenthau points out in his most popular and influential international relations text, both the United States and the Soviet Union should be condemned for the Cold War; it is their evangelistic, crusading belief in their own values that makes the East-West conflict so difficult to resolve. The following quotation from Morgenthau shows well this language of two-partyism:

> From the aftermath of the Second World War onwards, these two blocs [centered on the superpowers] have faced each other like two fighters in a short and narrow lane. They have tended to advance and meet in what was likely to be combat, or retreat and allow the other side to advance into what to them is precious ground....
>
> For the two giants that today determine the course of world affairs only one policy has seemed to be left; that is, to increase their own strength and that of their allies.... Either side must fear that the temporarily stronger contestant will use its superiority to eliminate the threat from the other side by shattering military and economic pressure by a war of annihilation.
>
> Thus the international situation is reduced to the primitive spectacle of two giants eyeing each other with watchful suspicion. They bend every effort to increase their military potential to the utmost, since this is all they have to count on. Both prepare to strike the first decisive blow, for if one does not strike it the other might. Thus, contain or be contained, conquer or be conquered, destroy or be destroyed, become the watchwords of Cold War diplomacy.[22]

This two-partyism is obvious in the peace research and related literature. There is no victim or aggressor, no right or wrong nation, but only two parties to a conflict. (When this two-partyism does break down, it is usually in terms of American or Western "imperialist aggression.") Consequently, to accept that the freedoms espoused by the United States and its democratic allies lead to peace, and that the totalitarian socialism fostered by the Soviet Union leads to violence and war, is to take sides. It is to be nationalistic. And this, for the internationalist, is ipso facto wrong.

Another psychological force toward two-partyism should not be underestimated. The statement that democratic freedom fosters peace seems not only nationalistic but inherently ideological. After all, freedom is one of the flags in the ideological Cold War. No matter that this is a scientific statement based on rigorous theory and empirical tests; no matter that the results come from researchers who themselves have conflicting ideologies. To accept it appears not only to take sides, but, what is worse, to be a right-wing cold warrior.

For these reasons there is a knee-jerk reaction among many peace researchers against any assertion that the democratic regimes of the West provide a path to peace. Is it any wonder, then, that there has been so relatively little empirical research directly and explicitly on this question,[23] as well as a strong resistance to the results of such research showing the inverse relationship between freedom and collective violence?

But, of course, there are peace researchers who reject two-partyism. For some of these researchers another factor is at work—an apparently strongly emotional factor, hinted at earlier. In the past two decades, there has grown within the peace research community a virulent anti-Westernism, often directed primarily against the United States. Rather than being neutral between East and West, evincing a studied internationalism, this view does take sides. It is fundamentally socialist, sometimes neo-Marxist and Third World in orientation. The West is seen as exploiting, lusting for profit and power, and forever struggling to dominate other countries; its alleged democratic values are viewed as a facade behind which it manipulates and controls poor nations. Violence is its means; the secret services, especially the CIA, its tool. In this view, which is held by a significant segment of the peace research community, there is nothing too evil for the West to do in grasping for power and profit. Seemingly, anything negative will be believed. For example, in a communication to the students and faculty of the Political Science Department at the University of Hawaii, the well-known peace researcher Johan Galtung alleged that the CIA has been guilty of "very much the same thing" as Hitler's "holocaust" against the Jews, insinuating that the CIA has "rubbed out" six million people throughout the world.[24] No peace researcher with these views could accept the possibility that Western, democratic freedoms promote peace.

Conclusion

Theoretical and empirical research establishes that democratic civil liberties and political rights promote nonviolence and provide a path to a warless world. The clearest evidence of this is that there has never been a war between democracies, whereas numerous wars have occurred between all other political systems; and that of the more than 119 million people genocidally killed in cold blood in our century, virtually all were killed by nondemocracies, especially totalitarian ones. That democracies are relatively nonviolent is not a new discovery. It was fundamental to seventeenth- and eighteenth-century classical liberalism. But this truth has been forgotten or ignored in our time.

The reasons are many and complex, but they reduce basically to these. First, nineteenth-century socialism and twentieth-century internationalism offered influential alternative explanations of war and ways to peace that seemed to fit the contemporary history of war better than the a priori speculations of the classical liberals. This history especially seemed to show that democracies not only made war on other nations, but were at least as aggressive as any. Second, for recent generations, ethical relativism (and its associated two-partyism) and anti-Westernism (or anti-Americanism) have caused many intellectuals to reject fundamental Western values, including the faith in classical democratic freedoms; this rejection has been accompanied by a rejection of any evidence that these freedoms could promote peace.

These ideological forces have been strengthened by several methodological errors. One is the tendency to see nations wholly in terms of their characteristics and behavior, and not in relation to each other. Thus peace researchers have overlooked the fact that democracies do not make war on one another, or that the less the democratic freedom in two nations, the more likely violence is between them. Other errors are to view history selectively, without systematic comparison of all cases or wars; to seek correlations atheoretically, thus ignoring the necessarily low, but significant inverse relationships between freedom and violence; and to treat all wars as the same, no matter how different the levels of their violence.

The final words to such a paper as this should be left to our foremost student of war, Quincy Wright, and his monumental *A Study of War*:

> To sum up, it appears that absolutist states with geographically and functionally centralized governments under autocratic leadership are likely to be most belligerent, while constitutional states with geographically and functionally federalized governments under democratic leadership are likely to be most peaceful.[25]

Discussion

Although commentator Elise Boulding shared R. J. Rummel's belief that democracy is a major resource for peaceableness in the international system, she disagreed with his assertion that peace researchers and leaders of the peace movement have ignored this point. These groups have been trying to understand the layers of structural violence in the international system, she said. The study of structural violence—defined as the damage that occurs to people because of discrepancies in access to resources within a social system—has shown how complicated applying nonviolent solutions to age-old international problems can be.

Boulding acknowledged that a small faction of the peace movement and research communities has condoned the use of violence to rectify a perceived social wrong, but she argued that that should not be considered a reflection of the vast majority of persons working in the peace community.

Although peace research has only recently begun to develop a strong foothold in the United States, its modern origins can be traced to Gandhi's India and post-World War II Norway, Holland, and Japan. In each of these cases, the major impetus behind the movement was the common goal of learning more about how nonviolent resistance can help the powerless to fulfill basic human needs. The effort was rooted in understanding that conflict resolution through political, social, economic, and psychological means, rather than through military force, was not only possible but vital if future generations were to be spared the horrors of another world war.

But the most important aim of peace research, Boulding said, is to challenge the traditional assumptions about the inevitability of international war and replace them with a new conceptualization of the international system.

How can the conditions be created under which the pacificity of democracies is better integrated into a fluid and dynamic international system? The first step, suggested Boulding, requires a change in the framework of analysis, not, as suggested by Rummel, from monadic to dyadic, but from dyadic to multilevel. This approach, which should be based on the principles of change and evolution, must include not only individual states but also alliance systems and the nonaligned movement.

Citing political scientist Karl Deutsch's work on the formation of pluralistic security relationships that can incorporate former adversaries, Boulding acknowledged that the task hinges on social and economic development within countries as well as heightened communication among them. Security communities, she added, are more complicated than alliance systems, but they share many of the same attributes.

Boulding suggested that research is needed to determine the kind of conflict resolution infrastructure necessary to foster dialogue, cross-cultural communication, and political accommodation with our traditional adversaries. The United States must begin to look to nondemocratic nations in the international system as potential partners in a pluralistic security community, rather than as probable enemies, and seize the opportunity provided by change in the Soviet Union to fashion a new era in East-West relations.

In the general discussion, William Kintner asked when the pacificity of democracies first emerged. He noted that the United States was a democracy in the nineteenth century, yet it initiated and fought the Spanish-American War. During the same period, Britain, also a leading democracy, was rapidly expanding and pursuing an aggressive colonial policy. Even France went on to accumulate a substantial empire after the democratic revolution of 1789. Is it not possible that the pacific nature of democracies has emerged only in the post-World War II era?

Prefacing his response by reminding the audience that he had not suggested that democracies never participate in violence or aggression, Rummel cautioned against measuring nineteenth-century America with the same democratic yardstick that we use today. In light of the fact that slavery was not abolished until 1863 and women did not get the right to vote until 1920, nineteenth-century America, it can be said, was still in the process of becoming a full democracy. Even so, Rummel said, this question illustrates the monadic type of inquiry that can be so misleading. The issue is not whether the United States fought an aggressive war with Spain during the nineteenth century, but how the United States compared in terms of participation in violent conflicts with the clearly less democratic autocracies of that period. Dyadic analysis bears out the hypothesis that democracies are less prone to domestic and international violence than are nondemocracies.

Suggesting that Rummel's assertion concerning the pacificity of democracies needed some qualification, Ted Gurr noted that, although democracies as a group do not tend toward violence, large democracies seem to use violence as much as their autocratic cousins do. Is it possible, he asked, that the relative peacefulness of democracies is a function of size?

Rummel responded that this apparent contradiction of his theory could be explained rather easily through a straightforward application of widely accepted international relations theory. Large democracies tend to be more powerful than smaller, like-minded states and are therefore called on more regularly to defend their interests and allies. But it is impossible to assess the relative bellicosity of democracies, large or small, by simply enumerating the incidences of participation in conflict while paying no heed to the historical conditions under which those conflicts were entered into or whether the actions were defensive or offensive. Otherwise, for example, one would have to equate the Spanish-American War with World War II, a clearly inappropriate comparison.

Boulding asserted that large democracies, like all powerful states, participate in international violence because they have the power to do so. This is indicative of what she termed the "culture of power" in the international system that results in the exertion of force in an almost reflexive fashion. The culture of power can be so intrusive as to weave its way into the fabric of a society, creating a situation in which force is employed as a matter of course rather than as an exception. What is needed, therefore, is a mechanism by which this acceptance of force is replaced in all societies by a nurturing and understanding culture that encourages the peaceful resolution of international disputes.

Francis Deng asked Rummel how the fundamental principles of democracy—namely, equality, reciprocity of rights and obligations, political and civil freedom, and tolerance—can be applied to the ethnically and culturally divided Third World, especially to former European colonies such as the Sudan, whose arbitrary borders and ethnic mix seem to make cooperative rule impossible.

Although acknowledging a lack of familiarity with the complexities of the Sudanese situation, Rummel suggested that the most workable solution might lie in the creation of two separate Sudanese states, one Christian and the other Islamic. Trying to force integration and unification may exacerbate rather than ameliorate the violent and costly war. Noting the experience of South Asia, Rummel suggested that the partition of India into separate Muslim and Hindu states has had a generally positive effect on the region as a whole. The Sudanese case may be similar in that continued efforts to force coexistence may prove futile, and peace might be better served by a partition agreement.

Boulding disagreed, noting that although every country must deal with the desire for ethnic autonomy, separation and partition are not the answer. What needs to be done in the Sudan, as in other regions of the developing world, she said, is to create conditions under which culturally relevant consensus-building processes can operate.

Amy Sherman asked whether the notion of structural violence introduced by Boulding could be addressed in much the same way that Rummel addressed peace and democracy. In other words, can it be shown that developing countries opting for a democratic-capitalist system of government exhibit less structural violence than developing countries following the socialist or totalitarian model of political organization?

Rummel responded affirmatively and reasoned that the freedom provided by democracies not only promotes nonviolence but enhances social justice as well. By ensuring greater political and economic rights and welfare for all members of the community, the democratic system of government prevents, to the greatest degree possible, the exploitation of populations by their own governments that Boulding described as structural violence. To promote democracy is to promote peace and social welfare.

Although Boulding agreed in principle with Rummel's response, she pointed out that structural violence was not a phenomenon restricted to the developing world. Modern Western states, even our own, she said, are susceptible to structural violence. In fact, she added, structural violence is on the rise in the West, and the problem cannot be dismissed by saying that there is less of this type of violence in democracies than in totalitarian states. We should work toward preventing its occurrence in every political system.

If democracies are less likely than totalitarian states to engage in domestic and international violence, asked one member of the audience, are they also less likely to pursue aggressively expansionist international policies?

The nature of state power, posited Rummel, is that it tends to perpetuate itself if left unchecked; it expands until it is prevented from doing so. By definition, totalitarian states have no effective internal checks of government power and therefore expand until prevented from doing so by external elements. Democracies, conversely, are based on the principles of political checks and balances and governmental responsibility to the electorate. Because aggressive expansion is politically, economically, and socially expensive, democratic governments tend not to opt for such policies for fear of substantial dissension among the populace.

Boulding took issue with Rummel's suggestion that there were no checks on government power in totalitarian societies. She said that every government must keep in mind the wants, needs, and goals of its people, and policies that run counter to the wishes of the population incur some cost. These costs vary widely, she noted, and it is up to peace researchers not only to determine the political checks and balances, even in closed societies, but also to examine the effect of ignoring them.

Notes

1. Michael Howard, *War and Liberal Consciousness* (New Brunswick, N.J.: Rutgers University Press, 1978), p. 31.

2. In my *Understanding Conflict and War*, Vol. 4: *War, Power, and Peace* (Beverly Hills, Calif.: Sage Publications, 1979), I surveyed all the systematic studies on this question and concluded that they supported a hypothesized inverse relationship between libertarian systems and foreign violence; in my "Libertarian Propositions on Violence Within and Between Nations: A Test Against Published Research Results," *Journal of Conflict Resolution* 29 (September 1985): pp. 419–55, I redid this survey, adding several refinements and tests of significance, and confirmed the earlier results.

3. In previous professional work, I have termed those nations that assure civil liberties and political rights *libertarian* rather than *democratic*. For one, the latter term has become blurred by its use in the battle for people's minds, as in "democratic centralism" or "people's democracy" and thus, it sometimes now stands for what used to be its opposite—dictatorship. Moreover, democracy technically does not stand for civil rights and political liberties but for majority rule, and such a majority within the historical meaning of democracy could eliminate minority rights and liberties. Although there is no one-to-one relationship between democracy on the one side and rights and liberties on the other, there is this identity for libertarian systems. A majority denying minority rights and liberties can still be democratic; it cannot be libertarian. These very rights and liberties create the conditions that reduce the likelihood of collective violence.

However, despite these problems, I must use the term "democratic" in this paper, understanding that it refers to libertarian systems. The reason is that it is the historically settled term for both the advocates and critics of such systems, the major subject matter here, and to replace it with "libertarian" would promote ambiguity and confusion.

4. Totalitarian and Communist systems should not be confused. Whereas most Communist systems are totalitarian, not all are (e.g., Poland); also, not all totalitarian systems are Communist, such as the Ayatollah Khomeini's Iran and Hitler's Germany.

5. For these figures and related analysis, see my "War Isn't This Century's Biggest Killer," *Wall Street Journal*, July 7, 1986; and my "Deadlier Than War," *IPA Review [Institute of Public Affairs Limited, Australia] 41 (August–October 1987):* pp. 24–30.

6. The words *enhance* and *foster* are carefully chosen to imply the use of the nonforceful, nonviolent arts of persuasion, facilitation, and encouragement. Any policy to spread democracy by force—to impose democratic institutions on others—would contradict the very essence of the policy, which is that people should be free to choose.

7. The ethical question whether this would be a socially just solution to violence is as important as whether there is an empirical relationship. I cannot treat this issue here, but, using the social contract approach to justice, I have concluded elsewhere that promoting the freedom of individuals to choose their way of life, consistent with a like freedom for others, would minimize violence and maximize social justice. See my *Understanding Conflict and War*, Vol. 5, *The Just Peace* (Beverly Hills, Calif.: Sage Publications, 1981).

8. Immanuel Kant, *Perpetual Peace*, trans. Lewis White Beck (New York: Library of Liberal Arts/Bobbs-Merrill, 1957), pp. 12–13.

9. Quoted in Howard, *War and Liberal Consciousness*, p. 29.

10. Of course, much of such writing was not self-consciously socialist or ideological, but the analyses and programs were in the socialist tradition. See, for example, the "world order" studies; in particular, Richard A. Falk, *A Study of Future Worlds* (New York: Free Press, 1975); and Richard A. Falk and Saul H. Mendlovitz, eds., *The Strategy for World Order*, Vol. IV: *Disarmament and Economic Development* (New York: World Law Fund, 1966).

11. Keep in mind that two kinds of freedom must now be distinguished. To the Marxist-Leninist, it is Communist freedom (in effect, anarco-communism) that creates peace; to the classical liberal, peace is fostered by individual freedom under a democratic government.

12. See Johan Galtung, "A Structured Theory of Aggressism," *Journal of Peace Research*, no. 2 (1964): pp. 95–119; and Johan Galtung, "Violence, Peace, and Peace Research," *Journal of Peace Research*, no. 3 (1969): pp. 167–91.

13. Based on Quincy Wright, *A Study of War*, 2d ed. (Chicago: University of Chicago Press, 1965), table 44, p. 650.

14. Hitler's Nazi party was self-consciously socialist: "Nazi" stood for the National Socialist German Workers' party. While not formally nationalized, big business was brought under complete Nazi government control and dictation, and the German economy was centrally directed by government ministries.

15. Kenneth Waltz, *Man, the State, and War: A Theoretical Analysis* (New York: Columbia University Press, 1954); by 1965 it had gone through six printings.

16. See, for example, E. Weede, "Democracy and War Involvement," *Journal of Conflict Resolution* 28 (December 1984): pp. 649–64; and S. Chan, "Mirror, Mirror, on the Wall...Are the Freer Countries More Pacific?" *Journal of Conflict Resolution* 28 (December 1984): pp. 617–48.

17. Rummel, *Journal of Conflict Resolution 29*.

18. The theoretical assumption is not that the data points for the violence versus freedom coordinate axes would lie close around a downward sloping regression line, which is required for a high correlation, but that the data points lie in a right triangle, whose base is the horizontal axis (freedom) and whose right angle is at the origin.

19. Note that this is even the way the question I was to answer in this paper was phrased by the conference organizers: "Can the relative bellicosity *of* states be measured and predicted as a function of *their* internal political system?" (emphasis added). Consider how different this monadic question becomes if "of" is replaced by "between," and "relative" is added after "their."

20. There are two minor exceptions to this: an "ephemeral republican France attacking an ephemeral republican Rome in 1849" (M. Small and J.D. Singer, "The War Proneness of Democratic Regimes, 1816–1965," *Jerusalem Journal of International Relations* I [Summer 1976]: p. 67), and barely democratic Finland joining Germany in fighting the Soviet Union in World War II. This put Finland formally at war with the democracies, but no actual hostilities occurred.

21. It has been alleged that the lack of war between democracies is due to chance or to lack of borders between most of them. Tests of significance show that both these possibilities are very improbable. See my "Libertarianism and International Violence," *Journal of Conflict Resolution* 27 (March 1983): pp. 27–71.

22. Hans J. Morgenthau, *Politics Among Nations: The Struggle for Power and Peace*, 6th rev. ed., ed. Kenneth W. Thompson (New York: Alfred A. Knopf, 1985), pp. 378–79.

23. Much of the accumulated evidence supporting the inverse relationship between democracy and violence comes from the empirical side results of research on other, often quite unrelated, topics.

24. Johan Galtung, "Memo to friends and colleagues," and published exchange of communications between Henry Kariel and Johan Galtung, Political Science Department, University of Hawaii, April 1988.

25. Wright, *A Study of War*, pp. 847–48.

Introduction to Chapter 15

In this chapter, Michael Nagler concentrates on how and why there has been a declining interest in world order theories, and how that interest could be reenergized and employed to reinvigorate the field of peace research. According to Nagler, much of the vitality that characterized peace research and the study of world order from the late 1950s to the 1970s has been lost as a result of an artificial separation of these two approaches into separate strands of inquiry. One of the main causes of this schism has been the unwillingness of many researchers to recognize the symbiotic relationship of the two.

In *City of God*, one of the Western world's first world order documents, Saint Augustine says, "Peace is the tranquillity that comes with the order of all parts." Therefore, to study peace is to study world order and vice versa. Nagler says that within the peace research community there is a consensus that peace should be defined not as the absence of war, but as the absence of violence, and violence should be defined as that which inhibits the fulfillment of the human being. Therefore, he says, one cannot make statements about peace until one determines what gives fulfillment to a human being.

The intellectual basis of all world order thinking—the theory that the surest path to peace rests with a single community—was first postulated, Nagler says, late in classical antiquity. The theory is grounded on the tension that evolved between the *oikos*, the extended-family-based system of political organization, and the *polis*, the territory-based political system that replaced it.

When the *polis* replaced the *oikos*, what had become a stable system based on the loose association of peoples was broken down into disparate groups defining allegiance as a function of geography, and the free association of the *oikos* was replaced by restricted association with those inside one's particular *polis*. According to Nagler, "Although the *polis* incorporated many *oikoi*, human beings in the particular global region were actually less united, in the newer, more formal, but also more superficial system of organization."

With this analysis in mind, it is understandable that theoreticians came to view the state as a major cause of international violence and sought to devise world order plans that avoided the supposed alienation resulting from the state structure. But Nagler argues that it is not the existence of the state that causes violence, but "the human habit of polarizing what is essentially one mankind, into 'self and other.'" The structure of political organization is not to blame; the rivalries that evolve between the structure's constituent elements cause the strife.

Why do people continue to seek enhanced association when it has been repeatedly shown to be fraught with problems? Nagler, again using Saint Augustine as his point of reference, views man's desire for fellowship and positive peace as an a priori drive of human nature. The essential question of world order, therefore, is how can federation be achieved without polarization? Traditional and historical theories of world order either constructed models that were based on polarization and the separation of traditional enemies such as Christians and non-Christians; or they based their models on force, military sanction, and death to defend the peace of their new world order. The answer lies instead, according to Nagler, in seeing man as a smaller-scale model of the whole, with every individual a bearer of some precious information from which one can unpack an entire world order. From this formulation, Nagler draws two conclusions: First, every human life is a sacred manifestation of the macrocosm that it represents and therefore must not be willfully taken for any reason. The second conclusion, again borrowed from Saint Augustine, is that there are fundamentally two world orders—the city of God, representing the ideal toward which all men strive, and the city of man, representing the actual world in which we live.

In Nagler's opinion, traditional world order theories have concentrated on structures but have not attempted to integrate the physical with the spiritual and motivational forces that could animate those structures for the desired ends. Nagler concludes that world order theory needs a structural design and a dynamic framework along the lines proposed by Gandhi: "He saw the ideal world as a system in which the individual would voluntarily serve the family, the family would serve the state, the state would serve the nation, and the nation would serve the world." Power would flow from the individual as both the representative and servant of the whole. The dynamic that would ensure the structure's integrity would be nonviolence.

The concept of humanity that underlies this theory emphasizes the diversity of the human species as a whole, and the necessary unity of the species in its parts. It demands what Gandhi called "heart unity" or the spontaneous desire for others' welfare.

15. Ideas of World Order and the Map of Peace

Michael N. Nagler

Notice that there can be life without pain but no pain without some kind of life. In the same way, there can be peace without any kind of war, but no war that does not suppose some kind of peace.

—Saint Augustine[1]

And if anyone saved a life, it would be as if he saved the life of the whole people.
—The Qur'an[2]

As the people of Eastern Europe break through the legacy of oppression left them by the world's most destructive war, as a great statesman takes the Soviet stage, as Western Europe once again picks up its task of finding community, and as in other ways a remarkable decade of danger and possibility opens, it seems timely to reconsider the age-old search for peace and world order—tasks that are in theory, and have often been in practice, complementary parts of the same project.

In Western thought, the first articulated discussion of peace occurs in what is also the first (and probably the most profound) document on world order, Saint Augustine's *City of God*,[3] which defines peace as "the tranquility that comes with the *order* of all parts [of a given system]."[4]

One can define peace as the absence of war, and world order as merely a description of the international system (or inverse of the "global problematique"). In these minimal, not to say reductionist, definitions, peace and world order are seen as overlapping but essentially different problems. Peace, for example, is one of four "world order values," in addition to justice, environmental integrity, and economic sufficiency, in the program of the former Institute for World Order. The closer we can get to essential definitions of peace and of world order—to a sense of why they have stirred passions since the beginning of history—the more they converge.[5] In what follows, I consider peace and world order alternate perspectives on the same human enterprise, and switch from one term to the other as is convenient for the discussion.

The formal study of world order seems to be languishing. It may be particularly symptomatic that the Institute for World Order has changed its name to the World Policy Institute and cut back its commitment to peace education. Peace research, always a fiendishly difficult endeavor, is also in decline after a renaissance, particularly in West Germany and Northern Europe, that inspired unprecedented hope and excitement from the late 1950s to the 1970s. Peace research and world order research seem to have wandered onto different maps, and both need new bearings. The amount of new research has declined, in part because previous research has not been used. The fifty or more world order models formally developed by world order scholars, like the more than two hundred perfectly good schemes catalogued by the *Bulletin of Disarmament Proposals* some ten years ago, are many paths not taken by policymakers or thought through by strategists. But the decline in and the drifting apart of peace and world order research also seem to have happened because the problems are not being sufficiently studied by scholars.[6] To illustrate, the European renaissance in peace research reached a consensus that peace is not so much the absence of war as it is the absence of violence,[7] defined by one influential scholar as "that which inhibits the fulfillment of a human being."[8] The challenging conclusion of this logic is that we cannot make any normative, prescriptive, valuative, or indeed any accurately descriptive statements about world order without knowing what gives fulfillment to a human being—which is tantamount to knowing what a human being *is*.

In the face of such a daunting prerequisite, it is perhaps not surprising that people are leaving the field, especially because the modern academic approach to research in both subjects is through the social sciences, where it is difficult to avoid the temptation to simplify one's existence by adopting the assumptions of rational actor theory. Rational actor theory really begs the question of human nature. When we forget that the theory is just a heuristic device and adopt its vision of human nature, it becomes difficult to remember why world order or peace should even be desired. I propose to address that question here and attempt to understand what has gone wrong, not only in the very recent and temporary decline but with the whole enterprise of world order research, taking up the challenge implicit in the logic of recent peace research to consider what fulfills a human being—and what a human being *is*.

Why World Order?

A sense that all humanity constitutes a single community, the ontological basis of all world order thinking, was first articulated late in classical antiquity (as far as the West is concerned). By Aristotle's time, this idea had taken hold among certain influential philosophical schools,[9] although, as is the case with philosophical schools everywhere, the implementation of the idea in the real political process was hardly impressive. It is worth noting the paradox between the great desirability of peace (as Saint

Augustine says, "nothing we can long for, talk about, or finally get is so desirable")[10] and the small amount of effort people have been willing to expend even thinking clearly about it, much less working for it. Einstein said that if 5 percent of the people would work for peace, we would have it; later he dropped the requirement to 2 percent.

If we ask ourselves what impulse lies behind the irrepressible curiosity about the nature of and possibilities for human community and the *quaestio perpetua* of how to give it greater solidarity in practice, one reason seems obvious: to escape from "the scourge of war." This need by itself, in a regime of pure reason, would account for the wish for a single world system, even without reference to the suspected single nature of the human family that began to surface in the utopian thinking of late antiquity.[11]

It is a perfectly natural second step to believe that, because war is something that states do to one another, we must reconsider the sovereignty of states and the dynamics of their "anarchical society"[12] to develop peace. And yet, this approach is inadequate in important ways. We recall Kant's surprising observation—accurate, if no longer applicable to modern conditions—that the very intolerance of human groups for one another has often kept them apart rather than at one another's throats; that is, nonassociation can create a negative kind of peace.[13] And the problems with large association, the idea of a single world state, do not end here.

Parable of the *Polis*

In a sense, the first document on world order in the West considerably antedates Augustine; in fact, it is virtually the first extensive document we possess from our tradition: Homer's *Odyssey*. Many classical scholars regard the mysterious lands Odysseus visits during his wanderings as making up a kind of early "world order modeling project," in which an exhaustive variety of social forms, every one inadequate for one reason or another, alternately tempt or threaten the hero until he arrives back in Ithaca. Ithaca—home—is a pre- or minimal-state kind of society based on the extended family, or *oikos*, which exists in a regime of almost unlimited potential for loose association among other family-based units (*oikoi*).[14]

Although the theory is not free of controversy, most scholars today believe that there is a tension in the Homeric poems between this *oikos* regime and that of the first experiment in state organization: the city-state, or *polis*, with new institutions based more on territory than on family and, in fact, destined to exist in constant tension with the earlier system and family rights. The difference was not unlike the progression from *Gemeinschaft* (community) to *Gesellschaft* (society). It seems that Homer did not agree with what we now call "*polis* ideology." What is more, fascinating evidence is buried here and there in linguistic usage indicating that he had good reason to dislike such ideology. Many forms of association that had sprung up and been sustained in long cultural tradition were simply discarded by the *polis* and replaced with a single rather stark principle: although the *polis* incorporated many *oikoi*, the human beings involved were actually less united in the newer, more formal but also more superficial system of organization; in fact, the *polis* polarized persons as belonging or not belonging to the state—nothing can be more divisive.[15] Bigger was not better. And should *poleis* form alliances, they could polarize the entire regime and create a setting for the destruction of civilization, which is exactly what happened in the Peloponnesian War.[16]

Given the problems of state organization, it is understandable that some modern world order thinkers have gone in the opposite direction, pointing not toward a superstate but toward a breakdown of the existing state to a human scale. This group has included people of many different persuasions: functionalists (David Mitrany), scale theorists (Leopold Kohr, Kirkpatrick Sale), and "green" bioregionalists of many shades (Sale, Peter Berg, Raymond Dasmann).[17] All these predecessors of E. F. Schumacher made "small" something that might not mean less. And yet scale theory by itself, however valuable, is incomplete.

The fact is, the pre-*polis* regime of ancient Greece was no paradise of stable peace either. Indeed, slightly earlier in mythological time than Odysseus's adventures, the catastrophe of the *Iliad* wars unfolded in precisely that prestate sort of regime, in which a loose association of *oikoi* (and some anachronistic souvenirs of a much earlier, Mycenaean-type palace state) came together long enough to destroy the entire civilization— not only the Trojans and their allies but, Homer hints,[18] the apparent victors also.

The nation-state cannot be the sole obstacle to world order, although certainly the "national security state,"[19] with its almost paranoid obsession with defense, constitutes a major obstacle. If the argument outlined here is correct, world order is consistent with the continued existence, but not the continued paranoia, of the nation-state or its assumption of mystical identity. The final realization of world order does not have to be, and indeed cannot be, in this view, exclusively a political achievement.[20]

So far, we have established two important points. First, it is not the existence of states, but the all-too-human habit of polarizing what is essentially one entity into "self" and "other" that tears the fabric of peace. Nation-states at worst institutionalize that habit. More accurately, the habit uses the state, as it does other group identities, making the state into an "actor," as we say today, into an institutional focus to act out deeply conditioned aggressions in its own drama of collective but divisive ego. The process may depend on such factors as the size or nature of a state's political regime. Bioregionalism combines smallness, which limits threat and damage, with the preservation of indigenous cultural forms. This is certainly an attractive school, but changes in structure can only be secured by deeper changes in ways of seeing:

The most naive fallacy in the field [of peace theory] is...to believe in global architectonics, that the structure can be...filled with any kind of actors,...to believe that structure is independent of culture. In addition to being simply empirically untenable this sheds more light on why balance of power theories...are among the most invalid of all approaches.[21]

The second point is that throughout the sawtoothed history of social evolution, human beings have never stopped desiring some form of federation, even when they have justifiably feared it. "At millennial intervals," Quincy Wright observed, "Western Civilization has made an attempt to organize itself as a world-empire, as a world-church, or as a world-federation,"[22] and neither Western nor global civilization (which must emerge as the next focus of concern) can cease making such attempts.

Why do human beings continue to desire association, given all its problems? I believe that an answer, the significance of which has long been overlooked, is in the text I mentioned at the outset, the *City of God*. Saint Augustine had the advantage over Homer of writing after the concept of an innate, fundamental unity of humankind had become, as Baldry said, a hallmark of being human, and the advantage of writing relatively soon after the coming of Christ, who can be said to have made that insight a living reality. In the passage to which I refer (XIX.12), Augustine has drawn attention to the phenomenon of sociability among animals, even the most ferocious, and he suddenly unfurls a banner that puts the question "Why world order?" on an entirely different footing: "It is even more so with man. By the very laws of his nature, he seems, so to speak, forced into fellowship and, as far as in him lies, into peace with every man."[23] Augustine's arguments about the primacy of the desire for peace and the innate human need for unlimited fellowship necessitate careful reading. These arguments have not been superseded by any modern understanding of human nature, and I accept them as the recognition of an a priori condition: human beings by nature desire world order, just as they desire "positive peace."

True world order, then, is not desired only for the absence of war, however marvelous that would be; war is only disorder's most impressive format. It is not even desired for the presence of world order values, although that is much closer to the mark. In the last analysis, world order is a good in itself, because human association is desired as such, despite the confusion imposed by the seemingly inevitable tendency of the mind to see difference and division.[24]

The idea that world order is desired in itself never appears in discussions of foreign policy in the mass media, whose imagination is limited to ruthless cost-benefit calculation by competing individual states; nor does it appear to surface in the decision-making processes of policy elites. I draw from this idea nothing less than a restructured concept of the relationship of the individual to the whole and argue that we can solve some critical dilemmas in world order thought with this concept, although it will pose challenges and problems of its own. However, this approach does not offer a simplistic, single-issue solution. It identifies not so much a single issue as a basic issue. As Johan Galtung pointed out with regard to structural models (and balance-of-power theory), the type of single solution rightly objected to for so vast a matter as world order is superficial. Anthropologist Bruce M. Knauft's brilliant study of homicide causality among New Guinea tribesmen[25] should put to rest single-factor explanations of an overdetermined behavior such as homicide, not to mention organized conflict.[26] If we take as a starting point the innate desirability of world order and the concept of human nature it implies, theories can emerge that are heuristically and esthetically simple but that can lead to appropriately rich and complex applications.

Order Without Paradox

The shift from *oikos* networks to a regime of *poleis* in the ancient world and the codification of the nation-state in seventeenth-century Europe—both cases of large formal association—led in similar ways to less peace in their respective systems. I suggest that this development took place because they swept aside valuable modes of association that had evolved in their respective cultures while creating a framework for even larger polarizations. Ways of posing the question of world order for our time are these: How can we take the next step forward without these costs? How can we have federation without polarization? How can we nourish indigenous processes of association while we build transnational institutions by conscious intervention (for there is no time left, of course, to depend on natural evolution alone)?[27]

The well-known European "perpetual peace" tradition, usually (although somewhat arbitrarily) dated from Pierre Dubois,[28] is instructive as an expression of the growing desire for world order and for the flaws in its suggested implementations. Two conceptual flaws marred this tradition from the outset, and Kant alone among its representatives avoided them. First, implementation would not cure but, again, only transfer the worst problem in the system, hostility, to a higher level of organization: the "peace" order was actually a federation of Christendom against the perceived pagan menace of the East.[29]

This error rests essentially on a negative definition of peace—peace as a mere absence of war—and, of course, has deeper roots in social thought than the perpetual peace tradition. It has impeded a workable construction of utopia since time immemorial. To quote René Girard:

> The building of the perfect city, entering into earthly paradise, has always been represented to us as based on the prior elimination or forced conversion of a Guilty Party.[30]

Closely linked to this error lies a second, which has been less readily recognized as significant: the question of means. Even Emeric Crucé provides for the "defenses of peace" by joint military sanction.[31] The world had to wait for Gandhi to maintain stridently that means are inseparable from ends ("Violent revolution," he said, "will bring violent *Swaraj* [independence]") and, more important, to demonstrate incontrovertibly that powerful nonviolent means are available.[32]

What Is Man?

Only one conceptual resource has allowed great thinkers to avoid these twin errors of the perpetual peace and other strands of utopian planning: the realization of or faith in a microcosmic conception of human beings. What is in a human being? How should we think of the individual for purposes of constructing, at least first in our minds, the possibility of a universal, seamless community?

The question might be framed and answered, for the purposes of world order thought, in terms of information theory, as the following anecdote illustrates. During a recent Senate hearing on an environmental issue, a biologist came forward to testify with a petri dish containing some rare microorganism. The "bug," as he put it, was an "endangered species" because someone cleaning his laboratory had been at the point of washing the last-known specimens down the sink. This organism later produced an enzyme that may help to cure cancer.

How much more we might say is man—not only as a species, but every single person in some way—the bearer of precious information for the construction of the world. The futurist Hazel Henderson once proposed making an index of all the indigenous cultures of the world before they disappear, because they contain precious information; but how much more is the individual. George Orwell, hardly a starry-eyed idealist, mused over the hanging of a young Hindu in one of his most famous essays and uttered a haunting line: "One life less; one world less."[33]

It seems to me that two conclusions arise from anthropology (perhaps we could call it a "person view" to parallel the concept of a world view). The first is prohibitive: each human life is beyond price and must not be taken. The grim fact of history is that no social order has ever been built on this value, built in a way that avoids the logic revealed by Girard, Weber, and others, that around some concealed bend of every polity lies the sanction of death, which is felt to be so fundamental to the social order that it cannot be sacrificed without undermining the order itself.[34]

But the second, or normative, conclusion is more unexpected and less moralistic than the first. This positive conclusion is implicit in the *City of God*. Its basic premise is that there are fundamentally two world orders. One is ideal and society has never experienced it (although a few individuals have). The other is far from perfect, and we are experiencing it right now. The ideal order is, of course, what Augustine calls the *City of God*: the divine plan for the universe. Although we have not experienced this as a reality, a "memory" of some kind draws us toward it through error after error.[35] It is the driving power behind all social experiments, and it will go on driving them until it is fully realized here on earth.

In identifying the basic cause of bipolarity, Augustine reaches a surprisingly modern conclusion: there are two types of social order because there are two *amores* (loves). By *amores* he means two fundamental dispositions or drives, deeply seated in and perpetually operating through human consciousness.[36] These two loves can be described, for world order purposes, as the drive toward community or wholeness (love of God) and the drive toward separate existence, ego, or the pursuit of self-interest (love of man).

Classically, as we have seen, world order theory has concentrated on social arrangements and not been overly concerned with the drives that bring those arrangements into existence or at least work through them to good or bad ends.[37] I believe that this focus is one of the reasons world order modeling has not become an intellectually or politically productive exercise. In the Augustinian view, the struggle between principles of order and disorder in individuals expresses itself in the orderliness of the resulting system; yet there is something more important. Given that the principle of order is inherently more real, more deeply rooted in ontology, the reality within the individual should be the prime resource for the reality without, even as far as world order. Gandhi believed this. He was fond of quoting the Sanskrit proverb, *Yatha pinde, tatha brahmande* (As in the particle, so in the cosmic whole), because it not only evoked a sense of awe *for* the individual but also hinted at Gandhi's method of soliciting social order *from* the individual.

World order thinking thus far has failed to come up with a system that can reconcile two values essential to human fulfillment: the free development of each individual and the meaninglessness of individual life without unlimited association with all life. In political thought, this is called the tension between autonomy and community, but its ontological origins lie deeper: no two development paths are identical for any person,[38] yet we are not fully human without community; our deepest individuality somehow demands fully articulated unity.

World order needs, then, both a structural design (or model) and a dynamic framework large enough to embrace these poles, which come into contradiction when considered separately or statically. Gandhi advocated this framework. He saw the ideal world as a system in which individuals would voluntarily serve the family, the family would serve the state, the state the nation, and the nation the entire world:

> In this structure composed of innumerable villages there will be ever-widening, ever-ascending circles. Life will not be a pyramid with the apex sustained by the bottom. But it will be an oceanic circle whose centre will be the individual always ready to perish for the village, the latter ready to perish for the circle of villages, till at last the whole becomes one life composed of individuals...sharing the majesty of the oceanic circle of which they are integral units.
>
> Therefore, the outermost circumference will not wield power to crush the inner circle, but will give strength to all within and derive its own strength from it.[39]

In this simple model, Gandhi emphasizes the process whereby order flows from individuals to the polities through service. Beginning with the living, conscious individual, Gandhi was able to develop a scheme that addresses our concern that such models not be thought of as empty constructs to be filled with nonentities or assumedly rational actors. What is more, the image actually solves—or it would, if applied—the most awkward problem of modern world order theory, the state. In the Gandhian vision, the state can remain as a servant of the world order; power flows from individuals to the whole through the state, as it does through other circles with which individuals identify and through and to which individuals feel responsibility and render service.

If the state fails to serve the global community (extrapolating from Gandhi's logic), individuals will serve it precisely by exercising their right of resistance in an effort to bring it (or, less metaphorically, their fellow citizens) back in line. If the state were seen in this way, the sacrificial aspect of the individual's relationship to it would not exist, for it would be recognized that the state, like the family and other entities, must "derive its own strength" from free individuals. Individuals would indeed serve the state and might even sacrifice themselves for the state, but the crucial difference is that they would do so freely, as a means of their own self-realization.[40] Finally, such a system would fully use indigenous networks of association that a culture had developed—in India's case, the village, on which Gandhi lavished so much thought and attention.

Elsewhere, Gandhi acknowledged the inherently violent character of the provisional state as we know it now, in the City of Man. "If India," he said, for example, "is to evolve along non-violent lines it will have to decentralize many things. Centralization cannot be sustained and defended without adequate force."[41] But his distinct genius lay in so clearly and articulately conceptualizing how the ideal city would work, namely, by mobilizing through service the positive love that resides, along with its negative counterpart, in every individual's consciousness.

Unity in Diversity

Underlying this theory is a different concept of humanity, but also a concept of order that articulates the individual and the whole differently from our familiar assumptions. An engineering colleague with a strong interest in philosophy and systems theory, who gave a guest lecture in my introductory course on peace and world order studies, posed a question none of us had considered. Why is it that biology, which began about the same time as physics, has had such a relatively poor development of theory? Because, he explained, our minds are well organized to operate in a framework of unity in uniformity; we cannot cope with a regime of unity in diversity. The essence of atomic theory is uniformity; every electron is like every other—which has something to do with the fact that it is an inanimate entity, or construct. No organism, no cell is exactly like any other.

It is appropriate to demand that an order be life sustaining in a sense extended from, but not contradictory to, the biological. Just as Gandhi insisted that nonviolence was a living force, latent in the individual but expressible on a mass and institutional scale, his world order model was that of a living system. There is a certain basis to this world view in biological reality, because the organism and the species exist in a way that no other functional unit—be it race, tribe, or family—exists in nature.[42] These two biological units, individual and species, correspond compellingly to the diversity and the unity that are the key terms in the Hegelian concept of order and the implicit values of Gandhi's centrifugal model.[43]

Going a step further, we can see our way to a resolution of the community/autonomy paradox. In the Gandhian model, the interests of the individual and the interests of the species are only perceived to be at variance. Because of the nature of human consciousness, a person's participation in unity does not have to be enacted in rituals or substantiated in taxes or formal security arrangements; still less does it have to be encoded in an artificially homogenized global culture. We are looking for (taking another apparently simple phrase from Gandhi) "heart unity," the spontaneous desire for others' welfare. This conceptual step does not come naturally, because we have grown so accustomed to thinking of life as a physical phenomenon, or a play of physical phenomena, in which neo-Darwinian competition is "natural." This again is a major issue—that the material commitment leading to technological triumphs may also have brought on the entire crisis of modern civilization. Without delving too deeply, we can say that this commitment to the physical deprives life of depth, or interiority. Thus, diversity and unity must compete at the same level of reality, and we indeed have a paradox. Depth resolves it: diversity is the law of the exterior person; unity the law of the interior person.

It follows that uniformity of customs or ideology is as antithetical to world order and peace as disunity of heart. The horror of a world state, whether cynically attempted by a Hitler or naively called for by a well-meaning Einaudi, is its uniformity. The idea of a world state is rejected not simply because it could be taken over by a selfish power, but because it is an inherently wrong expression of human order: it violates cultures and imposes uniformity on indigenous diversity, which is an outgrowth of the diversity of life itself.

War somehow always acts to suppress diversity, as Ivan Illich pointed out in a stunning and intuitive article;[44] war is much worse than hell; it is boring. Yet in their attempts to escape war, some world order enthusiasts have sinned against biocultural diversity, whether it be the Volapuk movement at the turn of the century or Esperanto today, and they must be considered single-issue enthusiasts who are off the mark. Remembering Galtung's definition of violence,[45] how is the person to develop under a conformist regime when the essence of life is biological or cultural diversity? In this model, a unifying culture is, oddly, the opposite of a uniform culture. Seen as an intellectual problem (which it is not—it is much deeper), world order necessitates nothing more or less than learning to disentangle diversity and unity and to apply each at the correct level of interpretation. War, or any form of conflict, is the result of a negative human drive precipitating around perceived differences. But some of the most fought-over differences are precisely those too precious to be sacrificed, and, in principle, nothing that supports life should be inimical to order. Fortunately, differences do not have to be sacrificed. Where there is unity of hearts, differences in custom are no threat; no amount of external diversity, recognized as external, provides an occasion for conflict. To paraphrase Saint Augustine, "Love one another, and decentralize to your heart's content."[46]

Conclusion

The foregoing discussion does not claim to sketch a complete world order or address all the obstacles that now prevent one. I propose that the next steps to investigate are the values that promote selfless participation and the technologies, primarily the mass media, that now play such an important role in manipulating values. Other serious questions will arise. However, the thinkers cited here seem to provide a framework and the beginnings of a process that might open the door to new, creative world order thought.

These thinkers establish that world order is not merely a necessity imposed on us by the dreadful capacity for violence we seem bent on facilitating; rather, world order responds to an innate, positive, deep human need.[47] From that principle, useful analysis and reorientation of prevailing assumptions follow, and three key assumptions emerge: that the best model for world order would be extended from biology rather than imposed on the whole-system level by political overviews; that the

Hegelian principle of unity in diversity is the appropriate concept of order to work out; and that only the principles of nonviolence, in which the individual is not smaller than the collective, can supply a methodology for the great transition. In this scheme, the nation-state may remain but the national security state must go. In other words, the cognitive regime—in which the state (or, for that matter, the economy) can become a symbolic focus of competition rather than a place to organize networks of association and a culture (or fulfill material needs)—must be dispersed.

We began by lamenting the fact that world order and peace had wandered onto different "maps." In the vocabulary of this chapter, world order is desired as a life-nurturing system of unity in diversity, and peace is the outward or most global expression of nonviolence. They do indeed seem to come closer in this perspective.

Human needs and consciousness are the key points of leverage at which an awakened society could begin moving again on the human task of world order. In his neglected 1923 classic, *War: Its Causes, Consequences and Cure,* Kirby Page called for all the traditional means of building a warless world order but emphasized "creation of an international mind."[48] We can take him to mean the development of a humanity so educated that the differences among people that now precipitate conflict are put into perspective, so trained that their psychic energies are more positively directed. This is what Gandhi must have meant when he said, "The structure of a world federation can be raised only on a foundation of non-violence."[49]

Gandhi was a prescient thinker. It is not surprising that the land of Shankara, Nagarjuna, and, in our own age, Chandrashekar and Ramanujan could produce a brilliant theorist in the area of world order. But Gandhi was much more and much less than a theorist; he never developed his theories as an intellectual would, in writing, without putting them into practice. It takes some acumen to derive out of his simple language and its concrete, everyday frame of reference the outlines of a brilliant theory on world order, but it is worthwhile to do just that. Millions join Einstein in believing that the Mahatma was a saint, far in advance of most of mankind in his ethical vision and power. However that may be, I have tried to show that he ranks as one of the great utopian thinkers of all time, and no one who wishes to avoid the dangers and realize the opportunities of the end of this millennium can afford not to take his thought and his achievement seriously.

Discussion

Commentator Lawrence Chickering endorsed Michael Nagler's association of the increasing size of social organization—from the *oikos* to the *polis* to the nation-state in seventeenth-century Europe—with the polarization or "enemy" definition that has set people against each other. He also pointed out the arresting paradox that the increasing concern for world order through the ages has been accompanied not by world order and peace, but by increasing polarization and war. Chickering suggested that advancing consciousness of the subjective self is the primary differentiating force underlying both the centuries-old movement away from small, personal forms of social organization to increasingly impersonal forms and the increasing polarization among people.

Summarizing Nagler's criticism of traditional world order theorists who focus only on the external manifestations of order while ignoring the qualities of spirit that make the external manifestations possible, Chickering explained why world order theorizing has yielded so little: the decline of the traditional forms of political, social, and psychological order has exhausted the spiritual and moral capital that sustained a sense of internal peace in earlier times.

Chickering contrasted the responses of modern conservatives and liberals to this state of affairs. Conservatives, seeing the consequences that have attended the decline of tradition, say the only conclusion is to respect tradition more—go back to it. Liberals say the traditions were corrupt, and they generally embark on ambitious new projects, usually in the form of large concentrations of government power. Nagler's approach, which Chickering endorsed, is to emphasize the importance of spirit and to call for regenerating a healthy spirit, which will, in turn, deliver order and secure the peace. The need, he says, is to "promote two values essential to human fulfillment which present themselves as a paradox: on the one hand, the free development of each individual; on the other, the meaninglessness of individual life without compact unlimited association with the whole." Chickering called the need to integrate freedom and order—in Nagler's terms, to work for unity in diversity—the central dilemma of modernity and said it was a natural consequence of the process of advancing consciousness of the self. Until this problem is solved, he said, the polarizing, differentiating processes of modernity will intensify.

Chickering said that although Nagler's analysis appeared abstract, the analysis can be an important guide to policy. For example, the analysis implicitly explains the special role that has been cast for the United States to play in world affairs. In broadest terms, this role is to be strong, a force for balance, but the United States cannot begin to fulfill its role in promoting peace without a real, bipartisan foreign policy. To be strong, the United States must be united, Chickering said, because strong policy must have a chance for continuity and predictability—things that are simply impossible in the present political environment.

Chickering questioned Nagler's reliance on Gandhi at two points in the discussion: in his embrace of Gandhi for holding the key to the solution of the paradox of integrating freedom and order and for his including nonviolence as a requirement complementary to integrating freedom and order in developing a new approach to order and peace.

Chickering said he saw no solution to the paradox of freedom and order in Eastern philosophies, which deny the ego and treat it as an illusion. The integration of individualism and values beyond the self is a problem because modern individualism has made it so.

Chickering also complained that Nagler's consideration of violence was somewhat hard to follow because he has two definitions of violence, one subjective ("that which inhibits the fulfillment of a human being") and the other objective (any action that results in physical harm to a person). Chickering said that his subjective definition is the only one consistent with Nagler's emphasis on spirit throughout the rest of his paper.

But a more fundamental problem, Chickering said, is this: having explained why violence has increased over the ages, Nagler abandons his logic, perhaps terrified by its implications, and retreats to throw nonviolence in with unity in diversity. He thus appears to abandon hope that a pure heart will deliver peace. Chickering suggested that the most interesting issue raised here is what uses of force are appropriate for someone who, for reasons implicit in this paper, sees fear and therefore aggression all around him.

In the general discussion, Goshu Wolde asked how the academic community foresees the evolution of the world's economic, social, security, and political systems. He also wondered how the superpowers are expected to react to the possible restructuring of the current security arrangements—away from the bipolar system that has maintained the sustained peace in postwar Europe and toward a multipolar, multicultural, and vigorously competitive new world order.

Nagler challenged Wolde's assertion that the bifurcation of the world into superpower blocs has been the primary reason a devastating war has not taken place in postwar Europe. Nagler argued that it is important to determine not only how peace has been maintained, but whether it is the kind of peace we desire for the future. Clearly, the present system is preferable to nuclear war, Nagler said, but he questioned whether bloc confrontation characterized by suspicion, terror, and social disintegration is the kind of peace we want. Nagler added that no all-inclusive and shared vision of the future exists among scholars.

Nagler said the question about how the superpowers will react to a shift from bi- to multipolarity was particularly important. How the United States will deal with the shift to a polycentric world will depend heavily on how the American people are culturally prepared for that shift. If the transition is communicated in such a fashion that it can be interpreted as America "losing" a high degree of prestige or power, it will most likely be fiercely resisted.

Chickering agreed that the traditional yardstick of American economic and military power has been pegged to the artificially high measure of both that the United States enjoyed immediately following World War II. The closer balance that exists today is much more reflective of the natural, symbiotic relationship that should exist among liberal democratic allies, yet still below the level of near-parity that multipolarity implies. The transition to real multipolarity, Chickering said, is inevitable and need not result in a dissipation of America's leadership role. But that relationship will increasingly depend less on American hardware and more on the vitality of the American spirit.

Alberto Coll challenged the last statement. The major reason the past forty-five years of Pax Americana has been successful, Coll said, is the international balance of power secured by American hardware. If there is a precipitous decline in the level of that hardware, there will most likely be a reciprocal decline in the West's ability to maintain the peace.

Chickering agreed that U.S. military capabilities are, and should continue to be, a major guarantor of the peace. In fact, he said, U.S. military preparedness was a major factor in the Soviet Union's decision to pursue the policy of glasnost. However, as the transition to a multipolar world becomes more of a reality, other nations' military capabilities will, by definition, take over some of the responsibilities now held by the United States.

Coll asked whether the humane and nurturing peace that Nagler covets might result from a coalition of like-minded, value-integrated, liberal capitalist states gaining a preponderance of power in the international system. Nagler responded that he believed we must move toward a world in which the power to support, to sustain, to nurture will be held in higher regard than the power to destroy.

Noting what he saw as a lack of prescriptive analysis in Nagler's paper, Edward Luck asked how humanity can make the transition from its present state to Nagler's more ideal condition. Nagler responded that the goal of the paper was to identify a major roadblock to achieving a more peaceful world and to suggest a conceptual framework to circumvent that roadblock. Chickering added that one practical application of Nagler's approach is that it reveals the possibility that the disagreements that erupt in the policy community over what constitute proper policy "ends" are more accurately described as divisions over the proper "means."

In conclusion, panel chairman Bruce Weinrod summarized four major drawbacks of Nagler's approach:

1. It fails to take into account the asymmetrical problems of application between open and closed societies. A closed or totalitarian society committed to the destruction of open democracies would be vastly more capable of that destruction if those democracies adopted Nagler's approach.

2. The role that Nagler sees for intermediate institutions, namely, serving the state, is precisely the opposite of the role that such institutions are meant to play, which is protecting against the state's usurpations of individual freedom. When one is put into the service of the other, personal freedom is sacrificed.

3. Voluntary utopian schemes such as Nagler's ultimately face the problem that certain persons will not want to participate in the process. What usually happens is that the few "renegades" are compelled to join, and once again personal freedoms are sacrificed.

4. If one believes that human beings are imperfect and that evil is an unchangeable fact of life, the only realistic goal is to seek to contain and manage unauthorized international violence. Ultimate and abstract nonviolent utopias are worthy of theoretical aspiration, but of little else.

Notes

1. Saint Augustine, *City of God* (Civitas Dei), XIX.13.

2. Qu'ran V.35. Interestingly enough, the Talmud states, "He who saves one life saves a whole world." *Mishue*, Sanhedrin, 37 A.

3. Augustine, *City of God*, XIX.12–ca.23. Abridged translation (useful but out of print): Gerald G. Walh et al. (New York: Doubleday, Image, 1958).

4. This is my translation and emphasis. The now-famous definition reads *pax est omnium rerum tranquilitas ordinis*. For reasons that will become clear later, we may compare a modern biologist's comment on the evolution of multicellular organisms: "This...step required, first and foremost, controls for the subordination of parts on behalf of the whole." See Robert B. Livingston, *Sensory Processing, Perception and Behavior* (New York: Raven, 1978), p. 6.

5. Myres S. McDougal, in chapter 6 of this volume, arrives at exactly the same conclusion regarding minimal or optimal definitions for peace and human rights.

6. As I prepared this chapter, I learned from *New Options* 52 (October, 1988) that a Committee for a Just World Peace had been formed by Saul Mendlovitz and Gerald and Patricia Mische, among others, to reinvigorate peace and world order studies along the lines I suggest. For more information contact the Committee for a Just World Peace, 777 United Nations Plaza, Fifth Floor, New York, NY 10017.

7. Heinrich Schneider, "Friedensverständniss in Vergangenheit und Gegenwart," in R. Weiler and V. Zsifkovits, eds., *Unterwegs zum Frieden* (Vienna: Herder, 1973), p. 149.

8. Johan Galtung, "Violence, Peace, and Peace Research," *Journal of Peace Research* 6, no. 3 (1969): pp. 167–91.

9. H. C. Baldry, *The Unity of Mankind in Greek Thought* (Cambridge: Cambridge University Press, 1965).

10. Augustine, *City of God*, XIX.11.

11. Louis Gernet, "The City of the Future and the Land of the Dead," in *The Anthropology of Ancient Greece*, trans. John Hamilton and Blaise Nagy (Baltimore, Md.: Johns Hopkins University Press, 1968), pp. 112–24.

12. Hedley Bull, *The Anarchical Society: A Study of Order in World Politics* (New York: Columbia University Press, 1977).

13. This is Galtung's "dissociative/direct violence" rubric, the weakest level of peace generation. See Johan Galtung, "Peace Theory: An Introduction," in E. Lazlo and J. Y. Yoo, eds., *World Encyclopedia of Peace* (Oxford: Pergamon, 1986), pp. 251–60.

14. Richard A. Posner, "Homer's Version of the Minimal State," *Ethics* 90 (1979): pp. 27–47 and Moses Finley, *The World of Odysseus* (New York: Viking, Compass, 1965).

15. Emile Benveniste, *Le vocabulaire des institutions Indo-Européennes* (Paris: Minuit, 1969), p. 95.

16. Jacqueline de Romilly, "Guerre et paix entre cités," in J. P. Vernant, ed., *Problèmes de la guerre en grèce ancienne* (The Hague: Mouton, 1968), pp. 207–20. Need I point out the parallel to our own strategic dilemma, which differs only in scale?

17. See David Mitrany, *A Working Peace System* (Chicago: Quadrangle, 1966); Leopold Kohr, *The Breakdown of Nations* (New York: Dutton, 1978); and Kirkpatrick Sale, *Human Scale* (New York: Putnam, 1982).

18. Michael N. Nagler, "Toward a Semantics of Ancient Conflict: ERIS in the Iliad," *Classical World* 82, no. 2 (1988): pp. 81–90.

19. Gerald and Patricia Mische, *Toward a Human World Order* (New York: Paulist, 1977).

20. There are several "islands" of world order in the global system already: Kenneth E. Boulding's "Triangles of Stable Peace," in Kenneth E. Boulding, *Stable Peace* (Austin, Tex.: University of Texas, 1978), p. 65 and ch. 2, generally; the Treaty of Raratonga (1985) which, with adjacent territories, declares 40 percent of the earth's surface nuclear-free zones—zones of formal transnational cooperation identified by Galtung and comprising eight hundred million inhabitants. These zones could "spread" but not without the evolution of peace culture to elicit the dynamism and desire to acknowledge and use them as such; in nonviolence theory, there is almost more of an opportunity for peace and order in the trouble spots, if conversion began within them.

21. Galtung, *World Encyclopedia of Peace*, p.259.

22. Quincy Wright, *A Study of War*, 2 vols. (Chicago: University of Chicago Press, 1965), p. 1043.

23. Augustine, XIX. 12. (emphasis added). See also XII.28, "There is nothing so social by nature, and so anti-social by sin, as man" and the famous observation of Einstein: "A human being is part of a whole, called by us the universe," in which subglobal identity is called "a kind of prison" (for full text and discussion, see Michael N. Nagler, *America Without Violence* [Covelo, Calif.: Island, 1982], p. 11.)

24. An extreme case of that polarization has been termed by ethologist Irenäus Eibl-Eibesfeldt "pseudo-speciation" conceptualizing people as nonhuman (See Irenäus Eibl-Eibesfeldt, *The Biology of Peace and War* [New York: Viking, 1979]). That it harms even the polarizer is evidenced by the intuition we all share: human dignity is bound up with human unity. As Gandhi said, "I have never understood how one human being can think he has gained by the humiliation of another."

25. Bruce M. Knauft, "Reconsidering Violence in Simple Human Societies: Homicide Among the Gebusi of New Guinea," *Current Anthropology* 28, no. 4 (1987): pp. 457–500.

26. Geoffrey Blainey's *The Causes of War* (New York: Macmillan, 1973) is a good example of how poorly single-factor analysis explains war.

27. Anthropologists have documented any number of "peaceful societies" (Matthew Melko, *52 Peaceful Societies* [Oakville, Ontario: Canadian Peace Research Institute, 1973]) that fell apart on contact with the larger, "civilized" world, often becoming more violent than the latter. This illustrates well the sawtoothed rhythm of social evolution, whereby what has been gained is sometimes partly lost on advances to a higher level of organization. I only argue here that now that advances can be made more consciously, they should be done with minimal brutality and loss of progress.

28. See S. J. Hemleben, *Plans for World Peace Through Six Centuries* (Chicago: University of Chicago Press, 1943) and W. Warren Wagar, *The City of Man* (Baltimore, Md.: Penguin, 1967), p. 40.

29. The only exceptions to the European tradition were Emeric Crucé and, implicitly, Kant. The role of the pagan chaos demon, of course, shifted to different players, but the ideology remained. For a much earlier example (the Attic orator Gorgias), see Baldry, *The Unity of Mankind*, p. 43. Note also that President François Mitterrand recently called for a stronger Europe to be united against the economic infidels across the Iron Curtain: can he be aware that he is perpetuating the error of his compatriot almost eight hundred years ago? Of course, many others, from Goethe to Einstein, have thought of "European" as a model of federation open to a progressively wider global community. Today that seems nearer the truth.

30. Or, as Girard later said, the conceptualization of *un dehors humain de toute société humaine* ("a human outgroup outside of all human society"). See René Girard, *Des choses cachées depuis la fondation du monde*, pp. 151, 466. Happily, this profound study of the contemporary condition and its deep historical roots has been translated by Michael Meteer and Stephen Bann (Palo Alto, Calif.: Stanford University Press, 1987). Girard's work illustrates, among other things, the importance of the humanities' contribution to world order thinking.

31. See Hemleben, *Plans for World Peace*. Note that "defenses of peace" assumes that the present condition *is* one of peace—the negative definition.

32. I believe that both Augustine and Kant, by accepting violence only provisionally within a developmental or evolutionary framework, are on Gandhi's spiritual wavelength in this regard, as in others.

33. George Orwell, "A Hanging," in *The Collected Essays, Journals, and Letters of George Orwell*, ed. Ian Angus and Sonya Orwell (London: Secker and Warburg, 1968), p. 46. Expressed positively in almost identical language in the Talmud and the Qur'an (V.35) is the expression, "Whoever saves a single life, [it is as though] he saves the whole world."

34. An excellent representation in fiction is Ursula LeGuin, "Those Who Walked Away From Omelas," in *New Dimensions*, vol. 3, ed. Robert Silverberg (New York: Signet, 1973), pp. 1–7. I understand that there is a Maoist conundrum, "If you could redress all social injustice by taking the life of one innocent child, should you do it?" To accept the terms of the question itself is to accept the sacrificial, pro-violent order.

35. On the paradox of a "memory" of the divine future, see Saint Augustine, *Confessions*, X.18. In a similar vein, a close associate of Gandhi's refers matter-of-factly to "the liberation of human unity" as something imminent; see A. Aranyanayakam, *Gandhi the Teacher* (Bombay: Bharatiya Vidya Bhavan, 1966), p. 2.

36. In Augustine's day, *amare* (to love) often had the connotation "to seek after," "to want," while *deligere* meant simply "to like" or "to love." Incidentally, we must distinguish between his view and classical dualism, for example, Jewish or Manichaean. For Augustine, the bedrock reality is one (and entirely good); see *Confessions* VII; and *City of God*, XIX.13 (exactly Gandhi's understanding of ultimate reality or truth, *satya*); see especially Gandhi, *Satyagraha in South Africa* (Madras: Triplicane, 1928), p. 433. It is only the world process, and underlying it the struggle in every human being between separateness and unity, that exhibits dualism. Thus the consciousness of the saint is an important exception: in the saint, all driving force has been converted or (in this view) restored to good.

37. An important example of the difference was Gandhi's acceptance of the caste system as an indigenous arrangement with certain legitimate uses, even while he spent his life fighting its misuse in categorizing persons hierarchically or polarizing them into "high" and "low," "in" and "out."

38. Note also the Hindu concept of *svadharma*, or one's own "natural law." As the Gita has it, "Better your own dharma, imperfectly performed, than another's carried off skillfully; better to die in the performance of your own dharma, so dangerous is someone else's" (III.35, my translation).

39. R. K. Prabhu and U. R. Rao, eds., *The Mind of Mahatma Gandhi* (Ahmedabad: Navajivan, 1967), p. 372. J. S. Mathur, the noted economist and editor of *Gandhi Marg*, has come to the same conclusion regarding the importance of Gandhi's apparently simple model of concentric circles.

40. On the centrality of self-realization (and its nonconflict with the common weal) in Gandhi's philosophy, see Arne Naess, *Gandhi and Group Conflict* (Oslo: Universitetsforlaget, 1974). This focus guarantees that we are not talking about blind devotion that is really an extension rather than an elimination of egoism and in which the will is mesmerized rather than mobilized. Psychologically, blind devotion to the state is probably a substitute for belonging to a tribe or village that is absent from modern industrial life.

41. Prabhu and Rao, *The Mind of Mahatma Gandhi*, p. 136.

42. On the unreality of "race" see Ashley Montagu, *The Concept of Race* (New York: Glencoe Free Press, 1964); for "tribe" and the like, see Colin Renfrew in J. Friedman and M. J. Rowlands, *The Evolution of Social Systems* (Pittsburgh, Pa.: University of Pittsburgh, 1977); in the same way, David I. Kertzer, *Ritual, Politics and Power* (New Haven, Conn.: Yale University Press, 1988) makes quite clear the construct nature (or what Richard Barnet once called the "mystique") of the nation-state.

43. We might say that if Western civilization has "at millennial intervals" tried organizing itself as a world empire, world church, and world federation, what was implicit in Gandhi's scheme (and almost explicit in Augustine's *City of God*, XIX.18) was the one notion we haven't tried: a world family.

44. Ivan Illich, "Delinking Peace and Development," *Alternatives* 7 (1981): pp. 409–16.

45. Galtung, *Journal of Peace Research* 6.

46. The phrase I have in mind is *Ama deum et fac quod velis* (Love God, and do what you want).

47. Is "world order" an adequate term for this need? Perhaps something like "human family order" or "earthly community" should replace it.

48. Kirby Page, *War: Its Causes, Consequences, and Cure* (New York: Doran, 1923), p. 191.

49. D.G. Tendulkar, *Mahatma: The Life of Mohandas Karamchand Gandhi* (New Delhi: Government of India, Publications Division, 1953), p. 158. He added, "The Congress...believes that true democracy can only be the outcome of non-violence. I do not believe in the possibility of establishing world peace through violence as the English and American statesmen propose to do."

Introduction to Chapter 16

At the conference banquet in honor of the participants, Ambassador Max Kampelman closed the proceedings with a mixed tone of optimism and caution. In his remarks, Kampelman encompassed ideas that had been touched on by all those in attendance. He reiterated the sentiment that "peace is not merely the absence of war," as he expressed the need to move beyond pacifism toward a peace qualified by "freedom, justice and the rule of law." He also took up such issues as "just war," the role of the pacifist versus the "moral architect," and the relationship of deterrence to peace. Kampelman concluded optimistically by encouraging all human beings to seek higher ideals and to aspire toward "genuine" peace.

Yet Kampelman's comments were distinguished from other participants' by a note of caution about ideology. Pointing to the Soviet Union, he acknowledged that the changes in that country should be recognized as a sign that the new Soviet leaders are "increasingly aware of its weaknesses and our strengths," but he warned that we must never lose sight of the "moral and practical differences between a dictatorship and a democracy."

Kampelman spoke of the pursuit of peace as a worthy, and even necessary, endeavor. But he offered a sober prescription for its achievement: the pursuit of peace must be accompanied by a keen sense of realism about the dangers of the international system—specifically, the dangers of repressive political systems that deny freedom. At the center of a genuine and desirable peace lie the very values that are denied by such regimes. Therefore, he cautioned, "we must maintain our vigilance, in order to maintain our values"—in order to achieve peace.

16. Beyond Pacifism Toward Peace

Max M. Kampelman

I was in my late teens, a college student, when I began reading and studying Gandhi, Tolstoy, Nehru, Shridharani, Thoreau, Richard Gregg, A. J. Muste, Evan and Norman Thomas. Pacifism had a strong appeal to the only son of a mother whose dearest brother had been killed in World War I, a draftee in the Austrian army. "Wars will cease when men refuse to fight" was the slogan justifying our conscientious objection. "Someday they'll give a war and nobody will come," wrote Carl Sandburg. Ethics and humanity and, yes, religion provided the unifying principles for moral behavior.

My school years had included Judaic studies. Each of us learns different lessons from schools, churches, family, experiences. My exposure taught me that the essence of Judaism could be found in a few words, words that Jewish martyrs cried out in prayer as they faced punishment for their beliefs: "Hear, oh Israel, the Lord our God, the Lord is One." If there is only one God, and monotheism was integral to the faith of the ancient Hebrew tribes, then aren't we all children of that one God and thus brothers and sisters to one another? Whether we were black or white, Jew or Christian, German or American, how could we engage in killing one another?

Much has been said about peace as the indispensable ingredient for the evolution of man from the species homo sapiens to the species "human being." And yet, there is the peace of the grave; the peace that reigns in a well-disciplined prison or gulag; the peace that may plant, with its terms, the seeds of a future war. Is peace synonymous with the absence of war? Is that an adequate definition for what our poets and dreamers have sought?

The discussion of war since the beginning of time has, in the main, been an ethical one. How does one justify the killings that take place in war? From Thucydides to Tolstoy to Churchill, this has been a recurring and dominant theme. Wars could not just be fought or won; except for those people like Bismarck, who asked, "Do I want war? Of course not, I want victory," man has tried to give moral meaning to the tragedy of war and the search for peace.

Ancient Greek philosophers accepted war as a necessary part of nature; Heraclitus said that "all things come into being and pass away through strife." Acceptance of war as a reality of our nature was also basic to early Christian writers. Thomas Aquinas regarded peace as the greatest of man's objectives, but he acknowledged a duty to defend the state. Theologians have long debated the concept of "just war." Thomas Hobbes asserted war to be part of nature, although he held out hope that the establishment of a single government with authority over all could abolish fighting. The views of philosophers such as Nietzsche, who glorified war as an instrument for refining the human race, also have had great influence on our history.

During the fifth century A.D., Saint Augustine considered the problem of how to reconcile Christian teaching with the use of violence, given the need to protect the Roman Empire from the Vandals. He posited a bystander observing a criminal attacking an innocent victim and concluded that the bystander had a right to protect the victim, using only the minimal force necessary to deter the criminal. The solution he reached had two important elements that remain in Western culture: first, that force—and by extension, war—may well be justified in some circumstances; and second, given that justification, there must be limitations governing the use and type of force.

Justification exists when there is "just cause," defined by Saint Augustine as intervention to protect the innocent; by Thomas Aquinas, to punish wrongdoers; for others, simply the notion of defense. Modern-day international law, reflected in the UN Charter, embraces the "inherent right of individual or collective self-defense."

There is a related question. If war is to be justified, must it not be authorized by a proper authority so that unrestrained warfare can be controlled? For war to be "right," there must be a "right authority"—a prince, a state. Control introduces the principle of proportionality. Lethal force should not be used against a criminal or aggressor if less force will suffice. Proportionality also suggests that force used in a just cause be directed only at those who perpetrate the injustice, not at innocent noncombatants. The issue is all the more real and difficult with the advances in modern technology.

Today, in a profound way, modern technology enters the discourse—and it must. Even before the full impact of nuclear weapons could be felt, Reinhold Niebuhr noted that "we have come into the tragic position of developing a form of destruction which, if used by our enemies against us, would mean our physical annihilation; and, if used by us against our enemies, would mean our moral annihilation." He noted "a moral dilemma for which there is no clear moral solution."

Two main moral approaches to war have been taken by those who make up the peace movements. Father Bryan Hehir of the U.S. Catholic Conference has described them as the position of the pacifist or the moral abolitionist, and the position of the moral architect. "The abolitionists sought to exorcise war, to expunge it from human history," through conscientious objection, nonviolent opposition to evil, and personal testimony. In that way, war would not be a part of their lives or the life of the society in which they lived. The moral architects, in contrast, "sought to build a moral framework in which war could be contained, restrained and, even though it stretches the imagination to think it could be, humanized."

Seeking to balance competing values, they accepted the legitimacy of force and its presence in human history. Persuaded that the eradication of war would require a change in human nature as well as structural political change, they were prepared to accept a more immediate remedy, a framework that justified some use of force, all within the moral universe.

The pacifist meets—some would say, avoids—the Niebuhr dilemma by declaring an absolute principle. War, he says, is a greater evil than any evil it would seek to correct. At this point, variations appear. For some, this principle is enough. It justifies yielding to the lesser evil in the faith that history or a higher moral authority will, in the end, set things straight. Regrettably, this perspective is also too often accompanied by a reluctance to accept unpleasant realities through a rationalization that the purported enemy or adversary is not evil at all. Thus, the sad alliance of many pacifists with politically motivated cadres who told us that Hitler was only reflecting rightful German grievances; or that the brutal excesses of Stalin and Mao were simply capitalist exaggerations; or that North Vietnam was seeking to unify and not subjugate the peninsula; or that the Sandinistas are idealistic liberals rather than totalitarian Communists. Thus, a "peace at almost any price" evolves. French President Mitterrand had this phenomenon in mind with his sardonic comment some years ago that the Soviet Union produces weapons while the West produces pacifists.

Other pacifists, symbolized by Gandhi, recognize the high moral duty to challenge and attempt to defeat evil. Their premise is that war does not serve that end. Instead, they focus on the power of love and nonviolent resistance to evil. Human beings, they argue, created in the image of God, have the capacity to respond more to the human force of love and conscience in their fellow human beings than to coercion and hate, which perpetuate conflict. As Abraham Lincoln, a champion of peace but not a pacifist, put it, the best way to defeat an enemy is to turn him into a friend. But Lincoln did conclude that a war, a costly one, was necessary to preserve the Union. Modern technology has undermined and bypassed the power of love by depersonalizing and automating the process of war, thereby destroying the opportunity for human beings to test the impact of their love on other human beings whom they do not see. Armed adversaries in modern war never see their victims. An individual has a right to suffer martyrdom for principle, but not to condemn others to that same fate. Here it is important to remember with Clausewitz that "the aggressor is always peaceloving. He would like to make his entry into our country undisturbed." The Russian proverb goes, "Make yourself into a sheep, and you'll meet a wolf nearby."

Human society, therefore, looks beyond pacifism for the peace with freedom we all seek. We have yet to find the way, but "the moral architects" continue their effort.

Nonintervention historically has had appeal. It was John Stuart Mill, however, who pierced the balloon of simplicity when he wrote,

The doctrine of nonintervention, to be a legitimate principle of morality, must be accepted by all governments. The despots must consent to be bound by it as well as the free States. Unless they do, the profession of it by free countries comes but to this miserable issue, that the wrong side may help the wrong, but the right must not help the right.

For many, however, the doctrine of nonintervention remains a comfort.

The policy of deterrence is appealing as consistent with the moral requirements of "just war." Deterrence, a defensive posture, meets a primary requirement of just war, even though it does not necessarily meet the requirements that the action be proportional and that innocent noncombatants be immune. Yet deterrence can work only in conjunction with a credible threat to engage in war in the event of attack. Therefore, at the strategic nuclear level, deterrence deliberately skates close to the edge of violence. What undermines this criticism, of course, is that it seems to be working. Deterrence has not led to mass, indiscriminate destruction. Rather, it has achieved stability. Michael Walzer, in discussing the ethics of nuclear peace, writes,

> Supreme emergency has become a permanent condition. Deterrence is a way of coping with that condition, and though it is a bad way, there may well be no other that is practical in a world of sovereign and suspicious states. We threaten evil in order not to do it, and the doing of it would be so terrible, that the threat seems in comparison to be morally defensible.

We continue to look for other and perhaps better alternatives to assure peace with dignity. The SDI is an alternative that must here be addressed. It is defensive in intent. It does not violate the requirements of proportionality and noncombatant immunity. With our SDI program, we are investigating whether we can strengthen deterrence through an increased ability to create effective defenses and thereby deny and deter aggressors from their objectives. People ask of their governments that they be protected from attack, not that their government be able only to avenge them after the attack. The possibility is a real one that defensive technologies, cost-effective at the margin and preferably nonnuclear, can be created.

The search, furthermore, is not ours alone. The Soviet Union has for many years been actively building up its defensive capabilities. It has the most comprehensive air defense system in the world; and it has spent enormous resources on passive defenses to protect its leadership, command and control system, industry, and population. It possesses the only operational antiballistic missile system in the world, which it has just modernized. It possesses the only operational antisatellite system in the world; and it was the first to destroy a satellite in space. The Soviets, furthermore, as General Secretary Gorbachev has acknowledged, are proceeding with an intensified program of research on their own version of SDI.

We will continue with our SDI research program, because it is not in our interest to permit the Soviets to have the field of strategic defense all to themselves. It would be highly imprudent for any American president not to pursue such an investigation with vigor. A coordinated effort, if one can be negotiated and devised, holds promise for greater stability and peace through mutual security.

Current U.S. policy is, furthermore, to reduce risks and tensions while maintaining the strategy of deterrence. We are negotiating to achieve verifiable reductions in nuclear arms, with numbers designed to enhance stability at lower levels of military forces. Simultaneously, we are engaged in a process to build realistic, constructive, and more cooperative relations with the Soviet Union. This effort calls for elaboration.

We have no illusions about the nature of the Soviet Union. The tensions that have characterized our relationship with the Soviet Union are real. Our differences are not based on mutual misunderstandings. To say that they are is a misleading, naive, and patronizing oversimplification. Soviet leaders are not crude peasants who need some reassurance about how well-intentioned we are. Our problems are too profound to be thought of as being resolved by quick fixes, super negotiators, a summit, or a master draftsman capable of devising language to overcome differences. The leadership of the Soviet Union is serious. Its diplomats are serious and well trained. Their response in a negotiation is motivated by one primary consideration: their perceived national self-interest.

The fundamental challenge to the free world is a principle that has governed Soviet international behavior: everything that has become Communist remains forever inviolate; everything that is not Communist is open to change by pressure, subversion, even terror. Gorbachev regrettably reaffirmed this dangerous Leninist principle in 1987 when he proclaimed in Warsaw that "socialist gains are irreversible" and warned that an effort to "undermine" the "international . . . socialist community" would threaten peace. And yet, in 1988 the Soviets finally began withdrawing their troops from Afghanistan—with bravado, but a pullback nevertheless.

No regime can be permitted to propagate its faith with the sword. A Soviet Union that desires to enter the twenty-first century as a respected and secure member of the international community must reject its old faith that the "irreconcilability" of our two systems means the "inevitability" of war and repudiate violence as the instrument to achieve its vision of a new society.

The Soviet Union is the last remaining empire of our day. Its empire consists of former states now absorbed within Soviet geopolitical boundaries, as well as states in different parts of the world over which it exercises control. But imperialism comes with a high price tag. The West learned that the price is too high. The Soviet elite may be reaching that conclusion as its

Third World clients become dependencies lining up for handouts. It is estimated that Vietnam costs the Soviets more than $3.5 billion annually; Cuba, $4.9 billion; Angola, Mozambique, and Ethiopia, $3 billion; and Nicaragua, close to $1 billion. The total cost to the Soviets may well reach more than $35 million a day.

The Soviet economy is working poorly, although it does provide a fully functioning military machine. Massive military power has provided the Soviets with a presence that reaches all parts of the world, but this military superpower cannot hide the fact that its economic and social weaknesses have Third World characteristics. The Soviet's awesome internal police force has provided continuity to its system of governance, but a Russia which, during Czarist days, exported food cannot today feed its own people. And no police can keep out the ideas and developments that are communicated by satellite to all parts of the world, any more than it can by fiat insulate the Soviet Union from the wind currents that circle our globe.

The economic growth rate of the Soviet Union is down to virtually zero; its standard of living is sinking; productivity is dropping. With absenteeism, corruption, and alcoholism widespread, internal morale is bad. Contrary to trends elsewhere in the world, life expectancy for Russian men is actually decreasing. It is estimated that a worker in the Soviet Union must work more than seven times as many hours as a Western European to earn enough money to buy a car.

The new leaders of the Soviet Union are fully aware of its problems. I suspect they are also aware of our strengths, reflecting the vitality of our values and the healthy dynamism of our system. It is increasingly evident to all that there are moral and practical differences between a dictatorship and democracy, even as both are powerful nuclear powers, just as there are differences between a prison yard and a meadow. In the past five years, we have seen 15 million new jobs created in the United States, a drop of five percentage points in our unemployment rate to its lowest level in eight years, a 17–percent increase in per capita gross national product, and a reduced inflation rate, which had been at double digits, to around 4 percent annually for the past six years. We have every reason to be proud of our system and of the human values that govern it.

Democracy works best. A closed, tightly controlled society tied in knots by a repressive bureaucratic system cannot compete in a world in which economic development and the power it produces are all important. Rapid technological change, stimulated by an information explosion that knows no national boundaries, requires the vitality that comes from freedom. Over the long term, human liberty, democracy, and economic well-being are inescapably linked.

We hope the time is at hand when Soviet authorities, looking at the energy of the West, comprehend that repressive societies in our day cannot achieve economic health, inner stability, or true security. We hope the leadership of the Soviet Union will come fully to accept that it is in its best interest to permit a humanizing process to take place. We hope it has come to understand the need to show the rest of us that cruelty is not indispensable to its system. We hope the ruling elite today realizes that its historic aim of achieving communism through violence has no place in this nuclear age. We hope Soviet authorities will join us in making the commitment that our survival as a civilization depends on the mutual realization that we must live under rules of responsible international behavior. We hope—but as yet we, regrettably, cannot trust.

But even as we cannot yet trust, we have a responsibility to ourselves to observe developments in the Soviet Union carefully and to do so with open eyes, an open mind, and an open heart. There have been changes within the Soviet Union. Gorbachev has shown himself in a dramatic way willing to reconsider past views. The words "glasnost" and "perestroika" have been repeated so extensively that the ideas they represent may well take on a meaning and dynamism of their own that could become internally irreversible. The political rehabilitation of Bukharin, a Communist party leader executed by Stalin in the 1930s, is of profound symbolic significance. It opens for discussion the very sensitive topic of Stalin's legacy. It also helps Gorbachev legitimate for today the principle of economic incentives that Bukharin himself favored in earlier times in the Soviet Union.

We are told that Gorbachev has internal difficulties and rivalries, with neither "reformers" nor their opponents able to gain a decisive victory and break a current stalemate. That may or may not be. It is good, however, to remind ourselves of Tocqueville's dictum that the most dangerous time for an authoritarian regime is when it begins to reform itself.

It is also a time when we must maintain our vigilance, in order to maintain our values. We must not forget that on two previous occasions we reached what seemed to be significant positive milestones in our relations with the Soviets, only to lose ground due to regional conflicts. In 1963, we signed an agreement with the Soviet Union banning nuclear tests in the atmosphere. President Kennedy called this agreement a "shaft of light" in the darkness, and some believed it marked the end of the Cold War. But not many months later, the Soviet client state, North Vietnam, began its aggression, and we were at war.

Again, in the early 1970s, "détente" with the Soviet Union was marked by the signing of SALT I and other arms control agreements. Again, regional conflicts—Soviet support for aggression against Israel, Angola, Ethiopia, Yemen, and, finally, and most chillingly, the Soviet invasion of Afghanistan—destroyed whatever was left of "détente." Today, we try again. The changes taking place within the Soviet Union seem to be real and are greatly encouraging. But having spent time talking to the Nicaraguan freedom fighters and internal opposition leaders, and visiting the democracies in Guatemala, San Salvador, Costa Rica, and Honduras, I urge that, as long as the Soviets continue to destabilize and undermine democracy in Central America, we must not lower our guard.

For us, peace is not merely the absence of war. A genuine and desirable peace is, to paraphrase Niebuhr, built only on the foundation of justice, freedom, and the rule of law. Our values are at the center of it all. The Nobel Committee shared this insight when it awarded the late Andrei Sakharov the Nobel Peace Prize.

All of us and our societies fall short of our aspirations. We grow by stretching to reach them. As we do so, however, let us be reassured by the conviction that the future lies with freedom, because there can be no lasting stability in societies that would deny it. Only freedom can release the constructive energies of men and women to work toward reaching new heights. A human being has the capacity to aspire, to achieve, to dream, and to do. We seek these values for all the children of God. Our task is to stretch ourselves to come closer to that realization. With its realization, we not only find the path to peace, we find peace.

Appendixes
A. Participants in the Intellectual Map Colloquia

Edward E. Azar, Director, Center for International Development, University of Maryland, March 24, 1988

Richard Bilder, Burrus-Bascom Professor of Law, University of Wisconsin-Madison, January 28, 1988

Coit Blacker, Senior Research Associate, Stanford University Arms Control Program, February 19–20, 1987

Lincoln Bloomfield, Professor of Political Science, Massachusetts Institute of Technology, January 28, 1988

Adda Bozeman, Professor Emeritus, Sarah Lawrence College, July 9, 1987

Inis Claude, Professor of Government and Foreign Affairs, University of Virginia, December 5, 1986

Harlan Cleveland, Professor of Public Affairs and Planning, Hubert H. Humphrey Institute of Public Affairs, University of Minnesota, January 28, 1988

Robert Conquest, Senior Research Fellow, Hoover Institution on War, Revolution and Peace, Stanford University, February 19–20, 1987

Anthony D'Amato, Professor, Northwestern University Law School, July 9, 1987

Daniel Druckman, National Academy of Sciences, November 19, 1987

Roger Fisher, Professor, Harvard University Law School, November 19, 1987

Arthur Hartman, Former U.S. Ambassador to the Soviet Union, November 19, 1987

Louis Henkin, Professor, Columbia University School of Law, July 9, 1987

G. Keigh Highet, President, American Society of International Law, July 9, 1987

Sidney Hook, Senior Research Fellow, Hoover Institution on War, Revolution and Peace, Stanford University, February 19–20, 1987

P. Terrence Hopmann, Professor, Brown University, November 19, 1987

Samuel P. Huntington, Director, Harvard University Center for International Affairs, March 5, 1987

James H. Laue, Lynch Professor of Conflict Resolution, George Mason University, March 24, 1988

Richard Ned Lebow, Director, Peace Studies Program, Cornell University, March 24, 1988

Monroe Leigh, Partner, Steptoe and Johnson, July 9, 1987

Edward N. Luttwak, Arleigh Burke Chair of Strategy, Center for Strategic and International Studies, December 5, 1986

Myres McDougal, Professor Emeritus, Yale University School of Law, July 9, 1987

Joseph V. Montville, Research Director, Center for the Study of Foreign Affairs, Foreign Service Institute, U.S. Department of State, March 24, 1988

David Newsom, Director, Institute for the Study of Diplomacy, Georgetown University, November 19, 1987

Robert North, Professor Emeritus, Stanford University, February 19–20, 1987

Robert Pickus, President, World Without War Council, February 19–20, 1987

Craig Ritchie, Board Member, Beyond War Foundation, February 19–20, 1987

Henry Rowen, Professor, Graduate School of Business, Stanford University, February 19–20, 1987

Jeffrey Z. Rubin, Professor, Department of Psychology, Tufts University, January 28, 1988

Robert Scalapino, Director, Institute of East Asian Studies, University of California at Berkeley, February 19–20, 1987

Steven Schwebel, Justice, International Court of Justice, July 9, 1987

Gene Sharp, President, Albert Einstein Institute, December 5, 1986

J. David Singer, Coordinator, World Politics Program, University of Michigan, March 24, 1988

Louis Sohn, Professor, University of Georgia School of Law, December 5, 1986

Helmut Sonnenfeldt, Visiting Scholar, Brookings Institution, November 19, 1987

John Stevenson, Partner, Sullivan and Cromwell, July 9, 1987

Donald Treadgold, Chairman, Russian and East European Studies Department, University of Washington, February 19–20, 1987

Gregory F. Treverton, Kennedy School of Government, Harvard University, March 5, 1987

Brian Urquhart, Scholar in Residence, Ford Foundation, January 28, 1988

Vamik Volkan, Professor of Psychiatry, University of Virginia Medical School, March 24, 1988

Carlos Warter, President, World Health Foundation for Peace, February 19–20, 1987

Charles Wolf, Senior Fellow, RAND Corporation, February 19–20, 1987

Herbert York, Director, Institute on Global Conflict and Cooperation, University of California at San Diego, February 19–20, 1987

I. William Zartman, Professor, Paul H. Nitze School of Advanced International Studies, Johns Hopkins University, November 19, 1987

B. Principal Participants and Attendees in the Airlie House Conference

Participants

Richard Bilder is Burrus-Bascom Professor of Law at the University of Wisconsin-Madison. Educated at Williams College and Harvard University Law School, Professor Bilder was a Fulbright scholar at Cambridge University and also a retired U.S. Navy Commander. He has also served as an attorney in the Office of Legal Adviser at the U.S. Department of State. His areas of expertise include international and foreign relations law, international organizations, admiralty law, contracts, and torts. Among other positions, Professor Bilder has served as vice president of the American Society of International Law, on the Board of Editors of the *American Journal of International Law*, as an arbitrator in international and domestic disputes, and on a number of U.S. delegations to international negotiations. He is the author of *Managing the Risks of International Agreement*.

Elise M. Boulding is professor emerita of Sociology at Dartmouth College and secretary general of the International Peace Research Association. She is a former member of the Governing Council of the United Nations University. Educated at Iowa State College and the University of Michigan, Dr. Boulding was research development secretary at the Center for Research on Conflict Resolution. Dr. Boulding also served as a member of the Commission on Proposals for the National Academy of Peace and Conflict Resolution, whose recommendations helped to shape the United States Institute of Peace. She is a founder of the Consortium on Peace Research, Education, and Development (COPRED) and a member of many international peace organizations. Dr. Boulding has authored a number of books, including *Building a Global Civic Culture: Education for an Interdependent World*; *Underside of History*; and *Bibliography on World Conflict and Peace*.

A. Lawrence Chickering is executive director of the Institute for Contemporary Studies and associate director of the International Center for Economic Growth. Educated at Stanford and Yale universities, he served as associate and assistant to the editor of the *National Review*, and as general counsel and director of research at the California State Office of Economic Opportunity. He is also a member of the Freedom House Advisory Council. Mr. Chickering has edited a number of books on behalf of the Institute for Contemporary Studies, including *Readings in Public Policy*.

Nazli Choucri is professor of political science at the Massachusetts Institute of Technology and associate director of its Technology and Development Program. She is also a faculty associate at the Center for Middle Eastern Studies at Harvard University. Educated at the American University in Cairo and Stanford University, she has held various academic and administrative positions where she specialized in the Middle East, international relations, and foreign policy. Dr. Choucri has published widely, including two recent articles, "Roots of War: the Master Variable" and "Lateral Pressure in International Relations: Concept and Theory."

Juergen Dedring currently serves as senior political officer in the newly created Office for Research and Collection of Information in the United Nations Secretariat. Educated at universities in West Germany, Berlin, and the United States, he holds a doctorate from Harvard University. Dr. Dedring taught at Harvard University and Dartmouth College, then served as research associate at the United Nations Institute for Training and Research (UNITAR), and in 1975, joined the United Nations Secretariat as political affairs officer in the Security Council Department. His 1976 UNITAR book, *Recent Advances in Peace and Conflict Research*, represents his research interests in international peace and security, particularly regarding questions of conflict resolution and prevention.

Roger D. Hansen is Andrew W. Mellon Professor of International Relations at the Paul H. Nitze School of Advanced International Studies, Johns Hopkins University. A Rhodes scholar, educated at Yale, Oxford, Princeton, and Johns Hopkins universities, he has served as a deputy assistant special trade representative and as a senior staff member of the National Security Council. Professor Hansen's publications include *The Politics of Mexican Development; Beyond the North-South Stalemate;* and *Rich and Poor Nations in the World Economy.*

Kenneth M. Jensen is director of the Research and Studies Program at the United States Institute of Peace, where he was previously director of the Grants Program. Dr. Jensen holds degrees in History, Russian, and Soviet Studies from the University of Colorado, University of Wisconsin, and Moscow State University, USSR. His doctoral research and subsequent scholarship has focused on Russian Marxist social and political thought. He is the author of *Beyond Marx and Mach*, and numerous articles, papers, and reviews in the Russian and Soviet field. He is consulting editor for *Studies in Soviet Thought*. Dr. Jensen is also editor (with Fred E. Baumann) of three recently published books on American policy issues: *American Defense Policy and Liberal Democracy; Crime and Punishment: Issues in Criminal Justice;* and *Religion and Politics.*

Max M. Kampelman is a partner in the law firm of Fried, Frank, Harris, Shriver, and Jacobson. He is also chairman of Freedom House, chairman of the Board of Governors of the United Nations Association, and chairman of the Jerusalem Foundation. Ambassador Kampelman formerly served as counselor of the U.S. Department of State and ambassador and head of the U.S. delegation to the negotiations on nuclear and space arms in Geneva. He is a trustee, by presidential appointment, of the Woodrow Wilson International Center for Scholars, where he previously served as chairman. Educated in law and political science at New York University and the University of Minnesota, Ambassador Kampelman has taught at Claremont College and Howard University, among others. He has also served on the governing boards of a number of universities, including the Hebrew University of Jerusalem.

Herbert Kelman is Richard Clarke Cabot Professor of Social Ethics at Harvard University and an executive committee member of Harvard's Center for Science and International Affairs. Educated at Yale University and the recipient of honorary degrees from a number of universities, including Harvard, Dr. Kelman was a lecturer in social psychology at Harvard and a research psychologist at the Center for Research on Conflict Resolution. He is the author of *A Time to Speak: On Human Values and Social Research*, as well as a number of articles in professional journals. Dr. Kelman was recently appointed Jennings Randolph Distinguished Fellow at the

United States Institute of Peace, where he is writing a book tentatively entitled *Interactive Problem Solving: Overcoming the Psychological Barriers to Resolution of International Conflicts.*

Geoffrey Kemp is a senior associate at the Carnegie Endowment for International Peace. Educated at Oxford University and the Massachusetts Institute of Technology, Dr. Kemp served on the faculty of the Fletcher School of Law and Diplomacy, Tufts University, and worked in the U.S. Department of Defense and on the staff of the U.S. Senate Committee on Foreign Relations. He has also served as a special assistant to President Reagan for national security affairs and as senior director for the Near East and South Asia on the National Security Council staff. Dr. Kemp is a founding member of the Committee on Present Danger and is the author or editor of many studies on political-military affairs, including *Projection of Power: Perspectives, Perceptions, and Problems.*

James H. Laue is Lynch Professor of Conflict Resolution at George Mason University; a senior consultant at the Conflict Clinic, Inc.; and vice chair of the National Peace Institute Foundation's Board of Directors. He was vice chair of the Matsunaga Commission that proposed the establishment of the United States Institute of Peace. Educated at the University of Wisconsin and Harvard University, Dr. Laue has held academic and administrative appointments at Washington University, Harvard Medical School, Emory University, Hollins College, and the University of Missouri at St. Louis. He has served in the U.S. Department of Justice Community Relations Service and was director of the Center for Metropolitan Studies before becoming president and executive director of the Conflict Clinic. Dr. Laue has written extensively on conflict resolution, including *Third Men in New Arenas of Conflict.*

Samuel W. Lewis became president of the United States Institute of Peace in November 1987, after thirty-one years as a foreign service officer. He was U.S. ambassador to Israel for eight years, first appointed by President Carter and then reaffirmed by President Reagan. He has become a prominent actor in Arab-Israeli negotiations, including the Camp David Conference, the Egyptian-Israeli Peace Treaty, and U.S. efforts to bring the Israeli invasion of Lebanon to a peaceful conclusion. He previously served as assistant secretary of state for international organization affairs, as deputy director of the Policy Planning staff, as a senior staff member of the National Security Council, as a member of the U.S. Agency for International Development mission to Brazil, and in lengthy assignments in Brazil, Italy, and Afghanistan. After retirement from the State Department in 1985, he was diplomat-in-residence at the Foreign Policy Institute, Johns Hopkins University, and a guest scholar at the Brookings Institution. A graduate of Yale and Johns Hopkins universities, Ambassador Lewis spent a year as a Visiting Fellow at Princeton University.

Edward C. Luck is president of the United Nations Association of the U.S.A. where he has also served as executive vice president and vice president for research and policy studies. Educated at Dartmouth College and Columbia University, Mr. Luck worked as a consultant in the Social Science Department of the RAND Corporation and was a fellow of the Russian Institute of Columbia University. Mr. Luck has written extensively on arms control, national security policy, and multilateral diplomacy. Most recently, he is the author of *Renewing the Mandate: The UN's Role in Peace and Security.*

Edward N. Luttwak currently holds the Arleigh Burke Chair of Strategy at the Center for Strategic and International Studies, and is a consultant to the Office of Secretary of Defense and the Department of State. He has served as adviser to the U.S. Army on force-structure development. Educated at the London School of Economics and Johns Hopkins University, Dr. Luttwak has taught at Johns Hopkins University (Baltimore and the Paul H. Nitze School of Advanced International Studies) and Georgetown University, and has been a guest lecturer at higher military schools in nine countries. He serves on the boards of a number of scholarly journals, including *Washington Quarterly, Journal of Strategic Studies,* and *The National Interest.* Dr. Luttwak is the author of *Coup d'Etat; The Grand Strategy of the Soviet Union;* and *Strategy: The Logic of War and Peace.*

Myres S. McDougal is Sterling Professor Emeritus at Yale University Law School. Educated at Yale Law School and a Rhodes scholar at Oxford University, Professor McDougal is former president of the American Society of International Law and of the Association of American Law Schools. He is a member of the Institute of International Law and has received the Hudson Medal from the American Society of International Law and the Read Medal from the Canadian Council of International Law. Professor McDougal served on the U.S. delegation to the 1969 Vienna UN Conference on the Law of Treaties and has been a member of the Permanent Court of Arbitration. Author and coauthor of many books on international law, including his current two-volume project *The Global Constitutive Process of Authoritative Decision,* Professor McDougal is a former United States Institute of Peace Jennings Randolph Distinguished Fellow.

Steven E. Miller is senior research fellow at the Stockholm International Peace Research Institute (SIPRI) in Sweden. Prior to his position at SIPRI, Dr. Miller was assistant professor of political science and research associate in the Defense and Arms Control Studies Program at the Massachusetts Institute of Technology's Center for International Studies. Educated at Occidental College and the Fletcher School of Law and Diplomacy, Tufts University, Dr. Miller was also coeditor of *International Security* and an adjunct research fellow at the Center for Science and International Affairs, Harvard University. He is the author or editor of many publications on foreign policy, nuclear weapons, and security, including *Military Strategy and the Origins of the First World War* and the forthcoming *Nuclear Arguments: The Major Debates on Strategic Nuclear Weapons and Arms Control.*

Joseph V. Montville is senior consultant on conflict resolution at the Center for the Study of Foreign Affairs, Foreign Service Institute, U.S. Department of State. Educated at Leigh, Harvard, and Columbia universities, Mr. Montville was also a Fulbright scholar at Cairo University in Egypt. He also previously served in diplomatic assignments at U.S. embassies in Iraq, Lebanon, Libya, and Morocco before working in the bureaus of Near Eastern and South Asian Affairs, intelligence, and research in the State Department. Mr. Montville is the author of *Conflict and Peacemaking in Multiethnic Societies.*

Fred L. Morrison is professor of law at the University of Minnesota Law School, a member of the U.S. State Department's Advisory Committee on International Law, and a part-time counselor with a Minneapolis law firm. A Rhodes scholar, Professor Morrison was educated at the University of Kansas, Oxford University, Princeton University, and the University of Chicago. He has served as a visiting professor at the universities of Bonn and Kiel in West Germany. He was counselor on international law for the U.S. Department of State and has been a member of the counsel for the United States in the International Court of Justice. Professor Morrison has published a number of articles, including most recently, "Treaties as a Source of Jurisdiction, Especially the U.S. Practice."

Michael N. Nagler is professor of classics and comparative literature at the University of California, Berkeley, and is a frequent speaker on global conflict and peace issues. Educated at Cornell University, New York University, the University of Heidelberg, and the University of California, Berkeley, Dr. Nagler co-founded the Peace and Conflict Studies Program at the University of California, Berkeley. Dr. Nagler has published widely, including *America Without Violence* and the prize-winning essay "Strength Through Peace."

David D. Newsom is director of the Institute for the Study of Diplomacy at Georgetown University's School of Foreign Service. Educated at the University of California, Berkeley, and Columbia University, he has had a distinguished career as a foreign service officer, including service as U.S. ambassador to Libya, Indonesia, and the Philippines, and as under secretary of state for political affairs. He has been widely published in major newspapers and is a regular contributor to the *Christian Science Monitor*.

Janne Nolan is a senior fellow at the Brookings Institution. Educated at Tufts and Stanford universities, she was contract manager at Science Applications International for the U.S. Department of Defense, senior adviser to Senator Gary Hart on defense and foreign policy in the U.S. Senate, and his designee to the Senate Armed Services Committee. She is the author of *Defense Industry in South Korea and Taiwan* and, most recently, *Guardians of the Arsenal: The Politics of Nuclear Strategy*.

Robert Pickus is founder and president of the World Without War Council. An initiator of the National Peace Research Council, the National Peace Intern Program, and the American Peace Initiatives Project, he is currently directing "Assessing the Public Effort for Peace in America: 1984–1988." Educated at the University of Chicago, Mr. Pickus was a Fulbright scholar at the London School of Economics. Author of *To End War* and *The ABM and a World Without War*, Mr. Pickus is also the chairman of the James Madison Foundation and a board member of the Alliance for Education in Global and International Studies and the Center for Democracy in the Soviet Union.

Jeffrey Z. Rubin is professor of psychology at Tufts University. He is also executive director of the Program on Negotiation at Harvard Law School. Educated in social psychology at Teachers College, Columbia University, Professor Rubin has written extensively on bargaining and negotiation, conflict resolution, decision making, and dispute resolution through third-party involvement. His books include *Social Conflict: Escalation, Stalemate and Settlement; The Social Psychology of Bargaining and Negotiation;* and *Dynamics of Third Party Intervention: Kissinger in the Middle East*.

R. J. Rummel is professor of political science at the University of Hawaii and president and founder of the Haiku Institute of Peace Research. Educated at the University of Hawaii and Northwestern University, Dr. Rummel has founded and directed international affairs-related organizations, including the Interpolimetrics Society, PATH Institute of Research on International Problems, and Political Economic Risk Consultants. Dr. Rummel is the author of a number of books and articles, including *Peace Endangered: The Reality of Detente* and, most recently, *In the Minds of Men: Principles Toward Understanding and Waging Peace.*

Bruce M. Russett is Dean Acheson Professor of International Relations and Political Science at Yale University. He is also editor of the *Journal of Conflict Resolution,* and former president of the International Studies Association and the Peace Science Society (International). Educated at Yale University, he is the author or editor of nineteen books, including most recently *Controlling the Sword: The Democratic Governance of National Security.*

Oscar Schachter is Hamilton Fish Professor Emeritus of International Law and Diplomacy at Columbia University. In addition to academic positions, his career has included various positions in the U.S. government and the UN where he served for fourteen years as director of its legal division. He is former president of the American Society of International Law, former editor-in-chief of the *American Journal of International Law,* and a member of the Institut de Droit International. His most recent book, *International Law in Theory and Practice,* is a comprehensive study of the relation of law and politics.

Richard N. Smith is an associate at the Center for Security Policy in Washington, D.C., where he deals with the conduct and direction of American national security policy. Formerly a project officer of the Research and Studies Program at the United States Institute of Peace, Mr. Smith was responsible for the organization and supervision of the Intellectual Map colloquia and conference.

W. Scott Thompson is professor of international politics at the Fletcher School of Law and Diplomacy, Tufts University, and a member of the Board of Directors of the United States Institute of Peace. A Rhodes scholar and graduate of Stanford and Oxford universities, Dr. Thompson has served as White House fellow, assistant to the secretary of defense, and associate director of the United States Information Agency. Author or editor of numerous books on foreign policy, Dr. Thompson is a founding member of the Council on Foreign Relations and the International Institute for Strategic Studies, and serves on the Board of the Institute for Strategic Trade.

Gregory F. Treverton is senior fellow and director of the Europe-America Project at the Council of Foreign Relations in New York. Educated at Princeton and Harvard universities, Dr. Treverton served on the staff of the Senate Select Committee on Intelligence (the Church Committee), as a staff member for Western Europe on the National Security Council during the Carter administration, as assistant director of the International Institute for Strategic Studies, and on the faculty of the Kennedy School of Government, Harvard University. He is the author of *The "Dollar Drain" and American Forces in Germany; Making the Alliance Work: The United States and Western Europe;* and, most recently, *Covert Action: The Limits of Intervention in the Postwar World.*

I. William Zartman is Jacob Blaustein Professor of International Organization and Conflict Resolution, and director of the African Studies and Conflict Management programs at the Paul H. Nitze School of Advanced International Studies, Johns Hopkins University. Professor Zartman has taught abroad and has written several works on Africa and the Near East. On the subject of negotiation, he has edited, authored, or coauthored *The 50% Solution; The Practical Negotiator; The Negotiation Process; Ripe for Resolution: Conflict and Resolution in Africa;* and *International Mediation in Theory and Practice.*

Attendees*

Lance Antrim, Sloan School of Management, Massachusetts Institute of Technology

Jeffrey H. Ashford, International Affairs Division, U.S. Office of Management and Budget

Orna Ben-Naftali, Peace Scholar, United States Institute of Peace

Bruce Berlin, Peace Fellow, United States Institute of Peace

David Birenbaum, Fried, Frank, Harris, Shriver & Jacobson

Mark Blitz, U.S. Information Agency

Julia Chang Bloch, Agency for International Development

John Burton, Center for Conflict Analysis and Resolution, George Mason University

Joanne Chang, School of Law, University of Maryland

Alberto Coll, U.S. Naval War College

Raymond Copson, CRS/FAND, Library of Congress

Robert H. Cory, Friends World Committee

Robin J. Crews, Kansas Institute of Peace and Conflict Resolution, Bethel College

Francis M. Deng, Distinguished Fellow, United States Institute of Peace

Daniel Druckman, National Academy of Sciences

Maire A. Dugan, Consortium on Peace Research, Education and Development, George Mason University

Gretchen Eick, National Impact

Evelyn Falkowski, World Federalist Association

Lily Gardner Feldman, Peace Fellow, United States Institute of Peace

Benjamin B. Ferencz, Pace Peace Center, Pace Law School

Clinton F. Fink, Consortium on Peace Research, Education, and Development, George Mason University

Allan Gerson, American Enterprise Institute

Patrick Glynn, American Enterprise Institute

Ted R. Gurr, Peace Fellow Designate, United States Institute of Peace

Christopher Hewitt, Department of Sociology, University of Maryland

George High, Bureau of Public Affairs, U.S. Department of State

Kent R. Hill, Institute on Religion and Democracy

David I. Hitchcock, Center for Strategy and International Studies

Walter Hoffman, World Federalist Association

Harry J. Hogan, Council for Advancement of Citizenship

Bill Hough, Institute for Peace Development

James T. Johnson, International Programs, Rutgers University

Whittle Johnston, Department of Government and Foreign Affairs, University of Virginia

Mark Katz, Peace Fellow Designate, United States Institute of Peace

Adrienne Kaufmann, School of International Service, American University

Ivan J. Kauffman, independent, Washington, D.C.

Richard Kauzlarich, Policy Planning Staff, U.S. Department of State

Edward L. Killham, U.S. Department of State

Paul R. Kimmel, Peace Fellow, United States Institute of Peace

Stanley Kober, independent, Arlington, Virginia

Ellie D. Krakowski, U.S. Department of Defense

Kathleen Lansing, National Peace Institute Foundation

Jay Lintner, United Church of Christ

David Little, Distinguished Fellow, United States Institute of Peace

John Marks, Search for Common Ground

Clifford McCarthy, National Peace Institute Foundation

John W. McDonald, Jr., Foreign Service Institute, U.S. Department of State

David Pabst, Atlantic Council

Hugh Pease, International Conference on Peacebuilding, Irish Peace Institute

Jerry Powers, U.S. Catholic Conference

Michael Privitera, Bureau of Public Affairs, U.S. Department of State

Gail Ranadive, American University

Robin Ranger, Peace Fellow, United States Institute of Peace

Betty Reardon, Peace Education Program, Columbia University

Maj. Gen. Indar Jit Rikhye, International Peace Academy

Eugene V. Rostow, National Defense University

Robert Rudney, National Institute for Public Policy

Louise Seeley, *Nuclear Times*

Amy Sherman, James Madison Foundation

Max Singer, Grantee, United States Institute of Peace

Robert F. Smith, U.S. Information Agency

W. Richard Smyser, independent, Washington, D.C.

Gregory Stanton, Law School, Washington and Lee University

Leonard Starobin, World Peace Association

John R. Stevenson, Sullivan & Cromwell

Charles T. Sweeney, Institute for National Strategic Studies, National Defense University

Robert F. Turner, Center for Law and National Security

W. Bruce Weinrod, Board Member, United States Institute of Peace

Leland Wilson, Church of the Brethren

Goshu Wolde, Peace Fellow, United States Institute of Peace

*Affiliations at time of conference (June 1988)

Research and Studies Program

To complement its research grants and fellowships for organizations and individuals, the United States Institute of Peace established its own Research and Studies Program in 1988.

Research and Studies projects are designed and directed by the Institute, which supervises their implementation with the assistance of expert consultants and contract researchers. Most projects are carried out through a process that includes the production of working papers on a selected topic and their discussion by experts in public session. Proceedings from the sessions are redrafted as papers, reports, articles, monographs, and books to assist scholars, educators, journalists, policymakers, and citizens' groups in understanding issues of peace and war.

Research and Studies activities fall into four main categories: study groups, public workshops, working-group projects, and studies. Study groups run from four to six months and involve a core group of expert participants in intensive examination of near-term international conflict situations. Public workshops are two- to three-hour events designed for group discussion around a discrete topic of current concern. Working-group projects run for one year or longer and proceed through four or more public sessions involving a core group of expert participants. Studies are conceived on the same scale as working groups, but with a changing cast of participants. In all these activities, the Institute strives to provide for representation of a wide range of viewpoints and to address its mandate to contribute to and disseminate knowledge about ways of achieving peace by doing as much work as possible in public session.

Kenneth M. Jensen
Director